criminal justice

BRIEF EDITION

Jay S. Albanese

VIRGINIA COMMONWEALTH UNIVERSITY

ALLYN AND BACON

Boston

London

Toronto

Sydney

Tokyo

Singapore

Editor-in-Chief, Social Sciences: Karen Hanson
Senior Developmental Editor: Mary Ellen Lepionka
Editorial Assistant: Sarah McGaughey
Senior Editorial-Production Administrator: Joe Sweeney
Editorial-Production Service: Colophon
Composition Buyer: Linda Cox
Manufacturing Buyer: Megan Cochran
Cover Administrator: Linda Knowles
Text Designer: Seventeenth Street Studios
Photo Researcher: PoYee Oster
Text Compositon: Omegatype Typography, Inc.

Copyright © 2001 by Allyn & Bacon
A Pearson Education Company
160 Gould Street
Needham Heights, MA 02494
www.abacon.com

Library of Congress Cataloging-in-Publication Data

Albanese, Jay S.
    Criminal justice / Jay S. Albanese—Brief ed.
      p. cm.
    Includes bibliographical references and index.
    ISBN 0-205-31811-8 (alk. paper)
      1. Crime—United States.   2. Crime—Government policy—United States.
   3. Criminal justice, Administration of—United States.   I. Title.

HV6789 .A366 2000
364.973—dc21

                                  00-055832

Printed in the United States of America
10 9 8 7 6 5 4 3 2 1   VHP   04 03 02 01 00

Photo Credits
p. 1, Laura Rauch/AP/Wide World Photos; **p. 7**, Bill Pugliano/Liaison Agency; **p. 9**, Photofest; **p. 11**, Corbis/Bettmann; **p. 18**, Adam Scull/Rangefielders/Globe Photos; **p. 23**, Jacques M. Chenet/Liaison Agency; **p. 26**, HO/AP/Wide World Photos; **p. 29**, PhotoDisc; **p. 39**, Pamela Salazar/Liaison Agency; **p. 45**, Prentice Hall, Inc.; **p. 47**, Columbia Tristar/ Shooting Star; **p. 48**, Brian Palmer/Corbis Sygma; **p. 52**, Courtesy of U.S. Census Bureau; **p. 56**, Susan Greenwood/Liaison Agency; **p. 57**, Jack Kurtz/Impact Visuals; **p. 62**, Chuck Pefley/Stock Boston;

Photo credits continued on page 441, which constitutes a continuation of the copyright page.

For my children

Thomas & Kelsey

who like this edition best

because it's "brief"

Contents

chapter three

Dealing with Sophisticated Crimes   70

chapter six

Officers of the Law   173

chapter seven

Issues in Law Enforcement and Police Behavior   210

chapter eight

Criminal Courts   247

chapter nine

Criminal Defense and Prosecution   277

chapter ten

Trials and Sentencing   307

chapter eleven

Prisons   **348**

chapter twelve

Corrections in the Community   **383**

Preface

The serious and personal nature of crime causes people to think viscerally and often emotionally about it. Facts are needed to determine whether the incidents we know about are typical or unusual. It is only in this way that we can properly gauge our fear, know which precautionary measures should to be taken, and whether or not we should support various new laws or policies.

Criminal Justice: Brief Edition provides these facts in systematic fashion by examining the nature of crime and the criminal justice system to reveal significant history, facts, and trends, tracing them from the past to the present and into the future. The phrase "criminal justice" refers to the operation and management of police, courts, and corrections agencies. The decision to punish certain behaviors as crimes, the arrest decision, charging decision, jury decision, and sentencing decision are a few of the far-reaching decisions made many times each day in criminal justice. The balance to be struck among public safety, concern for victims, and the protection of the accused is fundamental and is reflected throughout this book.

Surveys have reported for many years that the fear of crime is steadily increasing, especially among the poor and disenfranchised who often lack the ability to change the nature and condition of their communities. There is also evidence that this fear reduces the mobility of citizens, affects their social interactions (through increased fear of strangers), hurts the commercial sector (especially nighttime shopping), and generally affects the quality of life by which we judge our leaders, our communities, and our country.

This fear is intensified when reports of new crimes, new criminals, police problems, plea-bargaining, overcrowded courts, and ineffective prisons can leave the individual citizen with the feeling that little effort is being made to improve existing conditions and that life is becoming more dangerous. The consequences of such feelings include declining participation in the political process (by continuing drops in the percentage of eligible citizens who vote). People also react unexpectedly, and sometimes violently, to additional stresses placed upon them (by sporadic instances of workplace violence and road rage).

In the pages that follow, the issues of crime and justice that affect us all are clearly presented in the hope that readers, through greater understanding of these problems which have such far-reaching personal and social consequences, will be better able to participate in informed strategies for their amelioration.

Organization of the Book

Perhaps the most useful aspect of this book is that it is written like a book rather than an encyclopedia. The chapters read as a narrative, rather than an encyclopedia of facts too numerous for readers to learn, prioritize, or connect together. An emphasis is placed on fitting concepts and the criminal justice system together, rather than cramming in as many facts as possible onto each page. This is extremely important for students taking what might be their first course in criminal justice. This book is written so students are able to read with understanding and not be lost in an avalanche of facts and figures that serve to confuse rather than inform.

The topics are arranged logically beginning with a comparison of the fear of crime with other dangerous life events. Chapter 1 also defines crime and its causes and correlates, placing it in historical and political context. This is followed in Chapter 2 with a discussion of the differences among the various types of violent and property crimes, and how measuring crime accurately is more difficult than it might appear. Chapter 3 offers a unique look at the sophisticated crimes, including white-collar crime, computer crime, organized crime, and terrorism. The similarities among these crimes are presented as well as a typology to understand them more clearly. Chapter 4 explains the scope of the criminal law in how we define crime in precise terms, determine liability, and excuse conduct under certain circumstances. Chapter 5 provides an overview of the criminal justice system and criminal procedure, showing in exact terms how an individual case proceeds from arrest through disposition.

Chapters 6 and 7 address the history and organization of police, together with how police discretion is exercised and the legal limits on police conduct. Police are the gatekeepers of the criminal justice system; thus an understanding of police is central to the study of criminal justice. Chapter 8 explains how courts are organized in the United States and how they operate in practice. Innovations in dispute resolution are described. Chapter 9 offers a discussion of prosecutors and their role in criminal justice, plea-bargaining, and the conflicting pressures placed the prosecution. The role of defense counsel in criminal cases is also examined, including the important issue of the competing interests between seeking the truth versus winning criminal cases. Chapter 10 explains trials, judges, and sentencing and how the history and philosophy of sentencing has changed over the years. Chapter 11 discusses prisons and their role and purpose in dealing with offenders, including trends in prison populations. Chapter 12 introduces the reader to the concepts of authentic versus restorative justice and how alternatives to prison often can serve the dual purposes of deterrence and rehabilitation.

Features of the Book

There are four important features in this book; each adds to the book's usefulness as a source of information and as a tool for teaching and learning.

1. *Critical Thinking Exercises* are included in each chapter. These exercises describe an interesting issue, relate some facts, history, and research about it and then ask the reader two or three questions that query them to *think* about alternatives, rather than merely *recall* facts. The Critical Thinking Exercises force readers to think about issues of concern and come up with thoughtful responses rather than rehearsed answers. Examples of critical thinking topics included in the book are binge drinking, Justice on the Carolina frontier in 1764, terrorists on the Internet, chain gangs, and other topics.

2. *Contemporary Issues and Trends* are featured in each chapter that highlight a current issue, providing a jumping-off point for discussion, projects, or further reading. Examples include obscenity, carjackings, campus law enforcement, race and the death penalty, private prisons and liability, sex offender registries, cyber-theft, and other topics.

3. Each chapter has an illustrated *Media and Criminal Justice* feature that summarizes a film or television series dealing with criminal justice issues. Each media feature is followed by a question that requires the student to respond thoughtfully rather than give a prescripted response. Films in the media features include both contemporary and classic portrayals of fundamental issues of crime and justice.

4. This is the only book of its kind with a separate chapter on political and economic crimes. It addresses the growth of white-collar crime, organized crime, computer crimes, and terrorism, expanding the scope of criminal justice books from traditional street crimes. As technology advances and the economy changes to reflect that technology, these sophisticated crimes will continue to grow in number and in the severity of outcomes.

Supplemental Materials

Criminal Justice: Brief Edition is accompanied by an expansive package of supplementary materials to facilitate teaching and learning. These materials include:

INSTRUCTOR'S MANUAL AND TEST BANK   Each chapter of this valuable teaching tool includes a chapter summary, annotated chapter outline, learning objectives, key terms, class discussion questions, guest speaker suggestions, projects, and sample test questions. More than 1,000 test questions are included: approximately 40 multiple choice, 30 true-false, 15 fill-in, and 5 essay questions for each chapter of the text.

ALLYN AND BACON TEST MANAGER—COMPUTERIZED TEST BANK   The Test Bank is also available electronically: as a CD-ROM or disk for IBM (Windows) users, a disk for Mac users, and a DOS disk. This computerized version contains all of the questions from the Test Bank, plus you may customize it with your own questions. The Test Manager produces a variety of statistics that allow you to analyze the performance of test questions, students, an individual class or section, and assessment types such as homework and on-line tests.

ALLYN AND BACON DIGITAL MEDIA ARCHIVE FOR CRIMINAL JUSTICE   The Digital Media Archive was created as a tool to ease and enhance your lecture preparation. Allyn & Bacon provides you with one CD-ROM which conveniently houses a variety of resources giving you the power to create extensive multi-media presentations in a few simple steps. This CD-ROM contains four types of content: images, web links, audio clips, and video clips. The images are provided in several file formats that are compatible with most presentation software packages.

In addition, the Digital Media Archive contains a text-specific Power-Point presentation of approximately 500 graphic and text images.

ALLYN AND BACON INTERACTIVE VIDEO—PRIME TIME CRIME   This custom video covers a variety of major topics of interest to Criminology and Criminal Justice. The video segments are great to launch lectures, spark classroom discussion, and encourage critical thinking. The accompanying video user's guide provides detailed descriptions of each video segment, specific tie-ins to the text, and suggested discussion questions and projects. Prime Time Crime is organized as follows: predatory crimes; domestic violence; organizational crime; corporate crime; state crime; and crimes against humanity.

ALLYN AND BACON INTERACTIVE VIDEO FOR ALBANESE   This custom video covers a variety of topics in the field of criminal justice, which are linked tightly with the text. The up-to-the-minute video segments are great to launch lectures, spark classroom discussion, and encourage critical thinking. The accompanying video user's guide provides detailed descriptions of each video segment, specific tie-ins to the text, and suggested discussion questions and projects.

ALLYN AND BACON VIDEO LIBRARY FOR CRIMINAL JUSTICE   Qualified adopters may select from a wide variety of high quality videos from such sources as Films for the Humanities and Sciences and Arts and Humanities (A & B).

THE BLOCKBUSTER APPROACH: A GUIDE TO TEACHING CRIMINAL JUSTICE WITH VIDEO   This manual provides extensive lists, with descriptions, of hundreds of commercially available videos, and shows how they can be incorporated in the classroom. The videos are organized by topic and presented in an order common to most introductory textbooks.

CRIMINAL JUSTICE ON THE NET, 2001 EDITION   This handy reference guide contains a relevant discussion of Internet basics written for students in a language to which they can relate. It includes criminal justice Internet activities; a section on critical evaluation of Internet sources; proper electronic documentation guidelines for both MLA and APA styles; and a multitude of criminal justice-specific URLs.

CAREERS IN CRIMINAL JUSTICE   This supplement goes beyond the academic career path of the criminal justice major and explores careers in criminology and criminal justice, showing how people entered the field, and how a degree in criminal justice can be a preparation for careers in a wide variety of areas.

COMPANION WEBSITE WITH ONLINE PRACTICE TESTS   An extensive website has been developed for the *Brief Edition* at www.abacon.com/albanese. Features of the online study guide portion of the website include learning objectives; practice tests (interactive multiple choice, true-false, fill-in and essay questions); web destinations; exploring the Internet; chapter chats, etc. There are numerous non-text specific criminal justice resources included on this exciting site!

SUPERSITE FOR ALBANESE'S *CRIMINAL JUSTICE, BRIEF EDITION*   In addition, a new, content-rich website for the *Brief Edition* is available to students and instructors through the use of a pin code at www.abacon.com/albanese. Learning resources for every chapter are based on the following interactive and Internet-based media assets, grouped according to the sequence of main headings in the text:

> *Statistics and Graphs* activities with interpretation and assessment questions
> *Online Investigations* structured Internet explorations with URLs
> *Current Events* analyses with links and application questions
> *Contemporary Issues and Trends* more essays with critical thinking questions
> *Maps and Images* activities with interpretation and evaluation questions
> *Video* clips with critical thinking questions
> *Audio* files by Jay S. Albanese
> *Media and Criminal Justice* more movie reviews with questions
> *Matching Activities* for fun and self-testing
> *Crossword Puzzles* for self-testing and fun

Acknowledgments

This book is much more than a collection of several hundred thousand words. It took a significant portion of my life to gather the personal and social experience and knowledge that resulted in this manuscript. It began while a senior undergraduate at Niagara University when my sociology professor, Nicholas Caggiano, mentioned in class that Rutgers University was opening a new School of Criminal Justice. I applied there and was admitted to the only graduate school to which I applied. To this day, I do not believe I would have heard about Rutgers if I had cut that class.

After finishing my Master's degree at Rutgers and working as a criminal justice planner for a year, I considered attending law school. An emergency appendectomy the night before the law school admission test sidetracked those plans. Instead, I received a call from Don Gottfredson at Rutgers a few weeks later, inviting me to apply to their newly established doctoral program at the School of Criminal Justice. I entered the Ph.D. program that fall. I am indebted to Rutgers for starting the School of Criminal Justice when it did and also for supporting my studies with assistantships and fellowships along the way. I made a number of life-long friends with faculty and students there. I finished the Ph.D. in 1981, having obtained a variety of work experiences in the process. These experiences included research, consulting, and a great deal of teaching. The opportunity to teach enabled me to discover I enjoyed it, and that I improved with each class I taught.

I returned to Niagara University in fall, 1981 and taught there for 15 years. During that time I had the opportunity to revise the undergraduate curriculum in criminal justice, write the curriculum for a Masters program, and teach most of the courses there at one time or another. I have gained more knowledge through teaching than through any other activity because good teaching requires preparation. The lack of many good books in the field, especially during the early years of my career, forced me to look to primary sources. This instilled an appreciation of the history and philosophy that underlies the field of criminal justice that is reflected in this book. Teaching is a very important profession, and I am gratified to have the opportunity to do it for a living. I thank my students for providing the forum to do so.

I began research for the original manuscript while serving as president of the Academy of Criminal Justice Sciences and then moved to my current position as chair of the Department of Criminal Justice at Virginia Commonwealth University. These undertakings slowed my progress on this book somewhat, but they made it more interesting in light of a series of major events in criminal justice that have occurred in recent years, including major acts of domestic terrorism, dramatic growth in media coverage of criminals trials, and significant growth in international and sophisticated crimes.

The reviewers of this manuscript made many helpful suggestions on early drafts of this book. They include Nola Allen, University of South Alabama; Jennifer M. Balboni, Northeastern University; John K. Cochran, University of South Florida; Richard H. DeLung, Wayland Baptist University; David Friedrichs, University of Scranton; Herbert C. Friese, Burlington County College; Dennis Hoffman, University of Nebraska; Terrance W. Hoffman, Nassau Community College; Katherine Jamieson, University of North Carolina; William E. Kelly, Auburn University; JoAnne M. Lecci, Nassau Community College; Larry Rostintoski, Trident Technical College; Carl Russell, Scottsdale Community College; Jo Ann M. Scott, Ohio Northern University; Donald H. Smith, Old Dominion University; Gregory B. Talley, Broome Community College; and Angela D. West, Indiana State University. Their comments undoubtedly improved the quality of the final manuscript.

My editors deserve recognition for their help in seeing this project through to publication. Karen Hanson, editor-in-chief, thought the idea for this book was a good one and I thank her for her tactful yet persistent attention to details and deadlines. In a similar way Senior Developmental Editor Mary Ellen Lepionka provided invaluable editorial assistance, helping to organize and condense a large amount of information in a new and interesting way. (Mary Ellen also contributed photo captions asking students to think about images in terms of chapter concepts, and created content for a special pincoded website for the this text.) Denise Botelho and Joe Sweeney provided cheerful assistance in the book's production and marketing, and the many field representatives I have met impressed me with their knowledge of both publishing and the field of criminal justice. Casey Jordan also did fabulous work with the media boxes.

Like most families, mine wonders why projects like this take as long as they do to complete. Continual changes in the field of criminal justice, updates, and the production process prolonged completion but the book is better for it. I thank my family for giving up on asking when it would be over. Character-building exploits such as coaching a soccer team of 9- and 10-year-olds and teaching forensic science to middle school students provided welcome relief about the possibilities for constructive behavior by day, while I wrote about the dark side at night. Without all these experiences this book would have been quite different and probably not as good.

Jay S. Albanese

About the Author

JAY S. ALBANESE is professor and chair of the Department of Criminal Justice at Virginia Commonwealth University. He received the Ph.D. and M.A. degrees from Rutgers University and B.A. from Niagara University. He was the first Ph.D. recipient from the Rutgers School of Criminal Justice. He is author of books that include *Criminal Justice* (Allyn & Bacon, 2000), *Organized Crime in America* (3rd ed., Anderson, 1996), and *White Collar Crime in America* (Prentice Hall, 1995). He edited the book *Contemporary Issues in Organized Crime* (Willow Tree Press, 1995).

Dr. Albanese served as Interim Research Director to the National White Collar Crime Center during 1998–99. The Center is an investigative support and training agency funded by the U.S. Bureau of Justice Assistance in the Department of Justice. Dr. Albanese is author of several articles on the inter-relationship among casino gambling, law enforcement, and crime. He was consultant to the Ontario government (Canada) in 1993, and testified before the U.S. National Gambling Impact Study Commission in 1998. He is currently conducting a study of organized crime groups in Ukraine and the United States, sponsored by the National Institute of Justice.

Dr. Albanese is a past president of the Academy of Criminal Justice Sciences (ACJS) and Northeastern Association of Criminal Justice Sciences. He is recipient of the Teaching Excellence Award from the Sears Foundation (1990) and the Founders Award from ACJS (2000) for contributions to criminal justice education and to the Academy.

one
Crime and Violence

In a city and a location not

known for violent crime, a man opened fire in the Salt Lake City Family History Library, killing a security guard and a woman doing research. He wounded five others. A group of fourth graders on a field trip were briefly trapped in the library when the shooting broke out. The man was ultimately killed by police sharpshooters.[1] His wife said he suffered from mental problems and was not taking his medication.

In a separate incident Buford Furrow walked into the North Valley Jewish Community Center in Los Angeles carrying an Uzi machine gun, several handguns, and a large quantity of ammunition. He opened fire without provocation, spraying more than seventy bullets around the lobby. He left moments after he entered, leaving wounded a sixty-eight-year-old receptionist, a sixteen-year-old camp counselor at the day care center, and three children. Furrow then stole a car and drove to a residential area, where he shot a Filipino American postman who was delivering the mail. The postman was hit by at least three bullets and killed. Furrow turned himself in to authorities the next day. His actions apparently were motivated by hatred for the religious and ethnic backgrounds of the victims. He previously had been jailed for brandishing a knife at a psychiatric hospital.[2]

Are shocking incidents like these simply very rare tragedies, or are they increasingly typical? In the years 1997–1999 there were seven major school shooting incidents in the United States that resulted in thirty deaths and woundings of many others. Reports of homicides, thefts, robberies, and assaults typically are lead stories on television and in newspapers. Seven percent of U.S. households identify crime as a problem in their own neighborhoods. In public housing projects crime is identified as a neighborhood problem by up to 25 percent of households.[3]

How concerned about crime and violence *should* we be? Are the reports of crime we hear about on the news giving us an accurate reading of the true crime picture, or is there other information we need in order to assess our true risk?

Why Are Americans Fearful of Crime?

When one compares the actual risk of being victimized by crime to the risk of experiencing other negative events, crime does not appear so rampant. For example, each year about 242 of every 1,000 adults in the United States are hurt in accidents—nearly a 1 in 4 chance of injury in any given year. The odds of being struck by lightning are 1 in 9,100; those of dying from heart disease are almost 4 in 1,000; and those of dying from cancer are 2 in 1,000. These are all far higher than the risk of being victimized by crime. The top ten causes of death in the United States are presented in Table 1.1. As shown there, health problems and accidents are far more common causes of death than criminal homicide. A person is twenty-nine times more likely to die of a heart attack than to die as a homicide victim. Likewise, a person is twenty times more likely to die from cancer and six times more likely to die from a stroke than to die from homicide. In fact, you are almost twice as likely to die in a car accident as you are to die from homicide, and nearly four times more likely to die in some other kind of accident than you are to be a homicide victim. When one views homicide in context, therefore, it is clear that other risks, especially poor health and accidents, pose a much greater threat to life.

TABLE 1.1

Odds of Occurrence of Death

CAUSES OF DEATH	ODDS OF OCCURRENCE (PER 100,000 POPULATION)
1. Heart disease	276
2. Cancer	203
3. Stroke	60
4. Lung disease	40
5. Pneumonia and flu	32
6. Diabetes mellitus	23
7. All other accidents	19
8. Motor vehicle accidents	16
9. Suicide	12
10. Liver disease	9
11. Kidney disease	9
12. Homicide	8

SOURCE: National Center for Health Statistics, *National Vital Statistics Report* 47 (9) (November 10, 1998).

TABLE 1.2

How the Odds of Death Have Changed Since 1960

CAUSES OF DEATH IN 1996	1990 RANK	1980 RANK	1970 RANK	1960 RANK	% CHANGE 1960–97
1. Heart disease	1	1	1	1	−25%
2. Cancer	2	2	2	2	+36
3. Stroke	3	3	3	3	−44
4. Lung disease	4	4	9	10	+355
5. Pneumonia and flu	5	5	4	4	−14
6. Diabetes mellitus	6	8	7	7	−38
7. All other accidents	8	7	6	6	−39
8. Motor vehicle accidents	7	6	5	5	−25
9. Suicide	9	10	10	9	+13
10. Liver disease	10	9	8	8	−20
11. Kidney disease	12	12	12	11	+27
12. Homicide	11	11	11	12	+70

SOURCE: U.S. National Center for Health Statistics, *Vital Statistics of the United States* (Washington, DC: Pubic Health Service, published annually).

Perhaps our fear is related to the *direction* (up or down) in rates of certain causes of death, rather than to the odds themselves. Table 1.2 presents trends in the most common causes of death in the United States. As can be seen in the table, the rankings of the various causes of death have shifted only slightly since 1960. The largest jump has been in deaths from lung disease, the number 10 cause of death in 1960 and the number 4 cause in 1997. When calculated in deaths per 1,000 population, this represents an increase of 355 percent. The second-largest increase in risk of death is from homicide, which rose by 70 percent between 1960 and 1997. This increase is eight times higher than the increase in cancer deaths, which went up by 36 percent over the same period. Clearly, the risk of homicide has increased dramatically since 1960 and may account for some of the public's fear of crime.

RISKS OF HOMICIDE

This risk is amplified when one realizes the relative lack of control an individual has over homicide compared with other leading causes of death. Decreases in rates of death from heart disease, strokes, pneumonia and flu, and liver disease are due to changes in the lifestyle, exercise habits, and diet of U.S. citizens since the 1960s. Through research findings and public education regarding the links between personal habits and bad health, many people have gained increased awareness and adopted healthier lifestyles. The same is true for accidental deaths. Seat-belt laws, child bicycle helmets and car seats, air bags, and greater regulation of dangerous devices have done much to reduce the rate of deaths caused by accidents. Each of us can exert a certain amount of influence over the causes of bad health and accidents by changing our behavior. In contrast, homicide is thrust upon us by others. It is also sudden and violent, distinguishing it from most other causes of death. Fear of homicide, therefore, is justified to some extent by the significant increase in its occurrence in recent decades and our comparative lack of individual control over its occurrence.

Myths and Facts about Crime Rates and Criminal Victimization

Knowing the true crime rate would enable people to determine for themselves an appropriate level of fear and to know what precautions are reasonable. The true extent of crime is a subject of controversy, however. Sometimes victims do not call the police, and sometimes police do not apprehend the offender. This controversy led to the initiation of a national annual **victimization** survey of a representative sample of 50,000 U.S. households. This survey asks whether anyone in the household was the victim of a serious crime during the last year, and whether or not the crime was reported to the police. The results are used to estimate the incidence of crime across the entire United States with a high degree of accuracy.

Table 1.3 shows the results of these surveys from 1973 through 1998, illustrating that crime occurs with some frequency. Nearly 18 million larcenies occur each year, as do 4 million burglaries and 1.1 million automobile thefts. The crimes of violence occur less often, led by 1.7 million aggravated assaults, 886,000 robberies, and 110,000 rapes. Since 1973 the trend is generally downward. It can be seen that odds of being a rape victim in 1998, for example, are 0.5 per 1,000 population; the odds of being the victim of a serious assault are 7.5 per 1,000; and so on.

■victimization
Infliction of assault, theft, or other criminal behaviors on a person or household.

TABLE 1.3

Crime Victimization in the United States (Number and Rate per 1,000)

OFFENSES	1973	1980	1990	1998
Rape	156,000 1.0	174,000 0.9	130,000 0.6	110,000 0.5
Robbery	1,108,000 6.7	1,209,000 6.6	1,150,000 5.7	886,000 4.0
Aggravated assault	1,622,000 10.1	1,707,000 9.3	1,601,000 7.9	1,674,000 7.5
Household burglary	6,459,000 91.7	6,973,000 84.3	5,148,000 53.8	4,054,000 38.5
Larceny from the person	14,970,000 91.1	15,300,000 83.0	12,975,000 63.8	17,703,000 168.1 (All larcenies)
Household larceny	7,537,000 107.0	10,490,000 126.5	8,304,000 86.7	Combined with other larcenies beginning 1993
Motor vehicle theft	1,344,000 19.1	1,381,000 16.7	1,968,000 20.5	1,138,000 10.8

SOURCE: Lisa D. Bastian, Craig Perkins, Patsy Klaus, Michael Rand, Callie Marie Rennison, and Cheryl Ringel, *Criminal Victimization* (Washington, DC: Bureau of Justice Statistics, published annually).

The statistical odds of being a victim of these crimes are low. The most common crime is larceny, with nearly 1 in 5 persons victimized each year (168 per 1,000), whereas only one-half of 1 percent of the population is the victim of robbery each year (4 per 1,000). This compares to the odds of dying in a homicide of 8 per 100,000 (or .008 percent) and the odds of dying from heart disease of 2.76 per 1,000 (.276 percent), as shown in Table 1.1. Therefore, the most common crime (larceny) occurs about 20 percent of the time, while the other crimes occur considerably less often.

Another way to assess the impact that crime has on our lives is to examine injuries suffered (short of death). The National Center for Health Statistics annually compiles the reasons for visits to hospital emergency rooms. These are summarized in Table 1.4. Of the more than 35 million visits made each year to emergency rooms in the United States, 80 percent involve unintentional injuries such as falls, accidental collisions, traffic accidents, and cuts. Only 6 percent of emergency room visits involve intentional injuries (2.2 million each year), about two-thirds of which are for assaults (1.7 million). Therefore, crime accounts for a small but significant proportion (about 5 percent) of all injury-related visits to hospital emergency rooms each year.

TABLE 1.4

Injury-Related Emergency Room Visits

All injury-related visits	35,111,000	100%
Unintentional injuries	27,953,000	80%
Falls	6,383,000	18%
Collisions	4,806,000	14%
Traffic accidents	4,277,000	12%
Cuts	2,786,000	8%
Intentional Injuries	2,157,000	6%
Assaults	1,686,000	5%
Self-inflicted	401,000	1%
Other	70,000	0.2%

ODDS OF BEING
A VICTIM

PUBLIC
PERCEPTIONS
OF CRIME

SELF-DEFENSE?

Effects of Fear

In 1964 a Gallup poll asked, "What do you think is the most important problem facing this country today?" Forty-six percent of respondents cited international problems (mostly relating to the cold war); 35 percent cited racial problems; and 6 percent or fewer cited high cost of living, unemployment, or too much government control.[4] When asked the same question in the 1990s, respondents ranked the country's most pressing problems as health care (28 percent), the economy (26 percent), crime (16 percent), and poverty and education (6 percent each). The end of the cold war and concern about the national economy appear to have shifted public concern from international relations and domestic race relations to health care, the economy, and crime.

Table 1.5 traces changes in public perceptions of crime over the last three decades. It reveals that the 1960s saw a marked increase in the level of fear that has since leveled off. Approximately 39 percent of Americans are afraid to walk at night in areas near where they live.

A high level of fear can produce undesirable changes in behavior as well. A survey undertaken by the Metropolitan Washington, D.C., Council of Governments in the 1960s reflects concerns that continue today in many cities: "65 percent of the city's largely white suburban residents visit the downtown area less than once a month, and 15 percent come downtown less than once a year." When citizens are afraid to go downtown, stores close, restaurants close, and the economy and quality of life suffer.

Fear can also turn otherwise law-abiding citizens into outlaws. Perhaps the definitive example of what high levels of fear can do is the case of

TABLE 1.5

Levels of Fear of Crime: "Is there an area near where you live (within a mile) where you would be afraid to walk alone at night?"

YEAR QUESTION ASKED	PERCENTAGE AFRAID
1996	39
1993	43
1990	40
1983	45
1977	45
1972	42
1967	31
1965	34

SOURCE: George H. Gallup, *The Gallup Poll: Public Opinion, 1996* (Wilmington, DE: Scholarly Resources, 1997), p. 204.

EXAMPLE OF EFFECTS OF FEAR

Bernard Goetz. In 1984 Goetz, a thirty-seven-year-old white man, was riding on a New York City subway train when one of four boisterous black youths said to him, "How are ya?" Two of them approached Goetz, and one asked him for five dollars. Goetz asked him what he wanted, and he repeated, "Give me five dollars." Goetz proceeded to shoot at the youths five times, emptying his .38 revolver. He wounded each of the youths, paralyzing one of them.[5] The Goetz case illustrates what can happen when a citizen experiences high levels of fear over a prolonged period. Citizens arm themselves (sometimes illegally), focus on events that feed their fears, and sometimes act violently, convinced that they are acting in self-defense. Goetz was found guilty only of criminal possession of a weapon (his revolver), but it is clear that his actions pushed the rules of self-defense to their limit. Since the Goetz case, many states have passed laws making it easier for homeowners and battered spouses to employ force in self-defense, although the new rules apply to very few situations.[6]

The changes in behavior provoked by fear of victimization are not confined to individuals. Businesses also may alter their policies. For example, in an effort to prevent car jackings (in which criminals force their way into occupied vehicles, commandeering the car and sometimes robbing, assaulting, or killing the driver), car rental companies have removed their corporate logos and special license plates from rental cars in order to make it harder for car thieves and robbers to identify tourists.[7] Some are warning their customers *not* to stop when bumped from behind or when told that something is wrong with their car.[8] Similarly, after a series of thefts and violent crimes occurred in South Florida in the wake of Hurricane Andrew,[9] the level of fear and concern about crime led several Miami hotels to block local television news from TV sets in rooms to shield guests from "body-bag journalism."[10]

Even places that are usually considered safe, such as the workplace and the home, have been the scenes of serious violence in recent years. More than forty people were killed in post office shootings throughout the United States in the 1980s and 1990s.[11] Nearly one million individuals are victims of violent crimes while at work each year.[12] Nor do homes appear to be safe havens. In 1995 Susan Smith was convicted of murder in the killing of her two children in North Carolina. In Chicago a mother was sentenced to fifty-five years in prison for forcing her eleven-year-old daughter to have sex with a man in exchange for money. A man critically burned his girlfriend's ten-year-old son in an effort to find out who had taken $20 in food stamps. A Wisconsin high school teacher was convicted for hiring three students to kill her estranged husband. In Rochester, New York, four young teenagers were charged with spraying nail polish remover on

According to the latest research, what chances of being victimized do these neighbors face? What factors might affect their risk of victimization? In this case, what has been a significant behavioral effect of their fear of criminal victimization? In what other ways have Americans responded to fear of crime?

WORKPLACE CRIME

VIGILANTES AND SCAPEGOATS

CRIME IS NORMAL?

an eight-year-old boy and setting him on fire.[13] These are just some of the hundreds of shocking, bizarre, and violent crimes that have occurred throughout the United States in recent years. It does not take many such events to produce high levels of fear and resulting behavior changes. A Texas man formed an organization called Dead Serious that offered members $5,000 for legally killing a criminal who attacked them at home.[14] A relatively crime-free Chicago suburb has placed security checkpoints on the streets entering the area.[15] Throughout many parts of the nation, the perception that the government is not adequately protecting public safety has contributed to the arming of the citizenry. When this occurs, more people take the law into their own hands, and instances of wrongful shooting, vigilante activity, and lawlessness among otherwise law-abiding citizens increase.

Fear of crime also enhances fear of strangers and promotes stereotyping and scapegoating. Attacks against Japanese, Canadian, German, and other tourists, immigrants, and residents offer evidence of this problem.[16] This situation contributes to a self-fulfilling prophecy in which criminal incidents lead to fear, which then leads to more criminal incidents when people react incautiously to perceived threats to their well-being brought about by fear.

The prevalence of crime in societies throughout the world raises the question of whether crime is actually a "normal" part of modern life that we just have to live with. More than a century ago, the French sociologist Emile Durkheim observed that "Crime is present not only in the majority of societies of one particular species but in all societies of all types. There is no society that is not confronted with the problem of criminality."[17] Writing in 1895, Durkheim made the point that crime is "normal" inasmuch as every society has it; it would be abnormal to experience no crime. Nevertheless, crime is not a desirable phenomenon either. Although we cannot expect a society to have no deviance whatsoever, there is considerable variation among the rates of crime in different societies. As a result, it is not unrealistic to seek significant reductions in crime rates—at least for certain types of crimes.[18] Related to this issue is evidence that concern about crime may be a cyclical phenomenon. A presidential crime commission identified several historical periods in which concern about crime was at high levels: "A hundred years ago contemporary accounts of San Francisco told of extensive areas where no decent man was in safety to walk the street after dark; while at all hours, both day and night, his property was jeopardized by incendiarism and burglary." At that time it was widely believed that "crime especially in its more violent forms, and among the young, is increasing steadily and is threatening to bankrupt the Nation."[19]

The fact that concern about crime and violence may be cyclical does not mean, however, that its causes and its level remain the same. The nature and extent of crime differ widely from one time and place to another, and it is not unrealistic to search for ways to reduce current levels of crime and fear.

Media and Criminal Justice

TELEVISION CRIME DRAMAS AND THE CAUSES OF HOMICIDE

Crime-oriented programs are among the most popular forms of entertainment on television. TV newsmagazines, televised trials, "reality" police shows, and crime dramas can be found every night on many different channels. *NYPD Blue* and *Homicide: Life in the Streets* are two popular examples. Crime dramas are fictional and are created to entertain viewers. It is likely that fact-based crime shows also serve primarily to entertain rather than inform, given their propensity to feature the most sensational and violent cases. Many people, however, derive a significant part of what they know about crime from crime dramas; most people do not have personal experience with violent crime.[a]

Most crime dramas focus on homicides. This emphasis runs counter to the fact that homicide is by far the least common serious crime. Television crime dramas also devote very little time to the causes of the criminal behavior depicted, often resorting to "blind passions, crazy plots, and references to magic, if not to clinical madness,"[b] while simultaneously placing great emphasis on careful, scientific gathering and analysis of evidence. These contradictions between media images of crime and its reality have given rise to increasing criticism of the media's role in creating inaccurate public perceptions.

In 1997 a study was published on the content of all episodes of regularly scheduled network television crime dramas over a period of six weeks. A total of sixty-nine programs were studied. (Movies, news broadcasts, reruns, magazine shows, "reality" police shows, and comedies that dealt with crime were excluded.) The study found that most programs left viewers "with the impression that homicides were the consequences of idiosyncratic behavior; the result of vague and indeterminate causes, often perpetrated by 'people who were killers'; and generally unconnected to events of the past or present that might otherwise account for the behavior."[c] The programs made virtually no attempt to account for the homicidal behavior in terms of the offender's social background, past experiences, deprivations, or failure to develop moral values; nor did they consider the deterrent influences of the criminal law. In two-thirds of the crime dramas reviewed, the most common plot motives were greed, mental illness, self-protection, murder for hire, vengeance, or jilting by a friend or lover.

Such a portrayal suggests that homicide stems from individual characteristics and circumstances and that larger social factors are irrelevant. The viewer comes away with the notion that homicide offenders are different from the rest of us. Rarely is an effort made to provide insight into why most people, when placed in similar situations, do not commit (or even consider) homicide. The result over the long term may be to lead us to see law-abiding people as "us" and offenders as "them"—with no thought to the influences and motivations that are common to all of us.

If many people base their views about the causes and prevention of homicide on television crime dramas, what will be the impact of the increasing numbers of these programs that are being broadcast on an increasing number of channels?

NOTES

a. E. Mandel, *Delightful Murder* (Minneapolis: University of Minnesota Press, 1984), p. 43.

b. Ray Surette, *The Media and Criminal Justice: Images and Reality* (Pacific Grove, CA: Brooks/Cole, 1992).

c. David Fabianic, "Television Dramas and Homicide Causation," *Journal of Criminal Justice* 25 (1997), p. 200.

What Is Crime?

**FELONIES AND
MISDEMEANORS**

crimes
Forms of conduct that
society prohibits in order
to maintain order.

criminal law
A code that categorizes all
crimes and punishments
by type.

felonies
Serious crimes that are punishable by incarceration for
more than one year.

misdemeanors
Less serious crimes that are
punishable by imprisonment
for one year or less.

Crime is a natural phenomenon, because people have different levels of attachment, motivation, and virtue. If people are to live in society successfully, however, rules are required to make sure they can live together
peacefully with a high degree of order. Of course, there will always be some
people who do not obey the rules. Therefore, the rules must carry penalties
to serve both as a warning and as an enforcement mechanism. Rules that
prohibit certain forms of conduct so as to maintain social order identify a
set of behaviors termed **crimes,** which form the basis of the **criminal law.**
Violations of the criminal law are considered crimes against society because
they break rules designed for the common good. That is to say, the rules el-
evate the good of the community over the desires of any given individual.
Without such a system, anarchy would prevail as individuals competed to
fulfill their own wants and needs without regard for those of others.

The distinction between serious and nonserious crimes is related to the
possible sentences that can be imposed. Serious crimes that are punishable
by incarceration for more than one year are called **felonies** in most states.
Less serious crimes that are punishable by imprisonment for one year or less
are called **misdemeanors.**

As a general rule, criminal laws prohibit only acts or omissions of acts. Thus,
it is a crime to strike or steal from someone without a compelling justification. Omissions that constitute crimes are rare; they include forms of inaction
such as *failure to stop* for a stop sign or *failure to file* your income tax return.

Historical and Political Contexts of Crime

The history of U.S. criminal law is a history of change. Some acts that were
once against the law later became lawful (e.g., profanity, sale of alcoholic beverages after Prohibition). Other acts that were once lawful later
became illegal (e.g., possession of slaves, sale of alcoholic beverages
during Prohibition). Are such changes random, depending only on the
whims of legislators? Or do they reflect true changes in public views of
certain acts? Moreover, are there "fundamental" crimes that do not change
over time?

As a society grows larger, it becomes less and less feasible for all citizens
to participate in the daily operation of government. In a representative government, the people elect representatives to direct governmental affairs on
their behalf. These governmental affairs include the defining and punishing of crimes. It has been argued that government "creates" or selectively
enforces some crimes without the consent of the public in order to protect
the government from perceived threats to its existence. During times of

war, conflict, or civil unrest, the government has sometimes used its legislative and enforcement powers to persecute alleged enemies rather than to seek justice.

During the post–World War II era there were instances in which government overzealously identified crimes and criminals, causing several miscarriages of justice. In 1949 the infamous "Tokyo Rose" was convicted of treason for broadcasting propaganda to U.S. troops in the Pacific. She was sentenced to ten years in prison on the basis of dubious evidence.[20] During the 1950s, the era of McCarthyism, many reputations were destroyed through false charges of communist association by U.S. Senator Joseph McCarthy.[21] In 1951 this hysteria resulted in the trial of Julius and Ethel Rosenberg for allegedly giving U.S. nuclear secrets to the Soviet Union. On debatable evidence the Rosenbergs were convicted of espionage and sentenced to death.[22] The Vietnam War produced a similar outcry against perceived anti-American sentiment, with aggressive prosecutions of draft dodgers and antiwar protestors.[23]

The **criminalization** or **decriminalization** of certain behaviors, and the public's reaction to them, continue to make the application of the law controversial. Thus, when four Los Angeles police officers were acquitted in the beating of black motorist Rodney King, a riot erupted that lasted several days. When Timothy McVeigh was charged in the bombing of the federal office building in Oklahoma City in 1995, many believed that antigovernment militias were unfairly investigated and treated as suspects. In the Rodney King case, the *failure* of the government to treat questionable police behavior as criminal caused the public outcry. In the Oklahoma City case, it was the government's *action* to criminalize the activities of groups opposed to the government that caused division among the public. These debates have not been completely resolved, and the public is likely to remain divided and wary of the role of government in creating and administering the law.

Definitions of crime can therefore be viewed as evidence of development in social and political history, because they emerge from the public and political concerns that characterize different historical periods. For example, in 1920 the Eighteenth Amendment to the U.S. Constitution went into effect, banning the manufacture, transportation, or sale of alcoholic beverages to any person of any age. This policy, Prohibition, was enforced by the Volstead Act, passed by Congress in the same year. One can imagine what would happen if such a law were in effect today. Prohibition failed to recognize

CRIMINALIZATION AND DECRIMINALIZATION

■**criminalization**
The legislative decision to make a behavior a crime.

■**decriminalization**
The legislative decision to change a crime into a noncriminal act.

What factors led to the criminalization of the buying and selling of alcoholic beverages in the 1920s and the decriminalization of these acts in the 1930s? Did Prohibition reduce alcohol abuse? What unintended negative social consequences did Prohibition foster? Do you think Prohibition addressed a "victimless" crime? Why or why not?

SOCIAL AND
POLITICAL HISTORY

VICTIMLESS CRIMES

■victimless crimes
Offenses in which the
"offender" and "victim"
are the same individual
or in which behavior is
consensual.

the demand for liquor, and it is not surprising that millions of people manufactured, sold, and bought alcoholic beverages in violation of the law. In
1933 the Eighteenth Amendment was repealed by the Twenty-first Amendment, which permits the sale of alcoholic beverages under the regulated system that exists today.

What caused the outright prohibition of such a desired commodity? For
a brief period in U.S. history, the temperance movement's intolerance of *all*
liquor consumption garnered enough political support to bring about the enactment of Prohibition and the Volstead Act.[24] As the history of Prohibition
illustrates, however, laws passed without widespread public support are ultimately changed. Therefore, control of the political process results in only
temporary changes; it is necessary to have true public support for laws to
be effective.

Although it may be said that Prohibition did in fact reduce liquor consumption in the United States, there are no reliable estimates of the true
extent of the illegal manufacture and sale of alcoholic beverages from 1920
to 1933.[25] The criminalization of a desired product may have an impact on
when, where, and how one consumes it, but it usually does not affect
whether one consumes it. The law is remarkably ineffective when it comes
to so-called **victimless crimes** in which the "offender" and the "victim" are
the same individual.

Though laws without public support are sometimes passed (and invariably changed or left unenforced), such temporary attempts to mold social
history rather than to respond to it can exact a high price. Thousands of people were arrested and convicted during Prohibition. In 1924 alone, more than
22,000 cases related to liquor were pending in the federal courts.[26] When it
became apparent during the late 1920s that Prohibition was not working,
the government did what governments often do when a "crime" problem
appears out of control: It increased the penalties for violation (through the
Jones Act). The result was additional thousands of arrests for liquor law
violations.

An even more pernicious result of unpopular laws is the creation of black
markets. Studies have found that Prohibition was responsible for the creation of organized criminal syndicates, some of which still exist today. The
influence of Al Capone and Johnny Torrio in Chicago and the beginnings of
the Cosa Nostra in New York can be traced to Prohibition.[27] In addition, a
great deal of public corruption in Chicago, New York, and other cities was
rooted in Prohibition.

The Prohibition experience has been paralleled in many ways by the ebb
and flow of laws against gambling, drugs, and prostitution—the other consensual crimes in which the line between offender and victim is not clear
or does not exist at all. In different sociocultural contexts these "vices" have
alternatively been defined as crimes, highly regulated behaviors, or mere
leisure activities. The contemporary difficulties with the prosecution of the
"war on drugs" have many similarities to what occurred during the 1920s,
when alcohol was the drug of choice.

Mala in Se, Mala Prohibita, **and Criminal Harm**

Are there some behaviors that are objectively and inherently criminal, regardless of when and where they occur? It appears that there are. Although the criminal law had its origins among the ancient Greeks and Romans, the primary source of U.S. criminal law is England's common law. Under common law, crimes were seen as being of two types. Acts were considered either as ***mala in se*** (evil as themselves) or as ***mala prohibita*** (simply prohibited by law). *Mala in se* offenses include serious crimes of assault and theft, such as murder, rape, robbery, larceny, and burglary. *Mala prohibita* offenses are the result of legislative decisions to prohibit certain undesirable behaviors, such as alcohol use, drunkenness, drug use, and gambling.

■ ***mala in se***
Acts considered evil in themselves (e.g., assault and theft).

■ ***mala prohibita***
Acts considered undesirable although not inherently evil (e.g., drug use).

The number of *mala in se* offenses has remained fairly constant over the centuries. That is, acts that are identified as evil nearly always involve crimes against persons or property. In fact, crimes of assault (murder, rape, robbery) and theft (burglary and larceny) are illegal in societies of all types. This universality of certain serious crimes demonstrates that crime is not entirely a subjective phenomenon, nor is it arbitrarily defined by particular nations during particular historical periods. From the earliest years of recorded history, basic acts of assault and theft have been criminalized in most of their forms.

The reasons for this uniformity are fascinating. For example, if the law against murder were abolished tomorrow, it is unlikely that the murder rate would increase. This is because a strong moral force exists independently of the law. The law against murder merely reinforces a strongly held community sentiment. The same is true of all crimes of assault. It is doubtful that assault would become common if criminal laws against it did not exist. The same is true for crimes of theft, although thefts are perceived as less serious than assaults (which is probably why they are more common). Clearly, then, there exist crimes that transcend the boundaries of time and place.

It is sometimes argued that *no* acts are inherently criminal. For example, abortion is considered murder in Ireland but is not so defined in most other nations. Revenge killings also were permitted in some societies in earlier times.[28] But as governments became more competent and better able to protect citizens, the need for revenge killings disappeared. There is now consensus in most societies that the government's criminal justice system is able to determine justice more objectively and safely than revenge killings. Likewise, scientific knowledge regarding when human life begins in the womb (made possible through technological advances) has complicated the abortion debate, as has the need to balance the competing interests of the mother and child in light of society's long-term interests. So while the cases of abortion and revenge killings may *modify* the scope of the definition of murder, they do not cause it to appear or disappear from the criminal law.

MALA PROHIBITA

■**offenses against morality**
Acts that are seen as immoral, such as adultery and fornication, prostitution, and gambling.

■**political crimes**
Acts viewed as a threat to the government.

REGULATORY OFFENSES

■**regulatory offenses**
Activities of a business or corporate nature that are viewed as a threat to public health, safety, or welfare.

OVERCRIMINAL-IZATION

■**overcriminalization**
Blurring of the distinction between crime and merely inappropriate or offensive behaviors.

On the other hand, the number of *mala prohibita* offenses has grown dramatically in the United States. These offenses can be grouped into three general categories: crimes without victims, political offenses, and regulatory offenses. Crimes without victims are offenses in which the offender and the "victim" engage in the act voluntarily. This category of offenses has been increasing steadily in recent years. Sometimes called **offenses against morality,** these acts include adultery and fornication, prostitution, gambling, the use and selling of drugs, and drunkenness, among others. Another expanding category consists of **political crimes,** which include any act that is viewed as a threat to the government. These activities may involve treason, sedition, espionage, sabotage, and bribery. None of these political crimes are *mala in se* offenses, because they are not necessarily evil. Many of those who engage in these activities believe that they are acting justly against an unjust government. As the history of the United States illustrates, today's revolutionary can sometimes become tomorrow's hero. Therefore, political crimes are acts not necessarily bad in themselves.

A third type of *mala prohibita* offense that has grown dramatically in recent years is criminality produced through the powers delegated by Congress or state legislatures. These **regulatory offenses** are usually activities of a business or corporate nature that are viewed as a threat to public health, safety, or welfare. These offenses are violations of laws regulating pollution levels, workplace safety, the manufacture of unsafe products, and other aspects of business. They are crimes created by regulatory agencies as part of the agencies' effort to oversee certain activities of business enterprises. Regulatory offenses often change over time as acceptable levels of pollution, acceptable employee exposure to risk, and allowable margins for safety in consumer products evolve. Examples of regulatory agencies include the Federal Trade Commission, the Federal Communications Commission, the Consumer Product Safety Commission, the Food and Drug Administration, and the Environmental Protection Agency.

The increase in *mala prohibita* offenses has raised concern that the distinction between crime and merely inappropriate or offensive behaviors may be becoming blurred, a phenomenon called **overcriminalization.** Overcriminalization may dilute the moral force of the law if the law comes to be regarded as petty and intrusive rather than as a necessary means of social control.

It can be seen, therefore, that *mala in se* offenses are common to all societies. They differ only in regard to the breadth of their definitions (e.g., inclusion or exclusion of abortion from the definition of murder). *Mala prohibita* offenses vary widely over time, among societies, and sometimes even *within* societies. In the United States, for example, there is great variation in the extent to which gambling and marijuana use are considered crimes. Table 1.6 illustrates the three types of *mala prohibita* offenses and their differences.

Mala prohibita and *mala in se* offenses are distinct both in their substance and in the nature of the harm they cause. *Mala prohibita* offenses

TABLE 1.6

A Typology of *Mala Prohibita* Offenses

TYPE OF OFFENSE	NATURE OF OFFENSE	EXAMPLES
Victimless crimes	Offenses against morality involving consensual acts between offender and victim.	Gambling, prostitution, drug offenses.
Political crimes	Acts viewed as threats to the government.	Espionage, bribery, treason.
Regulatory offenses	Acts viewed as threats to public health, safety, and welfare.	Inadequate food and drug labeling or usage warnings, unsafe products.

cause harm that violates moral, business, or political principles. In the case of victimless crimes the offense is usually moral and consensual in nature. Gambling, prostitution, and most drug offenses are of this type. Unfairness in business is the typical harm in regulatory offenses. Price-fixing, bid rigging, and manufacturing shortcuts violate the principles of free markets. Betrayal of a government principle is the harm caused by political crimes. Treason and sedition are examples. In each of these cases of *mala prohibita* offenses, *violation of principles* is the focus of concern.

For *mala in se* offenses the harm is more personal and direct. All variations of assault, rape, and homicide result in physical harm to the victim in addition to violation of generally accepted moral principles. Burglary and theft involve loss and violation of property in addition to transgression of moral rules. Therefore, the seriousness of *mala in se* offenses is manifested by the physical loss or harm that they cause. *Mala prohibita* offenses involve violation of moral, business, or political principles, but they do not entail *direct physical loss or harm*. It is the harm caused by mala in se offenses that results in their central position in discussions of crime and justice.

Criminalization of Behavior

As the case of Prohibition makes clear, the ability to *create* crime through the actions of government is cause for concern. In assessing current events or historical ones, how can we determine the extent to which changes in the law truly reflect social consensus or are merely the fruits of lobbying efforts that try to shape political action? One way to determine this is to examine the enforcement of newly enacted laws. Take the 55-mph speed limit, for example. It was enacted in the 1970s in an effort to promote fuel economy; but it was not enforced, and eventually the speed limit was raised in most states. The point is that it is impossible to enforce a law if it is violated by large numbers of people. Other laws have had similar fates. Still others, however, are actively enforced because the public wants them to be enforced.

contemporary issues and trends

Obscenity: Sex or Violence?

bscenity and pornography constitute a "vice" with which the law has had difficulty over the years. To what extent should they be criminalized? And, more important, what precisely *are* they?

The First Amendment to the U.S. Constitution, ratified in 1791, protects freedom of religion, freedom of the press, the right to assemble peacefully, and the right to petition the government; it also states that "Congress shall make no law . . . abridging the freedom of speech." The Supreme Court held early on that the First Amendment did not apply to *all* speech. The case of obscenity has been troublesome, however, because obscenity is very difficult to define. As Justice Stewart of the Supreme Court remarked in 1964, "Perhaps I could never succeed in intelligibly" defining obscenity. "But I know it when I see it."[a]

THE MILLER CASE

The U.S. Supreme Court settled on the current legal definition of obscenity in the case of *Miller v. California*.[b] Marvin Miller had conducted a mass mailing to advertise four books titled *Intercourse, Man–Woman, Sex Orgies Illustrated*, and *An Illustrated History of Pornography*. The brochures consisted primarily of pictures and drawings "very explicitly depicting men and women in groups of two or more engaging in a variety of sexual activities, with genitals often prominently displayed." The legal action resulted from a complaint to the police from a person who had been sent five of these unsolicited brochures.

In its decision, the Supreme Court stated that obscenity exists when the average person, applying contemporary community standards, would find that the work *(a)* "taken as a whole, appeals to the prurient interest in sex"; *(b)* portrays sexual conduct (specifically defined by state law) in a "patently offensive way"; and *(c)* "taken as a whole, lacks serious literary, artistic, political, or scientific value." Examples of what state laws could define as obscene included "patently offensive representations of ultimate sexual acts, normal or perverted, actual or simulated" as well as "masturbation, excretory functions, and lewd exhibition of genitals."

The Court has decided more than thirty cases on obscenity-related issues since *Miller*.[c] These cases involved determinations of obscenity in adult films shown to an adult audience, the mainstream film *Carnal Knowledge*, a George Carlin monologue, child pornography cases, and reviews of state laws. But the Court has not uniformly applied such concepts as "serious value," "prurient interest," and "community standards" as set forth in *Miller*, illustrating the inadequacy of that definition of obscenity.

ALCOHOL

In the continuing effort to establish the limits of acceptable behavior, the *mala prohibita* offenses of alcohol consumption, commercialized sex, gambling, and drug use have drawn the most attention over the years. Throughout the nation's history, alcohol consumption has been viewed alternately as a vice, an evil, a crime, or a leisure activity. In the 1980s the attack on alcohol consumption began anew with the campaign mounted by Mothers Against Drunk Driving (MADD). MADD was founded by a mother whose teenage daughter had been killed in an automobile crash. The accident was caused by a man with two prior drunk driving convictions who was out on bail on a third charge. MADD became a powerful political lobbying group, because it addressed the already widespread belief that drunk driving was not adequately criminalized. The 1980s began an anti–drunk driving era in which some states increased penalties for drunk driving, establishing mandatory prison sentences and suspending the licenses of violators. In 1984 the federal government established rules that forced every state to raise

A NEW APPROACH
TO AN OLD PROBLEM

Two different approaches might be taken to unravel the continuing complexities in obscenity law. The first would legalize obscenity, prohibiting only its exposure to juveniles and nonconsenting adults. The second approach would be to move the focus of obscenity law from sex to violence.

The first approach was proposed by Justice Brennan in 1973 in his dissenting opinion (expressing the views of a four-justice minority) in *Paris Adult Theater I v. Slaton*.[d] Brennan proposed that the law not be permitted "to suppress sexually oriented material on the basis of their allegedly 'obscene' contents" unless the material was distributed or obtrusively exposed to juveniles or nonconsenting adults. This approach would protect the First Amendment right of free speech while avoiding the vagueness inherent in general tests for obscenity. A similar proposal was recommended by the U.S. Commission on Obscenity and Pornography in 1970.[e]

A second approach to obscenity law would be to prohibit the depiction of gratuitous *violence*, rather than sex.[f] Depictions of violent, assaultive behavior that is exhibited without legal justification would be held objectionable and punishable under law. Legal justifications for the use of force (e.g., self-defense, defense of others, etc.) are well defined in existing law, as are the definitions of assault. Such a test for obscenity might include photographs or broadcasts depicting assaultive behavior committed without legal justification. The only exception would be factual accounts of real events, which have informational or educational value. This definition of obscenity would avoid the problems inherent in efforts to determine the level of "offensiveness" of depictions of sex and would focus instead on depictions of *assaultive* conduct, making concern about depictions of sex secondary to concern about depictions of violence.

> The Court has decided more than thirty cases on obscenity-related issues since *Miller.*

NOTES

a. *Jacobellis v. Ohio*, 84 S.Ct. 1676 (1964).

b. 93 S.Ct. 1243 (1973).

c. Joseph F. Kobylka, *The Politics of Obscenity* (Westport, CT: Greenwood Press, 1991).

d. *Paris Adult Theatre v. Slaton*, 93 S.Ct. 2662 (1973).

e. U.S. Commission on Obscenity and Pornography, *Report* (Washington, DC: U.S. Government Printing Office, 1970).

f. Jay S. Albanese, "Looking for a New Approach to an Old Problem," in R. Muraskin and A. R. Roberts, eds., *Visions for Change: Crime and Justice in the Twenty-first Century*, 2nd ed. (Upper Saddle River, NJ: Prentice Hall, 1999), pp. 60–72.

---

its drinking age from eighteen to twenty-one. Drunk driving awareness programs became common throughout the United States.

The selling of sex for money has existed at least as long as alcohol consumption, gambling, and the other "vices." Historically, prostitution was seen as an undesirable behavior, and that view continues today. The only disagreement lies in opinions about whether criminalization is the best way to address it. Since the late 1960s the rise of the women's movement and the work of the National Organization for Women (NOW) have cast prostitution in a new light. NOW condemned the exploitation of women but in 1971 came out in favor of decriminalizing prostitution.[29] Today Nevada licenses prostitution on a county-by-county basis in jurisdictions with fewer than 400,000 residents, but other states have not followed suit. It appears that public sentiment still favors the criminalization of prostitution, although this sentiment may be due to the lack of noncriminal alternatives that do not appear immoral to a large segment of the public.

PROSTITUTION

Is prostitution considered a *mala in se* or a *mala prohibita* offense? Why? How could you argue that selling sex is or is not inherently criminal? What other behaviors are categorized today as offenses against morality? In any one case, under what circumstances might that behavior become inconsistently treated as criminal or even decriminalized at some time in the future?

GAMBLING

Gambling encompasses games of chance, in which the outcome is determined by luck rather than skill. Like prostitution, gambling has existed throughout recorded history. Biblical accounts of the Crucifixion include an anecdote about four soldiers who each wanted Jesus's robe. They resolved the dispute by saying, "Let's not tear it; let's throw dice to see who will get it."[30] Gambling was also popular among the Native Americans: The Onondaga and the Iroquois wagered using dice.[31] The Narragansett and the Chumash often gambled for days in games in which "the worldly goods of entire tribes might change hands."[32]

Lotteries were the most popular form of gambling in the American colonies. The Virginia Company of London was given permission to conduct lottery drawings in England to help fund its plantation in Virginia—yet at the same time it attempted to reduce gambling in Virginia. Reports of "gaming, idleness, and vice" were rampant, and antigambling ordinances became part of Jamestown's first legal code.[33] Nevertheless, gambling remained popular.

This particular dichotomy, in which gambling was encouraged for one purpose (public funding) but viewed as dissolute for another (recreation), provides an early illustration of how attitudes toward gambling have vacillated throughout history. The Puritans of Massachusetts saw gambling as an "appearance of evil" and therefore irreligious.[34] Like Virginia, Massachusetts and other colonies passed laws that attempted to limit or prohibit gambling; but despite these laws gambling (especially card and dice games) continued.[35] During the early 1700s, when funds were needed for public works (e.g., schools and roads), many northeastern colonies started lotteries to raise the required funds. This example shows again how gambling has been viewed as either a vice or a virtue, depending on how the profits are used.

Public sentiment toward gambling has been marked by indifference. Despite periodic scandals and moral crusades, the "now it's legal, now it's not" history of gambling reflects public attention or inattention to the issue, rather than indignation. Today gambling enjoys renewed popularity and legitimacy, largely as a way to boost local economies without raising taxes. Lotteries are legal in most states, and in a majority of the states casino gambling has been approved or is under active review. Like alcohol consumption, gambling is tolerated as a social vice largely because of the government's ability to profit from it (mostly through taxation). It appears that the only difference between legal and illegal gambling is whether or not the state is running the game.

NARCOTICS

Unlike gambling, narcotics distribution and use was generally not a crime until late in the nineteenth century. Although drug use was always considered a vice, during the 1800s the only laws addressing the consumption of drugs were those that criminalized opium use, which was associated largely with Chinese immigrants. Around the turn of the century, several states passed laws against morphine and cocaine use, but these laws were directed largely at pharmacists and physicians.[36]

The situation changed dramatically in the early twentieth century as intolerance for all the vices peaked. In 1914 Congress passed the Harrison Narcotic Drug Act, which added cocaine to the list of drugs whose use was subject to severe restrictions. Prohibition began in 1920, and during the following decade far fewer arrests were made for narcotics use than for violations of the liquor laws. However, evidence of continuing concern with narcotics can be seen in the establishment of the Federal Bureau of Narcotics (FBN) in 1930. The FBN led the crusade to add marijuana to the list of dangerous narcotics, a crusade that ultimately resulted in the Marijuana Tax Act of 1937.[37]

The prohibition of narcotics has continued ever since, highlighted by the formation of the Drug Enforcement Administration in 1973 and the creation in 1989 of the position of "drug czar" to head the Office of National Drug Policy. These initiatives further promoted the criminalization of narcotics, increasing the penalties for violations and emphasizing law enforcement approaches to controlling the problem. It is interesting that despite the moderation of public attitudes toward other vices during the late twentieth century, narcotics use is now criminalized more extensively than at any time in the nation's history (with the exception of marijuana laws in a few states).

The evidence suggests that drug usage decreased among most Americans in the 1990s but remains much worse among the poor and addicted.[38] Figure 1.1 shows that in 1997 11.4 percent of the population aged twelve to seventeen reported having used illicit drugs in the past month, compared to 14.7 percent of eighteen- to twenty-five-year-olds. Since 1985 the percentages of young people using drugs have declined, although there has been an upswing in drug use by youth since 1995. Ironically, the situation may well have been similar in the case of liquor usage during the Prohibition era. It is not clear that the intensive criminalization of narcotics has been responsible for changes in drug use, although it is undisputed that the illegal drug market has been exploited by organized crime—another unfortunate parallel to Prohibition. In the same way that alcohol use has declined in recent years as it has become a public health issue, drug use could also decline if it were defined as a health problem rather than as a crime.

In fact, several prominent conservatives have joined with liberals in advocating the legalization of drugs.[39] **Legalization** is unlikely to occur any time soon, however, because drugs still carry the same degree of stigma that prostitution does. It is difficult to imagine elected representatives

LEGALIZATION?

■**legalization**
Legislative action to remove a prohibited behavior from the criminal law.

FIGURE 1.1
Users of Cocaine, Marijuana, or Any Other Illicit Drug 1985–1997 by Age Group

SOURCE: 1997 National Household Survey on Drug Abuse.

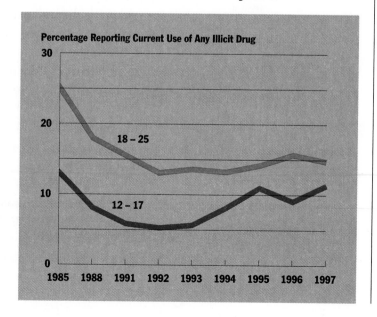

Percentage Reporting Current Use of Any Illicit Drug

voting in favor of any kind of legalization plan as long as they are afraid to give the appearance of supporting drug use. Nevertheless, this stigma has been overcome in the case of gambling, so legalization of drugs may be a matter of time. There is already abundant evidence of the ineffectiveness of police crackdowns, interdiction efforts, and attempts to eradicate drug production in source countries, as well as of the high economic and social costs of long-term imprisonment.[40] It is interesting to speculate as to whether today's war on drugs will be discussed seventy-five years from now in the same way that we now speak of the Prohibition era.

How Can Crime Be Explained?

Understanding the motives of criminal offenders is a central question in criminal justice, because all attempts to prevent and control crime are based on assumptions about its causes. Consider these questions, all of which arise from highly publicized actual crimes:[41]

- How can a mother kill her own children?

- How can children kill their own parents?

- How can a rapist be punished severely, released, and then do it again?

- How can young people commit brutal assaults without any provocation?

Questions such as these make it clear that we have a long way to go in understanding the causes of crime. During the twentieth century growing concern led to systematic study of the causes of crime, but this study has not discovered a uniform explanation. Some have argued that a single explanation should be able to account for all criminality, whereas others believe that different explanations are required for different types of crime and different offenders.[42] At present there are four general types of explanations of crime: classical, positivistic, structural, and ethical.

THE CLASSICAL SCHOOL

■ **classical school**
Perspective in criminology that sees crime as resulting from the conscious exercise of an individual's free will.

The **classical school** of thought in criminology sees crime as resulting from the conscious exercise of an individual's free will. Classicists see people as hedonists: They believe that all people pursue pleasure while attempting to minimize pain. Two of the best-known classicists, Cesare Beccaria and Jeremy Bentham, wrote during the eighteenth century.[43]

Classical thinking, sometimes called the free will school, dominated criminal codes during the nineteenth century because the law assumed that all people were equal in their capacity to guide their conduct rationally. If the law was violated, the punishment was based on the violation committed rather than on the type of person who committed it. This punishment was designed to deter future misconduct by the offender and by other members of society. Recent exponents of the classical explanation are Michael Gottfredson and Travis Hirschi; these criminologists believe that crime is a course of conduct chosen by individuals who have low self-control and are unable to defer immediate gratification of their desires.[44] Empirical studies continue to test the ability of classical explanations to account for the commission of crimes, but the results are inconsistent.[45]

Dissatisfaction with the classical school first appeared toward the end of the nineteenth century. Crime was seen as a growing problem, and punishment of violators apparently was not deterring others from committing criminal acts—a perception that remains widespread today, a century later. The late 1800s also witnessed the rise of the scientific method and the beginnings of social science. Charles Darwin developed his theory of evolution through natural selection, publishing it in his famous work *The Origin of Species*.[46] Emile Durkheim observed differences in rates of suicide in different regions of France. He used these observations to develop a theory of social factors in suicide.[47] Both Darwin and Durkheim were pioneers in the use of the scientific method, in which knowledge is advanced through observation rather than by theorizing without first gathering data.

This scientific approach to explanations gave rise to the positivist school of criminology. According to **positivism,** individual human behavior is determined by internal and external influences, which include biological, psychological, and/or social factors. Rather than seeing crime as the product of the rational exercise of free will, as classicists do, positivists see crime as largely determined by a variety of internal and external influences on a person. In many ways the positivist school in criminology emphasizes "nurture" (i.e., factors in the individual's environment), whereas the classical school emphasizes "nature" (i.e., a presupposed "natural" inborn tendency to seek pleasure and avoid pain).

Positivists believe that fundamental differences between criminals and noncriminals are based on these internal and external influences, which may include personality imbalances, family role models, and peer group pressure, among many others. From the positivist perspective all people are *not* equal, because the criminal act is seen as a symptom of an underlying problem rather than as the problem itself (the classicists' view). Instead of punishment, therefore, positivists see reform or rehabilitation of the offender as the best way to prevent future crime; they advocate changing the influences on an individual or changing how he or she reacts to those influences.

The **ethical view** sees crime as a moral failure in decision making. Simply stated, crime occurs when a person fails to *choose* the proper course of conduct; and this bad choice results from failure to appreciate an act's wrongfulness, rather than from lack of concern about being caught, as the classicists suggest. According to the ethical view, the positivist and classical

POSITIVISM

positivism
Perspective in criminology that sees human behavior as determined by internal and external influences, such as biological, psychological, and/or social factors.

THE ETHICAL VIEW

ethical view
Perspective in criminology that sees crime as a moral failure in decision making.

views are both inadequate. This is because external factors may play a role in influencing some people to engage in crime, but they do not *cause* crime (as positivists suggest). Although freely willed decisions lie at the base of virtually all criminal behavior, there is no hedonistic tendency to engage in crime that is controlled only through the possibility of apprehension (as classicists suggest). Instead, crime is caused by failure to appreciate the wrongfulness of criminal conduct; that is, the failure to appreciate its long-term impact both on the offender and on the community or victim.

In the ethical view, crime results when criminal acts bring pleasure rather than guilt. The key to understanding crime causation, then, lies in discovering *how* people make noncriminal choices. Stated another way, where do people learn to make decisions in accord with legal and ethical principles? Ethicists argue that most people are incapable of thinking through decisions in ethical terms, because ethical principles are rarely included in the educational process.[48] Lacking education or experience in ethical decision making, people often do what comes naturally: They base decisions on self-interest rather than on the greater interest of the community; they are concerned primarily with the short-term consequences of their decisions; and they confuse competing values such as honesty and loyalty. This tendency is shown by individuals who derive pleasure from short-changing a store clerk, shoplifting, participating in gang crimes, and engaging in vandalism and other crimes, rather than feeling guilt over their wrongful behavior or empathy for their victims. For example, a recent study of college students and prison inmates found the students were much more likely to feel bad or stressed about committing a crime, whereas the prison inmates were more likely to feel exhilarated or proud.[49] This finding suggests that greater appreciation of the wrongfulness of conduct (the basis for ethics) may be a bulwark against criminal behavior.

(handwritten margin note: crack = black people (poor))

THE STRUCTURAL/ CONFLICT VIEW

■ **structural/conflict view**
Perspective in criminology that sees the criminal law as reflecting the will of those in power and notes that behaviors that threaten the interests of the powerful are punished most severely.

A fourth approach to explaining crime, the **structural/conflict view,** focuses less on individual behavior and more on the behavior of law. That is to say, social, political, and economic conditions cause certain behaviors to be defined by the law as criminal. These conditions also cause the law to be applied in certain ways. As a result, those in power define a great deal of "marginal" behavior as criminal as a way to control people who are perceived as "undesirable." Laws against gambling, loan-sharking, and vagrancy are examples of the use of law as a tool of social control rather than as a means of protecting society from harm.

According to this structural or conflict view, the crime problem has roots deeper than the immediate environment or the pursuit of pleasure. This perspective sees the criminal law as reflecting the will of those in power, and notes that behaviors that threaten the interests of the powerful are punished most severely.[50] Thus, prisons are filled largely with poor and powerless people rather than with middle- and upper-class wrongdoers. According to conflict theory, there is little consensus within society on basic values, so the interests of the powerful are imposed through the criminal law and the manner in which it is enforced.[51] This explanation of crime clearly has merit in explaining politically or ideologically motivated crimes that are committed to protest some social, economic, or political condition. People who publicly refuse to pay their federal incomes taxes, or who protest mandated changes in the school curriculum by refusing to send their children to school, provide examples of the conflict view. In both cases it might be said that there is conflict regarding basic values and that the powerful (i.e., those who make the laws) have used their position to impose their values on society. On the other hand, the conflict view has less relevance in explaining murder, rape, robbery, assault, burglary, larceny, and many other crimes, which are rarely committed for ideological reasons.[52]

The tensions among the classical, positivist, ethical, and structural/conflict explanations of crime lie in their respective emphases. The positivist and structural explanations place most of the responsibility for crime on social factors that influence behavior. The classical and ethical explanations place most of the responsibility on individual decision making. The classicists place more emphasis on how the likelihood of apprehension and the threat of penalties (i.e., pain) control crime (i.e., the pursuit of pleasure), whereas the ethical view places more emphasis on the fact that crime (i.e., victimizing others) does not bring pleasure to ethical individuals.

Why is this person robbing this store and threatening people with personal harm and destruction of property? How might this crime be explained from the classical school of thought? How might a positivist explain it? What would be the ethical view? What would be the conflict view? Of these four explanations, which one or combination makes the most sense to you? Why?

Biological Determinism and Psychological Explanations

The earliest positivists saw the roots of criminal behavior in biological attributes, an approach known as **biological determinism.** Cesare Lombroso (1835–1909) took body measurements of offenders in Italian prisons and concluded that there were "born criminals" with distinctive body measurements and skull sizes. On the basis of his measurements, Lombroso developed a theory of *atavism* that suggested that "born criminals" were biological throwbacks to an earlier stage of human evolution.[53] In 1913, however, an English physician, Charles Goring, published the results of his measurements of 3,000 English convicts, which he had compared to similar measurements of a group of nonconvicts. Goring found no evidence of a distinct physical criminal type, thereby discrediting Lombroso's theory of atavism.[54]

Biological determinism did not die with Lombroso, however. Studies focusing on the body build of delinquents have been followed by investigations of chromosomal abnormalities, glandular dysfunction, chemical imbalances, and nutritional deficiencies. As measurement methods and techniques for assessing subtle biological differences have improved, interest in biological influences on crime has grown. Some criminologists now see links between certain biological features and a propensity to engage in crime.[55] Studies of twins raised separately, for example, have compared the incidence of their delinquent behavior, and studies of adopted children have compared their criminality to that of their biological parents. These studies suggest that genetic factors play some role in delinquency, but it is not clear that biological factors outweigh environmental factors.[56] A Panel on the Understanding and Control of Violent Behavior of the National Academy of Sciences concluded that biological studies have "produced mixed

■**biological determinism**
Positivistic view of criminal behavior as rooted in biological attributes.

remember

NATURAL-BORN CRIMINALS?

MALADJUSTED
PERSONALITIES?

■psychoanalytic theory
Freudian theory that behavior results from the interaction of the three components of the personality: id, ego, and superego.

results, suggesting at most a weak genetic influence on the chance of violent behavior."[57] Nevertheless, there is continuing interest in the interplay between biological predispositions and social influences on behavior. Such a biosocial approach attempts to link factors such as prenatal complications, malnutrition, brain dysfunction, poor attention span, hyperactivity, and low IQ with social "triggers," such as abuse, neglect, poverty, and antisocial role models, that may result in criminal violence.[58]

Psychological explanations of crime look inside the human psyche (or internalized controls) for the causes of crime. Instead of examining human physiology, psychologists look at how the human mind operates. The oldest and most influential psychological explanation of crime is based on the work of Sigmund Freud (1856–1939). Freud's **psychoanalytic theory** sees behavior as resulting from the interaction of the three components of the personality: id, ego, and superego. The id is defined as the primitive, instinctual drives of aggression and sex that everyone is born with. The superego acts as a person's conscience, reflecting the values one develops in the early years of life through interactions with family members. The ego mediates between the self-centered desires of the id and the learned values of the superego. The id, ego, and superego are theoretical constructs, of course; you cannot open someone's head and find them. Freud hypothesized their existence, attempting to demonstrate their presence through case studies of individuals' behavior.

Most explanations of crime based on Freud's theory see crime as resulting from faulty ego or superego structures that fail to control the id adequately. This results in personality imbalances, which produce deviant behavior. A weak or defective superego, for example, might result in "unsocialized aggressive behavior," in which a person has insufficient control over his or her aggressive or sexual instincts.[59] The conscience, in other words, is not sufficiently developed.

The ego and superego are said to develop by age six, and some psychologists believe it is difficult if not impossible to correct the damage caused when these components of the personality develop inadequately because of poor family relationships or other negative experiences during the early years.[60] Studies of juvenile murderers have found many to be "volatile" and "explosive" and some to be mentally ill as a result of personality problems that began during early childhood.[61] A study of 210 chronic delinquents found that those who committed violent crimes were more than twice as likely as their nondelinquent peers to have been exposed to serious physical abuse and to violence involving weapons between the adults in their household.[62] Prior exposure to violence may trigger psychological reactions that produce greater risk of delinquent behavior in the future.

Sociological Explanations

Sociological explanations of crime are more common than any other type. These approaches arose largely in response to the inability of biological and psychological explanations to account for many types of crime that appeared to be "normal" reactions of people raised in dysfunctional families or neighborhoods. Unlike biological or psychological explanations, which look at problems *within* the individual (whether physiological abnormalities or personality conflicts), sociological explanations look at *environmental* influences that affect the way people behave. Sociological explanations can be grouped into three types: theories based on learning, on blocked opportunity, or on the social bond to conventional society. I will summarize a leading theory of each type here.

THEORIES BASED ON LEARNING An influential sociological theory based on learning was proposed by Edwin Sutherland in 1939. Sutherland felt that delinquent behavior is learned in much the same way that people learn anything else: through observation, role modeling, and so forth. Sutherland called this learning process **differential association** and argued that a person becomes criminal or delinquent when he or she associates more with people who condone violation of the law than with people who do not. These attitudes toward the law are learned from intimate personal groups such as family, friends, and peers. Although everybody is exposed to procriminal and anticriminal attitudes, the *proportions* in which a person is exposed to these kinds of attitudes determine whether or not that individual will acquire those attitudes. Therefore, Sutherland does not speak of association with criminals or noncriminals but rather of association with those holding attitudes favorable to or tolerant of criminal behavior versus those who do not.[63] Subsequent researchers have investigated the link between juvenile associations and delinquency in order to determine how well the theory of differential association explains juvenile crime.[64] A study of chronic delinquents found that violent offenders were more likely to have experienced serious domestic violence and physical abuse. These juveniles were also more likely to believe that aggression has little impact on its victims and that it enhances one's self-image.[65] The results thus are mixed, suggesting that the differential association theory is a better explanation of the spread of delinquency than of its ultimate cause.

THEORIES BASED ON BLOCKED OPPORTUNITY Sociologists Richard Cloward and Lloyd Ohlin believed that delinquency and crime resulted from lack of access to legitimate means for achieving goals, or **blocked opportunity.** But they also felt that even illegitimate means are unevenly distributed in society. As a result, some lower-class neighborhoods provide greater opportunity for illegal gain than do others. Cloward and Ohlin did not believe that individuals substitute new goals; instead, they use illegitimate means to achieve accepted goals. Rather than getting a job and earning money to buy new shoes, for example, an individual may steal them. Cloward and Ohlin believed, however, that not all delinquents can attain their goals through illegitimate means, because the opportunities for doing so are not available to everyone—just as there are differences in the opportunities available to individuals to achieve these goals by legitimate means.

Cloward and Ohlin describe three types of **criminal subcultures** that develop when youths cease to adhere to middle-class standards.[66] Youths may

DIFFERENTIAL ASSOCIATION

■**differential association** Theory that a person becomes criminal or delinquent when he or she associates more with people who condone violation of the law than with people who do not.

ILLEGITIMATE MEANS

■**blocked opportunity** Theory that crime results from people's lack of access to legitimate means for achieving goals.

CRIMINAL SUBCULTURES

■**criminal subcultures** Different forms of deviance that result when youths cease to adhere to middle-class standards. Youths may become part of the adult *criminal* subculture, the *conflict* subculture, or the *retreatist* subculture.

LABELING DEVIANT BEHAVIOR

■ **labeling theory**
The view that adjudicating a juvenile as a delinquent serves to encourage future delinquency by generating a negative public identity or changed self-image.

■ **social bond**
An individual's attachment to society, which has four primary elements: attachment to others, commitment to conventional activities, involvement in conventional activities, and belief in widely shared moral values.

Take another look at the armed jewelry store burglar. Was he destined to commit this crime because of biological or psychological factors, or did environmental factors play a bigger role? What would Edwin Sutherland say caused him to become a criminal? What would Richard Cloward and Lloyd Ohlin say? According to Howard Becker, could his criminal behavior be the result of a self-fulfilling prophecy? According to Travis Hirschi, what failures of social bonding could account for his criminal behavior? Which of these four sociological explanations, or what combination thereof, makes the most sense to you? Why?

become part of the adult *criminal* subculture; they may participate in the *conflict* subculture by forming fighting gangs that emphasize violence and seek status by coercion; or they may become part of the *retreatist* subculture when either no opportunities exist in the criminal subculture or status cannot be obtained in the conflict group. Cloward and Ohlin maintain not only that legitimate opportunities for success are often blocked for lower-class juveniles but that illegitimate opportunities can also be blocked, leading to the creation of one of these types of delinquent subcultures.

LABELING THEORY Sociologist Howard Becker popularized **labeling theory** in his 1963 book *The Outsiders*. Originally put forth in 1951 by Edwin Lemert, labeling theory holds that "when society acts negatively to a particular individual (by adjudicating a person through the criminal justice system) by means of the 'label' (delinquent)—we actually encourage future delinquency." For Lemert and Becker the labeling process depends less on the behavior of the delinquent than on how others respond to delinquents' acts.[67] It is society's labeling of the individual (through adjudication of delinquency) that promotes deviant behavior, rather than any action by the juvenile. For example, a juvenile who is suspended from school or adjudicated in court as a delinquent gains a bad reputation. This bad reputation lowers the behavioral expectations of others (e.g., teachers, parents, friends). Also, the juvenile internalizes this reputation and acts in accord with it, resulting in more of the bad behavior everyone expects. According to this view, juveniles who are labeled as delinquents are actually encouraged to commit future acts of delinquency through the lowered expectations of others and their own changed self-image. The more frequent and prolonged the individual's contacts with the juvenile justice system, the more likely it is that he or she will ultimately accept the delinquent label as a personal identity and perhaps enter a life of crime.

STRENGTH OF THE SOCIAL BOND A third type of sociological explanation of crime is based on the individual's bond to society. When that bond is weakened or broken, the constraints that society places on the individual are also weakened or broken. As a result, this theory suggests, the person becomes more likely to break the law. A person's **social bond** has four primary elements: attachment to others, commitment to conventional activities, involvement in conventional activities, and belief in widely shared moral values.

In an attempt to test social bond theory, sociologist Travis Hirschi administered a self-report survey to 4,000 junior and senior high school students in California. He found that strong attachments to parents, commitment to values, involvement in school, and respect for police and law reduced the likelihood of delinquency. Replications of this study in Albany, New York, and elsewhere have generally supported Hirschi's results.[68]

It is clear that sociological explanations of crime far outnumber psychological or biological explanations. This is because a far greater number of social influences can be identified and measured. Also, each person's social environment is different and changes over time, making sociological explanations popular among positivists.

ATTACHMENT
THEORY

What Are Some Correlates of Crime?

Regardless of one's perspective on the causes of criminal activity, however, there is agreement that guns and drugs are frequent correlates of crime. The disagreement occurs in determining precisely how to counteract these dangerous associations among crime, guns, and drugs.

Guns

Few issues in criminal justice provoke more boisterous debate than the connection between guns and crime. The incidence of crimes involving guns is extremely high, but it is not clear whether the absence of guns would necessarily reduce the rates of violent crime. If all guns disappeared tomorrow, would violent crime disappear? Would it be significantly reduced?

Crime involves a decision by an individual. It is unlikely that a gun determines this decision, but it is possible that the presence of a gun may give a potential offender the "courage" to proceed with a crime he or she might not otherwise commit. This is what much of the **gun control** debate is about. To what extent would better control of guns result in better control of crime?

According to victimization surveys, 29 percent of victims of rape, robbery, and aggravated assault faced an offender with a firearm.[69] In 86 percent of these cases, the offender used a handgun. According to the Uniform Crime Reports, 70 percent of murders are committed with firearms,[70] and 81 percent of these involve handguns. It is clear that murder is the only crime of violence that is committed principally with guns, although handguns are the firearm of choice among criminals using weapons for all types of offenses.

Despite the relatively low rate of gun use for violent crimes other than murder, efforts to keep guns away from criminals are hotly debated. Proposals to reduce the availability of guns for criminal use most often involve one or more of the following: banning handguns altogether for most citizens; banning assault weapons; banning the carrying of weapons; banning certain kinds of bullets; and imposing mandatory sentences for crimes using guns. A brief examination of these alternative proposals illustrates why they have had limited success.

Several cities have banned handguns for nearly all citizens except police officers; Washington, D.C., is the largest of these cities. However, the impact

■gun control
Regulation of gun manufacturers, buyers, and sellers in an effort to minimize gun-related crime.

CRIMES WITH
HANDGUNS

GUN CONTROL?

on crimes committed with handguns has been negligible,[71] for two reasons. The first is that local gun control laws are unlikely to be effective when guns are readily available in bordering jurisdictions. The classic case is that of John Hinckley, who bought a gun in another jurisdiction, brought it to Washington, and shot President Reagan. The second reason is that there are an estimated 70 million handguns in the United States. Even though most are owned by law-abiding citizens, guns often find their way into the hands of criminals.

In the twentieth century more than 220 million guns were manufactured in or imported to the United States. Since 1973 alone, more than 40 million handguns have been produced in the this country.[72] It is not known what percentage of these guns have been lost, seized, stolen, or destroyed, but it is reasonable to believe that most are still in working order. A survey of inmates in state prisons found that 9 percent had stolen a gun and 28 percent had acquired a gun illegally from a fence or drug dealer.[73] Interviews with juvenile and adult inmates in other studies have found that between 10 and 50 percent have stolen a gun at some point in their criminal career.[74] In fact, the FBI's National Crime Information Center listed more than 300,000 *reported* incidents of stolen guns, ammunition, cannons, and grenades in a single year.[75] Of the guns stolen, almost 60 percent were handguns. Thus, other than increasing the black market price for stolen handguns, attempts to ban handguns will have little impact in the foreseeable future.

A second proposal is to ban assault weapons. Such a ban is even less likely to lower crime rates, because criminals rarely use these weapons to commit crimes. As noted earlier, 81 percent of murders with guns are committed with handguns, and most of the remainder do not involve assault weapons. A ban on assault weapons would have extremely little impact on gun crimes, even if the assault weapons now in circulation could be effectively monitored, something that is not currently possible. The National Firearms Act requires that all automatic weapons be registered with the Bureau of Alcohol, Tobacco, and Firearms. In 1995 more than 240,000 automatic weapons were legally registered, and nearly 8 percent of these were reported as stolen.[76]

A third approach is to restrict severely the unauthorized carrying of a handgun. The idea behind these laws is that handguns are easily carried and concealed. Interviews with convicted offenders show that many purchased a gun for self-defense, left home without intending to commit a crime, but ended up using the gun while committing a crime.[77] Many states have made it illegal to carry a handgun without a special license. The penalty is a mandatory sentence of one year in prison, simply for illegally carrying the weapon. In Massachusetts, gun crimes decreased after the handgun law was enacted, but assaults with other kinds of weapons increased, suggesting a "substitution effect" in weapon choice. Also, murders and robberies with guns decreased in Boston, but over the same period they also decreased in cities without such prohibitions.[78] These findings suggest that guns are an *accompaniment* to crime rather than a causal influence.

A fourth proposal is to ban bullets. Such bans have been proposed several times, mostly in relation to armor-piercing bullets that would be dangerous to police. Few criminals have been caught with such dangerous bullets, and no police officer has yet been killed with them, so it is not clear how common they really are.[79] The problem is that bullets are easily manufactured at home by the enterprising citizen, whether hunter or criminal. Therefore, a ban on bullets "would stimulate a sizable cottage industry" of bullet making.[80]

The fifth tactic is to impose mandatory sentences for crimes committed with guns. Many states and cities have passed laws increasing the penalties for these offenses. Evaluations of their impact reveal that these sentencing laws have had little effect, because the criminals involved were already receiving severe sentences.[81] Simply stated, offenders who commit crimes with guns already receive severe sentences (for the robbery, assault, or murder they committed). The impact of a gun law that adds a year or two in prison is insignificant in comparison.

It is clear that these five frequently heard proposals are flawed, for a variety of reasons. The debate could focus instead on one fundamental issue: How can we keep guns out of the hands of juveniles, criminals, and the mentally ill? Provisions for background checks at the point of sale are often minimal; the records that are supposedly checked (to determine criminality or mental illness) are incomplete; and many gun sales occur between private owners and hence are beyond the practical reach of regulation. But closer surveillance of gun sales would entail costs that U.S. society appears unwilling to pay. The gun control debate therefore focuses almost entirely on criminal penalties. Proposals to sue gun manufacturers, require gun insurance, and establish gun-free zones around schools tend to replace more serious discussion of the connection between guns and crime.[82] However, until point-of-sale checks (both retail and private) are monitored more effectively and the criminal and mental health records on which background checks are based are made more accurate, it will be impossible to keep guns away from criminals, juveniles, and the mentally ill.

Where did these youths get this weapon? What are the chances that they will commit violent crimes? Who will be their likely victims? What solutions have been proposed for keeping handguns and assault weapons away from juveniles, criminals, and the mentally ill? Which solutions do you favor? Do you think violent crime could be significantly reduced through gun control? Why or why not?

Drugs and Alcohol

Like guns, drugs are often raised in discussions of what to do about crime. The issue is twofold: To what extent are drugs linked to crimes of violence and crimes against property? And what is the best way to reduce the proportion of criminals who use drugs?

The number of adults arrested for violation of drug laws increased by 150 percent between 1980 and 1995.[83] Court commitments to state prisons for these violations rose to 21 percent of all state inmates in 1997.[84] These figures illustrate a dramatic escalation in public concern about drug offenses, but in themselves they do not demonstrate a connection between drugs and other forms of criminal conduct. This is because the total number and penalties for drug law violations increased over the same period, and those arrested may have been entrepreneurs catering to the public demand for drugs, rather than drug users.

DRUG USE
FORECASTING

■ **Drug Use Forecasting**
Program in many major
U.S. cities in which police
take urine specimens from
a sample of arrestees to
determine what proportion
of those arrested have
already used drugs.

In 1987 the National Institute of Justice began the **Drug Use Forecasting** (DUF) program in New York City. By 1998 this program had expanded to thirty-five cities. Police take urine specimens from a sample of arrestees in each city to determine what proportion of those arrested have already used drugs. More than half of all arrestees (male and female) test positive for drugs at the time of arrest, regardless of the crime for which they were arrested.[85] Although these figures do not necessarily mean that drugs *caused* the criminal activity in question, it suggests that drugs play a role in the lifestyle of arrestees. Better-controlled studies have found that criminals who use drugs commit robberies and assaults more often than non-drug-using offenders.[86] Another study found more than half of murders occurring in New York City to be drug related: (Thirty-nine percent involved drug trafficking; 8 percent, drug intoxication; 2 percent, a theft to buy drugs; and 4 percent involved more than one of these causes.[87]

It appears that alcohol also plays an important role in crime, particularly violent crime. It has been found, for example, that chronic drinkers are more likely than nondrinkers to have histories of violent behavior. Tests have shown that drinking immediately preceded half of all violent crimes studied by researchers.[88]

Among offenders in jail for any crime, more than 75 percent have used drugs in the past, about 60 percent use drugs regularly, and about 30 percent had used drugs at the time of the offense. More than 56 percent of inmates state that they were under the influence of drugs or alcohol at the time of the offense.[89] The evidence is quite strong, therefore, that use of drugs and alcohol is correlated with criminal behavior.

DRUG PREVENTION?

Proposals for reducing the use of drugs are intended to reduce either the supply of drugs or the demand for them. Strategies to reduce the supply of drugs include massive increases in arrests for drug crimes and prevention of the flow of drugs into the United States. Neither of these strategies has had any significant long-term impact. So-called police crackdowns or sweeps, in which many arrests are made in a specific geographic area, have been found to have little effect. Although these crackdowns often reduce drug trafficking for short periods in the targeted areas, studies have found that drug markets are simply moved, and customers go elsewhere to purchase the product.[90] Strategies to prevent the import of drugs have been unsuccessful for related reasons. Source countries have little incentive to substitute less profitable crops for drug-producing plants such as coca and poppies, and the immense borders of the United States are difficult to monitor effectively.[91]

Demand reduction strategies focus on drug education, treatment, and punishment as methods to reduce the public's appetite for drugs. These efforts have shown sporadic success. In Maricopa County, Arizona, for example, a zero tolerance program was instituted to hold all drug users accountable for their behavior. In two years of operation, a drug task force made 730 arrests, 32 percent of which were for marijuana possession. A large number of cases that previously would have been dismissed were referred for drug treatment, thus "widening the net" of the criminal justice system by including more offenders of all types. The program did succeed in increasing the use of treatment as an alternative to prosecution in some cases, and it fostered a communitywide consensus regarding the seriousness of the drug problem.[92]

The Drug Abuse Resistance Program (DARE) attempts to reduce drug use through educational programs for students in kindergarten through high school. More than half the nation's school districts have adopted this program in at least one of their schools. An evaluation of DARE programs found that they had little effect on drug use, attitudes toward drugs, attitudes toward the police, or self-esteem. On the other hand, DARE programs did increase student knowledge about substance abuse.[93] A revised DARE program was begun in 1993, and it appears that more interactive learning strategies in which students play roles and respond to case-based scenarios may prove more effective.

A study of drinking at college parties found that students who did not drink believed the risk of being caught was very high if they committed a crime. Those who drank most heavily condemned crime less strongly and believed the risk of being caught was low. A major implication of this research is that it may be possible to reduce crime by preventing heavy drinking.[94]

Treatment programs to reduce the drug-using population have had mixed results. Such programs are of two types: treatment with medications (i.e., other drugs, such as methadone), and behavioral programs that employ counseling and other techniques to reduce drug dependency. Perhaps the largest study of the impact of drug treatment tracked 10,000 patients receiving methadone maintenance, residential treatment, or outpatient treatment. Regardless of the type of treatment used, it was found that heroin use was reduced even three to five years after the treatment ended. The rate of serious crimes committed by these patients also dropped after treatment. Unfortunately, treatment for at least six months was necessary to overcome heroin addiction. In addition, no treatment program was found to have much success in reducing use of cocaine, which is more addictive than heroin.[95]

It appears that attempts to reduce drug use by reducing either supply or demand will require new ideas if they are to become more effective. Clearly, a reduction in demand would make a reduction in supply unnecessary. Even if the supply were somehow reduced, lingering demand would create new

DRUG TREATMENT PROGRAMS

criminal opportunities such as we now find in the domestic manufacture of synthetic drugs through chemical combinations.[96] Despite these roadblocks, efforts are under way to reduce both the demand and the availability of drugs. The central role of the family is made clear by the fact that inmates whose parents abused drugs began using drugs themselves by age thirteen. If the parents did not abuse drugs or alcohol, the child did not use drugs until age sixteen.[97] An examination of community antidrug campaigns in thirteen cities found that efforts with a broader scope (such as community education, family support, and security programs) and those that forged cooperative partnerships with the local police had some impact regardless of the type of neighborhood involved.[98] Much of the hope for reducing drug use in U.S. society is likely to emerge from these community efforts.

critical thinking exercise

Binge Drinking

Despite gains made in reducing alcohol-related traffic fatalities, other drinking behaviors remain a problem. Heavy episodic alcohol use, or binge drinking, has been identified by the Harvard School of Public Health as "the single most serious public health problem confronting American colleges."[a]

In 1993, the Harvard Alcohol Study surveyed a nationally representative sample of college students and found that 44 percent were binge drinkers—the men reporting that they consumed five or more drinks in a row and the women four or more drinks in a row at least once in the two weeks before the survey. Twenty percent of students were found to be frequent binge drinkers, and only 16 percent abstained from drinking alcoholic beverages.[b] A 1999 follow-up survey found the same proportion of binge drinkers (44 percent), and slight *increases* in both abstainers (19 percent) and frequent binge drinkers (23 percent). A major predictor of college binge drinking was found to be students' alcohol use while in high school.

Binge drinkers in both the 1993 and 1999 surveys were at least five times more likely than non–binge drinkers to experience alcohol-related problems such as missing classes, falling behind in their work, forgetting where they were or what they did, getting hurt or injured, damaging property, or driving after drinking. In addition, others experienced secondhand effects of students' binge drinking, including having their study or sleep interrupted (61 percent), having to take care of a drunken student (50 percent), or being insulted or humiliated (29 percent).

Despite a high level of public attention to responsible alcohol consumption, there appears to be little impact thus far on binge drinking by college students. For example, unchanged between the 1993 and 1999 Harvard surveys was the high rate at which residents of fraternities or sororities binge drink (81 percent).

CRITICAL THINKING QUESTIONS

1. Is binge drinking a crime? Why or why not?
2. What are the social, economic, political, and historical contexts of binge drinking?
3. What might be some consequences of criminalizing binge drinking?

NOTES

a. Henry Wechsler, Jae Eun Lee, Meichun Kuo, and Hang Lee, "College Binge Drinking in the 1990s: A Continuing Problem: Results of the Harvard School of Public Health 1999 College Alcohol Study," *Journal of American College Health* 48 (March 2000), pp. 199–210.
b. Henry Wechsler, George W. Dowdall, B. Moeykens, and S. Castillo, "Health and Behavioral Consequences of Binge Drinking in College. A National Survey of Students at 140 Campuses," *Journal of the American Medical Association* 272 (1994), pp. 1672–77.

Summary

WHY ARE AMERICANS FEARFUL OF CRIME?

- Public concern about crime has risen dramatically since the 1960s.
- Health problems and accidents are far more common causes of death than criminal homicide.
- Fear of death due to homicide is related to increased incidence since 1960 and the lack of control an individual has over homicide, compared with other causes of death.
- Polls have found that citizens rank feeling safe from crime ahead of job satisfaction, financial security, and health.
- Fear of crime leads many people to give up activities they would normally undertake, especially activities at night.
- High levels of fear can turn otherwise law-abiding citizens into outlaws.

WHAT IS CRIME?

- Crime of some type is present in all societies, but its nature and extent differ from one time and place to another.
- As a society becomes larger and more complex, more rules are required to ensure that citizens do not exploit one another.
- The criminal law punishes actions, not thoughts.
- The political view of crime leads to efforts to criminalize or decriminalize certain behaviors, depending on public sentiment at the time.
- The Prohibition era showed that it is necessary to have true public support for laws if they are to be effective.
- Criminal behaviors can be *mala in se* (acts bad in themselves) or *mala prohibita* (acts not inherently evil that are deemed undesirable).

HOW CAN CRIME BE EXPLAINED?

- The classical school of thought in criminology sees crime as resulting from the conscious exercise of an individual's free will—an exercise that is controlled by the threat of punishment.
- Positivism sees crimes as the result of internal and external influences on an individual.
- Structural explanations of crime focus on the selective formulation and application of the law rather than on the behavior of individuals.
- The ethical view sees crime as a moral failure in decision making.

WHAT ARE SOME CORRELATES OF CRIME?

- The incidence of crime involving guns is high, but it is not clear whether the absence of guns would necessarily reduce the rate of violence.
- There is strong evidence that use of drugs and/or alcohol is correlated with criminal behavior.

Key Terms

victimization	misdemeanors
crimes	criminalization
criminal law	decriminalization
felonies	victimless crimes

mala in se	structural/conflict view
mala prohibita	biological determinism
offenses against morality	psychoanalytic theory
political crimes	differential association
regulatory offenses	blocked opportunity
overcriminalization	criminal subcultures
legalization	labeling theory
classical school	social bond
positivism	gun control
ethical view	Drug Use Forecasting

Questions for Review and Discussion

1. Is there any justification for the public's increased fear of violent crime?
2. What are some psychological and behavioral effects of fear of crime?
3. In what sense can crime be considered "normal"?
4. What is the definition of a crime?
5. What is the role of intent in the definition of crime?
6. In what respects is crime political in nature?
7. What lessons can be drawn from the experience of Prohibition?
8. What is meant by the terms *mala in se* and *mala prohibita*?
9. What would be the possible effects of addressing alcohol and drug consumption as personal health issues rather than as crimes?
10. What is meant by "overcriminalization"? Do you think this phenomenon has occurred in the United States?

Notes

1. Joseph Galloway, "Shooting in the Stacks," *U.S. News & World Report* (April 26, 1999), p. 44.
2. " 'The Kids Got in the Way': All the Warning Signs Were There, but Still Buford Furrow Got His Hands on Guns and Went on a Rampage," *Time* (August 23, 1999), pp. 24–26; "Separatist in Federal Court," *United Press International* (August 31, 1999).
3. Carol J. DeFrances and Steven K. Smith, *Perceptions of Neighborhood Crime* (Washington, D.C.: Bureau of Justice Statistics, 1998).
4. George H. Gallup, *The Gallup Polls: Public Opinion, 1935–1971*, vol. 3 (New York: Random House, 1972), p. 2108.
5. George P. Fletcher, *A Crime of Self-Defense: Bernhard Goetz and the Law on Trial* (New York: Free Press, 1988).
6. William Wilbanks, *The Make My Day Law: Colorado's Experiment in Home Protection* (Lanham, MD: University Press of America, 1990).
7. Deborah Sharp, "Car-Jacking Trial Opens in Florida," *USA Today* (February 24, 1993), p. 3; "Life Sentence Given in Brutal Car-Jacking," *USA Today* (August 19, 1993), p. 3.
8. "Florida's Inroads to Rental Car Safety," *USA Today* (June 21, 1993), p. 5D.
9. Deborah Sharp, "In South Florida, Raising the Roof and the Crime Rate," *USA Today* (February 15, 1993), p. 3.
10. Deborah Sharp, "In Miami Hotels, Checkout Time for TV News of Violence," *USA Today* (June 6, 1994), p. 8.
11. Jonathan T. Lovitt, "California Postal Worker Held in Boss's Slaying," *USA Today* (July 10, 1995), p. 3; Carrie Dowling and Bruce Frankel, "Former Postal Worker Held in New Jersey Shootings," *USA Today* (March 23, 1995), p. 5; "Postal Feud Ends in Fatal Shootings," *Richmond Times-Dispatch* (December 20, 1997), p. 3.

12. Ronet Bachman, *Violence and Theft in the Workplace* (Washington, DC: Bureau of Justice Statistics, 1994).

13. "Murder for Hire," *USA Today* (May 22, 1995), p. 3; "Boy Burned," *USA Today* (March 27, 1995), p. 3; "Mom Sentenced," *USA Today* (October 25, 1993), p. 3; "Four Teens Charged After 8-Year-Old Is Set on Fire," *Buffalo News* (March 21, 1995), p. 14.

14. Mark Potok, "A Deadly Serious Call to Arms," *USA Today* (February 17, 1995), p. 3.

15. Kevin V. Johnson, "Chicago Suburb a Fortress against Crime," *USA Today* (July 5, 1995), p. 3.

16. Richard Price and Jonathan T. Lovitt, "Murder of Two Students Stuns Japan," *USA Today* (March 29, 1994), p. 1; Jeff Leen and Don Van Natta, Jr., "Canada Fears Escalating Crime While Miami Can Barely Keep Up," *Buffalo News* (September 11, 1994), p. 12.

17. Emile Durkheim, *The Rules of Sociological Method* (originally published in 1895) (New York: Free Press, 1964), pp. 65–66.

18. Freda Adler, *Nations Not Obsessed with Crime* (Littleton, CO: Fred B. Rothman, 1983); Jay S. Albanese, "Moving towards Utopia: Elements of a Crime-Free Society," in *Justice, Privacy, and Crime Control* (Lanham, MD: University Press of America, 1984), pp. 46–56.

19. President's Crime Commission, *Task Force Report: Crime and Its Impact—an Assessment* (Washington, DC: U.S. Government Printing Office, 1967) p. 19.

20. Stanley I. Kutler, *The American Inquisition: Justice and Injustice in the Cold War* (New York: Hill & Wang, 1982).

21. Melvin I. Urofsky, *A March of Liberty: A Constitutional History of the United States* (New York: McGraw-Hill, 1988), pp. 750ff.

22. Lawrence M. Friedman, *Crime and Punishment in American History* (New York: Basic Books, 1993), p. 372.

23. Steven E. Barkan, *Protectors on Trial: Criminal Justice in the Southern Civil Rights and Vietnam Antiwar Movement* (New Brunswick: Rutgers University Press, 1985).

24. Friedman, p. 341.

25. Mark H. Moore, in "Actually, Prohibition Was a Success," in R. L. Evans and I. M. Berent, eds., *Drug Legalization* (LaSalle, IL: Open Court Press, 1992) argues that Prohibition worked, citing a decline in cirrhosis deaths during the period. The unreliability of the data and reporting methods of the period make both the statistics used and the conclusions drawn suspect.

26. Ibid., p. 266.

27. Jay S. Albanese, *Organized Crime in America*, 3rd ed. (Cincinnati: Anderson, 1996); Samuel Walker, *Popular Justice: A History of American Criminal Justice* (New York: Oxford University Press, 1980).

28. Friedman, pp. 6–7.

29. Deborah Rhode, *Justice and Gender* (Cambridge, MA: Harvard University Press, 1989).

30. Mark 15:24; Luke 23:34; John 19:24.

31. Henry Chafetz, *Play the Devil: A History of Gambling in the United States from 1492 to 1955* (New York: Potter, 1960), p. 8.

32. John Rosecrance, *Gambling without Guilt: The Legitimation of an American Pastime* (Belmont, CA: Brooks/Cole, 1988), p. 12.

33. Ibid., pp. 12–13.

34. Gilbert Geis, *Not the Law's Business* (New York: Schocken, 1979), p. 223.

35. Chafetz, p. 17.

36. Friedman, pp. 137–38.

37. David F. Musto, *The American Disease: Origins of Narcotic Control* (New York, 1973).

38. Elliott Currie, *Reckoning: Drugs, the Cities, and the American Future* (New York: Hill & Wang, 1992); Lyle W. Shannon, Judith L. McKim, and Kathleen R. Anderson, *Alcohol and Drugs, Delinquency, and Crime: Looking Back to the Future* (New York: St. Martins Press, 1998).

39. Kurt L. Schmoke, "Decriminalizing Drugs: It Just Might Work—and Nothing Else Does," in R. L. Evans and I. M. Berent, eds., *Drug Legalization* (LaSalle, IL: Open Court Press, 1992); Ethan A. Nadelmann, Drug Prohibition in the United States: Costs, Consequences, and Alternatives," *Science* 245 (September 1989).

40. Lawrence W. Sherman, "Police Crackdowns: Initial and Residual Deterrence," in M. Tonry and N. Morris, eds., *Crime and Justice: An Annual Review of Research* (Chicago: University of Chicago Press, 1990); U.S. Comptroller General, *Drug Control: Interdiction Efforts in Central America Have Had Little Impact on the Flow of Drugs* (Washington, DC: U.S. General Accounting Office, 1994); Samuel Walker, *Sense and Nonsense about Crime and Drugs*, 3rd ed. (Belmont, CA: Brooks/Cole, 1994), pp. 260–63.

41. Alfred Blumstein, "Violence by Young People: Why the Deadly Nexus?," *National Institute of Justice Journal* (August, 1995), pp. 2–9; John M. Dawson and Patrick A. Langan, *Murder in Families* (Washington, DC: Bureau of Justice Statistics, 1994); John Ritter,

"Parent-Killers: A Deadly Streak," *USA Today* (March 8, 1995), p. 3; Kevin Johnson, "Woman Charged in Kids' Fire Deaths," *USA Today* (August 23, 1994), p. 3; Barry Meier, "Sexual Predator Finding Sentence May Last Past Jail," *New York Times* (February 22, 1995), p. 1.

42.   Compare the conclusions of Don C. Gibbons, "Talking about Crime: Observations on the Prospects for Causal Theory in Criminology," *Criminal Justice Research Bulletin* 7 (1992), pp. 1–10 with Michael R. Gottfredson and Travis Hirschi, *A General Theory of Crime* (Stanford, CA: Stanford University Press, 1990).

43.   For excerpts from the writings of Bentham and Beccaria, see Joseph E. Jacoby, *Classics of Criminology*, 2nd ed. (Prospect Heights, IL: Waveland Press, 1994).

44.   Michael R. Gottfredson and Travis Hirschi, *A General Theory of Crime* (Stanford, CA: Stanford University Press, 1990), pp. 90–91.

45.   Augustine Brannigan, "Self-Control, Social Control, and Evolutionary Psychology: Towards an Integrated Perspective on Crime," *Canadian Journal of Criminology* 39 (October 1997), pp. 403–31; T. David Evans, Francis T. Cullen, Velmer S. Burton Jr., R. Gregory Dunaway, and Michael L. Benson, "The Social Consequences of Self-Control: Testing the General Theory of Crime," *Criminology* 35 (August 1997), pp. 475–501.

46.   Charles Darwin, *The Origin of Species* (New York: Modern Library, 1936).

47.   Emile Durkheim, *Suicide* (New York: Free Press, 1951).

48.   Jay S. Albanese, *Dealing with Delinquency: The Future of Juvenile Justice*, 2d ed. (Chicago: Nelson-Hall, 1993), pp. 61–64; Jay Albanese, *White-Collar Crime in America* (Englewood Cliffs, NJ: Prentice Hall, 1995), pp. 105–9; Jay Albanese, *Organized Crime in America*, 3rd ed. (Cincinnati: Anderson, 1996), pp. 68–72.

49.   Peter B. Wood, "Nonsocial Reinforcement and Habitual Criminal Conduct: An Extension of Learning Theory," *Criminology* 35 (1997), pp. 335–66.

50.   Jeffrey Reiman, *The Rich Get Richer and the Poor Get Prison: Ideology, Class, and Criminal Justice*, 3rd ed. (New York: Macmillan, 1990).

51.   Jeffrey Reiman, *. . . And the Poor Get Prison: Economic Bias in American Criminal Justice* (Needham Heights, MA: Allyn & Bacon, 1996).

52.   Ronald L. Akers, *Criminological Theories*, 2d ed. (Los Angeles: Roxbury, 1997), pp. 157–58.

53.   Cesare Lombroso and Gina Lombroso-Ferrero, *The Criminal Man* (Montclair, NJ: Patterson Smith, 1972).

54.   Charles Goring, *The English Convict* (London: Her Majesty's Stationery Office, 1913).

55.   Richard J. Herrnstein, "Criminogenic Traits," and Patricia A. Brennan, Sarnoff A. Mednick, and Jan Voluka, "Biomedical Factors in Crime," in J. Q. Wilson and J. Petersilia, eds., *Crime* (San Francisco: ICS Press, 1995).

56.   Janet Katz and William J. Chambliss, "Biology and Crime," in Joseph F. Sheley, ed., *Criminology: Contemporary Handbook* (Belmont, CA: Wadsworth, 1991); Lee Ellis, "Genetics and Criminal Behavior," *Criminology* 20 (1982), pp. 43–66; William Gabrielli and Sarnoff Mednick, "Urban Environment, Genetics, and Crime," *Criminology* 22 (1984), pp. 645–53.

57.   Jeffrey A. Roth, "Understanding and Preventing Violence," *National Institute of Justice Research in Brief* (February 1994), p. 8; Albert J. Reiss and Jeffrey A. Roth, eds., *Understanding and Preventing Violence* (Washington, DC: National Academy Press, 1993).

58.   For a summary of this research, see Lee Ellis and Anthony Walsh, "Gene-Based Evolutionary Theories in Criminology," *Criminology* 37 (1997), pp. 229–76; Tim Friend, "Violence-Prone Men May Be Both Born and Made," *USA Today* (December 14, 1994), p. 5D; Robert Wright, "The Biology of Violence," *The New Yorker* (March 13, 1995), pp. 68–77.

59.   Richard Jenkins and Lester F. Hewitt, *Fundamental Patterns of Maladjustment* (Springfield, IL: Thomas, 1947).

60.   William McCord and Joan McCord, *Psychopathy and Delinquency* (New York: Grune & Stratton, 1956).

61.   James Sorrells, "Kids Who Kill," *Crime and Delinquency* 23 (1977), pp. 312–20; Richard Rosner, Melvin Widerlight, M. Bernice Horner Rosner, and Rita Reis Wieczorek, "Adolescents Accused of Murder and Manslaughter: A Five-Year Descriptive Study," *Bulletin of the American Academy of Psychiatry and the Law* 7 (1979), pp. 342–51.

62.   Steven Spaccarelli, Blake Bowden, J. Douglas Coatsworth, and Soni Kim, "Psychosocial Correlates of Male Sexual Aggression in a Chronic Delinquent Sample," *Criminal Justice and Behavior* 24 (March 1997), pp. 71–95.

63.   Edwin H. Sutherland, *Principles of Criminology* (Philadelphia: Lippincott, 1939).

64.   Jack Gibbs, "The State of Criminological Theory," *Criminology* 25 (1987), pp. 821–40; Mark Warr and Mark Stafford, "The Influence of Delinquent Peers: What They Think or What They Do?," *Criminology* 29 (1991), pp. 851–66.

65.   Spaccarelli et al., "Psychosocial Correlates," p. 92.

66.   Richard A. Cloward and Lloyd E. Ohlin, *Delinquency and Opportunity: A Theory of Delinquent Gangs* (New York: Free Press, 1960).

67. Howard Becker, *The Outsiders: Studies in the Sociology of Deviance* (New York: Free Press, 1963); Edwin M. Lemert, *Social Pathology: A Systematic Approach to the Theory of Sociopathic Behavior* (New York: McGraw-Hill, 1951).

68. Travis Hirschi, *Causes of Delinquency* (Berkeley: University of California Press, 1969); Michael J. Hindelang, "Causes of Delinquency: A Partial Replication and Exposition," *Social Problems* 20 (1973), pp. 470–87; LeGrande Gardiner and Donald Shoemaker, "Social Bonding and Delinquency: A Comparative Analysis," *Sociological Quarterly* 30 (1989), pp. 481–500.

69. Marianne W. Zawitz, *Guns Used in Crime* (Washington, DC: Bureau of Justice Statistics, 1995).

70. Federal Bureau of Investigation, *Crime in the United States, 1993* (Washington, DC: U.S. Government Printing Office, 1994).

71. Gary Kleck, *Point Blank: Guns and Violence in America* (New York: Aldine De Grytr, 1991); Edward D. Jones, "The District of Columbia's 'Firearms Control Regulations Act of 1975': The Toughest Handgun Control Law in the United States—or Is It?," *The Annals* 455 (May 1981), pp. 138–49.

72. Data from Bureau of Alcohol, Tobacco, and Firearms, cited in Zawitz (note 69 above), pp. 1–2.

73. Allen Beck et al., *Survey of State Prison Inmates, 1991* (Washington, DC: Bureau of Justice Statistics, 1993), pp. 18–19.

74. Joseph F. Sheley and James D. Wright, "Gun Acquisition and Possession in Selected Juvenile Samples," *Research in Brief* (Washington, DC: National Institute of Justice, 1993); James D. Wright and Peter H. Rossi, *Armed and Dangerous: A Survey of Felons and Their Firearms* (Hawthorne, NY: Aldine, 1986).

75. Cited in Zawitz, p. 4.

76. Cited in Zawitz, p. 5.

77. Wright and Rossi, op. cit.

78. Glenn L. Pierce and William J. Bowers, "The Bartley–Fox Gun Law's Short-Term Impact on Crime," *The Annals* 455 (May 1981), pp. 120–37.

79. Kleck, *Point Blank*, p. 82.

80. Samuel Walker, *Sense and Nonsense about Crime and Drugs*, 3rd ed. (Belmont, CA: Wadsworth, 1994).

81. Colin Loftin and David McDowall, "One with a Gun Gets You Two: Mandatory Sentencing and Firearms Violence in Detroit," *The Annals* 455 (May 1981), pp. 150–67; Alan Lizotte and Marjorie S. Zatz, "The Use and Abuse of Sentence Enhancement for Firearms Offenses in California," *Law and Contemporary Problems* 49 (1986), pp. 199–221.

82. Dennis A. Hennigan, "Gun Makers Are Liable," *USA Today* (March 27, 1995), p. 10; "Require Gun Insurance," *USA Today* (January 4, 1994), p. 10; Herb Kohl, "Keep Schools Gun-Free," *USA Today* (May 3, 1995), p. 10.

83. Federal Bureau of Investigation, *Uniform Crime Report—1996* (Washington, DC: U.S. Government Printing Office, 1997).

84. Allen J. Beck, and Christopher J. Mumola, *Prisoners in 1998* (Washington, DC: Bureau of Justice Statistics, 1999), p. 13.

85. *Annual Report on Drug Use among Adult and Juvenile Arrestees* (Washington, DC: National Institute of Justice, 1999).

86. Jeffrey A. Roth, *Psychoactive Substances and Violence* (Washington, DC: National Institute of Justice, 1994).

87. P. J. Goldstein, H. H. Brownstein, P. J. Ryan, and P. A. Bellucci, "Crack and Homicide in New York City, 1988: A Conceptually Based Event Analysis," *Contemporary Drug Problems* 16 (Winter 1989), pp. 651–87.

88. Roth, p. 2.

89. Caroline Wolf Harlow, *Drugs and Jail Inmates* (Washington, DC: Bureau of Justice Statistics, 1991).

90. David M. Kennedy, *Closing the Market: Controlling the Drug Trade in Tampa, Florida* (Washington, DC: National Institute of Justice, 1993); Lawrence W. Sherman, "Police Crackdowns: Initial and Residual Deterrence," in M. Tonry and N. Morris, eds., *Crime and Justice: A Review of Research* (Chicago: University of Chicago Press, 1990).

91. U.S. Comptroller General, *Drug Control: Interdiction Efforts in Central America Have Had Little Impact in the Flow of Drugs* (Washington, DC: U.S. General Accounting Office, 1994); U.S. Comptroller General, *Drug Control: Heavy Investment in Military Surveillance Is Not Paying Off* (Washington, DC: U.S. General Accounting Office, 1993).

92. John R. Hepburn, Wayne Johnston, and Scott Rodgers, *Do Drugs, Do Time: An Evaluation of the Maricopa County Demand Reduction Program* (Washington, DC: National Institute of Justice, 1994).

93. Christopher Ringwalt et al., *Past and Future Directions of the D.A.R.E. Program: An Evaluation Review* (Research Triangle Park, NC: Research Triangle Institute, 1994).

94. Lonn Lanza-Kadua, Donna M. Bishop, Lawrence Winna, "Risk Benefit Calculations, Moral Evaluations, and Alcohol Use: Exploring the Alcohol–Crime Connection," *Crime and Delinquency* 43 (1997), pp. 222–39; see also J. J. Thompson, "Plugging the Kegs: Students Benefit When Colleges Limit Excessive Drinking," *U.S. News & World Report* (January 26, 1998), pp. 63–67.

95. R. L. Hubbard, *Drug Abuse Treatment: A National Study of Effectiveness* (Chapel Hill: University of North Carolina Press, 1989).

96. Domestic Chemical Action Group, *Controlling Chemicals Used to Make Illegal Drugs: The Chemical Action Task Force and the Domestic Chemical Action Group* (Washington, DC: National Institute of Justice, 1993).

97. Harlow, p. 7.

98. Saul N. Weingart, Francis X. Hartmann, and David Osborne, *Case Studies of Community Anti-Drug Efforts* (Washington, DC: National Institute of Justice, 1994).

two
Defining and Measuring Crime

Eric Harris and Dylan Klebold

were high school students, typical in many ways. They were average students. They bowled on Saturday mornings; they worked together at a pizza parlor. Earlier, they had been Boy Scouts and played fantasy football. But then signs of trouble emerged. They were arrested in 1998 for breaking into a car. The parent of another student complained to the police about alleged death threats and bomb making. Eric and Dylan became part of a clique called the Trench Coat Mafia, whose members wore long black coats even in the hot weather. The two boys were insulted by some other students at school, and the jocks (student athletes) sometimes called them "fags" to their face. Eric and Dylan admired Hitler, sometimes spoke to each other in German, and wore swastikas, reveling in their status as outcasts whom most students, teachers, and parents ignored. They played war games with cards at lunch and wore armbands that said "I Hate People." Classmates reported how they always wrote and talked about killing people. Then they made a video for class that showed them walking down the halls of their school, pretending to shoot friends dressed as the hated jocks.

It all took a terrible turn into reality when Eric and Dylan walked into their school, Columbine High School in Littleton, Colorado, with a semi-automatic pistol, a carbine, and two sawed-off shotguns. They laughed as they shot at people at the school, ultimately killing twelve students and a coach. They also planted at least thirty pipe bombs and other explosives, discovered later, around the school.[1]

This tragedy at Columbine High School, perhaps the most calculated of any school shooting incident to date, occurred in an upper-middle-class neighborhood. Several copycat incidents occurred—and some were prevented—in the weeks that followed. To what extent does this case reflect new patterns and trends in crime in the United States?

What Are the Types of Crime?

Crimes are of three general types: crimes against persons, crimes against property, and crimes against public order. **Crimes against persons** are called violent crimes, because they involve the use of physical force. These crimes include criminal homicide, rape, assault, and robbery. **Crimes against property** are those in which property is taken unlawfully and misused. Examples include burglary, larceny, vandalism, and arson. **Crimes against public order** are acts that disrupt the peace in a civil society. Examples of these offenses include drug, liquor, and gambling law violations; disorderly conduct; weapons offenses; and loitering and prostitution violations. These three categories of offenses are summarized in Table 2.1.

Although these three categories of crime comprise the vast majority of the more than 15 million arrests made by police each year, there are other kinds of offenses that involve sophisticated fraud and deceit rather than

▪**crimes against persons**
Violent crimes involving the use of physical force.

▪**crimes against property**
Crimes in which property is taken unlawfully and misused.

▪**crimes against public order**
Acts that disrupt the peace in a civil society.

TABLE 2.1

Three General Categories of Crime

CRIMES AGAINST PERSONS	CRIMES AGAINST PROPERTY	CRIMES AGAINST PUBLIC ORDER
Criminal homicide	Larceny	Drug, liquor, and gambling law violations
Assault	Burglary	Disorderly conduct
Rape	Arson	Weapons offenses
Robbery	Vandalism	Loitering and prostitution violations

stealth or force. Chapter 3 examines these sophisticated crimes. In addition, specific acts of violence are perpetrated to achieve political, racial, ethnic, or religious objectives. These acts constitute terrorism or hate crime, also examined in Chapter 3.

How Are Violent Crimes and Property Crimes Classified?

VIOLENT CRIMES

CRIMES AGAINST PROPERTY

The violent crimes of homicide, rape, robbery, and assault lie at the heart of the public's fear of crime. Even though these constitute only 13 percent of all serious crimes reported to police, they can involve serious injury or death and are greatly feared. The crimes of rape, robbery, and assault make up nearly 20 percent of all crimes counted by victimization surveys (whether reported or not). Essential information about these crimes includes the specific types of actions they do and do not involve, as well as the nature of the circumstances under which they occur. Crimes against property account for the overwhelming majority (80 to 90 percent) of all serious crimes. It seems that stealing by stealth is more common than any other predatory crime. As a greater proportion of citizens have come to own more property of more kinds, burglary and larceny have come to be regarded as more serious crimes. The three main types of property crimes—burglary, larceny, and arson—are counted nationally each year. This section describes these categories of crime in detail.

MURDER AND MANSLAUGHTER

- **criminal homicide**
  Murder or manslaughter.

- **murder**
  All intentional killings, as well as deaths that occur in the course of dangerous felonies.

Homicide

Criminal homicides include both murder and manslaughter. **Murder** includes all intentional killings, as well as deaths that occur during dangerous felonies. A person who robbed someone on the street who then died from the shock would be held liable for felony murder, because he or she caused a death in the course of a dangerous felony. Likewise, if you aim to shoot a person but miss and kill his or her companion instead, you are liable for murder for the companion's death even though you had no intention of killing that person. This is because you *intentionally* took a person's life without lawful justification. All the criteria for the definition of murder are fulfilled. The law does not punish you less severely because you are a poor shot.

RECKLESSNESS AND NEGLIGENCE

- **manslaughter**
  A mitigated murder: causing a death recklessly, or intentionally under extenuating circumstances.

- **recklessness**
  Conscious disregard of a substantial and unjustifiable risk.

Manslaughter is a mitigated murder. It involves causing death recklessly, or intentionally under extenuating circumstances. An example of a reckless manslaughter would be killing a pedestrian with your car while drunk or speeding. In law, **recklessness** is conscious disregard of a substantial and unjustifiable risk. In this example, a reasonable person would know that it is difficult to control an automobile properly when one is speeding or drinking. This "reasonableness standard" is used throughout the criminal law to assess the culpability of an individual's conduct. Reckless manslaughter is punished less seriously than murder because of the "lower" state of mind involved (recklessness versus intention).

Recklessness is distinguished from **negligence,** which is failure to be aware of a substantial and unjustifiable risk. Negligence is not subject to criminal prosecution, although a person can be sued in civil court for damages caused by negligent conduct.

A middle ground between negligence and recklessness is gross negligence. **Gross negligence** is failure to perceive a substantial and unjustifiable risk when such a failure is a "gross deviation" from the standard of care a reasonable person would observe. The charge of gross negligence is usually applied in cases involving fatal car accidents in which conduct is seen as not serious enough to constitute recklessness but more blameworthy than negligence. Gross negligence is the borderland of the criminal state of mind and is the least severely punished form of criminal homicide.

In two very limited circumstances, intentional killings may be punished as manslaughter rather than as murder: "heat of passion" killings and imperfect self-defense. So-called "heat of passion" killings are treated as murder rather than manslaughter only when the offender responds to an unlawful act in the sudden heat of passion (without time to cool off). Imperfect self-defense occurs when a person kills another while responding to an unlawful act with excessive or unnecessary force. If a husband walks in on his wife in bed with someone else and shoots her, he has responded to an unlawful act (adultery) with excessive force (death is not the penalty for adultery). "Heat of passion" cases often occur in troubled marital or cohabitation situations.[2] Reduction of a charge from murder to manslaughter only reduces the length of the possible sentence; it does not excuse the conduct.

The incidence of criminal homicide does not fluctuate widely. The *number* of homicides has fluctuated over the years; but after peaking in the early 1990s, the *rate* of homicide (per 100,000 population) has been declining steadily (because of proportional increases in the population). Therefore, a person's risk of being the victim of a criminal homicide is slightly less today than it was in 1980.[3]

More than two-thirds of homicides are committed with guns, and 13 percent with knives. According to the FBI, about 25 percent of all criminal homicides in which the circumstances are known are related to the commission of a felony, as in robbery that results in death. Nearly 45 percent of all homicides result from arguments, romantic triangles, and drug- or alcohol-influenced brawls.[4]

Sexual Assault

Rape is sexual intercourse without effective consent. The term **sexual assault** is often used to accommodate homosexual rape; it includes both rape (forced vaginal intercourse) and sodomy (forced oral or anal sex). Victimization surveys include sodomy, and in the future the Uniform Crime Reports (UCR; discussed later in this chapter) will include it in the definition of rape.

■**negligence**
Failure to be aware of a substantial and unjustifiable risk.

■**gross negligence**
Failure to perceive a substantial and unjustifiable risk when such failure is a gross deviation from the standard of care a reasonable person would observe.

"HEAT OF PASSION" KILLINGS

RAPE AND STATUTORY RAPE

■**rape**
Sexual intercourse without effective consent.

■**sexual assault**
Forced sex, whether vaginal, anal, or oral.

■ **statutory rape**
Nonforcible sexual
intercourse with a minor.

Intercourse is defined as any penetration, however slight. Any kind of physical force, including "terrorizing of the senses," suffices to establish lack of effective consent. Effective consent also is not present if the victim is a minor, mentally ill, mentally retarded, or physically helpless.

Statutory rape is nonforcible sexual intercourse with a minor, an offense that the law provides as a way of protecting young people from exploitation by older ones. Statutory rape is not included in the UCR or victimization surveys because of its consensual nature.

According to victimization surveys, rapes of males accounted for 8 percent of all rapes. (Victimization surveys are conducted among the general public, so sexual assaults among the prison population are not included in this number.) In half of all cases of rape of a female, the victim knew the offender; in only 20 percent of all cases did the offender brandish a weapon. Just over half of female rape victims reported the incident to the police, a fact that was related to the presence of a weapon or injury rather than to the existence of a prior relationship. Most female victims who fought back through words or actions believed that their efforts helped the situation rather than aggravating it.[5]

SIMPLE AND
AGGRAVATED
ASSAULT

■ **simple assault**
A thrust against another
person intended to injure
that person.

■ **aggravated assault**
A thrust against another
person intended to cause
serious bodily harm or death.

Assault

Simple assault is distinguished from aggravated assault by the nature of the offender's intent. **Simple assault** is a physical thrust against another person intended to injure that person. **Aggravated assault** additionally involves the intention to cause serious bodily harm or death. A "thrust" can be a punch, a gunshot, a threatening action that causes fear and anxiety, or any form of "offensive touching." Assault has been charged in cases of spitting at another person and in cases of fondling an individual without his or her consent. Aggravated assault is a felony; simple assault is punished less severely as a misdemeanor.

Victimization surveys include data on simple assaults, accounting for some differences in the rates of assault reported in victim surveys as opposed to the rates indicated in the Uniform Crime Reports. Still, aggravated assault is the most common crime of violence, accounting for more than 1 million reports to the police each year and more than 500,000 arrests.[6] More than 20 percent of assaults of all kinds occur at or near the victim's home. Only about 7 percent occur inside a bar, restaurant, or nightclub. Only a third of aggravated assaults involve a gun; blunt objects cause more injury in assaults than any other type of weapon. As in the case of rape, more than 70 percent of victims who used words or actions in self-defense felt that their efforts helped the situation.[7] Therefore, victims who defend themselves often fare better in their own judgment.

■ **robbery**
Theft from a person involving
threats or force.

Robbery

Robbery is a combination of two other crimes: larceny (theft) and assault. **Robbery** consists of theft from a person involving threats or force. Threats must be serious enough to fulfill the element of assault and involve *im-*

mediate harm, such that the victim cannot call the police or take other action to prevent the crime. The number of victims in a robbery incident determines the total number of robbery charges that can be brought against a defendant. Robbery is punished according to the amount of force used.

After assault, robbery is the most common violent crime. It provokes high levels of fear, because 80 percent of robberies are committed by strangers. Approximately half of all robberies are committed by armed offenders (using guns about half the time). Nearly 35 percent of robbery victims are physically injured, although most who resisted the attacker report believing that it helped.[8]

Burglary

Burglary is unlawful entry into a building for the purpose of committing a crime while inside. Entry involves trespass, but breaking or force need not occur. In a case in Buffalo, a man entered a store during regular business hours and hid there when the store closed. After everyone had left, he "shopped" at his leisure in the empty store, leaving his selections in a bin near the loading dock. When the store reopened in the morning, he planned to pose as a new customer and simply leave through the back door. However, a security guard noticed his selections by the loading dock and was waiting for him as he attempted to leave. In this case the person's entry into the store was legal, but he remained behind surreptitiously, making his action criminal trespass.

Burglaries of dwellings cause the greatest concern among the public. Most burglaries have theft as their object, but burglaries can also occur for the purpose of assault. As noted earlier, there are about 5 million household burglaries per year, representing about 4 percent of all U.S. households. Therefore, the odds of household burglary are low. Only 30 percent of burglaries result in losses valued at $500 or more. More than 70 percent of burglaries with

■**burglary**
Unlawful entry into a building for the purpose of committing a crime while inside.

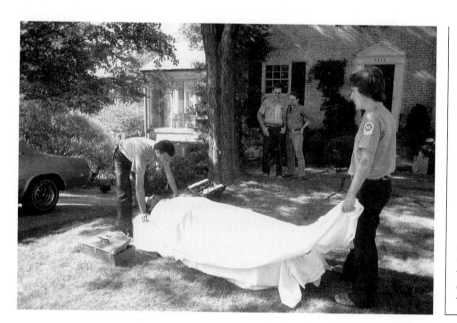

This is the scene of a crime involving a burglary with intent to commit larceny that turned into a robbery when a resident investigated a disturbance. How are these types of crimes against people and property distinguished? What are some other Part I offenses? Who are the victims of these types of crime? How are the rates of these crimes determined?

forced entry are reported to police, whereas only 42 percent of entries without force are reported.[9]

Larceny

Larceny is the most common serious crime in the United States. **Larceny** consists of taking the property of another person with the intent of depriving the owner. If force is used in a case of larceny, it becomes robbery. If deceit or trickery is used, the larceny becomes fraud, forgery, or embezzlement. The intention to deprive the owner is important, because moving companies take people's property all the time, as do valets, dry cleaners, and people who borrow books from libraries. These instances do not constitute larceny, because there is no intention to *deprive* the owner. Instead, the owner hands over the property for a short period, often in exchange for a service. Consent by the owner of the property is an absolute defense against charges of larceny.

"TAKING" UNDER THE LAW

The slightest movement of property may also be defined as "taking" under the law. If a shopper stuffs silk underwear under his jacket but is stopped before leaving the store, he has "taken" the property and can be charged with larceny, even though he never made it out the door.[10] Treating the silk underwear in a manner inconsistent with the buyer's right to inspect merchandise and the store's ownership of the property constitutes larceny in this case.

More than 20 million larcenies occur each year; 8 million of them involve property taken from households. Only about 333,000 involve pickpockets; 152,000 involve purse snatchings. Larceny is the offense least likely to be reported to police, according to national victimization surveys. The total loss from larceny each year is approximately $5.4 billion.[11]

Arson

Arson is burning of property without the lawful consent of the owner. As in the case of larceny, the lawful consent of the owner is an absolute defense against a charge of arson. Consent can be unlawful, however, if the owner is a minor or mentally incompetent, or if the owner gives consent with the intent of defrauding an insurance company.

Accidental fires do not constitute arson, although the law holds a person to the reasonableness standard in evaluating his or her decisions. A competent adult who started a bonfire at a school pep rally only ten feet from the gymnasium could be charged with reckless arson if the gym burned down. This is because a reasonable person would have had a higher standard of care. He or she would have recognized the substantial and unjustifiable risk of starting a large fire next to a building. Reckless arson are punished less severely than intentional arson.

More than 100,000 arsons are reported to police each year. Interestingly, only 56 percent of arsons occur in cities. Twenty percent occur in rural areas; the remainder, in suburban locations. About 25 percent of arsons involve

Media and Criminal Justice

he marked increase in the study of serial homicide has perhaps corresponded to an actual rise in incidents of serial killing, but nowhere is the public's fascination more evident than in commercial films. During the 1980s, slasher-style movies such as the *Halloween* and *Friday the 13th* series portrayed serial killers as bloodthirsty psychotic monsters out for revenge against wicked teenagers.

However, the 1991 Academy Award–winner *Silence of the Lambs* set a new standard for serial killer–themed films; instead of focusing on the senseless and gory activities of the killer, movies now began emphasizing the investigative and profiling techniques used to apprehend serial killers. Films of the 1990s such as *Copycat, Seven, Kiss the Girls, 8mm*, and *Resurrection* depicted forensic psychologists and specially trained law enforcement professionals striving to get inside the mind of the killer in order to stop him.

The 1999 film *The Bone Collector* continued this trend by presenting us with a character named Lincoln Rhyme, star forensics expert with the New York Police Department. A new angle in this movie is that our profiler, Lincoln, does not have the advantage of visiting the crime scenes or examining the bodies: Lincoln is completely paralyzed from an accident that has left him with—as he dryly puts it—"a finger, two shoulders, and a brain." It soon becomes clear that his brain is the most important tool available for catching a serial killer.

At the opening of *The Bone Collector,* a young female police officer, Amelia Donaghy, discovers a body buried next to the railroad tracks with only one hand protruding from the gravel. His ring finger has been amputated, and on its stump is his wife's wedding ring. Other clues, including a granular white powder and some pieces of paper lying on the track's rail, indicate to Amelia that this is no ordinary homicide. She literally stops the oncoming train in order to preserve the evidence, and she photographs the scene with a disposable camera before the investigative team arrives.

Amelia's intuitive actions convince Lincoln of her value as an investigator. Although she knows nothing of forensics, he recruits her to do his fieldwork by acting as his arms and legs at the crime scene while he ponders the evidence from the bed in his apartment. Not only is Lincoln a master of forensics, he knows his New York City history as well. When it is determined that the granular powder is ground oyster shells, he knows to look for the next victim near Pearl Street. The bits of paper found at the crime scene fit together to depict an old printing-house logo, which leads the investigators to an out-of-print book on torture techniques. The book is apparently inspiring the killer's acts, and by analyzing the vignettes depicted in each chapter, Lincoln and Amelia are able to predict the approximate locations and modus operandi for the forthcoming homicides.

While *The Bone Collector,* like other films of this genre, is based more on Hollywood formula than on homicide realities, it does serve to demonstrate the importance of analytical thinking and deductive logic in solving sophisticated crimes. By constantly asking the question, *According to similar crimes on record, what kind of person would do this?"* profilers use their expertise in criminal psychology and forensic evidence to assist law enforcement in solving serial homicide.

According to this chapter, how are the crimes of serial killers classified? What do you think are the likely characteristics of the perpetrators and victims of this kind of crime? What characteristics of serial murder does *The Bone Collector* depict? According to research, to what extent is this depiction accurate?

automobiles and 33 percent involve residences. The remainder involve commercial and community properties. The average loss in a typical incident of arson is about $11,000.[12] For arson to be charged, a structure or vehicle must be fire or smoke damaged intentionally or recklessly in some way by fire or explosion.

How Are Crime Rates Determined?

The Federal Bureau of Investigation tallies crimes reported to police and arrests made each year for eight types of offenses; the FBI counts only arrests for nineteen other types of offenses. These tallies are published annually in the FBI's Uniform Crime Reports (UCR). The offenses for which detailed information is collected are criminal homicide, forcible rape, robbery, aggravated assault, burglary, larceny, motor vehicle theft, and arson; these constitute the **FBI's Crime Index** and therefore are known as **Index crimes.** The offenses for which only arrests are counted (known as Part II offenses) are simple assault; forgery and counterfeiting; fraud; embezzlement; buying, receiving, or possessing stolen property; vandalism; weapons offenses; prostitution and commercialized vice; other sex offenses; drug law violations; gambling; offenses against the family and children; driving under the influence; liquor law violations; drunkenness; disorderly conduct; vagrancy; violations of curfew and loitering laws; and runaway cases.

Is the crime rate increasing or decreasing? The simplest questions are sometimes the most difficult to answer. To understand the difficulty of this seemingly straightforward question, visualize the sources of information for a typical criminal incident, such as the one illustrated in Figure 2.1.

How many sources of information are there in this incident? Perhaps three parties are involved: the offender, the victim, and the police. Perhaps there also are witnesses present. Police often are involved after the fact, however;

■ **FBI's Crime Index**
Tally of detailed reports on eight types of offenses: criminal homicide, forcible rape, robbery, aggravated assault, burglary, larceny, motor vehicle theft, and arson.

■ **Index crimes**
The eight offenses tracked by the FBI's Crime Index.

FIGURE 2.1
Sources of Information about a Crime

Victim
Data counted in *victimization surveys*

Police
Data counted in *uniform crime reports*

Offender
Data counted in *self-report studies*

How many potential sources of information are there about the nature and extent of crime in this incident? In what ways might the information vary depending on the availability and the nature of each source? How might data from the different sources affect our understanding of statistics on crime?

and victims and witnesses often are not able to provide precise information or to agree on what actually happened. Nevertheless, different surveys attempt to explore each of the three primary sources of information to see how well they capture the true extent of crime. Offenders' views are counted in self-report studies, victims' and witnesses' views are counted in victimization surveys, and police data are counted in the FBI Uniform Crime Reports.

The FBI Uniform Crime Reports

In the United States, national crime statistics have been collected since 1930. Every time a crime is reported to police, a notation of the incident is made. Data on these incidents are recorded by local police and sent to the FBI in Washington, D.C. Each year the FBI compiles these statistics and publishes them in its **Uniform Crime Reports (UCR).** Although this process was initiated in 1930 at the recommendation of the International Association of Chiefs of Police (IACP), it was not until 1958 that participation in this voluntary program by local (especially rural) police departments was sufficient to permit national crime estimates. The UCR system now covers virtually all of the U.S. population.

There are, of course, many ways to count crime—by incident, victimization, arrest, conviction, and so forth. The UCR system collects information only on *offenses known to police.* For many years, detailed information was collected for only seven types of offenses, selected on the basis of their seriousness, frequency of occurrence, and likelihood of being reported to the police: criminal homicide, forcible rape, robbery, aggravated assault, burglary, larceny, and motor vehicle theft. Arson was added to the list in 1979. Taken together, these eight crimes on the *Crime Index* indicate the extent of serious crime in the United States. For these crimes, information on the age, sex, and race of suspects is collected.

The UCR system also collects arrest data for nineteen other types of offenses, the "Part II" offenses mentioned earlier. Because the Uniform Crime Reports collect only arrest information for those offenses (not all the instances reported to the police), the utility of UCR data is limited, in that we know only about offenders who are caught.

If the Uniform Crime Reports were our sole source of information about the true extent of crime, it is likely that our picture of the crime rate would be incomplete. For example, many crimes are not reported to the police, but only crimes reported to the police are included in the UCR. Changes in reporting procedures by local police departments also can create artificial increases or decreases in apparent crime rates. In 1997, for example, the FBI announced that it was discarding the crime statistics submitted by the Philadelphia Police Department for the previous eighteen months. The statistics were inaccurate, and Philadelphia agreed to submit corrected figures to the Uniform Crime Reports.[13] Another disadvantage is that data on the Index crimes provide only partial coverage of all serious crime. Corporate price-fixing, illegal dumping, and the manufacture of unsafe products are examples of crimes that cause harm and loss to a much greater extent than

▪ Uniform Crime Reports (UCR)
Annual FBI compilations of all crimes reported to the police in the United States.

WAYS TO
COUNT CRIME

THE CRIME INDEX

NOT ALL CRIMES
ARE REPORTED

do the Index crimes; yet the impact of these crimes is overlooked by the UCR system. The true extent of crime in the United States thus is a bit more difficult to determine than one might think.

Table 2.2 provides a summary of crimes reported to police in the United States over a twenty-five year period. This table, taken from the UCR, includes both the number of crimes reported to the police and the crime rate (i.e., number per 1,000 population). In 1973, for example, a total of 420,650 aggravated assaults were reported to police. Twenty-five years later the number had increased to 974,400. The decimal numbers in Table 2.2, appearing under the number of reported offenses, indicate the rates. That is, the 974,400 aggravated assaults reported to police in 1998 meant that there were 3.61 aggravated assaults for every 1,000 people in the country.

Crime rates are a more reliable way to measure crime than raw numbers of crimes. This is because raw numbers do not account for changes in the population, which can greatly affect the degree of risk faced by an individual. For instance, if there are 100 people in your town and 10 Index crimes were committed last year, your chances of being a victim (on average) will be 1 in 10. However, if your town has 1,000 people living in it and 10 Index crimes are reported, the Uniform Crime Reports will show that the chances of being victimized are only 1 in 100. So even though the number of crimes is the same, each individual's **personal risk** of being the victim varies, depending on the population of potential victims.

Because the population of the United States has been increasing steadily (as displayed in the bottom row of Table 2.2), reports of numbers of crimes

CRIME RATES

■crime rates
The numbers of crimes committed in relation to the population at risk. Crime rates provide an indication of the risk of victimization per capita.

■personal risk
An individual's risk of being a victim of crime; determined through calculation of crime rates in relation to population.

TABLE 2.2

Serious Crimes Reported to Police in the United States (Number and Rate per 1,000 Population)

OFFENSE	1973	1980	1990	1998
Homicide	19,640 .094	23,040 .102	23,440 .094	16,910 .063
Rape	51,400 .245	82,990 .368	102,560 .412	93,100 .344
Robbery	384,220 1.83	565,840 2.51	639,270 2.57	446,630 1.65
Aggravated assault	420,650 2.00	654,960 2.98	1,054,860 4.24	974,400 3.61
Burglary	2,256,500 12.2	3,759,200 16.8	3,073,900 12.4	2,330,000 8.62
Larceny	4,347,900 20.7	7,112,700 31.7	7,945,700 31.9	7,373,900 27.3
Motor vehicle theft	928,800 4.43	1,114,700 5.02	1,635,900 6.6	1,240,800 4.59
U.S. population	209.9 million	225.3 million	249 million	270.3 million

SOURCE: Federal Bureau of Investigation, *Crime in the United States* (Washington, DC: U.S. Government Printing Office, published annually).

can be misleading. An actual example illustrates the point. Table 2.2 indicates that in 1973 there were 384,220 robberies reported to police in the United States—a rate of 1.83 per 1,000 people. Twenty-five years later this number had grown to 446,630, an increase of more than 60,000. However, the 446,630 robberies in 1998 resulted in a *lower* robbery rate: 1.65 per 1,000—because the overall population size was greater. What this means is that although the number of robberies increased, the population grew proportionately faster than the number of robberies taking place. The U.S. population grew from 209.9 million to 270.3 million between 1973 and 1998, a greater rate of growth than the rate of increase in the number of robberies. As a result, there was a slight reduction in an individual's personal risk of being a victim of a robbery. When comparing changes in the extent of crime, therefore, it is important to rely only on crime *rates*, because they account for changes in the population at risk. Measuring risk, after all, is the purpose of counting crimes.

Recently, efforts have been made to measure crimes that were not known to the police, because not all crimes are reported. For example, some victims may fear embarrassment, public disclosure, or interrogation by the police. Some victims may know the offender and not want to inform police of his or her identity. For property crimes, a victim may feel that the value of the property taken is not worth the effort to get police involved. Some may think the police cannot do anything about the crime. Further, some people simply fear or mistrust the police. Some are afraid of possible retaliation by the offender. Finally, some victims of crimes are engaging in criminal behavior themselves and therefore are reluctant to have any involvement with police. For all these reasons, police statistics reported in the Uniform Crime Reports provide an incomplete picture of the true extent of crime.

THE TRUE EXTENT OF CRIME?

The National Crime Victimization Survey

In 1967 the President's Crime Commission, recognizing the need for more accurate knowledge about the amount and kinds of crime, conducted the first national survey of crime victimization. In a survey of 10,000 households (containing 33,000 people), people were asked whether they had been the victim of a crime during the past year and, if so, whether the crime had been reported to the police.

Since 1973 the **National Crime Victimization Survey (NCVS)** has interviewed more than 100,000 individuals from 50,000 households throughout the nation each year. People are asked to report anonymously whether they have been the victims of certain crimes during the past year. Participants in the survey are selected through a representative sampling of households across the country; every household therefore has an equal chance of being included in the survey, so estimates of the true extent of crime can be given with a relatively small margin of error.

In each household surveyed, family members at least twelve years of age are interviewed individually. These surveys elicit much more information than is gathered by the Uniform Crime Reports, in that they include not only crime data but also information about each crime victim's age, sex, race, education level, and income; the extent of injury or loss suffered; any

■National Crime Victimization Survey (NCVS) An annual survey of a representative sample of the U.S. population that assesses the extent of victimization and the extent to which these incidents were reported to police.

PURPOSES OF NCVS DATA

relationship with the offender; and whether or not the crime was reported to the police. As a result, victimization surveys have many more potential uses than do police statistics. To date, NCVS data has been used for the following purposes:

1. To estimate the costs of victim compensation programs and thus help communities determine whether such programs are economically feasible.
2. To determine the kinds of special programs needed for elderly victims of crime. Older citizens' fear of crime remains high, even though victimization rates are low among the elderly.
3. To analyze the circumstance in cases of rape in order to provide better information on ways of preventing this crime.[14]

Victimization surveys thus provide a great deal of information about criminal incidents that can serve as a basis for crime prevention programs.

Victimization surveys also provide a more complete picture of the risk posed by crime than do UCR data, because they count both reported crimes and those not reported to police. For example, the 1967 survey consisted of interviews with 33,000 people and found only 14 rapes, 31 robberies, 71 aggravated assaults, 309 larcenies, and 68 motor vehicle thefts.[15] These numbers showed that crime was relatively rare even when one counted crimes not reported to police. Since 1973 the sample has included 100,000 people, and the survey has been conducted twice a year. The larger sample ensures that enough crime is uncovered so that precise estimates can be made. By contrast, most public opinion polls interview a sample of fewer than 2,000 people to determine nationwide opinion on a particular subject. Fortunately, crimes are much less common than opinions.

While the Uniform Crime Reports collect a little information about all crimes known to police, victimization surveys collect extensive information about a representative sample of the population, whether or not the vic-

COMPARING UCR AND NCVS DATA

One of the chief limitations of the Uniform Crime Reports is that the data are based on crimes reported to the police. Why is this a limitation in understanding crime rates? Why might crimes not be reported? The person in this photograph is being interviewed as part of a National Crime Victimization Survey. What questions will the person be asked? How is the NCVS different from the UCR as a source of data? How will information from this interview contribute to knowledge about crime in the United States?

timization was reported. Like the Uniform Crime Reports, the National Crime Victimization Survey collects information about forcible rape, robbery, assault, burglary, larceny, and motor vehicle theft. (Murder victims, obviously, are not included in victim surveys.) For victimization surveys, forcible rape is defined in the same manner as it is for the Uniform Crime Reports, although the UCR system counts only rapes of females. The NCVS, however, counts both simple (minor) assaults and aggravated assaults, whereas only aggravated assaults are recorded in the UCR.

The crimes of robbery, burglary, larceny, and motor vehicle theft are counted somewhat differently in victimization surveys than they are in the Uniform Crime Reports. The UCR system counts these crimes whether the victim is a private individual or a commercial establishment. The NCVS includes only households, however; so it does not count commercial robberies, burglaries, larcenies, and motor vehicle thefts. Therefore, bank and store robberies, nonresidential burglaries, and larcenies from commercial establishments are omitted from victimization estimates. Further, the UCR definition of motor vehicle theft includes snowmobiles and golf carts, but the NCVS definition does not.

Despite these differences, there is a fairly close correspondence between the definitions used in the UCR and NCVS. As a result, it is possible to gather nationwide crime information from two points of view: that of the victim and that of the police.

Table 2.3 is a summary of nationwide victimization rates over a twenty-five-year period. As in the Uniform Crime Reports, both numbers of crimes

VICTIM SURVEYS SHOW MORE CRIME

TABLE 2.3

Crime Victimization in the United States (Number and Rate per 1,000 population)

OFFENSES	1973	1980	1990	1998
Rape	156,000 1.0	174,000 0.9	130,000 0.6	110,000 0.5
Robbery	1,108,000 6.7	1,209,000 6.6	1,150,000 5.7	886,000 4.0
Aggravated assault	1,622,000 10.1	1,707,000 9.3	1,601,000 7.9	1,674,000 7.5
Household burglary	6,459,000 91.7	6,973,000 84.3	5,148,000 53.8	4,054,000 38.5
Larceny from the person	14,970,000 91.1	15,300,000 83.0	12,975,000 63.8	17,703,000 168.1 (All larcenies)
Household larceny	7,537,000 107.0	10,490,000 126.5	8,304,000 86.7	Combined with other larcenies beginning 1993
Motor vehicle theft	1,344,000 19.1	1,381,000 16.7	1,968,000 20.5	1,138,000 10.8

SOURCE: Lisa D. Bastian, Patsy Klaus, Craig Perkins, Callie Marie Rennison, and Cheryl Ringel, *Criminal Victimization* (Washington, DC: Bureau of Justice Statistics, published annually).

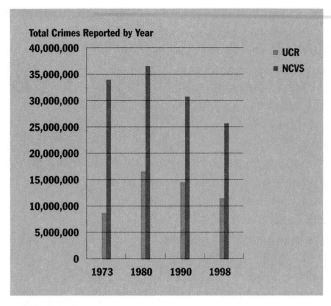

Total Crimes Reported by Year

FIGURE 2.2

The Level of Serious Crime as Measured by UCR and NCVS (Total Crimes Reported by Year)

SOURCES: FBI Uniform Crime Report and National Criminal Victimization Survey data published annually by the Federal Bureau of Investigation and Bureau of Justice Statistics.

REASONS FOR NOT REPORTING CRIMES

TABLE 2.4

Victimizations Reported to Police

TYPE OF CRIME	PERCENTAGE REPORTED IN 1973	PERCENTAGE REPORTED IN 1998
Crimes of violence (total)	46%	46%
Rape	49	32
Robbery	52	62
Aggravated assault	52	58
Simple assault	38	40
Crimes of theft		
Larceny	24	29
Household burglary	47	49
Motor vehicle theft	68	80
All crimes above (weighted average)	32%	38%

and rates of victimization are presented. For example, the NCVS estimates that 1,622,000 aggravated assaults occurred in the United States in 1973. This means that in 1973 there were approximately 10.1 aggravated assaults for every 1,000 citizens in the nation. In 1998 there were an estimated 1,674,000 aggravated assaults—an increase of about 52,000 over twenty-three years. Nevertheless, personal risk declined to 7.5 aggravated assaults per 1,000 citizens, because the population increased at a higher rate than did the number of aggravated assaults. The risk of being a victim of aggravated assault therefore declined by 25 percent. Once again, it can be seen that the use of raw numbers of crimes is misleading, because such numbers provide no indication of changes in degree of personal risk.

A comparison of the extent of crime as reported in police statistics and in victimization surveys reveals significant differences. For instance, the Uniform Crime Reports indicate that there were 93,100 reported cases of forcible rape in 1998, whereas victim surveys show 110,000—nearly 17,000 additional rapes! There were 446,630 reported robberies in 1998, but victim surveys uncovered 886,000 robberies: double the number reported to police. The same is true for all the other crimes counted by both the UCR and NCVS. In every instance, victim surveys show that there is significantly more serious crime than police statistics indicate. Taken as a whole, victim surveys annually uncover two to three times more crime than is reported in the Uniform Crime Reports.

This is clearly one of the most significant findings of the NCVS. As Figure 2.2 illustrates, the amount of crime discovered from interviews with the general public is much greater than the amount reported to police.

Table 2.4 provides a major part of the explanation for these differences. Victimization surveys reveal that, overall, 38 percent of all the crimes they count are reported to police, a percentage that has been generally increasing over the years. Larceny is the crime least likely to be reported (about 29 percent of the time), and motor vehicle theft is the crime most likely to be reported (about 80 percent of the time). The high rate of reporting of auto theft is undoubtedly due to mandatory automobile insurance, which usually requires that a police report be submitted before the owner can make a claim.

The reasons for reporting crimes to police have been found to vary according to the nature of the crime. Figure 2.3 presents the reasons given to interviewers in the National Crime Victimization Survey. The most common reasons for *not* reporting violent crimes are that the victim saw the incident as a private matter or that the offender was not successful in his or her attempt. The most common reasons for not reporting thefts are that the object was recovered, proof was lacking, the offender was unsuccessful, or the incident was reported to someone other than the police. For household crimes, the reasons are the same as those for thefts, with the additional reason that 10 to 12 percent of victims believed the police would not want to be bothered.

To make crime data more useful for purposes of crime analysis, law enforcement, and the design of prevention programs, the **National Incident-Based Reporting System** (NIBRS) is under development in the U.S. Department of Justice. This program collects data on each criminal incident for twenty-two different categories of offenses. The purpose is to gather more complete information about when and where crimes take place, and about the characteristics of the victims and perpetrators. By 1999 eighteen states were certified to submit this more comprehensive information about each criminal incident, and twenty-four more states are in various stages of implementation. Once the NIBRS program is implemented on a national basis, we will know a great deal more about every criminal incident, will understand some underlying factors behind crime trends, and can effectively target crime prevention initiatives.

Another way to assess crime trends is to look at crimes against households (i.e., apartments and homes). A household touched by crime is one that was victimized by burglary or theft, or in which a household member was robbed, raped, or assaulted or had property stolen (no matter where the crime occurred). Approximately 23 percent of households in the United States are touched by crime, and less than 5 percent of the incidents involve violent crimes. This reflects a steady decline in the risk of victimization since 1975, when these statistics were first gathered. Table 2.5 summarizes these changes. In 1975 approximately 1 in 3 households were

Crime	Most Frequent Reasons for Reporting Crimes to the Police
Violent Crime	
Rape	Prevent further crimes by offender, 23% Punish offender, 12% Prevent crime by offender against anyone,* 12%
Robbery	Recover property, 20% Prevent further crimes by offender, 12% Catch or find offender, 11%
Aggravated assault	Prevent further crimes by offender, 20% Stop or prevent this incident, 15% Because it was a crime, 14%
Simple assault	Prevent further crimes by offender, 25% Stop or prevent this incident, 17% Because it was a crime, 11%
Theft	
Personal larceny with contact	Recover property, 36% Because it was a crime, 18% Stop or prevent this incident, 9%
Personal larceny without contact	Recover property, 29% Because it was a crime, 19% Collect insurance, 9%
Household Crime	
Burglary	Recover property, 20% Prevent further crimes by offender, 13% Because it was a crime, 12%
Household larceny	Recover property, 27% Because it was a crime, 15% Prevent further crimes by offender, 11%
Motor vehicle theft	Recover property, 36% Because it was a crime, 12% Collect insurance, 12%

*Estimate is based on 10 or fewer sample cases.

FIGURE 2.3

Reasons That Crimes Are Reported to Police

SOURCE: Marianne W. Zawitz et al., *Highlights from 20 Years of Surveying Victims* (Washington, DC: Bureau of Justice Statistics, 1993).

■**National Incident-Based Reporting System**
Data-collection program designed to gather information on victims, perpetrators, and circumstances of crime.

THE NATIONAL INCIDENT-BASED REPORTING SYSTEM

TABLE 2.5

Households Victimized by Crime

OFFENSE	1975	1992	1995
Violent crimes (rape, robbery, assault)	5.8%	5.0%	2.6%
Burglary	7.7	4.2	4.1
Theft (from person or household)	26.6	16.9	16.4
Motor vehicle theft	1.8	2.0	1.5
Total (Any crime above)	32.1%	22.6%	23.4%

SOURCE: Michael R. Rand, *Crime and the Nation's Households, 1992* (Washington, DC: Bureau of Justice Statistics, 1993); Carol J. DeFrances and Steven K. Smith, *Perceptions of Neighborhood Crime, 1995* (Washington, DC: Bureau of Justice Statistics, 1998).

CRIMES AGAINST HOUSEHOLDS

touched by crime (6 percent involving violence). Twenty years later, fewer than 1 in 4 households were victimized.[16] Despite the increase in the total number of households, from 73.1 million in 1975 to 101.5 million in 1995, the risk of both violent and property crimes against household members dropped. In fact, the level of risk in 1995 was at its lowest point since this measure of victimization was first used in 1975. Naturally, individual risk is affected greatly by place of residence, income, and size of household; but for the nation as a whole, the risk of victimization declined steadily following 1975.

Investigation of the crime that touched this household could be used to provide data for the National Incident-Based Reporting System (NIBRS). What is the purpose of the NIBRS, and how is it different from the NCVS? What kinds of information are collected, and to what uses can these data be put? What have been the trends in the proportion of American households touched by crime over the past decade?

What Offenders Say

A third possible source of information about the extent of crime is the offenders themselves. Efforts to conduct self-report surveys of offenders date from the 1940s.[17] The first studies attempted to identify differences between offenders who were caught and those who were not apprehended. Many subsequent self-report studies have been undertaken, but most use small samples, rather than representative samples of the entire U.S. population as victimization surveys do.[18]

There have been only two national self-report surveys, and these were limited to young people.[19] These surveys were designed to investigate the causes of delinquency rather than to estimate national crime trends.[20] A **National Longitudinal Survey of Youth** begun in 1997, however, administers self-report surveys to a cohort of 9,000 youths aged twelve to sixteen every two years over an extended period of time.

The early results of the National Longitudinal Survey support the findings of early self-report studies. Information from these studies differs from statistics on crimes reported to police. Most important and consistent among the findings of the self-report studies is that virtually all juveniles break the law at one time or another, although only 10 to 20 percent are caught and arrested. Only a small proportion of all youth engage in serious or frequent criminal behavior. Self-report surveys usually do not include questions about many serious crimes, owing to the reluctance of respondents to report their involvement in such crimes. Therefore, they are weighted toward less serious offenses such as alcohol and drug use, truancy, and simple assaults. Also, the administration of self-reports has been confined mostly to schools and communities, environments that exclude some of the most serious and frequent offenders.

Self-reports have also suggested that offenders are more evenly distributed in terms of race and social class than police statistics indicate. To date,

SELF-REPORT SURVEYS OF OFFENDERS

- **National Longitudinal Survey of Youth**
Self-report study investigating extent of delinquency among young people.

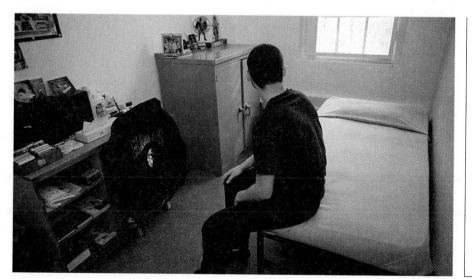

If this juvenile offender were part of a self-report study, what information would he give? What can we learn about crime in the U.S. from self-reports? How would this information complement data from the UCR and the NCVS? How could self-report studies contribute to the development of crime prevention programs? Is it true that most juveniles have engaged in criminal behavior whether or not they have been caught?

self-reports have dealt primarily with characteristics of offenders. Questions could be added about victim selection, victim description, and offenders' relationship to victims. Answers to these questions would help in the development of crime prevention programs that raise public awareness of the causes of victimization.

The Future of Crime in the United States

BEST PREDICTORS OF CRIME?

Trends in crime rates have shown a steady decline, especially since the early 1990s, which is reflected in both Uniform Crime Reports and the National Crime Victimization Survey. The three best predictors of the perpetration of crime are age, opportunity, and motivation. Most people who commit serious crimes are males who are between the ages of sixteen and twenty-four, poor, and from a central city. And victimization surveys show that most victims have the same characteristics as their offenders.

Age is one of the strongest predictors of serious violent and property crime, because these crimes involve force and/or stealth and hence are more likely to be committed by younger people. Few forty-year-olds rob convenience stores, because to do so you may have to be able to hop over the counter, hop back, and maybe outrun a pursuer. People between the ages of sixteen and twenty-four are strong and agile and therefore are the most crime-prone age group. Victims also tend to be in this age range: They are out more often, for more hours, later at night, and in a greater diversity of neighborhoods and settings. However, this is a shrinking age group in the U.S. population. In 1970 the median age in America was twenty-seven; in 2000 it was thirty-five; and by 2020 it is expected to rise past forty as life expectancy increases and birth and immigration rates remain low.[21] These facts and projections led one criminologist to conclude that "there is no evidence that violent or property crimes will increase dramatically over the next two decades, and all indications would seem to be that the rates will actually undergo an overall decline."[22] This view corresponds with the findings of victimization surveys, which show a general decline in the rates of serious crime in recent years.

OPPORTUNITIES FOR CRIME?

This forecast is subject to change, however, especially considering the possible impact of changes in opportunities and motivation for criminal activity in coming years. Opportunities for crime may increase. Serious crimes most often occur in central cities and involve people in poverty. Large pockets of low-income inner-city dwellers, who tend to be undereducated, unskilled, and underemployed, will contribute to serious crimes against persons and property. Twenty percent of all children in the United States are living below the poverty level.[23] Also, 15 percent of young people do not graduate from high school.[24] These facts do not bode well for the future of poverty, a factor closely associated both with serious criminal offenders and with victims.

Added to economic opportunities for crime are those provided by new technology. The popularity of portable equipment of all types—cellular telephones, computers and hand-held computer games, and tape and CD players, among many others—offers opportunities for theft, robbery, and misuse that did not exist even a decade ago. ATM machines, credit cards, and commerce via the computer also have created new opportunities for crime that are technology driven.

The third important factor, after age and opportunity, is motivation. If people are not motivated to be law-abiding, little can be done to stop them. Police now catch only 20 percent of offenders who commit reported serious crimes, a rate that has declined somewhat over the years. Thus, the odds of apprehension are low, have always been low, and are unlikely to increase any time soon. Law and order depends on the fact that most people choose not to break laws. Decisions to commit or to refrain from crime often are based on values and morals established early in life. Respect for others and their property is what keeps most of us law-abiding, whatever our economic background. We learn these values primarily through family and school role models.

MOTIVATION FOR CRIME?

Surveys of youth in custody have found that 70 percent of all juveniles in custody come from single-parent homes, 52 percent have a family member who has been incarcerated, more than half engage in regular drug or alcohol use, and more than 85 percent have been arrested at least twice before.[25] Surveys of high school youth have found that 4 in 10 have been involved in a physical fight and that 33 percent have had property stolen or vandalized at school; more than half of high school seniors have used illicit drugs.[26] A ten-year study tracked more than 1,000 children from age three to age fifteen. It found that preschool behavior problems were the single best predictor of antisocial behaviors' appearing at age eleven.[27] The best predictor of adult criminality is juvenile delinquency, and the best predictor of juvenile delinquency is behavior problems that date back to early childhood. These significant problems in the behavior and supervision of many juveniles may result in increased crime in the years ahead, despite the shrinking proportion of young people in the U.S. population.

Who Are the Perpetrators and Victims of Crime?

To evaluate the nature of criminal events, it is important to understand the types of people who are likely to become involved in such events either as victims or offenders. The Uniform Crime Reports include information about the age, sex, and race of those arrested. The National Crime

Victimization Survey also includes this information, as well as data regarding location, neighborhood, and other relevant factors. In this section we will consider the key sociological characteristics of crime victims and offenders.

Age

There is often little relation between an individual's fear of crime and the actual chances that he or she will be a victim of a crime. The elderly have been found to be most fearful of crime, yet they are victimized less often than any other age group. Figure 2.4 summarizes the distribution of crime victims by age. The figure indicates that in general, from age sixteen onward the younger the person, the greater the likelihood of being victimized by a violent crime (rape, robbery, assault). People age sixty-five or older are victimized by rape, robbery, aggravated assault, and personal larceny at a rate of less than 3 per 1,000. This is seventeen times lower than the victimization rate for the same crimes of sixteen- to nineteen-year-olds, the highest-risk group. It appears that one of the advantages of aging is a reduction in one's likelihood of being a crime victim. The risk is highest during the teenage and young adult years, but it drops dramatically after age twenty-five.

The reasons for these discrepancies by age are not difficult to understand. As noted earlier, young people are more active and mobile and expose themselves to risk more often. They also visit more dangerous places, at later hours, and take fewer security precautions than do older people. In fact, although they own considerably less property than older people, they expose themselves to risk much more often and hence are victimized more often.

According to the UCR, 18 percent of all persons arrested nationally are under eighteen and 45 percent are under age twenty-five. This age pattern does not vary much by type of crime, with 46 percent of violent crime arrests (including homicide) and 58 percent of property crime arrests involving people under age twenty-five.[28] This finding suggests that the majority of crimes are committed by young people, although not necessarily juveniles. Juveniles represent less than 20 percent of all arrests, a number that has been dropping steadily.

Figure 2.5 illustrates trends in arrests of those under age eighteen in the mid- to late 1990s. The graph illustrates that juvenile arrests dropped in every major crime category over the five years shown. Nevertheless, those aged eighteen to twenty-four were the most likely to be arrested. Violent and property crimes require some combination of force and/or stealth and therefore are most easily carried out by younger people. Older people disposed to violence or theft are much more likely to be arrested

JUVENILE OFFENDERS

FIGURE 2.4

Age Distribution of Crime Victims (Rate per 1,000 Persons Age Twelve and Older)

SOURCE: Compiled from Cheryl Rennison, *Criminal Victimization 1998* (Washington, DC: Bureau of Justice Statistics, 1999).

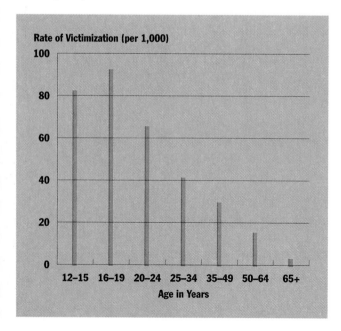

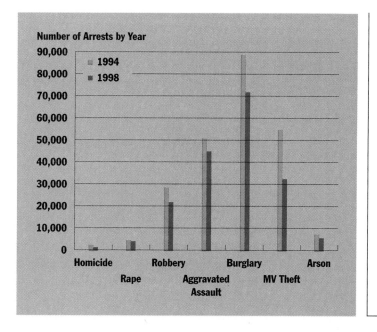

FIGURE 2.5
Five-Year Trends in Arrests of Juveniles (Number of Arrests by Year)

SOURCE: Federal Bureau of Investigation, *Uniform Crime Report* (Washington, DC: U.S. Government Printing Office, published annually).

for forgery, fraud, embezzlement, and offenses against the family, crimes in which the victims either are tricked or have little chance of escape.

Gender

Women make up 22 percent of all those arrested in the United States. Men are 83 percent of individuals arrested for violent crimes and 71 percent of those arrested for property crimes. Women are most frequently arrested for larceny, although they account for only 32 percent of all larceny arrests.[29] It is clear that serious crimes are far more likely to be committed by men than by women. Nevertheless, trends in female criminal activity are increasing. For the five-year period 1994–1998, female arrests rose 13 percent (compared to a 2 percent increase for males). Likewise, female arrests for violent crimes rose by 12 percent during that period, while male arrests for crimes of violence decreased by 12 percent. In general, although female involvement in crime has been increasing in recent years, males still are arrested five times more often than women.

The same is not true for victims, however. Victimization rates for men and women show that property crimes affect women almost as often as men. The rate of property crimes affecting men is 72 per 1,000 population; for women, 64 per 1,000. Women are victimized by violent crimes at a rate of 25 per 1,000 population, whereas the rate for men is 40 per 1,000.[30] Except for the crime of rape, however, women are significantly less likely than men to be victims of serious crime. This is illustrated in Figure 2.6, which shows that women suffer the vast majority of sexual assaults. For other types of assaults men are far more likely to be victimized. Women are only slightly more likely than men to experience thefts from their person with contact (i.e., purse snatching and pickpocketing). Overall, women are

VICTIMIZATION RATES FOR WOMEN

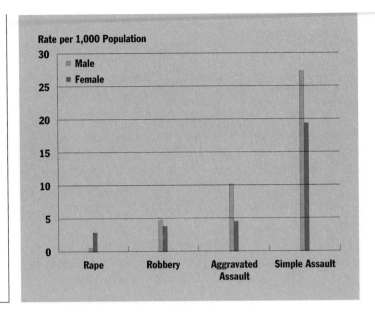

FIGURE 2.6

Gender and Victimization

SOURCE: Cheryl Rennison, *Criminal Victimization 1998* (Washington, DC: Bureau of Justice Statistics, 1999).

overrepresented among crime victims in relation to the rates of arrests of females. This suggests that for virtually all serious crimes, men victimize women in disproportionate numbers.

A significant factor in these patterns of victimization is the victim–offender relationship. More than half of violent crime victims know the offender. In cases of rape and sexual assault, 74 percent of victims knew the offender: Female victims of sexual assault are most likely to be victimized by friends/acquaintances (48 percent), intimates (18 percent), and relatives (8 percent).

What are the characteristics of people who are statistically more likely to become involved in criminal events, either as victims or as perpetrators? What characteristics of age, gender, race and ethnicity, and socioeconomic status relate both to risk of becoming an offender and risk of victimization? What is your risk of criminal victimization?

Race and Ethnicity

Whites account for 63 percent of all arrests for Index crimes—54 percent of arrests for violent crimes and 66 percent of arrests for property crimes. On the other hand, although whites and blacks are victimized by property crimes at the same rate, blacks are significantly more likely to be the victims of violent crimes than are whites.

These data are summarized in Table 2.6. The table makes it clear that blacks are victimized by violent crimes at a rate almost 17 percent higher than the rate for whites.[31] Younger black males are at even higher risk. Black males ages sixteen to nineteen are victimized by violent crime almost twice as often as white males. Nevertheless, the arrest rate for whites is higher than that for blacks for violent crimes. For property crimes, whites are arrested more than twice as often as blacks, although white and black victimization rates for these crimes are identical.

Blacks are more often victimized by rape, robbery, and aggravated assault than whites, although whites are more often victims of simple assault. When one examines the circumstances of these crimes, victimization surveys report that violent crimes involving black victims are twice as likely to be committed by offenders with guns as are violent crimes with white victims (20 percent versus 11 percent). Nevertheless, 80 percent of all victimizations involve white-on-white or black-on-black incidents.[32]

Hispanics constitute a small but growing segment of victims of serious crimes. People of Hispanic origin constitute about 8 percent of the U.S. population. They are immigrants from Spanish-speaking countries such as Mexico (62 percent), Puerto Rico (13 percent), and Central and South America (12 percent). Their rate of victimization by violent crimes is 40 per 1,000 population, 11 percent higher than the rate for whites but 5 percent lower than that for blacks. Hispanics are victims of thefts at a rate comparable to the rates for blacks and whites.[33]

VICTIMIZATION RATES FOR BLACKS AND HISPANICS

TABLE 2.6

Race of Victims and Offenders

RACE	OFFENDERS: VIOLENT CRIME	VICTIMS: VIOLENT CRIME	OFFENDERS: PROPERTY CRIME	VICTIMS: PROPERTY CRIME
White	54%	36 per 1,000	66%	61 per 1,000
Black	45%	42 per 1,000	32%	61 per 1,000
Other	2%	28 per 1,000	2%	52 per 1,000

NOTE: Offenders are percent of total arrests, victims are rate per 1,000 population age 12 and over.
SOURCES: Federal Bureau of Investigation, *Uniform Crime Report* (Washington, DC: U.S. Government Printing Office, published annually); Marianne W. Zawitz et al., *Highlights from 20 Years of Surveying Crime Victims* (Washington, DC: Bureau of Justice Statistics, 1993); Cheryl Rennison, *Criminal Victimization 1998* (Washington, DC: Bureau of Justice Statistics, 1999).

contemporary issues and trends

Carjackings in the United States

- A fifty-one-year-old driver of a Jaguar had her arm broken by a sixteen-year-old carjacker in San Mateo County, California.
- An eighty-year-old woman in Omaha foiled a carjacking attempt when she refused to surrender her car keys and began screaming.
- A cab driver in Ventura County, California, had his taxi stolen at gunpoint.

Reports of incidents like these seem to occur with alarming frequency. Are these events typical, or are they rare events?

Carjacking is defined as robbery of a motor vehicle by a stranger. It differs from other kinds of car thefts because the offender threatens force and the victim is present.

A federal study found that about 49,000 attempted or completed carjackings occurred each year between 1992 and 1996. No distinct upward trend was found. Surprisingly, it was found that nearly two-thirds of carjacking incidents occur within five miles of the victim's home.

Fear that some carjackers intend to kidnap infants led to an analysis of all newspaper accounts over a single year (1997–98). A total of eight infants (up to age two) were reported kidnapped as part of carjackings. Seven of the eight infants were found soon after the incidents. It appears that most offenders were unaware a baby was in the car (generally strapped into a car seat in the rear). After realizing an infant was inside, offenders usually left the infant or abandoned the car.

A law permits federal prosecution of carjackers in cases where there is intent to cause serious injury or death. An average of 229 carjacking cases were filed in federal court each year between 1992 and 1996, but more than half of these were not prosecuted federally; they were left to be adjudicated in state courts. The reason is that few carjacking victims are injured (16 percent), although in about half the cases the offender brandished a firearm.

> A law permits federal prosecution of carjackers in cases where there is intent to cause serious injury or death.

Ninety-two percent of carjacking incidents involved one person in a car, and victims were predominately black males aged twenty-five to forty-nine. Despite reports of carjackings of senior citizens, analysis of all carjackings over a four-year period found that those aged fifty and older were significantly less likely to be victims than any other age group.[a]

1. Explain why carjacking should be classified as a robbery, larceny, motor vehicle theft, or other crime.
2. How do the characteristics of victims of carjackings compare to those of victims of other crimes as found by the NCVS?
3. Given the circumstance of carjacking, what appears to be the offenders' motivation? How would you try to prevent these crimes?

NOTE

a. Patsy Klaus, *Carjackings in the United States* (Washington, DC: Bureau of Justice Statistics, 1999).

It should be kept in mind, of course, that race itself does not predispose a person to crime. In the United States, race and ethnicity are closely tied to age, income, and residence in cities (where crime rates are higher). Whites tend to be older and have higher incomes than blacks and Hispanics. Whites are also more likely to live outside cities. These factors contribute greatly to the differences in rates of victimization by race.

VICTIMIZATION RATES FOR LOW-INCOME HOUSEHOLDS

Socioeconomic Status

The influence of income on the risk of victimization is illustrated by the fact that the risk of household burglary declines as income rises. Households with incomes below $15,000 per year are more than 25 percent more likely to be burglarized than those with incomes above $15,000. Households with incomes of $50,000 or more have the lowest burglary rates (41 per 1,000 households). The same is true for victims of violent crime. People with incomes below $15,000 are 25 percent more likely to be victimized than those earning more. Likewise, rented dwellings are 75 percent more likely to be burglarized than homes that are owned by the resident (73 versus 42 per 1,000 households).

Household income is not related to motor vehicle theft rates, but the higher the annual household income, the higher the non–motor vehicle theft rate. In 1998, for example, households with annual incomes of more than $50,000 suffered about 30 percent more thefts than those with incomes under $15,000.[34] It appears that people with higher incomes lose more money through theft. This theme comes up again in the discussion of white-collar crimes in the next chapter.

critical thinking exercise

The Circumstances of Crime

Statistics merely summarize experience, and crime statistics summarize patterns that enable us to take preventive action. The table here presents crime data about robbery victims gathered through the National Crime Victimization Survey. On the basis of this information, answer the Critical Thinking Questions that follow.

CRITICAL THINKING QUESTIONS

1. You are involved with developing a robbery prevention program. Given the information in the table, what group of potential victims should you target?
2. Where would be a good place to pilot the program?
3. What points might you make and what issues might you address in your prevention program?
4. How could you assess the effectiveness of your program? What measures of this type of crime would you use? Which information would you favor more: UCR, NCVS, or self-report data? Why?

CHARACTERISTICS OF ROBBERY VICTIMS	FINDINGS FROM NATIONAL CRIME VICTIMIZATION SURVEY (1998)
Household income	Less than $7,500 = 6.5 victims per 1,000 population 12 and older
	$7,500–14,999 = 5.8
	$15,000–24,999 = 3.6
	$25,000–34,999 = 6.9
	$35,000–49,999 = 3.1
	$50,000 or more = 2.9
Marital status	Never married = 8.0/1,000
	Married = 1.3
Region of U.S.	Northeast = 3.2/1,000
	Midwest = 3.8
	South = 3.8
	West = 5.2
Residence	Urban = 6.5/1,000
	Suburban = 3.2
	Rural = 2.6
Relationship with offender	Stranger = 57%
	Friend/acquaintance = 21%
	Intimate = 12%
	Other relative = 8%
Weapon use by offender	None = 49%
	Gun = 21%
	Knife = 10%

The Columbine High School shooting incident that opened this chapter turned out to be one of ten shooting incidents that occurred in U.S. schools from 1997 through 1999. The incident at Columbine was the deadliest, but others involved more students and teachers who were wounded but escaped death. High levels of security and fear now grip many schools. In Oregon, for example, more than half the 1,100 students at Parkrose High School stayed out of school after graffiti was found on a bathroom wall saying, "If you think Columbine was bad, wait until Dec. 10, 1999."[35] Nothing occurred on that date, and it was not determined whether the message was a prank; but it is clear that many schools and communities are taking potential violence seriously. Fear of violent crime remains high. Despite falling rates of violent crime nationwide, crime remains a serious problem that is drawing significant attention. That attention increasingly is drawn to the highest-risk group—the young.

Summary

WHAT ARE THE TYPES OF CRIME?

- Crimes are of three general types: crimes against persons (violent crimes), crimes against property, and crimes against public order.

HOW ARE VIOLENT CRIMES AND PROPERTY CRIMES CLASSIFIED?

- Murder includes all intentional killings as well as deaths that occur in the course of felonies; manslaughter involves causing death recklessly, or intentionally under extenuating circumstances.
- Rape is sexual intercourse without effective consent; statutory rape is nonforcible sexual intercourse with a minor.
- Assault is a thrust against another person intended to injure that person.
- Robbery consists of larceny from a person involving threats or force.
- Burglary is unlawful entry into a building for the purpose of committing a crime while inside.
- Larceny consists of taking the property of another person with the intent of depriving the owner.
- Arson is burning of property without the consent of the owner.

HOW ARE CRIME RATES DETERMINED?

- Each year the FBI compiles statistics on crimes reported to the police and publishes them in its Uniform Crime Reports.
- The National Crime Victimization Survey provides information about crimes that are and are not reported to the police.
- Victimization surveys reveal that the amount of serious crime is much higher than police statistics indicate.
- Surveys of offenders show that virtually all juveniles break the law at one time or another.
- Victimization surveys can provide a precise estimate of the risk of crimes against households.
- Crime rates have generally been falling in recent years.

WHO ARE THE PERPETRATORS AND VICTIMS OF CRIME?

- Rates of victimization are higher among teenagers and young adults than among older people; offenders also are most likely to be teenagers or young adults.
- The majority of offenders are male.
- Blacks are much more likely to be victimized by violent crimes than whites.
- Female involvement in crime has been increasing in recent years, although males are arrested five times more often than women.
- People with lower incomes are more likely to be victims of crime than those with higher incomes.

Key Terms

crimes against persons
crimes against property
crimes against public order
criminal homicide
murder
manslaughter
recklessness
negligence
gross negligence
rape
sexual assault
statutory rape
simple assault
aggravated assault
robbery

burglary
larceny
arson
FBI's Crime Index
Index crimes
Uniform Crime Reports
 (UCR)
crime rates
personal risk
National Crime Victimization
 Survey (NCVS)
National Incident-Based
 Reporting System
National Longitudinal Survey
 of Youth

Questions for Review and Discussion

1. What is meant by recklessness? By negligence?
2. In what circumstances are intentional killings punished as manslaughter rather than as murder?
3. How does aggravated assault differ from simple assault?
4. What is the difference between larceny and robbery?
5. Why do the Unified Crime Reports present an incomplete picture of the true extent of crime?
6. What advantages does the National Crime Victimization Survey have over the UCR?
7. What are the most common types of crime as revealed by victimization surveys?
8. What reasons do people give for not reporting crimes to the police?
9. Why are both offenders and victims likely to be young?
10. What factors account for differences in rates of victimization by gender and by race?

Notes

1. Angie Cannon, Betsy Streisand, and Dan McGraw, "Why?," *U.S. News & World Report* (May 3, 1999), pp. 16–19; Brendan Koerner, "From Way Cool to Out of Control," *U.S. News & World Report* (May 3, 1999), pp. 20–21.

2. See *State v. Ott*, 297 Or. 375 (Supreme Ct. Oregon 1984) and *State v. Gounagais*, 88 Wash. 304 (Supreme Ct. Washington 1915).

3. James Alan Fox and Marianne W. Zawitz, *Homicide in the United States* (Washington, DC: Bureau of Justice Statistics, 1999).

4. Federal Bureau of Investigation, *Crime in the United States, 1996* (Washington, DC: U.S. Government Printing Office, 1997).

5. Ronet Bachman, *Violence against Women* (Washington, DC: U.S. Government Printing Office, 1994); Marianne W. Zawitz et al., *Highlights from 20 Years of Surveying Crime Victims* (Washington, DC: Bureau of Justice Statistics, 1993).

6. Federal Bureau of Investigation, *Crime in the United States, 1996* (Washington, DC: U.S. Government Printing Office, 1997).

7. Bachman, p. 10; Zawitz et al., p. 11.

8. Lisa D. Bastian, *Criminal Victimization in the United States, 1990* (Washington, DC: U.S. Government Printing Office, 1992); Zawitz et al., p. 10.

9. Zawitz et al., p. 12.

10. *Berry v. State*, 90 Wis. 2d 316 (Supreme Ct. Wisconsin 1979).

11. Zawitz et al., p. 13.

12. Federal Bureau of Investigation, 1996, p. 54.

13. "FBI Deleting Statistics on Philadelphia Crime," *Richmond Times–Dispatch* (October 20, 1997), p. 2.

14. Patsy Klaus, *Measuring Crime* (Washington, DC: Bureau of Justice Statistics, 1981).

15. James Garofalo and Michael J. Hindelang, *Introduction to the National Crime Survey* (Washington, DC: U.S. Government Printing Office, 1977).

16. Michael R. Rand, *Crime and the Nation's Households, 1992* (Washington, DC: Bureau of Justice Statistics, 1993).

17. Austin L. Porterfield, *Youth in Trouble* (Fort Worth: Texas Christian University Press, 1946); J. S. Wallerstein and C. L. Wylie, "Our Law-abiding Law-breakers," *National Probation* (March-April, 1947), pp. 107–12.

18. See Jay S. Albanese, *Dealing with Delinquency: The Future of Juvenile Justice*, 2nd ed. (Chicago: Nelson-Hall, 1993), pp. 26–31.

19. Delbert S. Elliott et al., *The Prevalence and Incidence of Delinquent Behavior, 1976–1980* (Boulder, CO: Behavioral Research Institute, 1983); Martin Gold, *Delinquent Behavior in an American City* (Belmont, CA: Brooks/Cole, 1970); Martin Gold and D. J. Reimer, "Changing Patterns of Delinquent Behavior among Americans 13–16 Years Old: 1967–1972," *Crime and Delinquency Literature* 7 (1975), pp. 483–517.

20. Robert M. O'Brien, *Crime and Victimization Data* (Beverly Hills, CA: Sage, 1985), pp. 63–79.

21. Gregory Spencer, *Projections of the Population of the United States by Age, Sex, and Race: 1988 to 2080*, U.S. Bureau of Census Current Population Reports, Series P-25, No. 1018 (Washington, DC: U.S. Government Printing Office, 1998).

22. Chester L. Britt, "The Nature of Common Crime in the Year 2010," in J. Klofas and S. Stojkovic, eds., *Crime and Justice in the Year 2010* (Belmont, CA: Wadsworth, 1995), p. 99.

23. Neil Bennett, Jiala Li, Younghwan Song, and Keming Yang, *Young Children in Poverty: A Statistical Update* (New York: National Center for Children in Poverty, 1999); Federal Interagency Forum on Child and Family Statistics, *America's Children: Key National Indicators of Well-Being, 1999* (Washington, DC: Office of Juvenile Justice and Delinquency Prevention, 1999).

24. "Progress Report on Educational Goals," *Associated Press Online* (December 2, 1999); Jerry Zremski, "State Gets Low Marks on Children," *Buffalo News* (February 2, 1991), p. 6.

25. Allen Beck, Susan Kline, Lawrence Greenfield, *Survey of Youth in Custody* (Washington, DC: U.S. Government Printing Office, 1998).

26. Howard N. Snyder and Melissa Sickmund, *Juvenile Offenders and Victims: 1999 National Report* (Washington, DC: Office of Juvenile Justice and Delinquency Prevention, 1999).

27. Jennifer L. White, Terrie E. Moffit, Felton Earles, Lee Robins, and Phil A. Silva, "How Can We Tell?: Predictors of Childhood Conduct Disorder and Adolescent Delinquency," *Criminology* 28 (1990), pp. 507–33.

28. Compiled from Federal Bureau of Investigation, *Crime in the United States* (Washington, DC: U.S. Government Printing Office, 1999), p. 210.

29. Ibid.

30. Ronet Bachman, *Violence against Women* (Washington, DC: U.S. Government Printing Office, 1994).

31. Lisa D. Bastian and Bruce M. Taylor, *Young Black Male Victims* (Washington, DC: Bureau of Justice Statistics, 1994).

32. Catherine J. Whitaker, *Black Victims* (Washington, DC: Bureau of Justice Statistics, 1990).

33. Lisa D. Bastian, *Hispanic Victims* (Washington, DC: Bureau of Justice Statistics, 1990).

34. Callie Marie Rennison, *Criminal Victimization 1998* (Washington, DC: Bureau of Justice Statistics, 1999).

35. "Oregon Students Absent after Threat," *Associated Press Online* (December 11, 1999).

three
Dealing with Sophisticated Crimes

Whereas most street crimes are

either random or involve very little planning, sophisticated crimes require planning or organization to succeed. Most street crimes take only a few minutes or even seconds to accomplish. Sophisticated crimes often take days, weeks, and sometimes months to plan and carry out. Take the case of Day-Lee Foods in California. The chief financial officer of this meat-packing firm began writing checks to himself from company accounts and depositing them into his automatic teller machine. To circumvent company audits, he used handwritten checks rather than computer-generated checks, which were routinely audited. He used lines of credit to replace the missing cash, then concealed the loans by manipulating other company accounts. These manipulations allowed him to pay his ex-wife $600,000 per year in family support payments, even though his annual salary was only $150,000! He was able to finance a lavish lifestyle for himself and his ex-wife until the Internal Revenue Service (IRS) arrested him in 1997. Ultimately, he embezzled $100 million. It took him seven years to carry out this crime, the largest embezzlement in U.S. history.[1]

Consider the similarities between the Day-Lee Foods case and another crime that occurred more than a half century earlier. The famous gangster Al Capone was widely believed to be involved in illegal gambling and bootlegging, but no one was able to prove it. Then the IRS examined his bank accounts and spending habits in Miami and Chicago and found that Capone had spent $7,000 for suits, $1,500 per week for hotel bills, $40,000 for a house on Palm Island, $39,000 on telephone calls, and $20,000 for silverware. This spending pattern suggested that he earned $165,000 per year. The IRS asked Capone to show how he lawfully earned this amount of money. Capone could not do so and was tried and convicted for failure to pay income taxes on $1 million of illegal income.[2]

In both cases it can be seen that planning and organization were central to the commission of the crimes, and that the crimes can be ongoing in nature. Sophisticated crimes are characterized by such planning.

Sophisticated crimes will reach new levels in the coming years. An aging population no longer suited to committing street crimes, more service industry jobs with access to cash and personal information, computers in most homes and workplaces, the ease of international travel and trade, and Internet communication for terrorists and hate groups—this combination of circumstances will promote new forms of white-collar, organized, and computer crime and will promote terrorism and hate crimes. Those who will exploit the opportunities and technologies of the era will be clever.

Sophisticated crimes are the most serious crimes occurring today, and they are the subject of this chapter. The following sections highlight several types of sophisticated crimes and their impact on our lives.

What Is Meant by Sophisticated Crimes?

CONSPIRACY

WHITE-COLLAR
CRIME

■ **conspiracy**
Agreement between two or more persons to commit a crime or to carry out a legal act in an illegal manner.

■ **white-collar crimes**
Crimes that are usually carried out during the course of a legitimate occupation; include crimes of fraud, crimes against public administration, and regulatory offenses.

Sophisticated crimes include white-collar crime, organized crime, computer crime, international and domestic terrorism, and some forms of hate crimes. The common behaviors that underlie these crimes links them together. The criminal law punishes the kind of criminal planning that underlies sophisticated crimes as **conspiracy.** Conspiracy takes places when two or more persons agree to commit a crime or to carry out a legal act in an illegal manner. Conspiracy, then, is essentially *preparation* or planning to commit a crime. The importance of making conspiracy a crime can be seen in virtually every case of white-collar, computer, and organized crime, in which authorities can punish the *planning* activities of sophisticated criminals, thereby thwarting their criminal designs.

White-collar crimes are crimes that are usually carried out during the course of a legitimate occupation. In place of the force or stealth that is inherent in violent and property crimes, white-collar crimes employ deceit in an effort to trick an unsuspecting victim. White-collar crimes are of three types: crimes of fraud, crimes against public administration, and regulatory offenses.[3] **Crimes of fraud** have money as their object and include embezzlement, extortion, forgery, and fraud. **Crimes against public administration** attempt to impede government processes. These include bribery, obstruction of justice, official misconduct, and perjury. **Regulatory offenses** are violations that circumvent measures designed to protect public health, safety, or welfare in business, industry, and government. It can be seen that *white-collar crime* is a generic term that encompasses several specific types of crimes.

How Can White-Collar Crimes Be Defined?

hite-collar crime goes beyond the crimes committed by business and professional people who often wear jackets, ties, and white shirts to work. It is easy to distinguish a mugging from an embezzlement, but what about the difference between simple theft and fraud? Or between assault and an injury caused by a defective product? The distinctions between white-collar and traditional street crimes are not always clear. These two categories of offenses are not distinguishable by the amount of harm they cause, because frauds or unsafe products can cause much more injury and harm than any number of street crimes. Nor are they distinguishable by the level of violence involved. Many street crimes, such as larceny and burglary, involve no personal confrontation, but conspiracy, extortion, or food and drug manufacturing violations can involve threats, injury, and even death. The distinctions between white-collar crime and more traditional forms of crime therefore do not lie in the nature of the victim, or in the amount of violence, or in the extent of injury. Instead, white-collar crime is distinguishable by the manner in which it is carried out, given available opportunities. The opportunity to commit such crimes is often determined by one's position in society. One cannot embezzle funds without first holding a position of financial trust, nor can one commit regulatory offenses without holding a particular position in business or industry. Thus, *access* to financial or governmental or institutional resources provides the *opportunity* to commit white-collar offenses.

Street crimes are characterized by the use of *force or stealth*, which is is required for homicide, rape, robbery, assault, burglary, larceny, or arson. In contrast, white-collar crimes are characterized by planning and deceit. *Planning and deceit* are required for successful conspiracy, fraud, extortion, embezzlement, forgery, or regulatory offenses. Thus, white-collar crime can be defined as:

> *planned illegal acts of deception committed by an individual or organization, usually during the course of legitimate occupational activity by persons of high or respectable social status, for personal or organizational gain that violates fiduciary responsibility or public trust.*[4]

- **crimes of fraud**
  Embezzlement, extortion, forgery, and fraud.
- **crimes against public administration**
  Attempts to impede government processes through bribery, obstruction of justice, official misconduct, or perjury.
- **regulatory offenses**
  Attempts to circumvent regulations designed to ensure fairness and safety in the conduct of business; include administrative, environmental, labor, and manufacturing violations as well as unfair trade practices.

ROLE OF PLANNING AND DECEIT

This definition highlights several facts about white-collar crime:

- It can be committed by an individual or by an organization or group of individuals.

- Deception, trickery, or fraud lies at the heart of white-collar crime.

- Most white-collar crimes emanate from otherwise legitimate occupational activity in which access to money or information makes possible the misuse of one or both of these resources.

- White-collar offenses sometimes lie on the border between illegal and unethical behavior, where what a company does may cause harm or even death without actually violating the criminal law. Many unethical offenses are adjudicated in civil proceedings that determine compensation, rather than in criminal court, which determines guilt.

Types of White-Collar Theft

EMBEZZLEMENT

EXTORTION

embezzlement
The purposeful misappropriation of property entrusted to one's care, custody, or control to which one is not entitled.

extortion
Purposeful obtaining of property from another person when his or her consent has been induced through wrongful use of force or fear or under the guise of official authority.

Table 3.1 shows a typology of white-collar crimes. As the table illustrates, white-collar crimes can be divided into three groups: theft, offenses against public administration, and regulatory offenses. White-collar thefts include embezzlement, extortion, forgery, and fraud. **Embezzlement** is the purposeful misappropriation of property entrusted to one's care, custody, or control to which one is not entitled. In some states this crime is called "misapplication of property" and is included under theft as a type of larceny. The essential element of embezzlement is violation of fiduciary (or financial) trust. An example is the former police chief in Rochester, New York, who was convicted of stealing $243,000 in police department funds over a three-year period.[5] Embezzlement is usually punished on the basis of how much money or property is misappropriated.

Extortion also involves theft, but it is accomplished in a different manner. It consists of purposely obtaining property from another person with

TABLE 3.1		
A Typology of White-Collar Crime		
CRIMES OF THEFT	**CRIMES AGAINST PUBLIC ADMINISTRATION**	**REGULATORY OFFENSES**
Embezzlement	Bribery	Administrative violations
Extortion	Obstruction of justice	Environmental violations
Forgery	Official misconduct	Labor violations
Fraud	Perjury	Manufacturing violations
		Unfair trade practices

SOURCE: Jay S. Albanese, *White-Collar Crime in America* (Englewood Cliffs, NJ: Prentice Hall, 1995).

his or her consent, when that consent is induced through wrongful use of force or threat of force or under the guise of official authority. Many states classify extortion as a type of larceny or theft. Extortion is sometimes called blackmail, as in the case of Sol Wachtler, chief judge of the New York State Court of Appeals, who was charged with telling his former lover that he would sell sexually explicit photos of her and her new boyfriend if she did not give him money.[6] The word *blackmail* is derived from European terms for money or payment (e.g., French *maille,* Gaelic *mal,* German *Mahl*). The "black" is believed to reflect the illegal nature of the payments and also may refer to the metal in which the payment historically was made. Copper or other base metal was usually used, rather than silver (a "white" metal). With the advent of paper currency, metal coins are now infrequently used as a form of payment, but the term *blackmail* continues to be used today.

A person who falsely makes or alters an official document with intent to defraud commits the crime of **forgery.** The penalty for forgery is often based on the type of document that is forged. For example, forging passports or currency usually carries a higher penalty. Forgery also includes other offenses that are sometimes defined separately under state law. Counterfeiting money, criminal possession of forged documents, and falsifying business records are all variations of the crime of forgery. In one forgery case, police found 250,000 fake social security cards, green cards, and counterfeit $20 bills in a suspected $8 million operation at a Los Angeles print shop.[7]

Another type of white-collar theft is **fraud,** or purposely obtaining the property of another person through deception. Fraud is at the heart of the concept of white-collar crime. Together with conspiracy, it forms the basis for many organized illegal acts. In many states bankruptcy fraud, false advertising, issuing a bad check, criminal impersonation, and theft of services are regarded as specific types of fraud. Fraud thus involves larceny by trickery or deceit. A common form of fraud is telemarketing scams. In a typical case, a New Jersey company used a 900 number to charge people up to $28 per call for responding to mail announcing that they had won a prize—which turned out to be worthless jewelry.[8] In a well-known 1998 case, American Family Publishers agreed to pay $1.25 million to thirty-two states over allegations of deceptive sales practices. This company sent more than 200 million mailings annually, using the names of well-known celebrities Ed McMahon and Dick Clark, to tell each recipient that he or she was one of a very small number of winners. The mailings suggested that if recipients ordered magazine subscriptions, their chances of winning a multimillion-dollar prize would be enhanced. The company agreed to make it clearer in future mailings that no purchase was necessary to enter or win the sweepstakes prize. This settlement was similar to one reached between Publishers Clearing House and fourteen states a few years earlier.[9] Although money is not obtained by theft in these cases, deceptive practices can trick a person into believing they are buying a chance at a million dollars through a magazine order. Obtaining money through deception is the essence of fraud.

FORGERY

▪**forgery**
False making or altering of an official document with the intent to defraud.

FRAUD

▪**fraud**
Purposeful obtaining of the property of another person through deception.

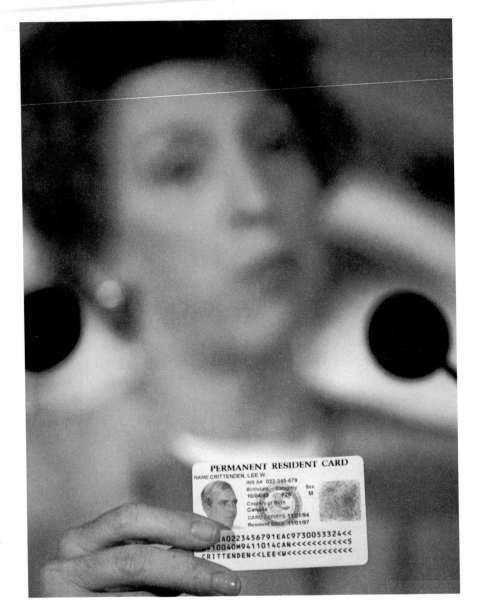

Forgery is the alteration of an official document with intent to defraud, and knowingly buying or selling forged documents also are criminal acts. What "documents" typically are found in forgery cases? What characteristics of forgery make it a white collar crime? What are some other types of white collar theft? Why is forgery a growing concern in the 21st century, and what solutions are being considered?

Economic and Political Crimes

Economic and political crimes involve misconduct by government officials and by individuals attempting to disrupt or corrupt government processes. The crimes in this category include bribery, obstruction of justice, official misconduct, and perjury. **Bribery** involves the voluntary giving or receiving of anything of value with the intent to influence the action of a public official. The more important the official act to be performed is, the more serious the penalty. For example, bribery of a judge in a criminal case carries a significant penalty. Bribery law works two ways: One can be convicted of bribery for offering the corrupt payment as well as for receiving it. In South Carolina, for example, fifteen legislators and six lobbyists were among those convicted after the FBI videotaped legislators taking cash from lobbyists in exchange for their votes.[10] Seven Arizona legislators were charged in a similar bribery scandal.[11]

Intentionally preventing a public servant from lawfully performing an official function is **obstruction of justice.** In the cover-up of the 1972 burglary of the Democratic party headquarters in the Watergate complex, for example, members of the White House staff refused to cooperate with investigations of alleged wrongdoing, and some were ultimately convicted of purposely concealing relevant information, which is obstruction of justice.[12] In 1993 three New York State troopers confessed to falsifying fingerprints in more than thirty criminal cases over a period of nine years in order to "solve" cases with adulterated evidence.[13] Lying about this evidence in court was obstruction of justice.

Official misconduct is a public official's unauthorized exercise of an official function with intent to benefit or injure another. Also, a person who uses an elected office for personal gain is guilty of official misconduct. Such misconduct can result from an act of omission (failure to perform legal duties) or commission (exercising powers in an unauthorized manner). People who use their public office to "fix" tickets, obtain permits without payment, or solicit sex are committing official misconduct. A police officer was convicted of this crime when he tried to get the driving records of a woman he was accused of raping.[14]

When someone makes a false statement under oath in an official proceeding, he or she is guilty of **perjury** or false swearing. The punishment for perjury is usually based on the nature of the proceeding. Perjury during a trial or grand jury proceeding is considered more serious than false swearing on an affidavit. John Poindexter, former national security advisor to President Reagan, was convicted of perjury when he was shown to have lied to Congress as part of the cover-up in the Iran–Contra affair.[15] In 1999 inside information provided by a former officer in the Los Angeles Police Department resulted in the dismissal of several cases due to confirmed instances of false testimony and planted evidence.[16]

Corporate Crimes

The third category of white-collar crimes is **corporate crimes**, also called regulatory offenses. The laws governing these offenses are designed to ensure fairness and safety in the conduct of business so that the desire for profits does not lead to dangerous or unjust actions. There are hundreds of types of regulatory offenses, but they can be grouped into five different categories: administrative, environmental, labor, and manufacturing violations, and unfair trade practices.

Administrative offenses involve the failure to comply with court orders or agency requirements. Failures to keep adequate records, submit compliance reports, acquire a valid permit, and the like are against the law where these procedures are required. For example, Equifax, a leading credit-reporting agency, settled a case brought by eighteen states alleging that it was issuing inaccurate credit reports. The company agreed to make credit reports easier to read, to explain to consumers how a credit rating is derived, and to resolve disputed reports within thirty days. Another credit-reporting agency, TRW, settled a similar case brought by nineteen states.[17] In the year 2000,

OBSTRUCTION

■**obstruction of justice**
Intentional prevention of a public servant from lawfully performing an official function.

MISCONDUCT

■**official misconduct**
A public official's unauthorized exercise of an official function with intent to benefit or injure another.

PERJURY

■**perjury**
Making a false statement under oath in an official proceeding.

■**corporate crimes**
Dangerous or unjust actions in the conduct of business, prompted by the desire for profits. Same as *regulatory offenses.*

ADMINISTRATIVE OFFENSES

In this photograph, what type of of regulatory offense has been committed by a corporation? What other types of regulatory offenses are involved in corporate crimes? Do you think corporate crimes are potentially as harmful as violent crimes and property crimes? Why or why not? What accounts for continuing increases in white collar crime in the U.S.?

ENVIRONMENTAL VIOLATIONS

LABOR VIOLATIONS

UNFAIR TRADE PRACTICES

Bayer agreed to pay $1 million over an inaccurate claim that nearly all adults could prevent heart attacks with aspirin.[18]

Environmental violations include emissions or dumping in violation of legal standards. Discharges of harmful substances into the air or water without a permit, failure to treat waste adequately before disposal, and deposit of hazardous waste in a landfill are examples of environmental violations. Rockwell International pleaded guilty to felony charges after it stored hazardous waste without a permit and the waste leaked into reservoirs outside Denver, Colorado. The company agreed to pay an $18.5 million fine.[19]

Labor violations can take several forms, including discriminatory hiring practices, exposure of employees to harm in the workplace environment, and unfair treatment of employees. Examples of unfair treatment include firing without cause, refusing employment, and ignoring complaints of sexual harassment. Imperial Food Products officials were charged in 1992 with twenty-five counts of involuntary manslaughter for locked exits and other safety violations that resulted in the deaths of twenty-five workers in a fire at Imperial's chicken-processing plant in Hamlet, North Carolina.[20] In 1999 a Boston contractor was fined by the Occupational Safety and Health Administration for repeated safety violations after a worker fell fifteen feet into a pit and was killed.[21]

The manufacture of unsafe products is the essence of the manufacturing violations category. Electric shock hazards, fire hazards, and lack of adequate labeling or directions on products are examples of such violations. In one case the Federal Trade Commission found that Kraft had falsely labeled its "Singles" cheese slice as containing the same amount of calcium as five ounces of milk; in fact, the calcium content was measurably lower than that.[22] In 1997, two members of the Pilgrim family of Mississippi received prison sentences for selling syrup and honey products that were labeled as pure but were not made from pure ingredients.[23]

Unfair trade practices prevent fair competition in the marketplace. Monopolization, price discrimination, price-fixing, and bid rigging are examples of unfair trade practices. In one case the state of Florida filed a lawsuit against three manufacturers of infant formula, claiming that they had conspired to raise the price of baby formula. The state pointed out that formula prices had risen 155 percent, whereas the price of milk, the primary ingredient, had risen only 36 percent over the same period.[24] Toys R Us and two other toy makers agreed in 1999 to pay $50 million to settle a multistate lawsuit claiming that they prevented other toy makers from selling popular toys to discount stores. The case arose from a complaint by the FTC that Toys R Us illegally used its size and domination of the toy market to force toy makers to supply toys to them and not to discount stores.

Media and Criminal Justice

In the 1999 hit movie *A Civil Action*, the viewer is presented with a familiar stereotype of the civil lawyer: the arrogant, money-hungry, egotistical ambulance chaser. For the dynamic Jan Schlichtmann, winning a case is only about making money, not about procuring justice. Schlichtmann is successful because he can assess, with calculator precision, the civil action value of a damaged human: A white male professional struck down in his prime is worth the most, but a dead child who has accomplished nothing is worth very little.

The viewer is surprised, then, when Schlichtmann travels to Woburn, Massachusetts, to visit a group of parents who have lost children to leukemia. As the Woburn residents began to recognize the extraordinarily high rate of cancer in their community, significant toxic pollutants were found in two of the town's water wells. Schlichtmann is not impressed with their case, because without the source of the toxins, he has no deep-pockets defendant to sue. But as he is leaving the little town, he stops on a bridge and notes a sudsy residue floating on the banks of the river beneath him. He follows the polluted water to its source, a tannery that surely has been dumping chemicals into the environment in order to avoid expensive toxic waste disposal regulations.

Schlichtmann's face lights up, not because he has determined the source of the polluted wells, but because he notices the corporate logos on the trucks that service the tannery: Beatrice Foods and W. R. Grace & Co. If these company names sound familiar, it is because they are real-life big-money corporations. Indeed, the story of Jan Schlichtmann and the civil action he instigates against these two industry giants is true, based on the book *A Civil Action* by Jonathan Harr.

While the film version of Harr's book does take some fictional liberties, it provides an excellent account of the real 1970s civil case against Beatrice Foods and W. R. Grace. In the movie we see a tannery foreman explaining that the process by which animal hides are cured involves pouring chemicals over the leather. Questions remain as to whether the chemical spillage from the process is responsible for the toxins

in the wells and to what extent the pollutants were spread knowingly or intentionally. Because the alleged environmental violations have been blamed for the illness and deaths of many Woburn residents, Schlichtmann has the responsibility of proving specific cause and effect in relation to the damages he is claiming.

Perhaps the most interesting aspect of the story is how the case humanizes the showboat lawyer Schlichtmann. He is clearly out for profit when he takes the case, but as he is faced with the suffering of the parents of Woburn's leukemia victims, his motive becomes more about justice than money. It is a position that will cost him the case: In his search for truth and justice, he turns down a $20 million offer from Grace and a $4 million offer from Beatrice. (The jury later would award $8 million from Grace, allocated almost exclusively for toxic cleanup, and would absolve Beatrice of liability). For the parents the civil action was obviously never about the money; but for Schlichtmann, the eye-opening experience has left his prestigious law firm bankrupt.

Currently there are many proposals in Congress that would limit the awards that plaintiffs can recover for personal injury. It is important to realize, however, than in civil actions against major corporations for regulatory crimes such as environmental dumping, the corporate giants always will have the hefty advantage of almost unlimited funds with which to finance their defense.

Is it possible that corporations are aware of their regulatory crimes but determine that it is more financially advantageous to pay damages than to fix the problem? Should there be a cap on how much injured parties can recover from regulatory crimes? Who ultimately pays for the damages that corporations must remit if they lose in a civil action brought against them?

In this way, Toys R Us was alleged to have unfairly reduced its competition in the toy market and to have artificially raised prices.[25]

As the offense categories for corporate crimes illustrate, regulations are designed to protect the public from unscrupulous or dangerous business practices. This type of white-collar crime is based on deviations from legitimate business activity. Penalties for violating regulations sometimes involve criminal sanctions; thus, regulatory offenses are part of the criminal law.

Trends in White-Collar Crime

An important question is whether white-collar crime is increasing or decreasing. An answer is not readily available, because there are no regularly collected data for white-collar crimes as there are for street crimes. Victimization surveys count only rape, robbery, assault, burglary, larceny, and motor vehicle theft. The Uniform Crime Reports, however, include forgery/counterfeiting, fraud, and embezzlement in their tallies of arrests (which represent only offenders who are caught). As Table 3.2 indicates, arrest rates for all these offenses have risen dramatically since 1970, even if we control for population growth (rate per 100,000 population). Both the number and the rate of arrests for fraud are higher than those for embezzlement and forgery, although arrest rates for the latter crimes have increased as well.

INCREASES IN
WHITE-COLLAR
CRIME

Increases in white-collar crime reflect employment trends. The proportion of the U.S. population employed in jobs that provide access to information and financial accounts is increasing, and as a result more people have access to criminal opportunities involving misuse of authority and funds.[26] As Americans move farther away from agriculture and manufacturing to jobs in service industries, high technology, and related professions, access to cash and account numbers by more employees will increase the opportunities for fraud.

Increases in white-collar crime also will reflect demographic trends. The average age of the U.S. population is rising. In 1970 the median age was 27,

TABLE 3.2

Arrests for White-Collar Crimes (Number and Rate per 100,000 Population)

OFFENSES	1970	1980	1995	1998	PERCENT CHANGE IN RATE
Forgery/ counterfeiting	43,833 28.9	72,643 34.9	91,991 46.8	81,254 43.7	+62%
Fraud	76,861 50.7	261,787 125.7	320,046 162.9	268,351 144.3	+124%
Embezzlement	8,172 5.4	7,885 3.8	11,605 5.9	12,215 6.6	+9%

SOURCE: Data compiled from Federal Bureau of Investigation, *Crime in the United States* (Washington, DC: U.S. Government Printing Office, published annually).

in 2000 it was 35, and by 2025 it will be about 40.[27] The aging of the U.S. population is due to a low birthrate combined with the fact that people are living longer than earlier generations did. The net result is more people in the "white-collar crime–prone" over-twenty-five age group. The majority of those arrested for forgery, embezzlement, and fraud are over twenty-five.

Why Is Computer Crime a Growing Threat?

The United States and much of the rest of the world has become completely dependent on computers and electronic telecommunications. Most U.S. households now have computers, as do the vast majority of governments, businesses, and schools. In the very near future, computers will become as central to our lives at home as they already are at work for most people. The opportunities for misuse of information systems and communication technologies grow daily.

The spread of the automobile early in the twentieth century nearly doubled the number of offenses named in the criminal codes of the United States, and the dominance of the computer is likely to have the same impact in the twenty-first century. Automobiles provided opportunities for illegal activity ranging from substandard manufacturing and repair frauds to auto theft. Computers will have a similar impact as computer viruses and cybertheft threaten people's property and the public order. Legal codes are being modified to eliminate opportunities for crime or misuse, much as changes were needed when automobiles became commonplace.

Types of Computer Crimes

COMPUTERS AS INSTRUMENTS AND OBJECTS OF CRIME

Computers are most often used to steal, but they can be used to commit other crimes as well. Different types of **computer crime** can be grouped into two basic categories: crimes in which computers are used as the *instrument* of the offense, and crimes in which computers are the *object* of the offense. Computers are used as an instrument in crimes of theft such as embezzlement, fraud, or larceny by computer. For example, the controller at Halifax Technology Services admitted embezzling $15 million by generating corporate checks to herself over a period of three years. In 1999 she was sentenced to six and a half years in prison, and she must make repayment at a rate of no less than $500 per month until the debt is repaid.[28] Computers can also be instruments of crime when they are used for purposes of extortion or harassment. The spread of computer viruses, hidden programs that annoy a user or threaten to alter a user's computer files, is an example. Thousands of Internet users received unsolicited e-mails stating that their orders had been processed and their credit card would be charged $300, but these people had not ordered anything. They were advised to call a phone number with a 767 area code if they had questions. The phone number

■**computer crime**
Crimes in which computers are used as the instrument of the offense, and crimes in which computers are the object of the offense.

turned out to be a phone sex line that incurred an automatic charge when connected. The number was located in the West Indies. The conspirators received their money from the phone companies who charged the customers for their connection to the phone sex line. At the end of 1999 the individuals behind the conspiracy had still not been located, but the FTC had obtained a court order to freeze the funds collected by phone companies for calls to the phone sex number.[29] This scheme illustrates the fact that criminal behavior in the new millennium will involve more sophisticated ways to steal and that the response of the criminal justice system will have to be more sophisticated as well.

Computers can be the object of a crime when the intention is to cause damage to computer hardware (machines) or software (programs). Data destruction and theft or vandalism of computers or programs are examples of such crimes. Likewise, computers can be the object of crime when the intention is to alter data stored in them. Attempts to alter financial statements, credit histories, or college grades are examples of this type of computer crime. In other cases, privileged or confidential information, such as software or company secrets, can be altered for purposes of sabotage or copied and sold for illicit profit. Table 3.3 illustrates the variations within the two general categories of computer crime.

Consequences of Computer Crime

The most common form of computer crime is theft by computer. The computer manager at King Soopers stores in Colorado was charged with stealing $2 million by manipulating computer records at the stores while he was supposed to be fixing "bugs" in the system.[30] Increasingly, computers and high-quality color printers are used to counterfeit U.S. currency. Of the $40 million in counterfeited money seized in 1998, $16 million was computer generated.[31] In these cases computers are used as an instrument to carry out thefts in the form of embezzlement and fraud.

TABLE 3.3	
Types of Computer Crime	
COMPUTER AS INSTRUMENT	COMPUTER AS OBJECT
Theft by computer (using a computer as a tool to steal)	Damage to software/hardware (physical or electronic damage to computers or computer programs)
Harassment/extortion (using a computer as a means for intimidation or threats)	Data alteration (changing information for undue advantage or revenge)

SOURCE: Jay S. Albanese and Robert D. Pursley, *Crime in America: Some Existing and Emerging Issues* (Englewood Cliffs, NJ: Prentice Hall, 1993).

Virus Alert

The Michelangelo virus is due to active on March 6th. This virus will destroy all data on floppy and hard disks. A recent survey found that almost 80% of NJIT's population may be infected with this virus. Please scan all of your disks for viruses. A shareware copy of virus scan is available from the software distribution system in all PC Labs.

Press any key to Continue

VICON

In the crime suggested by this photograph, is the computer the object or the instrument of the cime? What is the difference? What are some examples of each of these two types of computer crime? How is computer crime becoming a threat to individuals, businesses, national infrastructures, and global security? What impact do you think computer crime will have on criminal law and the American criminal justice system?

A onetime executive at Squibb and Sons, Inc., formerly one of the largest pharmaceutical firms in the United States, pleaded guilty to fraud in a scheme to steal more than $1 million of merchandise from the company. In one instance the executive arranged through a computer order to have $8,000 worth of merchandise shipped from a Massachusetts distribution center. Moments later he arranged to have the computer "kill" the invoice without leaving a trace. The goods were eventually sold to a middleman, who distributed them at a discount to drugstores.[32]

CYBERTHEFT

Examples of computer crimes abound. Kevin Mitnick was charged with four counts of fraud for using a friend's office computer to break into the computer system at Digital Equipment Corporation. Mitnick copied software that had cost Digital $1 million to develop. He was also charged with electronically entering the Leeds University computer system in England and transferring his telephone charges to a nonexistent MCI long-distance account. In 1999, Mitnick pled guilty to charges of penetrating business computer systems and causing millions of dollars in damage.[33] In another case, computer hackers apparently stole $12 million in telephone charges from NASA over two years, using long-distance credit card numbers.[34] These are examples of a trend toward using computers as a "burglar's tool" to conduct theft.

HACKER HARASSMENT

Another type of computer crime is the use of a computer to harass or extort a victim. Perhaps the most notorious case of this type is that of Donald Burleson, who inserted a virus (a program that continuously duplicates itself, interfering with the normal operation of computers) into the computer system at a brokerage firm from which he had been fired. The virus erased 168,000 sales commission records.[35] Robert Morris, a twenty-three-year-old graduate student, released a macrovirus that brought more than

6,000 university, research, and military computers to a standstill, although no information was taken or lost.[36] Many other viruses have been planted in computer programs. Some are relatively innocuous, flashing "Peace" or other messages on thousands of computer screens; others can be extremely harmful. The potential for damage has intensified efforts to improve security technology.

A twenty-one-year-old college student in New Jersey was charged when he sent 24,000 e-mail messages to two administrators, who promptly revoked his computer privileges.[37] In 1997 nine regional Internet service providers were infiltrated by hackers—individuals with sophisticated knowledge who go to great lengths to infiltrate computer systems.[38] In each of these cases the computer was used as an instrument to harass, invade privacy, or extort a victim. Hackers were detected in U.S. military computers more than 2,000 times during the 1990s, usually attempting to steal software or data or to leave viruses.[39] Although classified information has not been accessed, the potential threat is clear.

SOFTWARE PIRATING

Another type of computer crime involves damage to hardware or software. The damage can be physical or can exist in terms of competitive value. For example, Microsoft Corporation, working with U.S. marshals, seized more than $1 million in counterfeit software in Los Angeles that had been produced by ten illicit businesses.[40] Pirated software has been smuggled to Hong Kong and elsewhere, where copies of programs such as Windows are sold for only five dollars.[41] Printed matter and photographic images also are pirated in acts of copyright infringement.

In some computer crimes the object is acquisition or alteration of data for an unlawful purpose. During the 1980s a computer systems manager at Lawrence Berkeley Laboratory in California realized that an unauthorized user was looking at his computer files, so he set up a phony "Star Wars" computer file that the hacker could not resist. The suspect was eventually tracked to Hanover, West Germany, where three people were charged with selling secrets to the Soviet Union.[42] In the late 1980s the FBI's Computer Intrusion Squad found that 30 percent of large corporations and government agencies it surveyed admitted that their computer systems had been penetrated by outsiders during the previous year; 55 percent reported unauthorized access by insiders.[43]

Rates of computer crimes of all types are increasing, posing problems for law enforcement. A survey of 250 businesses found that the dollar value of losses from computer crimes totaled $137 million in 1997. Thefts of proprietary company information rose to approximately $1.7 million.[44] An FBI and Computer Security Institute survey of 163 businesses reported combined losses of $124 million during 1998.[45] Employees account for nearly two-thirds of suspected cases of computer crime, and some estimates place the number as high as 90 percent. In addition, many huge losses likely go unreported because companies wish to avoid bad publicity and embarrassment, especially if the value of their stock is likely to decrease as a result.

The impact of cybertheft on consumers is evident. In 1998 two members of a computer hacking group stole 1,749 credit card numbers.[46] This type of activity has resulted in growing numbers of instances of **identity fraud,**

▪identity fraud
Manufacture and use of false identification and credit cards based on personal information stolen without the victim's knowledge.

contemporary issues and trends

Avoiding Cybertheft

A twenty-eight-year-old California woman acquired a new $22,000 Jeep, five credit cards, an apartment, and a $3,000 loan. The problem was that she asked for none of it and never saw any of it. Another woman had impersonated her by obtaining personal information without the victim's knowledge. Generally, a social security number, employer's name, home address, and driver's license number are enough to equip a criminal for identity fraud. It took months of phone calls, court appearances, and legal expenses for the California victim to reclaim her identity and escape the bills in her name.[a]

An e-mail message sent to America Online subscribers was titled, "Important AOL Information." At the end of a purported letter from the chairman of AOL, subscribers were asked to enter their name, address, phone number, and credit card numbers to "update" AOL's new computers. The message, letter, and request were all fraudulent. They turned out to be part of a scam involving a thief who wanted to commit credit card fraud.[b]

These are examples of how criminals use computer technology to commit frauds that can have a devastating impact on victims. Despite such problems, however, companies and consumers remain anxious to make the Internet a secure forum in which to buy and sell merchandise.

To offer greater security in credit card transactions via computer, companies are installing firewalls and writing more and more sophisticated encryption software—programs that scramble transactions to make it difficult for hackers and others to eavesdrop or steal consumer information or credit card numbers.

The FBI fears that clever criminals will obtain similar encryption capabilities and use them to hide money laundering, drug distribution schemes, or terrorist plots. The Bureau has asked Congress to enact legislation to prohibit the private manufacture of encryption codes that the FBI cannot break, unless law enforcement agencies are given access to the codes for investigative purposes. According to the director of the FBI, "the widespread use of uncrackable encryption will devastate our ability to fight crime and prevent terrorism."[c] Others argue that dissemination of private manufacturers' encryption codes without the knowledge of consumers violates the right of privacy and will make electronic transactions even more vulnerable to forgery and fraud.[d]

These views reflect an important debate regarding what controls, if any, should be placed on technological advances in a free marketplace. Should law enforcement agencies respond to frauds only after they occur, or should they be granted access to all commercial encryption codes in order to take preventive actions? This debate involves at least the two significant questions presented below. The way these issues are resolved may shape the nature of criminal justice in the years to come.

> **The message, letter, and request were all fraudulent.**

1. Should potential threats to government security supersede threats to commercial security?
2. How should we balance the government's interest in preventing crime against the privacy of individual citizens and businesses on the Internet?

NOTES

a. T. Trent Gegax, "Stick 'Em Up? Not Anymore. Now It's Crime by Keyboard," *Newsweek* (July 21, 1997), p. 14.
b. "AOL Users Target of Cyberthief's E-Mail Scam," *Richmond Times–Dispatch* (August 26, 1997), p. 1.
c. Louis J. Freeh, "Let Law Keep Weapons," *USA Today* (September 26, 1997), p. 14.
d. Steven Levy, "Trying to Find the Key," *Newsweek* (October 14, 1996), p. 91; "Computer Privacy at Risk If FBI Gets the Codes," *USA Today* (September 26, 1997), p. 14.

in which false identification and credit cards are manufactured based on personal information stolen without the victim's knowledge. The criminal then uses the fake cards to spend lavishly, ruining in the process the victim's financial standing and credit rating. Although credit card insurance often covers much of the financial loss, victims of identity fraud must reestablish their credit ratings and personal reputation, a process that can take several

IDENTITY FRAUD

CAUSES OF
COMPUTER CRIME

years. The U.S. Secret Service reports that in 1997 alone actual identity fraud losses were $745 million.[47]

The causes of computer crime have not been studied extensively, but a survey of 600 university students found that 34 percent had pirated software and 16 percent had gained illegal access to a computer system. The study found that in many cases these behaviors were learned from others or imitated.[48] A complication in understanding the nature and scope of computer crime is the fact that businesses seldom want to admit to vulnerability and therefore tend to underreport breaches of computer security. In 1996 the Department of Justice established its Computer Crime and Intellectual Property Section to investigate and prosecute computer-related crimes. Thus far, the biggest challenge has been convincing businesses to report these offenses.[49]

THE NATIONAL
COMPUTER
CRIME SQUAD

Despite these problems, there have been some notable successes in efforts to combat computer crime. Many of these cases have resulted from work of the FBI's National Computer Crime Squad, which commenced operations in 1992. Undercover sting operations and the sharing of businesses' information about suspected computer hacking are the two most common methods of investigation. In 1996, for example, seventy-eight people were convicted for trading child pornography over the Internet in an FBI sting operation.[50] A thirty-seven-year-old computer repairman was found to have infiltrated Internet service providers and collected 100,000 credit card numbers. He was ready to sell a CD–ROM with these stolen numbers on it for $260,000 at San Francisco Airport but walked into an FBI sting operation.[51] Two raids on suspected Internet gambling operations in the Northeast found proceeds estimated at $56 million. In sum, it appears that computers are being used to commit both white-collar and organized crimes and that improved law enforcement sophistication is needed to combat them.

How Does Organized Crime Operate?

Organized crime has always fascinated people as a form of criminal behavior, yet its definition and true scope often are unclear. The President's Commission on Law Enforcement in the mid-1960s concluded that "our knowledge of the structure which makes 'organized crime' organized is somewhat comparable to the knowledge of Standard Oil which could be gleaned from interviews with gasoline station attendants."[52] A similar commission appointed by Ronald Reagan, reporting in 1987, also did not offer any clear definition of organized crime. One definition of **organized crime,** based on the work of researchers in the field, reads as follows:

Organized crime is a continuing criminal enterprise that rationally works to profit from illicit activities that are often in great public demand. Its continuing existence is maintained through the use of force, threats, monopoly control, and/or the corruption of public officials.[53]

■**organized crime**
A continuing criminal enterprise that rationally works to profit from illicit activities that are often in great public demand. Its continuing existence is maintained through the use of force, threats, monopoly control, and/or the corruption of public officials.

Even this definition is incomplete, however. For example, how does an otherwise legitimate corporation that collects toxic waste but dumps some of it illegally fit into this definition? Is a motorcycle gang that sells drugs as a sideline part of organized crime? What about a licensed massage parlor that offers some customers sex for money? The National Advisory Committee on Criminal Justice Standards and Goals has recognized that there are more similarities than differences between organized crime and so-called white-collar crime: "The perpetrators of organized crime may include corrupt business executives, members of the professions, public officials, or members of any other occupational group, in addition to the conventional racketeer element."[54]

ORGANIZED VERSUS WHITE-COLLAR CRIME?

At the same time, important differences exist between organized and white-collar crime. Perhaps the most significant distinction is the fact that white-collar crimes generally occur as a deviation from legitimate business activity. Organized crime, on the other hand, takes place through a continuing criminal enterprise that exists to *profit primarily from crime.*

It is important to keep in mind the fact that organized crime is not restricted to the activities of criminal syndicates. As Henry Pontell and Kitty Calavita concluded in their study of the savings and loan scandal of the 1980s, if we apply the term *organized crime* to continuing conspiracies that include the corruption of government officials, "then much of the savings and loan scandal involved organized crime."[55] In interviews with the Federal Bureau of Investigation, the Secret Service, and regulatory agencies, Pontell and Calavita found a "recurring theme" of conspiracies between savings and loan officials ("insiders") and accountants, lawyers, and real estate developers ("outsiders") that operated as a continuing criminal enterprise. If we compare these kinds of corrupt relationships with more traditional organized crime techniques such as no-show jobs at construction sites or payoffs for "protection," we find that they are more similar than different. Examples such as this illustrate that much of the crime committed by private corporations, politicians, and government agencies is as serious and harmful as the organized crimes of criminal enterprises.[56]

A Typology of Organized Crime

What types of illegal acts are we referring to when we speak of organized crime? Organized crime falls into three basic categories: provision of illicit services, provision of illicit goods, and infiltration of legitimate business. Within each of these categories are specific crimes that often come to the attention of the criminal justice system.

PROVISION OF ILLICIT SERVICES

Provision of illicit services involves attempts to satisfy the public's demand for certain services that may not be offered by legitimate society. Specific crimes in this category include loan-sharking, prostitution, and certain forms of gambling. Loan-sharking is the lending of money at an interest rate above that permitted by law. Organized prostitution offers sex for pay on a systematic basis. Numbers gambling is a type of lottery that operates without the approval of the state.

PROVISION OF
ILLICIT GOODS

INFILTRATION
OF LEGITIMATE
BUSINESS

racketeering
An ongoing criminal enterprise that is maintained
through a pattern of
criminal activity.

money laundering
"Washing" illegally obtained
money (e.g., money from
drug sales or gambling
proceeds) by making it
appear that the money was
earned legally as part of
a legitimate business.

Provision of illicit goods involves offering particular products that a segment of the public desires but cannot obtain through legitimate channels.
The sale and distribution of drugs and the fencing and distribution of stolen
property are examples of crimes in this category. There is a great demand
for drugs, such as marijuana, cocaine, valium, and heroin, that are either
illegal or distributed under very strict regulations imposed by government.
In a similar way, many people desire to buy products at the lowest possible price, regardless of how the seller originally obtained them. In response
to this demand, organized criminals fence stolen merchandise, buying
stolen property and then selling it to customers who do not care where it
came from.

The third category of organized crime is infiltration of legitimate business. This is often characterized by **racketeering,** which involves an ongoing criminal enterprise that is maintained through a pattern of criminal
activity. Labor racketeering and the takeover of waste disposal companies
are examples of this type of crime. Labor racketeering involves the use of
force or threats to employers or employees that if money is not paid, violence, strikes, and/or vandalism will result. In a similar way, organized
crime syndicates have taken over waste disposal companies by coercing
the legitimate owners to sell the business or have it operated by an out-
sider. Having the use of a legitimate business allows an organized crime
figure to engage in **money laundering.** This is a method of "washing" illegally obtained money (e.g., money from drug sales or gambling proceeds)
by making it appear that the money was earned legally as part of the legitimate business.

Table 3.4 illustrates this typology of organized crime. Provision of illicit
goods and services is distinguished from infiltration of legitimate business
by its consensual nature and by the lack of direct or inherent violence. That
is, organized crime figures who offer illegal betting, loan-sharking, or drugs
rely on the public's unsatisfied demand for these services. They also rely
heavily on return business, so they want the illicit transaction to go well. It
is very unusual for criminal syndicates to *solicit* business. Instead, those in-

TABLE 3.4		
A Typology of Organized Crime		
TYPE OF ACTIVITY	NATURE OF ACTIVITY	HARM
Provision of illicit goods and services	Gambling, loan-sharking, prostitution, distributing narcotics and stolen property	• Consensual activities • No inherent violence • Economic harm
Infiltration of legitimate business	Coercive use of legal businesses for purposes of exploitation	• Nonconsensual activities • Threats, violence, extortion • Economic harm

SOURCE: Jay S. Albanese, *Organized Crime in America*, 3rd ed. (Cincinnati: Anderson, 1996).

terested in illicit goods and services seek out the providers. But although violence plays no inherent role in the activities themselves, bad debts cannot be collected through the courts, as they can for loans and sales in the legitimate market. Therefore, violence or threats occur when one party to the transaction feels cheated or shortchanged and has no legal alternative for resolving the dispute. Violence also can occur when an organization attempts to control or monopolize an illicit market. If a group wishes to corner the market on illicit gambling in a particular area, for example, it may threaten or intimidate its illicit competitors. These threats are an enforcement mechanism rather than a part of the activity of providing illicit goods and services.

The infiltration of legitimate business is more predatory than the provision of illicit goods and services. In this case organized crime groups attempt to *create* demand for their services rather than exploiting an existing market. Demands for "protection" money or demands that employers provide no-show jobs in return for avoidance of property damage, work stoppages, or violence illustrate the predatory nature of this type of crime. In legal terms, organized crime uses coercion or extortion in the infiltration of legitimate business. "Protection" of prostitutes from robbery and assault in return for coerced payments to pimps is another example of the predatory nature of organized crime.

Organized Crime Offenders

Ethnicity is a common basis for categorizing organized crime, but this is misleading. A growing body of evidence shows that organized crime is not limited to the activities of a single, or even a few, ethnic groups. The President's Commission on Organized Crime in the 1980s described "organized crime today" as being carried out by eleven different groups:

- La Cosa Nostra (Italian)
- Outlaw motorcycle gangs
- Prison gangs
- Triads and Tongs (Chinese)
- Vietnamese gangs
- Yakuza (Japanese)
- Marielitos (Cuban)
- Colombian cocaine rings (drug cartels)
- Irish organized crime
- Soviet organized crime (the "Russian Mafia")
- Canadian organized crime.[57]

This curious mixture includes groups defined by their ethnic or national origin, by the nature of their activity (cocaine rings), by their geographic location (prison gangs), and by their means of transportation (motorcycle gangs). While such attributes may help describe a group, they are not very useful as explanations of behavior. Moreover, there is evidence that these and other organized crime groups sometimes work together.[58]

Ethnicity, therefore, is not a very powerful explanation for the existence or the causes of organized crime. This conclusion is supported by several studies of ethnically based organized crime. These studies show not only that no single ethnic group or combination of groups accounts for most organized crime, but also that as an explanation for organized crime, ethnicity is secondary to local opportunities for crime. A study by historian Alan Block of the illicit cocaine trade in New York City in the early twentieth century identified Jews as major players but also found evidence of considerable interethnic cooperation among New York's criminals. There was evidence of involvement by Italians, Greeks, Irish, and blacks, who did not always work within their own ethnic groups. Block described these criminals as "entrepreneurs" who were not part of one particular organization but were involved in a "web of small but efficient organizations."[59]

A study by Patricia Adler of the underground drug market in one community found that the market was largely competitive. Participants "entered the market, transacted their deals, [and] shifted from one type of activity to another" in response to the demands of the market rather than the dictates of any ethnically based organization.[60]

Similarly, in a study of illegal gambling and loan-sharking in New York, Peter Reuter found that economic considerations dictated entry into and exit from the illicit marketplace. Reuter concluded that these criminal enterprises were "not monopolies in the classic sense or subject to control by some external organization."[61] Instead, local market forces shaped criminal behavior—more so than ethnic ties or other characteristics of the criminal groups.

In a classic ethnographic study, Francis Ianni became a participant–observer of an organized crime group for two years; he also made observations of two other criminal groups. He found these groups to "have no structure apart from their functioning; nor do they have structure independent of their current 'personnel.' "[62] Joseph Albini's pioneering study of criminal groups in the United States and Italy reached a similar conclusion. Rather than belonging to an organization, those involved in organized crime formed relationships based on the particular activity they were engaged in at any given time. A **crime syndicate**, Albini concluded, is "a system of loosely structured relationships functioning primarily because each participant is interested in furthering his own welfare."[63] These studies suggest that the structure of organized crime groups is derived from the activities they are engaged in, rather than from preexisting ethnic ties.

■**crime syndicate**
A system of loosely structured relationships among groups and individuals involved in organized crime.

National and International Aspects of Organized Crime

The true extent of organized crime is unknown. Characteristic organized crimes such as conspiracy, racketeering, and extortion are not counted in any systematic way. Other offenses are known only when they result in arrests. The problems with relying on arrests as a measure of criminal activity are apparent: Much crime is undetected, some that is detected is not reported to police, and arrest rates go up or down depending on police activity and do not necessarily reflect levels of criminal activity. However, arrest data are the only available statistics, and they provide some indication of the amount of organized crime committed each year.

The Federal Bureau of Investigation tabulates arrests for several offenses that are characteristic of organized crime. Trends in these arrests from 1970 to 1998 are presented in Table 3.5. As can be seen, arrests for three of the four categories of offenses increased markedly over the twenty-eight years shown, whereas arrests for gambling dropped dramatically. These increases and decreases can be attributed to two primary factors: changes in law enforcement priorities and changes in the overall population and in the numbers of police. Both the U.S. population and the number of sworn police officers in the United States have grown significantly since 1970. Therefore, one would expect a "natural" increase in numbers of arrests, simply because there are more potential offenders and victims in the population, as well as more police looking for them.

At the same time, the public mood has shifted, especially with regard to gambling and drugs. Gambling in many forms has been legalized in a majority of the states in response to a shift from the perception of gambling as a vice to its perception as a form of recreation.[64] Conversely, public concern about drugs increased over the same period. The large increases in drug arrests (four times higher in 1998 than in 1970) are matched only by the huge decline in gambling arrests (eight times lower over the same period). These changes clearly indicate shifting public—and hence law enforcement—views regarding the seriousness of these forms of criminal behavior.

It is possible that the rates of these offenses have also changed over the years, but we cannot determine this from arrest statistics. The fact that prostitution and commercialized vice arrests increased over twenty-eight years, and that arrests for stolen property doubled from the 1970 level, suggests that more police, greater enforcement efforts, and increases in the numbers of cases combined to produce these large increases in arrests.

TABLE 3.5

Arrests for Crimes Related to Organized Crime

OFFENSE	1970	1980	1990	1998	28-YEAR CHANGE
Drug abuse violations	265,734	351,955	785,536	1,108,788	4 times higher
Gambling	75,325	37,805	13,357	9,216	8 times lower
Prostitution and commercialized vice	45,803	67,920	80,888	68,536	1.5 times higher
Stolen property (buy, receive, possess)	46,427	76,429	119,102	98,466	2 times higher

SOURCE: Data compiled from Federal Bureau of Investigation, *Uniform Crime Report* (Washington, DC: U.S. Government Printing Office, published annually).

In the future organized crime is likely to pose even greater problems than it has in the past. Technological change and economic globalization are likely to contribute to growth in organized crime. Organized crime groups increasingly are making use of stolen and forged credit cards, airline tickets, cell phones, and currency.[65] New Visa check cards and MasterMoney cards require only a signature and no personal identification number to withdraw funds, making it easy for forgers to withdraw large amounts of money quickly.[66] With each advance in technology, new criminal opportunities emerge. Gambling and pornography on the Internet and banking by telephone and by personal computer are examples of new opportunities for both organized crime and white-collar crime to grow in the future.

Just as advances in technology and the fall of Communism have made worldwide communication and travel much easier in recent years, they have also made the commission of crime much easier. Passenger miles flown on international commercial flights have increased by twenty times since 1970, to more than 600 billion miles per year. Global imports have increased by a factor of ten to $3,500 billion over the same period.[67] International smuggling, drug distribution, alien smuggling, hijacking, and political crimes have grown in proportion to the growth of international communication and movement among countries. As criminal justice researcher Jonathan Winer has observed, "the very networks that legitimate businesses use to move goods so cheaply are the same networks that criminals use to move illicit goods just as easily."[68]

INTERNATIONAL STOLEN VEHICLE TRADE One manifestation of **transnational crime** is the growing international trade in stolen vehicles. Of the 1.5 million vehicles stolen each year in the United States, approximately 200,000 are shipped overseas for resale. As recently as the mid-1980s, that international market barely existed.[69] In 1995 at the busiest seaport in the United States, Los Angeles–Long Beach, 225 stolen vehicles (valued at $10 million) were seized. This number was up from only 90 stolen vehicles two years earlier. To hide stolen cars from investigators, thieves often conceal them behind false container walls or in large steel containers bound for overseas shipping. A single ship holds as many as 4,000 steel containers, each as large as a semitrailer. Ten million containers leave the Los Angeles–Long Beach seaport alone each year, and the United States has 130 seaports. Criminals pay thieves to steal desired cars off the street; or criminals buy or rent the cars by using false identification and making a cash deposit, then drive away never to return. On the foreign end, buying and registering stolen vehicles is not very difficult. Some countries have no central registry of vehicles. In others, aspiring car owners can bypass registration requirements with cash payoffs. In some countries crimes of violence and political unrest are the focus of police attention, so police are not overly concerned with imports of stolen cars.

Major reasons why people in many countries do not simply buy the cars legitimately are lack of availability and huge import duties. In 1996 a $50,000 Lexus, for example, was selling in a Thailand showroom for $180,000.[70] The

∎**transnational crime**
Organized crime that takes place across two or more countries.

In what ways can organized crime often involve international, or transnational, crime? What exactly is organized crime? Does organized crime often involve white-collar crime? Why or why not? How can organized crime relate to political crime? According to statistics on international crime, what three kinds of contraband are most likely to be found on a vessel such as the one shown in the photo?

total cost of international vehicle smuggling is estimated at $1 to $4 billion annually. As a representative of the National Insurance Crime Bureau remarked, "It's getting to be of epidemic proportion."[71]

DRUG SMUGGLING The problem of international automobile smuggling is mirrored in international drug smuggling. Drug smuggling begins at a source country where coca or opium is grown, usually in Central or South America or Asia. Next, the raw plant must be processed. This can be done in the source country or in a nation where smuggling is relatively easy. Once the substance has been transformed into a consumable product, it must be smuggled to the consumer drug market; North America and Europe are the largest markets. After the drug has been sold to the consumer, money must be laundered through a legitimate business and transferred overseas; or else large amounts of cash must be physically smuggled by couriers back to the manufacturing and source countries. As discussed earlier, the laundering consists of reporting the drug money as part of the income from a legitimate business, such as a restaurant or other business that has a large number of cash transactions, making the money look as if it were lawfully earned as part of the legitimate business.

Here is an example of how the international drug trade works in practice. Nigerian heroin smugglers recruited non-Nigerian residents of Dallas to serve as couriers, smuggling heroin into the United States. The recruiters provided airline tickets and expense money for the couriers, in addition to a salary of $5,000 to $10,000 per trip. For each batch the first courier was sent to Thailand, the heroin source, and took the heroin from there to an intermediate nonsource nation (such as the Philippines, Kenya, Poland, or western Europe), where it was delivered to a second courier. The second courier concealed the heroin in a suitcase or strapped it to his or her body, and smuggled it into the United States. The strategy was designed to deceive

U.S. authorities, who would not suspect a courier who had not come from the source country.[72] This scheme capitalizes on multiethnic cooperation among criminals—and points to the need for international cooperation and surveillance by law enforcement agencies.

The two primary opportunities for preventing drug smuggling occur at the courier stages, when the finished product is being smuggled to the market or when the illicit cash is being returned from the consuming country. In the United States, profiles have been established for drug couriers and for "high-risk" and "source" nations and airports that lack effective controls on drug manufacturing or contraband. The profiles are descriptions of travelers who appear likely to be carrying drugs or cash, such as persons who are making short international trips, carry little luggage, appear in a hurry, and pay for their tickets in cash.[73]

ILLEGAL IMMIGRATION Illegal immigration is a third example of transnational crime. There are many people throughout the world who wish to come to the United States and other developed countries but have little chance of lawful immigration. Chinese smuggling rings have transported illegal immigrants to New York City by boat for a charge of $30,000 or more per person. Sometimes the "cargo" is smuggled by boat to Canada or Mexico and then transported by land to the United States.[74] Sometimes smugglers ship this human cargo in containers, causing injury and death.[75] The huge smuggling fee often turns the new arrivals into virtual slaves to their transporters.[76] Because they are illegal aliens, it is difficult for these immigrants to obtain legitimate employment, so they often are exploited in sweatshops by unscrupulous employers, become prostitutes or drug couriers, or become involved in criminal activity to raise the money to pay their smuggling fee.[77] The impacts are felt by the U.S. criminal justice system as well as by the illegal immigrants themselves. Nearly half of the non–U.S. citizens prosecuted in federal court are living in the United States illegally. Most have been charged with drug or immigration offenses, which have risen by more than 10 percent per year over the last decade. Nearly 20,000 noncitizens are now incarcerated in federal prisons.[78]

VICTIMIZATION OF IMMIGRANTS

Immigrants also continue to be victimized by their smugglers. In Los Angeles in 1995, for example, eight Thai nationals were arrested for enslaving fifty-six illegal immigrants. The smugglers extorted money from these people in exchange for safe passage to the United States, where they required the immigrants to work seventeen-hour days.[79] As William McDonald has remarked, "the problems of organized crime involved in the fraud, corruption, smuggling, and victimization associated with illegal immigration represent a growing area of need for transnational police cooperation which threatens to eclipse international drug trafficking as a social problem in the global village."[80]

U.S. authorities are able to identify only 5 percent of the vessels carrying illegal immigrants.[81] Given the vast extent of the nation's borders and the inability of any nation to search every person, car, boat, and plane that crosses its borders, there is a clear need for international cooperation and coordination of law enforcement efforts.

What Are the Impacts of Terrorism and Hate Crimes?

Terrorism and hate crimes are criminal acts committed for political or social purposes. They are distinguished from most other forms of crime in that these offenders usually have no personal financial motive. Instead, they attempt to make a "point" that goes beyond their own self-interest. Their purpose may be overthrow of the government, or they may wish to publicize an unpopular opinion. Hate crimes always involve prejudice in some form—usually racial or ethnic in nature. Terrorism sometimes entails prejudice, but more often it stems from political motives or causes. The FBI defines **terrorism** as

> *the unlawful use of force or violence against persons or property to intimidate or coerce a government, the civilian population, or any segment thereof, in furtherance of political or social objectives.*[82]

Hate crimes can also be defined in this way. The primary difference is the target: In the case of terrorism, the government is usually the target; in the case of hate crimes, a particular minority group is usually the target. Hate arises from prejudice against people's race, ethnicity, religious affiliation, or sexual orientation. In a particularly gruesome case in 1999, Aaron McKinney was convicted for the torture killing of gay college student Matthew Shepard in Wyoming.[83]

Both terrorism and hate crimes are new and growing concerns for the U.S. criminal justice system. Before the 1980s major acts of terrorism occurred almost exclusively in foreign countries, and hate crimes had not been defined as such and were not counted in any systematic way. This changed in 1993 with the bombing of the World Trade Center in New York City, which killed six people. The offenders were convicted and the mastermind was sentenced to 240 years in solitary confinement.[84] Subsequent terrorist events in the United States included the 1995 Oklahoma City bombing, which killed 168 people, making it the deadliest terrorist act in United States history. Acts of terrorism and hate crimes now occur regularly in the United States as well as in other parts of the world. Aircraft bombings, plots against government agents, church burnings, periodic random killings of minorities, and actions by hate groups founded on a premise of racial inequality illustrate the extent of the problem in the United States.[85]

■**terrorism**
Offenses designed to intimidate or coerce a government or civilians in furtherance of political or social objectives.

■**hate crimes**
Offenses motivated by prejudice, usually against a particular race, religion, or sexual orientation.

How is hate crime defined in criminal law in the U.S.? What are the causes of hate crimes, and what groups, institutions, and categories of persons are most commonly targeted? Why is hate crime identified as a type of sophisticated crime? How do hate crimes relate to domestic or international terrorism? On the basis of what you have read, how would you profile individuals or groups that perpetrate hate crimes?

Terrorism and Hate Crime Trends

The number of terrorist incidents in the United States has declined since the 1980s, but the crimes committed are becoming more deadly. Fears of Y2K-related sabotage resulted in heightened security around the world, and surveillance efforts resulted in several arrests of persons suspected of terrorist plots.[86] Law enforcement authorities are giving higher priority to terrorism investigations, with emphasis on the *prevention* of terrorist acts. Trends in the prevention of terrorism in the United States are illustrated in Figure 3.1. As the graph shows, a significant number of terrorist acts have been prevented or interrupted in recent years, and these preventions are increasing. This trend points to the importance of improved intelligence gathering on terrorist activities, which can anticipate and interrupt planned terrorist activity before it results in damage or death.

Statistics for hate crimes were not collected before the 1990s. In 1991 there were 4,755 reported incidents of hate crimes in the United States. By 1998 the number had risen to 7,755, an increase of 63 percent. More than 65 percent of these incidents are racial or ethnic in nature, and two-thirds of these involve antiblack motives. Nearly 18 percent of all reported incidents are religious in nature; 78 percent of these are anti-Semitic (anti-Jewish). More than 16 percent of all incidents involve sexual orientation; of these, two-thirds target homosexual males.[87] It is clear that minority groups are most likely to be the targets of hate crimes, and that prejudice against a particular race, religion, or sexual orientation motivates these offenders.

HATE CRIME STATISTICS

FIGURE 3.1
Terrorist Incidents and Prevention in the United States, 1987–1997

SOURCE: Federal Bureau of Investigation, *Terrorism in the United States* (Washington, DC: U.S. Government Printing Office, 1998).

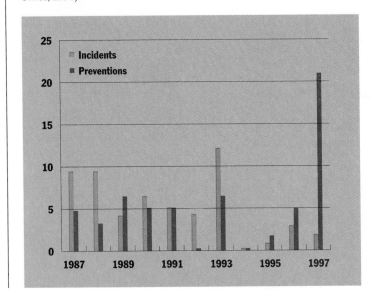

How Terrorism and Hate Crimes Merge

The following case illustrates how the problems of hate crime and terrorism merge. Two men belonging to an organization known as the Aryan Nations traveled from Idaho to Seattle, Washington, with the intent of exploding a bomb inside a gay bar. They were arrested after transporting the parts required for the bomb, but before they had assembled it. The arrest was based on evidence gathered by an undercover informant who had penetrated the Aryan Nations organization and had accompanied the two men on their trip to Seattle. The men were convicted of conspiracy involving interstate travel to kill or hurt human beings in violation of federal law.

The two men appealed their convictions, arguing that there was insufficient evidence of a conspiracy. They claimed that the government had failed to prove beyond a reasonable doubt that there existed an agreement to engage in the crimes charged.[88] However, the U.S. Court of Appeals found the testimony of the undercover informant, as well as tape-recorded statements of the conspirators, to be convincing evidence of a conspiracy. Before leaving for Seattle, the men had discussed obtaining a bomb from someone else. When that person could not be found, the defendants "actively participated in purchasing the components necessary to build another pipe bomb." Once in Seattle, they sought to borrow a drill from a friend to use in assembling the bomb. According to the testimony of the undercover informant, the two men had discussed the effect an explosion from a pipe bomb would have on a room full of people. In discussing the number of homosexuals that would be killed by such a bomb, they concluded that "the gravel and nails inside it would be lethal." One defendant also told the other that it would be best "to buy pipe and pipe caps for the bombs at various stores."[89] The court concluded that once a conspiracy has been shown to exist, evidence establishing a defendant's connection with it beyond a reasonable doubt "is sufficient to convict the defendant of knowing participation in the conspiracy," even though the connection may be slight.[90] This case demonstrates that the concerns about criminal organization and conspiracy that arise in hate crimes are nearly identical to concerns posed by terrorism. The planned and conspiratorial nature of the acts, and the political motives behind them, make terrorism and hate crimes serious threats to public safety and to law enforcement.

An infamous case of domestic terrorism is that of Theodore Kaczynski. Called the "Unabomber," Kaczynski pleaded guilty in 1998 to killing three people and injuring two others in five mail bombs. He also admitted to sending an additional eleven bombs that injured twenty-one other people. Kaczynski was a fifty-five-year-old mathematician who believed he was waging a struggle for individual autonomy against the forces of technology. He lived alone in a remote cabin in the woods for twenty-five years. His targets were university professors and others he believed represented the growth of technology. Kaczynski's motives can be viewed both as domestic terrorism and as hate crimes. He had a political agenda, and his choice of victims was based on a strong prejudice against people who advocated technological advancement. Kaczynski ultimately pleaded guilty and was sentenced to life in prison with no chance of parole.[91]

In place of the radicals of the earlier twentieth century, right-wing extremist groups have attracted supporters in recent years. These groups often adhere to an antigovernment or racist ideology. The FBI has found that recruits to these groups feel displaced by rapid cultural and economic changes and in some cases are "seeking some form of personal affirmation." As U.S. society continues to change, the FBI predicts that the potential for hate crimes by extremist right-wing groups will increase.[92]

In 1998 the federal government committed a record $6.7 billion to the fight against terrorism, and there is new coordination of multiagency

critical thinking exercise

Is the Internet an Avenue for Terrorists?

The Internet has come under fire for posting information that is inaccurate, inflammatory, and/or dangerous. A "police brutality" Web page admits to not verifying the facts posted. The publisher of the Web page said, "I don't think twice about bad-mouthing presidents, newspaper reporters, or other public officials."[a] In 1997 the Supreme Court struck down a law barring the posting of "indecent" material on the Internet because that term was too vague. Nevertheless, the government retains the right to prosecute individuals who post obscene material or child pornography on the Internet; these materials are more clearly defined in law.[b]

At the same time, the FBI has stated that some Internet sources "are repositories for inflammatory rhetoric which can influence extremists. Databases on the Internet contain recipes for bombs, dispense information on unconventional weapons, or offer computer viruses for download."[c] There are chat rooms for those who hold extremist, racist, sexist, and separatist views. Sometimes these people gather in person to engage in deviant activities. Occasionally these activities are unlawful. There is hate speech on the Internet as well as antigovernment postings, sites that advocate rape and violence, and many other sites that can be considered offensive. Those who spend time surfing the Internet can find a wealth of useful information posted there. But some of that information can also be used for destructive or illegal purposes.

CRITICAL THINKING QUESTIONS

1. Distinguishing harmless speech from harmful action is difficult. Should bomb recipes be barred from publication on the Internet? Why or why not?
2. Should inflammatory rhetoric that incites racial, ethnic, or government hatred be prohibited on the Internet? Why or why not?
3. Does a person have a right to post whatever he or she wants on the Internet, or should there be a standard for Internet content?

NOTES

a. Mark Johnson, "Lawsuits Spur New Rules for Internet," *Richmond Times-Dispatch* (September 9, 1997), p. 12.
b. *Reno, Attorney General of the United States v. American Civil Liberties Union*, No. 96-511 (decided June 26, 1997).
c. Federal Bureau of Investigation, *Terrorism in the United States* (Washington, DC: U.S. Government Printing Office, 1998), p. 14.

efforts to detect explosives, to gather intelligence, and to respond more effectively to terrorist incidents. This initiative is designed to organize more efficiently antiterrorism efforts that have been splintered among different agencies.[93]

Summary

WHAT IS MEANT BY SOPHISTICATED CRIMES?

- Sophisticated crimes are characterized by planning and organization. Criminal law punishes criminal planning as the crime of conspiracy.
- Conspiracy takes place when two or more persons agree to commit a crime, or to carry out a legal act in an illegal manner.

HOW CAN WHITE-COLLAR CRIMES BE DEFINED?

- White-collar crimes are distinguished by the manner in which they are carried out. Whereas street crimes are characterized by the use of force or stealth, white-collar crimes are characterized by planning and deceit.
- White-collar thefts include embezzlement (purposeful misappropriation of property entrusted to one's control, to which one is not entitled); extortion (purposely obtaining property from another person with his or her consent, when that consent is induced through wrongful use of force or official authority); forgery (falsely making or altering an official document with intent to defraud); and fraud (purposely obtaining the property of another person through deception).
- Offenses against public administration include bribery (the voluntary giving or receiving of anything of value with the intent of influencing a public official), obstruction of justice (intentional prevention of a public servant from performing an official function), official misconduct (unauthorized exercise of an official function with intent to benefit or injure another), and perjury (false swearing).
- Regulatory offenses, or corporate crimes, include administrative offenses (failure to comply with court orders or agency requirements), environmental violations (emissions or dumping in violation of legal standards), labor violations, manufacturing violations, and unfair trade practices.
- Arrest trends and demographic factors suggest that white-collar crime will increase in the future.

WHY IS COMPUTER CRIME A GROWING THREAT?

- Computers are the instrument in several types of crime. The most common of these is theft by computer.
- Other types of instrumental computer crime include use of a computer for harassment or extortion.
- Crimes in which computers are the object of the criminal act include causing damage to hardware or software, stealing trade secrets, and alterating data for an unlawful purpose.
- As computers proliferate and computer literacy increases, rates of computer crime can be expected to increase as well.

HOW DOES ORGANIZED CRIME OPERATE?

- Organized crime is a continuing criminal enterprise that rationally works to profit from illicit activities that are often in great public demand. Its continuing existence is maintained through the use of force, threats, monopoly control, and/or the corruption of public officials.
- In contrast to white-collar crimes, which generally occur as a deviation from legitimate business activity, organized crime takes place through a continuing criminal enterprise that exists to profit primarily from crime.
- The main types of organized crime are provision of illicit services (loansharking, prostitution, gambling), provision of illicit goods (drug dealing, fencing of stolen property), and infiltration of legitimate business (demands for "protection" money or no-show jobs).
- Research findings show that organized crime is not structured according to ethnic groups; rather, organized crime groups evolve around specific illicit activities.
- The true extent of organized crime is unknown, although there have been large increases in arrests for certain types of crime.
- Greater ease of travel and communication has made the commission of organized and transnational crime much easier.

- Among the most significant types of international crime are importation of stolen vehicles, drug smuggling, and illegal immigration.

WHAT ARE THE IMPACTS OF TERRORISM AND HATE CRIMES?

- Terrorism is the unlawful use of force or violence against persons or property to intimidate or coerce a government, the civilian population, or any segment thereof, in furtherance of political or social objectives.
- Hate crimes are similar to terrorist acts except that a particular minority group (defined by race, ethnicity, nationality, or sexual orientation) is usually the target.
- There has been a general decline in the number of terrorist incidents since the 1980s, but those that are still being committed are becoming more deadly.

Key Terms

conspiracy	official misconduct
white-collar crimes	perjury
crimes of fraud	corporate crimes
crimes against	computer crime
public administration	identity fraud
regulatory offenses	organized crime
embezzlement	racketeering
extortion	money laundering
forgery	crime syndicate
fraud	transnational crime
bribery	terrorism
obstruction of justice	hate crimes

Questions for Review and Discussion

1. What characteristics are common to all types of sophisticated crimes?
2. What factors must be present for conspiracy to be established?
3. What are the three main types of white-collar crime? Give an example of each.
4. Why is there reason to believe that white-collar crime will increase in the future?
5. In what kinds of crimes are computers the instrument? In what kinds are computers the object?
6. What is organized crime?
7. Give examples of each of the three basic types of organized crime.
8. What connection, if any, is there between organized crime and ethnicity?
9. What are some major types of international crime?
10. How is transnational drug smuggling carried out?
11. What is the distinction between terrorism and hate crimes?

Notes

1. Andrew Murr, "Living High on the Hog," *Newsweek* (October 27, 1997), p. 48.
2. James D. Calder, "Al Capone and the Internal Revenue Service: State-Sanctioned Criminology of Organized Crime," *Crime, Law and Social Change* 17 (1992), pp. 1–23; Laurence Bergreen, *Capone: The Man and the Era* (New York: Simon & Schuster, 1994).

3. Jay S. Albanese, *White-Collar Crime in America* (Englewood Cliffs, NJ: Prentice Hall, 1995).

4. Adapted from *Proceedings of the Academic Workshop* (Morgantown, WV: National White Collar Crime Center, 1996).

5. "Ex-Rochester Police Chief Is Guilty of Embezzlement," *Buffalo News* (February 26, 1992), p. 7.

6. John M. Caher, *King of the Mountain: The Rise, Fall, and Redemption of Chief Judge Sol Wachtler* (Buffalo: Prometheus Books, 1998); Bethany Kandel, "Top N. Y. Judge Faces Charges," *USA Today* (November 9, 1992), p. 2.

7. "Counterfeit Arrests," *USA Today* (September 26, 1991), p. 3.

8. "Mount Pleasant Suit," *USA Today* (February 28, 1992), p. 8.

9. Tom Lowry, "American Family to Settle," *USA Today* (March 13, 1998), p. 1B; Tom Lowry, "Settlement Won't End American Family Woes," *USA Today* (March 20, 1998), p. 1B.

10. Joseph Stedino with Dary Matera, *What's in It for Me?* (New York: HarperCollins, 1993); Mark Mayfield, "S. Carolina Bribery Scandal Widens," *USA Today* (March 21, 1991), p. 4.

11. "Bribery Plea," *USA Today* (February 20, 1991), p. 5.

12. Albanese, *White-Collar Crime in America*, pp. 47–51.

13. Jacques Steinberg, "Scars in a Proud Police Force," *New York Times* (October 12, 1993), p. B1.

14. "Albany: Ex-State Trooper," *USA Today* (January 23, 1992), p. 8.

15. Aaron Epstein, "Poindexter Guilty on All Counts," *Buffalo News* (April 8, 1990), p. 1.

16. "Cop Scandal May Affect 3,000 Cases," *New York Times* (December 15, 1999).

17. "Equifax Settlement," *USA Today* (July 1, 1992), p. 1B.

18. "Bayer to Pay $1 Million over Advertising Claim," *New York Times* (January 12, 2000) p. A21.

19. Jana Mazanec, "Rockwell Critics Hail Guilty Plea," *USA Today* (June 30, 1992), p. 3.

20. "Chicken Plant Executives Charged in Deadly Fire," *USA Today* (March 10, 1992), p. 3.

21. "Big Contractor Cited for Safety Violation," *Providence Business News* 14 (October 18, 1999), p. 16.

22. "Cheese Biz," *USA Today* (April 7, 1989), p. 3.

23. Paula Kurtzweil, "Sticking Public with Impure Products Puts Syrup Makers in Prison," *FDA Consumer* 31 (April 1997), p. 30.

24. "Baby Food Companies Fixed Price, Florida Says," *USA Today* (January 4, 1991), p. 3.

25. "Toys R Us, 2 Toy Makers to Pay $50 Million in Cash, Toys in Suit," *Richmond Times–Dispatch* (May 26, 1999), p. C1.

26. Edward Cornish, "92 Ways Our Lives Will Change by the Year 2025," *The Futurist* (January–February 1996), pp. 1–15; David E. Bloom and Adi Brender, "Labor and the Emerging World Economy," *Population Bulletin* 48 (October 1993), pp. 2–39.

27. U.S. Bureau of the Census, *Statistical Abstract of the United States*, 116th ed. (Washington, DC: U.S. Government Printing Office, 1998), p. 14.

28. Tom Campbell, "6½ years, $15 Million Payback Ordered in Theft," *Richmond Times–Dispatch* (April 6, 1999), p. 1.

29. Margaret Mannix, "Spammed and Scammed," *U.S. News & World Report* (May 31, 1999), p. 79.

30. Kim S. Nash, "PC Manager at Center of $2 Million Grocery Scam: Inside Job Spotlights Critical Security Threat," *Computerworld* (March 30, 1998), p. 1.

31. Fred Bayles, "Computers Aid Amateur Counterfeiters," *USA Today* (May 11, 1999), p. 3.

32. Robert Rudolph, "Ex-Drug Firm Computer Exec Admits Million-Dollar Product Bilk," *Star–Ledger* (Newark) (April 30, 1980), p. 32.

33. "Man on Most Wanted List Pleads Guilty to Hacking," *Richmond Times–Dispatch* (March 28, 1999), p. 2; Kathy Rebello, "'Sensitive Kid' Faces Fraud Trial," *USA Today* (February 28, 1989) p. 1B.

34. "Computer Security a Mess, Report Says," *USA Today* (December 6, 1990), p. 3; see also "Arrest in Hacking at NASA," *New York Times* (March 19, 1998), p. 19.

35. Mark Lewyn, "Computer Verdict Sets 'Precedent'," *USA Today* (September 21, 1988), p. 1.

36. Kathy Rebello and Leslie Werstein, "Brilliance Has Its Roots in Family Life," *USA Today* (November 10, 1988), p. 1B; Ted Eisenberg et al., "The Cornell Commission on Morris and the Worm," *Communications of the ACM* 32, no. 6 (June 1989), pp. 706–9; William Kates, "Cornell Student Convicted in Computer Case," *Buffalo News* (January 23, 1990), p. 3.

37. "Computer 'Bomb'," *USA Today* (November 27, 1995), p. 3.

38. Hoag Levins, "Hackers Devastate Texas Newspapers' Servers," *Editor & Publisher* (June 28, 1997), p. 45.

39. "Cyberwars," *USA Today* (April 24, 1998), p. 8.

40. "Bogus Software," *USA Today* (August 30, 1991), p. 1D.

41. Carroll Bogert, "Windows 95, 5 Bucks," *Newsweek* (May 26, 1997), p. 82.

42. Clifford Stoll, *The Cuckoo's Egg: Inside the World of Computer Espionage* (New York: Doubleday, 1989).

43. Brendan Koerner, "Can Hackers be Stopped?," *U.S. News & World Report* (June 14, 1999), pp. 46–52.

44. Laura DiDio, "Computer Crime Costs on the Rise," *Computerworld* (April 20, 1998), p. 55.

45. Koerner, "Can Hackers be Stopped?," pp. 46–52.

46. Ibid.

47. U.S. Comptroller General, *Identity Fraud* (Washington, DC: U.S. General Accounting Office, 1998); Margaret Mannix, "Getting Serious about Identity Theft," *U.S. News & World Report* (November 8, 1999), p. 88.

48. William F. Skinner and Anne M. Fream, "A Social Learning Analysis of Computer Crime among College Students," *Journal of Research in Crime and Delinquency* 34 (November 1997), pp. 495–519.

49. Wendy R. Leibowitz, "Low-Profile Feds Fashion Laws to Fight Cybercrime," *The National Law Journal* (February 2, 1998), p. 1.

50. Laura DiDio, "Special FBI Unit Targets Online Fraud, Gambling," *Computerworld* (April 27, 1998), p. 47.

51. Carol Levin, "Internet Capers," *PC Magazine* (October 21, 1997), p. 29.

52. President's Commission on Law Enforcement and Administration of Justice, *Task Force Report: Organized Crime* (Washington, DC: U.S. Government Printing Office, 1967), p. 33.

53. Jay S. Albanese, *Organized Crime in America*, 3rd ed. (Cincinnati: Anderson, 1996), p. 3.

54. National Advisory Committee on Criminal Justice Standards and Goals, *Report of the Task Force on Organized Crime* (Washington, DC: U.S. Government Printing Office, 1976), p. 213.

55. Henry N. Pontell and Kitty Calavita, "White-Collar Crime in the Savings and Loan Scandal," *The Annals* 525 (January 1993), p. 39.

56. See Albanese, *White-Collar Crime in America*.

57. President's Commission on Organized Crime, *The Impact: Organized Crime Today* (Washington, DC: U.S. Government Printing Office, 1987), pp. 33–128.

58. Alan A. Block, "The Snowman Cometh: Coke in Progressive New York," *Criminology* 17 (May 1979), pp. 75–99; President's Commission on Organized Crime, pp. 64, 81, 91.

59. Block, p. 95.

60. Patricia A. Adler, *Wheeling and Dealing: An Ethnography of an Upper-Level Drug Dealing and Smuggling Community* (New York: Columbia University Press, 1985), p. 80.

61. Peter Reuter, *Disorganized Crime: The Economics of the Visible Hand* (Cambridge, MA: MIT Press, 1983), p. 175–76.

62. Francis A. J. Ianni with Elizabeth Reuss-Ianni, *A Family Business: Kinship and Social Control in Organized Crime* (New York: New American Library, 1973), p. 20.

63. Joseph L. Albini, *The American Mafia: Genesis of a Legend* (New York: Irvington, 1971), p. 288.

64. See Jay S. Albanese, "Casino Gambling and Organized Crime: More Than Reshuffling the Deck," in Jay S. Albanese, ed., *Contemporary Issues in Organized Crime* (Monsey, NY: Willow Tree Press, 1995).

65. Kevin Johnson, "Cell Phone 'Cloners' Pushing the Law's Buttons," *USA Today* (June 21, 1996), p. 3.

66. Margaret Mannix, "Keeping a Check on Debit Card Liability," *U.S. News & World Report* (September 8, 1997), p. 7.

67. Richard Barnet and John Cavanagh, *Global Dreams* (New York: Simon & Schuster, 1995).

68. Jonathan M. Winer, "International Crime in the New Geopolitics: A Core Threat of Democracy," in William F. McDonald, ed., *Crime and Law Enforcement in the Global Village* (Cincinnati: Anderson, 1997), p. 41.

69. Carol J. Castaneda, "Car Thieves Wheeling and Dealing Overseas," *USA Today* (March 4, 1996), p. 3.

70. Ibid.

71. Ibid.

72. "Worldwide Nigerian Heroin Smuggling Ring Smashed," *Organized Crime Digest* (May 27, 1992), p. 3; "New Breed of Smugglers," *USA Today* (September 23, 1991), p. 3.

73. U.S. Comptroller General, *Drug Control: Interdiction Efforts in Central America Have Had Little Impact on the Flow of Drugs* (Washington, DC: U.S. General Accounting Office, 1994).

74. "Alien Smuggling Is the Dangerous New China Trade," *Organized Crime Digest* 14 (June 9, 1993), p. 10.

75. Sam Howe Verhovek, "Wretched Masses, Smuggled," *New York Times* (January 16, 2000), p. 2.

76. Bruce Frankel, "INS Getting Cagey in Cat-and-Mouse Game," *USA Today* (August 6, 1993), p. 10; "Chinese Smuggling," *USA Today* (September 1, 1993), p. 3.

77. William F. McDonald, "Illegal Immigration: Crime, Ramifications, and Control (The American Experience)," in William F. McDonald, ed., *Crime and Law Enforcement in the Global Village* (Cincinnati: Anderson, 1997), pp. 65–88.

78. John Scalia, *Noncitizens in the Federal Justice System* (Washington, DC: Bureau of Justice Statistics, 1996); Norman J. Rabkin, *Criminal Aliens: INS' Efforts to Identify and Remove Imprisoned Aliens Need to be Improved* (Washington, DC: U.S. General Accounting Office, 1997).

79. F. Swaboda, J. Webb, and M. Pressler, "U.S. Targets 'Slave Labor' Sweatshop," *Washington Post* (August 16, 1995), p. 1.

80. William F. McDonald, "Illegal Immigration," p. 83.

81. U.S. Comptroller General, *Immigration Enforcement: Problems in Controlling the Flow of Illegal Aliens* (Washington, DC: U.S. General Accounting Office, 1993).

82. Federal Bureau of Investigation, *Terrorism in the United States, 1995* (Washington, DC: U.S. Government Printing Office, 1997), p. 2.

83. Michael Janofsky, "Man Is Convicted in Killing of Gay Student," *New York Times* (November 4, 1999), p. A14.

84. Benjamin Weiser, " 'Mastermind' and Driver Found Guilty in 1993 Plot to Blow Up Trade Center," *New York Times* (November 13, 1997), p. 1; Gary Fields, "Yousef Sentenced to 240 Years in Solitary," *USA Today* (January 1, 1998), p. 4.

85. David E. Kaplan and Mike Tharp, "Terrorism Threats at Home: Two Years after Oklahoma City, Violent Sects Still Abound," *U.S. News & World Report* (January 5, 1998), pp. 22–27.

86. Warren P. Strobel, Kit R. Roane, Chitra Ragavan, "The Case of the Strange Conspiracy," *U.S. News & World Report* (January 17, 2000), p. 27.

87. Federal Bureau of Investigation, *Hate Crime Statistics* (Washington, DC: U.S. Government Printing Office, 1996); Kathleen Maguire and Ann L. Pastore, eds., *Sourcebook of Criminal Justice Statistics—1993* (Washington, DC: Bureau of Justice Statistics, 1994).

88. *U.S. v. Winslow, Nelson, and Baker*, 962 F. 2d 845 (9th Cir. 1992) at 849.

89. Ibid.

90. Ibid., and also *United States v. Stauffer*, 922 F. 2d 508 (9th Cir. 1990) at 514–15.

91. Gordon Witkin and Ilan Greenberg, "End of the Line for the Unabomber," *U.S. News & World Report* (February 2, 1998), p. 34; Ted Gest, "End of the Line," *U.S. News & World Report* (May 18, 1998), p. 37.

92. Gest, p. 11; Brent L. Smith, *Terrorism in America: Pipe Bombs and Pipe Dreams* (Albany, NY: State University of New York Press, 1994), p. 198–99.

93. "The Real Battle," *U.S. News & World Report* (April 27, 1998), p. 7; U.S. Comptroller General, *Combating Terrorism: Federal Agencies' Efforts to Implement National Policy and Strategy* (Washington, DC: U.S. General Accounting Office, 1997); U.S. Comptroller General, *Terrorism and Drug Trafficking: Responsibilities for Developing Explosives and Narcotics Detection Technologies* (Washington, DC: U.S. General Accounting Office, 1997).

four
Criminal Law

The proper role of law in regulat-

ing behavior is a subject of continuing debate. To what extent should the law be used to regulate behavior?

Consider the case of the father of a high school football player. Before a game he sharpened a buckle on his son's helmet. The buckle cut several opposing players, one of whom required twelve stitches. The reason the father gave for his action was that referees had not penalized opposing players for harming his son in an earlier game.[1] Is this conduct illegal, or simply a case of bad judgment? Should the son be held accountable, or were the injuries entirely the father's fault?

In Boston in the year 2000, a former FBI agent was awaiting trial on charges that he unlawfully protected organized crime informers. It was alleged that he tipped off his best informers by telling them about other pending investigations in which they were targeted.[2] Is this conduct illegal, or just a case of protecting an ongoing investigation? Should the agent be held responsible for the crimes of his informers, even though the informers were providing the FBI with information about "bigger fish"?

These questions are fundamental to an understanding of criminal justice, because the criminal law defines the outer boundaries of the criminal justice system. Police, courts, and the corrections system can take no action until a behavior has been criminalized under the law. Knowledge of the nature, elements, and sources of criminal law enables us to comprehend how acts become defined as crimes, and how liability is imposed or excused under various circumstances.

What Is Criminal Law?

civil law
Formal rules that regulate disputes between private parties.

criminal law
Formal rules designed to maintain social control.

The law can be divided into two basic categories: civil and criminal. **Civil law** is the set of formal rules that regulate disputes between private parties. Civil laws are concerned primarily with issues of personal injury and compensation. Most law is civil law, reflecting the large number and many types of disputes that can arise between individuals. **Criminal law**, on the other hand, is the set of formal rules for maintaining social order and control. Violations of criminal law are considered crimes against society, because they break rules that have been established for the common good of society. In civil law, in contrast, no general societal interest is at stake. Criminal cases are concerned primarily with issues of societal injury and the appropriate punishment of the offender.

The nature of punishment is one of the basic differences between civil and criminal law. Only the government, which represents society, can use legitimate force against a person. Civil penalties only provide compensation to an injured party. In the case of the football helmet, both the father and the son can be charged with assault. Their actions fulfilled the elements of a crime (discussed in Chapter 2) by unlawfully causing injury to others. The father sharpened the buckle for a specific illegal purpose, and the son used the buckle in a menacing and dangerous way. The father and son could be criminally punished by the government through fines or jail terms. In addition, players who were injured by the sharpened helmet buckle could bring civil suits to seek compensation for their injuries. The difference between the criminal and civil cases would be in their objectives: punishment in one case and compensation in the other.

SUBSTANTIVE AND PROCEDURAL LAW

substantive criminal law
Law defining specific behaviors that are prohibited.

procedural law
Rules for adjudication of cases involving prohibited behaviors.

The criminal law can be further divided into two types: substantive and procedural. **Substantive criminal law** defines behaviors that are prohibited, and **procedural law** provides the rules for adjudication of cases involving those behaviors. For example, the precise definitions of rape, robbery, burglary, or assault are included in the substantive criminal law. The rules of criminal procedure (discussed in Chapter 5) are specified in procedural law. These procedural rules are designed to ensure fairness in arrests, searches, preliminary hearings, arraignments, trials, and every other stage of the criminal justice process. All states, as well as the federal government, have both substantive and procedural criminal laws, which vary somewhat among jurisdictions. This chapter will focus on substantive criminal law.

Four Sources of American Criminal Law

Today criminal law in the United States has four main sources. The fundamental principles that guide the enactment of specific laws and the interpretations of courts are found in **constitutions.** The U.S. Constitution guides the formulation of federal law, and each state has a constitution that guides the passage of state law. If a contradiction arises between state and federal law, the U.S. Constitution supersedes any state law or constitution. For example, if Kansas passed a law making it a crime to criticize government officials, that law would be found unconstitutional by the courts. The First Amendment to the U.S. Constitution guarantees freedom of speech, and therefore such a law would be in violation of a constitutional principle and could not stand.

Another source of criminal law is statutes. **Statutes** are the specific laws passed by state legislatures or the U.S. Congress that prohibit or mandate certain acts. **Ordinances** are laws that apply only to a specific county, city, or town. Ordinances relating to crime are often systematically codified and compiled in a single volume called a **criminal code** or **penal code.** Legislatures can pass any law they desire as long as it does not violate a constitutional principle.

A third source of criminal law consists of court decisions. These decisions, often collectively called **case law,** involve judges' interpreting laws passed by legislatures to determine their applicability in a given case or to clarify their meaning. In the United States, judges are required to follow previous decisions, or **precedents,** in order to maintain consistency regarding what is deemed lawful or unlawful. This precedent rule—formally termed *stare decisis*—is occasionally broken when judges believe that a reversal or modification is necessary because of changing social values. For example, some courts have ruled in favor of "right to die" laws in recent years, reflecting changing social attitudes about the proper treatment of terminally ill patients. Reversals or modifications of earlier rulings are made by appellate courts.

Administrative regulations are a fourth source of criminal law. These regulations have the force of criminal law to the extent that they can provide for criminal penalties. They are written by regulatory agencies empowered by legislatures to develop rules governing specific policy areas. For example, many regulatory agencies were established during the second half of the twentieth century to protect public health, safety, and welfare in an increasingly complex marketplace. The Food and Drug Administration was established to screen products to protect consumers. Similarly, the Environmental Protection Agency, the Securities and Exchange Commission, and the Consumer Product Safety Commission were established to promulgate rules to promote safety and consistency in dealing with pollution and waste, stockmarket transactions, and potentially dangerous products, respectively. If a regulatory agency wishes to add new rules, it must provide public notice of its intention and hold public hearings before adopting the rules.

If you were to collect all fifty-one federal and state constitutions, all fifty-one sets of statutes, all state and federal court decisions, and all state

CONSTITUTIONS AND STATUTES

▪**constitutions**
The fundamental principles of societies that guide the enactment of specific laws and the application of those laws by courts.

PRECEDENTS

▪**statutes**
Specific laws passed by legislatures that prohibit or mandate certain acts.

▪**ordinances**
Laws that apply to a specific county, city, or town.

▪**criminal (penal) code**
A compilation of all the criminal laws of a jurisdiction.

▪**case law**
Judicial application and interpretation of law as it applies in a given case.

▪**precedents**
Previous court decisions that courts follow in current cases to ensure consistency in the application of the law.

ADMINISTRATIVE REGULATIONS

▪**administrative regulations**
Rules applied to organizations that are designed to protect public health, safety, and welfare in the marketplace.

and federal administrative regulations, you would have a complete collection of all the criminal law in the United States. Unfortunately, in addition
to covering several football fields, your collection would soon be out of
date—because court decisions are made every day, and some of these decisions alter existing law. Changes in statutes occur somewhat less often, and
constitutions are changed only rarely.

The criminal law can be said to arise from consensus or conflict. According to the **consensus view,** the criminal law reflects a society's consensus regarding behavior that is harmful enough to warrant government
intervention. Emile Durkheim, a founder of sociology, declared in 1893
that an act is criminal "when it offends strong and defined states of the col-
lective conscience."[3] This view suggests that the law reflects the moral
sense of the people about what actions ought to be prohibited.

The **conflict view** asserts that an act becomes a crime only when criminalizing it serves the interests of those holding positions of power. In this
view, the criminal law is used to protect the property interests of the ruling class. The conflict view has been used to explain laws against vagrancy,
loitering, and the vices. This view also attempts to explain the selective enforcement of laws against various racial, ethnic, and economic groups, suggesting that such enforcement protects the interests of the powerful rather
than promoting public safety in general.[4]

Examples can be found to support both consensus and conflict views.
Criminal laws that have existed for centuries, such as those barring murder, assault, and larceny, clearly reflect wide social consensus regarding
their harmfulness. Newer laws, on the other hand, such as those that severely penalize crack cocaine and juvenile offenders, may be directed primarily against the actions of poor or powerless groups in society.

Limits on Criminal Law

Debates regarding the proper role of criminal law arise when definitions of
crimes are not clear, are applied inconsistently, or appear to infringe on constitutionally protected areas. In a famous case in Jacksonville, Florida, two
men and two women riding in a car were detained by police after they
stopped near a used car lot that had been broken into several times. They
were charged with "prowling by auto."[5] The arrestees challenged this
charge, which was part of Jacksonville's vagrancy ordinance. The U.S.
Supreme Court held that the law was "void-for-vagueness." This phrase
means that the language in the law was so imprecise that a person of "ordinary intelligence" could not tell if his or her acts were prohibited. As a
result of this 1972 ruling, criminal laws must be written in very precise fashion, creating difficulties for cities attempting to legislate bans on "cruising"
and other vaguely defined behaviors.[6]

Another limit on the criminal law has to do with determining responsibility for applying it. One test of responsibility is **jurisdiction:** An act

Could these youths be held liable for violating state laws against cruising, prowling, or loitering by auto? Why or why not? What other specific conditions or tests place limits on the criminal law? What conflicts typically arise about who has responsibility for applying the law? What conflicts arise when the law criminalizes a behavior in an attempt to protect public health, safety, and morality?

JURISDICTION

must have been committed in the state, city, or county where the act is prohibited. Another test of responsibility in applying the law involves the balance of power between legislatures and the courts, and between the national and state governments. The Tenth Amendment to the U.S. Constitution gives states the power to pass laws. This "police power" enables a state to carry out its responsibility to protect health, safety, and morality, but there are limits on this power. One view is that the power to punish wrongdoers is vested in the legislature and that courts must stringently apply the law as written. Others argue that liberal, rather than strict, interpretation of statutes by the courts is necessary, because no law can anticipate all the possible circumstances that may arise. Courts must be given enough leeway, therefore, to apply the law to situations unforeseen by the legislature.

This debate continues today, as legislatures pass broader laws covering more types of behaviors but then complain about how courts apply those laws in specific cases. For example, consider laws that require motorcycle riders to wear helmets or automobile occupants to wear seat belts. Whom do these laws protect? Do they infringe on the right of private citizens to be left alone? Clearly, it is important to protect young people; but what about protecting adults from the consequences of their own actions? Do those consequences affect others who need the protection of the law? These are all valid questions that arise when the law attempts to protect "public health and safety" rather than dealing with a predatory harm (such as assault or larceny) where the distinction between offender and victim is clear.[7] Using the reasoning behind helmet and seat-belt laws, could not legislatures outlaw cigarette smoking or obscene gestures, as alcohol consumption was outlawed during Prohibition (see Chapter 1)?[8]

How Did the American System of Law and Justice Develop?

American criminal law is derived from British common law. Even though legal codes have existed for thousands of years in societies of all kinds, the structure of law in the United States today is modeled most closely on the British experience.[9] The **common law** was a body of unrecorded decisions made by judges in England during the Middle Ages. These decisions reflected the social values, customs, and beliefs of the period, and they were used as a basis for decisions in subsequent cases. As time went by, these decisions were recorded and followed more formally, so British legal decisions were guided by case law rather than by rules established by legislatures.

When America was first colonized, British precedents and procedures were followed. As in England, courts often relied upon biblical principles. Nevertheless, living as they did in a wilderness thousands of miles from Europe, the colonists faced certain problems that did not exist in England.[10] As a consequence, Americans came to rely on tighter legal rules created by local and state governments. This move toward regulating behavior by statute, rather than by court decisions, distinguishes American criminal law from its British foundations.

It is interesting that there is no mention of a "criminal justice system" in the U.S. Constitution or in federal or state law. In reality, the **criminal justice system** is a string of more than 55,000 independent government agencies that have been set up to deal with different aspects of crime and the treatment of offenders, including law enforcement, the courts, and corrections. These agencies often have failed to work together effectively because of a lack of systemwide thinking.[11] In fact, many of the problems of criminal justice throughout U.S. history have been caused by the failure of the various criminal justice agencies to act as a system. Yet it is important to keep in mind the idea of a system, because actions of one criminal justice agency invariably affect the others—and because agencies must attempt to act as a system if justice is to be achieved.

common law
The body of unrecorded decisions made by English judges in the Middle Ages, reflecting the values, customs, and beliefs of the period.

THE CRIMINAL JUSTICE "SYSTEM"

criminal justice system
The more than 50,000 government agencies in the United States that deal with aspects of crime including criminal law enforcement, the courts, and corrections.

Evolution of Lawful Justice

Over the course of history, societies have been fairly consistent in the way they handle criminal justice. First, the members of societies give a government authority to act on their behalf. When some members do not follow a society's codified rules—that is, its laws—the government usually establishes an agency whose responsibility is to make sure that the laws are obeyed. In U.S. society this enforcement function is performed by the police.

Next, societies often set up agencies to arbitrate in these matters. That is, if a person has an excuse or justification for violating the law, how do we determine whether it is a valid one? In U.S. society this arbitration function is performed by the courts.

Finally, when an assessment of blame or responsibility is made, a penalty or punishment is administered to the offender and compensation is sometimes given to the victim. In U.S. society this phrase is carried out by the corrections system. Thus, a system of justice evolves in a society to resolve disputes. A set of rules, a method to enforce those rules, a way to evaluate justifications for rule violations, and a way to administer penalties are all necessary to serve the common good. These fundamental components of criminal justice are required to resolve the sometimes conflicting or competing interests of individual citizens in ways that serve the wider public interest.

As stated previously, the United States has two levels of criminal justice systems: state and federal. Each state has its own set of criminal justice agencies, and the federal government has a criminal justice system that handles concerns that apply to some or all of the states. Therefore, there are actually fifty-one criminal justice systems in the United States. Our modern system of criminal justice has evolved as U.S. society has developed mechanisms for establishing rules, enforcing them, determining responsibility for violations, and deciding on appropriate remedies.

COLONIAL JUSTICE The American colonies occupied a sparsely populated domain that extended from New Hampshire to Georgia and was no more than 200 miles wide. In contrast to the situation today, in which paid professionals make, enforce, and adjudicate the law and carry out penalties, "colonial justice was a business of amateurs."[12] The first police force was not established until 1845; lawyers often played no role in the justice process; and cases were usually decided by lay magistrates. This made justice "democratic," in that it was communal in nature and aimed to protect the perceived shared rights of the community. This was unlike the system in England, which was dominated by aristocrats enforcing the law against the less privileged.[13]

Religion and the concept of sin played a significant role in colonial justice. Crime and sin were viewed as essentially the same. In many ways religion formed the basis for colonial laws. Colonial criminal codes often defined crime in biblical terms; and blasphemy, profanity, and violations of the Sabbath were seen as serious offenses and were punished severely. This religious orientation manifested itself in corrections as well. Rather than punishment or treatment, which characterize the modern era, shame and repentance were the goals of corrections of the colonial period. Punishments were used to "lead" a violator toward repentance and to serve as an example to others.[14] The stocks, whipping post, and ducking stool were used as methods of public shaming.[15] In the modern era we still expect offenders to express remorse for their actions, even though expressions of remorse

ROLE OF RELIGION

make little difference in terms of punishment or forgiveness. Over the years, with rapid population growth, geographic expansion, and a lessening of the role of religion in the lives of citizens, colonial communities gradually relied more and more on the law to enforce a standard of morality that previously had been the province of religion. The result was a dramatic increase in both the number of laws and the number of law violators, a trend that continues today.

REVOLUTIONARY JUSTICE The contemporary structure of law enforcement, courts, and corrections institutionalizes basic notions of how law should be enforced and adjudicated and how violators should be dealt with. The United States was founded in the aftermath of a revolution against the British government, which was seen as arbitrary, not representative of the people, and far too strong. This experience has guided the establishment of criminal justice agencies, which have been granted the power to intrude into the lives of citizens only under certain specified circumstances. Also, many criminal justice agencies exist on the local level, and local control prevents these agencies from becoming too powerful or abusive.

FRONTIER JUSTICE In early America, most of the country was rural and large population centers were few. The justice system was less formal than it is today: there were many fewer lawyers and judges and law enforcement officers, and many individuals did not wish to have their disputes formally adjudicated. Sheriffs had the authority, called *posse comitatus* (power of the county), to summon all males over fifteen years of age to assist them in ap-

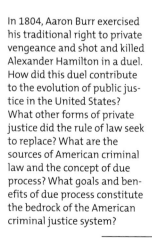

In 1804, Aaron Burr exercised his traditional right to private vengeance and shot and killed Alexander Hamilton in a duel. How did this duel contribute to the evolution of public justice in the United States? What other forms of private justice did the rule of law seek to replace? What are the sources of American criminal law and the concept of due process? What goals and benefits of due process constitute the bedrock of the American criminal justice system?

DUEL BETWEEN BURR AND HAMILTON.

prehending a suspected law violator. This was very important in the expansion westward because of the vast open spaces between towns and the small number of sheriffs.

The custom of dueling, which continued even into the twentieth century in some parts of the United States, was a way to settle disputes outside the formal justice process. Dueling involved two disputing parties who used guns or swords to resolve their disagreement. Dueling was seen as more direct and honorable way to resolve breeches of trust, property ownership disputes, and offenses against one's family or honor. The famous duel in which Aaron Burr killed Alexander Hamilton in 1804 was an incident that helped ultimately to end dueling and to encourage the use of the public justice system to resolve criminal and civil wrongs. Church ministers of that period used the Hamilton–Burr duel as a prime example of why such private vengeance was wrong: In the words of one sermon, "[Hamilton] was no less a murderer because he was deceived by the wickedness of the law of honor."[16]

Private settlement of disputes continues today in the form of vigilante groups. These groups sometimes attempt to enforce a standard of conduct by taking the law into their own hands. Shooting trespassers, assaulting unpopular members of the community, and using deadly force in cases in which the police should have been summoned are contemporary examples of private settlement of disputes—all of which undermine the effectiveness of the justice system in assessing the proper course of conduct and in determining responsibility for wrongdoing.[17]

PRIVATE JUSTICE

Evolution of Due Process

The criminal justice process is no longer an informal one run by amateurs. Many legal steps and procedures have been added, all with two goals: accuracy and fairness. These are the essential elements of **due process**, a legal protection included in the U.S. Constitution that guarantees all citizens the right to be adjudicated under established law and legal procedures. Both the Fifth and the Fourteenth Amendment prohibit all jurisdictions from depriving any person "of life, liberty, or property, without due process of law." Historically, this protection from arbitrary and unjust treatment became more important as the nation grew and became more urban, and as those making, enforcing, and adjudicating laws increasingly were strangers rather than neighbors. The growing size and diversity of the population also meant that a common core of religious values could no longer be counted on to promote conformity to laws.

due process
A legal protection included in the U.S. Constitution that guarantees all citizens the right to be adjudicated under established law and legal procedures.

In due process accuracy is a fundamental goal, because confidence in the outcome is pivotal if a criminal justice system is to work. If the public did not believe that the findings of the criminal justice process were accurate, people would lose confidence in the system, turn to private forms of justice, and eventually look for new forms of government.

**ACCURACY
AND FAIRNESS**

Fairness is closely related to accuracy. Fairness in the justice process is a matter of the balance between the government's interest in apprehending and punishing crime suspects and the public's interest in avoiding unjust punishments and unnecessary government interference in the lives of individuals. Thresholds for government intervention, such as probable cause, are designed to achieve a *fair* balance between the sometimes conflicting interests of the government and individual citizens.

Some have held that crime control is an important function of the criminal justice process,[18] despite the fact that there is little reliable evidence to suggest that the criminal justice system deters offenders or reforms those who pass through it. Proponents of the deterrence theory sometimes argue that overemphasis on accuracy and fairness interferes with the system's ability to deter or prevent crime.[19] It is unlikely, however, that a nation born only 225 years ago out of violent revolution would be willing to lower the legal thresholds established to preserve accuracy and fairness in the balance between government and citizen. Indeed, Americans have long been suspicious of government. This suspicion dates back to the Revolution and to the philosophy of John Locke, which holds that government exists not by divine right or by force, but only by the consent of the governed, who may alter or abolish the government if it acts in a manner inconsistent with the natural rights of citizens.[20] An important cause of the American Revolution was the widespread perception that British government procedures were arbitrary and unfair—another reason that the U.S. criminal justice process seeks to achieve impartiality and consistency in the application of the law.[21] Accuracy, fairness, and social control in the justice process would not have the continued support of the public unless applied consistently in an impartial manner.

The relative emphasis on these goals of due process remains relevant today. Criminal procedure, in which a citizen becomes a suspect and perhaps a defendant and a convicted offender, is a crucial part of criminal justice. The power of the government is vast compared to the resources of a private citizen, so it is extremely important that criminal procedures safeguard the rights of individuals in the adjudication process. An interesting example is the case of Terry Nichols, who was charged with conspiracy and murder for the planning and execution of the 1995 bombing of the federal office building in Oklahoma City. Nichols was associated with Timothy McVeigh, who was convicted of murder in the bombings. But Nichols was not in Oklahoma City at the time of the bombing.[22] In view of the horror of the most deadly terrorist act in the history of the United States, an objective presentation and evaluation of the evidence against Nichols was difficult but necessary under the law of criminal procedure. Without criminal procedure to guide the inquiry into guilt or innocence, public sentiment and outrage can result in unfair verdicts and gross injustices. In the case of Terry Nichols, the jury considered his role in the crime and convicted him of conspiracy and involuntary manslaughter, clearing him of murder charges. He was sentenced to life in prison.

IMPARTIALITY AND CONSISTENCY

Media and Criminal Justice

DOUBLE JEOPARDY

In 1946 and 1981, movie versions of the James M. Cain novel *The Postman Always Rings Twice* portrayed the story of an affair between a seedy drifter named Frank Chambers and the seductive Cora, wife of a roadside diner owner. The two hatch a plan to kill Cora's husband in a staged car accident. When Cora is tried for the murder, Frank corroborates her alibi as a "drunk driver who jumped from the car." Cora is found not guilty of murder, and instead pleads guilty to the much lesser charge of involuntary manslaughter; she is freed with a suspended sentence.

Later, when a private investigator blackmails them with the truth, Frank threatens to expose Cora's role in the murder if she doesn't help get rid of their blackmailer. Cora smugly replies: "Go ahead, Frank! That's the beautiful part. Once they just made it manslaughter, they can't do any more to me. It's in the Constitution or something."

Cora's constitutional guarantee—"nor shall any person be subject for the same offence to be twice put in jeopardy of life or limb" (Amendment V)—is the basis for the plot of the 1999 suspense thriller *Double Jeopardy*. The plot revolves around the conviction of a young wife for the murder of her rich husband and squarely depends on our idealized notion of due process and the procedural double jeopardy defense in presenting an interesting justification for murder.

The story begins when Libby Parsons goes on a sailing trip with her husband and is awakened in the middle of the night to find her husband missing from the boat. Her nightgown is covered with blood, and a bloody trail leads her to the deck, where she finds a knife—just as a Coast Guard rescue boat shines a spotlight on her. The viewer knows she's not the killer, but since there are no other suspects and she has no recollection of what happened, she is found guilty of the murder and sentenced to prison. Through a series of phone calls she is able to make from prison, Libby discovers that her best friend has run off with her husband and child while she remains incarcerated.

In prison Libby befriends another inmate, who—before killing her own husband—was once an attorney. This inmate gives her some interesting legal advice: Because Libby has already been tried and convicted for the murder of her husband, the due process guarantee against double jeopardy means that she cannot be tried for that crime again. Therefore, as her lawyer friend puts it: "You can walk right up to him in Times Square and pull the trigger and there's nothing anybody can do about it."

The rest of the film is a predictable continuation of the double jeopardy argument. After six years in prison for a murder she didn't commit, Libby does indeed get released and travel the country looking for her husband. When she finds him, she does exactly what the viewer is expecting her to do: She uses her constitutional rights to make sure justice is served.

The concept that Libby is "Teflon-coated" against punishment for committing a crime that she's already been convicted of and served time for is an interesting one and provides a fascinating plot for *Double Jeopardy*. In reality, however, double jeopardy was designed to protect those (like Cora) who have either been found guilty of a lesser crime or been found *not guilty* of any crime at all. Because Libby was found *guilty* of a murder she didn't actually commit, can she use her wrongful conviction and an interpretation of double jeopardy as a justification for murder? Shouldn't she be limited to filing a civil case for wrongful conviction? The question will remain part of the story's appeal, because there are no real-life documented cases like Libby's by which to test the movie's premise.

Should the concept of double jeopardy be limited to a due process protection for people found not guilty of a crime, or can it be used as a procedural defense to excuse later crimes of those found guilty? Do you think Libby's reasoning would hold up in a real court of law?

How Does the Law Define the Elements of a Crime?

hen a legislature decides to create a new criminal law, the crime in question must contain several defining elements. Without any one of these elements, a crime does not exist. If these elements are present, however, legislatures can make any undesirable behavior illegal so long as the new law does not violate a constitutional principle. Thus, it is important for citizens to be informed of proposed new laws so they can determine whether the social goal to be accomplished by the new law will justify the possible infringement on individual liberty.

The Three Elements of a Crime

MENS REA

■ *mens rea*
"Guilty mind": the conscious decision to commit a criminal act.

Perhaps the most important element of a crime is the *mens rea* or "guilty mind." The *mens rea* is a conscious decision to commit an unlawful act. This element consists of more than just criminal intent; it includes intention to commit *any* act that is illegal. For example, a person who intends to rob me and steal my criminal justice book might erroneously rob another person who happens to look like me. The original intent to rob meets the *mens rea* requirement, because the offender intended to rob someone and did so. Offenders will not be punished less severely merely because they victimize the wrong person, because their mistake does not negate their guilty mind. Thus, *mens rea* connotes a guilty state of mind rather than merely criminal intent.

ACTUS REUS

■ *actus reus*
The behavior that must be committed to meet the definition of a crime.

The second element of a crime is the act itself, the *actus reus*, the behavior that must be committed to meet the definition of the crime. No murder can occur without a death, for example, and no arson can occur without a fire or explosion. Thus, intent to commit a crime is not sufficient for criminal liability without a specific act taking place. *Actus reus* can take the form of an illegal act or can consist of the *omission* of an act one has a legal duty to perform.

ATTENDANT CIRCUMSTANCES

The third defining element of a crime is the attendant circumstances or causal link. That is, in order for a crime to occur, there must be a concurrence between the act and the harm that results. For example, taking the life of another person does not always constitute criminal homicide. Homicide by police officers in the line of duty or by citizens in self-defense is viewed as justifiable. Only the unlawful or unjustifiable taking of the life of another constitutes criminal homicide. Likewise, the harm caused must follow directly from the illegal act. Intervening or superseding causes can remove criminal liability. For example, in an assault that resulted in the victim's being taken away by ambulance, the offender might escape liability for the person's ultimate death if the victim were dropped by the ambulance crew or were left waiting in the emergency room for four hours before treatment was administered. In such a case the court would determine the extent to which the intervening or superseding causes independently resulted in harm apart from the original assault.[23]

In sum, the attendant circumstances or causation, together with the *actus reus* and *mens rea*, are referred to as the *elements of a crime*. Whenever a legislature defines a new form of criminal behavior, all three elements must be present. For example, a common definition of the crime of burglary is "the unauthorized entry or surreptitious remaining in a building or occupied structure for the purpose of committing a crime therein." The *actus reus* for this crime is entry into or the remaining in a building, while the *mens rea* is "for the purpose of committing a crime therein." The attendant circumstances prescribe that the entry must be "unauthorized" or the remaining "surreptitious." Without these circumstances there can be no burglary. The three elements of a crime, then, tell us the conditions that must exist before a person can be found guilty of a particular crime.

Characteristics of Criminal Acts

The three elements of a crime—act, guilty mind, and attendant circumstances—can be more difficult to establish than appears at first glance. For instance, *how much* of an act is necessary for criminal liability? Five characteristics of acts can incur **criminal liability** or punishable responsibility under criminal law: sufficiency, possession, status, voluntariness, and omission.

SUFFICIENCY In a Utah case, the defendant fell asleep in his car on the shoulder of the highway. Police stopped, smelled alcohol on his breath, and arrested him for driving while intoxicated. His conviction was reversed by the Utah Supreme Court, because the defendant was not in physical control of the vehicle at the time as required by the law.[24] The case against him failed because he was not violating the law at the time of the arrest and because it was also possible that he could have driven while sober, then pulled over, drank, and fell asleep. In short, the act observed by the police was not sufficient to confirm the existence of a guilty mind. If the car had been running, or had been parked on the traveled portion of the highway, this would have been sufficient for police to conclude that the defendant was operating the automobile while drunk, even though the police arrived after he had fallen asleep.

POSSESSION Possession alone is sufficient to fulfill the act requirement. In a New Jersey case, the defendant and his brother had marijuana and LSD

**FIVE CHARACTERIS-
TICS OF A CRIME**

■**criminal liability**
Punishable responsibility for a crime, determined by the presence of the elements of a crime in a given case. Criminal liability subjects the accused person to criminal penalties.

in a locked box in a closet. Both had access to the box, although both testified that the LSD did not belong to the defendant but to his brother. Should the defendant be held liable for items that were not on his person and did not belong to him? The court affirmed his conviction, holding that the elements of possession were fulfilled: The defendant knew of the existence and illegal nature of the object, and he had the opportunity to exercise control over it.[25] This concept is called **constructive possession.** Although distinguished from **actual possession,** in which a defendant has exclusive control over an object (such as a concealed weapon), constructive possession meets the act requirement.

STATUS   A particular status does not suffice to meet the act requirement. In a well-known California case, a man was convicted of a misdemeanor for being "addicted to the use of narcotics." His conviction was reversed on grounds that narcotics addiction has been held to be an illness, and people cannot be punished for being ill.[26] In other words, addiction is a status, not an act. A person can be convicted of buying, selling, or possessing narcotics, because these are *acts*. But the *status* of being an addict does not suffice for criminal punishment.

VOLUNTARINESS   A fourth feature of criminal acts is that they must be both voluntary and conscious. Unconscious and involuntary acts are not subject to criminal penalties. Sleepwalking and reflexive or convulsive acts are not voluntary, because they are not consciously carried out. "Shaken baby syndrome" cases, in which babies die from brain swelling after being shaken or struck, often involve questions of voluntariness. In the case of Louise Woodward in Massachusetts, the judge reduced a murder charge to involuntary manslaughter because he did not believe there was evidence that Woodward deliberately and voluntarily harmed the infant in her care.[27] The key legal challenge in these cases is to establish whether death resulted accidentally from normal activity or whether it was the outcome of malicious action.[28]

OMISSION   A fifth characteristic of a criminal act is that omission of an action meets the act requirement when there is a duty to perform it. In a child abuse case in Pennsylvania, a woman with a five-year-old daughter lived with her boyfriend, who regularly beat the child, ultimately causing her death. The court faced the question: Should the mother be held liable for failing to protect her child from the boyfriend's beatings? The court held that as a parent the mother had a legal duty to protect her child, which she had failed to do.[29] Omissions most often incur criminal penalties in situations in which there is a legal or contractual duty to act. Failure to file income tax returns and failure to obey traffic laws are two common examples.

■ constructive possession
A condition in which a person has the opportunity to exercise control over an object.

■ actual possession
A condition in which a person has exclusive control over an object.

What three elements of a crime are evident in or can be inferred from this photograph? Why are the elements of a crime often more difficult to establish than one might expect? How could you apply the five characteristics of criminal acts—sufficiency, possession, statuses, voluntariness, and omissions—in determining criminal liability for the act shown in the photo?

The State of Mind Requirement

The state of mind requirement separates criminal from civil law. Criminal law requires *mens rea*, or a guilty mind, which is not required in civil law. Punishments for violations of criminal law are based on assessment of degrees of *mens rea*. In New York State, for example, there are three degrees of assault. Third-degree assault is causing an injury *recklessly*; second-degree assault is causing *serious* injury recklessly; and first-degree assault is causing serious injury *with intent to cause* that injury. As explained in Chapter 2, *recklessness* connotes conscious disregard for a substantial and unjustifiable risk. It is punished because it fails to meet the standard of conduct of a *reasonable* person. The courts often use the behavior of a hypothetical "reasonable person" to assess whether a defendant's conduct is culpable or excusable. This standard of conduct is referred to as the **reasonableness standard.**

Intention characterizes conduct that is carried out *knowingly* or *purposely*; that is, the defendant either had a conscious intention to commit an act or at least was aware that the act would cause a certain result. In an Ohio case, the defendant was upset when another driver blew his car horn at him. The defendant took it upon himself to follow the other driver home and harass him, despite warnings that the other driver had a heart condition. The other driver had a heart attack and died. The defendant was charged with manslaughter, and his conviction was affirmed. The court held that the death could have been "reasonably anticipated by an ordinary prudent person."[30] The defendant, therefore, had acted recklessly in this case, and his actions were the proximate (immediate) cause of the victim's death.

An individual's state of mind, then, is central to a determination of criminal responsibility. The more an act reflects planning or deviates from the standard of a reasonable person, the more severe the punishment. This state of mind criterion distinguishes criminal law from civil law, in which the objective is to obtain compensation for private injury and the defendant's state of mind is less relevant.

THE REASONABLENESS STANDARD

■ **reasonableness standard**
A standard under which persons are culpable for their actions if they rationally understand the consequences of those actions. Young children and mentally ill individuals are generally not held culpable, because of their inability to reason effectively.

■ **intention**
Conscious purposiveness in conduct; a factor in the determination of criminal responsibility.

contemporary issues and trends

Crib Death or Maternal Infanticide?

cts that were formerly considered accidental are now sometimes determined to be criminal. Sudden infant death syndrome (SIDS) is increasingly seen as infanticide, a form of criminal homicide, and investigations are carried out to determine culpability. This shift in perception has occurred since the early 1980s as authorities have become increasingly reluctant to accept these incidents as accidents. For example, Brian Peterson, age nineteen, captured national headlines after he was accused, along with his girlfriend, of murdering their newborn son and dumping his body in a Delaware motel dumpster.[a] Peterson and his girlfriend, facing a murder trial, pleaded guilty to manslaughter in 1998.

More than 3,000 infant deaths each year are listed as resulting from sudden infant death syndrome. SIDS is said to be caused by prolonged sleep apnea, in which breathing stops repeatedly for periods of fifteen seconds or more. Studies have shown, however, that at least some SIDS deaths are the result of foul play. In England, a video camera in hospital rooms uncovered thirty-nine instances of mothers' trying to smother their babies after the infants had been admitted for interrupted breathing. Other studies suggest that SIDS is overdiagnosed, noting that SIDS cases fell 30 percent after pediatricians began recommending that babies sleep on their backs rather than on their stomachs.[b]

Videotaping is increasingly common in sleep apnea clinics, but no one knows for sure what goes on at home. SIDS support groups fear that families who suffer the loss of a baby will be placed under suspicion of murder, further aggravating their loss.[c]

Infanticides are among the rarest forms of homicide. According to the Uniform Crime Reports, there are approximately 600 homicides of children under age five each year. However, the U.S. Advisory Board on Child Abuse and Neglect estimates that nearly 2,000 infants and young children die from abuse or neglect each year.[d] Many of these cases involve maternal infanticide.

Postpartum psychosis is the medical label for irrational behavior that results from depression following childbirth, but little is known about the social circumstances that accompany such behavior.[e] In an important study, Martha Smithey interviewed fifteen Texas women who had been held legally responsible for the death of their own infants. She discovered that the women had been victims of prior sexual abuse or trauma at the hands of relatives and/or strangers. As mothers they had little or no emotional support, and the fathers of the infants were abusive, unsupportive, or antagonistic.[f] The fathers also provided very little economic support. The lack of emotional or economic support from the women's parents or the babies' fathers, combined with the fathers' antagonistic or abusive behaviors toward the mothers, resulted in significant emotional stress and substance abuse by the mothers, and ultimately in infanticide. The substance abuse occurred as a mechanism to cope with the stress, and it interfered with the mothers' rational judgment in their actions toward their children.

> ...authorities have become increasingly reluctant to accept these incidents as accidents.

1. How are the elements of a crime involved in infanticide?
2. What characteristics of criminal acts would be involved in determining criminal liability for infanticide?
3. How would the state of mind requirement apply?
4. What defenses do you think might be brought to bear?
5. If it is true that 2,000 young children die each year at the hands of their parents or caregivers, and if the parents are sometimes victims of abuse themselves, how do you think the criminal law should deal with this issue in determining legal responsibility?

NOTES

a. *State of Delaware v. Brian C. Peterson, Jr.*, Case No. 9611007811, Plea agreement, March 9, 1998; *State of Delaware v. Amy S. Grossberg*, Case No. 9611007818, Plea agreement, April 22, 1998.

b. Richard Firstman and Jamie Talan, *The Death of Innocents* (New York: Bantam, 1997).

c. Sharon Begley, "The Nursery's Littlest Victims," *Newsweek*, (November 22, 1997), pp. 72–73.

d. U.S. Advisory Board on Child Abuse and Neglect, *A Nation's Shame: Fatal Child Abuse and Neglect in the United States* (Washington, DC: U.S. Department of Health and Human Services, 1995).

e. C. Dix, *The New Mother Syndrome: Coping with Post-Partum Stress and Depression* (New York: Doubleday, 1985).

f. Martha Smithey, "Infant Homicide at the Hands of Mothers: Towards a Sociological Perspective," *Deviant Behavior* 18 (1997), pp. 255–72.

What Defenses against Criminal Charges Does the Law Recognize?

n criminal cases, police and prosecutors attempt to establish *criminal liability:* to establish the presence of the elements of the crime that subject the accused person to criminal penalties. Defendants, and defense lawyers working in their behalf, attempt to establish reasons why the act, guilty mind, or attendant circumstances do not apply. In many cases the defense will stipulate that although the act and harm were both caused by the defendant, there is a valid excuse for the defendant's conduct. Acceptable legal defenses are of three general types: defenses related to mental illness, defenses involving force, and defenses involving justification or excuse.

Defenses Related to Mental Illness

Mental illness can play a role in a criminal case in two ways. First, it must be asked whether the defendant is sane enough to be placed on trial. Second, it must be established whether the defendant was sane at the time of the act. A defendant must be mentally competent to stand trial so as to understand the legal proceedings against him or her. The legal standard for determining competency to stand trial was established back in 1960, when the U.S. Supreme Court held that a person is incompetent to stand trial if he or she lacks the ability to consult with a lawyer with a reasonable degree of understanding *and* lacks a rational and factual understanding of the legal proceedings.[31]

A defendant who is found incompetent to stand trial does not go free. He or she can be committed to a mental institution and can be tried after recovering competency. Courts have held that a person may be held in a mental institution for "a reasonable period" to achieve competency to stand trial. Some courts have interpreted this period to be no more than the maximum sentence that would be imposed for the crime if the person were convicted of it.[32]

COMPETENCY

A more controversial application of mental illness to criminal law occurs in the attempt to determine if a defendant was sane at the time of the act. A defense based on the claim that the defendant was not sane at the time of the act is referred to as the **insanity defense.** It is based on the principle that people who are not blameworthy should not be punished. Thus, the law treats young children and mentally ill individuals in the same way. Neither are held criminally liable for their actions, because they do not understand the consequences of those actions—another example of the reasonableness standard. The inability of young children or people with mental illness to reason or rationalize in a competent manner makes criminal punishment of their conduct both ineffective and unreasonable.

■insanity defense
A claim that the defendant was not sane under law at the time of the act.

Over the years the courts have adopted several different formulations of the insanity defense. None has been satisfactory, because in each instance the legal system finds itself asking a question that it cannot answer: What was the person's level of mental functioning at the time of the crime, and did that constitute insanity? This is ultimately a question of *mens rea* (or lack of it), and psychiatrists are unable to agree on a standard for determining the presence or absence of *mens rea* in any given case.

THE M'NAGHTEN CASE

He was plotted to be Killed.

The insanity defense originated in England in 1843 in the case of Daniel M'Naghten. M'Naghten suffered from the delusion that the British prime minister, Sir Robert Peel, was going to have him killed. To frustrate this imagined conspiracy against him, M'Naghten went to the prime minister's house in an effort to kill him first. He killed the prime minister's secretary by mistake. After a trial for murder, M'Naghten was found not guilty by reason of insanity. On appeal, England's highest court formulated the M'Naghten rule, which defined legal insanity for the first time. The definition of insanity focused on the *reasoning ability* of the defendant; it asked whether he understood the nature and quality of his act or was incapable of knowing that it was wrong "owing to a disease of the mind."[33]

In 1972 the federal courts adopted the test for legal insanity proposed by the American Law Institute in the Model Penal Code. In this formulation legal insanity exists when a defendant "lacks substantial capacity to appreciate the wrongfulness of his conduct or to conform his conduct to the requirements of the law." The Model Penal Code is now used in all federal courts and in about half the states.

PROBLEMS WITH THE INSANITY DEFENSE

In practice, the application of definitions of legal insanity is quite subjective. Prosecutors always seem able to find mental health experts who will argue that the defendant is mentally competent; experts for the defense always argue the reverse. Juries often are left to their own judgment in the battle of dueling experts in the courtroom.[34] To the public, the insanity defense often looks like a mechanism by which offenders get away with murder. Some have called for abolition of the insanity defense. Aside from the possibility that it may allow dangerous people to go free, the insanity defense also has created some ironic situations. During a trial a prosecutor might argue that the defendant was sane at the time of the act. However, if the defendant were found not guilty by reason of insanity, to obtain a civil commitment to a mental institution the prosecutor would then have to argue the opposite: that the defendant was insane.

In practice, the insanity defense has been seldom invoked. Studies have found that the insanity plea is used in only 2 percent of cases that go to trial.[35] Moreover, the insanity defense has rarely been successful. Judges and juries issue verdicts of not guilty by reason of insanity in only 2 to 5 percent of the cases in which the defense is attempted.[36] The number of people in mental hospitals who have been found not guilty by reason of insanity constitutes less than 1 percent of prisons inmates who were found guilty of the crime with which they were charged.[37] Interestingly, the debate over the insanity defense may be beside the point, as follow-up studies of insanity cases have found that the length of incarceration in prison of those found guilty was virtually the same as or even shorter than the length of incarceration in mental hospitals of those found not guilty by reason of insanity.[38] Nevertheless, dissatisfaction with the insanity defense has led to its abandonment in three states (Montana, Idaho, Utah). In general, however, defendants who are likely to plead insanity have been found incompetent to stand trial. The result is that they are confined indefinitely to the same mental hospitals to which they would have been committed if had been found not guilty by reason of insanity.[39]

In 1982 John Hinckley was found not guilty by reason of insanity in the attempted murder of President Reagan. Many believed that Hinckley "got away with murder," although he remains confined indefinitely at St. Elizabeth's Hospital in Washington, D.C. In response to public outrage over that case, seventeen states adopted a new type of verdict, "guilty but mentally ill." This wording means that the defendant was not legally insane at the time of the offense but suffered from a disorder that may have affected the commission of the crime. If found guilty but mentally ill, an offender is sentenced to prison but given psychological treatment. This is a troublesome alternative for two reasons. First, most prisons have no facilities for treating mental illness, and such treatment often is not guaranteed or implemented as directed by the court.[40] Second, "guilty but mentally ill" verdicts appear to constitute punishment without *mens rea* by holding a person criminally responsible for conduct despite finding that they are mentally ill.

In 1981 John Hinckley shot then President Ronald Reagan and others outside a Washington hotel. The Secret Service agents quickly pushed the President toward a limousine. Hinckley's plea was innocent by reason of insanity. What is the basis of the insanity defense? How did the insanity defense originate? What is the test for legal insanity? Why is the insanity defense so controversial? What do you think would have been the outcome for Hinckley if he had been judged sane? What do you think would have been the outcome if he had been judged sane but mentally ill?

Defenses Involving Force

Defenses involving force are of three types: self-defense, defense of others, and defense of property. A person may use force for self-protection or to protect others, but the extent of that force is limited by law. As a general rule, a person is permitted to use whatever force reasonably seems necessary, short of deadly force, to prevent immediate and unlawful harm to himself or herself. Killing in self-defense is permitted only to prevent imminent death or serious injury threatened by the attacker. Although the concept of self-defense is easily understood, problems can arise when the victim's *perception* of potential harm is not reasonable.

SELF-DEFENSE

In a Louisiana case, a bar patron weighing 215 pounds threatened to kill the bartender, who weighed only 145 pounds, for refusing to serve him drinks after he had become intoxicated. The unarmed patron started to climb over the bar, and the bartender shot and wounded him. Clearly, the extent of force used by the bartender exceeded that used by the patron. However, the court ruled that the shooting was lawful because of the circumstances. The size and age of the parties, the threat of weapons, and the aggressiveness of the assault are all relevant in determining the reasonableness of a defendant's behavior. In this case the court believed that the patron's large size and irrational, aggressive behavior were enough to justify the bartender's belief that his life was in danger.[41]

Some states require a person who can safely retreat from danger to do so before using deadly force, on the principle that it is not reasonably necessary to use extreme force if one can avoid danger by running away. Other states see the issue differently, basing their self-defense laws on the belief that a person should not be required to run away from an aggressor. In no state, however, is a person required to retreat from an attack in his or her own home.

The dual conditions of "reasonably necessary force" and "no requirement to retreat" in one's own home often conflict in cases of spouse abuse. In one case the defendant killed her husband by stabbing him with a pair of scissors. She was not in fear of immediate harm at the time of the act, but her husband had a history of assaulting her when he was drunk.[42] In another case a woman set fire to her husband's bed while he was sleeping, because he had beaten her severely and would not allow her to leave.[43] The ordinary rules of self-defense do not apply in these cases because of the absence of an immediate threat of harm. Nevertheless, many courts have permitted defendants in such cases to claim self-defense, on the grounds that an ongoing pattern of severe physical abuse constitutes a continual threat of harm. This pattern has been called the **battered woman syndrome.** Some states have changed their laws to expand the application of self-defense to situations in which women have been the victims of chronic physical abuse. In 1996 brothers Lyle and Erik Menendez received life sentences without possibility of parole for killing their parents.[44] This case was unusual because the brothers claimed that they had been abused by their parents throughout their childhood and that they had killed in retaliation for that abuse. The Menendez brothers were in their mid-twenties at the time of the crime,

BATTERED WOMAN SYNDROME

■ **battered woman syndrome**
An ongoing pattern of severe physical abuse that constitutes a continual threat of harm.

What is battered woman syndrome? How does the battered woman syndrome relate to defenses involving force, such as the law of self-defense? Could this woman be justified in assaulting her abuser at a time when she was not under immediate threat? Why or why not? Could she be justified in using deadly force? What legal criteria would be applied to try to determine the answers to these questions?

however, stretching a claim of self-defense to years after the abuse occurred. The trial jury rejected their argument.

Laws permitting the use of force in defense of others are designed to encourage citizens to come to the aid of others. A person may use reasonable force to defend another person against unlawful force, but the force used can be no more than what would be justified in self-defense. In one case an inmate in a Massachusetts prison attempted to rescue a fellow inmate from a severe beating by assaulting a corrections officer who was inflicting the beating. In determining that the inmate's intervention was legally justified, the court held that defense of others "does not necessarily stop at the prison gates."[45]

The right to defend one's property by force is narrowly limited. In general, reasonable force, short of deadly force, can be used to protect property or prevent a crime. Deadly force in defense of property is permitted only in one's own home during a burglary or other dangerous felony, such as rape, kidnapping, or robbery. In a California case, a man had tools stolen from his garage. To prevent further thefts he rigged a pistol that would fire at the door if it was opened slightly. This contraption shot a sixteen-year-old in the face during an attempted theft. The garage owner was convicted of assault, because "deadly mechanical devices are without mercy or discretion."[46] The owner's pistol placed at risk children, firefighters, and others who might have entered the garage for reasons other than theft. Thus, deadly force in defense of property is not permitted unless the victim is in imminent danger of serious bodily harm (in which case the rules for self-defense would apply).

DEADLY FORCE

Defenses Involving Justification or Excuse

In certain cases defendants admit to unlawful conduct but claim that an overriding justification or excuse makes their actions lawful. Five defenses involving justification or excuse are duress, necessity, mistake of fact, ignorance of law, and entrapment.

FIVE JUSTIFICATIONS OR EXCUSES

DURESS Three conditions must be met for a claim of **duress** (called *coercion* or *compulsion* in some jurisdictions). For duress to succeed as a defense, the defendant must have engaged in a criminal act because of a threat of serious bodily harm by another person. In addition, the threat must be immediate, and there must be no reasonable possibility for escape. In many jurisdictions the defense of duress is disallowed if the defendant intentionally or recklessly placed himself or herself in a situation subject to duress.

In a Washington, D.C., case, Clifford Bailey and James Cogdell escaped from jail, claiming that there had been "various threats and beatings directed at them." In addition, conditions at the jail were deplorable:

Inmates . . . and on occasion the guards . . . set fire to trash, bedding, and other objects thrown from the cells. According to the inmates, the guards simply allowed the fires to burn until they went out. . . . [And] poor ventilation caused the smoke to collect and linger in the cellblock.[47]

■duress
Defense in which a person claims to have engaged in criminal conduct because of a threat of immediate and serious bodily harm by another person.

The defendants also testified that the guards had subjected them to beatings and death threats and that medical attention was inadequate. In response to the charge of escape, they claimed the defense of duress, citing the horrible conditions they had endured in prison.

The U.S. Supreme Court held that duress was not applicable in this case, because the defendants had made no "bonafide effort to surrender or return to custody as soon as the claimed duress or necessity had lost its coercive force."[47] The defendants had been at large for a month or more. Criminal acts committed while under immediate, serious, and nonreckless duress are excused only while the coercive threats are in force. Once the duress has ended, no further criminal conduct is excused.

NECESSITY   In a classic case from the late 1800s, two men and an eighteen-year-old boy were shipwrecked and adrift at sea in a raft for twenty days. After a week without food or water, and with little hope of rescue, the two men decided to kill the boy and eat him so that they could survive. They reasoned that the boy was more expendable because he had no family responsibilities, whereas they did. The two men were rescued four days later.

> ■ **necessity**
> Defense in which a person claims to have engaged in otherwise criminal behavior because of the forces of nature.

Were the men guilty of homicide, or could their behavior be excused? They claimed the defense of **necessity,** which argues that a defendant has engaged in otherwise criminal behavior because of the forces of nature. In this case the men were convicted of homicide and sentenced to death—sentences that were later commuted to six months in prison. The court held that people may not save themselves at the expense of another.[48] The defense of necessity is successful only in cases in which the necessity is great, there is no reasonable alternative, and the harm done is less than the harm avoided. In this case a death was caused to prevent other deaths, so the defense was not applicable.

"CHOICE OF EVILS"

Necessity is called the "choice of evils" in the Model Penal Code. This phrasing conveys the principle that harm is done in these cases and that the defense is allowed only where the correct choice is made between degrees of harm. That choice must always be the lesser evil. In a Colorado case an attorney's claim of necessity in response to a charge of speeding was rejected. He claimed that he was late for a court hearing because of delays in a previous hearing elsewhere, but he "failed to establish that he did not cause the situation or that his injuries [penalties for speeding] would outweigh the consequences of his conduct."[49] Nevertheless, one can imagine a circumstance in which speeding might be excused, such as a medical emergency. Here again, the balance between two evils lies at the heart of the defense of necessity.

> ■ **mistake of fact**
> Defense in which a person claims that honest ignorance rules out the presence of a "guilty mind."

IGNORANCE OR MISTAKE OF FACT   **Mistake of fact** can serve as a defense if it neutralizes the "guilty mind" required for the commission of a crime. The mistake or ignorance must be both honest and reasonable. If a woman mistakenly picked up a purse very similar to her own and walked off with it, she could claim mistake of fact in response to a charge of larceny. In this case the mistake of fact would be a defense because it would negate the *mens rea* element of the crime of larceny. A court would assess the circumstances to determine whether the mistake was both honest and reasonable.

An interesting exception is the law against bigamy. Both English common law and rulings in some states in this country have upheld bigamy charges even when the defendant has been shown to have had a reasonable belief that a prior marriage ended in divorce or the death of the previous spouse.[50] This is because bigamy laws often are written as strict liability offenses, in which no *mens rea* is required. Strict liability offenses are exceptions to the guilty mind requirement and therefore are rare.[51] In cases such as bigamy, a person who engages in the criminal conduct, however reasonable the circumstances, still incurs a criminal penalty.

IGNORANCE OR MISTAKE OF LAW   **Ignorance of law** has rarely been sufficient to excuse criminal conduct. It is permitted as a defense only in situations in which the law is not widely known and a person cannot be expected to be aware of a particular law. These situations are not common; citizens generally are expected to know the law, and a claim of ignorance could be used to excuse virtually any type of illegal conduct. In a California case, Neva Snyder claimed that her conviction for possession of a firearm as a convicted felon should be overturned. She had mistakenly believed that her prior conviction for marijuana sales was only a misdemeanor. The court held that she was "presumed to know" what the law was, so her mistake was not reasonable.[52]

In another case an offender failed to register under a local ordinance requiring convicted persons to do so. The U.S. Supreme Court reversed the conviction, stating that ignorance of law could be used as an excuse in this case.[53] Thus, if the ignorance or mistake is reasonable under the circumstances, and if there is no evidence that the defendant should have known of the illegality of the conduct, ignorance or mistake of law can be a defense.[54]

> ▪**ignorance of law**
> Defense in which a defendant claims that a law is not widely known and that the person could not have been expected to be aware of it.

ENTRAPMENT   The traditional formulation of the defense of **entrapment** was established by the U.S. Supreme Court in 1932. The Court ruled that "entrapment exists if the defendant was not predisposed to commit the crimes in question, and his intent originated with the officials of the government."[55] Because this definition of entrapment focuses on the defendant's frame of mind, it is known as the *subjective formulation* of the entrapment defense.

The purpose of the entrapment defense is to prevent government agencies from "manufacturing" crime by setting traps for unwary citizens. The precise activities necessary for entrapment to occur have been the subject of much scrutiny, especially as police undercover tactics have become more common. It should be noted that the entrapment defense is aimed strictly at misconduct on the part of the government. If a private citizen, not associated with the government, entraps another into committing an offense, the entrapment defense is not available.

> ▪**entrapment**
> Defense designed to prevent the government from manufacturing crime by setting traps for unwary citizens.

SUBJECTIVE
AND OBJECTIVE
FORMULATIONS

A second formulation of the entrapment defense, adopted in the Model Penal Code in federal courts and in about half the states, focuses on the conduct of police and its potential to trap innocent persons. This standard is called the *objective formulation* and can be stated as follows: Entrapment occurs when government agents induce or encourage another person to engage in criminal behavior by knowingly making false representations about the lawfulness of the conduct or by employing methods that create a substantial risk that such an offense will be committed by innocent (i.e., unpredisposed) persons. The primary difference between the two formulations is that the objective standard shifts attention from the defendant's frame of mind to the conduct of the police.

The significance of this difference is made clear by an actual case. Keith Jacobson ordered two magazines from a bookstore containing photographs of nude preteen and teenage boys. Finding Jacobson's name on the bookstore's mailing list, the Postal Service and the Customs Service sent mail to him under the names of five different fictitious organizations and a bogus pen pal. The organizations claimed to represent citizens interested in sexual freedom and opposed to censorship. The proceeds from sales of publications were supposedly used to support lobbying efforts. Jacobson occasionally corresponded with the organizations, expressing his views of censorship and the "hysteria" surrounding child pornography.

The mail sent to Jacobson was designed to elicit a response that would violate the Child Protection Act of 1984, which bars individuals from receiving sexually explicit depictions of children through the mails. After receiving these mailings for more than two years, Jacobson ordered a magazine that depicted young boys engaging in sexual acts; he was arrested under the Child Protection Act. A search of his house revealed no sexually oriented materials except for the magazines and the government agencies' bogus mailings. Jacobson claimed entrapment. He was convicted at trial, but he appealed and had his conviction overturned. The appeal was heard by the U.S. Supreme Court, which based its decision on the subjective formulation of entrapment: The prosecution must prove beyond a reasonable doubt that the defendant was disposed to commit the criminal act *before* being approached by government agents. At the time Jacobson violated the law, he had been the target of twenty-six months of repeated mailings. His earlier bookstore order could not be used to show predisposition, because this act was legal at the time. Moreover, Jacobson's uncontradicted testimony stated that he did not know the magazines would depict minors until they arrived in the mail.

The Supreme Court had previously held that a person's sexual inclinations, tastes, and fantasies are "beyond the reach of the government." In Jacobson's case, the government provoked and aggravated his interest in illegal sexually explicit materials and "exerted substantial pressure" on him to purchase them under the pretense that his purchases would be part of a fight against censorship. Jacobson's conviction was reversed.[56] Government agents "in their zeal to enforce the law . . . may not originate a criminal design" that creates the disposition to commit a criminal act "and then induce commission of the crime so that the government may prosecute."[57] The entrapment defense is designed to prevent this. The split among the states in adopting the objective versus the subjective formulation of the entrapment defense is a primary reason why entrapment, and some police undercover tactics, remain controversial.

What Are Some Concerns about Applying Criminal Law?

The application of the law to actual cases is not always straightforward. Contemporary concerns in criminal law nearly always involve disagreements about how the law ought to be applied to new situations created by major incidents or by advancing technology. This section will examine one example of each type of situation. In each of these contexts the principles of criminal law must be brought to bear to determine the best way to deal with potentially dangerous conduct.

Controlling Animals or Owners?

Pit bulls, a breed of dog, were involved in several attacks on humans during the 1990s. Although accurate statistics do not exist, this type of dog is said to be especially aggressive and has a particularly harmful bite. Some localities have proposed ordinances that single out pit bulls for special licensing, registration, or banning.[58] Others have sought to label them as a "vicious breed," requiring that when on the street or in other public places pit bulls must be muzzled and kept on a six-foot chain with a 300-pound tensile strength. Proposed regulations would require owners of these dogs to carry liability insurance in the amount of $100,000.[59]

Do such ordinances violate the principles of due process set forth in the Constitution, or do they effectively balance the interests of all those involved—pit bull owners and those who might be bitten? It can be seen that the answer is not easy; it requires balancing a responsible owner's interest in possessing a dog against the public's need to be protected from dangerous animals. Questions that have to be answered include: Should the pit bull be singled out? Is it more dangerous than other breeds? Would it make more sense simply to hold owners liable for the actions of all dogs, regardless of breed? If so, under what circumstances should the law apply? What about a fenced or restrained dog that somehow manages to escape? Concerns about the application of the law to achieve due process in a given case are commonplace.

An analogous issue is the trend toward holding parents responsible for the criminal conduct of their children. In South Carolina, for example, a judge ordered a truant daughter and her mother to be tethered by a two-foot rope. Thus far, parental responsibility laws have been created in response to school vandalism and shootings. In some states parents are responsible for up to $300,000 in damages caused by their children. Criminal charges against parents are fewer, because they are difficult to prove. Nevertheless, in a 1996 case a father was sentenced to sixty days in jail and paid a fine after his son gave vodka to underage girls in his home while the father was asleep.[60] The boundary between young people's personal responsibility for conduct and the responsibility to be shared by parents is still being debated.

Assisted Suicide or Murder?

Determining the presence of the guilty mind required for criminal liability also can be difficult, as in the case of Dr. Jack Kevorkian. In the 1990s Kevorkian claimed to have provided deadly drugs to 130 terminally ill pa-

critical thinking exercise

Justice on the Carolina Frontier (1764)

Before the American Revolution the back country of South Carolina was a lawless place. Because of the remoteness of the region, criminals could operate with impunity. Following is an excerpt from a petition from the Reverend Charles Woodmason to the British government on behalf of the people of his community:

That for many years past, the back parts of this province have been infested with an infernal gang of villains, who have committed such horrid depredations on our properties and estates, such insults on the persons of many settlers, and perpetrated such shocking outrages throughout the back settlements as is past description.

Our large stocks of cattle are either stolen and destroyed, our cow pens are broken up, and all our valuable horses are carried off. Houses have been burned by these rogues, and families stripped and turned naked into the wood. Stores have been broken open and rifled by them. Private houses have been plundered. . . . Married women have been ravished, virgins deflowered, and other unheard of cruelties committed by these barbarous ruffians, who . . . have hereby reduced numbers of individuals to poverty . . .

No trading persons (or others) with money or goods, no responsible persons and traders dare keep cash or any valuable articles by them. Nor can women stir abroad but with a guard, or in terror. . . . Merchants' stores are obliged to be kept constantly guarded (which enhances the price of goods). And

thus we live not as under a British government . . . but as if we were in Hungary or Germany, and in a state of war . . . obliged to be constantly on the watch and on our guard against these intruders and having it not in our power to call what we possess our own, not even for an hour; as being liable daily and hourly to be stripped of our property.

Representations of these grievances and vexations have often been made by us to those in power, but without redress.[a]

CRITICAL THINKING QUESTIONS

1. What characteristics of colonial and frontier justice would you expect to find in South Carolina at the time Woodmason wrote his petition?
2. What ideas from English common law do you expect were already part of criminal law in the colony?
3. How would you respond to this petition to make the community a more just place, knowing that the population was small and could not afford a police force?
4. In the actual petition, Charles Woodmason requested the establishment of a better court system and local jails, a printed criminal code, the requirement that public officials carry out their duty under penalty of law, the founding of public schools, and the establishment of parishes with ministers. How might a printed criminal code and new laws for public officials have been expected to have an impact on the situation in South Carolina?

NOTE

a. Charles Woodmason, "Lawlessness on the South Carolina Frontier" (1764), in *The Annals of America*, vol. 2 (Chicago: Encyclopedia Britannica, 1976), pp. 185–95.

tients. His work has been alternately called "assisted suicide" and "murder." Many people believe that provision of these drugs allows for "death with dignity." Others believe Kevorkian is "playing God" and has no right to provide people with the means to hasten their death. The application of the criminal law to this kind of behavior is not uniform, because not all states include these acts in their definition of homicide. The ethics of assisted suicide are still being debated as communities evaluate a patient's right to determine his or her own destiny and the physician's role in that choice. After a highly publicized televised assisted suicide in 1999, Jack Kevorkian was convicted of second-degree murder in Michigan and sentenced to ten to twenty-five years in prison.[61] Application of the elements of a crime is complicated in these cases, both because the physician plays a passive role (does not administer the drug) and because the patient gives his or her consent or self-administers a lethal dose. Nevertheless, consent is not a valid defense to the crime of assault or homicide, because the law generally does not permit people to victimize themselves. As a result, the debate has focused on the role of the physician. The state of Oregon passed a law in 1998 that permits physicians to prescribe lethal medicines to terminally ill patients near the end of their lives. After the first year, only fifteen people had ended their lives with lethal medication; six others obtained the medications but died of their diseases.[62] The impact of a law is only one consideration in determining its desirability, of course, as the morality of the action also must be deemed acceptable.

Summary

WHAT IS CRIMINAL LAW?

- In contrast to civil law, the set of formal rules that regulate disputes between private parties, criminal law is the set of formal rules designed to maintain social control.
- Substantive criminal law defines behaviors that are prohibited; procedural law provides the rules for adjudication of cases involving those behaviors.
- The four main sources of criminal law are constitutions, statutes, case law, and administrative regulations.
- Criminal law arises from society's consensus about harmful conduct (consensus view) or is codified to advance the interests of those holding positions of power (conflict view).
- The scope of the criminal law is limited, in that laws must precisely define the behavior that is prohibited and must not contradict constitutional principles.

HOW DID THE AMERICAN SYSTEM OF LAW AND JUSTICE DEVELOP?

- Because there are more than 55,000 independent criminal justice agencies that often do not cooperate with one another, the American criminal justice "system" is often called a nonsystem.
- A system of justice evolves in a society in order to enforce rules, resolve disputes, and administer punishment. In the United States this occurred in the colonial period as small, religiously and culturally similar communities evolved into larger towns and cities with more diverse populations.
- The criminal justice process has two fundamental goals: fairness and accuracy.

- Colonial, revolutionary, and frontier justice was less formal than it is today because of the more sparse and homogenous population in early America.

HOW DOES THE LAW DEFINE THE ELEMENTS OF A CRIME?

- No crime can exist without three elements: *mens rea* ("guilty mind"), *actus reus* (a specific behavior), and attendant circumstances (a specific relationship between the act and the harm that results).
- Five characteristics of acts can invoke criminal sanctions: sufficiency, possession, status, voluntariness, and omission.
- Punishments for violations of criminal law are based on assessment of the offender's state of mind, including degree of recklessness (conscious disregard for a substantial and unjustifiable risk) and intention (whether the act was carried out knowingly or purposely).
- For an act to be considered a crime, the harm suffered must have occurred *because of* the act, and the act must be the proximate or direct cause of the harm.

WHAT DEFENSES AGAINST CRIMINAL CHARGES DOES THE LAW RECOGNIZE?

- A defense based on the claim that the defendant was not sane at the time of the act is referred to as the insanity defense. Although the Model Penal Code proposes a specific test for legal insanity, in practice the determination of insanity is highly subjective. Some states have adopted a finding of "guilty but mentally ill."
- Defenses involving force are of three types: self-defense, defense of others, and defense of property.
- Defenses involving justification or excuse include duress, necessity, mistake of fact, ignorance of law, and entrapment.
- The subjective formulation of the entrapment defense focuses on the defendant's state of mind; the objective formulation focuses on the conduct of police and its potential to cause innocent persons to engage in criminal conduct.
- What Are Some Concerns about Applying Criminal Law?
- Special concerns arise when the law must be applied to new situations, changing values, and new technologies.

Key Terms

civil law	due process
criminal law	*mens rea*
substantive criminal law	*actus reus*
procedural law	criminal liability
constitutions	constructive possession
statutes	actual possession
ordinances	reasonableness standard
criminal (penal) code	intention
case law	insanity defense
precedents	battered woman syndrome
administrative regulations	duress
consensus view	necessity
conflict view	mistake of fact
jurisdiction	ignorance of law
common law	entrapment
criminal justice system	

Questions for Review and Discussion

1. Distinguish between civil and criminal law and give an example of each.
2. Name and describe the four main sources of criminal law.
3. What is meant by *mens rea* and *actus reus*?
4. Describe the five characteristics of acts that can be sufficient to invoke criminal sanctions.
5. Define recklessness and intention. How do these terms relate to the determination of *mens rea*?
6. How has the legal definition of insanity changed since the M'Naghten case of 1843?
7. What degree of force is permitted in defense of property in one's own home during a dangerous felony?
8. What conditions must be met for a claim of duress to succeed as a defense?
9. Distinguish between the subjective and objective formulations of the entrapment defense.

Notes

1. "Father Says He Sharpened Son's Buckle," Associated Press (October 23, 1996).
2. Kit R. Roane, "FBI's Glitches with Snitches in Boston," *U.S. News & World Report* (January 31, 2000), p. 25.
3. Emile Durkheim, *The Division of Labor in Society* (New York: The Free Press, 1893), p. 80.
4. William J. Chambliss and Thomas F. Courtless, *Criminal Law, Criminology, and Criminal Justice* (Belmont, CA: Brooks/Cole, 1992), pp. 12–32.
5. *Papachristou v. Jacksonville*, 92 S. Ct. 839 (1972). See also *State v. Palendrano*, 120 N.J. Superior 336 (1972).
6. Deborah Sharp, "Cruising Taking a Bruising in Miami Beach," *USA Today* (September 1, 1993), p. 9; Richard Price, "Party May Soon Be Over for Dance on Wheels," *USA Today* (March 16, 1990), p. 7.
7. Richard Price, "Helmet Law Jolts Motorcyclists," *USA Today* (December 31, 1991), p. 3; Jeanne DeQuine, "Miami Case Tests Child Car-Seat Laws," *USA Today* (April 29, 1991), p. 3; Haya El Nasser, "Seat-Belt Case Takes Law to Limit," *USA Today* (October 16, 1990), p. 3.
8. Jonathan Schonsheck, *On Criminalization: An Essay in the Philosophy of Criminal Law* (Boston: Kluwer Academic, 1994).
9. Lawrence M. Friedman, *A History of American Criminal Law* (New York: Simon & Schuster, 1973).
10. Lawrence M. Friedman, *Crime and Punishment in American History* (New York: Basic Books, 1993), pp. 22–23.
11. Daniel L. Skoler, *Governmental Structuring of Criminal Justice Services: Organizing the Non-System* (Washington, DC: U.S. Government Printing Office, 1978).
12. Lawrence M. Friedman, *Crime and Punishment in American History* (New York: Basic Books, 1993), p. 27.
13. Ibid., p. 3; Peter Charles Hoffer and William B. Scott, eds., *Criminal Proceedings in Colonial Virginia* (Athens: University of Georgia Press, 1984).
14. Bradley Chapin, *Criminal Justice in Colonial America, 1606–1660* (Athens: University of Georgia Press, 1983).
15. See Herbert A. Johnson and Nancy Travis Wolfe, *History of Criminal Justice*, 2nd ed. (Cincinnati: Anderson, 1996).
16. Reverend James B. Britton, "The Practice of Dueling in View of Human and Divine Law," preached before the Congregation of Christ Church, Indianapolis, March 25, 1838. Cited in Susan Jacoby, *Wild Justice: The Evolution of Revenge* (New York: Harper Colophon, 1984).
17. Les Johnson, "What Is Vigilantism?," *British Journal of Criminology* 36 (spring 1996); "No Place for Vigilantism in Our Towns," *Hartford Courant* (May 22, 1998), p. 18.
18. Herbert Packer, *The Limits of the Criminal Sanction* (Stanford, CA: Stanford University Press, 1968).

19. Charles L. Gould, "The Criminal Justice System Favors Offenders," in Bonnie Szumski, ed., *Criminal Justice: Opposing Viewpoints* (St. Paul, MN: Greenhaven Press, 1987), pp. 33–39.

20. John Locke, *Concerning the True Original Extent and End of Civil Government* (Chicago: Encyclopedia Britannica, 1952).

21. George H. Smith, *The American Revolution* (Nashville, TN: Knowledge Products, 1979); Leonard W. Levy, *Seasoned Judgments: The American Constitution, Rights, and History* (New Brunswick, NJ: Transaction, 1995).

22. Jonah Blank, "Guilty—but Just How Guilty?," *U.S. News & World Report* (January 12, 1998), p. 21.

23. See Joel Samaha, *Criminal Law*, 4th ed. (St. Paul, MN: West, 1998); Thomas J. Gardner and Terry M. Anderson, *Criminal Law: Principles and Cases* (St. Paul, MN: West, 1996).

24. *State v. Bugger*, 25 Utah 2d 404, Sup. Ct. of Utah (1971).

25. *State v. McMenamin*, 133 N.J. Superior 521 (1975).

26. *Robinson v. California*, 82 S. Ct. 1417 (1962). See also *Powell v. Texas*, 88 S. Ct. 2145 (1968).

27. Commonwealth of Massachusetts Middlesex Superior Court Criminal No. 97–0433 v. Memorandum and Order Louise Woodward, (November 10, 1997).

28. Rob Parrish, "The Proof Is in the Details," *Shaken Baby Syndrome* (Winter 1998).

29. *Commonwealth v. Howard*, 265 Pa. Superior 535 (1979); *Jones v. United States*, 308 F. 2d 307, D.C. Cir. (1962).

30. *State v. Nosis*, 22 Ohio App. 2d 16, Ct. Appeals of Ohio (1969).

31. *Dusky v. United States*, 80 S. Ct. 788 (1960).

32. See *Jackson v. Indiana*, 92 S. Ct. 1845 (1972); Richard J. Bonnie et al., "Decision-Making in Criminal Defense: An Empirical Study of Insanity Pleas and the Impact of Doubted Client Competence," *Journal of Criminal Law and Criminology* 87 (fall 1996), pp. 48–62.

33. *M'Naghten's Case*, 8 Eng. Rep. 718 (1843).

34. David Rohde, "Insanity Defense Puts Big Burden on Juries," *New York Times* (October 11, 1999), p. 1; Ralph Slovenko, *Psychiatry and Criminal Culpability* (New York: Wiley, 1995).

35. Norval Morris, *Madness and the Criminal Law* (Chicago: University of Chicago Press, 1982).

36. See Henry J. Steadman, *Beating a Rap?* (Chicago: University of Chicago Press, 1979); Samuel Walker, *Sense and Nonsense about Crime*, 2d ed. (Monterey, CA: Brooks/Cole, 1989).

37. Norval Morris, *Insanity Defense* (Washington, DC: National Institute of Justice, 1979).

38. Henry J. Steadman, Margaret A. McGreevy, and Joseph P. Morrisey, eds. *Before and After Hinckley: Evaluating Insanity Defense Reform* (New York: Guilford Press, 1994); Steadman, *Beating a Rap?*; *Jones v. United States*, 103 S. Ct. 3043 (1983).

39. Gordon Witkin, "What Does It Take to Be Crazy?," *U.S. News & World Report* (January 12, 1998), p. 7.

40. Debra T. Landis, " 'Guilty but Mentally Ill' Statutes: Validity and Construction," *American Law Reports* 702 (1991).

41. *Mullin v. Pence*, 390 So. 2d 803, Ct. App. La. (1974).

42. *State v. Kelly*, 97 N.J. 178 (1978).

43. Faith McNulty, *The Burning Bed* (New York: Bantam, 1981).

44. Linda Deutsch, "Menendez Brothers Get Life," *Detroit News* (July 3, 1996).

45. *Commonwealth v. Martin*, 369 Mass. 640, Sup. Ct. (1976).

46. *People v. Ceballos*, 12 Cal. 3d 470, Sup. Ct. (1974).

47. *U.S. v. Bailey*, 100 S. Ct. 624 (1980). See *U.S. v. Webb*, 747 F. 2d 278, cert. denied 105 S. Ct. 1222 (1984).

48. *Regina v. Dudley and Stephens*, 14 Q.B.D. 273 (1884).

49. *People v. Dover*, 790 P. 2d 834 (Col. Sup. Ct. 1990).

50. *Crown v. Tolson*, 23 Q.B.D. 168 (1889); *Stuart v. Commonwealth*, 11 Va. App. 216 (1990).

51. Kenneth W. Simons, "When Is Strict Liability Just?," *Journal of Criminal Law and Criminology* 87 (1997), pp. 1075–1137.

52. *People v. Snyder*, 186 Cal. Rptr. 485 (Cal. 1982).

53. *Lambert v. California*, 78 S. Ct. 240 (1957).

54. Douglas Husak and Andrew von Hirsch, "Culpability and Mistake of Law," in S. Shute, J. Gardner, and J. Horder, eds., *Action and Value in Criminal Law* (New York: Oxford University Press, 1993), pp. 157–74.

55. *Sorrells v. United States*, 53 S. Ct. 210 (1932).

56. *Jacobson v. United States*, 112 S. Ct. 1535 (1992).

57. *U.S. v. Russell*, 93 S. Ct. 1637 (1973).

58. Kris Antonelli, "Fearing Attacks, Long Reach Residents Seek Ban on Pit Bulls," *Baltimore Sun* (December 13, 1999), p. 1B.

59. David, Plata, "Vicious Dog Law Is Being Opposed," *Sun Newspapers* (March 12, 1998).

60. Joanne M. Schrof, "Who's Guilty?," *U.S. News & World Report* (May 17, 1999), p. 40.

61. Joseph P. Shapiro, "Dr. Death's Last Dance," *U.S. News & World Report* (April 26, 1999), p. 44.

62. Joseph P. Shapiro, "Casting a Cold Eye on 'Death with Dignity'," *U.S. News & World Report* (March 11, 1999), p. 56.

five
The Criminal Justice System and Criminal Procedure

New York City experienced a

remarkable drop in the crime rate during the late 1990s. The drop was attributed in part to more aggressive police tactics against minor offenses that affect the quality of life: drinking in public, playing loud music, urinating in public, jumping subway turnstiles, loitering. It turned out that many of those arrested for these minor crimes were also wanted for more serious crimes. But these aggressive police tactics involved stopping people on the street and requesting identification, conducting drug sweeps of entire neighborhoods, and frisking people. These tactics drew considerable criticism, because they created at least temporary infringements on the privacy of many innocent persons.

As one neighborhood organizer said, "In the beginning we all wanted the police to bomb the crack houses, but now it's backfiring at the cost of the community. I think the cops have been given free rein to intimidate people at large."[1] Police were alleged to be pulling people out of cars at gunpoint, roughing up those who didn't speak English, frisking citizens for no clear reason, conducting searches in an abusive manner, selectively harassing minorities, and using force without provocation. These specific complaints against police all resulted from an effort to *reduce* crime in New York City.

Complaints against police grew considerably not only in New York, but in Pittsburgh, Charlotte, North Carolina, Washington, D.C., and elsewhere—in each case alleging overly aggressive police tactics in the effort to reduce crime.[2] These charges are serious, and they reflect a dilemma that lies at the heart of the American criminal justice system: What is the best way to balance the rights of individuals to be left alone against the community's interest in apprehending criminals? This dilemma is most evident in the activities of police, because of their continual interaction with the public.

This balance between individual and community interests also must be struck in the decision to formally charge a person with a crime, in the determination of guilt or innocence at trial, and in sentencing and prison release decisions. The entire criminal justice system is designed to provide a mechanism for achieving this balance in a just manner. This chapter will examine the agencies, laws, and procedures that are devoted to this task—even though they sometimes fall short of achieving their goal.

What Are the Agencies of Criminal Justice?

The contemporary structure of law enforcement, courts, and corrections institutionalizes basic notions of how law should be enforced and adjudicated and how violators should be dealt with. The nation's history as a democracy has guided the establishment of criminal justice agencies, which have been granted the power to intrude into the lives of citizens only under certain circumstances. In addition, many criminal justice agencies exist on the local level, and local control helps prevent these agencies from becoming too powerful or abusive. As a result, the United States has perhaps more criminal justice agencies than any other nation, including more than 12,000 police departments, 17,000 courts, and 6,000 correctional facilities centered largely in local government. These agencies have in common criminal law and criminal procedure, which specify the types of acts over which the system has jurisdiction and the precise way that individual cases are to be handled.

Law Enforcement

Law enforcement agencies exist at all levels of government: federal, state, and local. In each case, however, these agencies' duties are the same. We

Federal Law Enforcement
17 agencies
70,000 officers

State Law Enforcement
49 agencies
60,000 officers

Local Law Enforcement
19,000 agencies
500,000 officers

FIGURE 5.1
Law Enforcement
in the United States

■**policing**
Traditionally, enforcing the law by apprehending violators and thereby protecting citizens. Crime prevention and social services such as education of the public are more recent emphases in policing.

LIMITED, GENERAL, AND APPELLATE JURISDICTION

What three types of jurisdiction exist in state courts and in federal courts? How is a state supreme court like and unlike the United States Supreme Court? In what circumstances might a criminal case be referred to the U.S. Supreme Court for judgement?

generally expect law enforcement agencies to perform four tasks: protect people and their rights, apprehend those who violate laws, prevent crimes, and provide social services. The first two responsibilities are traditionally associated with the function of **policing;** that is, enforcing the law by apprehending violators and thereby protecting citizens. Crime prevention and social services such as education of the public are more recent emphases in policing.

The only difference between law enforcement agencies at different levels of government is in the types of laws they enforce. Federal law enforcement officers are charged with enforcing federal laws; state police enforce state laws; and local police must enforce both state and local laws. As Figure 5.1 shows, the majority of police agencies and police officers are at the local level of government, which includes towns, cities, metropolitan districts, and counties.

Courts

In criminal courts, legal responsibility is determined through interpretation of the law in relation to the circumstances of individual cases. More than 17,000 courts and related agencies operate in the United States, mostly at the state and local levels. These courts can be grouped into the federal court system (courts that interpret federal law) and a state court system (courts that interpret state and local laws). Both the state and the fed-

eral court systems have three basic types of jurisdiction. Courts of **limited jurisdiction** have narrow legal authority and may arbitrate only in certain types of disputes; these include family courts, municipal courts, and special courts such as tax courts. Courts of **general jurisdiction,** on the other hand, usually are referred to as trial courts. These are the courts in which felonies and civil cases go to trial. General jurisdiction courts across the country may be called county courts, circuit courts, and even supreme courts in some jurisdictions. The highest level of jurisdiction is **appellate jurisdiction.** Appellate courts review specific legal issues raised by cases in courts with general jurisdiction. An appellate court may uphold or reverse a conviction in a criminal case tried in a trial court. Figure 5.2 illustrates the court system structure. The sequence in which a case moves from a trial court to an appellate court occurs in every state and in the federal court system, although the names of the courts vary.

The U.S. Supreme Court is the appellate court of last resort in the United States. It has nine justices who are appointed by the president. The U.S. Supreme Court can hear on appeal any case involving federal law, suits between states, and cases involving interpretations of the U.S. Constitution. The decisions of the U.S. Supreme Court cannot be appealed further, and the Supreme Court can also choose *not* to review a case if it so desires. In fact, of the more than 5,000 cases that reach the U.S. Supreme Court each year, more than three-fourths are not heard. When the Supreme Court decides not to review a case, the previous court's ruling stands as the final decision.

The Court System

Courts of Appellate Jurisdiction

(e.g., Court of Appeals, Supreme Court)

Courts of General Jurisdiction
(e.g., county court, circuit court)

Courts of Limited Jurisdiction
(e.g., municipal court, tax court, etc.)

FIGURE 5.2
The Court Process

THE U.S. SUPREME COURT

- **limited jurisdiction**
  The jurisdiction of courts that have narrow legal authority over specific types of matters (e.g., family courts, municipal courts, tax courts).

- **general jurisdiction**
  The jurisdiction of trial courts: courts where most trials for felonies occur, as well as trials in major civil cases.

- **appellate jurisdiction**
  The jurisdiction of courts that review specific legal issues raised in trial courts.

- **local jails**
  Facilities used to detain adults awaiting trial and offenders serving sentences of one year or less.

Corrections

Like law enforcement, the correctional system exists at all three levels of government: local, state, and federal. There are more than 6,000 correctional facilities in the United States. Of these, nearly 3,400 are **local jails,** of which the vast majority are administered by counties. Usually operated by the county sheriff, a local jail is used to detain adults awaiting trial and offenders serving sentences of one year or less.

When offenders convicted in state courts are sentenced to periods of imprisonment, they usually are sent to the state correctional system. The state system includes prisons and prison farms and camps as well as community-based facilities such as halfway houses, work release centers, and drug and alcohol treatment facilities. About 95 percent of offenders sentenced to state correctional systems are incarcerated in prisons or other locked facilities. Nearly 60 percent of all persons incarcerated in the United States on a given day are held in state facilities.

■**probation**
A system under which a person convicted of a crime serves a sentence in the community under the supervision of a probation officer.

THE CRIMINAL JUSTICE PROCESS

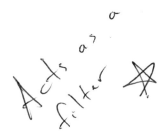

Many offenders are placed on **probation,** which involves serving a sentence in the community under the supervision of a probation officer. There are more than 3.4 million offenders on probation in the United States today, 600,000 in jail, and 1.3 million in prison.[3] These numbers are at record levels, indicating the extent to which the correctional system is used to deal with offenders.

The criminal justice system includes individuals and agencies that serve as links between law enforcement and the courts, such as prosecutors and defense counsel, and between the courts and corrections, such as parole agencies. These agencies will be considered in later chapters.

It is useful to think of the criminal justice process as a *filter*. The law, police, courts, and corrections each capture their share of law violators. The law itself casts the widest filter, reflecting the large number of behaviors that are illegal. The police arrest some law violators, depending on priorities, resources, public policies, and other factors. The courts find some offenders guilty and sentence them, and the corrections system carries out those sentences. As shown in Figure 5.3, decisions at the stages of arrest, preliminary hearing, grand jury, arraignment, trial, and sentencing represent the major decision points in the criminal justice process. Each step acts as a filter, pushing through serious cases that also have sufficient evidence to prove them. When cases are not serious, or when there is insufficient evidence for prosecution, the case is filtered out. Sometimes a serious case makes it a long way through the system, only to end in an acquittal at trial because the evidence was weak. At other times, a nonserious case may go on to a preliminary hearing or grand jury, where a judge or jury may determine that the case is not worthy of further prosecution. Thus, the filters provide multiple opportunities for the system to correct itself as a case moves through it. Because of the many actors involved (politicians, police, prosecutors, judges, and juries), there is room for confusion or error in any given case. The rules of criminal procedure provide a way to ensure that *most* offenders whose cases make it all the way through the system are actually guilty.

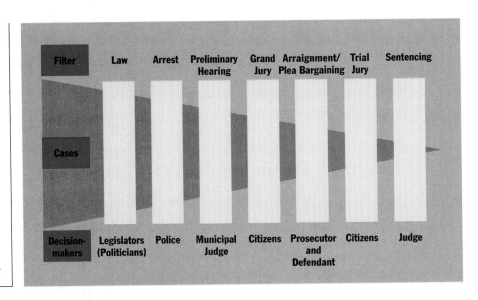

FIGURE 5.3
The Criminal Justice Filter

What Is Procedural Law?

Procedural law is a very important part of the criminal justice process, because it specifies how people accused of crimes will be treated. As in substantive law (see Chapter 4), the provisions of criminal procedure are guided by the principles of the U.S. Constitution. The **Bill of Rights**—the first ten amendments to the Constitution—details many of the requirements for adjudication, such as arrests, warrants, searches, trials, lawyers, punishment, and other important aspects of criminal procedure. The purpose of the Bill of Rights is to protect the individual citizen against arbitrary use of power by the government. Table 5.1 lists the Bill of Rights Amendments that relate directly to procedural law.

Although the Bill of Rights was added to the Constitution more than 200 years ago, it had little impact on the administration of justice until the 1960s. This situation existed because the majority of all criminal law is state law, whereas the Constitution is a federal document. For much of the nation's history the Bill of Rights was interpreted as protecting citizens against mistreatment by the federal government, rather than by state or local governments. After the Civil War, however, the Fourteenth Amendment was added to the Constitution. It states that

No State shall make or enforce any law which shall abridge the privileges or immunities of citizens of the United States; nor shall any State deprive any person of life, liberty, or property, without due process of law; nor deny any person within its jurisdiction the equal protection of the laws.

Most people have read the Fourteenth Amendment to mean that the Bill of Rights applies to the states, but it was not until the 1960s that the U.S.

THE BILL OF RIGHTS

▪**Bill of Rights**
The first ten amendments to the Constitution, which detail many of the requirements for adjudication, such as arrests, warrants, searches, trials, lawyers, punishment, and other important aspects of criminal procedure.

TABLE 5.1

Bill of Rights Provisions Relating to Procedural Law

AMENDMENT	GUARANTEE
Fourth	Protection against unreasonable searches and seizures.
Fourth	No warrants except upon probable cause.
Fifth	A person shall not be compelled to be a witness against himself or herself.
Fifth and Fourteenth	Life, liberty, and property shall not be taken away without due process of law.
Eighth	Cruel and unusual punishments shall not be inflicted.

Supreme Court interpreted it in this way. The important phrase in this amendment is "due process of law"; the due process clause means that individuals cannot be denied their rights as citizens without adjudication according to law.

Law, Investigation, and Arrest

The first requirement of the criminal justice process is, of course, a suspected violation of law, based on the existence of a specific criminal law. For example, an individual who possesses marijuana may come to the attention of police and be subject to the criminal justice process. If it is not illegal to possess marijuana, however, the criminal justice system plays no role. Thus, the law makes possible all the subsequent steps in the process by providing the raw material that feeds the criminal justice process. As the number of laws increases, so does the potential number of cases to be handled by the system.

Breaking the law, however, is no guarantee of becoming subject to the criminal justice process. Not only must lawbreaking occur; it must be made known to the police. If the police do not know of the criminal act, the perpetrator will not be subject to the criminal justice process.

POLICE INVESTIGATION

The first action to be taken by the police is an investigation, which may be the most important part of a case once it enters the criminal justice process. Although it seems obvious, the first fact to be ascertained is whether or not a crime has been committed. Naturally, if a police officer hears a gunshot, enters the room, and finds a body on the floor with a person standing over it holding a smoking gun, it is safe to assume that a crime may have been committed. In most instances, however, police respond to calls from citizens *after* a crime has been committed; only rarely do they see a serious crime in progress. As a result, police often must reconstruct an incident from the accounts of victims and witnesses in order to determine whether a crime was actually committed. As it turns out, many of the complaints to which police respond are unfounded: Property reported stolen is actually misplaced or lost, suspicious noises outside are not burglars, and suspicious persons reported to police have committed no crime.

The Fourth Amendment and Probable Cause

Perhaps the most intrusive authority possessed by police is their ability to search citizens and their belongings and to seize people's possessions. When a suspect is arrested, a search usually is conducted. Questions often arise regarding the scope of the police authority to search, its limits, and the circumstances in which a search may or may not be appropriate. When these questions are raised in a particular case, they inevitably refer back to a single source: the **Fourth Amendment** to the Constitution. This amendment

■Fourth Amendment
The amendment to the Constitution that prohibits searches without probable cause.

provides the guidelines and underlying principles for all law and policy regarding search and seizures by police:

The right of people to be secure in their persons, houses, papers, and effects, against unreasonable searches and seizures, shall not be violated, and no warrants shall issue but upon probable cause, supported by oath or affirmation, and particularly describing the place to be searched, and the persons or things to be seized.

Individuals thus are protected against searches and seizures conducted without a warrant specifying "probable cause." This provision goes back to the nation's early years. The ability of British soldiers to enter homes in America and seize property at will played a significant role in the colonists' movement toward independence. Without the protection of the Fourth Amendment, government agents could conduct searches in an arbitrary fashion. The Fourth Amendment created a standard—probable cause—by which the privacy of individuals would be protected.

Probable cause has been interpreted to mean a reasonable link between a specific person and a particular crime, given the "totality of circumstances."[4] It is a lower standard than that required for conviction at trial (proof beyond a reasonable doubt), but it is higher than the standard required for frisking of a suspect (reasonable suspicion). If police have evidence that establishes probable cause, they write it in a sworn statement, a statement supported by "oath or affirmation." When a judge signs this statement, it becomes a **warrant.** Issuance of a warrant indicates that the judge agrees with the officers' assessment of the evidence. It also means that there is little chance that the evidence will be thrown out of court at a later date, because the judge has approved the warrant *before* the search.

PROBABLE CAUSE

■**probable cause**
A reasonable link between a specific person and a particular crime; the legal threshold required before police can arrest or search an individual.

■**warrant**
A sworn statement by police that attests to the existence of probable cause in a given case; it is signed by a judge who agrees with the officers' assessment of the facts.

What is the first requirement of the criminal justice process, and what is the first action taken by police? What law protects the occupants of this dwelling against unreasonable search and seizure? Under what circumstances could these officers enter the dwelling to conduct a search to gather evidence to make an arrest? Under what circumstances could they search a student at school?

REASONABLE SUSPICION AND STOP AND FRISK For many years the police, the courts, and the public have been uncertain about the scope of a police officer's authority to stop a suspect when there are no grounds for arrest. Although it is common practice for officers to stop and question citizens, it was not clear until the late 1960s whether the police actually had this right—and, if they did, what its limits were. The case that established the legal authority and limits for a "stop and frisk" was *Terry v. Ohio*.[5] The case involved a Cleveland police officer who had been a plainclothes detective for thirty-five years and had patrolled a certain section of the downtown area for shoplifters and pickpockets for nearly thirty years.

The officer saw three men repeatedly walk slowly past a store window and suspected that they were casing the store for a robbery. He identified himself as a police officer and proceeded to ask them several questions, to which they "mumbled something" in response. The officer then grabbed one of the men, turned him around, and patted him down. He felt something in the man's left breast pocket and removed it; it was a .38 caliber revolver. He proceeded to pat down the outer garments of the other men and found another pistol on one of them. The men were charged with carrying concealed weapons in violation of the law.

In court, the men claimed that the officer had no probable cause to search them. Therefore, they argued, the search was illegal and the guns should not be admitted as evidence against them. On appeal, the U.S. Supreme Court agreed that the police officer did not have probable cause to conduct a search, but the gun possession charge was allowed to stand.

The Court distinguished between a "stop" and an "arrest" and between a "frisk" and a "search." A **frisk** was defined as a patting down of outer clothing, whereas a **search** is an exploration for evidence. **Seizure** of property occurs when there is some meaningful interference with an individual's possession of that property.[6] The Court held that a frisk is essential to the proper performance of a police officer's investigative duties, for without it "the answer to the police officer may be a bullet, and a loaded pistol discovered during the frisk is admissible [as evidence]." As a result, the two men were convicted of illegally carrying concealed weapons. The Court concluded that the experienced officer's observations were "enough to make it quite reasonable to fear that they were armed; and nothing in their response to his hailing them, identifying himself as a police officer, and asking their names served to dispel that reasonable belief." The officer's actions were not "the product of a volatile or inventive imagination, or undertaken simply as an act of harassment; the record evidences the tempered act of a policeman who in the course of an investigation had to make a quick decision as to how to protect himself and others from possible danger, and took limited steps to do so."

According to the Supreme Court, frisks are limited to a search for weapons that may pose an immediate threat to the officer's safety. The Court concluded that cases like these must be decided on the basis of their own facts; generally, however, police officers who observe unusual conduct that leads them to conclude that criminal activity may be involved and that

FRISK VERSUS SEARCH

- **frisk**
  A patting down of the outer clothing of a suspect, based on reasonable suspicion; designed to protect a police officer from attack with a weapon while an inquiry is made.

- **search**
  An exploratory inspection of a person or property, based on probable cause of law violation.

- **seizure**
  Meaningful interference with an individual's possession of property.

REASONABLE SUSPICION

the persons may be armed and dangerous are entitled to conduct "a carefully limited search of the outer clothing of such persons in an attempt to discover weapons" that might be used to assault them. Such a frisk was held to be reasonable under the Fourth Amendment, and any weapons seized may be introduced in evidence.

The decision in *Terry v. Ohio* lowered the standard determining when police could take action against a suspect. Before 1968, police could search only if they had probable cause. After *Terry*, police could conduct a frisk of a person's outer clothing to search for weapons if they had only "reasonable suspicion." **Reasonable suspicion** is a lower standard of evidence than probable cause, so the scope of the search permitted is less intrusive.[7]

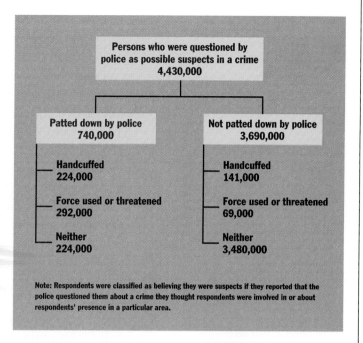

FIGURE 5.4
Prevalence of Frisks by Police

SOURCE: Lawrence A. Greenfeld, Patrick A. Langan, and Steven K. Smith, *Police Use of Force: Collection of National Data* (Washington, DC: Bureau of Justice Statistics, 1997).

■**reasonable suspicion**
A situation in which a police officer has good reason to believe that criminal activity may be occurring; this permits a brief investigative inquiry of the suspect.

Stop and frisk is now a common police practice. A survey asked citizens if they had been suspects in a police encounter in the past year. An estimated 4.4 million people reported having been questioned by police as possible suspects. Of this group, 740,000 (17 percent) had been patted down by police.[8] About 30 percent of those patted down by police were handcuffed, and nearly 40 percent of the encounters resulted in the use or threat of force. Figure 5.4 summarizes the results of the survey.

THE EXCLUSIONARY RULE The landmark case that applied the provisions of the Fourth Amendment to searches was decided in 1961. Three Cleveland police officers had arrived at Dolree Mapp's residence in response to information that a person wanted in connection with a recent bombing was hiding there. The officers knocked on the door and demanded entrance. After telephoning her attorney, Mapp refused to admit them without a search warrant. The police left the scene.

Three hours later the police (now numbering at least seven officers) again tried to enter Mapp's house. An officer knocked on the door, and when Mapp did not answer immediately, they forced one of the doors and gained entry. Mapp, who was halfway down the stairs, demanded to see a warrant. One of the officers held up a piece of paper that he claimed was a warrant. Mapp grabbed the paper and stuffed it into her blouse. After a struggle the police recovered the piece of paper and handcuffed Mapp because she had been "belligerent" during their recovery of the "warrant."

Meanwhile Mapp's attorney arrived, but the officers would not let him enter the house or see his client. Mapp was then forcibly taken upstairs to her bedroom, where the police searched a dresser, a closet, and suitcases. They also searched several other rooms, including the basement, where they found a trunk that contained obscene materials. Mapp was arrested for possession of those materials.

At trial it was discovered that the police had never obtained a search warrant for the search of Mapp's residence. Nevertheless, Mapp was convicted of illegal possession of obscene materials. The conviction was appealed, and the case eventually reached the U.S. Supreme Court.

The Supreme Court had ruled in 1914 that illegally seized evidence could not be used in federal prosecutions.[9] In 1949 the Court held that the Fourth Amendment protected individuals from both state and federal actions, but it did not extend the 1914 exclusionary rule to the states.[10] It was not until the Mapp case that the Supreme Court held that because the Fourth Amendment's right of privacy is enforceable in states through the due process clause of the Fourteenth Amendment, the exclusionary rule applies to both state and federal prosecutions. A growing interest in civil rights combined with concern for due process in police actions led to this decision.[11] The *Mapp v. Ohio* decision applied the exclusionary rule to the states.[12] The **exclusionary rule** holds that illegally seized evidence must be excluded from trials. Searches conducted without probable cause (or without a warrant where one is required) are illegal. Mapp's conviction in Ohio was reversed on the ground that her residence had been searched in violation of the Fourth Amendment. The Court explained, "Our holding that the exclusionary rule is an essential part of both the Fourth and Fourteenth Amendments is not only the logical dictate of prior cases, but it also makes very good sense. There is no war between the Constitution and common sense." In the *Mapp* case the police officers were required to possess a warrant in order to search Mapp's house legally. Because they did not have a warrant, their presence in her home was illegal under the Fourth Amendment. Therefore, any evidence they found was obtained illegally. No matter what the officers found in Mapp's house, it could not be used in court because their presence there was illegal.

THE GOOD FAITH EXCEPTION   The ruling in *Mapp v. Ohio* remained intact for nearly twenty-five years. During the 1980s, however, a trend toward greater conservatism in U.S. society resulted in a change in the composition of the U.S. Supreme Court through presidential appointments of new justices. The result was a shift in the balance between the individual's interest in privacy and the government's interest in apprehending criminals. Although the exclusionary rule still exists, the number of exceptions to the rule has grown.

The first and most significant exception was created in 1984 in the case of *U.S. v. Leon.*[13] Police in Burbank, California, initiated a drug-trafficking investigation of Alberto Leon on the basis of a tip from a confidential informant. After conducting a surveillance of Leon's activities, the police applied for a warrant to search three residences and Leon's cars for drug-related items. The warrant application was reviewed by several deputy district attorneys, and the warrant was signed by a state court judge. The searches

■**exclusionary rule**
Legal principle that holds that illegally seized evidence must be excluded from use in trials.

U.S. V. LEON

turned up large quantities of illegal drugs, and Leon was indicted for federal drug offenses.

A problem arose in that the surveillance of Leon had not actually produced the probable cause needed for a warrant or search. The original affidavit was therefore insufficient to establish probable cause, and the warrant application was signed by the judge in error. The case eventually reached the U.S. Supreme Court, which established a **good faith exception** to the exclusionary rule. The Court based the exception on three arguments. First, it held that "the exclusionary rule is designed to deter police misconduct rather than to punish the errors of judges." The rationale was that it did not seem fair to penalize police for the error of the state court judge who acted in good faith in signing the defective warrant. Second, the Court argued that a good faith exception would not defeat the purpose of the exclusionary rule. Police acted reasonably in this case, and the intent of the exclusionary rule is not to deter reasonable police conduct. Finally, the Court said that the exclusionary rule still applies if police act improperly. That is, if police misled a judge by using false information in a warrant application, the exclusionary rule would apply and any evidence seized on the basis of that warrant would be excluded at trial. In addition, the good faith exception would not apply if a judge were found to have "abandoned his detached or neutral role" or if police officers were "dishonest or reckless in preparing their affidavit" or did not reasonably believe that probable cause existed.[14]

Three justices dissented from this decision, and their opinion captures the essence of the ongoing debate over exceptions to the exclusionary rule. The dissent argued that an exception to the exclusionary rule for judicial errors is self-contradictory. How can a search and seizure be "reasonable" (because it was conducted in good faith) but at the same time "unreasonable" (because probable cause did not exist)? The Fourth Amendment does not address the role of intent in police decisions about search and seizure.

In subsequent cases the Court attempted both to refine the limits of the good faith exception and to create new exceptions for searches and seizures under law. For example, the Court held that inmates have no reasonable expectation of privacy in a prison cell and therefore are not protected by the Fourth Amendment:[15] Neither probable cause nor warrants are required for searches of inmates or seizures of their property. In a case involving the search of a high school student's purse, the Court held that the Fourth Amendment applies to school officials but not to students, because of a "substantial need" to maintain order in schools.[16] In a Maryland case, police mistakenly searched the wrong apartment without probable cause and found illegal drugs there; the evidence was allowed at trial, because the police error was an "honest mistake." Once again the Supreme Court relied on the intent of the officers rather than on the presence of probable cause, thereby creating what has been called the "honest mistake" exception.[17]

> ■**good faith exception**
> Exception to the exclusionary rule, stating that evidence seized with a defective warrant, not based on probable cause, is admissible in court if the police acted in good faith in presenting the evidence and the error was made by the judge.

OTHER EXCEPTIONS FOR LAWFUL SEARCH AND SEIZURE

[handwritten marginalia: - substantial need - Honest mistake.]

contemporary issues and trends

The Limits of Stop and Frisk

The Supreme Court is still wrestling with the question of limits on frisks of suspects. In the case *Illinois v. Wardlow,* decided in the year 2000, the Court ruled on a case from Chicago in which four police cars approached the sidewalk where Sam Wardlow was standing. Wardlow turned and ran down an alley. The police officers caught him, and when they frisked his outer garments they found a gun.

The issue in this case was whether the police had the requisite reasonable suspicion that criminal activity was afoot. In a five-to-four vote a divided Supreme Court held that Wardlow's presence in an area known for heavy narcotics trafficking, combined with his unprovoked flight, justified the search.[a] This ruling suggests that a suspect's flight at the mere sight of a police officer can be suspicious enough to justify a stop and frisk for weapons. Critics argued that the ruling encourages racial profiling of suspects based on prejudice rather than on evidence of criminal behavior. Police organizations, on the other hand, saw the decision as important for effective law enforcement.[b]

Other cases decided by the Supreme Court reflect this tension between the need to stop and question suspects and the evidence police must have to do so. For example, the Court has held that an automobile cannot be stopped unless there is a reasonable suspicion that the occupants are violating traffic or criminal law. It felt that random automobile stops could lead to arbitrary or discriminatory law enforcement—although the Court did not rule out the use of roadblock stops,

because such stops do not permit discriminatory use of police authority.[c] Nevertheless, in a 1995 case the Court upheld a traffic stop based on an erroneous computer readout stating that the person stopped was wanted by the police. A clerical error had caused the false report, and the result was a traffic stop without probable cause.[d] Criminal evidence was found in the vehicle, however. As in *U.S. v. Leon,* the Court held that exclusion of the evidence would penalize police for a clerical (or judge's) error, even though it is the suspect who is penalized in these circumstances.

These cases point to the difference between a stop for purposes of further investigation and a "seizure." In a 1997 case, police moved a bag from the overhead compartment on a bus to the seat to allow a drug-sniffing dog to smell it. This procedure took a short time and did not impair the owner's access to the bag, making the stop reasonable under the Fourth Amendment.[e] The Supreme Court has held that a twenty-minute investigatory stop without unnecessary delay is reasonable under the Fourth Amendment.[f] Therefore, physical movement of property does not constitute a seizure, although keeping it from the owner for an extended period, or destroying it, does.[g]

The U.S. Supreme Court held in *Minnesota v. Dickerson* that a frisk that goes beyond a pat-down search is not permissible, because of the limited purpose and scope of frisking. In this case an officer felt a small lump in a suspect's pocket;

the officer then examined the lump with his fingers and determined it to be cocaine wrapped in cellophane. The Court held that once the officer concluded that the lump was not a weapon, the continued examination constituted a search without probable cause. The search was disallowed, because it was unrelated to the purpose of the frisk: to protect an officer's safety.[h]

1. When does the line between a frisk and a search become blurred?
2. What is the difference between a stop and a seizure?
3. How are probable cause and reasonable suspicion different as grounds for search and seizure?
4. How might the Fourth Amendment and case law apply in cases of suspected computer crime?

NOTES

a. *Illinois v. Wardlow,* No. 98–1036 (decided January 12, 2000).
b. Linda Greenhouse, "Person's Flight Can Justify Police Stop and Search, Supreme Court Rules," *New York Times* (January 13, 2000).
c. *Delaware v. Prouse,* 99 S. Ct. 1391 (1979).
d. *Arizona v. Evans,* 115 S. Ct. 209 (1995).
e. *U.S. v. Gant,* 112 F. 3d 239 (1997). See also *U.S. v. Hary,* 961 F. 2d 1361 (1992) (cert. denied 113 S. Ct. 238).
f. *United States v. Sharpe,* 105 S. Ct. 1568 (1985).
g. *Fuller v. Vines,* 36 F. 3d 65 (1994) (cert. denied 115 S. Ct. 1361); *Bills v. Agetine,* 958 F. 2d 697 (1992) (cert. denied 116 S. Ct. 179).
h. *Minnesota v. Dickerson,* 113 S. Ct. 2130 (1993).

> ... presence in an area known for heavy narcotics trafficking, combined with his unprovoked flight, justified the search.

In these and other cases the U.S. Supreme Court has permitted the use of evidence seized by police that would have been excluded under the rule applied in *Mapp v. Ohio.* The Court's reliance on reasonable police activity, rather than on strict application of the probable cause standard of the Fourth Amendment, reflects the recent expansion of the authority of government officials to search citizens.

SEARCHES WITHOUT WARRANTS The ability of police officers to search suspects without a warrant emerged from the need for police to protect themselves and to prevent the destruction of evidence in street encounters. It is not practical, timely, or safe to obtain a warrant to search someone who has just been arrested for a violent crime. As a result, the U.S. Supreme Court has interpreted the Fourth Amendment clause "no warrants shall issue but upon probable cause" to mean that warrants must be based on probable cause, *not* that a warrant is the only way to establish probable cause. The Fourth Amendment as a whole has been interpreted to mean that citizens are protected against "unreasonable searches and seizures." Therefore, police are permitted to search without a warrant under circumstances in which it is "reasonable" to do so.

Over the years the Supreme Court has delineated five general types of situations in which searches can reasonably be conducted without a warrant. These exceptions to the warrant requirement include searches incident to a lawful arrest, searches with voluntary consent, searches of evidence in plain view, searches of automobiles and their contents, and searches of open fields and abandoned property.

Searches Incident to a Lawful Arrest The case that established the authority of police to conduct a warrantless search in a lawful arrest was *Chimel v. California.*[18] Police officers went to Chimel's home with a warrant to arrest him for the burglary of a coin shop. Chimel was not home, but his wife allowed the police to enter and wait for his return. When Chimel arrived, the police showed him the warrant, placing him under arrest, and proceeded to search the house. They found the coins that he was suspected of stealing and used them as evidence to convict him of burglary. On appeal, the U.S. Supreme Court overturned the conviction on the ground that the search of Chimel's entire house was unreasonable under the Fourth Amendment.

When an arrest is made, it is reasonable for the arresting officer to search the person arrested in order to remove any weapons the [suspect] might seek to use in order to resist arrest or effect his escape. Otherwise, the officer's safety might well be endangered, and the arrest itself frustrated. In addition, it is entirely reasonable for the arresting officer to search for and seize any evidence on the arrestee's person in order to prevent its concealment or destruction. And the area into which an arrestee might reach in order to grab a weapon or evidentiary items must, of course, be governed by a like rule. A gun on a table or in a drawer in front of one who is arrested can be as dangerous to the arresting officer as one concealed in the clothing of the person arrested. There is ample justification, therefore, for a search of the arrestee's person and the area "within his immediate control"—construing that phrase to mean the area from within which he might gain possession of a weapon or destructible evidence.

The Court's finding in *Chimel* allows for a search for only two purposes: to remove weapons and to seize evidence that might be concealed or destroyed. To accomplish these purposes, the police officer is permitted to search the arrestee and the area "within his immediate control." The difficulty of defining the area "within his immediate control" has resulted in a large number of cases that have attempted to delimit this area in different situations. Many of these have involved automobiles. In 1996 the Supreme Court summarized its current position in *Pennsylvania v. Labron*, stating that when there is probable cause for a belief that a car holds contraband and the car can move, the police have authority to search it without a warrant.[19]

Searches with Voluntary Consent   Another well-established exception to the warrant requirement occurs when a search is made with the consent of the suspect. The primary concern here is the voluntariness of the consent. In the landmark case of *Schneckloth v. Bustamonte*,[20] a police officer in Sunnyvale, California, stopped a car that had only one working headlight. Six men were in the car. The driver could not produce a driver's license. When the officer asked if he could search the car, the owner, who was present as a passenger, gave permission. Under the rear seat the officer found three checks that had previously been reported stolen from a car wash. The checks were used as evidence in a trial in which the owner and an accomplice were convicted of possessing stolen checks. The question on appeal was whether the consent to search was truly voluntary.

The distinction between a voluntary and an involuntary search is extremely important in this case, because the police did not have probable cause to conduct a search without consent. The car was stopped because of a burned-out headlight, for which the police could not make a custodial arrest (in which case a search would have been allowed).

The U.S. Supreme Court held that the search was legal and that the evidence discovered was therefore admissible in court. Consent was "voluntarily given, and not the result of duress or coercion, express or implied." The dissenting opinion in this case expressed concern about exploiting the ignorance of suspects who do not know this rule. Subsequent Supreme Court decisions on this issue culminated in the 1996 decision in *Ohio v. Robinette* that people stopped for traffic violations do not have to be told they are free to go before their consent to a search can be recognized as voluntary.[21]

Plain View Searches The right of police to search without a warrant items that are in "plain view" is another well-established exception to the warrant requirement. This exception was explained in the Supreme Court's decision in *Coolidge v. New Hampshire.*[22] The Court specified two conditions for a plain view search: (1) The police officer's presence where the plain view search is made must be lawful, and (2) the discovery must be inadvertent. That is, if police have probable cause before the search, they must obtain a warrant.

The Court established a third condition for plain view searches in *Texas v. Brown* and other cases.[23] It held that police do not have to be "absolutely certain" that evidence is incriminating before making a plain view search. In this case, during a routine traffic stop a police officer seized an opaque green party balloon (which was knotted) together with several small vials, white powder, and empty balloons that were in the automobile. The Court held that the circumstances established probable cause for arrest for possession of an illegal substance, even though the officer was not certain that the balloon he had seized contained an illicit substance.

Evidence seized in a plain view search must be "open to view."[24] In a 1995 case, however, the Court held that a person has no reasonable expectation of privacy in the visible interior of his or her car, even if the interior is inspected by police with a flashlight from outside the car. As in other types of searches with and without warrants, it can be seen that in recent years the Court has relaxed earlier restrictions and allowed police to search under a wider variety of circumstances.[25]

Searches of Automobiles and Their Contents The so-called "automobile exception" to the warrant requirement was established in 1925 in the case of *Carroll v. United States.*[26] The defendants were arrested and convicted of transporting sixty-eight quarts of whiskey and gin in an automobile in violation of the National Prohibition Act. They challenged their convictions on the ground that the search and seizure was conducted in violation of the Fourth Amendment. The defendants claimed that because the search was made without a warrant, the evidence discovered in the search should be excluded. In ruling on the appeal, the Supreme Court clarified a legal point it had made in 1914, stating that once a person has been lawfully arrested, "whatever is found upon his person or in his control which it is unlawful for him to have and which may be used to prove the offense may be seized and held as evidence in the prosecution."[27]

In the cases of *Chambers v. Maroney*[28] and *Michigan v. Thomas,*[29] the Supreme Court expanded the power of police to search an automobile without a warrant. It held that police do not have to obtain a warrant to search a car that is stopped on a highway and impounded, if they have probable cause. Therefore, a vehicle does not necessarily have to be "moving" or even capable of moving for a warrantless search to be lawful. In recent years the scope of the automobile exception has been expanded further to vehicles that have already been impounded.[30] In *Ross v. United States* the U.S. Supreme Court held that "if probable cause justifies the search of a lawfully stopped vehicle, it justifies the search of every part of the vehicle and its contents that may conceal the object of the search."[31]

Open Fields and Abandoned Property The fifth exception to the warrant requirement allows for searches of open fields and abandoned property, which have been found not to be protected by the Fourth Amendment. The open fields exception was first recognized in 1924 in the case of *Hester v. United States*.[32] Police officers suspected that liquor was being manufactured illegally at Hester's home. Fleeing from police across an open field, the suspects dropped bottles they were carrying. The bottles contained the evidence that a crime had occurred. Although the officers did not have a search warrant or an arrest warrant, the Supreme Court upheld the men's convictions, holding that "there was no seizure in the sense of the law when the officers examined the contents of each bottle after it had been abandoned."

Since this decision, the meaning of "house" under the Fourth Amendment has been extended to include the grounds and buildings immediately surrounding a home, known as the "curtilage." However, there are no precise guidelines for determining where curtilage ends and open fields begin.[33] In *California v. Ciraolo* police flew an airplane over private property at 1,000 feet in response to an anonymous tip that marijuana was being grown in the yard. A search warrant was obtained on the basis of an aerial photograph in which marijuana plants could be easily identified. The Supreme Court upheld this search and seizure, holding that "the Fourth Amendment simply does not require the police traveling in the public airways at this altitude to obtain a warrant in order to observe what is visible to the naked eye."[34] Like other decisions of federal courts in the 1980s and 1990s this ruling expanded the authority of police to conduct searches without judicial warrants.[35]

Arrest

Once it is established that a crime has been committed, evidence is collected to support the case and a search for the offender is begun. If the police do not find a suspect, no arrest is made; the case remains "open" until a suspect is found. Continuing investigations are conducted by police detectives. One of the most serious problems facing police is their low rate of solving (or "clearing") crimes by making arrests. For the criminal justice process to continue, however, a suspect must be found, and he or she must be placed under arrest. An **arrest** involves taking a suspected law violator into custody for the purpose of prosecution. To carry out a valid arrest, a police officer must have probable cause to believe that a specific person committed a particular illegal act. This requires a reasonable link between the person and the crime. The police officer must have more than mere suspi-

arrest
Process of taking a suspected law violator into custody for the purpose of prosecution.

cion as a basis for linking a person to an act but does not need to be certain beyond a reasonable doubt.

Following an arrest, the suspect is booked. **Booking** is a procedure in which an official record of the arrest is made. Fingerprints and photographs of the suspect are usually taken at this point. For minor offenses, such as traffic violations, a citation is issued and the suspect is not taken into custody. A **summons** or citation or is a written notice to appear in court. It documents the offense charged, the person suspected, and the time and place at which the person must appear in court. If the person charged signs the citation, thereby agreeing to appear in court, he or she is entitled to be released pending the court appearance.

The Fifth Amendment and the *Miranda* Warning

After an arrest and search have been carried out, the police have the authority to interrogate the arrested person. Interrogations are not specifically mentioned in the Constitution, but the limits of official interrogations are implied in the **Fifth Amendment:**

No person shall be held to answer for a capital, or otherwise infamous crime, unless on a presentment or indictment of a Grand Jury, except in cases arising in the land or naval forces, or in the Militia, when in actual service in time of War or public danger; nor shall any person be subject for the same offense to be twice put in jeopardy of life or limb; nor shall be compelled in any criminal case to be a witness against himself, nor be deprived of life, liberty, or property, without due process of law; nor shall private property be taken for public use, without just compensation.

The Fifth Amendment mentions interrogations when it states that no person can be "compelled in any criminal case to be a witness against himself." The inclusion of this phrase in the Fifth Amendment was a reaction to the Court of the Star Chamber, which was established by Henry VII in 1487. Sedition and heresy trials were conducted in this court, which allowed for forced testimony. This inquisitional system resulted in confessions due to torture rather than guilt. It was not until the seventeenth century that England guaranteed individuals protection from forced testimony against themselves. This history of arbitrary and malicious accusatory practices led the framers of the U.S. Constitution to include in the Fifth Amendment specific provisions for protection against self-incrimination.

The Fifth Amendment has had its greatest impact on interrogations and confessions obtained by the police. The landmark case in which the U.S. Supreme Court applied the Fifth Amendment to specific police procedures was *Miranda v. Arizona.*[36] Ernesto Miranda was arrested at his home and taken to the Phoenix police station. A rape victim identified Miranda as her assailant. He was then taken into a police interrogation room and questioned

BOOKING AND CITATION

booking
Procedure in which an official record of an arrest is made.

summons
Written notice to appear in court; also called a citation.

Fifth Amendment
The amendment to the Constitution that includes protection against self-incrimination.

MIRANDA V. ARIZONA

Media and Criminal Justice

THE STAR CHAMBER

he name of the 1983 film *The Star Chamber* comes from an English court in the fifteenth and sixteenth centuries that was composed primarily of lawyers and judges to supplement the regular common law courts. Popular in its day, the Star Chamber was eventually abolished because in meting out arbitrary justice, it undermined the protections of democracy.

In the film, a modern-day star chamber is established by a group of judges who meet in a secretive backroom court and reevaluate rape and murder cases that they have had to dismiss based on legal "technicalities." Like the cynical cops whose innocent blunders necessitate that the guilty go free, these judges are frustrated with the limits of the law.

In one case, a perpetrator tosses the gun used in a crime into a garbage can as he flees from the police. The police see the gun go into the trash container but, trained in procedural law, they know that the contents of the container are the property of the owner and are thus protected from a warrantless search and seizure. Luckily, a sanitation truck is on its way up the street; the officers cleverly wait for the trash can to be routinely emptied into the city's garbage truck, then remove the evidence from the garbage in the truck's rear trough. But at the trial the perpetrator's lawyer successfully argues that evidence from the search should be excluded, because the truck's scoop had not been lowered before the removal of the gun. The judge has no choice but to admit that the garbage in the trough had not been mixed with all the other garbage; thus, the police action constituted an illegal search of private property.

In another case, seasoned patrol officers find themselves pulling over a suspicious van, using a radio report of unpaid parking tickets on the license plate as their probable cause. Citing the phatom smell of mar-

ijuana smoke as their basis for searching the vehicle they find the bloody sneaker of a recently missing child and immediately arrest the van's occupants for the child's murder. In court it is learned that the defendant's parking tickets were indeed paid on time, but that a backlog in computer data entry caused the dispatcher to relay outdated information on the vehicle to the arresting officers. Once the basis for the pullover is excluded, the consequent fruits of the illegal search also have to be excluded.

These vignettes provide the basis for the movie's panel of judges' creation of their own star chamber. The participants believe that justice has been lost to the stacks of law books and the case precedents to which they must adhere. To the judges, the legal system isn't working anymore, and it is up to them to make sure true justice prevails. They collectively rule that the accused they have set free in a court of law are indeed actually guilty, and dispatch professional hit men to serve the interests of justice.

The Star Chamber does not consider the ultimate question: What if the judges of the star chamber are wrong? In the end, the film allows that any system of justice in our complex society has flaws, but that due process is a necessary evil in balancing the costs.

Are the police searches in *The Star Chamber* legal or illegal under current law? Explain. What aspects of criminal court procedure does the judges' star chamber circumvent? What weakness or criticism of the American criminal justice system does this star chamber address? Do you feel a body like the English Star Chamber is the solution to problems of justice?

---

by two officers. (The layout of a typical interrogation room is shown in Figure 5.5.) Two hours later the officers emerged from the room with a written confession signed by Miranda. A typed paragraph at the top of the confession said that it has been made voluntarily "with full knowledge of my legal rights, understanding any statement I make may be used against me."

At his trial, the officers admitted that Miranda had not been told that he had the right to have an attorney present during the interrogation. Nevertheless, the written confession was admitted into evidence. Miranda was found guilty of kidnapping and rape and was sentenced to twenty to thirty years in prison. He appealed his conviction, but the appeal was denied on the ground that he did not specifically request legal counsel at the interrogation. The case was finally appealed to the U.S. Supreme Court.

The Supreme Court took special notice of the typed paragraph at the top of Miranda's signed confession stating that it had been made "with full knowledge of my legal rights." As the Court noted, Miranda

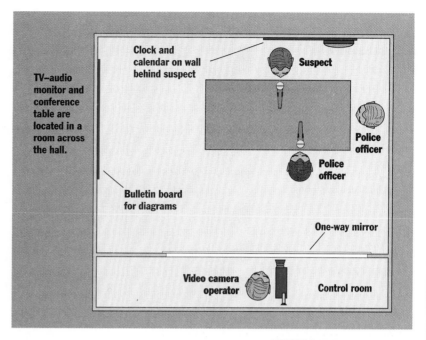

FIGURE 5.5
Layout of the Interview Room in the Denver Police Department

SOURCE: William A. Geller, *Videotaping Interrogations and Confessions* (Washington, DC: National Institute of Justice, 1993), p. 8.

was uneducated, indigent, and "a seriously disturbed individual with pronounced sexual fantasies." Moreover, no one other than the police had been present during his interrogation. The Court felt that these circumstances cast doubt on whether the confession was truly voluntary.

The current practice of incommunicado interrogation is at odds with one of our nation's most cherished principles—that an individual may not be compelled to incriminate himself. Unless adequate protective devices are employed to dispel the compulsion inherent in custodial surroundings, no statement obtained from the defendant can truly be a product of free choice.

Using this rationale, the Supreme Court overturned Miranda's conviction, stating that the confession was inadmissible as evidence. To ensure protection from self-incrimination in future cases, the Supreme Court said that once a suspect is taken into custody, he or she must receive the five-point warning now known as the **Miranda warning** (see Figure 5.6). This warning is required when an individual is taken into custody and is subjected to questioning, because this is when the protection against self-incrimination is jeopardized.

Although the *Miranda* decision set specific guidelines for the conduct of police interrogations, it did not prohibit them in any way. The Court's only objective was to ensure fairness in nonvoluntary interrogations. As the Court observed, "there is no requirement that police stop a person who enters a police station and states that he wishes to confess a crime, or a person who calls the police to offer a confession or any

THE MIRANDA WARNING

■ *Miranda* warning
 Five-point warning derived from the case of *Miranda v. Arizona*. Its purpose is to give crime suspects fair notice of their basic constitutional rights.

FIGURE 5.6
The Miranda Warning

The Miranda Warning

- The suspect must be warned prior to any questioning that he or she has the right to remain silent.

- Any statements made by the person can be used in a court of law.

- The suspect has the right to the presence of an attorney.

- If the person cannot afford an attorney, one will be appointed prior to any questioning.

- Opportunity to exercise these rights must be afforded to the suspect throughout the interrogation. After such warnings have been given, a person may knowingly and intelligently waive these rights and agree to answer questions or make a statement.

These youths were stopped and frisked on the street and were arrested for carrying concealed illegal weapons. What rules of law did law enforcement officers observe in making a legal stop and frisk? What procedures did officers follow in making the legal arrests? What will happen next to the arrestees? What law protects them from illegal interrogation and self-incrimination?

ESCOBEDO V. ILLINOIS

RHODE ISLAND V. INNIS

other statement he desires to make. Volunteered statements of any kind are not barred by the Fifth Amendment and their admissibility [as evidence] is not affected by our holding today."

The *Miranda* decision ensures that those who are ignorant of the law will be given the same understanding of their constitutional protections as those who already understand their rights under the law. The decision added specific legal protections beyond the right to an attorney—a right that was guaranteed to a suspect in custody by the Supreme Court's 1964 decision in *Escobedo v. Illinois*.[37] In that case the suspect, Danny Escobedo, was interrogated by police for fifteen hours, released, and rearrested eleven days later. Escobedo's attorney arrived at the police station for the second interrogation, but the police would not allow the attorney to see his client until the police had finished their questioning. It was during this second interrogation that Escobedo made self-incriminating statements. The Supreme Court reversed Escobedo's conviction, holding that Escobedo was in custody as a suspect in a crime, was interrogated by police, had requested to speak with his lawyer, but was denied access. The Supreme Court's decision in *Miranda* two years after the *Escobedo* decision added specific warnings required at police interrogations to deter this kind of police conduct.

The definition of interrogation was the subject of a 1980 case, *Rhode Island v. Innis*, in which the Supreme Court used police intent to determine if a violation of *Miranda* had occurred. In this case a suspect who indicated that he wanted to speak with a lawyer before talking to police inadvertently incriminated himself during casual conversation with police officers. An issue was whether the officers had conducted the functional equivalent of an interrogation, thereby violating the suspect's *Miranda* rights.

The Supreme Court found that the suspect's rights has not been violated; but the Court also made it clear that the *Miranda* warnings apply during the "functional equivalent" of questioning, which consists of words or questions by police that are "reasonably likely to elicit an incriminating response from the suspect." The Court concluded that for a violation of *Miranda* to take place, "It must also be established that a suspect's incriminating response was the product of words or actions on the part of the police that they should have known were reasonably likely to elicit an incriminating response."[38] This decision narrows the scope of the *Miranda* warning by applying it only to direct questioning by police or to situations in which police actions are "reasonably likely" to result in self-incrimination.

THE PUBLIC SAFETY EXCEPTION   In a landmark New York case, a woman approached two police officers on patrol and told them that she had just been raped. She described her assailant and said that he had just entered a nearby supermarket and was carrying a gun. While one of the officers radioed for assistance, the other entered the store and spotted a man named Benjamin Quarles who matched the description of the assailant. The suspect spotted the officer and ran to the rear of the store as the officer pursued him with his gun drawn. The officer momentarily lost sight of the suspect but soon saw him again. He then ordered the suspect to stop and put his hands over his head. He frisked the suspect and discovered that he was wearing an empty shoulder holster. After handcuffing him, the officer asked him where the gun was. The suspect nodded toward some empty cartons and said, "the gun is over there." The officer retrieved the gun, arrested the suspect, and read him his *Miranda* rights.

The case reached the U.S. Supreme Court because the officer's first question to the handcuffed suspect was likely to be incriminating. If the suspect's statement, which gave the location of the gun, was obtained illegally (i.e., without benefit of the *Miranda* warning), it should be excluded from trial, as should the gun that was discovered as a result of the illegally obtained statement. A majority of the justices held that "overriding considerations of public safety justify the officer's failure to provide *Miranda* warnings before he asked questions devoted to locating the abandoned weapon."[39] This decision created the **public safety exception** to the *Miranda* warning. The exception was justified on the ground that it would be allowed only in cases involving "questions reasonably prompted by a concern for public safety."

public safety exception
Rule stating that police do not have to provide the *Miranda* warning to suspects when circumstances indicate that public safety would be jeopardized.

INTERROGATIONS AND CONFESSIONS   Beginning in the 1980s the Supreme Court decided many cases that provided additional exceptions to

This officer is reading the arrestee his *Miranda* rights. What are the *Miranda* warnings, and on what case were they based? When is this procedure required, and why? What more recent rulings have made exceptions to *Miranda*? Whose interests are in conflict in *Miranda* rulings? Do you think the rule impedes police in doing their job? Do you think the rule protects citizens from unfair police practices?

the *Miranda* rule. In *South Dakota v. Neville,* the Court held that it is not "fundamentally unfair" to use a defendant's refusal to take a blood- alcohol test as evidence of guilt. In other words, this refusal, if used as evidence, does not violate the protection against self-incrimination.[40] In *Oregon v. Bradshaw,* the Court held that if the accused waives the right to counsel and then initiates further conversation, his or her statements may be used as evidence.[41] In another case the Court found that a probation officer seeking incriminating evidence is not required to give the *Miranda* warning to a probationer.[42] And roadside questioning of a motorist detained in a routine traffic stop was determined not to constitute a "custodial interrogation" for the purposes of *Miranda.*[43] In still another case, police arrested a man for purchasing stolen firearms but questioned him about a murder. The Supreme Court held that "mere silence by law enforcement officials as to the subject matter of an interrogation is not 'trickery' sufficient to invalidate a suspect's waiver of *Miranda* rights." The constitutionality of the interrogation was upheld.[44]

VIDEOTAPING INTERROGATIONS

These cases characterize the direction of U.S. Supreme Court decisions in recent years, which have given police greater latitude to stray from the strict language of the *Miranda* finding.[45] In addition, the many conditions and exceptions to the *Miranda* rule have created uncertainty in its application. This uncertainty regarding confessions has prompted many police departments to videotape interrogations and confessions. Videotaping provides an objective record of the interrogation that prosecuters can use in responding to challenges from defense attorneys and in proving that confessions are voluntary. One study estimates that more than 60 percent of large police agencies in the United States now videotape interrogations or confessions in at least some types of cases. About 85 percent of police departments surveyed believe that videotaping improves the quality of interrogations.[46]

What Is Involved in Criminal Court Procedure?

Criminal procedure provides the legal linkage among the agencies of the criminal justice system. It specifies the rules by which individual cases are to be adjudicated. Once a suspect is arrested, his or her liberty is at stake, so criminal court procedure is designed to safeguard the rights of the suspect while also protecting the interests of the community at large.

Initial Appearance and Preliminary Hearing

After an arrest and booking, the suspect must be brought before a judge within a reasonable period of time. In many states the time limit is forty-eight hours, excluding Sundays and holidays. This limit was established in response to past injustices in which arrestees were held in jail for long periods without knowledge of the charges against them and without an opportunity to post bail. At the initial appearance, which usually takes place in municipal court, the arrestee is given formal notice of the charge(s) for which he or she is being held. The suspect is also informed again of his or her legal rights, such as the right to legal counsel and the protection against self-incrimination.

The judge also sets **bail** at the initial appearance in order to ensure that the arrestee will appear in court for trial. An arrestee who posts bail remains free pending the court appearance. Bail is posted in the form of cash or its equivalent, which is refunded when the arrestee appears for trial. For instance, if the judge sets bail at $1,000, a person with access to that amount of money or a property owner with equity of $2,000 will go free until trial. Most arrestees do not have sufficient money or property to make bail, however, and must rely on bail posted by a bail bondsman; this is known as a **surety.** For a fee, the bail bondsman will post bail for the arrestee. When the arrestee appears for trial, the court gives the money back to the bondsman, who charges the arrestee 10 percent of the amount for the use of the money.

Sometimes, if the risk of forfeiture appears too great, a bail bondsman will refuse to post bail. In such cases, unless the arrestee can obtain money from other sources, he or she will be held in custody until the criminal proceedings have been completed. Because the bail system relies exclusively on cash or its equivalent, it can be said to discriminate against poor people. And in fact, the overwhelming majority of people in jail awaiting trial are poor.

Most states allow judges to release suspects *on their own recognizance.* This means that a judge can release a suspect pending trial after receiving the suspect's written promise to appear in court. It is within the judge's discretion, however, later to require bail or to increase the bail amount. In setting bail the judge may consider the seriousness of the crime charged as well

THE BAIL SYSTEM

■**bail**
Money or property held by a court to ensure that an arrestee temporarily released before trial will appear for the trial.

■**surety**
Bail posted by a bondsman on behalf of an arrestee.

ARRAIGNMENT AND PRELIMINARY HEARING

plea
A statement of innocence or guilt.

arraignment
A hearing where the defendant is informed of the charges and of his or her rights and enters a plea.

information
A formal accusation filed by a prosecutor based on the findings of a preliminary hearing.

grand jury
A group of citizens who hear the evidence presented by a prosecutor to determine whether probable cause exists to hold a person for trial.

as the arrestee's prior criminal record, employment history, family ties, and financial burdens or obligations.

If the crime charged is within the jurisdiction of a municipal court, the arrestee may also be asked to make a **plea,** a statement of innocence or guilt, at the initial appearance. For minor crimes this appearance is sometimes called an **arraignment.** The judge then sets a date for trial in municipal court.

In the case of a serious crime, the criminal procedure is more extensive and the trial is heard in a higher (general jurisdiction) court. Following the initial appearance, the next step of criminal justice procedure is the preliminary hearing (or "probable cause" hearing): an appearance in court at which a judge determines whether there is probable cause to hold the arrestee for trial. On behalf of the police, the prosecutor presents evidence against the accused person. The arrestee is present and may be represented by an attorney, who has the right to cross-examine witnesses and present evidence showing that the defendant is innocent. If the judge is convinced that there is probable cause to believe that a crime has been committed and that the person charged committed it, the case is bound over for trial. If the judge does not find the evidence convincing enough to establish probable cause, the complaint is dismissed and the defendant is released.

Before trial a defendant must be formally accused based on a determination of probable cause. This formal step occurs in either of two ways: through an **information,** which is a formal accusation filed by a prosecutor based on the findings of a preliminary hearing, or through an indictment, discussed in the next section.

Grand Jury, Indictment, Arraignment

A **grand jury** consists of a group of citizens who hear the evidence presented by a prosecutor to determine whether probable cause exists to hold a person for trial. The grand jury system was originated in England to prevent the holding of accused persons without justification. Following this common law tradition, grand juries in the United States consist of sixteen to twenty-three people, who are usually selected from voter registration rolls in the same way as members of trial juries. Evidence is presented by the prosecutor, and members of the grand jury can question witnesses. The defendant is not permitted to attend grand jury proceedings, and all grand jury hearings are secret.

The secrecy of grand jury proceedings, together with the absence of defense counsel, can lead to abuses. Grand juries often act as a "rubber stamp" for prosecutors, according to Abraham Blumberg, "since in practice grand juries tend to ratify the charges that are presented to them."[47] The prosecutor's evidence and arguments are unopposed, and questions about a suspect's political beliefs or associations can be used to influence a grand jury.[48] These criticisms were renewed in 1998 with the grand jury investigation of President Clinton's alleged liaison with a White House intern. The intern's mother and Secret Service agents assigned to the White House were *subpoenaed* (given a written order to appear in court) to testify before the grand jury. Numerous leaks to the media about the content of secret grand jury testimony suggested efforts to attack the President and to intimidate certain individuals rather than to discover the truth.[49]

If a majority of the members of a grand jury believe there is probable cause to hold the accused for trial, the grand jury issues a "true bill," or **indictment**, in which the accused is formally charged with the crime. If a majority of the grand jury members believe there is not enough evidence against the accused to establish probable cause, the charges are dismissed. It is possible, however, for a grand jury proceeding to begin before a person has even been arrested. If the grand jury votes to indict, a judge can issue a warrant for the person's arrest based on the grand jury's finding of probable cause. This proceeding, called a *secret indictment*, is carried out when knowledge of a pending investigation would cause a suspect to flee the jurisdiction or to alter his or her conduct.

Grand juries are still used in about half the states, although the Supreme Court has permitted the states to use preliminary hearings in place of grand juries. Until grand jury proceedings attain greater public confidence, visibility, and consistent fairness, they will be seen by some as "serving more as an adjunct of prosecutorial power" than as a buffer between the power of the state and the interests of those suspected of crimes.[50]

After a grand jury votes to indict, or after an information has been drawn up on the basis of a preliminary hearing, the defendant is arraigned. An arraignment takes place before a judge, who reads the information or indictment to the suspect, formally notifying him or her of the charge or charges. The judge again formally notifies the defendant of his or her constitutional rights, such as the right to a trial by jury, the right to have legal counsel at trial, and the right to cross-examine witnesses. If relevant to the case, the defendant's competency to stand trial is assessed, and the court appoints legal counsel for the defendant if he or she cannot afford to retain a lawyer. Finally, the judge asks the defendant to make a plea.

Defendants generally have four alternatives in making a plea: They can plead guilty, *nolo contendere,* no plea, or not guilty. If a defendant pleads guilty (which rarely occurs without negotiations with the prosecutor), the judge will set a date for sentencing. *Nolo contendere* means "no contest" and is treated as a plea of guilty. In states where *nolo contendere* pleas are permitted, the judge accepts or disallows the plea.

A *nolo* plea may not be used against a defendant in a later civil suit. Former Vice President Spiro Agnew provides a well-known example. Agnew's plea of "no contest" to charges of accepting illegal kickbacks as governor of Maryland protected him from having his plea used against him in civil suits brought by residents of Maryland or other injured parties. Those seeking damages had to offer independent proof that he had accepted kickbacks; they could not rely on his plea alone.[51]

If a defendant chooses to make no plea, the case is treated as if he or she had pleaded not guilty. "No plea" is sometimes entered when a defendant has not yet had an opportunity to discuss the case with his or her attorney. Finally, when a defendant pleads "not guilty" (which most accused people do at their arraignment), the judge sets a date for trial. A defendant can change his or her plea to guilty at any time, however, waiving the right to trial.

INDICTMENT

indictment
A formal accusation of a crime based on the vote of a grand jury.

FOUR KINDS OF PLEA

Susan Smith has just been convicted of a felony to which she ultimately pled guilty. What were her other options for a plea? What happened to her next in the criminal justice process? What correctional options did the judge consider in her case? What are her chances of winning a mistrial on appeal?

Trial and Conviction

bench trial
Trial in which the judge determines guilt or innocence.

jury trial
Trial in which the jury determines guilt or innocence.

**BEYOND A
REASONABLE DOUBT**

THE JURY TRIAL

acquittal
A finding of not guilty following a trial.

conviction
A finding of guilt beyond a reasonable doubt.

After the arraignment a trial takes place in one of two formats. In a **bench trial** the prosecutor and defense counsel make their arguments to a judge, who determines guilt or innocence. A **jury trial** is similar except that guilt or innocence is determined by a jury. In a jury trial the judge is present only to rule on issues of law or procedure.

Whether a case is heard at a bench trial or a jury trial, the standard of proof is the same. To arrive at a verdict of guilty, a judge or jury must believe "beyond a reasonable doubt" that the defendant committed the crime.[52] This is the highest standard of proof in American jurisprudence. While "beyond a reasonable doubt" is not the same as 100 percent certainty, it is a much higher standard than probable cause. The precise meaning of "beyond a reasonable doubt" has been the subject of much debate. Some jurisdictions define reasonable doubt as "a serious and substantial doubt," whereas others define it as "a doubt based on reason." In *Victor v. Nebraska* the judge used "actual and substantial doubt" to explain the meaning of "beyond a reasonable doubt" to a jury. On appeal, the U.S. Supreme Court agreed that the Nebraska definition was ambiguous but upheld the constitutionality of the judge's explanation.[53] The definition of "reasonable doubt" is critical, because it has a bearing on jurors' comprehension of the burden of proof when a defendant's liberty is at stake. The Supreme Court has been reluctant to prescribe a uniform definition, and the result is wide disparity in terminology and meaning among the states.[54]

Unlike a grand jury, a trial jury most often consists of twelve citizens, who in most states must unanimously agree on a verdict of guilt. That is, if only eleven of the twelve agree that the evidence indicates guilt beyond a reasonable doubt, then the verdict must be "not guilty." A finding of not guilty is an **acquittal,** and acquittal means that no further legal action can be taken against the accused person on the charge in question. A finding of guilt by a judge or jury is a **conviction.** Only at this point can a defendant be termed an *offender.* An offender can challenge his or her conviction only by appealing to a higher court, attempting to show that errors have been made in law or procedure in the case. While most appeals are unsuccessful, those that succeed usually result in a new trial.

Sentencing and Appeals

sentencing
A judge's decision as to the most appropriate punishment for a convicted offender, within a specified range established by law, given the type of crime and type of offender.

Upon a finding of guilt, the judge sets a date for sentencing. In **sentencing** the judge decides what he or she believes to be the most appropriate punishment, given the type of crime and type of offender. The judge's discretion is guided only by the minimum and maximum sentence for the crime as set by law. If the penalty established by law for a certain crime is one to ten years in prison, a judge can sentence a convicted offender to any term between one and ten years. A sentence outside this range would be a violation of law and would require resentencing.

Before deciding on an appropriate sentence, the judge often will ask the probation department to conduct a **presentence investigation** of the offender. This investigation seeks information regarding the offender's personal and social background, his or her criminal record, and any other information that may help the judge match the sentence to the offender. For example, information indicating a history of drug or alcohol abuse or knowledge that an offender has dependents may influence the judge's decision.

At the sentencing hearing, the judge can fine the offender, impose a sentence of incarceration, or place the offender on probation, depending on the type of crime involved. In probation the offender is placed under the supervision of a probation officer employed by the court. Although the use of incarceration has been increasing steadily in recent years, probation remains the most widely utilized sentencing alternative in criminal court. **Incarceration** segregates offenders from the rest of the community in jails or prisons to rehabilitate, incapacitate, or punish them and to deter others from committing similar crimes.

After serving part of a sentence of incarceration, an offender may be placed on **parole.** In this phase of the criminal justice process, an offender is released before completing his or her sentence and serves the remainder of the term under the supervision of a parole officer in the community. Parole is designed to assist the offender in readjusting to life and work in society after he or she has served time in prison. Parole is not available in all states or to all types of offenders.

Appeals are an often misunderstood part of the criminal justice process. Appellate courts never hear new trials or sentence offenders; once convicted, however, an offender can appeal the conviction to an appellate court. The appeal is a written statement, called a *brief,* which explains the alleged legal errors made during the trial. The appellate court, consisting of a panel of several judges, reviews the brief and the trial transcript. If the court finds that there is no basis for the appeal, the appeal is dismissed. Otherwise, the court holds a hearing in which the defense attorney and the prosecutor present arguments on the issue raised in the brief. This is not a retrial but a hearing on a particular legal issue. For example, the appeal in *Victor v. Nebraska* dealt only with the legal meaning of proof "beyond a reasonable doubt."[55] The evidence presented at trial, the defendant's background, the length of the sentence, and all other aspects of the case were not relevant to the appeal and were not argued.

Sometime after the hearing, the appellate court **justices** discuss the issue and vote either to affirm the conviction by leaving it undisturbed, or to reverse the conviction by overturning it on the grounds that a significant legal error was made during the trial. Occasionally an appellate court will find "harmless error," meaning that a legal error was made during the trial but was not serious enough to affect the fairness of the trial.[56]

Most appeals are unsuccessful. The defendant usually has little recourse but to accept the trial court's verdict, unless a violation of a constitutional

PRESENTENCE INVESTIGATION

■**presentence investigation**
An investigation by the probation department that seeks information regarding an offender's personal and social background, his or her criminal record, and any other information that may help the judge match the sentence to the offender.

PROBATION OR INCARCERATION AND PAROLE

■**incarceration**
Segregation of offenders from the rest of the community in jails or prisons to rehabilitate, incapacitate, or punish them and to deter others from committing similar crimes.

■**parole**
Phase of the criminal justice process in which an offender completes the end of a prison sentence under supervision in the community.

■**appeals**
Review of lower-court decisions by a higher court that looks for errors of law or procedure.

THE APPEAL PROCESS

■**justices**
Judges of an appellate court.

REVERSAL OF CONVICTION AND RETRIAL

right is alleged. In that case the defendant may appeal to the federal courts. Here again, however, appeals usually are unsuccessful. In the rare event that a conviction is reversed, the case usually is retried in the original court of general jurisdiction. For example, if a confession is ruled to be defective on appeal, a new trial may occur, but the confession used in the original trial may not be used in the retrial. Other evidence of guilt, independent of the confession, must be produced. The reversal of the conviction renders the initial trial a **mistrial,** and the retrial is treated as the first trial under law. Thus, a retrial is not considered a violation of the *double jeopardy clause* of the Fifth Amendment, which prohibits a defendant from being tried twice for the same crime.

mistrial
A trial that has been declared invalid because of a substantial error in law or procedure.

What Are Some Concerns about the Criminal Justice System?

The criminal justice system faces continuing challenges to its successful operation. Two of the most pressing concerns involve (1) its cost and (2) the effect of the rules of criminal procedure on efforts to obtain truth and justice in the criminal justice process. The cost of justice is escalating, and the impact of the rules of criminal procedure can be deleterious if the rules are oppressive or obscure the search for truth.

The Cost of Justice

Justice is expensive. Each year, federal, state, and local governments spend $112 billion on civil and criminal justice system agencies. The largest share goes to police ($49 billion), followed by corrections ($40 billion), which includes jails, prisons, probation, and parole. Nearly 2 million people are employed in the justice system, including about 900,000 police employees, 656,000 in corrections, and 401,000 in judicial posts, prosecution, defense, and legal services. As you have seen, most law is on the state and local level, so most expenditures for the criminal justice system also occur there. State and local governments spend an average of $354 per capita each year on justice activities, and their justice expenditures account for 87 percent of all justice dollars.[57] All this money, of course, is provided by taxpayers.

Why is the cost of justice so high? The primary reason is increased spending on prisons and police. Legislatures appropriate funds to these agencies because the public either actively encourages them or does not object strongly. The high levels of fear of crime, documented in Chapter 1, have put pressure on legislators to "do something" about crime. Spending on police and prisons is a popular way to "do something" because these agencies already exist and have clear legal mandates. Spending on more innovative programs, such as delinquency prevention and family intervention initiatives, is less popular because these are not established political institutions.

Despite the apparently high cost of justice, outlays in this area pale in comparison to other expenditures by government. Of the more than $2.7 trillion spent by governments in this country, only about 4.4 percent goes to criminal justice. Much higher amounts go toward social security (24.4 percent), education and libraries (15 percent), national defense and international relations (12 percent), interest on government debt (11 percent), public welfare (9 percent), and environment and housing (5.5 percent). As Figure 5.7 shows, then, many other government priorities outpace criminal justice in terms of total expenditures. It is true that the costs of crime in terms of physical harm, the costs of doing business, the need for locks and alarms, and related human costs are difficult to quantify. It is clear, however, that successful crime prevention initiatives might avert the human losses caused by crime and the fear it creates. This, in turn, might ultimately lower the cost of the justice system, because we would turn to it less often. The rising cost of the justice system, an increase of 73 percent since 1990 in constant dollars, is not likely to be reduced in the near future, however. Calls for police service have increased; jails are filled beyond their capacity; police departments are increasing staffing; and prosecutors report that they are unable to keep up with caseloads.[58] Prosecutors, public defenders, judges, trial court administrators, and probation, parole, and correctional administrators all believe that the current system is not achieving its goals. The time appears ripe for innovations in crime prevention, policing, adjudication, and sentencing so that we can be assured that our expenditures are being put to their best possible use.

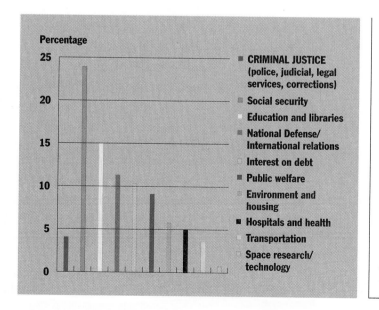

FIGURE 5.7

Expenditures on Criminal Justice Compared to Other Government Spending (Percentages of Total Government Expenditures: Federal, State, and Local)

SOURCE: Lea Gifford and Sue A. Lindgren, *Justice Expenditure and Employment in the United States, 1995* (Washington, DC: Bureau of Justice Statistics, 1999).

Impacts of Procedural Law on Law Enforcement

Since the U.S. Supreme Court's 1961 decision in *Mapp v. Ohio*, there has been much debate over the desirability of the exclusionary rule. Supporters of the rule maintain that the *Mapp* case illustrates how citizens need the rule if they are to be protected against police misconduct. Without the protection provided by the exclusionary rule, there would be nothing to prevent police from making illegal searches in the hope of finding some kind of incriminating evidence. The potential for harassment of citizens would be great. On the other hand, opponents argue that the exclusionary rule makes it possible for criminals to go free. Just because a search is conducted illegally, all the evidence found is excluded from use at trial. Such a sweeping rule may "handcuff" the police in their efforts to obtain evidence against criminals.

STUDIES ON EFFECTS OF THE EXCLUSIONARY RULE

This debate has prompted empirical investigations aimed at determining the relative merits of the exclusionary rule. Are many suspects released because searches are found to be illegal? Is there any evidence that the exclusionary rule deters police from making illegal searches? Sheldon Krantz and his colleagues examined the effect of the exclusionary rule in 512 drug and gambling cases in Boston. They found that the rule was used to exclude evidence in only 2 percent of those cases.[59] The U.S. General Accounting Office assessed the impact of the exclusionary rule in federal court. A review of 2,804 cases found that the rule had been invoked successfully in only 1.3 percent of the cases.[60]

A National Institute of Justice study examined felony cases over three years and found that once cases reached trial, fewer than one-half of 1 percent (0.4 percent) were dismissed because of the exclusionary rule, although there was some variation by jurisdiction and by type of crime.[61] Thus, as one expert noted, the impact of the exclusionary rule on prosecution of violent crime was "infinitesimal."[62] Nevertheless, the rule appeared to have some effect in drug cases, in which police rarely have a complainant whom they can rely on to establish probable cause for search and arrest.

The debate over the desirability of the exclusionary rule has continued, and the Supreme Court anticipated this controversy in its decision in the *Mapp* case:

> *Because [the Fourth Amendment protection of privacy] is enforceable in the same manner and to like effect as other basic rights secured by the Due Process Clause, we can no longer permit it to be revocable at the whim of any police officer who, in the name of law enforcement itself, chooses to suspend its enjoyment. Our decision, founded on reason and truth, gives to the individual no more than that which the Constitution guarantees him, to the police officer no less than that which honest law enforcement is entitled, and, to the courts, that judicial integrity so necessary in the true administration of justice.*

The Court argued that the exclusionary rule guarantees a constitutional right to individuals and grants to the government only the authority it needs if it is to carry out police functions with integrity. Since the 1980s, however, the composition of the Supreme Court has changed, resulting in a shift in the Court's views regarding the proper balance between the right to privacy and the government's desire to apprehend crime suspects. The Court has moved from adhering to a clear exclusionary rule to creating various exceptions, as noted earlier in this chapter, in which police may conduct searches without a warrant under a variety of circumstances.

Also at issue are laws governing police procedures. Law enforcement officials initially criticized *Miranda v. Arizona* for limiting their ability to obtain evidence through interrogation. Many believed that officers would no longer be able to conduct interrogations of suspects without lawyers present, and that suspects who understood that they had the right to remain silent would always invoke this right and refuse to talk to the police.

What has been the impact of the *Miranda* warning on contemporary police interrogations? One study of this question was carried out in Connecticut by Richard Ayres two years after the *Miranda* decision. Ayres placed ten observers in the New Haven Police Department for eleven weeks. Working around the clock, they observed all interrogations and interviewed detectives, defense counsel, prosecutors, and suspects after the interrogations. On the basis of these observations and interviews, Ayres concluded that the *Miranda* decision "had virtually no effect on police investigation."[63] Ayres also discovered that detectives often found ways to reduce the effect of the *Miranda* warnings by changing the words in subtle ways: "Whatever you say may be used *for* or against you in a court of law," or "You don't have to say a word, but you ought to get everything cleared up," or "You don't have to say anything, of course, but you can explain how. . . ." The U.S. Supreme Court has ruled that the *Miranda* warnings do not have to be stated in their exact form.[64]

Interestingly, suspects rarely reacted to the *Miranda* warnings when they were given. Most suspects chose not to exercise their rights to have counsel present or to remain silent. They appeared not to grasp the importance of the warnings and felt compelled by the circumstances to talk with the police. Subsequent investigations in Oakland, Los Angeles, Washington, D.C., and an unnamed midwestern city have yielded similar results: Police often fail to inform suspects of their rights, and few suspects exercise their rights under *Miranda* when they are informed of them.[65]

On the other hand, studies by Paul Cassell in the 1990s concluded that thousands of cases had not been prosecuted because suspects did not make statements after being given the *Miranda* warning. Cassell found that more cases were pled to a lesser charge and that confession rates by suspects also had dropped since *Miranda*.[66] These conflicting findings are difficult to reconcile.

The importance of confessions to police work may be overstated, however. Police rarely take a suspect into custody without some kind of evidence, and a confession rarely forms the basis for a conviction without other corroborating evidence. Likewise, guilty suspects who are taken into custody usually have a story, excuse, or alibi to sell the police; and innocent suspects are eager to talk with police to establish their innocence. Therefore, remaining silent when in police custody is difficult to do under most circumstances.

STUDIES ON EFFECTS OF THE MIRANDA WARNING

critical thinking exercise

Civil Suits against Police

In 1998, New York City agreed to pay nearly $3 million to settle a lawsuit filed by the family of a man who died after being held in an illegal choke hold by a police officer. The officer was acquitted of negligent homicide but was convicted in federal court of violating the man's civil rights.[a] The officer faces a prison sentence.

Clearly, the consequences of police conduct on both civil and criminal liability can be significant. Police officers and their departments are increasingly being sued for damages. This trend is due in part to a general tendency in the United States to seek compensation through lawsuits. Police are especially susceptible to lawsuits because of their authority over the liberty of others and their ability to use force to ensure compliance with the law under certain circumstances. Most lawsuits against police involve claims of false arrest, negligence, or excessive use of force.

The U.S. Supreme Court has held that a police officer can be sued for false arrest or false imprisonment "when a reasonably well-trained officer, under the same circumstances" would have known that probable cause did not exist for the arrest. This liability holds even if the officer has a warrant signed by a judge, because the judge's incompetence in not recognizing the lack of probable cause cannot excuse the officer's conduct.[b]

Police have been sued for negligence when they have failed to be aware of a substantial and unjustifiable risk posed by their conduct. Many of these lawsuits involve high-speed pursuits for nonserious crimes in which bystanders or suspects have been injured or killed; in other cases a lack of adequate training "amounts to deliberate indifference to the rights of persons" police encounter. The Supreme Court has held that when poor training is the result of a conscious or deliberate choice, police may be held liable for civil damages.[c] In a 1997 decision the Supreme Court made it clear that only deliberate indifference to obvious consequences can result in a successful civil suit against police.[d]

Lawsuits brought in federal court often allege violation of Section 1983 of Title 42 of the United States Code. This law prohibits anyone from denying others their constitutional rights to life, liberty, or property without due process of law. This type of suit has occurred most often in cases of alleged excessive use of force. The consequences of the use of deadly force have spurred a move toward development of nonlethal methods to stop and subdue suspects, such as chemical sprays, tranquilizer darts, and electric shock devices.[e] As these new devices are developed, it will be important for police to receive extensive training in their proper use, for they may open another avenue of litigation against police.

A 1998 study investigated what police administrators might do to avoid civil lawsuits against their departments. This survey of 248 police departments discovered three factors that are associated with fewer civil suits lodged against police departments: community policing, minority recruitment, and citizen review. As community-oriented policing programs were adopted, lawsuits declined quite markedly in those departments. Also, stronger interest in minority recruitment of police officers and citizen involvement in handling complaints against police were associated with fewer civil suits. As study author John Worrall concluded, research like this can help police agencies arrive at "preemptive and preventive administrative decisions" that make a difference in the lives of both police and the public.[f]

CRITICAL THINKING QUESTIONS

1. Why do you believe lawsuits against police have been increasing in recent years?
2. What kinds of Supreme Court decisions regarding searches and seizures might best protect police from future lawsuits?

NOTES

a. "New York Pays $3 Million to Police Victim Kin," Associated Press Online (October 2, 1998).
b. *Malley v. Briggs,* 106 S. Ct. 1092 (1986).
c. *City of Canton, Ohio v. Harris,* 109 S. Ct. 1197 (1989).
d. *Board of the County Commissioners of Bryan County, Oklahoma v. Brown,* 117 S. Ct. 1382 (1997).
e. Steven M. Edwards, John Grainfield, and Jamie Ormen, *Evaluation of Pepper Spray* (Washington, DC: National Institute of Justice, 1997).
f. John L. Worrall, "Administrative Determinants of Civil Liability Lawsuits against Municipal Police Departments: An Exploratory Analysis," *Crime and Delinquency* 44 (April 1998), p. 295.

Summary

WHAT ARE THE AGENCIES OF CRIMINAL JUSTICE?

- The main types of criminal justice agencies are law enforcement agencies, courts (including trial and appeals courts), and correctional systems. All three types are found at all three levels of government: federal, state, and local.
- The criminal justice process acts like a filter in which the agencies of criminal justice each capture a share of law violators.

WHAT IS PROCEDURAL LAW?

- Many important aspects of criminal procedure are detailed in the Bill of Rights, the first ten amendments to the U.S. Constitution.
- Only since the 1960s have the provisions of the Bill of Rights been applied to the states as well as to the federal government.
- The criminal justice process begins with a violation of the law that is made known to the police. The police conduct an investigation, which may or may not lead to the arrest and booking of the suspect.
- The Fourth Amendment protects individuals from searches and seizures conducted without a warrant specifying probable cause.
- A frisk is a patting down of an individual's outer clothing on the basis of a reasonable suspicion, whereas a search is an exploratory quest for evidence. Frisks are limited to a search for weapons that may pose an immediate threat to the officer's safety. Automobiles may be searched without probable cause if officers possess a reasonable belief that the occupant is armed.
- The exclusionary rule holds that illegally seized evidence must be excluded from trials. The "good faith" exception to this rule occurs when police conduct a search on the basis of a warrant that is later found to be defective.
- Searches may be conducted without a warrant if they are incident to a lawful arrest, are conducted with voluntary consent; or involve evidence in plain view, automobiles and their contents, or open fields and abandoned property.
- The Fifth Amendment provides for grand juries, protection against double jeopardy, and protection from self-incrimination. It has had its greatest impact on interrogations and confessions obtained by the police.
- To ensure protection against self-incrimination, suspects taken into custody must be read the *Miranda* warning, which states that the suspect has the right to remain silent and to have an attorney present during questioning.
- The Supreme Court has established some exceptions to the *Miranda* rule. These include the public safety exception, in which a suspect may be asked questions prompted by concern for public safety before being read the *Miranda* warning.

WHAT IS INVOLVED IN CRIMINAL COURT PROCEDURE?

- At the initial appearance the arrestee is given formal notice of the charge(s) for which he or she is being held and is informed of his or her legal rights; in addition, the judge sets bail. This step is followed by a preliminary hearing to determine whether there is probable cause to believe that a crime has been committed and that the person charged committed it.
- A grand jury consists of a group of citizens who hear the evidence presented by a prosecutor in order to determine whether probable cause exists to hold a person for trial. If the grand jury finds probable cause, it will issue a true bill or indictment formally charging the accused person with the crime.
- At an arraignment a judge reads the information or indictment and notifies the defendant of his or her constitutional rights. The defendant then makes a plea.

- In a bench trial the prosecutor and defense make their arguments to a judge, who determines guilt or innocence. A jury trial is similar except that guilt or innocence is determined by a trial jury. A finding of not guilty is an acquittal; a finding of guilty is a conviction.
- In the case of a guilty verdict the judge sets a date for sentencing and may ask the probation department to conduct a presentence investigation of the offender. At the sentencing hearing the judge can fine the offender, impose a sentence of incarceration, or place the offender on probation.
- A convicted offender can appeal the conviction to an appellate court consisting of a panel of several justices, who may vote either to affirm the conviction or to reverse it—that is, to overturn it because a significant legal error was made during the trial.

WHAT ARE SOME CONCERNS ABOUT THE CRIMINAL JUSTICE SYSTEM?

- Criminal justice is expensive. A major reason for the cost of justice is a significant increase in spending on prisons and police in recent years.
- Debate continues about the benefits of the exclusionary rule and *Miranda* for citizens and for law enforcement, reflecting continuing conflict in the balance to be struck among the interests of government, the public interest, and the rights of private citizens.

Key Terms

policing	*Miranda* warning
limited jurisdiction	public safety exception
general jurisdiction	bail
appellate jurisdiction	surety
local jails	plea
probation	arraignment
Bill of Rights	information
Fourth Amendment	grand jury
probable cause	indictment
warrant	bench trial
frisk	jury trial
search	acquittal
seizure	conviction
reasonable suspicion	sentencing
exclusionary rule	presentence investigation
good faith exception	incarceration
arrest	parole
booking	appeals
summons	justices
Fifth Amendment	mistrial

Questions for Review and Discussion

1. Name the three basic types of criminal justice agencies and their primary functions.
2. What criminal justice processes are defined by procedural law?

3. What limits does the Fourth Amendment place on searches and seizures by police?
4. What is the difference between a frisk and a search?
5. What is meant by the "reasonable suspicion" standard? How is it different from the "probable cause" standard?
6. What is the exclusionary rule, and what are some exceptions to that rule?
7. In what kinds of situations may a search be conducted without a warrant?
8. What protections are provided by the Fifth Amendment?
9. What is the *Miranda* rule, and what exceptions to the rule have been allowed by the Supreme Court?
10. What basic sequence of events is involved in criminal court procedure?
11. Why has the cost of justice risen dramatically in recent years?
12. Why are the impacts of procedural law on law enforcement controversial?

Notes

1. Larry Reibstein, "NYPD Black and Blue," *Newsweek* (June 2, 1997), p. 67.
2. Bob Herbert, "Attention Must Be Paid," *New York Times* (September 30, 1999), p. A31.
3. Thomas P. Bonczar and Lauren E. Glaze, *Probation and Parole in the United States* (Washington, DC: Bureau of Justice Statistics, 1999); Allen J. Beck and Christopher J. Mumola, *Prisoners in 1998* (Washington, DC: Bureau of Justice Statistics, 1999).
4. *Illinois v. Gates*, 426 U.S. 318 (1982).
5. 88 S. Ct. 1868 (1968); see also the related cases of *Sibron v. New York*, 88 S. Ct. 1902 (1968) and *Peters v. New York*, 88 S. Ct. 1904 (1968).
6. *Saldal v. Cook County*, 113 S. Ct. 538 (1992).
7. *Alabama v. White*, 496 U.S. 325 (1990); see also *Ornelas v. United States*, 116 S. Ct. 1657 (1996).
8. Lawrence A. Greenfeld, Patrick A. Langan, and Steven K. Smith, *Police Use of Force: Collection of National Data* (Washington, DC: Bureau of Justice Statistics, 1997), p. 13.
9. *Weeks v. United States*, 34 S. Ct. 341 (1914).
10. *Wolf v. Colorado*, 338 U.S. 25 (1949); Henry J. Abraham, *Freedom and the Court: Civil Rights and Liberties in the United States* (New York: Oxford University Press, 1977).
11. *Rochin v. California*, 342 U.S. 165 (1952); *Rea v. United States*, 350 U.S. 214 (1956).
12. *Mapp v. Ohio*, 367 U.S. 643 (1961).
13. *U.S. v. Leon*, 104 S. Ct. 3405 (1984) and *Massachusetts v. Sheppard*, 104 S. Ct. 3424 (1984).
14. Robert L. Misner, "Limiting *Leon*: A Mistake of Law Analogy," *Journal of Criminal Law and Criminology* 77 (fall 1986), pp. 507–45.
15. *Hudson v. Palmer*, 104 S. Ct. 3194 (1984).
16. *New Jersey v. T. L. O.*, 105 S. Ct. 733 (1985).
17. *Maryland v. Garrison*, 107 S. Ct. 1013 (1987).
18. 89 S. Ct. 2034 (1969).
19. 116 S. Ct. 2485 (1996).
20. 93 S. Ct. 2041 (1973).
21. *U.S. v. Matlock*, 94 S. Ct. 988 (1974); *U.S. v. Watson*, 96 S. Ct. 820 (1976); *Florida v. Jimeno*, 111 S. Ct. 1801 (1991); *Ohio v. Robinette*, 117 S. Ct. 417 (1996).
22. 91 S. Ct. 2022 (1971).
23. 103 S. Ct. 2317.
24. *U.S. v. Roblem*, 37 F. 3d 1260 (1994); *United States v. Jacobson*, 104 S. Ct. 1652 (1984).
25. *Arizona v. Hicks*, 107 S. Ct. 1149 (1987); *Horton v. California*, 496 U.S. 120 (1990); *U.S. v. Hatten*, 68 F. 3d 257 (1995) (cert. denied 116 S. Ct. 1026).
26. 45 S. Ct. 280. (1925).
27. *Weeks v. United States*, 34 S. Ct. 341 (1914).
28. 90 S. Ct. 1975 (1970).
29. 102 S. Ct. 3079 (1982).
30. *South Dakota v. Opperman*, 96 S. Ct. 3092 (1976); *Pennsylvania v. Mimms*, 98 S. Ct. 330 (1977); *Colorado v. Bertine*, 107 S. Ct. 738 (1987); *California v. Acevedo*, 111 S. Ct. 1982 (1991); *Brown v. United States*, 116 S. Ct. 1769 (1996); *Florida v. Meyers*, 104 S. Ct. 1852 (1985); *United States v. Johns*, 105 S. Ct. 881 (1985).
31. 102 S. Ct. 2586 (1982).

32. 44 S. Ct. 445 (1924).

33. *Oliver v. United States*, 104 S. Ct. 1735 (1984); *U.S. v. Gorman*, 104 F. 2d 272 (1996); *U.S. v. Van Damme*, 48 F. 3d 461 (1995).

34. 106 S. Ct. 1809 (1986).

35. *U.S. v. Gorman*, 104 F. 3d 272 (1996); U.S. v. Van Damme, 48 3d 461 (1995).

36. 86 S. Ct. 1602 (1966).

37. *Escobedo v. Illinois*, 378 U.S. 478 (1964).

38. *Rhode Island v. Innis*, 100 S. Ct. 1682 (1980).

39. *New York v. Quarles*, 104 S. Ct. 2626 (1984).

40. 103 S. Ct. 916 (1983).

41. 103 S. Ct. 2830 (1983).

42. *Minnesota v. Murphy*, 104 S. Ct. 1136 (1984).

43. *Berkimer v. McCarty*, 104 S. Ct. 3138 (1984).

44. *Colorado v. Spring*, 107 S. Ct. 851 (1987); see also *Clabourne v. Lewis*, 64 F. 3d 1373 (1995).

45. *Oregon v. Elstad*, 105 S. Ct. 1285 (1985); *Moran v. Burbine*, 106 S. Ct. 1135 (1986); *Colorado v. Spring*, 107 S. Ct. 851 (1987); *Illinois v. Perkins*, 111 S. Ct. 1121 (1990).

46. William A. Geller, *Videotaping Interrogations and Confessions* (Washington, DC: National Institute of Justice, 1993).

47. Abraham S. Blumberg, *Criminal Justice: Issues and Ironies*, 2nd ed. (New York: New Viewpoints, 1979).

48. Marvin E. Frankel and Garry P. Naftalis, *The Grand Jury* (New York: Hill & Wang, 1977).

49. Judy Keen and Gary Fields, "Deal Sought on Guards' Testimony," *USA Today* (February 13, 1998), p. 1; Walter Shapiro, "Loneliest Job in the World—Except for All the Lawyers," *USA Today* (February 13, 1998), p. 6.

50. Blumberg, p. 144.

51. See Spiro T. Agnew, *Go Quietly . . . or Else* (New York: Morrow, 1980).

52. Ronald L. Carlson, *Criminal Justice Procedure*, 5th ed. (Cincinnati: Anderson, 1996), p. 177.

53. *Victor v. Nebraska*, 114 S. Ct. 1239 (1994).

54. Craig Hemmens, Kathryn E. Scarborough, and Rolando V. Del Carmen, "Grave Doubts about 'Reasonable Doubt': Confusion in State and Federal Courts," *Journal of Criminal Justice* 25 (1997), pp. 231–54.

55. *Victor v. Nebraska*, 114 S. Ct. 1239 (1994).

56. Gilbert B. Stuckey, *Procedures in the Justice System*, 5th ed. (New York: Macmillan, 1996), p. 242.

57. Lea S. Gifford and Sue A. Lindgren, *Justice Expenditure and Employment in the United States* (Washington, DC: Bureau of Justice Statistics, 1999).

58. Barbara A. Webster and J. Thomas McEwen, *Assessing Criminal Justice Needs* (Washington, DC: National Institute of Justice, 1992); Tom McEwen, *National Assessment Program: 1994 Survey Results* (Washington, DC: National Institute of Justice, 1995).

59. Sheldon Krantz, Bernard Gilman, Charles G. Benda, Garol Rogoff Hallstrom, and Gail J. Nadworny, *Police Policymaking* (Lexington, MA: Lexington Books, 1979).

60. U.S. Comptroller General, *The Impact of the Exclusionary Rule on Federal Criminal Prosecutions* (Washington, DC: U.S. Government Printing Office, 1979).

61. Robert W. Burkhart, Shirley Melnicoe, Annelsely K. Schmidt, Linda J. McKay, and Cheryl Martorana, *The Effects of the Exclusionary Rule: A Study in California* (Washington, DC: National Institute of Justice, 1982).

62. James J. Fyfe, "The NIJ Study of the Exclusionary Rule," *Criminal Law Bulletin* 19 (May–June 1983), pp. 253–60.

63. Richard Ayres, "Confessions and the Court," *Yale Alumni Magazine* (December 1968), p. 287.

64. *Duckworth v. Eagan*, 492 U.S. 195 (1989).

65. Alan Carlson and Floyd Feeney, "Handling Robbery Arrestees: Some Issues of Fact and Policy," in F. Fenney and A. Weir, eds., *The Prevention and Control of Robbery*, vol. 2. (Davis, CA: University of California Center on Administration of Justice, 1973); R. J. Medalie, L. Zeitz, and P. Alexander, "Custodial Police Interrogations in Our Nation's Capital: The Attempt to Implement Miranda," *Michigan Law Review* 66 (May 1968), pp. 1347–1422; David W. Neubauer, *Criminal Justice in Middle America* (Morristown, NJ: General Learning Press, 1974).

66. Paul G. Cassell, "Miranda's Social Costs: An Empirical Reassessment," *Northwestern Law Journal* 387 (1996).

six
Officers of the Law

On a November night in Phila-

delphia, more than twenty separate calls were made to 911 to report a teen rumble. But the police did not arrive for forty-five minutes. When police appeared at the scene, Eddie Polec, a sixteen-year-old, lay dying on the steps of a church with his head crushed. This incident prompted outrage and concern around the nation about slow police response to emergency calls. In addition, some 911 operators were found to be both curt and hostile to callers. An audit of the emergency system in Philadelphia discovered that there were not enough officers on duty to handle the volume of 911 calls—and that at the same time the system was overloaded with abandoned vehicle reports and non-emergency calls for requests for hospital transportation.[1]

At the other end of the policing spectrum, the FBI announced in 1999 its upgrade of the National Crime Information Center, which is expected to revolutionize police work. Within a few years this new system should permit equipped police officers to see photos of missing or wanted persons on laptop computers in their patrol cars. Fingerprints will be able to be taken electronically at the scene to be compared to a national database within seconds.[2]

These examples reflect the disjunction in our images of police—from slow and incompetent to highly efficient and effective. This chapter will survey the evolution of law enforcement in the United States as a context for understanding the growing sophistication of police work. This sophistication has backfired in some ways, making the public overreliant on the police for help with a growing array of social and personal problems.

How Did Policing Evolve?

Long before police departments were formally established, less formal measures of self-protection were used by property owners who could afford them. These measures are illustrated by the **mutual pledge system** that was prevalent in Britain during the middle ages. Alfred the Great (who ruled approximately 870–900) established an organized system of community self-responsibility in which everyone in the community was responsible for everyone else. Communities were divided into ten-family groups called "tithings." Cities as we know them did not exist, so each tithing was responsible for maintaining peace within its own boundaries. "It was each citizen's duty to raise the 'hue and cry' when a crime was committed, to collect his neighbors and to pursue a criminal who fled from the district. If such a group failed to apprehend a lawbreaker, all were fined by the Crown."[3] This system of mutual responsibility and shared penalties was designed to ensure that all members of the community made a conscientious effort to control crime.

Every ten tithings, or hundred families, constituted a "hundred" and was headed by a **constable** (who was appointed by a local nobleman to be in charge of weapons and equipment). The hundreds, in turn, were grouped together to form a "shire" (about the equivalent of a county). For each shire the Crown appointed a supervisor called a **shire reeve,** from which the modern term "sheriff" is derived.

The Watch and Ward System

The Statute of Winchester, enacted in 1285, established the **watch and ward system** to aid constables in their law enforcement efforts.[4] This system also emphasized community responsibility for crime control. Men from each town were required to take turns standing watch at night. If any criminals were apprehended, they were turned over to the constable for trial the following day. In 1326 Edward II established the position of **justice of the peace.** The justice of the peace assisted the sheriff in enforcing the law. Eventually the role of the justice of the peace shifted to adjudication of cases in court, while the sheriffs retained their local peacekeeping function.

This system of law enforcement, based on the mutual pledge and supplemented by the watch and ward, was in effect for several hundred years, but

CONSTABLES AND SHERIFS

- **mutual pledge system**
  System of community self-responsibility that existed in Britain during the Middle Ages, in which residents were held responsible for the conduct of their neighbors.

- **constable**
  A citizen in charge of weapons and equipment for one hundred families in his geographic area. In England constables were appointed by a local nobleman beginning around the year 900.

- **shire reeve**
  Official appointed by the British Crown who was responsible for overseeing the constables and several hundred families in a given area (called a "shire"). The modern word *sheriff* is derived from this term.

- **watch and ward system**
  System established in England in 1285 to aid constables in their law enforcement efforts. Men from each town were required to take turns standing watch at night. Crime suspects were turned over to the constable.

- **justice of the peace**
  An office established by Edward II in 1326 to assist the sheriff in enforcing the law. Eventually the role of the justice of the peace shifted to adjudication, while the sheriffs retained their local peacekeeping function.

gradually it lost community support and declined. This happened because citizens who were required to take their turn at the watch started evading this duty by paying others to do it for them. These substitutes were usually poorly paid and ignorant, and often too old to be effective.[5] In the sixteenth century "bellmen," who watched for fires, relieved the watchmen of that duty. However, this did little to prevent crime. Watchmen were generally incompetent, sometimes drank on the job, and eventually came to be ridiculed. Consider the situation as it existed in London at that time:

> *During the 16th and 17th centuries, there was no question in the minds of Londoners that they lived in a dangerous place which was ill-protected by their watchmen. . . . The watchmen generally were considered to be incompetent and cowardly. By the mid-17th century they had acquired the derisive name of "Charlies." It was a common sport of rich young men of the time to taunt and terrorize them, to wreck the watchhouses, and occasionally to murder the watchmen. The large rattles they carried to signal for help were little comfort since they knew their colleagues were not dependable; the watchmen spent a good deal of time discreetly concealed from the public.*[6]

Jonathan Rubinstein describes the citizens' reactions to these circumstances, noting that there was no public outcry to change the watch and ward system. There were no lights in the city, so home owners were required to place a candle on the street in front of their homes at night. This rule was not enforced, however, and as a result the streets were dark and considered dangerous. Those who could afford to do so hired guards and armed themselves. Women never went out on the street unaccompanied. Those who could not afford these self-protective measures were often victimized. Given this situation, in which the rich could buy protection for themselves and the poor were being victimized in unsafe streets, a catalyst was needed—some unanticipated influence or event that would galvanize the poor to act. That catalyst was gin.

PUBLIC SAFETY
VERSUS GIN

The catalyst that provoked a more organized effort toward the establishment of public policing was the invention of gin by a Dutch chemist during the seventeenth century. The British government encouraged the manufacture of gin as a way to deal with grain surpluses while also making a profit. Gin was much cheaper than brandy and much more potent than beer, wine, or ale. Sales of gin skyrocketed; by 1725 more than 7,000 gin shops operated in London, and gin was sold as a sideline by many other shopkeepers. Between 1727 and 1743 consumption more than doubled. According to one historian, London became "awash in an orgy of drinking which has probably not been matched in history."[7] For a penny a person could drink all day, and public drunkenness became commonplace. Drunken mobs often roamed through the city. The streets of London became filled with people who engaged in unpredictable and occasionally violent behavior.

In response, the government "got tough" on offenders. Street lighting was improved; more watchmen were hired; and the penalties for many crimes were dramatically increased. Individual citizens also began arming themselves and stayed off the streets at night. In addition, the rich began to move away from areas where poor people lived.

The Gin Act, passed in 1736, attempted to limit the availability of gin by establishing extremely high licensing fees for all gin sellers and manufacturers and providing rewards for information leading to the conviction of unlicensed distillers or retailers. These measures had little positive effect. Constables overlooked violations; informers were beaten or murdered; and although the act was in force for seven years and resulted in 10,000 prosecutions, only three licenses were sold. There was no reduction in the consumption of gin.[8] Consumption fell only when taxes were increased, resulting in higher prices.

The problems associated with gin were alleviated, but fear of crime did not decline correspondingly. Members of Parliament continued to be accompanied by bodyguards, and bulletproof coaches were advertised to thwart the highwaymen (robbers) who victimized travelers on the roads to the city. The Lord Mayor of London was robbed at gunpoint, and the Duke of York and the Prince of Wales were mugged as they walked in the city during the day. During the same period the Great Seal of England was stolen from the house of the Lord Chancellor and melted down for the silver. There was a growing demand for protection from crime, and private police organizations flourished.[9]

In 1748, in response to growing concern, Henry Fielding proposed that the watch and ward system be centralized. He organized a private agency that patrolled the streets rather than staying at the watch boxes. He also organized a mounted patrol, the Bow Street Runners, to guard highways. The Runners quickly established a reputation for their ability to catch criminals.[10] Although this system declined after Fielding's death, he is credited with being the first person to propose the idea of a mobile police force.

Despite the success of the Bow Street Runners, fear of crime continued to increase. The Gordon Riots of 1780 produced serious mob violence in London, but the notion of a centralized police agency still was not widely accepted. There was fear, particularly among the wealthy (who controlled the constables), that a centralized police agency would become too strong and abuse its power.

← GIN

THE BOW STREET RUNNERS

The New Police Bobbies

In response to the urging of legal reformer and philosopher Jeremy Bentham and the lobbying of English statesman Sir Robert Peel, the Metropolitan Police of London was established in 1829. The force, also referred to as the New Police or the **preventive police,** was seen as "a civilizing instrument whose effort and example would make possible more harmonious relations among city people."[11] The popular English name for police officers, "bobbies," comes from the name of the founder of the Metropolitan Police, Robert Peel.

■preventive police
The first organized police department in London, established in 1829. The popular English name for police officers, "bobbies," comes from Sir Robert Peel, a founder of the Metropolitan Police.

Where did models for the American system of policing come from? What historical and social factors forced cities and states to replace the watch and ward system with formal police forces? Why were these "Keystone Cops" (Hollywood's tag for uniformed metropolitan police) objects of ridicule? What cultural factors delayed the modernization of law enforcement in the United States? What events then encouraged the professionalization of policing?

BRITAIN'S NEW POLICE

The basis of this new police force was very different from that of the watch and ward system. The city was to be patrolled by officers who were assigned specific territories (or beats). The watch and ward system had made it clear that strict supervision was required to ensure that officers would actually perform their duties and not sleep, drink, or loaf on the job. Robert Peel sought to provide inspiration by employing military principles in organizing what had traditionally been a civilian force. Thus, the Metropolitan Police were distinguished by their patrolling of specific areas and by their paramilitary organization, which was designed to maintain discipline.

The New Police were not without problems, however. Poorly supervised patrol officers often drank or slept on the job, and there was a general lack of discipline. The first police commissioner was Colonel Charles Rowan, a former military officer. In order to maintain discipline, he instituted severe penalties for even minor infractions. For most violations the officer was dismissed from the force. As a result, during the early years of the Metropolitan Police more than a third of the force was discharged each year.[12]

Metropolitan Police in American Cities

Despite the problems experienced in England, the American colonies repeated the British experience. As early as 1636 Boston had night watchmen to protect warehouses and homes. This approach was imitated in other eastern cities. As in England, the night watch was supervised by constables at the local level and by sheriffs at the county level.

The night watchmen were poorly paid, poorly supervised, and known for drinking and falling asleep on the job. Perhaps the most widespread criticism, however, was the same one that plagued the British watch and ward system: The watchmen did nothing to prevent crime.[13]

After the American Revolution there were no further efforts to establish a full-time police force. Because the British had used their army to enforce their laws in the colonies, most Americans saw a police force as the equivalent of a standing domestic army. This was an important issue at the Constitutional Convention.[14] It was believed that a police force would lead to the same kinds of oppression and abuse that the colonists had come to America to escape.

It was not until 1838 that Boston created a daytime police force to supplement the night watch. This occurred only after major riots in 1834, 1835, and 1837.[15] The day and night police forces were separate agencies, however, and there was intense rivalry between the two Boston forces. New York was the first city to create a unified day and night police force (and to abolish the night watch). The New York City Police Department, established in 1845, was unique in its payment of (low) salaries, its use of uniforms to distinguish police officers from other citizens, and its paramilitary organization. New York's example was soon followed by other cities, including Chicago (1851), New Orleans (1852), Cincinnati (1852), Philadelphia (1855), Newark (1857), and Baltimore (1857). By 1900 nearly every U.S. city of any size had established a full-time police force.

Most of the new police forces assigned officers to specific territories. At first the officers resisted wearing uniforms, because they felt demeaned by them. There were other, more serious problems as well:

UNIFORMED POLICE IN THE UNITED STATES

> These first formal police forces in American cities were faced with many of the problems that police continue to confront today. Police officers became objects of disrespect. The need for larger staffs required the police to compromise personnel standards in order to fill the ranks. And police salaries were among the lowest in local government service, a factor which precluded attracting sufficient numbers of high standard candidates. It is small wonder that the police were not respected, were not notably successful, and were not noted for their visibility and progressiveness.[16]

These problems of low pay, disrespect, and ineffectiveness existed for a number of reasons. First, the military model of organization was not well suited to police work. Unlike the soldier, the police officer is primarily a solitary worker, and military discipline is most effective for people who work together in a group. Second, police officers have the contradictory tasks of both protecting and arresting their employers—the public. Citizens expect the police to protect them, but they become irate when they are stopped, questioned, or arrested. Third, police forces were often used as a source of political patronage and control, and police work therefore became associated with corrupt politics.[17]

Efforts to improve police efficiency and discipline were impeded by problems of communication. During much of the 1800s there were no police telephones or call boxes, and those that existed could be sabotaged by officers who did not wish to be bothered by their superiors.[18] In fact, it was not until 1929 that the first two-way radio was installed in a patrol car.

Crime Commissions and the Professionalization of Policing

The early decades of the twentieth century saw the beginnings of a movement toward police professionalism. The Progressive Era was marked by renewed concern about crime, because the passage of the Eighteenth Amendment (Prohibition) led to extensive illegal manufacturing and distribution of alcoholic beverages. This period was characterized by criticism of corruption and inefficiency in social institutions, and by recommendations for change that centered on better management and training. Government concern was manifested as early as 1919, which saw the formation of the Chicago Crime Commission; similar commissions were created to investigate crime in twenty-four states. In addition, two national **crime commissions** were established: the National Crime Commission in 1925 and the Wickersham Commission in 1931. These commissions focused on improved operation of the criminal justice system as the best way to reduce crime. They recommended a number of reforms in police operations.

The dominant concern of the crime commissions was to find ways to bring criminals to justice more swiftly and certainly. The first agency in the criminal justice system responsible for this task was the police. Professionalization of the police came to be defined in terms of those changes in police organization, administration, and technology that would improve the efficiency of the police in the deterrence and apprehension of criminals. Police officials measured progress toward police professionalism in terms of expansion of police services, development of scientific methods of criminal investigation and identification, police training, communications, transportation, police records, police selection, executive tenure, and police organizational growth.[19]

In short, the themes of **progressivism** in policing were efficiency, professionalism, and improved technology.

During this period a dedicated effort was made to transform police work from an undesirable job into an attractive career. A leader in the movement to improve police professionalism was August Vollmer, chief of police in Berkeley, California, from 1905 to 1932. Vollmer established the first crime detection laboratory in the United States, and John Larson invented the polygraph (lie detector) while working for him. This period also saw the inauguration of investigative techniques such as fingerprint identification, firearms identification, toxicology, document examination, and other methods that had not been not used in policing in the United States before 1900.[20]

Police **professionalization** also included improved selection and training procedures. In 1900 the only criteria used in the selection of police officers were physical fitness and political influence. After World War I psychological and intelligence tests began to be employed; these "revealed a shockingly low level of intelligence and psychological fitness among police personnel."[21]

■crime commissions
Commissions that focus on improved operation of the criminal justice system as the best way to reduce crime. Early twentieth-century crime commissions included the Chicago Crime Commission (1919), the National Crime Commission (1925), and the Wickersham Commission (1931).

POLICING IN THE PROGRESSIVE ERA

■progressivism
Early twentieth-century era in policing that focused on efficiency, professionalism, and improved technology.

■professionalization
Changes in police organization, administration, and technology aimed at improving the efficiency of the police in the deterrence and apprehension of criminals.

A 1934 survey estimated that only 20,000 of the 134,000 police officers in the country had participated in any kind of training program. As Vollmer pointed out, however, twenty-five years earlier training programs for police had not existed at all.[22] The problem continues today, as classroom training and written testing of police recruits are chronically under fire. These training and assessment methods turn out not to be good predictors of successful performance on the job. As a result, there is now a move toward "authentic assessment," which consists of rating police candidates' ability to carry out actual job-related tasks.[23] This movement reflects a continuing emphasis on the progressive idea of improved professionalism and training.

Innovations in equipment also contributed to improved police work during the twentieth century. In 1930 there were fewer than 1,000 patrol cars in the entire country. By 1966 there were more than 200,000 radio-equipped cars. The advent of the patrol car, the two-way radio, and the telephone had dramatic effects on policing in the United States.[24] These technological advances enabled police to patrol much larger geographic areas, respond to calls more quickly, and generally increase their accessibility to the public.

The Law Enforcement Assistance Administration

The growing reliance on technology, coupled with the increasing demand for police services, began to peak during the 1960s, when concern about crime was also at an all-time high.[25] This concern manifested itself in a series of government investigations. Between 1967 and 1973 there were no fewer than seven national crime commissions. Among their recommendations were improvements in police professionalism, training, and technology. In 1968 the **Law Enforcement Assistance Administration (LEAA)** was set up within the U.S. Department of Justice to allocate money to improve the efficiency and effectiveness of the criminal justice system. Between 1968 and 1977 the LEAA spent more than $6 billion on crime control programs and college education for police officers. Much of the money was spent on weaponry, riot control equipment, helicopters, SWAT (Special Weapons and Tactics) equipment, and other equipment for police. This occurred despite the fact that use of such equipment had resulted in violent outcomes and widespread criticism of the police during the civil rights and antiwar protests of the late 1960s and early 1970s.[26] A 1977 article from the *New York Times* illustrates the problem:

> *The Attorney General has publicly criticized such LEAA-financed activities as the $250,000 development of a shoe to accommodate a pistol that could be shot through the toe. And [the attorney general] was reportedly upset when he learned that the agency, which is financing about 55,000 programs, was planning to spend $2.5 million for a brochure telling local police departments how to apply for agency funds.*[27]

The expenditure of money on questionable items, coupled with poor or nonexistent evaluations to assess the effectiveness of the programs funded, led to growing criticism of the LEAA. By the late 1970s there was a move to abolish the LEAA and discontinue federal aid to local law enforcement.

THE POLICE AND URBAN RIOTS

■**Law Enforcement Assistance Administration (LEAA)**
Agency established in 1968 within the U.S. Department of Justice to allocate money to improve the efficiency and effectiveness of the criminal justice system. Between 1968 and 1977 the LEAA spent more than $6 billion on crime control programs and college education for police officers.

How did the Law Enforcement Assistance Administration (LEAA) influence the development of policing in the United States? How could you explain the historical context of this development from a sociological perspective? Why was the LEAA later abolished, and with what consequences for American law enforcement? To what extent or in what ways do you think the federal government should be involved in local law enforcement today?

The LEAA was finally abolished in the early 1980s. Law enforcement now is almost entirely the responsibility of local governments, although the federal government plays a role in the allocation of funds. For example, federal highway and transportation funds are increasingly allocated to states on the basis of their enforcement of laws involving drunk driving, acceptable blood-alcohol levels, and speed limits in keeping with standards imposed by the federal government. In this way the federal government manages to control some aspects of local law enforcement.

What Is the Organization of Law Enforcement?

As a result of the fear of a strong central government that existed at the time of the nation's founding, the U.S. Constitution has no provision for a national police force with broad enforcement powers. Most other countries have large, centralized national police forces. The United States, in contrast, has many different agencies at each level of government that specialize in the enforcement of certain types of laws. The result is a patchwork of law enforcement agencies with differing types of jurisdictions in terms of the types of laws they enforce and the level of government they work for.

On the local and state levels, most police are generalists, responsible for the enforcement of most criminal laws. On the federal level there is much more specialization in the types of crimes different agencies handle. These distinctions are illustrated in Table 6.1.

TABLE 6.1

Career Opportunities in Law Enforcement

lawenforcementjob.com http://www.lawenforcementjob.com	Free employment information on over 3,500 municipal police, state police and patrol, sheriff, federal, international, corrections, and university and college departments.
Federal Bureau of Investigation (FBI) http://www.fbi.gov/employment.htm	Largest federal law enforcement agency, responsible for enforcing all federal laws not assigned to other agencies. *Qualifications:* Bachelor's degree; skills in police work, teaching, foreign languages, engineering, accounting, computer sciences, chemistry, or law.
Drug Enforcement Administration (DEA) http://www.usdoj.gov/dea/employ/ employ.htm	Enforces all federal narcotics laws. *Qualifications:* Bachelor's degree; skills in law, accounting, piloting aircraft, and/or foreign languages.
U.S. Marshals Service http://www.usdoj.gov/marshals/careers/ career.html	Provides security in U.S. courtrooms, transports federal prisoners, operates the federal witness protection program. *Qualifications:* Bachelor's degree and work experience.
U.S. Customs Service http://www.customs.ustreas.gov/careers/ career.htm	Involved with narcotics interdiction and illegal currency violations at the nation's borders; investigates fraud and imports and exports. *Qualifications:* Bachelor's degree and prior law enforcement experience.
Immigration and Naturalization Service (INS) http://www.ins.usdoj.gov/graphics/workfor/ index.htm	Investigates illegal immigration and handles deportations from the U.S. *Qualifications:* Bachelor's degree and prior experience.
Border patrol http://www.ins.usdoj.gov/graphics/lawenfor/ bpatrol/bpcareer/index.htm	Patrols areas between points of entry into the U.S. from Mexico to guard against illegal immigration. *Qualifications:* Bachelor's degree or work experience and competency in Spanish.
State police http://www.statetrooper.net/	In each state, enforces laws on state roads and investigates crimes that cross county lines or cannot be handled by local police. *Qualifications:* Two years of college or more.
Local police Use a search engine for "[*city*] Police Department"	In each city and town, county and municipal police enforce laws. *Qualifications:* Passage of competitive entrance examinations; college preferred.
Regulatory Enforcement http://www.epa.gov/ http://www.atf.treas.gov/jobs/jobs.htm http://www.mrps.doi.gov/ http://www.notes.dol.gov/vacancy.nsf	Specialized law enforcement for government regulatory agencies, such as environmental protection; alcohol, tobacco, and firearms; gambling; postal system; forests and parks; wildlife protection; occupational health and safety. *Qualifications:* Bachelor's degree.
Private Security http://www.securitymagazine.com/	Protects private property for banks, airports, college campuses, insurance companies, hospitals, and corporations; investigates crimes by employees and customers. *Qualifications:* Law enforcement background.

Local Police

The vast majority of police agencies exist at the local level of government. Of the nearly 19,000 police agencies in the United States, more than 17,000 are operated by municipal and other local governments.[28] Most of these are the police departments of municipalities, but local law enforcement also includes county sheriffs and special police agencies such as park, airport, transit, and university police. Local police departments have nearly 522,000 full-time employees, about 80 percent of whom are police officers. The remaining 20 percent are civilian employees of police departments who perform specific tasks, such as communications specialists, evidence technicians, crime analysts, and people involved in victim assistance.[29]

■**local police**
Police departments of municipalities; local law enforcement also includes county sheriffs and special police agencies such as park, airport, transit, and university police.

Local police primarily enforce applicable state laws, but they also enforce local ordinances and traffic laws and investigate accidents and suspected crimes. Sheriffs provide police protection and investigate crimes in jurisdictions within their county that lack their own police forces; they also serve court papers, maintain order in courtrooms, and operate county jail facilities.[30]

The local nature of American policing is further illustrated by the fact that nearly two-thirds of local police and sheriffs' departments employ fewer than ten full-time officers. Of this number, nearly 2,000 departments have only one full-time officer or only part-time officers.[31] The number of officers is related to the size of the population served. In towns with populations of 2,500 or less, the typical police department has 3 sworn full-time officers. As towns develop into cities, their police departments also grow: Towns with populations of 2,500 to 10,000 have police departments with an average of 10 full-time sworn officers, and the numbers are higher in cities with populations of 100,000 to 250,000, which average 266 full-time sworn officers.[32]

In large metropolitan areas, police agencies sometimes perform law enforcement tasks for both the city and surrounding jurisdictions. The Boston Police Department, for example, is assisted by the Metropolitan District Commission, which patrols public parks, parkways, and related areas. In New York City, the police department has taken over policing public housing projects and subway law enforcement tasks by merging smaller agencies into the NYPD. Other large metropolitan areas have similar arrangements, in which local police tasks have been consolidated into larger police efforts to serve the overlapping needs of surrounding communities with a growing list of law enforcement demands and responsibilities.

LOCAL PARAMILITARY UNITS

An interesting trend is the growth of police paramilitary units at the local level. These units function as military special-operations teams to respond to hostage situations, bomb threats, and similar situations that require a showing of force. Paramilitary units are typically equipped with submachine guns, semiautomatic shotguns, sniper rifles, flash-bang grenades, night vision equipment, and battering rams. A national survey of small cities with 25,000 to 50,000 residents found that 65 percent of departments had a SWAT team, often outfitted with the latest armor and weaponry.[33] Between 1985 and 1995 the number of paramilitary units within small city police departments increased by 157 percent. These units averaged only 106 hours of formal training per officer per year, compared to an average of 225 hours of formal training in medium-sized to large police

COMMUNITY POLICING

departments.[34] The need for paramilitary units in smaller jurisdictions is infrequent, and the low level of training poses a serious hazard, given the destructive potential of high-powered weaponry.

Recently there has been a trend back toward **community policing.** The central tenet of community policing is a service-oriented style of law enforcement, as opposed to the traditional focus on serious street crimes. Table 6.2 summarizes the major differences between community

■**community policing**
A service-oriented style of law enforcement that focuses on disorder in the community, crime prevention, and fear reduction, as opposed to the traditional focus on prosecution of serious street crimes.

TABLE 6.2

Traditional versus Community-Based Policing

	TRADITIONAL CRIMINAL JUSTICE SYSTEM	COMMUNITY-BASED PREVENTION
The crime problem	Index crime: The more serious the crime, as determined by traditional measures, the more energy criminal justice agencies should expend dealing with it.	Disorder, fear, serious crime. Seriousness determined by context, neighborhood priorities, and the extent to which problems destabilize neighborhoods and communities.
Priorities in crime control	Apprehend and process offenders.	Prevent and control crime, restore and maintain order, reduce citizen fear.
Role of citizens	Aid police: Because crime control is best left to criminal justice professionals, citizens "aid" professionals in controlling serious crime by calling police, being good witnesses, and testifying against wrongdoers; all else is vigilantism.	Citizens are key: Control of disorder, fear, and crime has its origins in the "small change" of neighborhood life; citizens set standards for the neighborhood and maintain order; police and other criminal justice agencies support and aid citizens, especially in emergencies.
Police, prosecutors, courts, and corrections: structure	Centralized organization.	Decentralized agencies allow for flexible responses to local problems and needs.
Methods	Process individual cases when crimes occur.	Problem-solving approach: Identify and solve larger problems within which individual cases are embedded.
Use of discretion	Discouraged, unrecognized. Assumption that little guidance is needed for law enforcement processing; clear and precise rules and regulations developed as required; attempt to limit/eradicate discretion with mandatory arrest and prosecution policies, determinate sentences.	Fundamental and important to crime control efforts. Controls developed through statements of legislative intent; carefully crafted laws that address the complexity of issues; formulation of guidelines, procedures, rules, and regulations with input from citizens and line police officers.
Order vs. liberty interests	Individual liberty interest predominate: Most nonviolent deviance should be tolerated in the name of individual liberty interests.	Balanced: Liberty interests not absolute, but balanced against need to maintain basic levels of order for neighborhoods and communities to function.
Public–private relationship	Police neutral and removed: Should intrude into community life as little as possible.	Police act on behalf of community; are intimately involved in local life but also act justly, equitably, in accord with established legal principles.

SOURCE: George M. Kelling and Catherine M. Coles, *Fixing Broken Windows: Restoring Order and Reducing Crime in Our Communities* (New York: Touchstone, 1997).

policing and traditional law enforcement. As the table shows, community-based policing differs from the traditional approach in eight distinct ways.[35]

Community policing focuses more broadly on disorder in the community, crime prevention and fear reduction, and community support in organized prevention and enforcement efforts. Traditional policing, in contrast, focuses exclusively on serious crime and the apprehension of offenders; citizens are involved only to the extent that they can help police carry out their law enforcement role. Traditional policing responds to crimes after they occur, whereas community policing attempts to solve underlying problems that ultimately result in crimes. Perhaps most important is the difference in the attitudes of police officers: Officers are detached in the traditional model, but in the community policing model they act in conjunction with citizens in an involved way.

Despite this trend, national surveys have found that police departments continue to embrace the crime control model of enforcement. Most states continue to view law enforcement as more important than community service.[36] A survey of police departments employing one hundred or more officers found that an announced change to a community policing philosophy did not change the departments' organizational structure in any significant way.[37] In addition, it is not clear whether the role of the media will help or hinder community policing, because the media seek up-to-the-minute news and pay less attention to community trends than to immediate crises.[38]

The **Weed and Seed** program is an example of a popular community policing initiative of the 1990s. It is a federal program that provides funds to cities to help prevent and control crime and to improve the quality of life of high-crime neighborhoods.[39] It began in only 3 cities in 1991 and grew to 200 sites nationwide by 1999. Weed and Seed programs combine enforcement with community services. The "Weed" part of the program concentrates law enforcement by coordinating the efforts of police and prosecutors to identify, arrest, and prosecute violent offenders and drug traffickers in targeted areas. The "Seed" portion coordinates neighborhood revitalization efforts designed to prevent future crime.

Figure 6.1 shows the distribution of Weed and Seed programs around the United States. Typical efforts include weekend and after-school activities for youth, adult literacy classes, and parental counseling. Police officers and prosecutors in Weed and Seed cities attempt to gain community and business support for their efforts by involving them in the problem-solving effort. An evaluation of the impact of the Weed and Seed program in eight cities found varied results so far. However, the most effective efforts "were those that relied on bottom-up, participatory decision-making approaches, especially when combined with efforts to build capacity and partnership among local organizations."[40] It appears that following the principles of community policing have produced positive results for the Weed and Seed program.

WEED AND SEED PROGRAMS

■ **Weed and Seed**
Federal program that provides funds to help cities combine enforcement with community services in an effort to reduce crime in targeted neighborhoods.

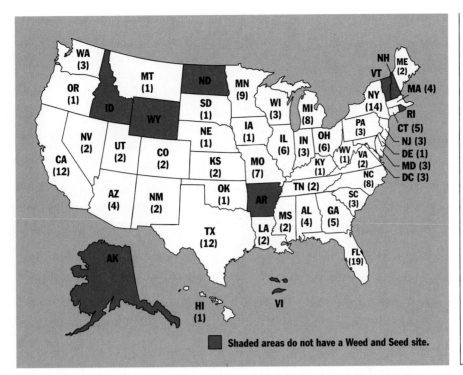

FIGURE 6.1

Location and Numbers of Weed and Seed Program Sites in the United States

SOURCE: U.S. Comptroller General, *More Can Be Done to Improve the Weed and Seed Program Management* (Washington, DC: U.S. General Accounting Office, 1999).

State Police

Every state except Hawaii has a state police force. These agencies were created in response to the need for law enforcement on roads that pass between municipalities. **State police** are different from local and federal police agencies in that they enforce state laws exclusively. Most states also have specialized law enforcement agencies similar to those at the federal level, such as state departments of environmental protection, alcohol control, and other specialized units.

In all, state police departments have approximately 84,000 full-time employees, of whom about 70 percent are sworn officers. These departments vary widely in size. The largest state police department is the California Highway Patrol, with 6,200 sworn officers; the smallest is the North Dakota Highway Patrol, with 120 full-time officers.[41]

All state police departments are responsible for traffic law enforcement and accident investigation. Nearly all are engaged primarily in highway patrol activities. Only about half have the authority to conduct investigative work. The focus on patrol work is evidenced by the fact that in the nation as a whole there are ninety-eight police cars (marked and unmarked) for every hundred sworn state police officers.[42]

Approximately 70 percent of all state police are uniformed officers whose primary duty is patrolling roads and responding to calls for service. Fifteen percent of state police are investigators, who attempt to solve crimes once they are reported. Other state police personnel have administrative or training

■ **state police**
Agencies that enforce state laws exclusively. Primarily engaged in highway patrol activities; about half of state police agencies also have the authority to conduct investigative work.

HIGHWAY PATROL

How would you describe the differences between policing at the local level and policing at the state level? What is "community policing"? For instance, how might a "Weed and Seed" program in this community help prevent auto theft? What are some other trends in the organization of law enforcement in the U.S.? What do you think are the advantages and disadvantages of having a number of separate jurisdictions in which police work is conducted? What are some areas of jurisdictional competition and cooperation?

tasks. Fifteen states have more than 1,000 state police officers; the largest is the California Highway patrol, with 9,132 employees all told. The smallest state police agency is the North Dakota Highway patrol, with a total of 186 employees.[43]

Federal Law Enforcement Agencies

There are nearly 70,000 federal law enforcement officers in the United States, and they are employed by seventeen different agencies. These officers are authorized to carry firearms and make arrests in investigating violations of federal law. Unlike state police agencies, few federal agencies engage in patrol work; most perform exclusively investigative functions.

Federal law enforcement agencies can enforce only laws enacted by Congress. Congress has the power to coin money, for example, and hence has delegated law enforcement authority to the U.S. Treasury Department. The Treasury Department is responsible for the printing of currency and therefore is also responsible for enforcing federal laws against counterfeiting and forgery. This function is performed by the Secret Service (which has the ancillary task of protecting the president). In addition, the Treasury Department is responsible for collecting federal income taxes; preventing contraband from entering the United States; and regulating the sale and distribution of alcohol, tobacco, and firearms. As a result, the Treasury Department houses the enforcement division of the Internal Revenue Service; the Customs Service; and the Bureau of Alcohol, Tobacco, and Firearms.

Four federal agencies employ 58 percent of all federal law enforcement officers. The largest agency is the Immigration and Naturalization Service (INS), with 12,400 agents and officers who protect the nation's borders against illegal immigration. Within the INS is the Border Patrol (4,200 offi-

■**federal law enforcement**
Seventeen different agencies that investigate violations of federal law; most perform exclusively investigative functions.

FEDERAL AGENCIES

cers), which monitors 145 border stations around the country.[44] The U.S. Customs Service has nearly 10,000 agents and is responsible for investigating contraband entering or leaving the United States. The Federal Bureau of Investigation (10,400 agents) is responsible for enforcing more than 250 federal laws that are not specifically designated to other federal agencies. The FBI is thus a catchall agency and has the widest jurisdiction of any federal law enforcement agency. Finally, the Federal Bureau of Prisons employs more than 11,000 corrections officers, who maintain security at all U.S. correctional facilities for convicted offenders and for defendants awaiting trial.

The remaining federal law enforcement agencies employ fewer than 4,000 officers each; the smallest is the U.S. Fish and Wildlife Service, which employs only 620 agents. Table 6.3 presents a summary of all federal law enforcement agencies employing more than 500 full-time officers with authority to carry firearms and make arrests.

TABLE 6.3

Federal Law Enforcement Agencies

AGENCY	NUMBER OF OFFICERS	PRIMARY RESPONSIBILITY
U.S. Customs Service	9,700	Investigates contraband entering or leaving country.
Federal Bureau of Investigation	10,400	Enforces 250 federal laws not specifically designated to other agencies.
Federal Bureau of Prisons	11,300	Corrections officers in federal jails and prisons.
Immigration and Naturalization Service	12,400	Border patrol and investigation of illegal aliens at ports of entry.
Administrative Office of U.S. Courts	2,800	Federal probation and parole officers.
Internal Revenue Service	3,800	Investigates tax fraud.
U.S. Postal Inspection Service	3,600	Investigates crimes committed using the mails.
Drug Enforcement Administration	2,900	Investigates federal narcotics crimes.
U.S. Secret Service	3,200	Investigates counterfeiting and federal computer fraud; provides security for federal officials.
National Park Service	2,100	Police services for the U.S. park system.
U.S. Marshals Service	2,700	Provides security in federal courtrooms; finds fugitives; transports prisoners; manages witness security program and federal forfeitures.
Bureau of Alcohol, Tobacco, and Firearms	1,900	Investigates illegal firearm, explosive use; enforces federal alcohol, tobacco regulations.
U.S. Capitol Police	1,000	Police services for U.S. Capitol.
Tennessee Valley Authority	740	Police services for TVA facilities.
U.S. Forest Service	619	Protects national forest land, animals, natural resources, and visitors.
General Services Administration— Federal Protective Services	643	Security for federal buildings and property.
U.S. Fish and Wildlife Service	869	Enforces federal laws relating to hunting and fishing.

SOURCE: Adapted from Brian A. Reaves, *Federal Law Enforcement Officers* (Washington, DC: Bureau of Justice Statistics, 1994), and Brian A. Reaves, *Federal Law Enforcement Officers* (Washington, DC: Bureau of Justice Statistics, 1997).

Because the historical evolution of policing in America began at the local level, and because most federal agencies do not engage in patrol work, the organization of police in the United States is skewed heavily toward local police. For example, the New York Police Department, with more than 28,000 officers, is nearly three times the size of the FBI. Likewise, the Chicago Police Department (12,000 officers), the Los Angeles Police Department (7,700), the Philadelphia Police Department (6,000), the Houston Police Department (5,000), and other large city police departments are larger than most federal law enforcement agencies.

INTERPOL AND EUROPOL

■ **transnational law enforcement**
International agreements and law enforcement efforts that attempt to serve the interests of all nations in the face of developments such as the growth of international travel, the transnational nature of the Internet, and the threat of international organized crime and terrorism.

■ **Interpol**
The International Criminal Police Organization, which assists 177 member nations' law enforcement agencies by providing information about crimes or criminals of a transnational nature.

Transnational Law Enforcement

Transnational law enforcement is not centrally organized, because individual nations around the world have sovereignty and resent other nations that attempt to enforce their laws outside their own borders. Nevertheless, the growth of international travel, the transnational nature of the Internet, and the threat of international organized crime and terrorism have combined to bring about international agreements and law enforcement efforts that attempt to serve the interests of all nations.

Interpol, the International Criminal Police Organization, was begun in 1923 and took its current name in 1956. Interpol assists the law enforcement agencies of its 177 member nations by providing information about crimes or criminals of a transnational nature.[45] It provides information in four languages: Arabic, English, French, and Spanish. The U.S. National Central Bureau (USNCB) is the point of contact between Interpol and police agencies in the United States. The USNCB is located within the U.S. Department of Justice and is jointly managed with the U.S. Treasury Department. All requests from federal, state, or local police are transmitted to Interpol through the USNCB.[46]

The importance of Interpol will increase as internal and external security concerns merge. As Malcolm Anderson has observed, "State security is now threatened by political violence which falls short of conventional military operations but which arises from complex criminal conspiracies—areas formerly considered squarely in the domain of policing."[47] Organized crime, drug trafficking, corruption, and other traditional concerns of law enforcement are becoming national security concerns in many nations. The demise of the Soviet Union has freed intelligence agencies and the military to focus more on transnational crime than on military threats. Evidence that reliance on Interpol is increasing can be seen in the fact that the USNCB staff grew from six to eighty-one between 1979 and 1995. This rise reflects an increase in transnational criminal activity as well as greater attention to international criminal matters on the part of U.S. agencies.[48]

Another effort to combat transnational crimes is Europol, which was established in 1991 to share information about drug trafficking among member countries of the European Union. Europol emerged out of growing concern over drug trafficking and money laundering, as well as a growing awareness of the need for better coordination among European police agencies and customs officials. The removal of many of the barriers to free trade and economic growth in Europe since the late 1980s has made it easier to communicate and travel among the European nations. This situation also makes it easier for criminals to smuggle stolen property and drugs across borders. Europol was seen as a mechanism for organizing international law enforcement activities.[49]

The need for shared information is paralleled by the need for trained law enforcement personnel. Efforts are being made to professionalize law enforcement agencies around the world. The Federal Bureau of Investigation now trains law enforcement officials from other nations in a program sponsored by the U.S. State Department. These officials come to the United States to be trained in modern law enforcement and prosecution techniques. In addition, the FBI opened an international police training academy in Budapest 1995 and an office in Moscow in 1994. As FBI Director Louis Freeh observed, there is a need for "a centrally located school where we can develop a network of police partners in countries where we do not now have those relationships."[50]

There are now more than 1,600 American law enforcement personnel working overseas. Nearly a third of these are agents with the Drug Enforcement Administration, which has agents in thirty nations. The U.S. Immigration and Naturalization Service, Customs Service, and Coast Guard each have law enforcement personnel in more than twenty countries. The FBI; Internal Revenue Service; Secret Service; and Bureau of Alcohol, Tobacco, and Firearms also have agents assigned overseas.[51] This high level of international law enforcement activity points to the growth in international crime and the need for coordination of law enforcement activities.

In the 1990s the United Nations held several conferences on themes of concern to international law enforcement, such as international money laundering and transnational organized crime. The purpose of the meetings was to examine existing international standards, legislation, and models for cooperation in dealing with international organized crime. The conferences were attended by representatives from 142 countries, reflecting the high level of interest and concern about these problems.[52] Such meetings permit open discussion of the problems posed by international criminal behavior, along with exploration of possible solutions.[53] This is extremely important when so many U.S. law enforcement agencies are working in other countries. Nations can feel threatened when there is not consensus about the seriousness of a problem or about the appropriateness of the measures taken. It is through such efforts that international law enforcement trust, cooperation, and professionalism are improving. International cooperation also is a mechanism for placing pressure on nations that are not diligent in their efforts to thwart transnational crime.

GLOBALIZATION OF LAW ENFORCEMENT

What are some mechanisms for cooperation between local, state, federal, and transnational law enforcement agencies? Under what circumstances might local and state police be involved in police operations at the federal or transnational levels? What agencies are involved in transnational and overseas police work? What crimes in the global community are their greatest concerns? What do you predict will be the future of international law enforcement?

Who Are the Police?

People in law enforcement in the United States are a diverse group totaling more than 1 million sworn officers and civilians. In 1987 the Bureau of Justice Statistics began the Law Enforcement Management and Administrative Statistics (LEMAS) program, which is a nationwide survey of state and local police agencies employing one hundred or more officers that is conducted every three years. According to the most recent survey, municipal police departments employed an average of 23 officers per 10,000 city residents, but varied from 2 to more than 100 officers per 10,000 residents.[54] This shows that the relative size of police departments varies considerably.

In addition, a growing proportion of these officers are women. Until recent decades, women and those of certain heights, weights, and backgrounds were excluded from police work. The 1972 amendments to Title VII of the Civil Rights Act of 1964 made its provisions applicable to *both* public (e.g., police) and private sector employers. The act prohibits discrimination on the basis of gender, and it also mandates that gender must be shown to be a "bona fide occupational qualification" if females are not hired or promoted on the same basis as men. Therefore, an employer must prove that there is a significant difference in the performance of men versus women if they are not to be hired or assigned in the same manner.

Although the idea of females in police work is more than a century old, it has only been during the last forty years that women have been hired and assigned in the same manner as men. The guidelines of the Equal Employment Opportunity Commission (EEOC) also have helped to eliminate discrimination on the basis of gender. Under these guidelines both public and private employers "must demonstrate that any requirement for employment or promotion is specifically related to some objective measure of job performance."[55] Although there has been criticism of the EEOC for a sluggish enforcement record, the guidelines have helped to eliminate arbitrary police qualifications such as minimum height requirements, unless they can be shown to affect job performance.[56]

The result of these trends is that police officers are increasingly diverse. Female officers now make up 9 percent of all local police, African Americans more than 11 percent, and Hispanic Americans more than 6 percent of the total. These figures vary by type of police agency. For example, women make up 5 percent of all state police, but 15 percent of all sheriff's departments.[57] Police recruits are increasingly college graduates (as discussed in the next section), and many have had internship experiences within police agencies.[58] In addition, many larger police departments now recruit prospective officers from outside their own jurisdiction, in an attempt

Media and Criminal Justice

Although women have been police officers since the early 1900s, their advent into modern policing began in the 1970s, when various court decisions offered women equal opportunities in hiring and policing responsibilities. The media's portrayal of women in policing, however, has often been outpaced by actual progress. For many, outdated TV series such as *Charlie's Angels, Get Christy Love, Policewoman,* and *Cagney and Lacey* have served as the primary— although least accurate—media portrayal of female police officers. Historically, women in law enforcement have been depicted as police*women* rather than as female police *officers,* and media portrayals have tended to suggest women's foibles as females instead of their strengths as cops.

An exception to the policewoman stereotype can be found in the 1990 movie *Blue Steel.* In this film Megan Turner decides to join the New York Police Department (NYPD) despite her father's objections. A prospective boyfriend says, "You're a good-looking woman. Why would you want to be a cop?" To which Megan replies, " I like to slam people's heads up against walls."

Her comment is only half joking, but it prompts the question: Is Megan interested in policing because she already has the attitudes or traits required of the profession, or is she acknowledging the necessity of acquiring those traits if she wants to be successful? Megan is an intelligent cop with a badge and a gun, but she knows that people see her gender before they see her uniform.

Her police training is put to the test only a day after she graduates from the academy. Megan finds herself in the middle of a convenience store holdup and fatally shoots the robber when he turns toward her with a gun. But the perpetrator's gun is lost in the melee that follows; and without eyewitnesses to corroborate her story, Megan is suspended pending an investigation. She knows the shooting was justifiable, but she also knows her superiors are not going to give a rookie female cop the benefit of the doubt—and they don't.

The movie's plot deepens as the viewer realizes that at the time of the robbery, a bystander in the store, a stockbroker named Eugene, actually pocketed the robber's gun. Eugene appears normal on the surface, but he is actually quite demented, and the sight of the strong and powerful Megan reducing the robber to a corpse sets him on a path of destruction. A string of homicides begin to plague the city, and next to each body is a shell casing inscribed with Megan Turner's name. Suspended from the force and seeking solace and support, Megan finds herself becoming romantically involved with the sympathetic Eugene.

The viewer is not surprised when Megan eventually finds herself in a showdown with the serial killer Eugene, who has orchestrated the whole scenario in an effort to get Megan to kill him. The irony is that it is not hatred or disdain for the "policewoman" that has caused him to pick her, but his admiration for her as a female police officer. Having witnessed her heroic handling of the store robbery, Eugene considers Megan the perfect officer to justifiably take his life.

The plot of *Blue Steel* may border on ridiculous, but the movie's real value is in its breaking of the "vixen with gun" stereotype of the female police officer. There is a defiant edge to the movie in its presentation of Megan's male superiors, who are such slaves to their preconceptions about women in general, and female officers in particular, that they can't even assess the facts of the case. Although Megan is set up in the movie to be a likely victim, she is never portrayed as helpless or insipid. Instead, she fights back with her intelligence, her police training, and her physical strength—just as male officers in the movies have done for decades.

Based on your readings on the status of women in policing, do you think much has changed for female officers since *Blue Steel* was made? Does the male officers' attitude toward female officers in this movie provide an accurate picture of most men's attitudes?

to obtain better-qualified recruits and have their department more closely reflect the makeup of their community.

A detailed job analysis of the tasks performed by New York City police officers, for example, identified forty-two distinct tasks that police officers carry out. As a result, all police exams, interviews, and other testing must be based on these performance criteria.[59] This requirement ensures that the officers chosen will conform to the qualifications for the job, rather than to stereotypes not based in fact. Nevertheless, job expectations change. The growth of community policing, for example, requires police to work with the noncriminal public more than ever before and makes crime prevention as important a goal as the apprehension of law violators. Police researcher Stephen Mastrofski has identified six characteristics that summarize current expectations of "good service" from police officers:[60]

- Attentiveness—vigilance and accessibility to the public and to their concerns.

- Reliability—predictable and error-free police service when called upon.

- Responsiveness—"client-centered" service that always provides a good faith effort by police.

- Competence—use of police legal authority and discretion in acceptable ways.

- Manners—interaction with the public in a respectful way.

- Fairness—enforcement of the law and treatment of suspects in an even-handed manner.

These six characteristics reflect the belief that police work requires much more than the application of the law in the community. The quality of police service is increasingly scrutinized, because the manner in which police tasks are carried out is considered as important as the tasks themselves. This situation has placed increased emphasis on the way in which police officers are selected and trained.

Training and Education

Selection processes vary somewhat among police departments, but most agencies require applicants to pass a written test, a physical agility test, a drug test, a medical exam (including visual and hearing tests), an oral interview, a psychological assessment, a polygraph test, and a background investigation. There are questions about the utility of some of these requirements. Research has shown, for example, that written tests do not always provide a valid indication of who will be a successful police officer. Police departments are looking for better ways to screen recruits;[61] some of these methods include scenario-based testing, which requires physical and verbal responses by an applicant to simulated situations.

Police training has improved dramatically over the years. The typical police agency requires more than 800 hours of classroom training for new recruits. This training includes detailed knowledge of diverse subjects, such as criminal law, traffic law, patrol function, criminal investigation, ethics, first aid, and related subjects. In addition, police agencies require an average of more than 400 hours of field training in subjects such as defensive driving, use of firearms, arrest and control of suspects, and general physical fitness. Wide variations in these training requirements continue to exist around the nation. Likewise, the criminal law and rules for its enforcement change continually, as you have seen; yet requirements for in-service training for police vary widely, from none (e.g., Fort Collins, Colorado, and Washington, D.C. Metropolitan Police) to more than 100 in-service hours per year (e.g., Santa Cruz County Sheriff, California, and Fort Myers, Florida).[62]

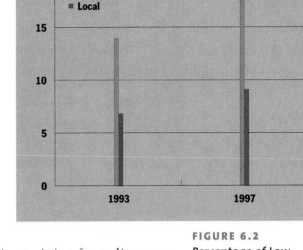

FIGURE 6.2

Percentage of Law Enforcement Agencies Requiring New Officers to Have a Two-Year or Four-Year College Degree

SOURCE: Brian A. Reaves and Andrew L. Goldberg, *Law Enforcement Management and Administrative Statistics, 1997: Data for Individual State and Local Agencies with 100 or More Officers* (Washington, DC: Bureau of Justice Statistics, 1999).

IMPROVEMENTS IN POLICE TRAINING

POLICE SALARIES

The basic education required of most new police officers is a high school diploma, but that is changing. Sixteen percent of state police agencies now require a two-year college degree, and 4 percent require a bachelor's degree. Virtually all federal law enforcement agencies require a bachelor's degree. Similar to the state police, 16 percent of county police departments require either a two-year or four-year degree, followed by 9 percent of large municipal police departments. These percentages have increased in recent years and will continue to do so as higher salaries and benefits make police work a more desirable profession. Figure 6.2 illustrates the significant increase in education requirements for police from 1993 to 1997.

Police salaries vary by jurisdiction and are related to the size of the police department and the cost of living in different parts of the country. The average starting salary in large municipal police departments (with more than one hundred officers) is $29,859, according to the most recent data published (1997), which is slightly more than the average paid by county and state police agencies. Officer salaries increase by an average of 10 percent after one year of experience on the job, and more than half of all police agencies provide educational incentive pay to encourage officers to further their education. At all levels of experience, the median pay for state, county, and large local police agencies is between $70,000 and $80,000.[63]

Issues of Gender and Race

The human element of police professionalism has not always kept pace with organizational and educational changes. Female officers, minority officers, and new tactical approaches to policing have not always won ready acceptance. A 1997 study in a midwestern city found de facto segregation of officers by race, as well as sexual harassment and marginalization of women. Although no single factor was found to cause the lack of integration of women and minorities, entrenched attitudes and organizational policies appeared to be implicated.[64] Studies in other locations also find that female officers often struggle for acceptance and do not receive equal treatment from male officers and superiors.[65] These findings provide context for the cases that come to public attention when lawsuits are filed. In Southborough, Massachusetts, for example, a police dispatcher was awarded $250,000 in settlement for a claim of sexual harassment. A female police sergeant in Florida was awarded $100,000 after a jury found that her chief had used racial slurs when calling her. An Illinois county settled a discrimination suit for $444,000 and agreed to make significant changes in its hiring practices when an investigation found it had not hired a female patrol officer in seventeen years. In similar fashion, the Bureau of Alcohol, Tobacco, and Firearms agreed to pay $5.9 million in damages and overhaul its hiring and promotion system in response to a suit by African American agents who claimed they had been assigned to lower-ranking positions and lower salaries.[66] In 1999 fourteen minority officers sued the New York City police department, alleging discrimination in disciplinary practices.[67]

Discrimination on the basis of gender occurs despite the fact that numerous objective studies have demonstrated that women perform police tasks as well as men. In St. Louis, New York City, and many other jurisdictions, it has been found that female officers perform police tasks as competently as male officers do. No significant difference has been found between men and women in the time it takes to handle an incident, the way threatening situations are handled, the proportion of arrests that result in prosecution, injuries on the job, citizen satisfaction with the way that an incident is handled, or other important aspects of the job.[68] Yet female officers in the United States encounter barriers and "gendered images that establish them as outsiders, sexual objects, targets of men's resentment, and competitors who threaten to change the rules of officer interaction."[69] Despite the satisfactory performance of female officers, these attitudes may be responsible for the slow assimilation of women in policing.

Analogous attitudes may be responsible for lingering instances of racism within police departments. Studies have found that minorities are more likely than whites to have unfavorable attitudes towards police in general, although the race of crime victims or the race of police officers handling a case has been found to make no difference in the degree to which victims feel the police fulfilled their expectations in a given incident.[70] In sum, race and gender images appear not to hold up when one looks at specific cases and makes objective comparisons.

PERSISTING SEXISM AND RACISM

What kind of training and amount of education are police officers required or encouraged to have? What are the demographic characteristics of people who tend to choose police work as their profession? What perennial issues of gender and race compromise police professionalism? Would you consider law enforcement as a career? Why or why not? If you did, how would technology and the media influence your work?

Findings like these have led to growing emphasis on ongoing research within police agencies and promotion of the concept of police departments as "learning organizations" that are more dynamic and better able to respond to both social and technological changes. Researchers examine, for example, changes in the behaviors of both police and society; and they study the impact of those changes to ensure that efforts to improve police professionalism are not subverted by negative attitudes or archaic organizational policies.[71]

What Are Some Concerns about Policing in the United States?

This nation's historical ambivalence about establishing an organized police system and reluctance to centralize it and make it more efficient has hampered the ability of police to apprehend criminals and reduce the fear of crime. On one hand is the need to organize law enforcement efforts more efficiently. On the other hand is society's reluctance to provide the resources, technology, and authority that are required if a system of property protection and personal safety is to be effective. Concerns about policing include jurisdictional cooperation, the impacts of high technologies on police work, and the privatization of policing.

The Dilemma of Jurisdictions and Need for Cooperation

As you have learned, law enforcement is carried out by municipalities. In the United States today, only 1 percent of the 19,000 law enforcement agencies in the nation are state or federal agencies. As the President's Commission stated in 1967, "A fundamental problem confronting law enforcement today is that of fragmented crime repression efforts resulting from the large number of uncoordinated local governments and law enforcement agencies."[72] A 1996 investigation came to a similar conclusion regarding federal police, citing a "need for greater coordination of the numerous agencies involved in federal law enforcement."[73] The need for coordination has been a problem throughout the history of policing in the United States, even though the amount of resources devoted to the task has increased dramatically in recent years. The growing police presence must be organized efficiently to be fully effective.[74]

An example of this problem is the enforcement of drug laws. A person who sells crack cocaine in any city could be under surveillance by, and arrested by, the city police, the state police, the FBI, or the DEA. Other agencies also

MULTIJURISDICTIONAL CRIMES

could be involved if certain other circumstances are present, such as the possession of weapons, terrorist purposes, or affiliation with organized crime. Overlapping jurisdictions sometimes result in several law enforcement agencies investigating the same suspects for the same crimes. Because of the ease with which people, planes, cars, and electronic communications can traverse local boundaries, multijurisdictional crimes are becoming more common. Police agencies tend to respect geographic boundaries, but criminals do not. The creation of **multijurisdictional task forces** allows for different levels of enforcement to pool evidence, personnel, and expertise while reducing unnecessary duplication of effort. A study of eight cities found that each had a combined federal, state, and local law enforcement task force that focused on some combination of drug crimes, weapons, and violent crimes.[75] The Metropolitan Richmond Task Force in Virginia includes detectives from the DEA; the Richmond Police Department; the Virginia State Police; the Henrico, Chesterfield, and Hanover County Police; and the City of Petersburg. Two major task force investigations culminated in 1995 with the conviction of twenty members of two drug-trafficking organizations. Similarly, the Cold Homicide Task Force involves the FBI, Virginia State Police, and Richmond Police Department. The task force identified an East Coast drug organization as responsible for twelve homicides in New York City and Virginia.[76] Such task forces, although they deal with only a small proportion of all the crimes that occur in an area, often pursue complicated cases requiring resources that no single agency can devote.

Thus, additional resources alone have not improved the efficiency of policing. It will take greater recognition of the limits of political boundaries and jurisdictions to make law enforcement more effective.

The Impacts of Technology and the Media on Police Work

In recent decades improvements in police communications and technology have backfired to a certain extent. Following the lead of police in other countries, police in the United States have made it easier to contact them through the introduction of the 911 emergency phone number, nontoll telephones, and remote communications equipment. The public makes use of these innovations so frequently that police efficiency has suffered. As one observer commented in the 1970s,

These efforts have been so successful that they threaten to overturn the traditional conceptions of police work and to undermine the efficiency and purpose of street patrols. Since New York City introduced its emergency number in July 1968, the average number of calls each day to the police has risen from 12,000 to 17,000, and it is still climbing. In Philadelphia, a city one-fourth the size of New York, during a 14-hour period of a Friday in June 1971, more than 8,000 emergency calls were received. During peak periods, patrolmen are often unable to handle all of their as-

signments. They are so busy answering calls that they have no time to patrol these territories.[77]

During the 1990s this problem became even more serious. The number of 911 calls made each day in the United States is estimated at 268,000. By the year 2005 New York City alone will receive an estimated 12.5 million 911 calls annually.[78]

The problem lies not only in the growing volume of calls to the police. An increasing proportion of 911 calls do not involve emergencies. Also, the growing use of cellular phones has resulted in 18 million additional 911 calls each year from locations that are difficult to trace; and undertrained and poorly paid dispatchers have contributed to several tragedies due to failure to respond.[79] Better training of dispatchers, new fiber-optic systems designed to handle a higher volume of calls, and the use of alternate nonemergency numbers are some recent initiatives designed to address the dramatic increase in emergency calls.

Technology will make some aspects of police work more efficient. In 1999 the FBI upgraded the National Crime Information Center (NCIC), a system of 39 million computer records that contains criminal histories and lists of missing persons, wanted persons, and stolen property. Called NCIC 2000, the new system includes electronic mug shots and a fingerprint of each wanted person. The FBI's goal is for all police agencies to have laptop computers, miniature fingerprint scanners, and video cameras in patrol cars to allow police officers to see photos of wanted or missing persons on computer screens in their cars, and to permit them to take fingerprints from suspects at the scene and compare them instantly to the NCIC database. It is expected to cost about $2,000 to equip a patrol car with this equipment, but this system should dramatically improve the ability of police to screen suspects quickly and accurately.[80]

The National Commission on the Future of DNA Evidence was created in 1998 by U.S. Attorney General Janet Reno in response to concern about wrongful convictions in rape and homicide cases. The Commission found unrealized potential for the use of DNA evidence in crime scene investigations.[81] Historically, DNA has been used in laboratory testing and as courtroom evidence to link a suspect with a crime by using his or her unique DNA "genetic fingerprint" obtained from blood, saliva, semen, or other body tissue found at a crime scene. The FBI's DNA Index System (CODIS) was authorized in 1994, and since then every state has enacted legislation establishing a CODIS database, requiring that DNA profiles be entered into the system for offenders convicted of serious crimes. Currently there are more than 300,000 DNA profiles in the CODIS system, permitting police who have found body fluids or residue from a crime scene, but no suspects, to compare it to the CODIS database. Thus far, police have had hundreds of "cold hits" in which suspects were identified from the DNA database without other evidence of their involvement in the crime. Police also have been able to include or exclude suspects based on the results of DNA testing.[82]

CALLING 911

DNA EVIDENCE
AND CODIS

As the CODIS database continues to grow, more crimes will be solved by means of DNA evidence.

The influence of the mass media on police work has been dramatic. The ability of media to access police records (through the Freedom of Information Act) and the use of remote video cameras, automobiles, and even helicopters to film police in action have all contributed to changes in the way police behave. According to police researcher Peter Manning, police demonstrate "reflexivity," in which their choices are influenced by the anticipated responses of others. Those responses, in turn, are shaped by how police decisions are portrayed in the media.[83] For example, news footage of police beating a motorist, as in the Rodney King incident, is repeated and analyzed on television many times, blurring the distinction in people's minds between unusual and everyday police actions. Misrepresentations of this kind can confuse or mislead both the public and policy makers. According to Manning, the police are countering extensive media coverage with media of their own. They are using surveillance videos and video cameras mounted in patrol cars to record actual police conduct, including pursuits and arrests. This police footage sometimes is aired as entertainment on network television. Thus, the boundaries between police and public tend to merge as the mass media (for better or for worse) become partners in police work.

The impact of the media clearly involves more than public image. "Reality" television programs follow police on the job—but feature episodes of violent action and high-speed pursuits as if they were typical. *America's Most Wanted* also features the most gruesome unsolved cases, then advertises for leads from the general public. The result of these media portrayals is public misunderstanding about the true nature of police work, the success of police in solving crimes, and the true level of crime and violence in society. There is an increase in unrealistic expectations of police when television alternately portrays them either as a fearsome force that always catches the offender or as an agency hopelessly trying to deal with an extremely violent society—when the true situation is somewhere in between.

The Movement toward Private Policing

private security
Law enforcement agencies that protect private property and are paid by private individuals and corporations.

Private security is growing at an incredible rate. There are twice as many private security officers as there are police officers in the United States (see Figure 6.3). In an interesting reversal of history, public policing, which arose because of the ineffectiveness of private security measures, is now faced with a movement back toward privatization. Historically, private security has taken on law enforcement tasks when public police forces have not adapted quickly to major social or technological changes. These changes have resulted in new manifestations of crime, spurring private entrepreneurs to offer protective services to those who can afford them.

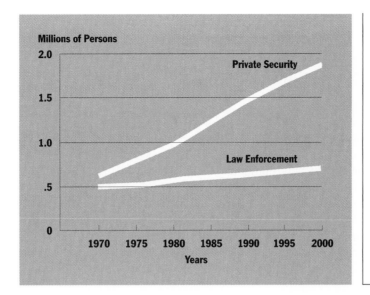

FIGURE 6.3
Trends in Private Security and Law Enforcement Employment

SOURCE: William Cunningham, J. Strauchs, Clifford W. VanMeter, *The Hallcrest Report II: Private Security Trends 1990–2000* (Boston: Butterworth–Heinemann, 1990); Charles P. Nemeth, *Private Security and the Investigative Process*, 2nd ed. (Boston: Butterworth–Heinemann, 1999).

This response has played a significant role in the continuing growth of private security.[84]

An early example was the need for multijurisdictional law enforcement. The development of an interstate railroad system during the mid-1800s created new opportunities for theft, robberies, and vandalism that were beyond the capacity of public police agencies to control. Regional policing and regulatory enforcement agencies were not yet developed, and local police agencies were not well equipped to deal with multijurisdictional crimes. In 1855 Allan Pinkerton was hired by six railroads to provide police protection over a five-state region. Within the next few years Pinkerton extended his activities into areas normally the responsibility of municipal police, providing detective services and an evening patrol for businesses in the Chicago area.[85]

In 1844 Samuel Morse invented the telegraph, which not only revolutionized communication but also provided the means to detect burglaries electronically through the use of relays. In 1858 an entrepreneur named Edwin Holmes seized the opportunity to establish the first central office burglar alarm. He later founded Holmes Protection, Inc., a private security agency that is still operating today. In 1874 American District Telegraph (ADT) was established to provide protective services through the use of messengers and telegraph lines.[86] Today private security agencies continue to manage a larger proportion of the central burglar alarm market than do police departments.

The 1850s also saw social changes resulting from an expanding population and increasing distance between population centers. Robberies, thefts, and unreliable delivery of goods led Perry Brink to form a truck and package delivery service in 1859. Brink later expanded into armored car services, delivering his first payroll in 1891; today Brink's is the largest agency of its kind in the United States.[87]

PINKERTON'S AND BRINK'S

contemporary issues and trends

Campus Law Enforcement

Campus security has grown as an industry as crime on college campuses has become a national concern. This attention has been aroused by highly publicized homicides at universities as well as by the more common problems of binge drinking, rape, and reckless deaths on college campuses. Today, three-fourths of four-year colleges and universities with more than 2,500 students employ sworn police officers who have general arrest powers under state or local law. There are nearly 11,000 full-time sworn officers serving these colleges and universities, plus 9,000 additional full-time campus security personnel who are not sworn officers.

The backgrounds and training requirements of campus security officers vary widely. Most sworn campus police officers are armed, including 95 percent of security per-

sonnel serving campuses with 20,000 or more students. One-fourth of campuses contract for private security services, most involving private security companies. Training for new officers ranges from less than 400 to more than 900 hours. Similarly, 30 percent of campus security agencies require that new officers have some college education, but only 2 percent require a four-year degree.

Campus security officers engage in a variety of tasks, from investigation of serious crime to enforcement of parking regulations. The tasks of campus security personnel are summarized in Figure 6.4. As the figure indicates, most campus security agencies are responsible for alarm monitoring, building lockup, investigation of serious crimes, personal safety escorts, stadium security, parking, and traffic enforcement. A smaller number handle medical center or nuclear facility security.

The vast majority (85 percent) of campus law enforcement agencies operate general crime prevention programs. These programs are designed to increase awareness of

> Two-thirds of campus police agencies have education programs for date rape prevention

criminal opportunities and reduce the risk of victimization. Two-thirds of campus police agencies have education programs for date rape prevention, for example, and half have programs for prevention of drug and alcohol abuse.[a]

1. What aspects of local law enforcement have come to your attention as a member of your college community? How do you rate your campus security?
2. If cities and towns placed the same degree of emphasis on crime awareness and prevention programs as campus police do, do you think levels of crime would be as low there as they are on college campuses?

NOTE

a. Brian A. Reaves, *Campus Law Enforcement* (Washington, DC: Bureau of Justice Statistics, 1996); Verna A. Henson and William E. Stone, "Campus Crime: A Victimization Study," *Journal of Criminal Justice* 27 (July–August 1999).

FIGURE 6.4

Tasks Performed by Campus Law Enforcement Personnel

SOURCE: Brian A. Reaves, *Campus Law Enforcement* (Washington, DC: Bureau of Justice Statistics, 1996).

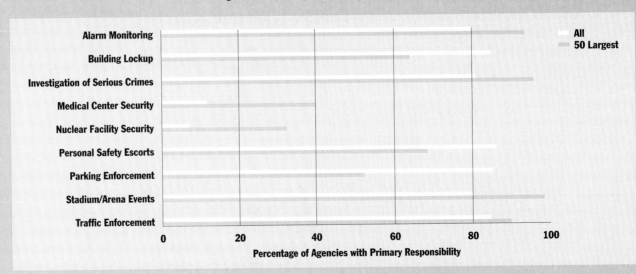

During the 1960s the deterioration of central cities caused many urban residents to move to the suburbs. The resulting changes in public shopping patterns accelerated the development of enclosed shopping malls in suburban locations. This trend, in turn, led to the utilization of private protective services on a large scale. Virtually all enclosed malls now have private security forces.

The late 1960s also witnessed widespread demonstrations and uprisings on college campuses. These protests were not handled adequately by local police. According to a RAND Corporation study, many colleges and universities have doubled or tripled their expenditures on private security since then.[88] The increasing incidence of robberies, assaults, and theft on college campuses, together with new national requirements for reporting of campus crime, have kept campus security forces at the forefront of a growing industry. Today campus law enforcement expenditures average $109 per student.[89]

During the late 1960s and early 1970s there was a dramatic increase in the number of people using air transportation, largely owing to the increasing capacity of the airline industry and the decreasing cost of air travel. Between 1963 and 1967 there were only 4 attempted skyjackings in the United States, but between 1968 to 1972 there were 134 such attempts. In addition, a large number of bomb threats were made against aircraft in the United States and elsewhere. In response to this situation, the Federal Aviation Administration (FAA) began compulsory point-of-departure screening of airline passengers in 1972. This screening for weapons and explosives is the responsibility of the airlines and is carried out primarily by contract security firms. Similar procedures have been established in other countries, where they also are conducted by private security agencies.[90]

The expanding frontiers of international business have increased the scale and influence of U.S. multinational corporations—and the number of terrorist threats and kidnappings of corporate executives and their families. It is estimated that in the 1990s there were more than 30,000 kidnappings of Americans overseas.[91] As a result, more than 20,000 private security personnel are involved in executive protection.[92] This protection has been extended to computer networks to protect them from acts of sabotage and theft of company secrets.[93]

There is every reason to believe that private security will continue to grow and to assume tasks that were previously the responsibility of public law enforcement. Increasing reliance on computer networks, greater frequency of terrorist acts, and transnational organized crime are creating opportunities for new forms of crime that police are ill equipped to control. The ultimate result of these trends may be continued shrinkage of the domain of public police and increased reliance on private protection services. In addition, the relatively high cost of public police forces may lead to consolidation and, in some cases, elimination of these agencies.[94] It remains to be seen whether public law enforcement agencies will embrace aspects of privatization that can benefit their communities, and whether private security agencies can perform police tasks in a consistently efficient, effective, and accountable manner.

PRIVATIZATION IN BUSINESS AND INDUSTRY

critical thinking exercise

The Cyclical Nature of Community Policing

Before the establishment of full-time police in the 1800s, private citizens were largely responsible for protecting their own property. With advances in police professionalism and technology, the public has come to rely on the police for this service. The dramatic growth in calls for police service over the years testifies to this reliance.

Increased calls to police have diminished their effectiveness in solving crimes; fewer than 20 percent of serious crimes are now "closed" by an arrest. Community policing attempts to reintroduce the public as a significant player in crime control. Community policing has been defined as "a collaboration between the police and the community that identifies and solves community problems."[a] Recognizing that crime often plagues poor and disorganized neighborhoods, community policing is designed to incorporate members of the community as "active allies in the effort to enhance the safety and quality of neighborhoods" so that police are "no longer the sole guardians of law and order."[b] It is ironic that in 150 years the United States evolved from a crime prevention system in which private citizens fended for themselves to one in which they are almost totally dependent on police—and that the trend is now being reversed.

The nature of community policing varies in different jurisdictions, but the theme is the same: assigning a neighborhood patrol officer who gets to know the local residents, building trust between police officers and citizens, devoting time to solving problems before they develop into crimes. This approach to law enforcement makes citizens partners with the police in controlling crime rather than passive recipients of police services.

Evaluations of the effectiveness of community policing strategies have found mixed results thus far. On the positive side, citizens in many neighborhoods have reported a more positive view of police and of the crime situation in their area. On the negative side, community policing has had no uniform effects on crime rates; it has proved difficult to involve neighborhood organizations in the programs; and within police departments there appears to be some resistance to community policing strategies.[c]

CRITICAL THINKING QUESTIONS

1. Why do you believe the public's attitude toward police often improves in neighborhoods where community policing is practiced?
2. What forces within police departments (and within police officers themselves) may provoke resistance to the idea of community policing?
3. How might changes in the impacts of the mass media and telecommunications technologies affect community policing?
4. At what point do you think the involvement of private citizens in policing could go too far?

NOTES

a. Bureau of Justice Assistance, *Understanding Community Policing* (Washington, DC: Office of Justice Programs, 1994), p. vii.
b. Ibid.
c. Gary W. Cordner, "Community Policing: Elements and Effects," *Police Forum* 5 (July 1995), pp. 1–8; Susan Sadd and Randolph M. Grinc, *Implementation Challenges in Community Policing: Innovative Neighborhood-Oriented Policing in Eight Cities* (Washington, DC: National Institute of Justice, 1996); Wesley G. Skogan, *Community Policing in Chicago: Year Two* (Washington, DC: National Institute of Justice, 1995); Jerome H. Skolnick, *On Democratic Policing* (Washington, DC: Police Foundation, 1999).

SUMMARY

HOW DID POLICING EVOLVE?

■ Before police departments were formally established, less formal measures of self-protection were used. In the mutual pledge system, everyone in the community was responsible for everyone else. In the watch and ward system, men from each town were required to take turns standing watch at night.

■ The invention of gin was a catalyst for the establishment of public policing. Although the gin craze abated, the fear of crime did not. This led to the creation of the Bow Street Runners, a private agency that patrolled the streets.

■ The first police force was established in London in 1829. Police officers patrolled specific areas and were organized in a paramilitary fashion to maintain discipline.

■ The first daytime police force in the United States was established in Boston in 1838; New York was the first city to create a unified day and night police force. By 1900 nearly every city of any size had established a full-time police force.

■ Urban police forces were plagued by problems of low pay, disrespect, and ineffectiveness. During the Progressive Era there was a movement toward police efficiency, professionalism, and improved technology.

■ Police effectiveness was increased through improved investigative techniques and better selection and training procedures.

WHAT IS THE ORGANIZATION OF LAW ENFORCEMENT?

■ The vast majority of police agencies are found at the local level of government. Local police enforce applicable state laws, local ordinances, and traffic laws; they also investigate accidents and suspected crimes.

■ State police agencies enforce state laws and investigate accidents. They include specialized law enforcement agencies for such purposes as alcohol control.

■ There are seventeen different federal law agencies that enforce laws enacted by Congress. The largest federal agencies are the U.S. Customs Service, the Federal Bureau of Investigation, the Federal Bureau of Prisons, and the Immigration and Naturalization Service.

■ The growth of international travel, the transnational nature of the Internet, and the threat of international organized crime and terrorism have combined to bring about international agreements and law enforcement efforts that serve the interests of all nations.

WHO ARE THE POLICE?

■ Police selection processes vary among police departments, but most agencies require applicants to pass a written test, physical agility test, drug test, medical exam (including visual and hearing test), oral interview, psychological assessment, polygraph test, and background investigation. The typical police agency requires more than 800 hours of classroom training for new recruits.

■ Police officers are increasingly female and minorities, although there continue to be cases of harassment and discrimination within some police departments, despite the fact that performance studies and victim interviews show that females and minority officers perform well and are accepted by the public.

WHAT ARE SOME CONCERNS ABOUT POLICING IN THE UNITED STATES?

■ Policing faces a dilemma: There is a need to organize law enforcement efforts in a more efficient way. However, there is also reluctance to provide the necessary resources and authority.

■ Innovations in equipment have contributed to improved police work. However, the introduction of 911 lines led to unanticipated problems due to an extremely high volume of calls.

■ Reliance on technology in policing is increasing with the updated National Crime Information Center, which will allow for police to access criminal histories, wanted person files, and fingerprint comparisons via computers in their patrol cars. DNA banking is enabling police to compare human tissue found at crime scenes with a database of known offenders to solve more crimes.

- Media images of police work often distort the true nature of policing, providing the public with an unrealistic view of the capabilities and performance of police.
- Private security is a burgeoning industry, taking on law enforcement tasks in areas where public police forces do not adapt sufficiently to social and technological changes.

Key Terms

mutual pledge system
constable
shire reeve
watch and ward system
justice of the peace
preventive police
crime commissions
progressivism
professionalization
Law Enforcement Assistance
   Administration (LEAA)

local police
community policing
Weed and Seed
state police
federal law enforcement
transnational law
   enforcement
Interpol
multijurisdictional task
   forces
private security

Questions for Review and Discussion

1. What systems for community protection evolved before the establishment of formal police departments?
2. Why did the invention of gin act as a catalyst for the establishment of public policing?
3. What were some of the problems faced by early police forces?
4. How was police professionalism enhanced in the early decades of the twentieth century?
5. Why is growing reliance on technology a problem for police operations today?
6. Why is law enforcement carried out largely by municipalities in the United States?
7. What are the primary activities of local and state police forces?
8. What are the major federal law enforcement agencies, and what are their responsibilities?
9. What are important issues facing transnational law enforcement?
10. Explain the growing diversity among police officers in recent years.
11. How is the growth of private security related to the police?

Notes

1. Tracy Lenzy, "The November Night When 911 Didn't Work," *U.S. News & World Report* (June 17, 1996), p. 36.
2. Gary Fields, "Upgraded Database to Aid Patrol Officers," *USA Today* (July 12, 1999), p. 3.

3. President's Commission on Law Enforcement and Administration of Justice, *Task Force Report: The Police* (Washington, DC: U.S. Government Printing Office, 1967), p. 3.

4. Harold T. Amidon, "Law Enforcement: From 'The Beginning' to the English Bobby," *Journal of Police Science and Administration* 5 (September 1977), pp. 355–67.

5. President's Commission, p. 4.

6. Jonathan Rubinstein, *City Police* (New York: Ballantine, 1974), pp. 4–5.

7. Rubinstein, p. 6.

8. M. Dorothy George, *London Life in the Eighteenth Century* (New York: Capricorn, 1925).

9. Rubinstein, pp. 8–9.

10. Amidon, p. 366.

11. Rubinstein, p. 10.

12. Rubinstein, p. 11.

13. Center for Research on Criminal Justice, *The Iron Fist and the Velvet Glove*, revised ed. (Berkeley, CA: Center for Research on Criminal Justice, 1977), p. 22.

14. George Smith, *The United States Constitution* (Nashville, TN: Knowledge Products, 1987).

15. Roger Lane, *Policing the City: Boston, 1822–1885* (Cambridge, MA: Harvard University Press, 1971); Center for Research on Criminal Justice, *The Iron Fist and the Velvet Glove.*

16. President's Commission, p. 5.

17. Carl B. Klockars, *The Idea of Police* (Beverly Hills, CA: Sage, 1985).

18. Rubinstein, pp. 15–20.

19. Nathan Douthit, "Enforcement and Nonenforcement Roles in Policing: A Historical Inquiry," *Journal of Police Science and Administration* 3 (September 1975), p. 339.

20. Harry Soderman, "Science and Criminal Investigation," *The Annals* 146 (1929), pp. 237–48.

21. Douthit, p. 341.

22. August Vollmer, "Police Progress in the Last Twenty-Five Years," *Journal of Criminal Law, Criminology, and Police Science* 24 (1933), pp. 161–75.

23. Clifford E. Thermer, "Authentic Assessment for Performance-Based Police Training," *Police Forum* 7 (July 1997), pp. 1–5.

24. See Samuel Walker, *A Critical History of Police Reform* (Lexington, MA: Lexington Books, 1977).

25. James O. Finckenauer, "Crime as a National Political Issue: 1964–76, from Law and Order to Domestic Tranquility," *Crime and Delinquency* 24 (January 1978), pp. 1–23.

26. See National Advisory Commission on Civil Disorders (1968) and President's Commission on Campus Unrest (1970).

27. Wendell Rawls, "Justice Department May Seek Special Revenue Sharing to Replace Anti-Crime Grants," *New York Times* (June 30, 1977), p. 30.

28. Brian A. Reaves, *Census of State and Local Law Enforcement Agencies* (Washington, DC: Bureau of Justice Statistics, 1998).

29. Ibid.

30. Brian A. Reaves, *State and Local Police Departments* (Washington, DC: Bureau of Justice Statistics, 1998); Brian A. Reaves, *Sheriffs' Departments* (Washington, DC: Bureau of Justice Statistics, 1992).

31. Reaves, *Census of State and Local Law Enforcement Agencies*, p. 9.

32. Reaves, *State and Local Police Departments*, p. 2.

33. Peter B. Kraska and Louis J. Cubellis, "Militarizing Mayberry and Beyond: Making Sense of American Paramilitary Policing," *Justice Quarterly* 14 (December 1997), pp. 607–29.

34. Peter B. Kraska and Victor E. Kappeler, "Militarizing American Police: The Rise and Normalization of Paramilitary Units," *Social Problems* 44 (1997), pp. 1–18.

35. George L. Kelling and Catherine M. Coles, *Fixing Broken Windows: Restoring Order and Reducing Crime in Our Communities* (New York: Touchstone, 1997), pp. 240–41.

36. Jihong Zhao and Quint C. Thurman, "Community Policing: Where Are We Now?," *Crime and Delinquency* 43 (July 1997), pp. 345–57; Velmer Burton, James Frank, Robert Langworthy, and Troy Barker, "The Prescribed Roles of Police in a Free Society: Analyzing State Legal Codes," *Justice Quarterly* 10 (1994), pp. 683–95.

37. Edward R. Maguire, "Structural Change in Large Municipal Police Organizations during the Community Policing Era," *Justice Quarterly* 14 (September 1997), pp. 547–76.

38. Joanne Ziembo-Bogl, "Exploring the Function of the Media in Community Policing," *Police Forum* 8 (January 1998), pp. 1–12.

39. U.S. Comptroller General, *More Can Be Done to Improve Weed and Seed Program Management* (Washington, DC: U.S. General Accounting Office, 1999).

40. Terence Dunworth and Gregory Mills, *National Evaluation of Weed and Seed* (Washington, DC: National Institute of Justice, 1999).

41. Reaves, *State and Local Police Departments*, p. 10.

42. Ibid., p. 12.

43. Ibid.

44. U.S. Comptroller General, *Border Patrol: Staffing and Enforcement Activities* (Washington, DC: U.S. General Accounting Office, 1996).

45. Fenton Bresler, *Interpol* (Toronto: Penguin, 1993); Michael Fooner, *Interpol* (New York: Plenum, 1989).

46. Interpol web page.

47. Malcolm Anderson, "Interpol and the Developing System of International Police Cooperation," in William F. McDonald, ed., *Crime and Law Enforcement in the Global Village* (Cincinnati: Anderson, 1997), p. 101.

48. Ethan A. Nadelmann, "The Americanization of Global Law Enforcement: The Diffusion of American Tactics and Personnel," in McDonald, ed., *Crime and Law Enforcement in the Global Village*, p. 124.

49. John Benyon, "The Developing System of Police Cooperation in the European Union," in McDonald, ed., *Crime and Law Enforcement in the Global Village*, p. 115.

50. Ordway P. Burden, "Law Enforcement Agencies Working Overseas," *CJ International* 11 (November–December 1995), p. 17.

51. Ibid.

52. "The World Ministerial Conference on Organized Transnational Crime," *United Nations Crime Prevention and Criminal Justice Newsletter*, nos. 26/27 (November 1995).

53. See Gary T. Marx, "Social Control across Borders," in McDonald, ed., *Crime and Law Enforcement in the Global Village* pp. 23–39.

54. Brian A. Reaves and Andrew L. Goldberg, *Law Enforcement Management and Administrative Statistics, 1997* (Washington, DC: Bureau of Justice Statistics, 1999).

55. Theresa M. Melchionne, "The Changing Role of Policewomen," *The Police Journal* 47 (October 1974), 340–58.

56. Nancy E. McGlen and Karen O'Connor, *Women's Rights* (New York: Praeger, 1983).

57. Reaves and Goldberg.

58. Kevin W. Dale, "College Internship Program: Prospective Recruits Get Hands-On Experience," *The FBI Law Enforcement Bulletin* 65 (September 1996), p. 21.

59. *Guardians Association of New York City Police Department v. Civil Service Commission of New York*, 23 FEP 909 (1980).

60. Stephen D. Mastrofski, *Policing for People* (Washington, DC: Police Foundation, 1999).

61. Larry K. Gaines and Steven Falkenberg, "An Evaluation of the Written Selection Test: Effectiveness and Alternatives, *Journal of Criminal Justice* 26 (May–June 1998), p. 175.

62. Reaves and Goldberg.

63. Ibid.

64. Robin N. Haarr, "Patterns of Interaction in a Police Patrol Bureau: Race and Gender Barriers to Integration," *Justice Quarterly* 14 (March 1997), pp. 53–85.

65. James Daum and Cindy Johns, "Police Work from a Woman's Perspective," *Police Chief* 61 (1994), pp. 46–49; Mary Brown, "The Plight of the Female Officer: A Survey," *Police Chief* 61 (1994), pp. 50–53.

66. "The High Cost of Discrimination," *Law Enforcement News* (December 31, 1996), p. 19; see also Benjamin Weiser, "14 Minority Officers Sue Police Force, Alleging Bias on Disciplinary Practices," *New York Times* (September 10, 1999), p. B3.

67. Weiser, "14 Minority Officers."

68. Susan Ehrlich Martin and Nancy C. Jurik, *Doing Justice, Doing Gender: Women in Law Enforcement Occupations* (Thousand Oaks, CA: Sage, 1996), p. 73; Lewis J. Sherman, "An Evaluation of Policewomen on Patrol in a Suburban Police Department," *Journal of Police Science and Administration* 3 (December 1975), pp. 434–38; Joyce L. Sichel, Lucy N. Friedman, Janet C. Quint, and Michael E. Smith, *Women on Patrol: A Pilot Study of Police Performance in New York City* (Washington, DC: U.S. Department of Justice, 1978).

69. Anthony V. Bouza, "Women in Policing," *FBI Law Enforcement Bulletin* 44 (1975), pp. 2–7; Susan Ehrlich Martin, *Breaking and Entering: Policewomen on Patrol* (Berkeley: University of California Press, 1980); Bernadette Jones Palombo, "Attitudes, Training, Performance and Retention of Female and Minority Police Officers," in G. T. Felkenes and P. C. Unsinger, eds., *Diversity, Affirmative Action and Law Enforcement* (Springfield, IL: Thomas, 1992), pp. 76–79; Donna C. Hale and Stacey M. Myland, "Dragons and Dinosaurs: The Plight of Patrol Women," *Police Forum* 3 (April 1993); Daniel Bell, "Policewomen: Myths and Reality," *Journal of Police Science and Administration* 10 (March 1982), pp. 112–20; Peter Horne, *Women in Law Enforcement*, 2nd ed. (Springfield, IL: Thomas, 1980); Sean A. Grennan, "Findings on the Roles of Officer Gender in Violent Encounters with Citizens," *Journal of Police Science and Administration* 15 (1987); Kerry Segrave, *Policewomen: A History* (Jefferson, NC: McFarland, 1995); Susan Ehrlich Martin, "Women on the Move?: A Report on the Status of Women in Policing," *Women and Criminal Justice* 1 (1989), pp. 21–40.

70. Ronald Weitzer and Steven A. Tuch, "Race, Class, and Perceptions of Discrimination by the Police," *Crime and Delinquency* 45 (October 1999), pp. 494–507; Meghan Stroshine Chandek, "Race, Expectations and Evaluations of Police Performance," *Policing: An International Journal of Police Strategies and Management* 22 (1999), pp. 675–95.

71. William A. Geller, "Suppose We Were Really Serious about Police Departments Becoming 'Learning Organizations'?," *National Institute of Justice Journal* 234 (December 1997), pp. 2–8.

72. President's Commission, p. 68.

73. U.S. Comptroller General, *Federal Law Enforcement* (Washington, DC: U.S. General Accounting Office, 1996), p. 8.

74. Mahesh K. Nalla, Michael J. Lynch, and Michael J. Leiber, "Determinants of Police Growth in Phoenix, 1950–1988," *Justice Quarterly* 14 (March 1997), pp. 115–43.

75. Pamela K. Lattimore et al., *Homicide in Eight U.S. Cities: Trends, Context, and Policy Implications* (Washington, DC: National Institute of Justice, 1997).

76. Lattimore et al., pp. 125–29.

77. Rubinstein, p. 22.

78. Gordon Witkin with Monika Guttman, "This is 911 . . . Please Hold," *U.S. News & World Report* (June 17, 1996), pp. 31–38.

79. Ibid.

80. Gary Fields, "Upgraded Database to Aid Patrol Officers," *USA Today* (July 12, 1999), p. 3A.

81. See Victor Walter Weedon and John W. Hicks, *The Unrealized Potential of DNA Testing* (Washington, DC: National Institute of Justice, 1998).

82. Christopher H. Asplen, "Forensic DNA Evidence: National Commission Explores Its Future," *National Institute of Justice Journal* (January 1999), pp. 17–24.

83. Peter K. Manning, "Policing and Reflection," *Police Forum* 6 (October 1996), pp. 1–5.

84. Jay S. Albanese, "The Future of Policing: A Private Concern?," *Police Studies: The International Review of Police Development* 8 (1986), pp. 86–91.

85. Samuel Walker, *A Critical History of Police Reform* (Lexington, MA: Lexington Books, 1977), p. 30.

86. National Advisory Committee on Criminal Justice Standards and Goals, *Report of the Task Force on Private Security* (Cincinnati: Anderson, 1977).

87. James S. Kakalik and Sorrel Wildhorn, *The Private Police: Security and Danger* (New York: Crane Russak, 1977), p. 75.

88. Kakalik and Wildhorn.

89. Brian A. Reaves, *Campus Law Enforcement Agencies* (Washington, DC: Bureau of Justice Statistics, 1996), p. 2.

90. Hilary Draper, *Private Police* (Atlantic Highlands, NJ: Humanities Press, 1978), pp. 85–89.

91. Tom Carter and Jasminka Sktlec, "Americans Easy Targets for Greedy Kidnappers," *Insight on the News* (April 26, 1999), p. 42.

92. William C. Cunningham and Todd H. Taylor, *Crime and Protection in America: A Study of Private Security and Law Enforcement Resources and Relationships* (Washington, DC: U.S. Government Printing Office, 1985), p. 7.

93. Steve Rigney, "Thinking about Security," *PC Magazine* (January 4, 2000), p. 191; Jim Kerstetter, "Hackers Stake Out New Turf," *PC Week* (January 10, 2000), p. 1.

94. John T. Krimmel, "The Northern York County Police Consolidation Experience: An Analysis of Consolidation of Police Services in Eight Pennsylvania Rural Communities," *Policing: An International Journal of Police Strategies and Management* 20 (1997), pp. 497–507.

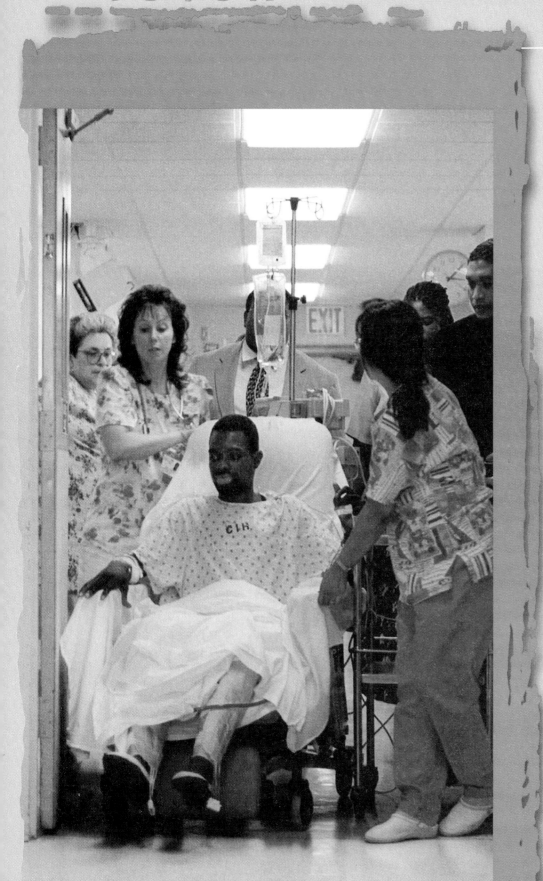

In 1999 a New York City police

officer pleaded guilty to torturing a Haitian immigrant by sodomizing the man with a broken broom handle while he was in custody at the police station. The victim suffered severe internal injuries, including a ruptured bladder and colon, and spent two months in the hospital. At sentencing the judge called this a "barbarous misuse of power" and said that "it would be difficult to overstate the harm that [the officer] inflicted on [the victim], the police department, and society at large."[1] The police officer was sentenced to thirty years in prison. Three other officers also were found guilty of conspiring to cover up the involvement of another officer in this crime.[2] Shocking incidents such as this one receive extensive media coverage; is it surprising, then, that public perceptions of police are shaped by such occurrences, even though they are rare?

Is There Such a Thing as a Police Personality?

Police must impose themselves into the lives of citizens in order to do their job. They make traffic stops, question loiterers, stop suspicious persons, help those in need of assistance, and apprehend suspected criminals. The police chief in Richmond, Virginia, asserts that police must address crime and disorder "respectfully but aggressively"—a paradoxial assignment that is not always easy to accomplish.[3] The need to be helpful to the public, yet always on the lookout for law violators, requires an even-handed approach and an objective attitude in all interactions with citizens.

Police officers are sometimes accused of cynicism or of having a "bad attitude" toward the public they serve. These attitudes are thought to influence police stop and arrest decisions and to contribute to poor community relations, corruption, and brutality. To what extent do police officers acquire personality characteristics that are unique to their job? Are police different from the general public? And, most important, do certain personality characteristics affect a police officer's discretion and performance on the job?

Myths and Stereotypes about Police

The police are the focus of a wide range of public opinion. Many people have strong views about what police ought to be doing and openly express their praise or criticism of police officers and police work. Everyone agrees that police should attempt to prevent crime and apprehend offenders, for example; but few enjoy being stopped, questioned, or ticketed by police. This debate about the proper role of police is reflected in state legislatures, where lawmakers debate about such questions as whether police should be permitted to stop a driver for nothing more than failure to wear a seat belt.[4]

racial profiling
Alleged tacit or explicit police guidelines that lead officers to stop and search minorities for minor violations significantly more often than whites.

There also is concern about underlying attitudes that contribute to apparent **racial profiling** in some jurisdictions, where police are alleged to stop and search minorities for suspected minor violations significantly more often than they stop and search whites.[5] Specific incidents of racial profiling have been discovered that reflect police misconduct, but it is not clear that these incidents characterize police in general or merely the attitudes, practices, or personalities of a small group of officers or departments. There also is the problem of determining if racial profiling has occurred. For example, when the St. Louis Police Department responded to the problems caused by teenagers "cruising" around town in cars by treating the teens' behavior as a form of loitering, critics argued that black teenagers were selectively targeted. Although it was not established that targeting of minorities actually occurred, there was a community perception that racial bias motivated the police.[6]

Perceptions of the police and their attitudes are extremely important, because they affect the level of citizen cooperation with police, the reporting of crimes, and people's willingness to share responsibility for crime prevention in the community. The news and entertainment media play a role in forming attitudes toward the police by portraying various police actions.[7] Media portrayals have a significant impact, because most citizens have little direct contact with police and form their attitudes about police through incidents they experience vicariously through the media.

What positive and negative preconceptions about law enforcement officers and police work might these children have? Where do those preconceptions come from? Why is public image a concern to police, especially in local law enforcement? How do public perceptions of police and police attitudes toward the public affect law enforcement? What do you think the officer should be saying to these children in a police outreach educational program?

Police are taking a more proactive role in developing public attitudes by working with communities in crime prevention programs. In Hampton, Virginia, for example, the local police department developed the KEEPS program (Knowledge, Enforcement, and Enhancement for Public Safety) to establish police–community action committees. These committees design and carry out strategies to improve the quality of life in specific neighborhoods.[8] Police agencies also use mass media and the Internet to encourage positive views. The U.S. Department of Justice has an Internet site designed to inform children about police work, drugs, and safety.[9] These efforts indicate the importance of public image in police work and illustrate how the police are working to improve that image.

KEEPS

Three Styles of Policing

Management of police decision making is a major concern of police supervisors. It is difficult to balance the competing goals of protecting the community and avoiding undue interference in the lives of citizens. Three "styles" of policing have been identified that characterize different approaches to the management of police discretion: the watchman style, the legalistic style, and the service style.[10]

The watchman style of policing emphasizes the maintenance of order. Order is threatened by both serious crimes and nonserious but disruptive offenses. Therefore, police may use both formal methods (arrest) and informal methods (warnings or threats) to maintain order. The watchman style is characteristic in lower-class neighborhoods, where police intervention is

WATCHMAN STYLE

What are the three main styles, or modes, of policing? Which style seems most relevant to the situation in this photograph? According to research, what are some common attitudes and values of people who are attracted to and do well in police work? How might the scene in the photograph be interpreted from the viewpoint of "police cynicism"? How do you think police performance in this incident should be evaluated?

LEGALISTIC STYLE

SERVICE STYLE

"POLICE PERSONALITY"

seen as necessary to control behavior. The Christopher Commission, which investigated the Los Angeles Police Department after the beating of Rodney King by police officers, observed that the police in Los Angeles emphasized crime control over crime prevention, thereby distancing themselves from the community they served.[11]

The legalistic style of policing focuses more strictly on law violations than on the maintenance of order. This more limited approach to policing is largely reactive. The police respond to calls for service, act only if there is probable cause to suspect serious law violation, and generally avoid intervention in problems that do not constitute violations. This approach to policing is becoming rare as police take on responsibilities for tasks other than law enforcement.

The service style of policing approaches law enforcement from a broad problem-solving perspective. Police seek to correct problems that are correlated with crime, such as loitering, public intoxication, delinquency, and domestic arguments. Police departments address these social problems both through direct intervention and through referrals to other social agencies.[12] This style of policing is found most often in middle- and upper-class neighborhoods; it avoids legal processing of minor offenses as much as possible.

To reflect their different emphases, the three styles also have been termed the neighbor (watchman), soldier (legalistic), and teacher (service) styles.[13] The style of policing employed by a department depends largely on the chief's preferences and, in larger cities, on those of the precinct commander, as well as on the responsiveness of the neighborhood. The nature of the public's reaction to local police often corresponds to the style of policing employed.[14] Public hostility is more common in watchman-style police departments, for example, because of their emphasis on order rather than service. Nevertheless, the personalities of the officers involved also play a significant role in the use of discretion, regardless of the style of policing characteristic of the department.

Current Research on Police Attitudes toward Their Jobs

In a classic study Jerome Skolnick examined police attitudes and discretion in a medium-sized city that he called Westville. Skolnick believed that the police officer's "working personality" grows out of his or her social environment rather than being a product of preexisting personality traits. Skolnick maintained that the "police personality" emerges from several aspects of police work—in particular, danger, isolation, and authority. He felt that danger causes police officers to become more wary of people in general. They grow more suspicious and tend to isolate themselves from others. Skolnick recognized that police have authority to direct and restrain citizens, but noted that this authority often is challenged. This questioning of legitimate authority by some members of the public reinforces officers' perception of danger and further isolates them from the rest of society.

According to Skolnick, this link between danger and suspicion, coupled with constant challenges to their authority, can lead police officers to over-react to "vague indications of danger suggested by appearance." These perceptions are reinforced by the police system, which encourages sensitivity to danger. Skolnick found that confining and routine jobs were considered least desirable by police officers, whereas the potentially most dangerous jobs were preferred. He concluded that officers "may well enjoy the possibility of danger, especially its associated excitement, while fearing it at the same time."[15] A similar observation was made in a survey of officers from five different police departments, which found that "even though the officers surveyed did not perceive physical injury as an everyday happening . . . nearly four-fifths of the sample believed that they worked at a dangerous job"—despite that fact that they had not faced dangerous situations themselves.[16]

Skolnick found that police officers believe that their biggest problems are relations with the public and racial issues, and that the public generally has negative, or at least nonsupportive, views of them. This feeling of isolation may increase solidarity among police officers, making them more likely to associate with one another than with people in other occupations. Isolation increases as police officers are called upon to direct ordinary citizens or restrain their freedom of action (as in traffic stops or in the questioning of citizens). The average citizen resents this intrusion and thinks or says something like "Why are the police bothering me? They should be catching crooks."[17]

Despite this conflicting and difficult task of trying to protect the public via intrusions and restraint, recent studies have found that commitment to the job remains high for police officers, even after the idealism of the early years in the profession has passed.[18] At the same time it has been shown that police officers who become alienated from the public because of personal experiences of antipolice sentiment feel less confident in their decision making and show declining motivation.[19] Despite the effects of lack of citizen support, however, police dedication to the job remains high.

Current Research on Police Attitudes toward the Public They Serve

Police officers often are viewed as cynical; that is, as believing that human conduct is motivated entirely by self-interest. A cynical person attributes all actions to selfish motives and has a pessimistic outlook on human behavior. The pioneering study of police **cynicism** was conducted by Arthur Niederhoffer, a twenty-year New York City police officer who earned a Ph.D. in sociology and began a teaching career. He was the first researcher to attempt to quantify police cynicism and explain its origins and variation among police officers.

According to Niederhoffer, cynicism is a by-product of "anomie" in the social structure. The term **anomie** was coined by sociologist Emile Durkheim

■**cynicism**
Belief that human conduct is motivated entirely by self-interest. A cynical person attributes all actions to selfish motives and has a pessimistic outlook on human behavior.

■**anomie**
A "normlessness" or lack of attachment felt by some people toward their society.

in the late 1800s to describe a "normlessness" or lack of attachment felt by some people toward their society. As Niederhoffer explained,

> As the cynic becomes increasingly pessimistic and misanthropic, he finds it easier to reduce his commitment to the social system and its values. If the patrolman remains a "loner," his isolation may lead to psychological anomie and even to suicide.[20]

Niederhoffer supported his view by pointing out that suicide rates are 50 percent higher among police officers than in the general population.

According to Niederhoffer, all police officers enter a law enforcement career with an attitude of professionalism and commitment, but all soon ex-

---

TABLE 7.1

Niederhoffer's Police Cynicism Questionnaire

For each of the following items, please place the letter of the statement which, in your opinion, is most nearly correct on the line at the left.

_____ 1. The average police superior is . . .
   a. Very interested in the welfare of his subordinates.
   b. Somewhat concerned about the welfare of his subordinates.
   c. Mostly concerned with his own problems.

_____ 2. The average departmental complaint is a result of . . .
   a. The superior's dedication to proper standards of efficiency.
   b. Some personal friction between superior and subordinate.
   c. The pressure on superior from higher authority to give out complaints.

_____ 3. The average arrest is made because . . .
   a. The patrolman is dedicated to perform his duty properly.
   b. A complainant insisted on it.
   c. The officer could not avoid it without getting into trouble.

_____ 4. The best arrests are made . . .
   a. As a result of hard work and intelligent dedication to duty.
   b. As a result of good information from an informer.
   c. Coming from the "coop."

_____ 5. A college degree as a requirement for appointment to the police department . . .
   a. Would result in a much more efficient police department.
   b. Would cause friction and possibly do more harm than good.
   c. Would let into the department men who are probably ill-suited for police work.

_____ 6. When you get to know the department from the inside, you begin to feel that . . .
   a. It is a very efficient, smoothly operating organization.
   b. It is hardly any different from other civil service organizations.
   c. It is a wonder that it does one half as well as it does.

_____ 7. Police Academy training of recruits . . .
   a. Does a very fine job of preparing the recruit for life in the precinct.
   b. Cannot overcome the contradictions between theory and practice.
   c. Might well be cut in half. The recruit has to learn all over when he is assigned to a precinct.

_____ 8. Professionalism of police work . . .
   a. Is already here for many groups of policemen.
   b. May come in the future.
   c. Is a dream. It will not come in the foreseeable future.

_____ 9. When a patrolman appears at the police department Trial Room . . .
   a. He knows that he is getting a fair and impartial trial with legal safeguards.
   b. The outcome depends as much on the personal impression he leaves with the trial commissioner as it does on the merits of the case.
   c. He will probably be found guilty even when he has a good defense.

_____ 10. The average policeman is . . .
   a. Dedicated to high ideals of police service and would not hesitate to perform police duty even though he may have to work overtime.
   b. Trying to perform eight hours of duty without getting into trouble.
   c. Just as interested in promoting private contacts as he is in performing police work.

_____ 11. The Rules and Regulations of police work . . .
   a. Are fair and sensible in regulating conduct on and off duty.
   b. Create a problem that it is very difficult to perform an active tour of duty without violating some rules and regulations.
   c. Are so restrictive and contradictory that the average policeman just uses common sense on the job, and does not worry about rules and regulations.

perience failure and/or frustration on the job. The resulting disenchantment leads to cynicism for some but renewed commitment for others. Niederhoffer believed the degree of cynicism experienced by an officer increases with age and length of experience on the job.

Niederhoffer developed a questionnaire to assess levels of cynicism and administered it to 220 male officers in the New York Police Department at various stages of their careers. The questionnaire, shown in Table 7.1, contained twenty statements, each with three response choices. Choice *a* was the **altruistic** or selfless, noncynical response; choice *b* was a neutral response; and choice *c* indicated a cynical response. The altruistic response received a score of 1, the neutral response a score of 3, and the cynical response a score of 5. Therefore, the lowest possible score one could receive

■ altruistic
Selflessly helpful and giving toward others.

_____ 12. The youth problem is best handled by police who are . . .
  a. Trained in a social service approach.
  b. The average patrolman on post.
  c. By mobile, strong-arm Youth Squads who are ready to take strong action.

_____ 13. The majority of special assignments in the police department . . .
  a. Are a result of careful consideration of the man's background and qualifications, and depend on merit.
  b. Are being handled as capably as you could expect in a large civil service organization.
  c. Depend on whom you know, not on merit.

_____ 14. The average detective . . .
  a. Has special qualifications and is superior to a patrolman in intelligence and dedication to duty.
  b. Is just about the same as the average patrolman.
  c. Is a little chesty and thinks he is a little better than a patrolman.

_____ 15. Police department summonses are issued by policemen . . .
  a. As part of a sensible pattern of enforcement.
  b. On the basis of their own ideas of right and wrong driving.
  c. Because a patrolman knows he must meet his quota even if this is not official.

_____ 16. The public . . .
  a. Shows a lot of respect for policemen.
  b. Considers policemen average civil servants.
  c. Considers policemen very low as far as prestige goes.

_____ 17. The public . . .
  a. Is eager to cooperate with policemen to help them perform their duty.
  b. Usually has to be forced to cooperate with policemen.
  c. Is more apt to obstruct police work, if it can, than cooperate.

_____ 18. Policemen . . .
  a. Understand human behavior as well as psychologists and sociologists because they get so much experience in real life.
  b. Have no more talent in understanding human behavior than any average person.
  c. Have a peculiar view of human nature because of the misery and cruelty of life which they see every day.

_____ 19. The newspapers in general . . .
  a. Try to help police departments by giving prominent coverage to items favorable to police.
  b. Just report the news impartially whether or not it concerns the police.
  c. Seem to enjoy giving any unfavorable slant to news concerning the police and prominently play up to police misdeeds rather than virtues.

_____ 20. Testifying in court . . .
  a. Policemen receive real cooperation and are treated fairly by court personnel.
  b. Police witnesses are treated no differently from civilian witnesses.
  c. Too often the policemen are treated as criminals when they take the witness stand.

SOURCE: From *Behind the Shield: Police in Urban Society* by Arthur Niederhoffer. Copyright © 1967 by Arthur Niederhoffer. Used by permission of Doubleday, a division of Bantam Doubleday Publishing Group, Inc.

TABLE 7.2

Cynicism and Police Experience

EXPERIENCE	CYNICISM SCORE
Controls on first day	42.6
Recruits 2–3 months on job	60.3
Patrolmen 2–6 years on job	64.1
Patrolmen 7–10 years	69.1
Patrolmen 11–14 years	62.9
Patrolmen 15–19 years	62.5

SOURCE: Arthur Niederhoffer, *Behind the Shield* (Garden City, NY: Anchor, 1967).

THE SOCIALIZATION MODEL

socialization model
The view that holds that police officers learn their attitudes and values from socializing experiences such as education and experience on the job.

predispositional model
The view that the attitudes and values of police officers are developed before entry into the law enforcement profession.

was 20, while the highest (i.e., most cynical) was 100. As Table 7.2 indicates, the most cynical group consisted of patrol officers with seven to ten years of experience (a score of 69.1). The least cynical group consisted of officers on their first day on the job; even a small amount of experience seemed to increase cynicism. As Table 7.2 suggests, however, cynicism is not strictly a function of experience on the job. Superiors were less cynical than patrolmen; also, college-educated patrolmen were more cynical than other patrolmen, and officers approaching retirement became less cynical.

Niederhoffer's cynicism scale was a pioneering effort—the first attempt to quantify police cynicism. Subsequent efforts in Detroit, Washington State, Idaho, and elsewhere have both validated and challenged his model. The mixed results suggest that cynicism is a multidimensional attitude caused not only by police work but by other factors.[21]

Police attitudes can come from one of two sources. One group of investigators, including Niederhoffer and Skolnick, base their work on the **socialization model:** They view the police personality as a product of learning—of education and of experience with the demands of police work. An alternative explanation, the **predispositional model,** holds that the police personality is a product of the values of individual officers.[22]

To assess the validity of the predispositional model, Richard Bennett and Theodore Greenstein administered a survey asking people to assign priorities to the values that served as guiding principles in their lives.[23] The list included choices such as a comfortable life, an exciting life, a sense of accomplishment, equality, freedom, and happiness. The respondents, all students at a state university, were divided into three groups: police officers, police science majors, and non–police science majors. Bennett and Greenstein expected that the police officers and the police science majors, who were seriously contemplating careers in law enforcement, would have similar value orientations. Interestingly, however, the opposite was the case. They found that the police science majors had value systems that were "nearly identical" to those of students majoring in other subjects but markedly different from those of experienced police officers.[24] Therefore, the researchers rejected the idea that individuals are predisposed to (enter the job with) a police personality.

These findings gained further support in a study conducted in England that compared three groups: male constables with more than two years of experience, new recruits with less than seven days on the job, and working-class male civilians. The researchers found that "police recruits have similar values to those of the population from which they are recruited, whereas there are more differences between the values of experienced policemen and the community."[25] As in the earlier study, the researchers found no empirical support for the predispositional model.

It appears from these and other studies that police officers acquire their attitudes from their work environment and that people who choose a po-

lice career do not differ from the general population in personality characteristics.[26] Despite these findings, most police departments continue to
use psychological tests and interviews as part of their recruitment process.[27]
Popular screening tests, such as the Minnesota Multiphasic Personality Inventory (MMPI) and the California Psychological Inventory (CPI), generally
have been unable to predict the on-the-job success of police applicants.[28]
Similarly, other personality screening devices have been unable to identify
the reasons that some people become police officers or to explain why some
are successful and some are not.[29]

Many investigators have tried to identify influences that prevent the development of cynical or suspicious attitudes. The most commonly recommended strategy for reducing undesirable police attitudes is college
education.[30] Alexander Smith, Bernard Locke, and William Walker conducted a series of studies on the influence of education on attitudes at John
Jay College of Criminal Justice in New York City. They looked specifically
at the effect of college education on **authoritarianism.** An authoritarian person is one prone to blind obedience to authority and strong reliance on authority—characterized by statements such as "You should listen to me
because I tell you to." The researchers compared the attitudes of officers who
were college graduates with the attitudes of police who had not attended college and with those of students who were not police officers. College education made a significant difference.[31] Police officers attending college were
less authoritarian than nonpolice at the same educational level, and police
officers graduating with a bachelor's degree were less authoritarian than officers of similar age and experience lacking a college education.

A study of one hundred officers of the Royal Canadian Mounted Police
(the federal police of Canada) provided another test of the role of education
in the formation of authoritarian attitudes. Senior police officers who were
not college graduates had more authoritarian, conservative, and rigid attitudes than did college-educated officers.[32] These studies reveal the relationship between higher education and attitudes, although they leave open
the question of whether a police officer's attitudes make a difference in his
or her performance.

Dogmatism is closely associated with authoritarianism. A dogmatic person is positive about his or her opinions even though they may be unwarranted. A dogmatic viewpoint is often based on insufficiently examined
premises. An important study examined officers' level of education, score on
a dogmatism scale, and job performance as measured by ratings on a standard police evaluation form. The researchers considered twenty factors ranging from attendance to effectiveness on the job. The results showed that
officers with higher levels of education had more open belief systems and performed in a more satisfactory manner than did those with less education.[33]
Age, length of experience, and college major did not affect this relationship.

This finding is extremely important, because it reveals the links among education, attitudes, and performance and shows how a college education plays
a direct role in this relationship. The more college education officers had at-
tained, the less dogmatic their attitudes were and the higher their job performance was rated by their supervisors. Numerous studies have corroborated

PSYCHOLOGICAL
TESTING

■**authoritarianism**
A tendency to favor blind
obedience to authority.

THE ROLE OF
EDUCATION

■**dogmatism**
An attitude characterized
by tenacious adherence to
one's opinions even though
they may be unwarranted
and based on insufficiently
examined premises.

the relationship between attitudes and performance. Most have focused on successful performance in the police training academy or in the early years on the job and have shown that higher educational levels are associated with better performance.[34] This finding is consistent with the socialization model: Education serves to change attitudes and values that form the police personality in a way that results in better performance on the job.

How Should Police Performance Be Evaluated?

Most people agree that the primary job of police is law enforcement, but police have other tasks as well. If police performance is to be evaluated, what should be the criteria? Police are expected to question citizens and make stop, frisk, and arrest decisions both quickly and accurately. Clearly, mistakes sometimes will be made, given that police often must make quick and important decisions in a small amount of time and with incomplete facts at their disposal.

To what extent should these errors be classified as poor performance? Should we hold police responsible for increases in the crime rate, or for decreases in total arrests? Should conviction rates and community service be considered? These are all significant issues if the job of policing is to be evaluated fairly and consistently, and if public expectations of police are to be realistic.

Police Discretion and Police Misconduct

For many people, the police are the closest contact they ever have with the criminal justice system. It is not surprising, therefore, that when the system is examined or criticized, police take a central role. The primary task of police is law enforcement, but that job description is not as clear as it may seem. Should police give a ticket to anyone who does not make a full stop at a stop sign? What about people who drive at 35 mph in a 30 mph zone? Should teenagers hanging out in a mall be arrested for loitering? What soon becomes evident is that although the laws in the criminal code are quite specific, it is far less clear how the police should act in practice in concrete situations.

More than forty years ago, Joseph Goldstein recognized that a police officer's decision to place a suspect under arrest "largely determines the outer limits of law enforcement."[35] Today, renewed interest in this claim is based on the observation that police have greater latitude in deciding whether to make an arrest than was once believed. Although police officers are sworn to enforce the law, they choose to take official action only part of the time. This is the essence of **police discretion:** the ability to choose between arrest and nonarrest solely on the basis of one's own judgment as a police officer. In many instances an officer warns, reprimands, or releases a person rather than making an arrest. Traffic violations, gambling offenses, prostitution, violations of liquor laws, and minor assaults are examples of crimes about which police often exercise discretion.

police discretion
An officer's ability to choose between arrest and non-arrest solely on the basis of his or her own judgment.

Police discretion upsets some people, who feel that the police are not performing their job as they should. Other people believe that full enforcement of the laws is not desired by the public (who would feel harassed), the courts (which are already overloaded), the police (who would be bogged down by court appearances), or the nation's legislatures (which may not have intended certain laws to be enforced fully). In addition, police do not have the resources that they would need in order to process each case, even if an arrest were made every time one was possible. As a result, police engage in an unofficial policy of **selective enforcement,** meaning that not all laws are fully enforced.

As Goldstein pointed out, "the mandate of full enforcement, under circumstances which compel selective enforcement, has placed the municipal police in an intolerable position" in which some laws are enforced and some are not, depending on the police officer involved, the situation, the offense, and other, possibly arbitrary, factors.[36] Whenever discretion is exercised in important matters—such as the denial of a person's liberty through arrest—without clear or consistent objectives, there is the possibility of unfairness and discrimination.

Since the issue of discretion came to prominence, researchers have focused largely on the range and appropriateness of factors that influence a police officer's decision to arrest. For example, Nathan Goldman examined 1,083 contacts between police and juveniles in four Pennsylvania cities and found that most resulted in no legal action, although arrest rates varied widely among the cities.[37] Irving Piliavin and Scott Briar found that the demeanor of juveniles—their attitude and conduct toward the officer—was the most important factor in a police officer's decision as to whether to take them into custody.[38] In Washington, D.C., Donald Black and Albert Reiss found that the complainant's preference—whether the complainant was insistent on or indifferent to arrest of the suspect—was the most important factor.[39] This study was replicated in an unnamed large midwestern city with the same results.[40] More recent studies find conflicting results regarding the impact of a suspect's demeanor in arrest situations, but the complainant's preference is clearly influential.[41] Studies assessing the type of offense and the age, education, experience, race, and gender of the officer, as well as similar attributes of the offender, have yielded inconsistent results.[42]

Although these studies help us understand the nature and scope of police discretion, they do not explain how or why discretion is used in some situations and not in others. There are several reasons for this:

- Most studies examine only a few factors that may influence police decision making and do not attempt to explain it comprehensively.

- Most do not cover a wide enough range of offenses to account adequately for discretion in serious versus nonserious crimes.

- Findings on factors influencing police decisions in one city may not hold true for police decisions in other cities.

- Many studies rely on responses to hypothetical scenarios rather than actual observations of police work.

- Even factors found to be important in police discretion do not accurately predict behavior more than 25 percent of the time.

selective enforcement
An unwritten policy under which police are not required to fully enforce all laws as written.

RESEARCH ON POLICE DISCRETION

REASONS FOR INCONCLUSIVE FINDINGS

STANDARDS
FOR POLICING

The Task Force on Police of the 1965 President's Commission noted that the arrest decision "continues to be informal, and, as a consequence, may very well serve to complicate rather than solve important social problems."[43] The commission recommended that police departments "should develop and enunciate policies that give police personnel specific guidance for the common situations requiring police discretion."[44]

In 1973 the National Advisory Commission on Criminal Justice Standards and Goals also called for specific guidelines, recommending "comprehensive policy statements that publicly establish the limits of discretion, that provide guidelines for its exercise within those limits, and that eliminate discriminatory enforcement of the law."[45] In 1974 the American Bar Association and the International Association of Chiefs of Police (ABA–IACP) jointly published standards for policing in urban areas. Their report stated that police administrators should "give the highest priority to the formulation of administrative rules governing the exercise of discretion, particularly in the areas of selective enforcement, investigative techniques, and enforcement methods."[46] According to President's Commission, the advantages of systematically drafting policy in this manner "would remove from individual [officers] some of the burden of having to make important decisions ad hoc, in a matter of seconds":

> It would create a body of standards that would help make the supervision and evaluation of the work of the individual [police officer] consistent. It would help courts understand the issues at stake when police procedures are challenged and lessen the likelihood of inappropriate judicial restriction being placed on police work.[47]

Criticisms of police arrest decisions are common. Researcher David Klinger argues that police discretion is tied to local crime rates; as crime increases, deviant acts must be more serious to result in formal action by police.[48] Thus, decision-making guidelines or policy should be developed on the basis of current practice. This idea is not new. Corresponding efforts have been made in parole decision making and in sentencing policy.[49] Although police decision making often requires spontaneous judgments, a properly developed policy based on an understanding of current practice, together with guidelines on factors that departments believe police also should consider, promotes consistent and defensible police decisions.

Police Pursuits

Police traditionally have had considerable discretion in the decision to pursue a suspect. This discretion has come under increasing scrutiny in recent years, however, because of incidents in which police chases resulted in accidents and the deaths of suspects, police, and innocent bystanders.

In 1998 the U.S. Supreme Court supported police discretion in pursuits by deciding in *Sacramento v. Lewis* that police officers can be held liable only for activities that "shock the conscience."[50] In this case a motorcyclist fled after ignoring a police order to stop. In a chase that lasted less than two minutes but reached speeds of 100 mph, the motorcycle skidded and fell. The pursuing officer was unable to stop his car in time, hitting and killing the motorcyclist. The police department was sued for the wrongful death of the motorcyclist. The U.S. Supreme Court held that the cyclist's "outrageous behavior" caused the accident and that imposing liability on the police would fail to take into account the need for split-second decision making.

It is still not clear, however, when police officers should undertake a pursuit, what the best pursuit strategies are, or when a pursuit should be terminated. An investigation of pursuits in six jurisdictions, shown in Table 7.3, found that most incidents do not involve fleeing or pursuits and that the nature of pursuits varies. A review of the circumstances of **police pursuits** found that many are unnecessary. In Miami–Dade County, a review of all 488 police pursuits occurring over five years found that only 35 percent involved suspected felonies. Forty-five percent of the pursuits were initiated for traffic violations.[51] The findings in other cities were similar: In Omaha, only 40 percent of pursuits involved suspected felonies; in Aiken County, South Carolina, 43 percent were felony pursuits.

The average time devoted to driving training at police academies is less than fourteen hours, and in-service training adds three hours per year. This training, however, focuses on the mechanics of police pursuit and defensive driving, not on the decision to engage in a pursuit. As police expert Geoffrey Alpert has observed, "It is shameful for our law enforcement agencies to expect their officers to make proper and appropriate decisions with minimal or no training."[52]

Although nearly all police departments have written policies governing pursuits, few have collected pursuit statistics to assess the effectiveness of

SACRAMENTO V. LEWIS

police pursuits
Police chases of suspects immediately after crimes have been committed.

PURSUIT MANAGEMENT TASK FORCE

TABLE 7.3			
Suspect Flight and Police Pursuits (Six Jurisdictions)			
TYPE OF FLIGHT BY SUSPECT	PERCENTAGE OF ARRESTS (N = 7,512)	TYPE OF PURSUIT BY POLICE	PERCENTAGE OF ARRESTS (N = 7,512)
No flight	93.5	No pursuit	94.4
Flee on foot	4.7	Pursue on foot	3.0
Flee in car	1.7	Pursue in car	2.4
Other	0	Pursue in helicopter	0.3

SOURCE: Joel H. Garner and Christopher D. Maxwell, "Measuring the Amount of Force Used by and against Police in Six Jurisdictions," *Use of Force by Police* (Washington, DC: National Institute of Justice, 1999).

their policy.[53] A Pursuit Management Task Force (PMTF) was created in 1996 by the National Institute of Justice to help define police practices and to see if technology might be used to protect police officers and citizens in pursuit situations. A public opinion survey has found strong support for "reasonable pursuits," but reasonableness can be difficult to define, especially in cases where pursuits continue for a long period.[54] Currently, a variety of technological alternatives are being developed and tested in an effort to both reduce and shorten police pursuits. These include helicopter support, electrical devices that stall a suspect's vehicle, and other mechanisms that hamper the ability of a suspect in a car to flee.[55]

Crime Response and Clearance Rates

One common indicator of police performance is the crime rate. If the crime rate is going up in a town, residents may claim that the police are not controlling crime effectively. Is the crime rate a fair indicator of police performance?

Police are primarily a *reactive* force. In the vast majority of cases, police are informed of an incident *after* it occurs by a complaining victim, a witness, or an alarm. (A study of police response time found that only about 6 percent of callers reported crimes while they were in progress.[56]) In addition, the National Crime Victimization Survey (NCVS) reveals that only about a third of serious crime is reported to police. It is difficult to hold police responsible for increases in the crime rate when they are not called for most crimes or are called after the incident has ended. Several other factors may cause the crime rate to rise, such as an increase in the proportion of young people in the population, higher rates of long-term unemployment, and the criminalization of drug use. Police have no control over these conditions. Thus, the crime rate is really not a useful indictor of police effectiveness.

The number of officers in a jurisdiction also is inadequate as an indicator. Police forces in the United States range in strength from 1 to 55 officers per 1,000 residents. In cities with populations of 250,000 or more, police departments vary in size from 1.7 to 7 officers per 1,000 citizens. For example, San Diego has 1.7 officers per 1,000 residents, yet has a much lower crime rate than Baltimore, with 4.6 officers per 1,000, or Houston, with 3.1 officers per 1,000 residents.[57] There is no evidence that the mere presence of more officers has any effect on the crime rate in a city.

Another common measure of police performance is the proportion of crimes cleared by arrest—that is, the proportion of "open" cases that are "closed" or solved by an arrest. This proportion is called the **clearance rate.** It could be argued that because we know the number of crimes reported, we should be able to determine how well the police perform by looking at the number of cases they clear. Table 7.4 lists police clearance rates for Index crimes. These figures show that approximately 21 percent

MEASURES
OF POLICE
EFFECTIVENESS

clearance rate
The proportion of crime cases that are "closed" or solved by an arrest.

or one in five of all Index crimes were cleared by arrest. But clearance rates, too, have drawbacks as an indicator of police performance. Low clearance rates may be due to factors other than poor police work. For example, some crimes remain "open" because police cannot spend an unlimited amount of time on an unsolved case. New crimes occur every day, and the police are forced to move on. Moreover, note that clearance rates are lowest for property offenses. Because burglary, larceny, motor vehicle theft, and arson generally occur without the knowledge or presence of the owner, a significant lag occurs between the crime and the time police are informed of it. Analyses of police investigations have found that the older the crime, the lower its chances of being solved.[58]

TABLE 7.4

Crimes Cleared by Arrest

TYPE OF CRIME	PERCENT CLEARED
Murder	69%
Forcible rape	50
Robbery	28
Aggravated assault	58
Burglary	14
Larceny	19
Motor vehicle theft	14
Arson	16
Overall clearance rate	21%

SOURCE: Federal Bureau of Investigation, *Uniform Crime Report, 1998* (Washington, DC: U.S. Government Printing Office, 1999).

Arrest and Conviction Rates

If clearance rates are not a good measure of police performance, why not use arrests as an indicator of effectiveness in controlling crime? In a given year there are more than 12 million arrests in the United States. But if there are 100 arrests in your town in a year, what does that tell you? It could be that 100 people were arrested once, or it could be that one person was arrested 100 times. Moreover, arrests provide no indication of how many cases were dismissed in court because of insufficient evidence, illegal searches, or other problems. Thus, arrests alone do not offer a good measure of police performance.

Even the number of arrests resulting in convictions is not a good indicator. In a typical year about 80 percent of all arrests are prosecuted. Of these, about 25 percent are acquitted or dismissed, and approximately 75 percent (or 60 percent of those arrested) are convicted on the same or a lesser charge.[59] The reasons for acquittals, dismissals, or reduced charges may have nothing to do with police work, however. They may involve reluctant victims or witnesses, incompetent counsel, errors in court procedure, or any number of circumstances that are beyond police control.

A superior indicator of police performance is *arrests resulting in prosecutions.* Prosecutors will not bring a case to court unless it involves a meaningful charge resulting from a legal arrest and is based on sufficient evidence. Beyond this, further criminal justice processing is the responsibility of the prosecutor. Therefore, using arrests resulting in prosecutions as a measure of police performance overcomes the limitations of using number of arrests or number of arrests resulting in convictions. In sum, the

ARRESTS RESULTING
IN PROSECUTIONS

contemporary issues and trends

Responding to Spouse Abuse

ne of the important lessons of the O. J. Simpson trial was the need for improved police response to domestic violence. Yet at the time of the Simpson case, many experts believed that the police response to these incidents had already been greatly improved.

The watershed was an incident that resulted in the 1985 judgment in *Thurman v. The City of Torrington, Connecticut.*[a] In this case a woman had been repeatedly and severely abused and threatened by her former husband, who was no longer living with her. The Torrington Police Department failed to enforce a court order prohibiting the husband from harassing her. After an attack in which her husband nearly killed her, Ms. Thurman sued the police department for negligence and for violation of her civil rights. She won the case and was awarded a settlement of $2 million.

But the question remained: How *should* police handle domestic violence cases?

The Torrington case dramatically changed the way police exercised discretion in cases of domestic violence. Police departments, and their insurers, realized that their potential legal accountability made a new policy mandatory. But the question remained: How *should* police handle domestic violence cases? As one former police chief remarked, "The chief's responsibility is to take whatever legal measures he believes wisest, based on something other than seat-of-the-pants feelings."[b]

Today 93 percent of large local police agencies and more than three-fourths of sheriff's departments have written policies concerning domestic disputes. Nearly half of these agencies also have special units to deal with domestic violence.[c]

> But the question remained: How *should* police handle domestic violence cases?

The precise actions taken by police vary by state, and sometimes even by locality. Fourteen states now have laws requiring that arrests be made in domestic violence situations. These laws were passed in response to a study in Milwaukee that found that when police made arrests there was a reduction in the number of subsequent complaints. This finding is controversial, however, because it has not been found to hold in other locations; the decline in subsequent complaints may have been due to intimidation by the arrested spouse rather than to the deterrent impact of an arrest.[d]

Victims report that police respond to more than three-fourths of domestic incidents by coming to the scene, although they appear to respond more quickly to victimizations by strangers than to victimizations by intimates.[e] This fact points to a

evaluation of police performance is an important concern and should be based only on valid, reliable, and representative indicators of police efforts to control crime.

Community Service

Evaluation of overall police performance by arrests that result in prosecutions assumes that the police spend most of their time making arrests. This is not the case, however. Examinations of calls for police service in cities as varied as Tampa, Rochester, and St. Louis have found that the vast majority of police time is devoted to noncriminal matters. It is not unusual for police to spend more than three-fourths of their working day responding to calls that have nothing to do with crime.[60]

problem in current police policies. Even in jurisdictions where police are required to arrest the offender when responding to episodes of domestic violence, they often do not do so. Some officers feel that they will place the victim in more danger by making an arrest. In other cases police departments may give these types of situations low priority or may assume that the victim will not follow through with a complaint.[f] Therefore, many cases of domestic violence continue to be handled informally.

It has been observed that police are aware of households that are at high risk of a serious domestic assault (owing to a history of complaints), but that their focus on case-by-case responses prevents effective police action *prior* to such an assault.[9] It appears that paying greater attention to problem *households*, rather than just responding to assaultive *incidents*, may hold the best prospects for long-term prevention.

1. How do you explain the different results found in various studies of the impact of arrests in domestic violence cases?

2. How do you explain the fact that 90 percent of all domestic violence cases involve men assaulting women? Why is the proportion not closer to 50 percent?

3. Why do you think society is reluctant to target problem households rather than simply having police respond to specific incidents of domestic assault?

NOTES

a. 595 F. Supp. 1521 (1985).

b. Anthony Bouza, "Responding to Domestic Violence," in M. Steinman, ed., *Woman Battering: Policy Responses* (Cincinnati: Anderson, 1991), p. 201.

c. Marianne W. Zawitz, *Violence between Intimates* (Washington, DC: Bureau of Justice Statistics, 1994).

d. Jannell D. Schmidt and Lawrence W. Sherman, "Does Arrest Deter Domestic Violence?," in Eve S. Buzawa and Carl G. Buzawa, *Do Arrests and Restraining Orders Work?* (Thousand Oaks, CA: Sage, 1996), pp. 43–53; Jeffrey Fagan, *The Criminalization of Domestic Violence: Promises and Limits* (Washington, DC: National Institute of Justice, 1996); Loretta J. Stalans and Arthur J. Lurigio, "Responding to Violence against Women," *Crime and Delinquency* 41 (October 1995), pp. 387–98; J. W. E. Sheptycki, *Innovations in Policing Domestic Violence* (Brookfield, VT: Avebury, 1993).

e. Zawitz, *Violence between Intimates*, p. 5.

f. See Eve S. Buzawa, Thomas L. Austin, and Carl G. Buzawa, "The Role of Arrest in Domestic versus Stranger Assault: Is There a Difference?," in Buzawa and Buzawa, *Do Arrests and Restraining Orders Work?*, p. 152.

g. Lawrence W. Sherman, Jannell D. Schmidt, and Daniel P. Rogan, *Policing Domestic Violence: Experiments and Dilemmas* (New York: Free Press, 1992); Shelly Feuer Domash, "Putting the Cuffs on Domestic Abusers," *Police* (January 1998), pp. 46–47.

There are two major reasons for this heavy preponderance of noncrime work: (1) Often police are the only social service agency available twenty-four hours a day, and (2) the police will deal with the social problems of the poor and disadvantaged, groups that may be underserved by other agencies. As a result, police devote the majority of their time to social service tasks. This role has expanded as problem-oriented or community policing has become popular as a means of addressing underlying problems that lead to criminal incidents.[61] For example, a concentration of burglaries, larcenies, loiterers, or vandalism in a particular neighborhood may relate to poor lighting, a local school problem, or community difficulties that can be remedied with proper analysis of the problem.[62] Public satisfaction with the police in their community service role is an important part of a valid evaluation of police performance.

What Are Some Forms of Police Corruption?

■ **police corruption**
Illegal acts or omissions by police officers in the line of duty who, by virtue of their official position, receive (or intend to receive) any gain for themselves or others.

■ **nonfeasance**
A form of police corruption involving failure to perform a legal duty.

■ **misfeasance**
A form of police corruption involving failure to perform a legal duty in a proper manner.

■ **malfeasance**
A form of police corruption involving commission of an illegal act.

In this scene, former Police Commissioner Patrick Murphy testifies before the Mollen Commission on police corruption in 1993. What are the different forms of police corruption? How can police corruption be explained? According to research, what seem to be the principal causes of police corruption? What measures against corruption have been proposed? What measures have proven most effective when undertaken? Corrupt practices are negative indicators of police performance. What are some positive indicators of police performance that can be measured objectively and systematically? What other indicators might you include?

In 1998 forty-two police officers from northern Ohio were arrested on cocaine distribution charges—the largest number of officers ever arrested in a single day in U.S. history. In the late 1990s more than 500 convictions resulted from federal investigations of police corruption in only five years.[63] How common is police corruption, and why does it occur?

Police corruption consists of illegal acts or omissions by police officers in the line of duty who, by virtue of their official position, receive (or intend to receive) any gain for themselves or others. The important elements of this definition are the illegal acts or omissions, the fact that they occur while the officer is on duty, and the intent to receive a reward for these acts. Fundamentally, police corruption is misuse of authority for personal gain.

Every encounter between a police officer and citizen involves a decision. As discussed earlier, if the behavior is serious enough, the officer will arrest the offender. In the majority of cases, however, the officer has considerable discretion in choosing a course of action. Sometimes police are offered money or other inducements to take no official action or to release a suspect. If a police officer accepts money or favors in exchange for performing or omitting a specific legal duty, he or she has committed an act of corruption.

Police corruption can take three forms: nonfeasance, misfeasance, and malfeasance. **Nonfeasance** involves failure to perform a legal duty; **misfeasance** is failure to perform a legal duty in a proper manner; and **malfeasance** is commission of an illegal act. For example, an officer who sees a car swerving down the road can legitimately pull it over. If the driver hands the officer his license with a $50 bill clipped to it and the officer takes the money, does not write out a ticket, and then proceeds to search the driver by tearing off his clothes, the officer is guilty of nonfeasance (in failing to write a ticket), misfeasance (in conducting a search improperly), and malfeasance (in accepting a bribe).

You can see that corruption is always malfeasance, whereas nonfeasance and misfeasance do not always involve corruption. For example, many police departments set enforcement priorities and ignore petty offenses in favor of serious crimes. Under these circumstances nonfeasance in certain situations represents department policy rather than an individual failure to perform a legal duty. Likewise, misfeasance is not always considered corruption. An officer's search in violation of legal rules may reflect improper understanding of the law rather than a willful attempt to circumvent it. A general definition of police corruption thus should reflect the possibility of various types of official wrongdoing.

Explanations of Corruption

Several investigators have offered useful explanations of the existence of police corruption. Some explanations focus on individual officers, some on departmental problems, and others on problems external to the department.[64]

Explanations focusing on individuals see the particular officer as the primary problem. Supporters of this view claim that if a few "rotten apples" were eliminated, police corruption would disappear. For example, some officers are seen as having "low moral caliber." If they feel underpaid, unjustly maligned by the public, or unrecognized for good work, this moral weakness may make them corruptible. Another type of corrupt officer may misuse authority for selfish ends, thinking, "I might as well make the most of the situation," actively seeking opportunities for illicit payoffs, and justifying this activity with a rationalization such as low pay or lack of recognition.[65] The case of Michael Dowd of the New York Police Department is an example of a "bad apple." Dowd was found to be organizing raids on the apartments of drug dealers to steal cash and narcotics.[66] His behavior was featured in the Mollen Commission's investigation of corruption in New York City during the mid-1990s.

Although explanations that focus on the individual officer are popular, most experts reject the "rotten apple" theory of corruption. It fails to explain how individual officers become corrupt or why police corruption is so widespread. Nor does it explain differences between departments or within a particular department over time. As one investigator notes, if corruption is to be explained in terms of a few "bad" people, then some departments must have attracted a disproportionately high number of rotten apples over long periods.[67] Michael Dowd was one of nearly fifty officers who were arrested in New York City during 1994 and 1995 on charges of brutality, drug trafficking, extortion, and civil rights violations.[68] Another drawback to the rotten apple theory, noted by the Knapp Commission in its investigation of corruption in the New York Police Department during the 1970s, is that the theory can become an excuse for command officers to deny that a serious problem exists.[69] This kind of thinking delayed FBI self-policing initiatives. In 1998 the FBI disciplined 301 employees and fired 32 of them for sexual harassment, unprofessional conduct, misuse of their position, or theft of government property. And of those punished, 44 percent had previous recorded rule violations.[70]

A second type of explanation of police corruption is the "departmental" explanation. If corruption cannot be explained in terms of a few bad apples, then the barrel itself must be examined. An example of this approach is the **deviant police subculture hypothesis.** According to this view, small groups of officers within a department have a similar outlook regarding their commitment to the job and the support they receive from superiors. If these officers feel uncommitted and unsupported, their outlook and values are reinforced by others in the group and may lead to cynicism, opening the door to corruption.[71] In New Orleans, for example, more than fifty police officers were charged with offenses including rape, assault, drug trafficking, and murder committed during the mid-1990s.[72] Group corruption in that instance suggests the existence of an organized subculture within the department that condoned illegal behavior.

■ **deviant police subculture hypothesis**
The view that some police departments have groups of officers who place loyalty to one another above obedience to the law.

Another version of the "bad barrel" explanation focuses on loyalty and secrecy within the department. A questionnaire administered by William

Westley revealed that three-quarters of the officers surveyed said they would not report on partners who engaged in a corrupt activity. Moreover, officers would perjure themselves rather than testify against their partners. When Westley asked respondents for their reasons, he found that an officer who violated the unwritten code of secrecy within the police organization was regarded as a "stool pigeon," "rat," or "outcast," even if he or she reported illegal behavior.[73]

Departmental explanations have been investigated in several studies, which have shown that certain conditions within a department can be conducive to corruption.[74] As the Pennsylvania Crime Commission found in its investigation of corruption in the Philadelphia Police Department, "Systematic corruption does not occur in a vacuum. Officers succumb to pressures within the department" such as illegal conduct by fellow officers and failure by superiors to take action against "open and widespread violations" of the law and of department policy.[75] The 1994 Mollen Commission in New York City found that beyond merely overlooking the illicit behavior of other officers, groups of officers were acting as criminal gangs.[76] A federal study of drug-related police corruption found a pattern of "small groups of officers who protected and assisted each other in criminal activities."[77] In 2000 a major police corruption scandal in the Los Angeles Police Department resulted in reversals of more than forty criminal convictions because of planted evidence and false testimony. City officials estimate that civil damages for the wrongfully convicted suspects could exceed $125 million.[78]

OUTSIDE FACTORS

A third explanation of corruption focuses on factors external to the department, especially government actions that make honest policing more difficult. For example, laws prohibiting such behaviors as gambling, personal drug use, and prostitution are difficult to enforce, because there is no complainant except the government (represented by the police). As a result, police are mandated to enforce laws that neither the offender nor the "victim" wish to have enforced. In the words of one book on the subject, "the law enforcement system is placed in the middle of two conflicting demands. On the one hand, it is their job to enforce the law, albeit with discretion; on the other hand, there is considerable disagreement as to whether or not certain particular activities should be declared criminal."[79] In this situation police may "look the other way"—or be paid to do so. Also, when arrests are made in gambling, drug, or prostitution cases and the offenders are treated leniently in the courts, it is easier for police to be drawn into corruption, because neither the public nor the criminal justice system appears to be serious about enforcing the law.

A second category of externally caused corruption stems from weak or ineffectual local government. When government is unwilling or unable to oversee or manage its police force, the operation of the department becomes haphazard, and corruption often results. In addition, corruption in the local government can spread to the police department through calls for the "protection" of illegal activities. A study of police corruption in three cities found that corruption was made possible by informal systems allowing politicians to influence personnel decisions within the police

Media and Criminal Justice

COPLAND

Traditionally, films focusing on police brutality and corruption have ultimately held the police officer's working personality to blame. However, high-profile cases alleging abuses of power and authority among officers indicate that such problems stem from a culture of police solidarity and professional privilege to which only some officers fall prey.

The movie *Copland* (1997) offers a new perspective on police culture by pointing out that cops may see policing not only as "us versus them" but perhaps also as "us against other kinds of us." The story revolves around a local sheriff of a small New Jersey town where the majority of residents are New York Police Department (NYPD) cops. A certain group of detectives from the 37th Precinct consider their bedroom community as just another jurisdiction in which to exercise their power; and Sheriff Heflin, in awe of their "supercop" reputations, is obsequious to their every whim. Even when being defeated in a video game at the local diner, Heflin hears the metallic voice inform him that "you have no authority."

It seems that Heflin had wanted to be part of the NYPD elite; but, because of hearing loss suffered when he heroically rescued a drowning motorist as a teen, he didn't qualify as a police officer. Heflin's reality—that he cannot be a "real" cop because of a demonstration of courage and sacrifice that would otherwise have made him a "good cop"—causes him great frustration as he deals with the corrupt police residents of his town. Cowed by their status, Heflin limits his career to writing traffic citations to nonresidents and settling recurring domestic disputes.

When one of the NYPD cops, Babitch, accidentally guns down a bunch of joyriding black teenagers on a bridge, his friends arrive to help him cover up his mis-

take. Within seconds Babitch is gone—presumed to have jumped off the bridge to his death, devastated by his mistake. In truth, Babitch has been smuggled back to his New Jersey "Copland," where he will stay hidden until the Internal Affairs (IA) investigation is concluded.

Heflin is soon recruited by the IA investigator, Tilden, to help infiltrate the tight-knit culture of Copland. Tilden challenges Heflin to work with him in exposing the crooked cops and finding Babitch, appealing to his deep need to do "real" police work. Questioning of the locals reveals that some of the so-called "bad" cops are genuinely torn by the ambiguity of their situation. The film offers a telling reminder that the lines between good and bad are rarely easy in police work and that even truly "good" cops can, when entrenched in the cop culture, make bad decisions.

In the end, Heflin's honesty and integrity prevail over the power-hungry police culture that has dismissed his virtues as weakness. In refusing to acquiesce to the notion of solidarity as power, Heflin proves that Copland's police culture is merely the product of individuals—who always have the ability to choose right over wrong.

Is the corruption depicted in *Copland* individual, departmental, or external/governmental? What can be done to combat the abuse of authority by officers in their residential neighborhoods? What are the dangers of extending professional courtesy to all officers based on the notion of "fraternity"?

department. "By determining who will occupy key positions of power within a department, and by making as many members of the . . . department as possible obligated to the politicians, political leaders can impose their own goals on the department—including protection of vice for the financial benefit of the political party in power or of the party leaders themselves."[80]

Other investigators have found that corruption can result from the "political climate" of the city.[81] An example is the case of Chicago. In 1998, when a new police chief was appointed, the Chicago Police Department faced accusations that police brutality was endemic. The previous chief had been forced to resign after it was discovered that he had maintained a close friendship with a convicted felon. In addition, officers had been charged with taking bribes and selling drugs. When this pervasive culture of corruption came to light, the police union blamed local politicians for placing political interests above the law.[82] In a similar vein, the City of Philadelphia also appointed a new police chief in 1998 to "improve the performance of a 7,000-officer force that has been troubled over the years by numerous accusations of brutality, graft and . . . ineptitude."[83] Both cities had a long history of political interference in department affairs and higher-than-average incidences of police brutality against citizens and corruption involving the vices.

Preventing Corruption

The most effective strategies for preventing police corruption are those based on carefully identified causes. If corruption in a particular department involves only a few officers, several control strategies may be appropriate. Examples include closely monitoring complaints against the police, making all police hirings and dismissals more visible to serve as examples and deterrents, and making sure police officers do not get into debt. Other, longer-term strategies include more exhaustive background checks of recruits; periodic retraining of all police; and measures aimed at enhancing professionalism, such as leaves for study or specialized training. These longer-term strategies are designed to improve the commitment of individual officers to the ideals and values of a law enforcement career.

If corruption is found to be due to problems in the department itself, a different set of control strategies will be appropriate. For example, establishing civilian review boards to hear complaints against the department and enhancing career mobility within the department may help prevent hidden corruption. Likewise, procedures to ensure the fair and confidential hearing of personnel matters within the department and to guarantee that promotions are based on qualifications, rather than on patronage, can help prevent political considerations from inhibiting honest police work.

When corruption is due to external, governmental factors, the most fruitful strategies involve both supervision of police and legislative decision making. A jurisdiction can improve supervision of officers by making sure that only qualified police and government officials are given supervisory responsibilities. Political reform through legislation may be needed to eliminate government interference with police department operations. Similarly, decriminalization of minor undesirable behaviors can eliminate opportunities for corruption by removing "victimless" crimes from police jurisdiction.

In its New York City investigation, the Knapp Commission found that the most important source of police corruption was control of the city's illegal gambling, narcotics, loan-sharking, and sex-related enterprises. The next most important source was "legitimate business seeking to ease its way through the maze of City ordinances and regulations."[84] In this case changes in laws and regulations could have a substantial impact on police corruption. As the Knapp Commission noted, "The laws against gambling, prostitution, and the conduct of certain business activities on the Sabbath all contribute to the prevalence of police corruption."[85] One expert has concluded that without "a public commitment . . . to realistic vice laws . . . the elimination of police corruption will not occur."[86]

THE "FLEEING FELON" RULE

■**deadly force**
The use of lethal force by police against a suspect.

■**"fleeing felon" rule**
The now obsolete common-law rule that police can use deadly force against any felon who flees the scene of a crime.

What Is Legitimate Use of Deadly Force?

There is growing controversy about the legitimate use of **deadly force** by police against citizens. When is the shooting of a suspect by police reasonable? When should the use of lethal force be prohibited? Do police discriminate in their use of force? In this section we will examine the extent of police shootings, the nature of the victims, and the constitutionality of deadly force laws.

The legal justification for police use of deadly force stems from English common law. Under common law an arresting officer could use deadly force to prevent the escape of a fleeing felon, but *not* to prevent the escape of a fleeing suspect who had committed a misdemeanor. The reason for this distinction was that in the fifteenth century most felonies were punishable by death. Death sentences could be imposed for the crimes of arson, murder, manslaughter, rape, robbery, burglary, sodomy, escape from prison, and larceny, among other offenses.

This common-law **"fleeing felon" rule** was adopted in the early years of the United States. Since then, however, the number of crimes defined as felonies has risen dramatically, whereas the use of capital punishment has dropped significantly. As a result, by the late nineteenth century the historical justification for the "fleeing felon" rule had disappeared. Also, for many offenses, the distinction between misdemeanor and felony is no longer obvious. The difference between felony larceny and misdemeanor larceny, for instance, is the value of the property taken. A police officer operating under the "fleeing felon" rule cannot readily determine whether a larceny suspect has stolen enough property to be a fleeing felon rather than a fleeing misdemeanant.

If these officers were to use deadly force in the course of their investigation, by what standards would their actions be judged? Under what circumstances would their use of deadly force be legitimate? Under what circumstances would their use of deadly force be judged illegal? What if they encounter a felon who attempts to flee from the scene? What if they see a suspect they think might have a gun to use against them?

Victims of Violent Crime Control

The National Center for Health Statistics collects information on "deaths by legal intervention"; that is, on civilian fatalities caused by police. During the 1950s there were 240 homicides by police in the nation as a whole. Between 1968 and 1976 this number was 342.[87] In the 1990s a survey of city police departments found that citizens were shot and killed at a rate of nearly 1 person for every 1,000 sworn officers.[88] Homicides by police may be underreported by 25 to 50 percent, however, because medical authorities may inaccurately determine the cause of death or omit mention of police involvement. Upon examination of death records from the California Department of Health over a seven-year period, Lawrence Sherman and Robert Langworthy found official records of 257 homicides by police. To check this number, they asked the police departments themselves for the number of police homicides that had occurred in each jurisdiction. This yielded a total of 544 homicides for the same period. As a result, the actual number of civilian deaths caused by police shootings may be significantly higher than "official" statistics indicate.[89]

The Violent Crime Control and Law Enforcement Act of 1994 requires the U.S. attorney general to obtain data on the use of excessive force by law enforcement officers. To gather this information, the Justice Department conducted a national survey of citizens ages twelve and older during 1996. This survey made it possible for the first time to estimate the prevalence of the use of force in police–citizen encounters. The results indicate that nearly 21 percent of Americans ages twelve and older (45 million people) had face-to-face contact with a police officer during 1996. Figure 7.1 summarizes these results. Of these people, an estimated 500,000 persons reported being handcuffed, hit, held, pushed, choked, threatened with a flashlight, restrained by a police dog, threatened or sprayed with a chemical or pepper spray, or threatened with a gun. That is, about 1 in 430 of all people surveyed alleged that police threatened or used force against them. About 60 percent of these individuals had aroused police suspicion, according to their own admission.[90] Future surveys will allow the study of trends in police use of force over time.

A primary objection to use of deadly force by police is that police appear to shoot blacks significantly more often than whites, leading to charges of racial discrimination. Investigations in different cities have found that blacks are shot by police two to four times more often than one would expect, given their proportion of each city's population.[91] Arnold Binder and Peter Scharf suggest that a better indicator of discrimination in police shootings would be the rate of police shootings of blacks in relation to blacks' arrest rate for violent felonies (compared to the same rates for whites). Binder and Scharf argue that "police as a general rule do not shoot college professors [white or black], physicians [white or black], infants [white or black], shopkeepers [white or black], and so on." Police do, however, shoot at

VIOLENT CRIME
CONTROL ACT

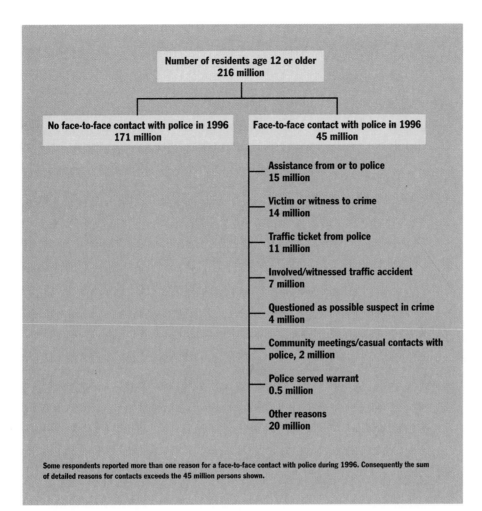

FIGURE 7.1

Persons Age Twelve or Older with Face-to-face Contact with Police in 1996

SOURCE: Lawrence A. Green-field, Patrick A. Langan, and Steven K. Smith, *Police Use of Force: Collection of National Data* (Washington, DC: Bureau of Justice Statistics, 1997).

felons, white or black. Binder and Scharf examined arrest rates for violent crimes and found that the proportion of black suspects shot by police closely mirrored the proportion of people arrested for serious crimes who were black.[92] More recent studies have found that race of officers and suspects "played no role" in predicting police use of force.[93]

Another way to determine possible racial discrimination is to examine the situational factors present in police shootings of all types. Studies have found no situational differences between white and black shooting victims in Atlanta, Kansas City, or New York City.[94] On the other hand, studies in Los Angeles, Chicago, and Memphis found police more likely to shoot blacks than whites under similar circumstances.[95] As Blumberg has noted, this variation in findings among cities "underscores the need to examine this issue on a city-by-city basis."[96] Potential discrimination in police shooting decisions remains an important issue for study and policy. These efforts will be assisted by further national surveys of police–citizen encounters conducted under the mandate of the Violent Crime Control and Law Enforcement Act of 1994.

"Fleeing Felon" and "Prowler Inside" Laws

For many years a significant element in the controversy over police use of deadly force was the lack of a uniform national standard governing the use of force by police. In 1980 a review of state laws found that eight states allowed deadly force only in defense of life or when the suspect threatened deadly force or showed a substantial likelihood of doing so. Ten states permitted deadly force by police only against individuals suspected of violent crimes. Thirty-two states, however, allowed police to shoot any "fleeing felon," including unarmed suspects fleeing from nonviolent felonies.[97]

The primary rationale given by supporters of the "fleeing felon" rule is deterrence. It is argued that the authority of police to shoot unarmed, non-violent suspects will deter future felonies. Researchers have tested this belief by comparing crime rates in cities with differing rates of police shootings. A review of these investigations concluded that "nothing in the research to date suggests that a high frequency of police shooting reduces crime rates in any way."[98] A further justification for the "fleeing felon" rule is that it increases the rate of apprehension of nonviolent felony suspects who might otherwise escape. But shootings are extremely rare in nonviolent circumstances. Given the large number of nonviolent felonies, one investigator estimated that in order to apprehend by shooting even 1 percent of nonviolent felony suspects in a year, police would have to "increase the rate at which they shot people during that year by fifty-fold."[99]

TENNESSEE V. GARNER

The debate over the use of deadly forced changed dramatically in 1985 with the ruling of the U.S. Supreme Court in *Tennessee v. Garner*. Responding to a "prowler inside call," two Memphis police officers saw a woman standing on her porch and gesturing toward an adjacent house. She told them that she had heard glass breaking and that "they" or "someone" was breaking in next door. While one officer radioed the police station, the other went behind the house. The officer heard a door slam and saw someone run across the backyard. The fleeing suspect, Edward Garner, stopped at a six-foot-high chain-link fence at the edge of the yard. The officer was able to see Garner's face and hands with his flashlight. He saw no sign of a weapon and was "reasonably sure" that Garner was unarmed. While Garner crouched at the base of the fence, the officer called out "police, halt!" and took a few steps toward him. Garner then began to climb over the fence. Convinced that Garner would escape if he made it over the fence, the officer shot him. The bullet hit Garner in the back of the head and killed him. Ten dollars and a purse taken from the house were found on his body.

The Supreme Court held in *Tennessee v. Garner* that the use of deadly force is subject to the Fourth Amendment, because such a use of force "restrains the freedom of a person to walk away," and that person is therefore "seized." Using the rationale employed in all search and seizure cases, the Court attempted to evaluate the constitutionality of the officer's action by balancing the extent of the intrusion (deadly force) against the government's interest in apprehending people suspected of crimes. The Court found the "fleeing felon" law to be unconstitutional.

> *The use of deadly force to prevent the escape of all felony suspects, whatever the circumstances, is constitutionally unreasonable. It is not better that all felony suspects die than that they escape. Where the suspect poses no immediate threat to the officer and no threat to others, the harm resulting from failing to apprehend him does not justify the use of deadly force to do so. . . . A police officer may not seize an unarmed, nondangerous suspect by shooting him dead.*[100]

This decision struck down all "fleeing felon" laws in the United States. Police are constitutionally justified in using deadly force to stop a fleeing suspect only "if the suspect threatens the officer with a weapon or there is probable cause to believe that he has committed a crime involving the infliction or threatened infliction of serious physical harm," the Court said. In the latter instance, police may use deadly force to prevent the suspect from escaping after some warning has been given "where feasible."

The Supreme Court admitted that there are practical difficulties in assessing the suspect's dangerousness, but pointed out that "similarly difficult judgments must be made by the police in equally uncertain circumstances [such as stop and frisk]." The justices also found evidence showing that during the previous ten years "only 3.8 percent of all burglaries involved violent crime." As a result, they felt that burglars cannot be presumed to be dangerous and therefore be subjected to deadly force unless additional aggravating conditions are present.

Today the use of deadly force by police has been greatly reduced. Many police departments have enacted policies that restrict the use of force according to *Tennessee v. Garner* and define "dangerousness" in specific terms to guide the decisions of police officers. The frequency with which deadly force is used now appears to be related to the extent to which departments help their officers by limiting use of force to specifically defined circumstances.[101]

Police Brutality

The case of the Haitian immigrant in New York City who was sodomized and tortured while in police custody produced a new public outcry about police brutality in the United States. Earlier, the videotaping of the 1991 Rodney King beating had done more to focus public attention on police use of force against an individual than had any previous incident. King, a twenty-five-year-old black man, was stopped by Los Angeles police for alleged violation of motor vehicle laws. He was subjected to a beating that lasted several minutes, in which he was shocked twice with stun guns and struck numerous times with nightsticks and fists by four officers while twenty-one others watched. King suffered multiple skull fractures, a crushed cheekbone, lost teeth, and a broken ankle. What made this incident vivid was the fact that a private citizen had captured it on a home video camera. The video footage was replayed numerous times on news broadcasts.

In an era of growing police professionalism, this incident looked like a step backward and a clear instance of police brutality. **Police brutality** occurs when police use excessive physical force in carrying out their duties. Many observers, including some police officials, saw the Rodney King beating as a case of excessive and intolerable behavior on the part of police.[102] Other sensational cases have resulted in heightened public concern about excessive force by police. In 2000 four New York City police officers were put on trial for killing an unarmed African immigrant, using forty-one bullets.[103] These highly publicized cases have far-reaching consequences. In the Rodney King case, the first trial ended in acquittal of the police officers, but the announcement of this verdict was followed by several days of rioting in Los Angeles. The New York City cases resulted in protests and ill will that will take years to overcome.[104]

In practice, however, the use of force by police in making arrests is relatively low. A recent study in six large metropolitan areas found that of 7,512 adult arrests, fewer than 1 in 5 involved police use of physical force in any form (use of weapon, weaponless force, or use of severe restraints).[105] These findings are presented in Figure 7.2. The study also found that when police use force, they rarely use deadly force, although the level of force usually is related to the amount of resistance offered by the suspect. One

■police brutality
Use of excessive physical force by police carrying out their duties.

In 1991 national television networks aired this video footage of police brutality in Los Angeles. The name of the victim, Rodney King, became a household word, and what happened to him sparked a wave of riots and calls for reform. What was at issue in the Rodney King case? What standards can be applied to protect police officers using reasonable force while protecting suspects from excessive force? Do you think successful civil suits against perpetrators of police brutality are the answer? What other reforms might you propose?

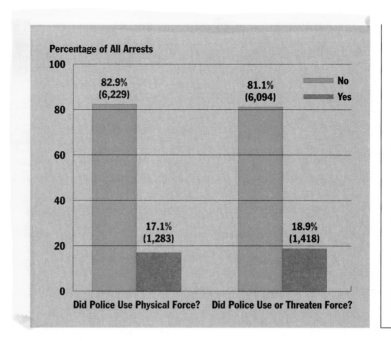

FIGURE 7.2

Arrests of Adults that Involve Force (Six Jurisdictions)

SOURCE: Joel H. Garner and Christopher D. Maxwell, "Measuring the Amount of Force Used by and against Police in Six Jurisdictions," *Use of Force By Police* (Washington, DC: National Institute of Justice, 1999).

study has found that officers are more likely to be injured when they use less force than that of a resisting suspect.[106] Nevertheless, widely publicized incidents of excessive force command the attention of both the public and policy makers.

In all cases of this kind the question is the same: What should be the limits on the use of force by police in arresting and subduing citizens? The U.S. Supreme Court addressed this issue in the 1989 case *Graham v. Connor*. It held that police officers may be held liable under the Fourth Amendment when they use excessive force.[107] In this case police handcuffed a suspect, refusing to allow him to explain that he had passed out because he was diabetic. While he was in their custody, the officers attacked him and inflicted injuries, including cut wrists, ear damage, and a broken foot. This use of force was held to be excessive according to an "objective reasonableness" standard: the perspective of a hypothetical reasonable officer on the scene. In the Rodney King case, many citizens found it difficult to accept explanations by police that the officers' use of force was "reasonable" and necessary to subdue the suspect, because the videotape appeared to speak for itself. In 1993, in a second trial, two Los Angeles police officers were ultimately convicted for violating King's constitutional rights. The following year, the City of Los Angeles settled a civil suit for damages suffered by King, who was awarded $3.8 million.

The Supreme Court's decision in *Graham* sets forth four kinds of factors that police must consider in evaluating the reasonableness of use of force: the immediacy of the threat to the officer, the severity of the crime alleged, whether the suspect is resisting arrest, and whether the suspect is attempting to escape from custody. When applied objectively, these standards protect a reasonable police officer from harm while also protecting suspects from unreasonable use of force by police.

GRAHAM V. CONNOR

critical thinking exercise

An Appropriate Remedy for Police Misconduct?

Much of the controversy over improper police searches, interrogations, and use of force focuses on the question of appropriate remedies. Should police be criminally punished, be civilly sued, have their cases thrown out of court, or suffer some other consequence if they are found to have engaged in misconduct?

Some argue that police officers should be punished as individuals for engaging in improper conduct in the course of their duties. In view of the extensive screening of police applicants, their training requirements, and the authority they hold over the liberty of other citizens, police should be held to a high standard of conduct. On the other hand, police are often asked to make quick decisions without knowing all the facts. Is it fair to punish them for decisions that seem reasonable at the time but are incorrect?

Over the years court decisions have attempted to reach a middle ground. It has been held that government officials (including police) enjoy "qualified immunity" when performing discretionary functions on the job. This means that they are shielded from liability "if their conduct does not violate clearly established statutory or constitutional rights of which a reasonable person should have known."[a]

It has also been argued that the exclusionary rule (see Chapter 5) is too permissive, because it can allow a guilty person to go free, as in the *Miranda* case. Should police misconduct benefit the suspect? One alternative is to fine or suspend a police officer who makes improper decisions that a "reasonable" officer would not make under the same circumstances. This leads to the question of whether fines or suspensions are appropriate or sufficient punishment for improper conduct.

In a majority of states, police officers who abuse their powers may be subject to "decertification proceedings" that strip of them of the ability to work as police unless they are recertified at a later date.[b] Decertification might serve as a deterrent to future police misconduct, but it does not directly address the effects of past misconduct.

CRITICAL THINKING QUESTIONS

1. Would it be a good idea to allow new court rulings (such as the *Miranda* warning) to apply only to *future* cases, rather than allowing a guilty person to go free?
2. If police officers were fined, suspended, or decertified for making certain kinds of improper decisions, how would such punishments serve the interests of justice?
3. What do you think should be done with police officers who make reasonable but incorrect decisions?

NOTES

a. *Harlow v. Fitzgerald*, 457 U.S. 800 (1982).
b. Roger Goldman and Steven Puro, "Decertification of Police: An Alternative to Traditional Remedies for Police Misconduct," *Hastings Constitutional Law Quarterly* 15 (1987), pp. 45–80; Steven Puro, Roger Goldman, and William C. Smith, "Police Decertification: Changing Patterns among the States, 1985–1995," *Policing: An International Journal of Police Strategies and Management* 20 (1997), pp. 481–96.

Summary

IS THERE SUCH A THING AS A POLICE PERSONALITY?

- Many myths and stereotypes about police develop because most people have comparatively little contact with police and tend to generalize from media images of incidents that are not typical.
- There are three styles of policing: the watchman, legalistic, and service styles.
- Current research on police attitudes toward their jobs shows that police develop these attitudes through job experiences rather than through preexisting personality traits.

- Authoritarian attitudes are more likely to be found in officers without a college education who have been on the job a long time. Officers with less education have also been found to be more dogmatic than those with higher levels of education.
- Current research on police attitudes toward the public indicates that police are affected by citizens' negative sentiment toward them but that they remain dedicated to the job.

HOW SHOULD POLICE PERFORMANCE BE EVALUATED?

- Various measures of police response to crime have been used, but most have problems stemming from the fact that the police are primarily reactive and cannot spend unlimited time on unsolved cases.
- The number of arrests resulting in prosecutions is, however, a useful indicator of police performance.
- Police spend a great deal of time on noncriminal matters, and their community service function should be taken into account in evaluations of their performance.

WHAT ARE SOME FORMS OF POLICE CORRUPTION?

- Police corruption takes three forms: nonfeasance (failure to perform a legal duty), misfeasance (failure to perform a legal duty in a proper manner), and malfeasance (commission of an illegal act).
- Some explanations of police corruption focus on individual "rotten apples," whereas others focus on the "barrel"—the whole department. Most experts reject individual explanations and suggest that there is a deviant police subculture or that corruption results from secrecy within departments.
- Still other explanations look to external factors such as laws that are difficult to enforce or a weak local government.
- Prevention of corruption depends on careful identification of its causes.

WHAT IS LEGITIMATE USE OF DEADLY FORCE?

- Research on civilian fatalities due to police shootings has found that such incidents are underreported.
- The Supreme Court has ruled that police may use deadly force to stop a suspect only if the suspect threatens the officer with a weapon or there is probable cause to believe that the suspect is dangerous.
- Police brutality occurs when police use excessive physical force in carrying out their duties.
- Police officers may be held liable under the Fourth Amendment when they use excessive force.

Key Terms

racial profiling	clearance rate
cynicism	police corruption
anomie	nonfeasance
altruistic	misfeasance
socialization model	malfeasance
predispositional model	deviant police
authoritarianism	subculture hypothesis
dogmatism	deadly force
police discretion	"fleeing felon" rule
selective enforcement	police brutality
police pursuits	

Questions for Review and Discussion

1. What is meant by selective enforcement?
2. Why is it difficult to formulate a clear policy to guide police decision making?
3. What are the key findings of research on police cynicism?
4. What factors were identified by Skolnick as leading to the development of police attitudes?
5. Why has the predisposition hypothesis been discredited as an explanation of the formation of the police personality?
6. In what way does college education influence authoritarianism in police officers?
7. How do police officers' attitudes affect their performance?
8. What are the three forms of police corruption? Give an example of each.
9. What are the three main types of explanations of police corruption?
10. What can be done to prevent police corruption?
11. What numerical measure is the best indicator of police performance in crime control?
12. What can be done to relieve police of noncriminal tasks so that they can devote more time to crime control?
13. What justification is there for the use of deadly force by police?
14. What actions have police departments taken to prevent incidents of police brutality?

Notes

1. Joseph P. Fried, "New York Officer Gets 30-Year Term in Man's Torture," *New York Times* (December 14, 1999), p. A1.
2. "Three Cops Convicted in Louima Coverup," Associated Press (March 6, 2000).
3. Jerry Oliver, "Police Target Most Likely Criminals of All Races," *Richmond Times–Dispatch* (January 30, 2000), p. C5.
4. Michael Hardy and Pamela Stallsmith, "House Kills Stricter Law on Car Belts," *Richmond Times–Dispatch* (February 10, 2000), p. 1.
5. "A New Flap over Racial Profiling," *U.S. News & World Report* (May 3, 1999), p. 10; Jeffrey Goldberg, "The Color of Suspicion," *The New York Times Magazine* (June 20, 1999), p. 50; Tammerlin Drummond, "It's Not Just in New Jersey," *Time* (June 14, 1999), p. 61.
6. Charles L. Klotzer, "Perception—Not Intent—Is What Counts," *St. Louis Journalism Review* 30 (October 1999), p. 4.
7. Haven Simmons, "Media, Police, and Public Information: From Confrontation to Conciliation," *Communications and the Law* 21 (June 1999), p. 69.
8. Pat G. Minetti and Jacqueline Stephan, "Playing for Keeps: The Importance of Strong Citizen–Police Relationships," *The Police Chief* 66 (October 1999), p. 133.
9. The URL is http://www.usdoj.gov/kidspage/
10. James Q. Wilson, *Varieties of Police Behavior* (Cambridge, MA: Harvard University Press, 1968).
11. Independent Commission on the Los Angeles Police Department, *Report of the Independent Commission on the Los Angeles Police Department* (1991).
12. Robert C. Davis and Bruce G. Taylor, "A Proactive Response to Family Violence: The Results of a Randomized Experiment," *Criminology* 35 (May 1997), pp. 307–33.
13. Roy R. Roberg and Jack Kuykendall, *Police Organization and Management: Behavior, Theory, and Process* (Pacific Grove, CA: Brooks/Cole, 1990), p. 41.
14. Douglas W. Perez, *The Paradoxes of Police Work* (Incline Village, NV: Copperhouse, 1997).
15. Jerome H. Skolnick, *Justice without Trial: Law Enforcement in Democratic Society,* 3rd ed. (New York: Macmillan, 1994), p. 46.
16. Francis T. Cullen, Bruce G. Link, Lawrence F. Travis, and Terrence Lemming, "Paradox in Policing: A Note on Perceptions of Danger," *Journal of Police Science and Administration* 11 (December 1983), pp. 457–62.
17. Skolnick, *Justice without Trial,* p. 54.

18. James C. McElroy, Paula C. Morrow, and Thomas R. Wardlow, "A Career Stage Analysis of Police Officer Work Commitment," *Journal of Criminal Justice* 27 (1999), pp. 507–16.

19. Robert C. Ankony and Thomas M. Kelley, "The Impact of Perceived Alienation on Police Officers' Sense of Mastery and Subsequent Motivation for Proactive Enforcement," *Policing: An International Journal of Police Strategies and Management* 22 (1999), pp. 120–32.

20. Arthur Niederhoffer, *Behind the Shield: The Police in Urban Society* (Garden City, NY: Anchor, 1967), p. 101.

21. G. Marie Wilt and James D. Bannon, "Cynicism or Realism: A Critique of Niederhoffer's Research into Police Attitudes," *Journal of Police Science and Administration* 4 (March 1976), p. 40; Robert M. Regoli, Eric D. Poole, and John D. Hewitt, "Refining Police Cynicism Theory: An Empirical Assessment, Evaluation, and Implications," in D. M. Peterson, ed., *Police Work: Strategies and Outcomes in Law Enforcement* (Beverly Hills, CA: Sage, 1979), pp. 59–68; John P. Crank, Robert G. Culbertson, Eric D. Poole, and Robert M. Regoli, "The Measurement of Cynicism among Police Chiefs," *Journal of Criminal Justice* 15 (1987), pp. 37–48; Robert H. Langworthy, "Police Cynicism: What We Know from the Niederhoffer Scale," *Journal of Criminal Justice* 15 (1987), pp. 17–35.

22. Richard S. Bennett and Theodore Greenstein, "The Police Personality: A Test of the Predispositional Model," *Journal of Police Science and Administration* 3 (1975), pp. 439–45.

23. Milton Rokeach, *The Nature of Human Values* (New York: Free Press, 1973).

24. Bennett and Greenstein, p. 444.

25. Raymond Cochrane and Anthony J. P. Butler, "The Values of Police Officers, Recruits, and Civilians in England," *Journal of Police Science and Administration* 8 (June 1980), pp. 205–11.

26. S. J. Saxe and M. Reiser, "A Comparison of Three Police Applicant Groups Using the MMPI," *Journal of Police Science and Administration* 4 (December 1976), pp. 419–25; L. S. Schoenfeld, J. C. Kobos, and I. R. Phinney, "Screening Police Applicants: A Study of Reliability with the MMPI," *Psychological Reports* 47 (1980), pp. 419–25; Edward E. Johnson, "Psychological Tests Used in Assessing a Sample of Police and Firefighter Candidates," *Journal of Police Science and Administration* 11 (December 1983), pp. 430–33; Jack Aylward, "Psychological Testing and Police Selection," *Journal of Police Science and Administration* 13 (Spring 1975), pp. 201–10; Bruce W. Topp and Frederic A. Powell, "A Short-Form Dogmatism Scale for Use in Field Studies," *Social Forces* 44 (December 1965), pp. 211–14; George Pugh, "The California Psychological Inventory and Police Selection," *Journal of Police Science and Administration* 15 (June 1985), pp. 172–77.

27. Beth Sanders, Thomas Hughes, and Robert Langworthy, "Police Office Recruitment and Selection: A Survey of Major Police Departments in the U.S.," *Police Forum* 5 (October 1995), pp. 1–4; Philip Ash, Karen B. Slora, and Cynthia F. Britton, "Police Agency Selection Practices," *Journal of Police Science and Administration* 17 (1990), pp. 258–69.

28. Bruce N. Carpenter and Susan M. Raza, "Personality Characteristics of Police Applicants: Comparisons across Subgroups and with Other Populations," *Journal of Police Science and Administration* 15 (March 1987), pp. 10–17; Joseph Putti, Samuel Aryee, and Tan Seck Kang, "Personal Values of Recruits and Officers in a Law Enforcement Agency: An Exploratory Study," *Journal of Police Science and Administration* 16 (1988), pp. 249–54; Stephen B. Perrott and Donald M. Taylor, "Attitudinal Differences between Police Constables and Their Supervisors," *Criminal Justice and Behavior* 22 (September 1995), pp. 326–39; Jennifer M. Brown and Elizabeth A. Campbell, *Stress and Policing* (New York: Wiley, 1994).

29. David Lester, "Why Do People Become Police Officers?: A Study of Reasons and Their Predictions of Success," *Journal of Police Science and Administration* 11 (June 1983), pp. 170–74; Deirdre Hiatt and George E. Hargrave, "Predicting Job Performance Problems with Psychological Screening," *Journal of Police Science and Administration* 16 (1988), pp. 122–25; Joyce I. McQuilkin, Vickey L. Russell, Alan G. Frost, and Wayne R. Faust, "Psychological Test Validity for Selecting Law Enforcement Officers," *Journal of Police Science and Administration* 17 (1990), pp. 289–94.

30. Matt L. Rodriguez, "Increasing Importance of Higher Education in Police Human Resource Development Programs," *CJ The Americas* 8 (April–May, 1995), pp. 1–9.

31. Alexander B. Smith, Bernard Locke, and William F. Walker, "Authoritarianism in College and Non–College Oriented Police," *Journal of Criminal Law, Criminology, and Police Science* 58 (spring 1967), pp. 128–32; Alexander B. Smith, Bernard Locke, and William F. Walker, "Authoritarianism in Police College Students and Non-Police College Students," *Journal of Criminal Law, Criminology, and Police Science* 59 (fall 1968), pp. 440–43; Alexander B. Smith, Bernard Locke, and Abe Fenster, "Authoritarianism in Policemen Who Are College Graduates and Non-College Police," *Journal of Criminal Law, Criminology, and Police Science* 61 (summer, 1969), pp. 313–15.

32. A. F. Dalley, "University vs. Non-University Graduated Policemen: A Study of Police Attitudes," *Journal of Police Science and Administration* 3 (December 1965), pp. 458–68.

33. Roy R. Roberg, "An Analysis of the Relationship among Higher Education, Belief Systems, and Job Performance of Patrol Officers," *Journal of Police Science and Administration* 6 (September 1978), pp. 336–44; Milton Rokeach, *The Open and Closed Mind* (New York: Basic Books, 1960).

34. Elizabeth J. Shusman, Robin E. Inwald, and Hilary Knatz, "A Cross-Validation Study of Police Recruit Performance as Predicted by the IPI and MMPI," *Journal of Police Science and Administration* 15 (June 1987), pp. 162–68; Gerald Gruber, "The Police Applicant test: A Predictive Validity Study," *Journal of Police Science and Administration* 14 (June 1986), pp. 121–29; George E. Hargrave and Deirdre Hiatt, "Law Enforcement Selection with the Interview, MMPI, and CPI: A Study of Reliability and Validity," *Journal of Police Science and Administration* 15 (June 1987), pp. 110–17; Anthony R. Moriarty and Mark W. Field, *Police Officer Selection* (Springfield, IL: Thomas, 1994). See also Mary Ann Wycoff and Timothy N. Oettmeier, *Evaluating Patrol Office Performance under Community Policing* (Washington, DC: National Institute of Justice, 1994); Joseph E. Talley and Lisa D. Hinz, *Performance Prediction of Public Safety and Law Enforcement Personnel* (Springfield, IL: Thomas, 1990).

35. Joseph Goldstein, "Police Discretion Not to Invoke the Criminal Process: Low-Visibility Decisions in the Administration of Justice," *Yale Law Journal* 69 (1960), p. 543.

36. Ibid., p. 580.

37. Nathan Goldman, *The Differential Selection of Juvenile Offenders for Court Appearance* (Hackensack, NJ: National Council on Crime and Delinquency, 1963).

38. Irving Piliavin and Scott Briar, "Police Encounters with Juveniles," *American Sociological Review* 70 (September 1964), pp. 206–14.

39. Donald J. Black and Albert J. Reiss, "Police Control of Juveniles," *American Sociological Review* 35 (1970), pp. 63–77.

40. Richard J. Lundman, Richard E. Sykes, and John P. Clark, "Police Control of Juveniles: A Replication," *Journal of Research in Crime and Delinquency* 15 (1978), pp. 74–91.

41. David A. Klinger, "More on Demeanor and Arrest in Dade County," *Criminology* 34 (February 1996), pp. 61–82; Robert E. Worden and Robin L. Shephard, "Demeanor, Crime, and Police Behavior: A Reexamination of the Police Services Study Data," *Criminology* 34 (February 1996), pp. 83–105; Richard E. Sykes, James E. Fox, and John P. Clark, "A Socio-Legal Theory of Police Discretion," in Arthur Niederhoffer and Abraham Blumberg, eds., *The Ambivalent Force*, 2nd ed. (Hinsdale, IL: Dryden, 1976), pp. 171–83.

42. James O. Finckenauer, "Higher Education and Police Discretion," *Journal of Police Science and Administration* 3 (1975), pp. 450–65; Wayne R. LaFave, *Arrest: The Decision to Take a Suspect into Custody* (Boston: Little, Brown, 1965); James O. Finckenauer, "Some Factors in Police Discretion and Decisionmaking," *Journal of Criminal Justice* 4 (1976), pp. 29–46; Imogene L. Moyer, "Demeanor, Sex, and Race in Police Processing," *Journal of Criminal Justice* 9 (1981), pp. 235–46; Dennis D. Powell, "A Study of Police Discretion in Six Southern Cities," *Journal of Police Science and Administration* 17 (1990), pp. 1–7; Stephen D. Mastrofski, Robert E. Worden, and Jeffrey B. Snipes, "Law Enforcement in a Time of Community Policing," *Criminology* 33 (1995), pp. 539–63; David A. Klinger, "Demeanor or Crime?: Why 'Hostile' Citizens Are More Likely to Be Arrested," *Criminology* 32 (1994), pp. 475–93; Richard J. Lundman, "Demeanor or Crime?: The Midwest Police–Citizen Encounters Study," *Criminology* 32 (1994), pp. 631–56.

43. President's Commission on Law Enforcement and Administration of Justice, *Task Force Report on Police* (Washington, DC: U.S. Government Printing Office, 1967), p. 22.

44. President's Commission on Law Enforcement and Administration of Justice, *The Challenge of Crime in a Free Society* (Washington, DC: U.S. Government Printing Office, 1967), p. 103.

45. National Advisory Commission on Criminal Justice Standards and Goals, *Report on Police* (Washington, DC: U.S. Government Printing Office, 1973), p. 21.

46. American Bar Association, *The Urban Police Function* (Gaithersburg, MD: International Association of Chiefs of Police, 1974), p. 8.

47. President's Commission on Law Enforcement and Administration of Justice, *The Challenge of Crime in a Free Society*, p. 271.

48. David A. Klinger, "Negotiating Order in Patrol Work: An Ecological Theory of Police Response to Deviance," *Criminology* 35 (May 1997), pp. 277–306.

49. Don M. Gottfredson, Leslie T. Wilkins, and Peter B. Hoffman, *Guidelines for Parole and Sentencing Policy: A Policy Control Method* (Lexington, MA: Lexington Books, 1978).

50. *Sacramento v. Lewis*, 118 S. Ct. 1708 (1998).

51. Geoffrey P. Alpert, "Pursuit Driving: Planning Policies and Action from Agency, Officer, and Public Information," *Police Forum* (January 1997), pp. 1–12.

52. Alpert, "Pursuit Driving," p. 3.

53. Geoffrey P. Alpert, "Analyzing Police Pursuit," *Criminal Law Bulletin* 27 (July–August 1991), pp. 358–67.

54. *Pursuit Management Task Force* (Washington, DC: National Institute of Justice, 1998).

55. Geoffrey P. Alpert, *Helicopters in Pursuit Operations* (Washington, DC: National Institute of Justice, 1998).

56. Marianne W. Zawitz, ed., *Report to the Nation on Crime and Justice,* 2nd ed. (Washington, DC: Bureau of Justice Statistics, 1988).

57. Brian A. Reaves and Andrew L. Goldberg, *Law Enforcement and Administrative Statistics, 1997* (Washington, DC: Bureau of Justice Statistics, 1999).

58. Peter Greenwood, Jan M. Chaiken, and Joan Petersilia, *The Criminal Investigation Process* (Lexington, MA: Lexington Books, 1977); John E. Eck, *Solving Crimes: The Investigation of Burglary and Robbery* (Washington, DC: Police Executive Research Forum, 1983).

59. Jacob Perez, *Tracking Offenders* (Washington, DC: Bureau of Justice Statistics, 1991).

60. George Autunes and Eric J. Scott, "Calling the Cops: Police Telephone Operators and Citizen Calls for Service," *Journal of Criminal Justice* 9 (1981); David H. Bayley, *Police for the Future* (New York: Oxford University Press, 1994), ch. 2; Elaine Cumming, Ian Cumming, and Laura Edell, "Policemen as Philosopher, Guide and Friend," *Social Problems* 12 (1965).

61. William Spelman and John E. Eck, *Problem-Oriented Policing* (Washington, DC: National Institute of Justice, 1987).

62. Lorraine Green Mazerolle and William Terrill, "Problem-Oriented Policing in Public Housing: Identifying the Distribution of Problem Places," *Policing: An International Journal of Police Strategies and Management* 20 (1997), pp. 235–55; Richard H. Ward, "On the Cutting Edge: Policing Research Shows Changes," *Criminal Justice: The Americas* 1 (August–September, 1988), p. 1.

63. Warren Cohen, "The Feds Make a Cop Drug Bust," *U.S. News & World Report* (February 2, 1998), p. 36; Kevin Johnson, "42 Law Officers Arrested in Sting," *USA Today* (January 22, 1998), p. 3.

64. Mark Pogrebin and Burton Atkins, "Probable Causes for Police Corruption: Some Theories," *Journal of Criminal Justice* 4 (1976), pp. 9–16; Samuel Walker, *The Police in America* (New York: McGraw-Hill, 1983).

65. Herman Goldstein, *Policing in a Free Society* (Cambridge, MA: Ballinger, 1977); Virgil Peterson, "The Chicago Police Scandals," *Atlantic* (October 1960), pp. 58–64; Howard S. Cohen and Michael Feldberg, *Power and Restraint: The Moral Dimension of Police Work* (New York: Praeger, 1991); Edwin J. Delattre, *Character and Cops: Ethics in Policing*, 2nd ed. (Washington, DC: AEI Press, 1994); Steve Herbert, "Morality in Law Enforcement: Chasing 'Bad Guys' with the Los Angeles Police Department," *Law and Society Review* 30 (1996), pp. 799–817.

66. Gordon Witkin, "When the Bad Guys are Cops," *Newsweek* (September 11, 1995), pp. 20–22; Mike McAlary, *Good Cop Bad Cop* (New York: Pocket Books, 1994).

67. Walker, *The Police in America*, p. 181.

68. Witkin, "When the Bad Guys are Cops," pp. 20–22; Tom Morganthau, "Why Good Cops Go Bad," *Newsweek* (December 19, 1994), p. 34.

69. Knapp Commission, *Report on Police Corruption* (New York: Braziller, 1972), p. 6.

70. Michael Hedges, "Lawbreakers among Law Enforcers," *Richmond Times–Dispatch* (August 10, 1999), p. 3.

71. John Kleinig, *The Ethics of Policing* (New York: Cambridge University Press, 1996).

72. Witkin, p. 22.

73. William A. Westley, *Violence and the Police* (Cambridge, MA: MIT Press, 1970).

74. Albert J. Reiss, *Police and the Public* (New Haven: Yale University Press, 1971); J. Roebuck and T. Barker, "A Typology of Police Corruption," *Social Problems* 21 (1974), pp. 423–27; E. Stoddard, "The Informal Code of Police Deviancy: Group Approach to Blue Coat Crime," *Journal of Criminal Law, Criminology, and Police Science* 59 (1968), pp. 201–13.

75. Pennsylvania Crime Commission, *Report on Police Corruption and the Quality of Law Enforcement in Philadelphia* (St. Davids: Pennsylvania Crime Commission, 1974).

76. Morganthau, "Why Good Cops Go Bad," p. 34.

77. U.S. Comptroller General, *Information on Drug-Related Police Corruption* (Washington, DC: U.S. General Accounting Office, 1998).

78. James Sterngold, "Police Corruption Inquiry Expands in Los Angeles," *New York Times* (February 11, 2000), p. A16; "L. A. Mayor: Use Tobacco Funds to Pay Police Suits," *USA Today* (February 18, 2000), p. 3.

79. William Chambliss and R. Seidman, *Law, Order and Power* (Reading, MA: Addison-Wesley, 1971), p. 490.

80. Lawrence W. Sherman, *Scandal and Reform: Controlling Police Corruption* (Berkeley: University of California Press, 1978), p. 35.

81. John A. Gardiner, *The Politics of Corruption: Organized Crime in an American City* (New York: Russell Sage, 1970); Chambliss and Seidman, *Law, Order, and Power*; Knapp Commission, *Report on Police Corruption*.

82. Dirk Johnson, "Popular Detective Will Head Chicago Police," *New York Times* (February 19, 1998), p. 2.

83. B. Drummond Ayres, Jr., "Former New York Official to Lead Philadelphia Police," *New York Times* (February 19, 1998), p. 16.

84. Knapp Commission, *Report on Police Corruption*, p. 68.

85. Ibid., p. 18.

86. Edward A. Malloy, *The Ethics of Law Enforcement and Criminal Punishment* (Lanham, MD: University Press of America, 1982), p. 45.

87. Gerald D. Robin, "Justifiable Homicide by Police Officers," *Journal of Criminal Law, Criminology, and Police Science* (June 1963), pp. 225–31; Arthur L. Kobler, "Police Homicide in a

Democracy," *Journal of Social Issues* 31 (1975), pp. 163–91; Cynthia G. Sulton and Phillip Cooper, "Summary of Research on the Police Use of Deadly Force," in Robert N. Brenner and Marjorie Kravitz, eds., *A Community Concern: Police Use of Deadly Force* (Washington, DC: U.S. Government Printing Office, 1979).

88. Anthony M. Pate and Lorie A. Fridell, *Police Use of Force: Official Reports, Citizens Complaints, and Legal Consequences* (Washington, DC: Police Foundation, 1993).

89. Lawrence W. Sherman and Robert H. Langworthy, "Measuring Homicide by Police Officers," *Journal of Criminal Law and Criminology* (winter 1979), pp. 546–60; Tom McEwen, *National Data Collection on Police Use of Force* (Washington, DC: Bureau of Justice Statistics, 1996).

90. Lawrence A. Greenfeld, Patrick A. Langan, and Steven K. Smith, *Police Use of Force: Collection of National Data* (Washington, DC: Bureau of Justice Statistics, 1997).

91. James J. Fyfe, *Shots Fired: An Examination of New York City Police Firearms Discharges* (Albany: State University of New York at Albany Ph.D. Dissertation, 1978); Richard W. Harding and Richard P. Fahey, "Killings by Chicago Police," *Southern California Law Review* (March 1973), pp. 284–315; Marshall W. Meyer, "Police Shooting at Minorities: The Case of Los Angeles," *The Annals* (November 1980), pp. 98–110; C. H. Milton, J. W. Hallack, J. Lardner, and G. L. Abrecht, *Police Use of Deadly Force* (Washington, DC: Police Foundation, 1977); Robin, "Justifiable Homicide."

92. Arnold Binder and Peter Scharf, "Deadly Force in Law Enforcement," *Crime and Delinquency* 28 (January 1982), pp. 1–23.

93. Joel Garner, John Buchanan, Tom Schade, and John Hepburn, *Understanding the Use of Force by and against Police* (Washington DC: National Institute of Justice, 1996).

94. Mark Blumberg, "Race and Police Shootings: An Analysis in Two Cities," in James J. Fyfe, ed., *Contemporary Issues in Law Enforcement* (Beverly Hills, CA: Sage, 1981); James J. Fyfe, "Blind Justice: Police Shootings in Memphis," *Journal of Criminal Law and Criminology* 83 (summer, 1982).

95. Jerome H. Skolnick and James J. Fyfe, *Above the Law: Police and the Excessive Use of Force* (New York: Free Press, 1993); William A. Geller and Hans Toch, eds., *And Justice for All: Understanding and Controlling Police Abuse of Force* (Washington, DC: Police Executive Research Forum, 1995); Geoffrey P. Alpert and Lorie A. Fridell, *Police Vehicles and Firearms: Instruments of Deadly Force* (Prospect Heights, IL: Waveland Press, 1992).

96. Mark Blumberg, "Research on Police Use of Deadly Force: The State of the Art," in Abraham Blumberg and Elaine Niederhoffer, eds., *The Ambivalent Force: Perspectives on the Police*, 3rd ed. (New York: Holt, Rinehart, and Winston, 1985), p. 344.

97. Lawrence W. Sherman, "Execution without Trial: Police Homicide and the Constitution," *Vanderbilt Law Review* (January 1980), pp. 71–100.

98. James J. Fyfe, "Observations on Police Deadly Force," *Crime and Delinquency* 27 (July 1981), pp. 376–89; Brenner and Kravitz, eds., *A Community Concern.*

99. Fyfe, 1981, p. 381.

100. *Tennessee v. Garner*, 105 S. Ct. 1694 (1985).

101. Skolnick and Fyfe, *Above the Law*; James J. Fyfe, "Police Use of Deadly Force: Research and Reform," *Justice Quarterly* 5 (June 1988), pp. 165–205; U.S. Comptroller General, *Use of Force* (Washington, DC: U.S. General Accounting Office, 1996).

102. Lance Morrow, "Rough Justice," *Time* (April 1, 1991), pp. 16–17; Richard Lacayo, "Law and Disorder," *Time* (April 1, 1991), pp. 18–21.

103. Kit R. Roane, "Are Police Going Too Far?," *U.S. News & World Report* (February 7, 2000), p. 25.

104. Nicholas Stix, "Liberal Community Activists Attack Aggressive, 'Racist' Police as the Enemy in Crime-Ridden Cities," *Insight on the News* (April 26, 1999), p. 29; John O'Sullivan, "Black and Blue: New York Erupts over a Race-Tinged Killing—Again," *National Review* (April 19, 1999), p. 33; David Dante Troutt, "Screws, Koon, and Routine Aberrations: The Use of Fictional Narratives in Federal Police Brutality Prosecutions," *New York University Law Review* 74 (April, 1999), pp. 18–122.

105. Joel H. Garner and Christopher D. Maxwell, "Measuring the Amount of Force Used by and against the Police in Six Jurisdictions," in *Use of Force by Police* (Washington, DC: National Institute of Justice, 1999).

106. Geoffrey P. Alpert and Roger G. Dunham, "The Force Factor: Measuring and Assessing Police Use of Force and Suspect Resistance," in *Use of Force by Police* (Washington, DC: National Institute of Justice, 1999).

107. *Graham v. Connor*, 490 U.S. 396 (1989).

eight
Criminal Courts

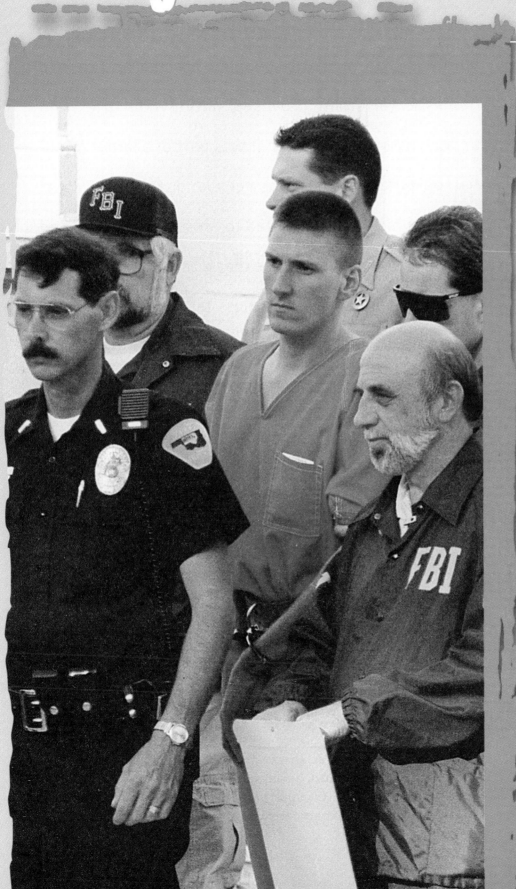

Timothy McVeigh was convicted

in 1997 for the Oklahoma City federal office building bombing that killed 168 people. This shocking case of domestic terrorism provoked nationwide grief and anger—as well as fear that it was part of a larger criminal conspiracy. The case was a challenge to the U.S. court system, which was mandated to prosecute, defend, and adjudicate objectively a case that was on the front page of newspapers and in countless television reports for weeks. How do U.S. courts come to fair and impartial decisions in sensational cases such as this one?

How Were Criminal Courts Similar and Different in the Past?

Of the more than 11 million arrests made in the United States each year, far fewer than 1 percent are for murder. The overwhelming majority of court cases involve misdemeanors, because those are the offenses that are most often committed and for which suspects are most often arrested. If we examine the historical record of both misdemeanor and felony trials and compare it to contemporary court proceedings, we find both striking similarities and significant differences.

For example, compare the O. J. Simpson case with one that occurred two centuries ago. In 1995 O. J. Simpson, a successful and popular former football player, was charged with brutally killing his estranged wife and another man with a knife. There was circumstantial evidence, such as shoe prints and blood, that tended to incriminate him. On the other hand, there were no eyewitnesses; no murder weapon was recovered; there was no apparent motive; and questions were raised about whether the physical evidence had been tampered with. The O. J. Simpson case was unique in many ways. Most notably, it is rare for such a popular celebrity to be a defendant in a murder trial. It is also rare to have so little conclusive physical evidence linking a particular person with a murder of this nature.

In the year 1800 the body of Gulielma Sands was found in a well. Her cousin, Catherine Ring, was suspected of the crime because she lived with Sands. A coroner had concluded that the death was due to willful murder, and there were no other suspects. Ring was indicted for the crime, but she had an alibi and the assistance of a "dream team" of defense attorneys that included Alexander Hamilton and Aaron Burr, who were among the most well-known Americans at that time. It was a long trial involving seventy-five witnesses. The trial procedure was similar to today's procedure, though less cumbersome; and, in a striking similarity to the Simpson case, the jury returned a verdict of acquittal in five minutes.[1] The historical record shows that both the Ring and Simpson trials are atypical, because murders are uncommon, murder trials are rare, and long, celebrated murder cases are rarer still.

A major difference between trials today and trials in earlier centuries is the absence of lawyers in times past, even in felony trials. Defense attorneys were not required in most types of cases until 1963, when the U.S. Supreme Court ruled in *Gideon v. Wainwright* that indigent defendants charged with felonies were guaranteed the right to an attorney at trial—a right that has since been expanded to most other stages of criminal procedure. It took the Supreme Court nearly 200 years to interpret the Sixth Amendment "right to counsel" as applying to all defendants, even poor ones. Most earlier trials, for both felonies and misdemeanors, took place without the accused being represented by a lawyer.

Misdemeanor cases historically have tended to be handled in an "amateur" or nonprofessional fashion. As in today's TV *People's Court* series, individuals, often neighbors, brought small claims against one another without benefit of legal counsel on either side. Minor criminal cases were treated the same way until the late twentieth century. A century ago many cities had local aldermen or justices of the peace who would hear and decide cases for a fee. Their role was similar to that of today's local judges, except that aldermen were untrained in the law and were not paid a salary. As one historian has written, "In some ways a [minor] criminal case was not much more than a civil suit with a government subsidy." And although there was no such penalty as banishment, the historical record has frequent references to local alderman and magistrates telling minor offenders to "get out of town."[2]

The nature of justice was indeed informal in cases involving minor crimes; and in many ways this is still true, although the presence of legal counsel in these cases has expanded dramatically since the 1960s. In typical felony cases (robbery, burglary, larceny, and assault), however, the court system has always been more formal and the criminal procedure more elaborate. The United States initially modeled its grand jury system on England's, which required that a group of citizens find probable cause before a

felony case could go to trial. This rule resulted in greater deliberation on the merits of a case. Since then, the U.S. Supreme Court has granted states the right to determine probable cause using other procedures, such as preliminary hearings.[3] Thus, the right to a trial by jury is guaranteed in the Bill of Rights but until recently was reserved for serious cases.

Historically, juries consisted of white males. Even after the Civil War, some states excluded blacks from juries until the U.S. Supreme Court specifically ruled against this practice in 1879.[4] In the past, as today, people generally were reluctant to serve on juries. Historical records reveal that people have routinely attempted to evade jury service despite believing that a jury system is fundamental to fair trial.[5]

Another change is the role of the defendant in criminal cases. Until the late 1800s a defendant had no say in his or her own case. A defendant could not act as a witness or take the stand in his or her own defense. Beginning just over a century ago, both the states and the federal government permitted defendants to testify under oath. This made the role of defendants and defense counsel more significant, because a defendant could take an active role rather than being limited to reacting indirectly to prosecution's allegations. Today, defendants are expected to testify and those who do not are often seen as having something to hide.

How Did the State and Federal Court Systems Develop?

Before the nation's founding, each colony had its own court system. Under the Constitution the states retained significant powers, including the powers to create, enforce, and apply laws. During the colonial period punishments generally were more severe, and the death penalty was permitted for virtually all felonies, including crimes such as stealing crops, sacrilege, sodomy, and trading with Indians.[6] The severity of punishment may have stemmed both from the uncertainty and dangerousness of frontier life and from the association of crime with sin. Civil laws often were used to enforce moral and religious behavior. Fines and imprisonment also were used to punish blasphemy, failure to attend church, and violation of accepted religious practices.

During the American Revolution the courts increasingly were used as a forum to dispute "unjust" laws imposed by England, such as laws that taxed the colonies for paper, tea, various other imports, and trade with non-English nations. Because of shortages of desired goods and the high prices people had to pay when these goods were obtained by legitimate means, smuggling became common. Customs officials often were harassed, threatened, and beaten, but few juries were willing to convict alleged assailants. It was argued in court that taxation on the colonies without representation in the British Parliament was unjust. Unlike juries today, juries at that time were permitted to address the legitimacy of a law rather than the illegal act alone.[7] The establishment of the United States in the late eighteenth century, the rapid growth of a population that included immigrants from many nations, and rapid urbanization created a need for more courts with specialized tasks. Differing legal and social cultures often clashed, requiring court systems to decide disputes neutrally.

State Court Systems

The majority of criminal cases are heard in state courts, because most felonies are defined by state laws. For example, murder generally is a violation of state law—unless one kills the President of the United States. Robbery also is a violation of state law, unless it is a robbery of a federally insured bank. In these cases, the murder or robbery would be adjudicated in a federal court as a violation of federal law. As you read in Chapter 2, the definitions of murder, robbery, and other crimes are quite similar among the states, but often there are significant differences as well: in the variations and degrees of these crimes, in aggravating or mitigating circumstances, and in the penalties that may be imposed. These differences are permitted under the Tenth Amendment to the Constitution, which grants police power to the states.

State courts interpret only state law. Courts in all states are organized in a similar manner, with three levels of jurisdiction: limited, general, and appellate. Each state determines how its system is organized, however, so the names of the state courts and their precise jurisdictions vary.

As an example, Figure 8.1 diagrams the court system in the Commonwealth of Virginia. Cases flow from the lower courts (at the bottom of the diagram) up through the court of last resort. General district courts and juvenile and domestic relations courts have restricted jurisdiction over a specific range of matters; circuit courts are the general trial courts; and the court of appeals and Supreme Court of Virginia are the two appellate courts in the state.

STATE COURTS INTERPRET STATE LAW

MUNICIPAL COURTS

FIGURE 8.1
Virginia Court Structure

SOURCE: http://www.courts.
state.va.us/cib/cib.htm

LIMITED AND GENERAL JURISDICTIONS As you read in Chapter 5, in all states, the lowest (i.e., most restricted) courts are the courts of limited jurisdiction, such as municipal courts. Their legal authority is restricted to certain specific types of cases. For example, small claims courts hear only civil cases involving amounts less than $10,000. Surrogate courts hear cases involving probate of wills and administration of estates. Family courts hear matters involving children and the family, such as cases of juvenile

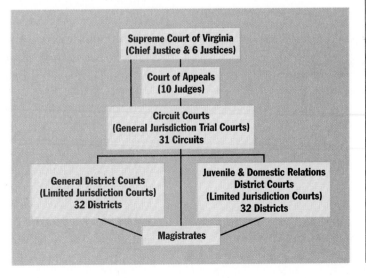

What are the origins of the American criminal court system? How are the courts organized in terms of jurisdictions and the types of cases they hear? Where are most cases heard? What is the purpose of courts of appeal? What is the purpose of U.S. Supreme Court? How does the court system reflect American history and government?

TRIAL COURTS

delinquency, child protection, status offenders, foster care placement, paternity suits, family offenses, support of dependent relatives, and adoptions. Municipal courts include all city, town, village, and district courts. These courts handle trials for minor criminal and civil cases, traffic and motor vehicle violations, and ordinance violations, and conduct probable cause hearings for felonies. Each type of limited jurisdiction court is permitted to hear only a narrow range of alleged offenses involving mostly civil cases.

Courts of general jurisdiction often are referred to as trial courts. Most felony trials are held at this level. In sixteen states general jurisdiction courts are called circuit courts. Fifteen states call them district courts, twelve call them superior courts, and the balance use a combination of names or other names. Each county usually has one felony court, making a nationwide total of 3,235.[8] General jurisdiction courts hear felony trials and civil suits involving amounts that are too large to be handled in small claims court.

APPELLATE COURTS At the highest level of state court systems are appellate courts, which hear appeals from courts of general jurisdiction. Appellate courts usually have a panel of three to nine judges (justices) who hear arguments in cases that are referred to them from lower courts. Trials are not held in appellate courts, only arguments on specific legal issues. For example, in the *Miranda* case the appellate courts heard arguments about whether or not the defendant's confession was obtained voluntarily. Other aspects of the case that were part of the trial were not reconsidered, because they were not a basis for the appeal. As explained in Chapter 5, if the justices of an appellate court believe an error was made in law or procedure in a court of general jurisdiction, they refer the case back to that court for retrial. Most states also have a higher appellate court known as a supreme court. The state supreme court is the court of last resort for appeals from lower courts in that state.

The Federal Court System

The federal court system parallels the state court systems. Federal courts exist at three levels of jurisdiction, but they hear only cases involving alleged violations of federal laws. In most cases federal laws are designed to adjudicate misconduct that occurs in more than one state. Interstate transportation of stolen property, kidnapping across state lines, and some forms of drug trafficking are examples. Figure 8.2 diagrams the federal court system in the United States. As in state courts, there is a case flow from courts of limited jurisdiction to courts of general jurisdiction to appellate courts.

The U.S. Court of Claims, U.S. Customs courts, and the U.S. Tax Court are examples of federal courts. The titles of these courts indicate their limited jurisdictions. Many of these courts were created by Congress and are therefore called legislative courts. Congress has greater control over courts it has created than over courts created by the Constitution. The jurisdiction of legislative courts and the terms of office for judges can be changed by an

EXAMPLES OF FEDERAL COURTS

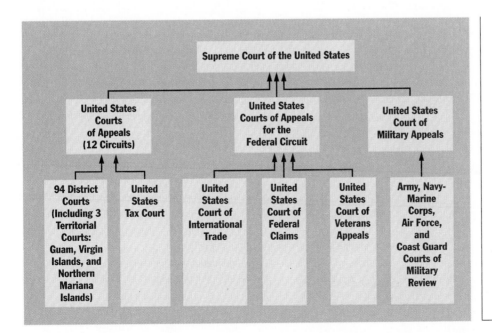

FIGURE 8.2
The Federal Court System

SOURCE: http://www.uscourts.gov/understanding_courts/gifs/figure1.gif

act of Congress. In constitutional courts, in contrast, the authority of the courts does not rely on legislative acts.

DISTRICT COURTS AND COURTS OF APPEALS   The federal courts of general jurisdiction are the **U.S. district courts.** These courts have unlimited jurisdiction in both civil and criminal matters, and most federal trials are conducted in them. The trials in the Oklahoma City bombing case occurred in a U.S. district court, because the bombing was an attack on a federal building and resulted in the death of federal agents. In addition, district courts also hear appeals from the courts of limited jurisdiction. There are ninety-four U.S. district courts in the United States, with at least one in each state. They can hear cases involving alleged violations of federal law wherever they may occur. Larger states may have several federal district courts.

Above the courts of general jurisdiction are the appellate courts. In the federal system, as in many states, there are two levels of appellate courts. The first level is the intermediate appellate court, which reviews judgments handed down in the federal trial courts. These intermediate appellate courts are the **U.S. courts of appeals.** There are thirteen of these courts, located in federal judicial districts throughout the United States. Figure 8.3 illustrates the composition of the federal judicial districts or circuits. Each district groups three or more states, and all federal appeals from those states are directed to the court of appeals in that circuit. The courts of appeals were created in 1891 to take some of the burden off the nation's court of last resort, the U.S. Supreme Court.

THE U.S. SUPREME COURT   The **U.S. Supreme Court** can hear on appeal any case involving federal law, suits between states, and cases involving interpretations of the U.S. Constitution. The decisions of the U.S. Supreme

■ **U.S. district courts**
Federal trial courts of general jurisdiction.

■ **U.S. courts of appeals**
Intermediate federal appellate courts.

■ **U.S. Supreme Court**
The highest court in the United States, which hears final appeals in cases involving federal law, suits between states, and interpretations of the U.S. Constitution.

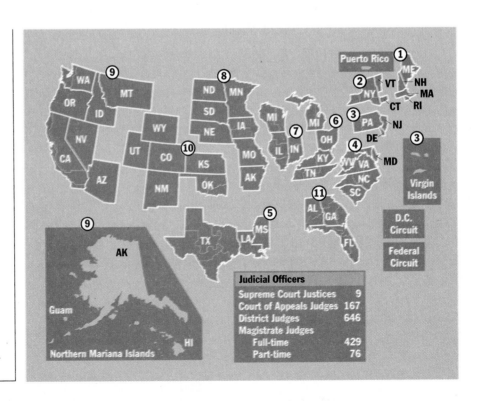

FIGURE 8.3
The Number and Composition of Federal Judicial Circuits

SOURCE: http://www.uscourts.gov/understanding_courts/gifs/map.gif

Judicial Officers	
Supreme Court Justices	9
Court of Appeals Judges	167
District Judges	646
Magistrate Judges	
Full-time	429
Part-time	76

Court cannot be appealed further, and the Supreme Court also can choose *not* to review a case if it so desires. In fact, of the more than 5,000 cases that reach the U.S. Supreme Court each year, and more than three-fourths are not heard. When this happens, the previous court's ruling stands as the final decision.

There are four types of cases in which the U.S. Supreme Court *must* render an opinion, and all involve interpretations of the U.S. Constitution:

FOUR TYPES OF CONSTITUTIONAL CASES

1. When an act of Congress has been found unconstitutional in a lower federal court

2. When a state supreme court has found a federal law unconstitutional

3. When a U.S. court of appeals has found a state law unconstitutional

4. When a constitutional challenge of a state law has been upheld by a state supreme court

The U.S. Supreme Court's ability to choose which cases it will hear is known as *certiorari*. This term is derived from the **writ of certiorari,** which is a legal order from the U.S. Supreme Court stating that a lower court must "forward the record" of a particular case for review. Such a writ is issued when four or more justices on the U.S. Supreme Court believe that the legal issues presented in the case merit review.

The decisions of the Supreme Court are made by a majority vote of the nine justices, who are appointed for life by the president with the consent of the Senate. The far-reaching powers of the Supreme Court were not included in Article III of the U.S. Constitution, which created the Court. The powers were established in the 1803 case of *Marbury v. Madison,* in which the Court claimed the authority to review the constitutionality of acts of Congress.[9] After Thomas Jefferson defeated incumbent John Adams in the presidential election of 1800, the Congress and President Adams created many new federal judgeships, appointed new judges, and reduced the number of U.S. Supreme Court justices. This partisan strategy limited Jefferson's ability to appoint judges of his own choosing when he took office. Chief Justice John Marshall led the U.S. Supreme Court in ruling that Congress had exceeded its power, however, and had acted unconstitutionally. This case established the principle known as **judicial review** of legislative acts. The *Marbury* ruling is considered one of the most significant court decisions in U.S. history, for it specifies how the balance of powers operates and clarifies the extent of the Supreme Court's authority.

■ writ of certiorari
A legal order from the U.S. Supreme Court stating that a lower court must forward the record of a particular case for review.

MARBURY V. MADISON

■ judicial review
The U.S. Supreme Court's authority to review the constitutionality of acts of Congress.

Who Are the Participants in the Judicial Process?

The court system lies at the heart of the American system of justice. It is through the judicial process and the courts that police, prosecutors, and victims square off against defendants and defense counsel to determine liability for crimes. Before a case comes to trial, only allegations and suspected crimes exist. The only proof required to initiate a trial is probable cause. As explained in Chapter 5, the probable cause requirement was set forth in the Fourth Amendment to the Constitution, which was added to protect the privacy of citizens from warrantless searches. To convict a defendant at trial, however, prosecution must meet a higher standard of proof, usually requiring the concurrence of a jury. The purpose of this higher standard is to ensure that only those who in fact *are* guilty are punished, not those who we believe *might be* guilty. A higher standard of proof also maintains public confidence in the accuracy and fairness of the system and of the government it represents.

Five main groups of participants in the judicial process are prosecutors, defense counsel and defendants, judges, victims and witnesses, and juries. The roles of these participants and their interactions determine the nature and quality of the justice that results from the adjudication process. It is important, therefore, to understand how these participants can and should convict the guilty, exonerate the innocent, and protect the community.

PARTICIPANTS IN THE JUDICIAL PROCESS

Prosecutors

■ prosecutors
Elected or appointed officials who represent the community in bringing charges against an accused person.

Prosecutors also are called district, county, state, commonwealth, or U.S. attorneys, depending on the jurisdiction. Whatever the title, the task of prosecutors is the same: to represent the community in bringing charges against an accused person. The job of the prosecutor is constrained by political factors, caseloads, and relationships with other actors in the adjudication process.

CONSTRAINTS ON PROSECUTORS

First, most prosecutors are elected (although some are appointed by the governor), so it is in their interests to make "popular" prosecution decisions—and in some cases these may run counter to the ideals of justice. For example, prosecution "to the full extent of the law" of a college student caught possessing a small amount of marijuana may be unwarranted, but failure to prosecute may be used by political opponents as evidence that the prosecutor is "soft on crime." Likewise, a prosecutor may not believe that a first offender deserves the maximum penalty for a robbery or assault, but uninformed public or political pressure may encourage the prosecutor to pursue the maximum sentence anyway. Thus, a prosecutor must be able to deal effectively with demands for action that may not be in the best interests of justice. As the standards of the American Bar Association state, the "duty of the prosecutor is to seek justice, not merely convict."[10]

A second constraint on the job of prosecutor is caseload pressures, which often force prosecutors to make decisions based on expediency rather than justice. A prosecutor in a jurisdiction where many serious crimes occur may have to choose which cases to prosecute to the full extent of the law and which ones to plea-bargain (as discussed in Chapter 9). There may not be enough prosecutors to handle all the cases being filed in criminal court. Therefore, priorities must be set, meaning that some cases will be given superficial attention in order to free prosecutors to focus more fully on others. The result is that violent crimes, which are relatively rare, usually

Marcia Clark was the prosecutor in the sensational O. J. Simpson murder trial, which ended in acquittal. At the beginning of the trial, Clark wore a pin to show support for the victims' families, but the judge asked her to remove it because it created confusion about her role as the prosecuting attorney. What is the prosecuting attorney's role in criminal court? Under what other restrictions do prosecutors operate?

receive full attention, whereas the more common crimes against property are handled outside the courtroom in plea bargains. Caseload problems can lead to accusations of "assembly-line justice," in which cases often end in reduced sentences.

Third, prosecutors must maintain good relationships with the other participants in the adjudication process: police, judges, juries, defense attorneys, victims, and witnesses. Cases typically are brought to prosecutors by the police, and police officers usually serve as witnesses. Prosecutors need the police to provide valid evidence and to serve as reliable witnesses. Cases in which the evidence is weak ultimately result in dismissal or acquittal, so prosecutors must work closely with police to ensure that time and effort is not wasted by either party. Prosecutors also need judges to rule on the admissibility of evidence, to decide guilt or innocence in nonjury trials, and to follow their recommendations in sentencing decisions. Prosecutors must maintain good relationships with defense counsel, because most

contemporary issues and trends

Independent Counsel and Prosecutorial Misconduct

In the early 1980s Congress passed legislation creating the Office of the Independent Counsel. This federal office was formed in response to allegations of misconduct by officials in the executive branch of the federal government. Several officials within the Reagan administration were convicted of lying to Congress through the efforts of independent counsel Lawrence Walsh, who spent $35 million in the Iran–Contra investigation.[a] Since then, numerous independent counsel investigations have been authorized. The most well known is that headed by Kenneth Starr, whose investigation of President Clinton's real estate dealings as governor of Arkansas expanded into an investigation of alleged sexual misconduct in the White House. Concern about the scope of the broad authority of the independent counsel grew when Starr had the friend of a targeted White House intern wear a concealed microphone to surreptitiously tape conversations, then subpoenaed the intern's mother to testify before a grand jury about her con-

versations with her daughter. The independent counsel was seeking evidence of presidential involvement in obstructing justice or in encouraging perjury, but these intrusive tactics were widely criticized.[b] It has been suggested that the strong-arm tactics prosecutors used in this case would have resulted in disciplinary proceedings if they had been used by a private attorney representing a client.[c] The law that created the independent counsel mandates that any evidence gathered is given to Congress, but no guidance is provided about when evidence should be provided or in what form.[d] Starr was criticized for an investigation that lasted more than five years and cost more than $40 million. Ultimately, Congress chose in 1999 not to reauthorize the independent counsel statute.

Across the nation, the conduct of prosecutors in handling criminal cases has been a growing concern. In one well-known murder case a prosecutor concealed from the jury the

> the conduct of prosecutors in handling criminal cases has been a growing concern.

fact that red stains on the defendant's clothing were paint, not blood.[e] In some instances prosecutors have attempted to sway juries by appeals to inadmissible evidence, appeals to prejudice, or inflammatory statements.[f] In other cases prosecutors retried defendants after the case had been earlier dropped or dismissed. In a Louisiana case a man was tried five times for a murder.[g] Nevertheless, the U.S. Supreme Court has granted prosecutors absolute immunity from being sued for misconduct in the courtroom, even if the misconduct is intentional. The Court made this ruling in a case in which a prosecutor was sued for knowingly using perjured testimony that resulted in an innocent person's being convicted and incarcerated for nine years.[h] The Supreme Court held that without absolute immunity prosecutors risked "harassment by unfounded litigation" that would make it difficult for them to carry out their duties effectively.

cases end in plea bargains and both sides must be willing to reach an agreement. Prosecutors also must communicate well with juries, victims, and witnesses. Victims and witnesses provide evidence that may be crucial in determining guilt or innocence; so it is important that they understand the judicial process, are forewarned about what they may face in court, and receive support throughout the process.

THE PROSECUTOR'S ROLE   The prosecutor is the only actor in the criminal justice system who is involved in all aspects of criminal justice processing from arrest through disposition. He or she makes decisions that greatly affect the outcome of a case. The scope of prosecutors' discretion is rarely defined by statute, but it dramatically affects the operation of the criminal justice system.

Nevertheless, prosecutors have only limited immunity from being sued for actions taken outside the courtroom. For example, when one prosecutor was sued for deciding to authorize a warrantless wiretap, he was not granted absolute immunity.[i] In another case a prosecutor was found to have fabricated evidence by shopping around for a favorable expert witness and to have made false statements to the press. Here again, the prosecutor was not granted absolute immunity.[j] The pattern in these cases shows that prosecutors enjoy absolute immunity in courtroom actions but only qualified immunity for investigative actions (such as advice and direction to the police).[k] One former prosecutor has recommended imposing civil penalties on prosecutors for professional misconduct and has encouraged appellate courts to discipline prosecutors as they do defense attorneys to curb unethical actions.[l] It is unethical for a prosecutor to bring a case to trial when he or she knows that the defendant is innocent. Closer scrutiny and enforcement of ethical standards can serve as a way to control prosecutorial misconduct.

1. Whom did the federal independent counsel represent? Why did Congress create and then abolish this role?
2. How can the role and duties of a prosecutor lead to misconduct or abuse of power?
3. Why did the U.S. Supreme Court grant prosecutors absolute immunity? What are the limits on that immunity?
4. How do you think ethical standards should apply to the other players in the U.S. court system?

NOTES

a. Constance Johnson, "High Crimes and Special Prosecutors," *U.S. News & World Report* (November 8, 1993), p. 47.
b. Mortimer B. Zuckerman, "Has Mr. Starr No Shame?," *U.S. News & World Report* (April 6, 1998), p. 74; Barry A. Bohrer, "President Clinton Is No Mafia Chieftain," *The National Law Journal* 20 (March 2, 1998), p. 23; Paul Glastris, " 'False Statements': The Flubber of all Laws," *U.S. News & World Report* (March 30, 1998), pp. 25–26.
c. Harvey Silvergate, "Prosecutors Tread Where Defenders Daren't Go," *The National Law Journal* 20 (February 16, 1998), p. 21.
d. Douglas Stanglin, "Starr Weighs His Options," *U.S. News & World Report* (May 4, 1998), p. 9.
e. *Miller v. Pate,* 386 U.S. 1 (1967).
f. See Alschuler, "Courtroom Misconduct by Prosecutors and Trial Judges," *Texas Law Review* 50 (1972), pp 627–35.
g. Pamela Coyle, "Tried and Tried Again: Defense Lawyers Say the D.A. Went Too Far Prosecuting a Louisiana Man Five Times for Murder," *ABA Journal* 84 (April, 1998), p. 38.
h. *Imbler v. Pachtman,* 424 U.S. 409 (1976).
i. *Mitchell v. Forsyth,* 472 U.S. 511 (1985); 515 U.S. 304 (1995).
j. *Buckley v. Fitzsimmons,* 509 U.S. 259 (1993).
k. Erwin Chemerinsky, "Prosecutorial Immunity: The Interpretation Continues," *Trial* 34 (March, 1998), p. 80.
l. Bennett L. Gershman, "Why Prosecutors Misbehave," in P. F. Cromwell and R. G. Dunham, eds., *Crime and Justice in America: Present Realities and Future Prospects* (Upper Saddle River, NJ: Prentice Hall, 1997), pp. 192–200.

Whether they work at the federal, state, or county level, prosecutors represent the public in their actions. Because violations of the criminal law are crimes against society, prosecutors represent their jurisdictions, not the victims or other individuals. Federal prosecutors are called U.S. attorneys; state prosecutors are called state, district, or commonwealth attorneys; and local prosecutors are called **district attorneys** or county prosecutors. Most prosecutions are conducted at the state or county level. Of the nearly one million felony convictions each year in the United States, only about 6 percent occur in federal courts.[11]

PROSECUTORS REPRESENT THE PUBLIC

■**district attorneys**
City and county prosecutors (called by this title in many jurisdictions, but not in all).

SELECTION OF PROSECUTORS The more than 24,000 state, county, and local prosecutors in the United States handle felony cases in state trial courts, and most also have jurisdiction for misdemeanor cases and traffic violations.[12] Most prosecutors are county-level officials, and approximately three-quarters of chief prosecutors hold full-time salaried positions. The typical prosecutor's office has three assistant prosecuting attorneys in addition to the chief prosecutor, although this number varies widely according to the size of the jurisdiction. Large cities with populations of 1 million or more average 163 assistant prosecutors, whereas smaller cities with populations of 250,000 to 999,999 average 41 assistant prosecutors.[13]

**APPOINTMENT
VERSUS ELECTION
OF PROSECUTORS**

In all but five states, prosecutors are elected. Supporters of *appointed* prosecutors point out that appointment reduces the possibility of overzealous or lackluster prosecutions of unpopular or controversial cases for election-related reasons. According to this argument, for example, prosecutors may pursue more cases involving high-profile defendants during election years.[14] Or they may try to match public expectations of being the "toughest" prosecutor. The best prosecutors, however, do their best to see that justice and fairness are sought in every case, which may have little to do with being "tough."

Supporters of *elected* prosecutors believe that elections provide regular opportunities for the public to express their approval or disapproval of a prosecutor's policies—and that appointments to the position of prosecutor may be based on political considerations. According to this line of thought, political patronism can result in appointments of individuals who may not have the background or experience to be effective prosecutors on behalf of a jurisdiction.

**SPECIAL
PROSECUTORS**

In some states special prosecutors can be appointed to investigate extraordinary crimes. Special prosecutors are appointed by the governor to investigate multijurisdictional crimes that involve a potential conflict of interest on the part of the state attorney general (who is part of the state government). In these cases the offense usually involves allegations of misconduct on the part of a government official or a government agency. Therefore, an outside special prosecutor is appointed to conduct an independent objective evaluation of the evidence.

Defense Counsel and Defendants

defense attorneys
Attorneys who represent the legal rights of persons accused in criminal or civil proceedings.

Defense attorneys represent the legal rights of accused persons in criminal proceedings. Unlike the image that has emerged from some notorious cases, the reality is that defense attorneys' task is not to get the best deal for their client but to ensure that their client's legal rights are protected. Defense attorneys provide this protection by examining the evidence used to establish probable cause and questioning whether the evidence proves guilt beyond a reasonable doubt. This role sometimes brings defense counsel into conflict with police and prosecutors, and with victims and witnesses who may believe they are being "attacked" by the defense. An effective defense attorney, however, uses his or her skills to examine the reliability and validity of the evidence produced by police, prosecutors, victims, and witnesses; the attorney does not attack anyone *as an individual*. Attaining this neu-

Prominent Defender Alan Dershowitz once said, "The vast majority of criminal defendants are in fact guilty of the crimes with which they are charged. Almost all of my own clients have been guilty." Does this mean that defense attorneys must lie to try to get their clients acquitted? Should a lawyer defend a guilty person? What exactly is the defense lawyer's role in criminal court? Under what other restrictions do defense attorneys operate?

trality is difficult, however. Strong advocacy of the legal rights of a defendant can become blurred with the desire to win at all costs. Nevertheless, the role of a defense attorney is crucial, because it increases certainty about outcomes of the adjudication process. Without high levels of certainty in court findings of guilt or innocence, the public might lose faith in the justice system and in the government it represents.

CRIMINAL LAWYERS

The majority of lawyers are not criminal lawyers. Of the more than 800,000 lawyers in the United States (with an additional 30,000 graduating from law school each year), only about 6 percent practice criminal law. The reasons that most defense attorneys are not involved in criminal law are many. As defense attorney Seymour Wishman reports, "You spend most of your time with monsters," "you're in and out of depressing places like prisons all day long," "the pay isn't extraordinary," and "you're looked down upon."[15] Some defense lawyers dislike visiting police stations, jails, and prisons; and because most defendants are poor, comparatively little money is made defending crime suspects. In addition, the public sometimes views defense attorneys as trying to subvert justice by successfully defending guilty people.[16] Public opinion polls show little confidence in lawyers, especially defense lawyers.[17] As a result, lawyers who choose careers as criminal attorneys, especially as public defenders, are in a distinct minority. Dramatic increases in the number of attorneys graduating from law schools in recent years may change this situation.

Most defendants in criminal cases are poor, and three-fourths of prison inmates were represented by court-appointed attorneys.[18] The case that most increased the availability of defense counsel to the poor was *Gideon v. Wainwright* in 1963. The Supreme Court ruled that indigent persons who are charged with felonies but cannot afford counsel must be appointed counsel at trial. In 1972, in *Argersinger v. Hamlin,* the Court extended the right to counsel to indigent defendants charged with misdemeanors for which imprisonment can be the penalty.[19] Other decisions have further extended the right to counsel to most stages of the criminal justice process. To meet the representation requirement, most states provide assigned counsel, contract attorney programs, or public defender services to indigent individuals charged with crimes. **Assigned counsel** is a private attorney appointed by the court on a case-by-case basis from a list of available attorneys. In **contract attorney programs,** private attorneys, firms, or local bar associations—professional associations of lawyers—provide legal representation to indigent defendants for a specific period under a contract with the county. **Public defender** programs are usually public nonprofit arrangements in which salaried attorneys are paid by the government to represent indigent defendants. About half of all counties in the United States have assigned counsel systems, and contract programs are found in about 11 percent of counties. Public defenders exist in 37 percent of all counties, including most of the largest jurisdictions, serving two-thirds of the U.S. population.[20] Eighty-one percent of all felony defendants receive appointed counsel, either public defenders or assigned counsel. Only 18 percent can afford to hire their own lawyer.

■**assigned counsel**
Private attorney appointed by the court on a case-by-case basis from a list of available defense attorneys.

■**contract attorney programs**
Programs in which private attorneys, firms, or local bar associations provide legal representation to indigent defendants for a specific period under contract with the county.

■**public defender**
Salaried attorney paid by the government to represent indigent persons charged with crimes.

■**judge**
Person who objectively assesses the strength of a case, rules on issues of law and procedure, and in many cases determines the disposition of a case.

METHODS OF SELECTING JUDGES

Judges

Judges play a pivotal role in the criminal justice process in upholding the rights of the accused and arbitrating between the prosecution and the defense in criminal cases. From the initial appearance through sentencing, the task of the **judge** is to objectively assess the strength of a case, rule on issues of law and procedure, and sometimes determine the ultimate disposition of a case.

Judges, sometimes called magistrates in courts of limited jurisdiction, are selected in one of five ways, depending on the state. In six states judges are appointed by the governor, usually with the consent of the state legislature; this method is similar to the selection process for federal judges, who are appointed by the president with the approval of the U.S. Senate. In two states judges are selected by the state legislature alone. Nonpartisan elections (in which candidates are not affiliated with any political party) are held in thirteen states, and eight other states elect judges in partisan elections. In ten states judges are chosen by a merit selection process. Eleven states use various combinations of these five methods, depending on the type of judicial vacancy to be filled.

Strengths and weaknesses are associated with each method of selection, and the diversity of methods indicates a lack of consensus on which method is best. Selection of judges by election gives the political party or the public direct input in the selection process, but it may pressure a judge seeking election or reelection to make "popular" decisions rather than ones based on principles of justice. Political appointment by the governor or the legislature sometimes results in the selection of a judge who is well connected politically but lacks some of the credentials one might wish to see in a judge.

Merit selection was designed to overcome the drawbacks of both election and appointment of judges. The Missouri **merit selection** plan was initiated in 1940. When a judicial vacancy occurs, a nominating commission composed of citizens and attorneys recommends three candidates to the governor. The governor must appoint one of the three candidates. After the appointed judge has served on the bench for a year, a public referendum is held in which the voters are asked, "Shall Judge Z remain in office?" If a majority vote "yes," the judge completes his or her term of office; a "no" vote starts the process all over again. The merit selection system was designed to remove judicial candidates from the political arena while allowing the public to confirm or unseat a judge after one year. Although it is not a foolproof system, the procedure has been approved by both the American Bar Association and the American Judicature Society.

Whatever selection method is used, judges play a significant role in the adjudication process. They serve as an informed, neutral party, ruling on issues of fact and law throughout the court process. Even in cases in which the evidence of guilt appears overwhelming, the judge must ensure that the defendant's legal rights have been adequately safeguarded by the defense and that the community's interests have been effectively represented by the prosecution.

In recent decades two important reform movements, state court unification and the establishment of U.S. magistrates, have increased the quality of the judicial system. Courts had been criticized for the use of nonlawyers in judicial roles, especially in local "justice of the peace" courts in small jurisdictions. Local court procedures were idiosyncratic, giving unfair advantages to local attorneys practicing in those courts. Local courts also were found to be more interested in generating revenue by imposing fines than in seeking justice.[21] During the 1960s and 1970s several national commissions recommended the abolition of many local courts and the creation of unified lower courts of limited and general jurisdiction. Uniform procedures for these courts were developed to reduce confusion about legal rules; additional recommendations mandated legal training for judges, provided for the rotation of judges among courts, and specified other reforms.[22] Many states have streamlined their court systems to some extent, but few have completely unified their courts. Texas, for example, still has more than 2,000 courts of limited jurisdiction. Nevertheless, the court unification movement has helped standardize court jurisdiction, procedure, and personnel qualifications in many states.

The second important reform movement was the establishment of **U.S. magistrates** by Congress in 1968. These magistrates are appointed by U.S. district court judges; they hold pretrial hearings as well as trials for minor civil and criminal offenses. They replaced U.S. commissioners, who were not required to be trained lawyers (and in many cases were not). Like the court unification movement in the state courts, the establishment of

■merit selection
A method for selecting judges that involves a combination of appointment and election.

JUDICIAL REFORMS

■U.S. magistrates
Judges appointed by U.S. district court judges to conduct pretrial hearings and trials for minor civil and criminal offenses in federal court.

legally trained magistrates served to enhance and standardize the quality of justice in the lower federal courts.

Judges are better qualified now than at any time in the nation's history. Virtually all are required to hold law degrees, and legal education is more standardized today than in the past. The Federal Judicial Center, established in 1967, is responsible for judicial education and research in the federal courts, but not all states have a similar organized system of regular judicial training.[23] Standardized judicial training is important for maintaining high levels of competence and for fostering public confidence in the adjudication process.

THE VICTIM'S RIGHTS MOVEMENT

Which of the many participants in the criminal judicial process are evident in this photograph? What are the roles of victims and witnesses? How would this scene change if it were taken in a specialized court, such as a felony drug court? How would the scene change in a community court for resolving disputes? Do you think community dispute resolution is an appropriate and effective way to ease overcrowding in the courts? Why or why not?

Victims and Witnesses

Victims and witnesses have sometimes been called the "forgotten players" in the criminal justice process, because no one specifically represents them. The police and prosecutor represent the community at large, the defense counsel represents the accused, and the judge is a neutral third party. The adjudication process is designed in this manner because violations of criminal law are viewed as violations of the rules of social order. It is society at large, not just the victim, that is harmed by an assault or robbery. Therefore, the prosecutor represents the entire jurisdiction and not just the victims or witnesses in a particular case.

Recent years have seen efforts to give victims and witnesses a greater role in the criminal justice process, usually at sentencing and at parole hearings, where they are permitted to voice their concerns. However, the criminal justice process is not designed to settle private disputes between victims and offenders; that is the purpose of civil law. It can be argued that greater input by victims and witnesses in criminal proceedings blurs the distinction between criminal and civil proceedings.

Nevertheless, victims and witnesses sometimes are not appropriately informed of the progress of criminal proceedings or of the pending release of offenders from prison. Also, until recently the impact of crime on victims has received little recognition.[24] In gang-dominated neighborhoods, for example, there are high levels of victim and witness intimidation.[25] Intimidation occurs most often in connection with violent crimes and often involves people with some previous connection with the defendant; many such people are young, and many are illegal immigrants. Explicit threats, physical violence, and property damage have been reported in these cases.

In response, prosecutors have requested high bail and initiated aggressive prosecution of reported attempts at intimidation. In recent years new strategies have been developed, such as emergency relocation and support of victims and witnesses, more extensive pretrial and courtroom security measures, and coordination with other agencies that provide support services.[26] These measures are part of what has been called the

"victim's rights movement," which is a grassroots effort to make the criminal justice system more responsive to the perspective and suffering of crime victims. More than 8,000 organizations now provide counseling, transportation to court, temporary housing, and advocacy services for victims.[27] To the extent that the victim's rights movement has helped keep victims informed, aware, and protected in the adjudication process, it has accomplished a useful public service.

The criticism that victims are not adequately represented in the criminal justice process peaked during the 1980s, when a presidential Task Force on Victims of Crime recommended a more formal role for crime victims in criminal proceedings.[28] In 1991 the U.S. Supreme Court permitted judges and juries to consider **victim impact statements** in arriving at sentencing decisions. Before that time statements made by victims after the trial were considered inflammatory and prejudicial and were not considered in sentencing hearings. A majority of states have now made victim impact statements a mandatory part of criminal procedure.

The effect of victim impact statements on actual sentences is not clear. Several studies have found these statements to have little influence.[29] Other analyses indicate that victim impact statements foster sentencing based on perceptions of the victim's worth rather than on the seriousness of the crime.[30] The inclusion of these statements is new, however, and changes in sentencing laws to accommodate the requests of victims are still occurring. It is too early, therefore, to determine the full effect of victim impact statements.

In addition to this trend toward providing a greater voice and more services to victims, there is a national push for a constitutional amendment to protect victims' rights during criminal proceedings.[31] Sometimes crime victims and families are excluded from trials where they may be called as witnesses, and there is a perception that defendants' rights are given more attention than the concerns of victims. More than half the states have enacted some form of a **Victim's Bill of Rights,** giving formal legal recognition to the role of victims in the justice process in state courts. And a proposed amendment to the U.S. Constitution would guarantee victims nationwide the right to restitution and the right to be heard during plea bargaining, at trial, at sentencing, and at parole hearings.

One version of the proposed constitutional amendment is presented in Figure 8.4. This version would give victims legal authority to object to plea bargaining, would guarantee a speedy trial, would require full restitution by the offender, and would provide for "reasonable measures" to protect the victim where necessary. Some prosecutors fear that this amendment, if passed, would give victims "veto power" over their decisions. Others have expressed concern about victims being present during trials in which they later appear as witnesses. They might then be able to shape their testimony according to the version of events presented by earlier witnesses.[32] The proposed constitutional amendment has languished in Congress for years but has not

■**victim impact statements**
Statements made by victims to the judge before sentencing about how the crime has harmed them.

■**Victim's Bill of Rights**
Legal changes that formally recognize the role and rights of victims in the justice process.

FIGURE 8.4
Proposed Constitutional Amendment to Guarantee Victims' Rights

As a matter of fundamental rights to liberty, justice and due process, the victim shall have the following rights:

to be informed of and given the opportunity to be present at every proceeding in which those rights are extended to the accused or convicted offender; to be heard at any proceeding involving sentencing, including the right to object to a previously negotiated plea, or a release from custody; to be informed of any release or escape; and to a speedy trial, a final conclusion free from unreasonable delay, full restitution from the offender, reasonable measures to protect the victim from violence or intimidation by the accused or convicted offender, and notice of the victim's rights.

(Proposed by U.S. Senators
John Kyl, R-Arizona, and
Dianne Feinstein, D-California, 1997)

reached a vote, because many lawmakers believe crime victim rights can be achieved through new federal laws that do not require a constitutional amendment.[33] Despite these problems, continuing concern with fair and equal treatment of victims in the criminal justice process will keep the victim's rights movement alive for years to come.

Juries

When a trial takes place, it begins with the selection of a jury. The right to a jury dates from the signing of the Magna Carta in 1215, and it is incorporated into both Article III of the Constitution and the Sixth Amendment—which states that "in all criminal prosecutions, the accused shall enjoy the right to a speedy and public trial by an impartial jury." The jury pool typically is selected from voter registration records, property tax rolls, or motor vehicle records. This selection process has been widely criticized, because it excludes from the jury pool those who do not vote, own property, or drive cars.[34] Nevertheless, experiments with other methods of sampling have not found a completely effective way to choose a jury pool representative of the entire community.[35] The U.S. Supreme Court has held that it is not necessary for every jury to contain a representative cross-section of the community by race, gender, religion, economic status, or other attributes. Instead, the Court has held that jurors may not be *excluded* on the basis of these characteristics and has overturned convictions in cases where blacks or males were purposely excluded from juries.[36] In a 1994 paternity suit in which the mother was suing the purported father, nine of the prosecutor's ten "peremptory challenges" (challenges without a reason required) were used to strike males from the jury panel, thus biasing the jury toward the plaintiff. The Supreme Court held that this use of peremptory challenges was unconstitutional, because it attempted to exclude an entire class of potential jurors.[37]

A strategy lawyers use to assist juries in their decision making is to call an **expert witness.** This person is called to testify because of his or her special expertise in an area at issue in the case. A common expert witness in criminal trials is the coroner or medical examiner. Coroners are appointed or elected officials who investigate the causes of suspicious deaths in the jurisdiction. Over the years the position of coroner came to be filled politically by laypersons who were not competent at the job. The office of medical examiner has now been established in many jurisdictions, taking the place of the coroner. Medical examiners must be physicians with training in pathology, the study of the causes of death. The role of the medical examiner and of forensic science in solving criminal cases of all types has grown dramatically since the early 1990s. This growth has been largely the result of the invention and increasing sophistication of DNA testing, which allows very small samples of body tissue or fluids from evidence to be matched against those of a suspect. Sim-

■expert witness
A person called to testify because of his or her special expertise in an area at issue in a legal proceeding.

This juvenile is being tried as an adult in criminal court. Why was the decision made to accord him the status of an adult in this case, and what is at stake? What difference would it make in court procedures? What difference could it make in the disposition of the case? What trends in criminal justice does this treatment of a juvenile offender reflect?

ilarities or differences in the genetic coding of the samples can implicate or exclude suspects in cases. Similar advances have been made in drug testing in recent years, helping juries sort through sometimes conflicting testimony of victims and witnesses at trial.

In 1997 the Office of the Inspector General in the U.S. Department of Justice released a 500-page report charging the FBI forensic lab with errors in its forensic testing. It was widely believed that thousands of convictions might be overturned, but only twenty defendants tried to overturn their convictions. This inaction was due in part to the lack of legal counsel to enable prisoners to challenge their convictions and to the fact that federal law permits a prisoner only one year to file a petition challenging a conviction after new evidence is discovered.[38] Nevertheless, FBI and other forensic lab procedures have improved greatly with the assistance of a laboratory accreditation program of the American Society of Crime Lab Directors, which imposes minimum standards on laboratory equipment, conditions, and staffing.

The Courtroom Work Group

In many ways, prosecutors, defense counsel, and judges form a **courtroom work group.** They represent distinct interests but share the goal of shepherding large numbers of cases through the adjudication process. As one observer put it, "The client, then, is a secondary figure in the court system . . . a means to other ends of the organization's incumbents."[39] A defense attorney who is perceived as pushing too hard in a case may be informally sanctioned by inconvenient scheduling or contrary rulings from judges or by reluctance on the part of prosecutors to share reports or to plea-bargain in good faith.[40] Defense attorneys also need to maintain good relations with all other court personnel in order to maintain and build their law practice.[41] Thus, the actors in the courtroom work group must "get along," even if cooperation places some defendants at a disadvantage.

■**courtroom work group**
The prosecutors, defense counsel, judges, and other courtroom personnel, who represent distinct interests but share the goal of shepherding large numbers of cases through the adjudication process.

In addition to prosecutors, defense attorneys, and judges, the courtroom work group includes sheriffs, court clerks, stenographers, and witnesses. *Sheriffs* or *bailiffs* are responsible for maintaining order in the courtroom. They most often track and ensure the appearance of defendants, and they sometimes also handle general court security tasks and handle witnesses. The *court clerk* keeps track of the cases pending before the court. The clerk does this by preparing the court's calendar of cases, calling each case as scheduled, and maintaining court records of case status and judicial rulings. Many court clerks are lawyers. A *court stenographer* or *court reporter* makes a transcript of each court appearance. *Witnesses* are also an important part of the courtroom work group, because they are involved in every case. Most witnesses are police officers. Laypersons who are crime victims or witnesses rely on guidance from the attorneys, court clerk, and sheriff's officers to understand the proceedings. The ability of a defense attorney to work successfully with all these players can improve the treatment of his or her client in court and in jail.

Media and Criminal Justice

THE COLOR OF JUSTICE

Four black youths from the Bronx are kicked off a subway train for disruptive behavior. When they come above ground they realize that they are on the upper west side of Manhattan: "Whitey-Land," as they call it. The ringleader, Kenny, has a gun and notes that "Whitey got the protection of the Five-O here; we do anything and Blue will be all over us!" So begins the 1997 Showtime original movie *The Color of Justice*, a story that focuses on conflicts of race, ethnicity, age, gender, geography, and politics in the system's process of seeking justice.

The movie's plot unfolds when the four black youths steal a car in an effort to get back home to the Bronx. They make a wrong turn and find themselves crossing the George Washington Bridge into New Jersey. As they attempt to exit the bridge and turn around, the stolen car runs out of gas, leaving them stranded on the ramp. Another car approaches behind them; its driver is a white suburban housewife on her way home from self-defense classes. She is alarmed by the youths approaching her car, and reaches for her mace. In the ensuing struggle, Kenny strikes her with his gun and leaves her on the side of the highway while the four youths escape in her car. When they are apprehended at the end of the George Washington Bridge on the New York side, the police pull Kenny and his friends from the car, shouting "Where is it?" to which Kenny replies "I don't got nothing! Are you my lawyer?" When the police find the gun under the seat of the car, the boys are arrested, read their *Miranda* rights, and taken off to jail.

What follows is a complex tale of criminal procedure. The district attorney from New York is pitted against the DA from New Jersey, because each wants jurisdiction of the case for political purposes. Meanwhile, a Bronx preacher and community activist attempts to use the media to his benefit, depicting the boys as victims of a vindictive white system and arguing that "an African American cannot get a fair trial in this country."

In the opening of the trial of the boys, dubbed the "GW4," their public defender argues that by questioning Kenny before reading him his rights, the police violated due process; therefore, the consequent discovery of the gun that linked them to the crime should be suppressed under the exclusionary rule. The lawyer then attempts to discredit the arresting officer by pointing out that the officer was dis-

honorably discharged from the military for racist behavior. He concludes that the boys acted in self-defense against a racist woman who attacked them with mace because they were black.

As the details are revealed, it is clear that Kenny is the most culpable of the gang but that his younger cousin Kamil was truly in the wrong place at the wrong time and is gen-
uinely remorseful for his role as an accomplice. Should Kamil be held as responsible as Kenny? Should they all be tried as adults? Should the case be tried by the New York DA who is using it as leverage  to run for mayor, or sent to New Jersey, where there is less racial tension? These questions become fodder for the media circus that ensues, obscuring the facts of the case in a cloak of presumptions known as the "race card."

Worried about the defense's claims of procedural wrongdoing, fearful that the court won't be able to convene a jury without a large number of blacks, and knowing that a panel of minorities might well ignore the letter of the law because of the media's portrayal of the case, the DA agrees to a plea bargain. In a matter of minutes, the GW4 are remanded to juvenile court, agree to lesser charges of assault, and are released with a sentence of time served.

But this is not the end of the case. The distraught husband of the victim waits outside the courtroom with a gun. As the players exit the courtroom, he fires at the Bronx preacher responsible for the media blitz but mistakenly kills Kamil. The white shooter is immediately subdued by a bailiff, who tells him with certainty: "Take it easy. No jury in the world would convict you for that."

What are the similarities between the fictional case of the GW4 and the real-life cases of the LA4—the four black youths charged with beating motorist Reginald Denny in the aftermath of the Rodney King riots—or the four white NYPD officers charged in the shooting death of Amadou Diallo? What can be done to limit media influence in high-profile cases? Are there measures we can take to make sure that truly guilty defendants don't get off on procedural technicalities?

HOW ARE SPECIALIZED AND ALTERNATIVE COURTS CHANGING THE COURT SYSTEM?

269

How Are Specialized and Alternative Courts Changing the Court System?

The court system lies at the center of the justice system, for it is here that justice is most clearly carried out. Police and prosecutors work to assemble evidence of guilt. Defense attorneys closely scrutinize this evidence on behalf of the accused. Only in court, with a judge serving as referee and a jury sitting in judgment, does an objective assessment of the facts and law occur. Without neutral and detached courts and judges, there would be no forum in which the rights of the community could be balanced against the rights of the accused. The future of the court system will reflect improved judicial quality, discussed above; it will also reflect the development of specialized courts and alternatives to the courtroom for certain kinds of cases, which we will consider in this section.

Felony Drug Courts

Specialized courts have emerged as a way for society to deal more effectively with the problem of drug-related crime. The drug court movement began during the late 1980s in response to the dramatic growth in drug-related cases. As Figure 8.5 illustrates, the most frequently charged felonies in the nation's seventy-five largest counties are drug offenses, accounting for more than a third of all defendants. The purpose of **felony drug courts** is to hold the defendant or offender "personally and publicly accountable for treatment progress."[42] Drug courts began in Miami and are now found in nearly 200 jurisdictions. Each drug court is coordinated by the judge, who works with the prosecutor, defense counsel, and drug treatment personnel. Members of this team select an appropriate treatment; address issues of housing, employment, or other barriers to progress; and monitor the offender's progress.[43] Figure 8.6 illustrates the two different models of drug courts: treatment after adjudication and treatment while prosecution is deferred.

An evaluation of Miami's felony drug court found that fewer defendants were incarcerated but also that fewer drug cases were dropped during adjudi-

■felony drug courts
Courts that handle only drug offenses and attempt to correct underlying causes of the illegal conduct.

EVALUATING
DRUG COURTS

FIGURE 8.5
The Most Frequently Charged Offenses of Felony Defendants in the Seventy-five Largest Counties

SOURCE: Brian A. Reaves, *Felony Defendants in Large Urban Counties* (Washington, DC: Bureau of Justice Statistics, 1998).

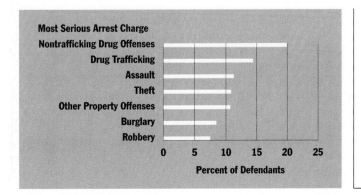

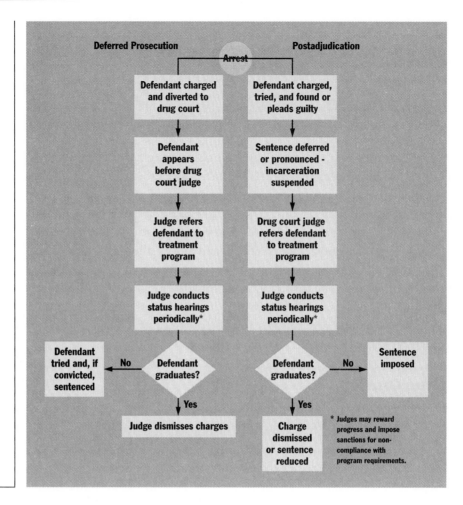

FIGURE 8.6

Two Drug Court Approaches

SOURCE: U.S. Comptroller General, *Drug Courts: Overview of Growth, Characteristics, and Results* (Washington, DC: U.S. General Accounting Office, 1997).

cation and offenders were re-arrested less frequently.[44] Remaining challenges include obtaining accurate information about defendants, ensuring proper screening of drug offenders, and providing different treatments for different kinds of drug abuse. In 1994, Congress passed the Violent Crime Control and Law Enforcement Act to support specialized local and state drug courts.

The drug court movement has built on the experiences of night courts and expedited case processing for drug cases in selected cities. Through night courts and expedited case processing, various jurisdictions responded to expanding drug caseloads by increasing hours of operation and handling these cases more efficiently.[45] Drug courts concentrate cases and expertise in a single courtroom, thereby reducing the time from arrest to disposition while relieving the caseload in general felony courts.[46] Goals are consistency in the handling of drug cases, timeliness in adjudication, and reduction of offender recidivism through treatment of underlying drug addictions.

Dispute Resolution and Community Courts

The use of alternatives to the formal adjudication process is a growing trend. Mediation and pretrial intervention programs have been instituted partly in response to high caseloads, but they also reflect a change in philosophy from "adjudication at any cost" to "justice at lower cost." Through these alternatives courts permit defendants to complete programs of restitution or rehabilitation in exchange for holding their cases in abeyance. After the restitution or rehabilitation is completed, the charges are dropped. In other programs, the victim and the accused mutually agree on an appropriate remedy outside of court.[47]

RESOLVING CONFLICT CREATIVELY PROGRAMS

Taking this trend one step farther are efforts to prevent disputes from arising in the first place. The Resolving Conflict Creatively Program (RCCP) in New York City is a school-based program designed to teach young people how to resolve conflicts peacefully. The goal is to reduce violence, delinquency, and court appearances by young people by equipping youth with the skills they need in order to make more rational decisions in dealing with conflict. Workshops teach young people about cooperating, appreciating diversity, and being aware of bias, and provide specific skills for avoiding and de-escalating conflicts.[48] An evaluation found that most students in the program "learn the key concepts and are able to apply them when responding to hypothetical conflicts." In addition, the students report fewer fights and less name-calling behavior compared to a matched group of nonparticipants. Finally, teachers in the program have been found to be "more willing to let students take responsibility for solving their own conflicts."[49] Efforts like RCCP may offer a long-term solution to crowded courts by disseminating the skills people require for avoiding conflicts or resolving them *before* civil or criminal misconduct occurs.

A predictable response to increasing court caseloads has been to resolve more disputes outside the courtroom. Historically, this has meant reliance on plea bargaining; but this approach still involves the full adjudication process, from prosecution and defense representation to sentencing. **Dispute resolution,** in contrast, involves handling complaints outside the judicial process entirely. The goal of this practice is to get both sides to agree to a settlement facilitated by a mediator or arbiter who is appointed by the court. The incentives for dispute resolution are three: A dispute is resolved more quickly, less expensively, and often with a settlement more mutually agreeable than one likely to emerge from the normal adjudication process. For example, a teenager who spray-paints his name on the walls of a school gymnasium can be charged with vandalism, taken to court, and placed on probation or perhaps incarcerated. Alternatively, a dispute resolution procedure might involve a "teen court" made up of students from the teenager's school who would suggest penalties proportional to the offense. Or a dispute resolution procedure could involve an advisory committee of local citizens who would impose a sentence, such as cleaning up the paint, attending counseling, or other remedies. The purpose is to permit the community to address its problems in ways it sees as fair, proportional, and locally controlled.[50]

dispute resolution
Method of handling complaints outside the judicial process through a mediator appointed by the court.

Dispute resolution works most effectively for first and minor offenders who commit "disorderly" offenses—offenses that are nonviolent yet disruptive and sometimes threatening to the community, such as loitering, vandalism, thefts, and public nuisance offenses. In Hawaii, for example, it was found that different cultural, ethnic, and neighborhood groups sometimes have different views regarding appropriate responses to these types of misconduct.[51] Dispute resolution gives neighborhoods a greater voice in dealing with misconduct that occurs in their own communities.

■community prosecution
A program in which pros-
ecutors intervene in all
disorderly behavior that
affects the quality of life
in neighborhood.

A variation on dispute resolution is **community prosecution,** which has been used on an experimental basis in several counties around the nation. Responding to the demands of community groups, assistant district attorneys (ADAs) are assigned to specific neighborhoods, where they intervene in disorderly behavior (vandalism, prostitution, drug sales, loitering, etc.). The ADAs work to bring affected parties together to negotiate solutions, to make it easier for property owners to arrest trespassers and use civil eviction to remove undesirable tenants, and to close properties that are found to violate local ordinances.[52] Community prosecution efforts force prosecutors to work on a neighborhood level, acting as problem solvers rather than only as proces-

critical thinking exercise

Limiting Criminal Appeals

The adjudication process is undermined when there are long delays between the commission of the crime and imposition of a sentence. Growth in the number of appeals filed by convicted offenders may be seen as an example. As noted in Chapter 5, an appeal simply argues that an error of law or procedure was made and that a new trial is warranted. Although 80 percent of appeals are unsuccessful, appeals delay punishment while they are heard by an appellate court.[a] A common kind of appeal is a writ of habeas corpus, which requires that a prisoner be brought before a judge and that the judge determine whether he or she is incarcerated lawfully (i.e., whether no legal error has been made). The number of habeas corpus petitions filed has increased dramatically over the years, even though few result in a new trial or the release of an offender. This large volume of appeals from criminal trials adds to already mushrooming caseloads.

During the 1990s the U.S. Supreme Court made rulings that limit an offender's right to appeal. The Court has held that an offender is entitled to federal appeal from a state court finding only when bias or unfairness would result from a failure to appeal or "when a fundamental miscarriage of justice would result" without a review of the case.[b] This ruling limits the circumstances in which an offender can have a state case reviewed in federal court for legal errors.

In 1993 the Court held that an offender sentenced to death for murder is not necessarily entitled to a federal order for a new state trial if new evidence emerges, because new evidence is not automatic

grounds for a new trial.[c] This holding also makes it more difficult for an offender to have a state court conviction reviewed by a federal court.[d] The outcome in practice has been fewer appeals accepted for review. In death penalty cases, in which numerous appeals are common, the ruling has resulted in more executions per year than at any time since the 1930s.

CRITICAL THINKING QUESTIONS

1. What are the positive and negative consequences of limiting the number of appeals made by convicted offenders?
2. How would you evaluate the relative strengths of the positive and negative consequences of limiting criminal appeals?
3. Why do you believe the Supreme Court ruled that new evidence is not always sufficient grounds for a new trial of a person sentenced to death?
4. Do you think rights to appeal should be further limited or abolished? Why or why not?

NOTES

a. Dwight Aarons, "Getting Out of This Mess: Steps toward Addressing and Avoiding Inordinate Delay in Capital Cases," *Journal of Criminal Law and Criminology* 89 (Fall 1998); Joy A. Chaper and Roger A. Hanson, *Understanding Reversible Error in Criminal Appeals* (Williamsburg, VA: National Center for State Courts, 1989).
b. *Kenney v. Tamayo-Reyes,* 504 U.S. 1 (1992).
c. *Herrera v. Collins,* 113 S. Ct. 853 (1993).
d. Arleen Anderson, "Responding to the Challenge of Actual Innocence Claims after *Herrera v. Collins,*" *Temple Law Review* 71 (Fall 1998); Robert D. Pursley, "The Federal Habeas Corpus Process: Unraveling the Issues," *Criminal Justice Policy Review* 7 (1995), pp. 115–41.

sors of criminal cases. These efforts have helped local communities respond more effectively to crimes that erode the quality of life in the neighborhood.

A parallel development is **community courts,** decentralized courts that respond directly to neighborhood concerns rather than waiting for serious crimes to occur. Community courts are being instituted in localities around the country. Many have "satellite" courtrooms in problem neighborhoods, facilities designed to forge a stronger connection between unruly conduct and the adjudication process. Many courts have formed citizens' advisory committees; use citizen volunteers; and have established teen courts, school outreach programs, and other programs that involve the community more closely in the adjudication process.[53]

Dispute resolution, community prosecution, and community courts are related ideas that attempt to accomplish three key objectives: address more quickly nonserious crimes that affect community order, permit organized community input into the adjudication and sentencing processes, and establish a court presence and understanding at the neighborhood level. These initiatives, if widely adopted, will increase confidence in the judicial process and its outcomes by reflecting the values of the local community.

community courts
Decentralized courts that respond to neighborhood conditions using citizen advisory committees, volunteers, and teen courts.

Summary

HOW WERE CRIMINAL COURTS SIMILAR AND DIFFERENT IN THE PAST?

- Although celebrated cases have occurred on occasion in the past, in many cases lawyers were absent from the trial. Misdemeanor cases were handled in a nonprofessional fashion; the processing of felonies tended to be more formal, as it is today.
- Until the late 1800s a defendant could not act as a witness or take the stand in his or her own defense. Today defendants are permitted to testify under oath.

HOW DID THE STATE AND FEDERAL COURT SYSTEMS DEVELOP?

- The vast majority of criminal cases are heard in state courts, because most felonies are defined by state laws.
- There are three levels of jurisdiction: limited, general, and appellate. These are found in all state court systems, but each state determines how its system is organized.
- The legal authority of courts of limited jurisdiction is restricted to certain specific types of cases. Courts of general jurisdiction are often referred to as trial courts, and most felony trials are held at this level. Appellate courts hear appeals from courts of general jurisdiction.
- The federal court system parallels the state court systems. There are courts of limited jurisdiction such as the U.S. Court of Claims. There are also courts of general jurisdiction, the U.S. district courts; these are located throughout the country and hear cases involving alleged violations of federal law.
- There are two levels of federal appellate courts. The intermediate level consists of U.S. courts of appeals. The highest level is the U.S. Supreme Court.
- All cases heard by the Supreme Court involve interpretations of the U.S. Constitution. The Court can choose which cases it will hear through a procedure termed certiorari; a writ of certiorari is issued when four or more justices believe that the legal issues presented in a case merit review.
- The decisions of the Supreme Court are made by a majority vote of the nine justices, who are appointed for life by the president with the consent of the Senate.

WHO ARE THE PARTICIPANTS IN THE JUDICIAL PROCESS?

- Prosecutors represent the community in bringing charges against an accused person. Most prosecutors are elected officials and therefore may feel pressure to make "popular" prosecution decisions. Other influences on prosecutors' decisions include caseload pressures and the need to maintain good relations with other actors in the adjudication process.
- Defense attorneys represent the legal rights of the accused in criminal proceedings. They examine the evidence used to establish probable cause and assess the strength of the evidence to be used to prove guilt.
- The duties of judges are to objectively assess the strength of a case, to rule on issues of law and procedure, and sometimes to determine the ultimate disposition of a case. Judges are selected in a variety of ways, including appointment, nonpartisan election, and merit selection.
- Two recent reform movements—state court unification and the establishment of U.S. magistrates—have increased the quality of the judicial system.
- Victims and witnesses are not represented by specific actors in the adjudication process. In recent years there have been efforts to give victims a greater role in the process, usually at sentencing and at parole hearings.
- A proposed constitutional amendment would give victims legal authority to object to plea bargaining, guarantee a speedy trial, require full restitution by the offender, and provide protection of victims where necessary.
- The right to a jury trial is stated in the Constitution, but historically it has been difficult to obtain a jury that represents the community. Expert witnesses are used to help a jury understand technical issues.
- Prosecutors, defense counsel, and judges can be viewed as a courtroom work group. Although they represent distinct interests, these actors share the goal of moving large numbers of cases through the adjudication process.

HOW ARE SPECIALIZED AND ALTERNATIVE COURTS CHANGING THE COURT SYSTEM?

- Improved judicial quality, specialized courts such as felony drug courts, and alternatives to the courtroom are good news for the future of the court system.
- Dispute resolution, community prosecution, and community courts are three alternatives to formal adjudication in criminal court; all three of these approaches attempt to achieve dispositions that match the offense and will prevent crimes in the future.

Key Terms

U.S. district courts
U.S. courts of appeals
U.S. Supreme Court
writ of certiorari
judicial review
prosecutors
district attorneys
defense attorneys
assigned counsel
contract attorney programs
public defender

judge
merit selection
U.S. magistrates
victim impact statements
Victim's Bill of Rights
expert witness
courtroom work group
felony drug court
dispute resolution
community prosecution
community courts

Questions for Review and Discussion

1. What are some of the most important differences between the way trials were conducted in the past and the way they are conducted today?
2. How are state court systems organized?
3. What are U.S. district courts?
4. What kinds of cases are heard by the U.S. Supreme Court?
5. Describe the five main groups of participants in the judicial process.
6. What are some of the ways in which judges are selected in different states?
7. What is meant by state court unification?
8. What initiatives have been taken to give victims and witnesses a greater role in the criminal justice process?
9. What are the major challenges facing the justice system in the future?

Notes

1. Julius Goebel, Jr., ed., *The Law and Practice of Alexander Hamilton: Documents and Commentary* (New York: Columbia University Press 1964).
2. Lawrence M. Friedman, *Crime and Punishment in American History* (New York: Basic Books, 1993), p. 239.
3. *Hurtado v. California,* 110 U.S. 516 (1884).
4. *Strauder v. West Virginia* (1879).
5. Friedman, pp. 245–50.
6. Herbert A. Johnson and Nancy Travis Wolfe, *History of Criminal Justice,* 2nd ed. (Cincinnati: Anderson, 1996), p. 81, 112.
7. Peter Hoffer, *Law and People in Colonial America* (Baltimore: Johns Hopkins University Press, 1992).
8. Patrick Langan, *State Felony Courts and Felony Laws* (Washington, DC: Bureau of Justice Statistics, 1987).
9. *Marbury v. Madison,* 1 Cr. 138 (1803).
10. American Bar Association, *ABA Standards for Criminal Justice* (Washington, DC: American Bar Association, 1992), Standard 3-1.
11. Steven K. Smith and John Scalia, Jr., *Compendium of Federal Justice Statistics* (Washington, DC: Bureau of Justice Statistics, 1999); Patrick A. Langan, *Felony Sentences in the United States* (Washington, DC: Bureau of Justice Statistics, 1996).
12. Carol DeFrances and Greg W. Steadman, *Prosecutors in State Courts* (Washington, DC: Bureau of Justice Statistics, 1998).
13. Ibid., p. 2.
14. Comments of several defense attorneys appearing on *Rivera Live* on CNBC television, May 29, 1997, in reference to the sexual harassment case of Paula Jones against President Clinton and the prosecution of sportscaster Marv Albert.
15. Seymour Wishman, *Confessions of a Criminal Lawyer* (New York: Penguin, 1982), p. 231.
16. Charles M. Sevilla, "Criminal Defense Lawyers and the Search for Truth," *Harvard Journal of Law and Public Policy* 20 (winter 1997), pp. 519–28.
17. Stephen Budiansky with Ted Gest, "How Lawyers Abuse the Law," *U.S. News & World Report* (January 30, 1995), pp. 50–56.
18. Steven K. Smith and Carol J. DeFrances, *Indigent Defense* (Washington, DC: Bureau of Justice Statistics, 1996).
19. *Argersinger v. Hamlin,* 92 S. Ct. 2006 (1972).
20. Carla K. Gaskins, *Criminal Defense Systems* (Washington, DC: Bureau of Justice Statistics, 1984); Smith and Defrances, *Indigent Defense,* p. 2.
21. Thomas Henderson and Cornelius Kerwin, *Structuring Justice: The Implications of Court Unification Reforms* (Washington, DC: National Institute of Justice, 1984).
22. American Bar Association, *ABA Standards Relating to Court Organization* (Chicago: American Bar Association, 1990).
23. U.S. Comptroller General, *The Federal Judiciary: Observations on Selected Issues* (Washington, DC: U.S. General Accounting Office, 1995).

24. Ted R. Miller, Mark A. Cohen, and Brian Wiersema, *Victim Costs and Consequences: A New Look* (Washington, DC: National Institute of Justice, 1996).

25. Kerry Murphy Healey, *Victim and Witness Intimidation: New Developments and Emerging Responses* (Washington, DC: National Institute of Justice, 1995).

26. Ibid.

27. Office for Victims of Crime, *Victims of Crime Act Crime Victims Fund* (Washington, DC: U.S. Department of Justice, 1996).

28. President's Task Force on Victims of Crime, *Final Report* (Washington, DC: U.S. Government Printing Office, 1982).

29. Robert C. Davis and Barbara E. Smith, "The Effects of Victim Impact Statements on Sentencing Decisions: A Test in an Urban Setting," *Justice Quarterly* 11 (September 1994), pp. 453–69; Edna Erez and Pamela Tontodonato, "The Effect of Victim Participation in Sentencing on Sentence Outcome," *Criminology* 28 (1990), pp. 451–74.

30. Wayne A. Logan, "Through the Past Darkly: A Survey of the Uses and Abuses of Victim Impact Evidence in Capital Trials," *Arizona Law Review* 41 (spring 1999); Amy K. Phillips, "Thou Shalt Not Kill Any Nice People: The Problem of Victim Impact Statements in Capital Sentencing," *American Criminal Law Review* 35 (fall 1997), pp. 93–118.

31. Tony Mauro and Bill Nichols, "Obligation of a Fair Trial vs. Victims' Rights," *USA Today* (June 26, 1996), p. 8.

32. Ibid.

33. Marlene A. Young and Roger Pilon, "Should We Amend the Constitution to Protect Victims' Rights?," *Insight on the News* (August 31, 1998), p. 24; "Senate Panel Approves 'Victims' Rights' Amendment," *CongressDaily/A.M.* (October 1,1999).

34. James P. Levine, *Juries and Politics* (Pacific Grove, CA: Brooks/Cole, 1992); Charles J. Ogletree, "Just Say No! A Proposal to Eliminate Racially Discriminatory Uses of Peremptory Challenges," *American Criminal Law Review* 31 (1994), pp. 1099–1151.

35. Hiroshi Fukurai, Edgar W. Butler, and Richard Krooth, "Cross-Sectional Jury Representation or Systematic Jury Representation? Simple Random and Cluster Sampling Strategies in Jury Selection," *Journal of Criminal Justice* 19 (1991), pp. 31–48.

36. *Thiel v. Southern Pacific Company*, 328 U.S. 217 (1945); *Batson v. Kentucky*, 106 S. Ct. 1712 (1986); Audrey M. Fried, "Fulfilling the Promise of Batson: Protecting Jurors from the Use of Race-Based Peremptory Challenges by Defense Counsel," *University of Chicago Law Review* 64 (fall 1997), pp. 1311–36.

37. *J. E. B. v. Alabama ex rel. T. B.*, 55 CrL. 2003 (1994).

38. David E. Rovella, "Predictions of Big Effects from Ills in FBI Lab Prove False," *Fulton County Daily Report* (April 23, 1998), pp. 1–5.

39. Abraham S. Blumberg, "The Practice of Law as a Confidence Game," in George S. Bridges, Joseph G. Weis, and Robert D. Crutchfield, eds., *Criminal Justice* (Thousand Oaks, CA: Pine Forge Press, 1996), p. 269.

40. James Eisenstein, Roy Fleming, and Peter Nardulli, *The Contours of Justice: Communities and Their Courts* (Boston: Little, Brown, 1988).

41. Blumberg, "The Practice of Law as a Confidence Game," p. 269.

42. *The Drug Court Movement* (Washington, DC: National Institute of Justice, 1995).

43. U.S. Comptroller General, *Drug Courts: Overview of Growth, Characteristics, and Results* (Washington, DC: U.S. General Accounting Office, 1997).

44. John S. Goldkamp and Doris Weiland, *Assessing the Impact of Dade County's Felony Drug Court* (Washington, DC: National Institute of Justice, 1993).

45. American Bar Association, *Drug Night Courts: The Cook County Experience* (Washington, DC: Bureau of Justice Assistance, 1994).

46. Steven Belenko and Tamara Dumankovsky, *Special Drug Courts* (Washington, DC: Bureau of Justice Assistance, 1993).

47. David Rottman and Pamela Casey, "Therapeutic Jurisprudence and the Emergence of Problem-Solving Courts," *National Institute of Justice Journal* (July 1999), pp. 11–19.

48. William DeJong, *Building the Peace: The Resolving Conflict Creatively Program* (Washington, DC: National Institute of Justice, 1996); Donna Crawford and Richard Bodine, *Conflict Resolution Education* (Washington, DC: Office of Juvenile Justice and Delinquency Prevention, 1996).

49. DeJong, *Building the Peace,* p. 11.

50. Daniel McGillis, *Resolving Community Conflict: The Dispute Settlement Center of Durham, North Carolina* (Washington, DC: National Institute of Justice, 1998).

51. Sharon Rodgers, "The Future of Cultural Forms of Dispute Resolution in the Formal Legal System," *Futures Research Quarterly* 9 (Winter 1993), pp. 41–49.

52. Barbara Boland, "What Is Community Prosecution?," *National Institute of Justice Journal* (August 1996), pp. 35–40.

53. David B. Rottman, "Community Courts: Prospects and Limits," *National Institute of Justice Journal* (August 1996), pp. 46–51.

nine
Criminal Defense and Prosecution

In 1998 Darrell Harris was placed

on trial for killing three people and seriously wounding a fourth at a Brooklyn social club. It was the first capital punishment case to be tried after New York State reinstated the death penalty in 1995. Harris was charged with robbing the victims of $200 and then killing them because he wanted no witnesses. His defense attorney claimed that Harris "lost control and snapped" during this incident because he suffered from posttraumatic stress disorder, having endured "combatlike" work conditions in jails when he worked as a corrections officer.[1] In addition, Harris's attorney argued that Harris's mental health was affected by a chaotic and abusive childhood, spinal meningitis that caused brain damage, cocaine and alcohol abuse, and failure to hold a job. Harris had resigned from his job as a corrections officer in 1991 after failing a drug test. Two days before the homicides occurred, Harris had been fired from his job as a security guard. He also had discovered his car had been towed.

Most of these claims bore little relationship to the charges filed, and such arguments feed the perception that defense attorneys focus less on seeking truth than on exoneration of their client at any cost. Cases such as this one raise other questions as well: What is the proper role of a defense attorney? What is the scope of a defendant's right to have counsel? And what are the limits of proper representation?

What Are the Rights of the Accused?

The Sixth Amendment to the U.S. Constitution deals specifically with the rights of people accused of crimes. It states:

In all criminal prosecutions, the accused shall enjoy the right to a speedy and public trial, by an impartial jury of the State and district wherein the crime shall have been committed, which district shall have been previously ascertained by law, and to be informed of the nature and cause of the accusation; to be confronted with the witnesses against him; to have compulsory process for obtaining witnesses in his favor, and to have the Assistance of Counsel for his defense.

THE SIXTH AMENDMENT

The right "to have the assistance of counsel" has drawn a great deal of attention over the years. Do all defendants have this right? Does it apply to all crimes? At what stage of criminal procedure does this right become effective? What kind of counsel does it guarantee?

The Sixth Amendment also guarantees the rights to "a speedy and public trial" and to "an impartial jury." The definition of "speedy" has been the subject of much debate. In 1999, for example, a prisoner on death row asked the court for a speedy execution but was denied until his appeals were exhausted.[2] Jury trials date back in history nearly 800 years, but the scope of a defendant's right to choose a jury trial has been subject to U.S. Supreme Court interpretation of the Sixth Amendment.[3]

- Right to counsel
- applied narrowly at first

Right to Counsel

The scope of the **right to counsel** has been defined by the U.S. Supreme Court in a series of cases involving the interpretation and application of the Sixth Amendment. The Supreme Court applied the right to counsel narrowly at first but has expanded it significantly over the years. In 1931 the Court held in *Powell v. Alabama* that legal counsel is guaranteed to defendants who are charged with a capital crime, are indigent, or are unable to represent themselves due to ignorance, illiteracy, or low intelligence.[4] The case involved nine young black men accused of raping two white women. The Supreme Court reversed their convictions, although they were retried with the assistance of counsel and four of the nine defendants were convicted (even though one of the victims recanted the charges of rape). Six years after the

■**right to counsel**
A Sixth Amendment protection that guarantees suspects the right to representation by an attorney when their liberty is in jeopardy.

POWELL V. ALABAMA

Powell decision, in *Johnson v. Zerbst*, the Supreme Court extended the right to counsel to *all* indigent felony defendants in *federal* cases, but did not extend the right to state cases (where most felony trials take place).[5] The Court justified this position in the 1942 case *Betts v. Brady*, stating that the right to counsel "is not a fundamental right" in noncapital cases unless special circumstances such as lack of education or mental illness are present.[6] Many states did not follow the guidelines of *Betts*, however, and often failed to provide attorneys even in cases that warranted provision of defense counsel. In 1963 this situation culminated in the case *Gideon v. Wainwright*, one of the Supreme Court's most significant decisions.

GIDEON V. WAINWRIGHT   Clarence Earl Gideon was charged with breaking into a poolroom in Panama City, Florida. A witness claimed to have seen Gideon through the broken poolroom window at 5:30 A.M. A cigarette machine and jukebox were broken into and coins were taken. A "small amount of beer and some wine" were also taken.[7] This offense was a felony under Florida law. Appearing in court without funds and without a lawyer, Gideon asked the court to appoint counsel for him, whereupon the following exchange took place:

The Court: *Mr. Gideon, I am sorry, but I cannot appoint counsel to represent you in this case. Under the laws of the State of Florida, the only time the Court can appoint Counsel to represent a Defendant is when that person is charged with a capital offense. I am sorry, but I will have to deny your request to appoint Counsel to defend you in this case.*

The Defendant: *The United States Supreme Court says I am entitled to be represented by Counsel.*

Gideon was forced to conduct his own defense at trial. As the Supreme Court later said, he performed "about as well as could be expected from a layman. He made an opening statement to the jury, cross-examined the State's witnesses, presented witnesses in his own defense, declined to testify himself, and made a short argument emphasizing his innocence to the charge."

Nevertheless, the jury returned a verdict of guilty, and Gideon was sentenced to five years in state prison. From prison Gideon filed a handwritten habeas corpus petition challenging his conviction and sentence on the ground that the trial court's refusal to appoint counsel for him denied him rights "guaranteed by the Constitution and the Bill of Rights of the United States Government."

In considering the petition, the Supreme Court noted that the government spends large amounts of money on lawyers to prosecute defendants and that defendants who have money hire the best lawyers they can find to represent them. The Court concluded:

That government hires lawyers to prosecute and defendants who have money hire lawyers to defend are the strongest indications of the widespread belief that lawyers in criminal courts are necessities, not luxuries. The right of one charged with crime to counsel may not be deemed fundamental and essential to fair trials in some countries, but it is in ours. From the very beginning, our state and national constitutions and laws have laid great em-

phasis on procedural and substantive safeguards designed to assure fair trials before impartial tribunals in which every defendant stands equal before the law. This noble ideal cannot be realized if the poor man charged with crime has to face his accusers without a lawyer to assist him.[8]

The Court went on to quote Justice Sutherland's opinion from the 1932 *Powell v. Alabama* case. That opinion held that the right to be heard in court would be "of little value if it did not comprehend the right to be heard by counsel":

Even the intelligent and educated layman has small and sometimes no skill in the science of law. If charged with crime, he is incapable, generally, of determining for himself whether the indictment is good or bad. He is unfamiliar with the rules of evidence. Left without the aid of counsel he may be put on trial without a proper charge, and convicted upon incompetent evidence, or evidence irrelevant to the issue or otherwise inadmissible. He lacks both the skill and knowledge adequately to prepare his defense, even though he have a perfect one. He requires the guiding hand of counsel at every step in the proceedings against him. Without it, though he be not guilty, he faces the danger of conviction because he does not know how to establish his innocence.[9]

Following this line of argument, the Court made the right to counsel during felony trials binding on all the states. The case of *Gideon v. Wainwright* proved to be a precedent-setting case in establishing the scope of the right to counsel.

EXTENSIONS OF THE RIGHT TO COUNSEL After the *Gideon* decision, questions remained regarding its scope. Would it extend to misdemeanor cases? What about nontrial proceedings? Beginning in 1963, the same year as the *Gideon* decision, the Court extended the right to counsel

This person has been accused of committing a violent crime. In the American criminal justice system he is entitled to a trial by jury that is speedy, public, and impartial or fair. What provisions will be made to achieve this kind of a trial? How will his case be conducted and who will be involved in it?

to other stages of the criminal justice process to ensure fair and impartial treatment of those accused of crimes. The Sixth Amendment right to counsel now extends to crime suspects questioned while in police custody[10] or during preliminary hearings,[11] to first appeal after conviction,[12] to police lineups,[13] to juvenile delinquency proceedings,[14] and to those charged with misdemeanors when imprisonment may result.[15] The decision in the last case referred to, *Argersinger v. Hamlin*, held that in situations in which a person can be deprived of liberty, the right to counsel exists, even when imprisonment for only one day can result.[16]

The impact of these legal decisions on practice illustrates their importance. Table 9.1 summarizes the findings of a survey of jail inmates awaiting trial in the United States. As Table 9.1 indicates, of those who hired their own legal counsel, 69 percent first spoke with their attorney either before they were jailed or during the first week in jail. Of those for whom counsel was provided by the government, only 47 percent spoke with a lawyer that early in the process. The timing of access to legal counsel can be critical, because interrogations and statements often are made early in the process and can influence the outcome of a case. This survey of jail inmates also shows the significance of the Supreme Court decisions guaranteeing legal counsel to indigent defendants. More than 77 percent of all inmates received appointed counsel, illustrating the large proportion of defendants who are poor.

Right to *Effective* Counsel

■ effective counsel
Competent representation by a defense attorney. It is ineffective assistance of counsel when unprofessional errors would have changed the outcome of the case.

A defendant is entitled not only to legal counsel, but to **effective counsel.** In 1970 the Supreme Court ruled that defendants are entitled "to the effective assistance of competent counsel."[17] But in 1999 litigation was still alleging that effective assistance of counsel is often lacking—because of an inadequate supply of experienced lawyers in some jurisdictions, poor court supervision of the conduct of defense counsel, and jurisdictions' lack of funds to pay good lawyers.[18] The fundamental question in many instances is whether the legal advice given to a defendant is defective to such a degree that a defendant's case is hampered.

TABLE 9.1

When Jail Inmates Awaiting Trial First Talked with a Lawyer

FIRST MET WITH LAWYER	HIRED COUNSEL	APPOINTED COUNSEL
Before admission to jail	28%	13%
First week after admission	41%	34%
Second week after admission	10%	15%
More than 2 weeks after admission	19%	34%
Don't know	3%	4%
Number of inmates	68,409	230,599

SOURCE: James J. Stephan and Louis W. Jankowski, *Survey of Jail Inmates* (Washington, DC: Bureau of Justice Statistics, 1992).

STRICKLAND V. WASHINGTON

An actual case, *Strickland v. Washington*, illustrates the issue. Over a ten-day period David Leroy Washington committed a series of crimes, including theft, kidnapping, assaults, torture, and three brutal stabbing murders. After his two accomplices were arrested, Washington surrendered to police and gave a lengthy statement in which he confessed to one of the criminal incidents. The State of Florida indicted Washington for kidnapping and murder and appointed an experienced criminal lawyer to represent him.

Washington's appointed counsel subsequently learned that, against his advice, Washington had confessed to another of the murders. Washington waived his right to a jury trial, again acting against his counsel's advice, and pleaded guilty to all charges, including three capital murder charges.

When entering his plea Washington told the judge that he had no significant prior criminal record and that at the time of the crime spree he was under extreme stress caused by his inability to support his family. He also stated that he accepted responsibility for the crimes. The judge told Washington that he had "a great deal of respect for people who are willing to step forward and admit their responsibility," but he postponed sentencing.

In preparing for the sentencing hearing, Washington's lawyer spoke with his client about his background; he also spoke on the telephone with Washington's wife and mother, but did not seek any other character witnesses for him. The lawyer did not request a psychiatric examination, as his conversations with Washington gave no indications of psychological problems. He successfully excluded Washington's criminal record from consideration in sentencing by not requesting a presentence report. Such a report would have found that Washington did indeed have a significant criminal history.

At the sentencing hearing, the defense counsel argued that Washington's surrender, confession, offer to testify against a codefendant, and remorse and acceptance of responsibility justified sparing him from the death penalty. He characterized Washington as "fundamentally a good person who had briefly gone badly wrong in extremely stressful circumstances."[19] In determining whether the death sentence was appropriate, the judge found that all three murders had been cruel, involving repeated stabbings; all had been committed during the course of robberies; and all had been committed to avoid detection and arrest. The judge held that Washington was not suffering from extreme mental or emotional disturbance, and that his participation in the crimes was significant and not dominated by an accomplice. Washington was sentenced to death.

On appeal, Washington argued that he had received ineffective assistance of counsel in violation of the Sixth Amendment. He argued that his attorney's failure to request a psychiatric report, present character witnesses, or seek a presence report had adversely affected his chances of receiving a less severe sentence. The Supreme Court ruled that when ineffective assistance of counsel is claimed, "the defendant must show that counsel's representation fell below an objective standard of reasonableness." In addition, the defendant must show "that there is a reasonable probability that, but for counsel's unprofessional errors, the result of the proceeding would have been different." In reviewing the facts of Washington's case, the Court determined that his lawyer's conduct was reasonable. Moreover, it held that even if his attorney's

This is a public defender's office. What laws and judicial rulings guarantee Americans accused of crimes the right to be represented by free and effective legal counsel? At what stages of the criminal justice process are defendants entitled to defense counsel's assistance? Who are public defenders, and what services do they provide? Whose interests do they serve? Do you think that public defenders are more likely to provide better representation than assigned counsel? Why or why not?

STUDIES OF
DEFENSE QUALITY

INDIGENT DEFENSE

conduct was unreasonable, the case was not affected to the extent that would warrant setting aside his death sentence.[20]

In sum, under current law crime suspects and defendants are permitted to consult attorneys at most stages of the criminal justice process. The level of assistance provided must be "objectively reasonable, considering all the circumstances"; and for an appeal to be sustained, it must be shown that without counsel's errors the outcome of the trial would probably have been different. Different outcomes are difficult to prove, and grave errors of legal counsel are insufficient to prove that counsel's assistance was ineffective.

Several studies have attempted to assess objectively the quality of defense counsel. Each study has focused on whether someone who retains his or her own counsel receives better legal representation than someone represented by assigned counsel or a public defender. A few facts are clear: Caseloads are high, funding for indigent defense is low, and there are no national data that compare funding of prosecution to funding of defense in criminal cases. More than $1.3 billion is spent on indigent defense services annually in nearly 5 million cases, although the average expenditure per case is only $223.[21] This low case preparation cost has led to criticism of how indigent defense works in practice. Critics believe that government reimbursement for assigned counsel is too low, leading to poor-quality representation and inadequate investigations by defense lawyers of the charges against their clients.[22]

States vary in how they pay for indigent defense. In twenty states the state government funds the defense of indigent persons; in ten states the county does; and in twenty jurisdictions funding is shared by the county and state. Most counties (75 percent) require the defendant to repay a portion of his or her defense costs, but this money is difficult to collect, because of the indigent status of most defendants. Overall spending is much higher for prosecutors' offices than for public defenders' offices, and it is likely that expenditures per case (on investigations, witness interviews, expert opinions, and legal research) are also significantly higher. The state of Mississippi, for example, leaves indigent criminal defense funding to the individual counties, a fact that has caused concern about uniformity in the funding and quality of legal representation.[23] A study of legal representation in Chicago found that public defenders obtained more guilty pleas than did private or assigned counsel.[24] However, a subsequent study discovered that this difference may have been due to the types of cases that public defenders handle. Ninety percent of the public defender caseload in one city consisted of burglary, forgery, robbery, and theft cases, but only 66 percent of defendants with private counsel were charged with these crimes.[25] Because criminality is strongly related to opportunities to commit crime, it is not surprising that indigent offenders commit different types of offenses than do middle-class offenders. On the basis of the available information, therefore, no definite conclusions can be drawn from this debate—except that perhaps we cannot gauge the quality of defense lawyers by looking at the proportion of guilty pleas they obtain.[26]

Media and Criminal Justice

PRIMAL FEAR

Many of the most famous American defense attorneys have said that they never ask their clients whether or not they are guilty, because it doesn't matter. The job of a defense attorney is a simple mission: Consider the case against the accused and do one's utmost to test the strength of that case on any grounds available.

The 1996 psychological thriller *Primal Fear* features an arrogant but aggressive defense attorney named Martin Vail who is torn between the fight for justice and his own need for fame. When Vail sees an evening TV news story about a Catholic archbishop who has been found murdered in his underwear, he immediately seeks to defend the shy young man accused of the crime. His new client, Aaron, insists that he is innocent—that he was in the room shortly before the cleric was murdered, but that he also remembers someone else being there. He claims to have blacked out, perhaps having been attacked by the murderer. As a good defense attorney, Vail doesn't care. He explains to Aaron that whether or not he committed the murder is immaterial to the defense of the case.

To prepare his defense, Vail launches an investigation that reveals that the murdered archbishop was involved in land deals that lost millions of dollars and left many powerful investors angry. The priest had received many death threats. Is it possible that Aaron is being framed for what was actually a mob hit?

At first Vail's motivation is to grab headlines and bolster his image. As the facts unfold, however, Vail begins to realize that he may actually be defending a truly innocent person. It is discovered that the murdered archbishop was involved in sexually exploitative relationships with Aaron and other young men at the orphanage where the murder occurred, and Vail finds himself emotionally involved in the case, suddenly determined to help the innocent boy find justice.

Vail's defense must take a sudden turn, however, when the court-appointed psychologist discovers that Aaron has a dual-personality disorder and that a "bad" Aaron may have committed the crime. Unfortunately for Vail, the trial has already begun and his defense strategy has been launched; it is too late to enter a plea of insanity. The movie's climax occurs when Vail manages to coax the unsuspecting Aaron into revealing his "bad" alter  ego on the witness stand: In a sudden violent outburst, Aaron's dark side is exposed to the jury, and a mistrial is declared.

The most riveting scene of *Primal Fear*, however, is not Vail's successful Perry Mason–style defense of Aaron in the courtroom. Rather, it is the last scene of the movie, in which Vail must face the truth about who actually killed the archbishop. After one final meeting with the vindicated Aaron, Vail is shown leaving the courthouse in shock, trying to absorb the ramifications of what he has done.

Primal Fear was made to be more entertaining than educational, but it still offers insight into a situation that defense attorneys must face every day: defending a person who may or may not be guilty, and living with the consequences of doing so.

Should the guilt or innocence of a defendant affect how a defense attorney handles the case? What are the roles and goals of the prosecutor and the defense attorney in a criminal trial? How does the system of prosecution, defense, judge, and jury attempt to ensure justice?

A related issue in evaluations of the effectiveness of indigent defense is the nature of attorney–client relations. Defendants usually cannot choose their lawyers, and the feeling that "you get what you pay for" often leads to suspicion, lack of cooperation, and guarded exchanges of information.[27] These circumstances may have a significant but unmeasured impact on the quality of legal representation and may account for continuing suits by defendants claiming they received ineffective assistance of counsel under the Sixth Amendment.[28]

How Are Cases Settled without Trial?

Police are called to the scene and find an inebriated husband assaulting his wife. They arrest the man and charge him with assault, possession of narcotics, and possession of a weapon. After they complete the arrest report, it is forwarded to the prosecutor for his or her evaluation. The prosecutor may decide to prosecute on all the arrest charges, drop some of them, reduce the charges, or not prosecute the case at all. A decision not to prosecute may be based on errors in the conduct of the police in the case or on a high volume of felony cases in the area where the offense took place, an overload that forces the prosecutor to set priorities in deciding which cases will be adjudicated to the full extent of the law. If the prosecutor decides not to prosecute a case, the judge and jury cannot serve any function and the arrest is meaningless.

The scope of a prosecutor's discretion is broad. As noted in Chapter 8, the prosecutor's ability to select the charge on which a case will be prosecuted, or whether the case will be adjudicated at all, can have dramatic effects on the suspect, on the community, and on the criminal justice system. In recent years this role has expanded further, as half the states now permit prosecutors to select a trial by jury even if the defendant prefers a bench trial.[29]

Prosecutorial Discretion

Prosecutors have few limits on how they carry out their role. Consider a Manhattan district attorney in New York City who has established a narcotics eviction program. In response to complaints of tenants in poor neighborhoods, the DA asks landlords to begin eviction proceedings against tenants who are using drugs or allowing others to use their apartment to sell drugs. If the landlord does not act, the DA initiates eviction proceedings under New York's real estate law, which prohibits the use of any premises for the conduct of illegal activity. Police searches of the premises produce evidence that support allegations of illegal use. In one case a sixty-eight-year-old woman was living with two daughters who were selling drugs. The judge allowed the mother to remain in the apartment but barred the daughters from returning there. In six years the program removed more than 2,000 drug users and dealers from both residential and commercial buildings.[30] This example illustrates the broad powers of prosecutors.

PROSECUTORIAL POWERS

Prosecutors are granted considerable discretion in the manner in which they enforce the law.[31] They can set priorities, concentrate on certain types of cases, and avoid other cases entirely. A good way to assess the extent of prosecutorial discretion is to trace the effects of a prosecutor's decision on a single case as it proceeds through the system. Assume that police have arrested a suspect on a charge of armed robbery. They turn the case over to the prosecutor, who decides (1) whether the case will be prosecuted and (2) what charges will be pressed. In the case of armed robbery, for example, assault, larceny, and weapons charges could be filed in addition to the robbery charge. These additional charges are called **necessarily included offenses** (or "lesser" included offenses) because they are, by definition, included as part of the other (more serious) offense.

After charges have been filed, the prosecutor can decide not to press the charges any farther or to reduce the charge in exchange for a guilty plea. When the charge is not pressed farther, it is called **nolle prosequi** (or nol. pros.). Such a decision is entirely within the prosecutor's discretion. Exchanging a reduced charge for a guilty plea is a form of plea bargaining (discussed below). After a defendant has pleaded guilty or been convicted in court, the prosecutor usually recommends a particular sentence to the judge. Thus, the prosecutor has considerable discretion at virtually all important decision points in the criminal justice process: determining whether the police decision to arrest was appropriate, determining the charge, recommending bail, playing a role in whether or not a defendant goes to trial, and influencing the judge's sentencing decision.

The scope of a prosecutor's discretion continues to expand as the adoption of mandatory minimum sentence laws and truth-in-sentencing laws (discussed later in this chapter) has reduced judges' flexibility in decisions about sentencing. For example, many states have gun-carrying laws that attach mandatory sentences of one year of more for persons who possess a handgun without a proper permit. A prosecutor may choose to prosecute a first offender for a lesser crime, such as disorderly conduct or trespass, that does not carry a mandatory sentence. Alternatively, the prosecutor may wish to charge the first offender with the greater offense—whether for deterrence or for political leverage in a campaign. This shifting of sentencing authority away from judges and toward the prosecutors has been criticized for placing too much power in the hands of individuals.[32] Prosecutors have opportunities to misuse their discretionary powers.[33]

Diversion of Cases

Another important decision made by prosecutors is to divert some offenders out of the adjudication process. **Diversion programs** are alternatives to the formal criminal justice process, implemented after a suspect has been charged but prior to adjudication. These programs attempt to achieve a noncriminal disposition of the case. Sixty-three percent of all prosecutors' offices in the United States have a diversion program for first-time offenders.[34]

A common type of diversion program is **pretrial intervention (PTI).** Where PTI programs exist, any offender can apply to the prosecutor for admission to the program. If the nature of the offense and the offender's background are such that little risk will be posed to the community, the prosecutor suspends prosecution of the case for one year. During this time the prosecutor can require the offender, for example, to make restitution to the victim, attend a drug or alcohol treatment program, or participate in voluntary service to the community. After one year, if the offender has not gotten into further legal trouble, the prosecutor will move to dismiss the case. If the offender fails to live up to the prosecutor's expectations, the case is resumed and passes through the normal adjudication process. Pretrial intervention

■ necessarily included offenses
Offenses that are, by definition, included in a charge as part of another (more serious) offense; also called "lesser" included offenses.

■ nolle prosequi
Decision by a prosecutor not to press charges; also known as nol. pros.

EXPANDING
DISCRETIONARY
POWERS

■ diversion programs
Alternatives to the formal criminal justice process that are implemented after charging but prior to adjudication; they attempt to achieve a noncriminal disposition of the case.

■ pretrial intervention (PTI)
A type of diversion program in which a prosecutor suspends prosecution of a case pending the fulfillment of special conditions by the defendant. If these conditions are met, the case is dismissed.

CRITICS OF
DIVERSION
PROGRAMS

INTERMEDIATE
SANCTIONS

■plea bargaining
Agreement by a prosecutor
to press a less serious charge,
drop some charges, or recommend a less severe sentence
if the defendant agrees to
plead guilty.

FIGURE 9.1
Adjudication of Felony
Arrests in the Seventy-
five Largest Counties
in the U.S.

SOURCE: Compiled from
Timothy C. Hart and Brian A.
Reaves, *Felony Defendants in
Large Urban Counties* (Wash-
ington, DC: Bureau of Justice
Statistics, 1999).

gives first-time offenders, property offenders, and people who have committed misdemeanors an opportunity to show that they should not be prosecuted. Such programs increase the possibility that an offender will be
rehabilitated. They also reduce court costs and caseloads.

Some critics of diversion programs believe that offenders do not deserve
a break and that PTI programs weaken the deterrence effect of the law.
Other critics feel that diversion programs do not go far enough and that prosecutors, in order to compile a good record of success for their office, may
recommend diversion only to the offenders with the greatest chance of
completing the program successfully. As a result, people who could benefit from the treatment may be denied access to PTI. Also, prosecutors may
be tempted to encourage participation in diversion programs when the case
is weak or when they otherwise would not have prosecuted the case. In this
sense, diversion may *increase* rather than decrease the number of people
who are subjected to the criminal justice process.[35]

Diversion also takes the form of conditional sentences. Most prosecutors
now recommend a wide range of "intermediate sanctions" that involve
neither incarceration nor probation. More than three-fourths of prosecutors'
offices nationwide report resolving some cases by recommending alcohol or
drug rehabilitation, community service, counseling, or restitution.[36] These
kinds of dispositions are designed to deter future misconduct more effectively by addressing the underlying causes of the unlawful behavior.

Evidence indicates, however, that most felony cases result in prosecution.
An analysis of prosecutions in the seventy-five largest counties in the
United States found that for every 100 persons arrested for a felony, 29
went to court but were dismissed; only 55 were convicted of a felony. Of
these, 38 received jail or prison sentences, and only 17 were imprisoned for
more than one year.[37] This case shrinkage is illustrated in Figure 9.1. What
is not clear is why some of the cases were not prosecuted and why so many
suspects escaped conviction and prison sentences.

Plea Bargaining

Plea bargaining occurs when a prosecutor agrees to press a less serious
charge, drop some charges, or recommend a less severe sentence if the de-

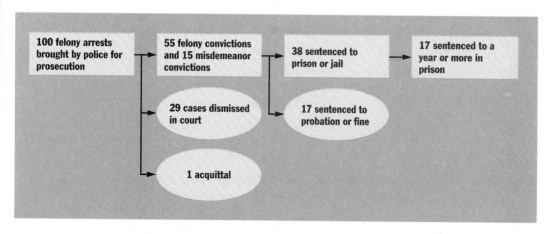

In this negotiating session, the prosecuting attorney is offering to press a less serious charge or drop some charges, or to recommend leniency in sentencing, in exchange for the defendant's guilty plea. The defense attorney is advising his client to take the deal. This kind of arrangement is common in the American court system. What is it called? What are its advantages and disadvantages for the operation of the courts? for defendants? for justice?

fendant agrees to plead guilty. Prosecutors often claim that plea bargaining is a necessary evil that enables them deal with large caseloads. Others claim that it is merely an administrative convenience. To understand this debate, it is important to know the history, nature, and extent of plea bargaining.

Milton Heumann conducted a classic study to determine how recently plea bargaining became a common practice in the United States. He looked at trial rates for felonies in Connecticut Superior Court from 1880 through 1954 and found that the percentage of cases that went to trial averaged about 9 percent throughout this seventy-five-year period.[38] That is to say, only 9 percent of all dispositions were the result of a trial—meaning that about 9 in 10 cases were resolved through guilty pleas. Heumann then looked at Connecticut trial rates from 1966 to 1973, and found the same low rate of trials and high incidence of guilty pleas.

High rates of plea bargaining also have been found in other studies of plea-bargaining practices in other locations. Abraham Blumberg examined trial rates in a metropolitan court over a period of twenty-five years. Blumberg found no significant variation in the frequency of trials over the years, and never did the trial rate exceed 10 percent.[39] Another study looked at fourteen different counties and found that pleas outnumbered trials by eleven to one.[40] Similarly, a study of felony defendants in the seventy-five largest U.S. counties found that more than 90 percent pleaded guilty and did not go to trial.[41] Recent national surveys of prosecutors' offices in the United States found that the proportion of guilty pleas changed little in the period studied, averaging 90 percent of all felony convictions.[42] It appears, therefore, that plea bargaining is not a recent phenomenon and that it is widely used to resolve cases in jurisdictions of all types. Table 9.2 illustrates that the proportion of pleas to trials does not

THE HEUMANN STUDY

TABLE 9.2

Trial Rates for Convicted Felony Offenders in the Seventy-five Largest U.S. Counties

OFFENSE	TOTAL CONVICTED	PLEA	TRIAL
Murder	62%	32%	29%
Rape	57	50	7
Robbery	57	51	6
Assault	33	29	4
Burglary	62	58	5
Larceny	55	52	3
Drug Offenses	63	61	3
All Offenses	55%	52%	4%

SOURCE: Timothy C. Hart and Brian A. Reaves, *Felony Defendants in Large Urban Counties* (Washington, DC: Bureau of Justice Statistics, 1999).

contemporary issues and trends

Selective Prosecution of High-Rate Offenders

Many of the most serious offenders are also repeat offenders. Often these persons are habitual, high-rate, and/or dangerous offenders who commit a larger proportion of crimes than their numbers would warrant. Selective prosecution of repeat offenders ensures that their cases receive special attention, charges are not reduced, and long sentences are recommended in order to incapacitate problem defendants.

In a growing number of jurisdictions, prosecutors have established formal or informal guidelines under which these offenders are prosecuted on an individualized basis. The TARGET program in Ocean County, California, for example, is a collaborative effort of the district attorney's office, the police department, and the probation department. The program targets the most dangerous gangs and their leadership, using an assessment of gang members' past conduct to predict which one is most likely to offend next. Police place this person under surveillance in an effort to

catch him committing even a nonserious crime. The district attorney then aggressively prosecutes the gang member and seeks a long sentence in order to incapacitate the offender and disrupt the gang. In two-thirds of all prosecutors' offices nationwide, a system known as *vertical prosecution* is employed for specialized prosecutions like these. For at least certain kinds of cases (such as sexual assault, gun, or drug cases), a prosecutor stays with the same case through sentencing in order to develop expertise about the offenders involved and legal developments in the area.[a]

A national survey found that a significant proportion of prosecutors' offices deal with serious cases involving repeat offenders, including cases of domestic violence (88 percent repeat offenses), stalking (68 percent), elder abuse (41 percent), hate crime (29 percent), or environmental pollution (26 percent).[b] A

> There exist many repeat offenders: two-thirds of felony defendants have a felony arrest record.

problem arises, however, when prosecutors attempt to determine which offenders are "dangerous" or "high-rate" early in their criminal careers.

An examination of selective prosecution efforts in several counties found that written criteria defining what constitutes a "career criminal" serve to "promote consistency" in prosecutors' judgments about which cases to handle differently.[c]

Some factors that are commonly believed to be associated with high-rate offending actually are not. Display of a weapon, alcoholism, prior arrests for drug offenses, prior probation or parole revocation, and previous incarceration have been found not to be associated with high-rate offending.[d] On the other hand, some defendants arrested for less serious offenses (such as larceny or burglary of an empty building) have prior records indicating a high rate of violent offenses. These defendants cannot be selectively

---

fluctuate widely by type of offense. These data from the seventy-five largest U.S. counties found that trial rates are 7 percent or less for all offenses except murder, for which 29 percent of cases are tried.

Contrary to what you might expect, courts with low caseloads have been found to have higher plea rates than courts with high caseloads.[43] In an analogous way, counties with high rates of plea bargaining often were found to have lower caseloads than counties with low rates of plea bargaining. To try to explain this, Heumann interviewed prosecutors, judges, and defendants. He discovered that most cases have no substantial legal or factual issues, and that the risks entailed in going to trial (and possibly losing) are quite high. Therefore, many prosecutors, defense counsel, and suspects feel that a guilty plea is a more advantageous path than going to trial. Thus, plea bargaining appears to result from factors other than high caseloads.

prosecuted, because the most recent offense does not carry a severe penalty.

To be effective, then, selective prosecution must overcome at least two major hurdles: obtaining accurate knowledge of which factors are in fact associated with repeat and violent offenses, and arresting the repeat offender as early as possible in his or her career for a serious offense that warrants selective prosecution. There exist many repeat offenders: two-thirds of felony defendants have a felony arrest record, and more than a third are on bail, probation, or parole at the time that they are charged with a new crime.[e] Nearly 20 percent of felony offenders are sentenced for convictions for two or more felonies arising from a single case, indicating that there exists a significant proportion of serious offenders.[f] Multiple felonies in a single case might include a robbery and murder; kidnapping and assault; burglary, theft, and assault; or some other combination of crimes that occur as part of a single incident. In addition, more than 96 percent of all prosecutors' officers use a defendant's criminal history during the course of pretrial negotiations and at sentencing.[g]

Continuing research into criminal offending patterns is needed to ensure that typologies of career criminals are based on factual data and not on inaccurate or outdated "folk wisdom." Also, there must be safeguards to ensure that individuals who are predicted to be high-rate offenders are not handled differently without proof that they have committed prior offenses. The criminal justice system permits punishment only for crimes committed in the past, not for crimes contemplated in the future. Yet, if they are armed with reliable information about past patterns of criminal activity, prosecutors have a strong argument for enhanced sentencing based on the offender's past and on the behavior of other criminals with similar backgrounds.

1. Given the broad scope of prosecutors' discretion, what safeguards exist to make sure that they do not fail to prosecute career criminals to the full extent of the law?
2. How might plea bargaining work against selective prosecution of high-rate offenders?
3. How can defense attorneys ensure that clients are not unjustifiably prosecuted as suspected or predicted career criminals?

NOTES

a. Heike P. Gramckow and Elena Tompkins, *Enabling Prosecutors to Address Drug, Gang, and Youth Violence* (Washington, DC: Office of Juvenile Justice and Delinquency Prevention, 1999).

b. Carol J. DeFrances, Steven K. Smith, and Louise van der Does, *Prosecutors in State Courts* (Washington, DC: Bureau of Justice Statistics, 1996).

c. Marcia R. Chaiken and Jan M. Chaiken, *Priority Prosecution of High-Rate Dangerous Offenders* (Washington, DC: National Institute of Justice, 1991), p. 4.

d. Ibid., p. 6.

e. Brian A. Reaves and Pheny Z. Smith, *Felony Defendants in Large Urban Counties* (Washington, DC: Bureau of Justice Statistics, 1995).

f. Patrick A. Langan and Jodi M. Brown, *Felony Sentences in State Courts* (Washington, DC: Bureau of Justice Statistics, 1997), p. 6.

g. DeFrances et al., 1996, p. 6.

What Are Some Problems of the Court System?

Courts face problems that arise from increasing arrests and higher caseloads, a more litigious society, and overreliance on pleas. These problems have created delays in the adjudication process, growing backlogs of cases to be heard, and claims of unfairness in the way cases are handled.

Courts adjudicate a large volume of cases each year, and the number is growing. This increased volume reflects the growth of the U.S. population, increases in arrests, and increases in the use of lawsuits to resolve disputes.

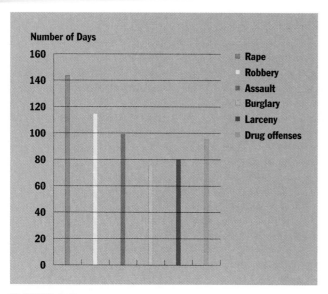

FIGURE 9.2

Time from Arrest to Adjudication for Felony Defendants in the Seventy-five Largest U.S. Counties

SOURCE: Timothy C. Hart and Brian A. Reaves, *Felony Defendants in Large Urban Counties* (Washington, DC: Bureau of Justice Statistics, 1999).

ADJUDICATION
STATISTICS

■Speedy Trial Act
Legislation requiring that all criminal cases be brought to trial within one hundred days.

■caseloads
The numbers of cases to be adjudicated in the courts of various jurisdictions.

TABLE 9.3

Criminal Cases Filed
in U.S. District Courts

YEAR	NUMBER OF CASES FILED
1980	27,910
1985	38,546
1990	47,962
1995	45,053
1998	57,023

SOURCE: Administrative Office of the United States Courts, *Annual Report to the Director* (Washington, DC: U.S. Government Printing Office, 1999).

The dramatic growth in caseloads has placed tremendous strain on many courts. The situation was aggravated in 1974 when Congress passed the **Speedy Trial Act.** This act requires that all criminal cases be brought to trial within one hundred days; if they are not, they will be dismissed.

The rationale for the Speedy Trial Act is that the Sixth Amendment requires "a speedy and public trial" and that delays in court often work against the interests of the accused, who may be in jail awaiting adjudication of the case. The result of the act has been an increase in the speed with which criminal cases are brought to trial, but a dramatic slowing in the processing of civil cases, which are not covered by the act. This is why it often takes several years for a civil case to reach the trial stage. In addition, criminal cases take up a great deal of court time. Every criminal case requires an initial appearance, a preliminary hearing or grand jury, arraignment, and possibly a trial and an appeal. Courts must be highly organized to handle so many court appearances and to determine the need for and availability of judges, courtrooms, court clerks, stenographers, sheriff's deputies, and other participants in the adjudication process.

Figure 9.2 displays the median time from arrest to adjudication for felony defendants in the seventy-five largest counties in the United States. The typical felony is now adjudicated in 89 days, although it varies considerably by offense, from 142 days in rape cases to 70 days in burglary cases. Murder cases usually take considerably longer, because of the time it takes to analyze physical evidence and obtain expert witnesses, which are used often in cases of homicide. Cases are permitted to exceed the 100-day limit only when the court agrees that the defense needs additional time to prepare its case.

Caseloads

The problem of rising **caseloads** is serious in federal courts; the volume of cases in federal district courts has nearly tripled since 1980. In 1991 the average federal trial judge handled 401 cases. In 1997 the number was 470. Part of the problem arises because of judicial vacancies: More than 100 positions for federal judges remain unfilled because of disagreement between the president and the Senate (controlled by the opposing political party) about suitable candidates. In 1994 101 new federal judges were approved; in 1996 and 1997 combined, only 53 were confirmed. Another contributing factor to high federal caseloads is the "federalizing" of crimes previously handled by the states.[44] Since 1980 Congress has dramatically increased the number of federal crimes, especially drug and gun offenses. Therefore, crimes once handled exclusively in state courts are increasingly being tried as violations of federal law. Table 9.3 illustrates the dramatic increase in criminal cases filed in U.S. district courts. In 1980 27,910 cases were filed; by 1998 the number had more than doubled to 57,023.

Both new criminal charges and appeals from adjudicated cases have increased tenfold in recent decades, and there is no end in sight. In state courts, which handle more than 95 percent of the total volume of cases, nearly 90 million new cases are filed each year. Since 1970 the largest increases have been in criminal cases (up 35 percent), juvenile cases (up 60 percent), and domestic relations cases (up 65 percent).[45] Despite a growing trend toward the use of mediation and pretrial intervention programs, new cases far outstrip the capacity of these programs to deal with them.

As the U.S. population grows, it is reasonable to expect the numbers of arrests and cases filed to increase as well. One of the largest sources of higher caseloads is drug cases. The increase in laws and law enforcement in this area in recent decades has led to thousands of arrests and prosecutions throughout the nation. As noted in Chapter 8, specialized drug courts have been created in some areas, but it is clear that more judges and more courtrooms and courtroom personnel will be needed for the foreseeable future. Table 9.4 outlines some growing career opportunities in adjudication.

TABLE 9.4

Career Opportunities in Adjudication

Prosecuting attorney http://www.abanet.org/lsd/jobopp.html http://www.ndaa-apri.org/	Represents a jurisdiction (district or commonwealth) in bringing charges against accused persons arrested by the police. *Qualifications:* Law school graduation and passage of the bar examination.
Legal assistant http://www.paralegals.org http://www.nala.org/	Paralegal employed by prosecutors, defense attorneys, and law firms to assist in the preparation of civil and criminal cases. *Qualifications:* Completion of ten or more college-level courses at a certified school.
Defense attorney http://www.abanet.org/lsd/jobopp.html http://www.law.indiana.edu/law/v-lib/criminal.html http://www.uscourts.gov/	Represents accused persons in court proceedings. Public defenders are salaried attorneys who work on behalf of indigent defendants. Attorneys in private practice also represent clients accused of crimes. *Qualifications:* Law school graduation and passage of the bar examination.
Victim and witness assistant http://www.ilj.org/programs.html http://www.ojp.usdoj.gov/ovc/	Coordinates and provides services to victims and witnesses by providing information, counseling, or other support services.
Forensic scientist http://www.cl.state.ut.us/ http://www.ganet.org/gbi/labsci.html http://dpa.state.ky.us/~rwheeler/evidence.htm	Studies and reports on criminal evidence used in adjudication (DNA, drugs, blood, hair, fingerprints, fibers, documents, residue from bullets and explosives). *Qualifications:* Master's degree preferred; background in chemistry and biology lab work.
Judge or magistrate http://www.ajs.org/ http://www.fjc.gov/ http://www.ncsc.dni.us/ http://www.ncjfcj.unr.edu	Upholds rights of the accused, arbitrates between the prosecution and the defense in a criminal case. Instructs juries, rules on issues of law and procedure, may decide on a sentence. *Qualifications:* Attorneys are elected or appointed to the office.

Case Mortality

In a controversial case prosecutors in Ontario, Canada, offered a plea bargain to the wife of Paul Bernado, who was charged with the abduction, rape, torture, and murder of two teenage girls inside the couple's home. Despite evidence that the wife participated in the killings, and despite the fact that a judge found the plea bargain "distasteful," the plea was accepted as possibly the only way to make a case against the husband.[46] Sixteen months after the plea bargain was struck, however, videotapes were discovered that depicted the wife's active participation in the brutal rape and torture of the victims. More than 300,000 citizens signed petitions protesting the plea-bargain agreement, but it could not be changed after the fact. The wife received a twelve-year sentence and Paul Bernado received a life term.[47] Plea bargaining can backfire if prosecutors carry it out before conducting a thorough investigation, and sensational cases, although rare, inflame the public belief that offenders are getting a "deal" and that prosecutors are not representing the interests of the community effectively.

Few people are satisfied with plea bargaining, and many examples justify this skepticism. In 1999, author Stephen King was hit by a car as a pedestrian and was seriously injured. The driver plea-bargained to receive a suspended six-month jail sentence for dangerous driving. Stephen King publicly expressed his dissatisfaction that the driver was able keep his driver's license.[48] Critics have called plea bargaining "injustice for all."[49]

Public officials often have claimed that if prosecutors had smaller caseloads, the number of trials relative to pleas would increase. However, a survey by the U.S. Bureau of Justice Statistics found that only about 1 percent of all felony cases were decided by a jury trial regardless of the size of the prosecutor's office or the jurisdiction. An even smaller number of felony defendants had a bench trial, while all the other defendants pleaded guilty. Prosecutors' offices in jurisdictions of 1 million or more population handle an average of nearly 40,000 cases per year. In jurisdictions of less than 250,000, an average of 900 cases are prosecuted per year, yet the trial rate remains the same.[50] A study of federal prosecutions found that 93 percent of those convicted pleaded guilty, while 7 percent were convicted at trial.[51]

Studies of criminal case processing have found high levels of **case mortality,** or attrition. An investigation by Boland, Brady, Tyson, and Bassler examined felony arrests in fourteen counties across the country. They found that 50 percent of all cases were either dismissed or rejected by the prosecutor because of lack of sufficient evidence or for other reasons. Forty-five percent ended in guilty pleas, and only 5 percent went to trial.[52] Table 9.5 presents findings from a similar study conducted in the nation's seventy-five largest urban counties. The table indicates that, on average, the likelihood that a case will go to trial is between 4 and 8 percent. It also shows that 36 percent of violent crimes and 22 percent of property crimes are either rejected by the prosecutor or dismissed by the judge before trial. In federal cases the numbers are similar: Thirty-seven percent of violent crimes

**STUDIES OF
CRIMINAL CASE
PROCESSING**

■**case mortality**
Case attrition, in which, for
various reasons, arrests do
not result in convictions.

TABLE 9.5

Processing of Felony Cases

CRIMINAL PROCEDURE	VIOLENT CRIME	PROPERTY CRIME
Total felony defendants	100%	100%
Cases rejected by prosecutor or dismissed by court	36%	22%
Diversion from prosecution	2%	2%
Guilty pleas	52%	72%
Trials	8%	4%
Acquittal	2%	1%
Jail or prison sentence	76% of those convicted	63% of those convicted

SOURCE: Compiled from Brian A. Reaves, *Felony Defendants in Large Urban Counties* (Washington, DC: Bureau of Justice Statistics, 1998).

and 49 percent of property crimes are prosecuted.[53] The question that remains is: Why are so many cases lost along the way?

One of the first studies to address the reasons for case mortality was conducted by the Vera Institute of Justice. In this study, randomly selected case files of felony arrests in New York City were followed to their ultimate disposition. For a small subsample of those cases, participants were interviewed. Of the 53 robbery cases examined in detail, only 1 went to trial, and only 15 resulted in felony sentences.[54] Although it might appear at first glance that justice was not carried out in these cases, a closer look reveals that 23 of the 53 robberies (36 percent) involved a prior relationship between the victim and the defendant—a situation that reduces the possibility of a conviction at trial. In cases involving prior relationships, juries tend to suspect victims of using the court to seek revenge against a former spouse or lover. Of the 30 robberies that remained, 26 (88 percent) resulted in convictions and 20 (77 percent) in a jail or prison sentence. Offenders who managed to avoid felony sentences by pleading guilty to a lesser charge did so primarily because of lack of interest on the part of the victim or because the victim had a criminal record or was engaging in criminal conduct (such as prostitution or drug dealing). In a national survey of prosecutors' offices, the most frequent reasons given for case dismissals were search and seizure problems (52 percent of offices) and unavailability of witnesses (44 percent). In a large proportion of these cases, prosecutors declined to prosecute because of reluctance on the part of the victim (74 percent) or of a witness (58 percent).[55]

In cases that were prosecuted, 98 percent of offenders with a criminal record were sentenced to jail, despite the fact that serious injury occurred in only 7 of the 53 cases and only six offenders had threatened their victims with guns. These findings were confirmed in studies of different counties, which also found a high incidence of cases involving prior relationships between defendant and victim (45 percent); again, the primary factors preventing prosecution were evidence- and witness-related problems.[56]

VERA INSTITUTE OF JUSTICE STUDY

The Vera Institute study also found that court congestion caused pretrial delays that induced some defendants to plead guilty who probably would have been acquitted if they had gone to trial, because of weak evidence in the case. Subsequent studies in different cities have uncovered similar findings.[57] Judges tend to equalize the impact of lesser pleas by imposing a relatively longer sentence on the reduced charge, raising the question of whether plea bargaining benefits the defendant. Likewise, some courts have permitted longer sentences in plea bargains by taking dismissed charges into consideration.[58]

"FAKE" PLEA
BARGAINS

OVERRELIANCE ON PLEA BARGAINING Overreliance on plea bargaining can result in its abuse. A prosecutor in Ulster County, New York, authorized a "fake" plea bargain with a kidnapping defendant in which the prosecutor asked the defendant to lead them to the kidnapped girl, who was found dead. The prosecutor claimed that because the girl had been killed during the kidnapping, the plea bargain was voided. The ethics and constitutionality of rescinding a plea bargain have been questioned.[59] Similarly, some courts have allowed defendants who plea-bargained to be reindicted if their sentence is subsequently overturned on other grounds. These courts view the plea bargain as an obligation to serve the full sentence rather than an obligation to plead guilty.[60] Thus, you can see that the contractual nature of plea bargains is called into question when the plea deal changes after the agreement has been made.

REASONS FOR
PLEA BARGAINING

In sum, a growing body of evidence suggests that plea bargaining is not due to overcrowded courts or overburdened prosecutors, and that it usually does not result in lenient sentences. In reality, plea bargaining appears to result from two overriding factors: (1) Most cases have few issues of fact or law to be established at trial, because the evidence against the defendant is or is not present. And (2) the risks of going to trial are high for both sides; at trial even an "open-and-shut" case can be lost because of victims and witnesses who may be poor witnesses, and at trial even a case with weak evidence can be decided in favor of the prosecution. Therefore, plea bargaining occurs so often because it assists both prosecution and defense in obtaining a predictable outcome in an otherwise uncertain process.[61]

Plea bargaining has many undesirable features, however. Plea negotiations are conducted in private; the rights of the accused and the interests of the community are not visibly balanced (as occurs in trials); and the public may believe that justice is not achieved. In 1973 these features led the National Advisory Commission on Criminal Justice Standards and Goals to recommend that "as soon as possible, but not later than 1978, negotiations between defendants and prosecutors concerning concessions to be made in return for guilty pleas be abolished."[62] This recommendation formed the basis for several ill-fated efforts to eliminate plea bargaining entirely. Perhaps the best-evaluated effort involved New York State's drug laws. Under these laws the possession or sale of heroin or other narcotics was punished by mandatory minimum prison sentences of 1 to 15 years, with maximums ranging up to life imprisonment. If released, offenders were placed on parole for the rest of their lives, and pleas to lesser charges were not permitted.

Undesirable
Features
Of
↓
ELIMINATE PLEA
BARGAINING?

In the 1970s the New York City Bar Association conducted an evaluation of the impact of this law on drug offenders. Researchers compared arrests, indictments, and convictions a year before the law was passed and several years after it had taken effect. Surprisingly, arrests decreased, indictments fell, the proportion of arrests leading to indictments fell, and the number of convictions fell by almost one-half, indicating that the law has had the opposite of its intended effect.[63] Knowing that arrests, indictments, and convictions can lead to very severe penalties, police officers, grand juries, and trial juries are more reluctant to arrest, indict, or convict offenders who they believe do not deserve such harsh penalties.

Nevertheless, the New York experience has been repeated elsewhere, and for other crimes other than drug possession or sale. Studies have evaluated the effects of establishing mandatory penalties for drunk driving and gun law violations.[64] The results are remarkably consistent. When discretion is removed from one part of the system, it is replaced by greater use of discretion in other parts.

IMPACT OF MANDATORY SENTENCES ON PLEA BARGAINING

Mandatory sentences are designed to require a certain penalty upon conviction in order to guarantee that offenders do not escape punishment. When combined with policies forbidding plea bargaining, however, mandatory sentencing appears simply to shift discretion to other parts of the criminal justice system. As Arthur Rosset and Donald Cressey have observed, "efforts to eliminate discretionary decisions or to limit them substantially seem bound to fail because there must be a place in the courthouse both for the rule of law and for discretion."[65]

Perhaps the best-known examples of mandatory sentence laws are the **"three strikes" laws** in which conviction for a third felony results in a life sentence. These laws have increased prison populations, but they incarcerate many nonviolent offenders. In New York State, for example, nearly 80 percent of drug offenders who receive prison sentences have never been convicted of a violent crime.[66] In California, the "three strikes" law has not reduced the crime rate.[67] In Michigan, former Republican Governor William Milliken called the "650 Lifer Law" his biggest mistake. The law mandated life terms for offenders possessing 650 grams of heroin or cocaine. As a result, 86 percent of the offenders prosecuted under this law received life sentences when they had never been to prison before.[68]

Given the consistent findings about the effects of mandatory sentences and policies prohibiting plea bargaining, some general conclusions can be drawn. First, a restrictive plea-bargaining policy usually leads to a restrictive case-screening policy, so fewer cases—the stronger ones—are prosecuted. Second, when sentences are mandatory, the bargaining focuses on the charges against the accused. Third, a combination of no-plea-bargaining polices *and* mandatory sentences leads to fewer arrests, fewer indictments, fewer convictions, and more dismissals, trials (versus pleas), and appeals. Fourth, researchers have not found that harsh penalties have a deterrent effect on the commission of the offenses covered by these policies. Nevertheless, calls for the abolition of plea bargaining continue. These pro-

■ **mandatory sentences**
Requirements that certain penalties be imposed upon conviction in order to guarantee that offenders do not escape punishment.

■ **"three strikes" laws**
Laws under which conviction for a third felony results in an extended sentence, even life imprisonment.

CONSEQUENCES
OF NO-PLEA-
BARGAINING RULES

posals, in turn, are leading to proposals to change the way negotiations are conducted.[69]

CHANGING PLEA NEGOTIATIONS   The difficulty of eliminating plea bargaining has provoked efforts to find ways of reducing unfairness in existing plea-bargaining practices. Various ways to eliminate the undesirable aspects of plea bargaining have been suggested, among them public negotiations, time limitations, better case-screening procedures, and reviews of plea agreements by judges and victims. The National Advisory Commission called for a time limit on all plea negotiations; after a certain period, only pleas to the original charge filed would be permitted. In the commission's view, such a procedure would prevent unnecessary delays, which sometimes result in unwise pleas by defendants in jail awaiting trial. Felony cases typically are concluded in four to seven months, which can be a long time for a defendant serving that period in jail.[70]

pretrial settlement conference
A meeting of the prosecutor, the defendant, the defendant's counsel, and the judge to discuss a plea before a trial is held. No plea negotiations can take place outside this setting.

Several cities use a **pretrial settlement conference,** in which the prosecutor, the defendant, the defendant's counsel, and the judge meet before a trial to discuss a plea. The arresting officer and the victim are invited to attend these sessions. No plea negotiations can take place outside this setting; and no plea negotiations are admissible as evidence if a trial eventually results, so as not to prejudice a judge or jury. Therefore, trials are reserved for the few cases in which no pretrial settlement can be reached. This procedure makes the plea-bargaining process more visible, and a neutral party (the judge) is present to ensure that the rights of the defendant and the need to protect the community are properly balanced. Experimentation with this procedure has produced encouraging results.[71]

EFFECTIVE SCREENING

Another proposal is that prosecutors adopt more effective screening procedures to eliminate cases unlikely to be prosecuted successfully. A national survey of prosecutors found that inadequate evidence gathering by police and poor preparation of crime reports caused case dismissals, which proper screening might have prevented.[72] Better case screening is becoming mandatory as court caseloads include more drug offenders. Throughout the nation more than 30 percent of the felony court caseload consists of cases involving drug traffickers (19 percent) and possessors (13 percent).[73] Screening can help prosecutors distinguish between major and minor drug cases so as to use criminal justice resources more effectively.

Adjudicate the Offender or the Act?

Sensational cases in recent years have drawn attention to the defendant rather than to the crime. Although the adjudication process is designed to assess responsibility for the criminal act, media portrayals and the tactics of some defense attorneys have shifted the focus to the criminal. Defendant Colin Ferguson, for example, asked to represent himself at his trial. He was accused of engaging in a shooting rampage on a Long Island Railroad train car in which six people were killed and nineteen others wounded. Legal and psychiatric experts argued that Ferguson was paranoid and delusional, but the judge ruled that he was competent to represent himself in court. Ferguson later appealed his conviction, arguing that he was mentally incompetent to stand trial in the first place.[74] This series of events reflects confusion between granting defendants the legal right to represent themselves and the need to maintain the integrity of court proceedings by focusing on the act.

In the Menendez case and others of a similar nature, the defense has argued that the defendants should be excused because of abuse they suffered as children.[75] Although some observers consider this argument outrageous, several states have extended the excuse of self-defense to battered women who kill their husbands out of fear after a history of physical abuse, even though the husband might be sleeping at the time of the murder.[76] It can be argued that the Menendez "child abuse" defense is simply an extension of the "battered woman syndrome" defense created in the 1980s. Both attempt to employ the principle of self-defense in situations that fall outside the traditional scope of this principle.[77] On one hand, self-defense is being expanded well beyond its logical limits when the defendant is successfully portrayed as a "victim."

These brothers killed their parents, allegedly because of abuse they had suffered as children years earlier. What defense was extended in this case on the grounds that the perpetrators actually were victims? Is this kind of defense an anomaly or a trend in homicide cases today? How does it result in the adjudication of offenders rather than their crimes? Why is the shift in the target of adjudication a concern for the criminal justice system?

On the other hand, less sympathetic defendants, such as those convicted of assault and manslaughter for shooting trespassers, are treated according to the traditional rules of self-defense. Again, the focus shifts from the crime to the criminal.

The same trend can be seen in the "urban survival defense," in which defendants who take lives unlawfully are portrayed as victims.[78] Timothy McVeigh's argument that the Oklahoma City bombing was necessary as "retaliation" against the government for its actions at Waco, Texas, was an effort to stretch "self-defense" to new dimensions. Applying the logic of self-defense in these cases is a slippery slope, yet defendants and their attorneys increasingly are doing so.

After the media onslaught that surrounded the O. J. Simpson trial, courts in Los Angeles proposed new rules to ban hallway interviews during trials.[79] Attorneys in that case often held impromptu news conferences after each day's proceedings in an effort to shape public opinion about the case. Such posturing can indirectly influence the jury, which may learn of the lawyers' statements through the media. Similarly, guidelines have been proposed for lawyers who appear on television as legal commentators during subsequent civil cases, as in O. J. Simpson's civil trial. In these appearances attorneys can accidentally broadcast client confidences or distort information because of their prior involvement in a related criminal case.[80] Here again, it appears that defense attorneys focus on building the image of the defendant rather than on responding to the crimes charged. In a shocking example of this phenomenon, former assistant district attorney Steven Pagones was accused in 1987 of raping Tawana Brawley. The accusation was made by three prominent individuals from the New York City area, including the Reverend Al Sharpton.

OFFENDERS AS VICTIMS

Mr. Pagones was cleared of the charge in 1988, and he then successfully sued his accusers on charges of defamation of character. This civil suit was tried in 1998 in a case marred by name-calling, contempt citations, and other disorderly behavior in the courtroom. A defense lawyer served a night in jail for contempt in refusing to obey a judge's order.[81] Although atypical, misbehavior on the part of defense attorneys fuels the perception that they abuse the process in order to draw attention away from the facts of the case.

Crime Control or Due Process?

Among the most compelling questions for criminal defense in the future is, What do we want the criminal justice system to accomplish? The answer to this question is not straightforward and can involve quite different perspectives on the justice process.

Criminologist Herbert Packer described two ideal models of criminal justice operations that are useful when we try to evaluate the system and its operations. According to the **crime control model,** repression of criminal conduct is the most important function of the criminal justice system. To accomplish this, the system must achieve maximum speed, efficiency, and finality in criminal justice processing. Proponents of this model argue that deterrence of crime is achieved when the penalty is imposed quickly and with certainty. Quick and certain punishment cannot occur when a prolonged series of pretrial hearings, continuances and other delays, and appeals distance the connection between the crime and the punishment. In contrast, the **due process model** treats the preservation of individual liberties as the most important function of the criminal justice system. Therefore, according to this view, accuracy, fairness, and reliability in criminal procedure are keys to a properly functioning system.[82] Proponents of the due process

■ **crime control model**
The perspective that views the repression of criminal conduct as the most important function of the criminal justice system, thus calling for speed, efficiency, and finality in criminal justice processing.

■ **due process model**
The perspective that considers preservation of individual liberties to be the most important function of the criminal justice system, thus emphasizing accuracy, fairness, and reliability in criminal procedure.

What is the criminal justice system really supposed to accomplish? Do you favor the crime control model of criminal justice operations, or the due process model? How do you defend your choice? What issues about justice are inherent in efforts to achieve a balance between crime control and due process? How would you describe the differences between the ideal and the real cultures of the court process?

model believe that careful attention to the rights of individuals—when individuals are prosecuted by a much more powerful government—is essential to ensure that only the guilty are convicted and that the public has a high level of confidence in the system. This attention cannot be given when so many cases are plea bargained, defendants are encouraged to waive their constitutional rights, and the outcomes of cases are determined by invisible negotiating behind closed doors rather than in court.

These two ideal models allow us to clarify the assumptions we make about criminal justice operations. For example, someone who claims that the largest problem in criminal justice is legal restrictions on the police in stopping, questioning, and searching suspicious individuals probably believes that extensive police powers are necessary to control crime. This person probably subscribes to the crime control model and believes that repression of crime is the criminal justice system's most important function. On the other hand, someone who argues that widespread use of plea bargaining results in unfairness in the adjudication and sentencing process probably sees accuracy and fairness as the primary objectives of the criminal justice system—and believes that the due process model best describes the ideals of criminal justice.

Achieving a balance in practice between crime control and due process is not always easy. For example, the federal government spent several million dollars on the defense of Timothy McVeigh in the Oklahoma City bombing case. This amount was criticized as excessive by some observers. The underlying question, however, is: Is speed and finality more important or is accuracy and reliability more important in this case? The question is not about money, therefore, but about which model of justice should be paramount. Most people want both speed and accuracy, but these goals are difficult to achieve simultaneously. Given the constraints imposed by limited resources, the emphasis placed on one or the other of these goals will depend on the philosophy of justice that dominates in a particular case or jurisdiction.

The balance between crime control and due process is complicated also by perceptions. Public perceptions include widespread beliefs to the effect that due process protections frustrate justice rather than advance it. Two examples are the belief that defense lawyers lie to exculpate their clients and the belief that lawyers use legal technicalities to free defendants.[83] The facts generally do not support these beliefs; but the perception is reinforced when a prominent defense attorney shockingly states that "the vast majority of criminal defendants are in fact guilty of the crimes with which they are charged. Almost all of my own clients have been guilty."[84] What is the relevance of the due process model when defendants are admittedly guilty?

From a due process perspective, however, the guilt or innocence of the defendant is secondary to ensuring that the process is carried out with fairness and accuracy to reduce the *possibility* that an innocent person will be convicted unjustly. Thus, a primary difference between the two models lies in where errors are made. From the crime control perspective, the potential for wrongful conviction of a small number of innocent persons is offset by the deterrent impact of more swift and certain punishment of offenders in general. From the due process perspective, it is more egregious to punish an innocent person than it is to let a small number of the guilty go free.

ACHIEVING
A BALANCE

critical thinking exercise

Should a Lawyer Defend a Guilty Person?

Many college students wish to go on to law school but do not want to become defense attorneys. Many argue that they do not want to represent guilty people. According to one account, "What many people want to know is how defense attorneys can live with themselves after they help a guilty person escape punishment."[a] This view overlooks the fact that defense attorneys represent only the *legal rights* of defendants; not their past, their personality, or their guilt or innocence. In fact, it is "not [defense counsel's] job to decide who is guilty and not. Instead, it is the public defender's job to judge the quality of the case that the state has against the defendant."[b] According to the standards of the American Bar Association, "the defense lawyer is the professional representative of the accused, not the accused's alter ego."[c]

In a murder case that was appealed to the U.S. Supreme Court, *Nix v. Whiteside*, a defense attorney did not permit his client to testify falsely about whether he had seen a gun in the hand of the victim. The defendant claimed that he was deprived of effective assistance of counsel because of the lawyer's refusal to permit him to perjure himself. The Supreme Court disagreed and held that the defense lawyer's duty "is limited to legitimate, lawful conduct compatible with the very nature of a trial as a search for truth." As a result, "counsel is precluded from taking steps or in any way assisting the client in presenting false evidence or otherwise violating the law."[d] The proper role of a defense attorney is to represent a defendant in an honest way that seeks the truth in the case.

Nevertheless, there are those who claim that defense attorneys do not act honestly. It has been argued that the defense attorney "is a person who is more concerned with appearance and perceptions than with underlying facts; who puts greater reliance in 'personality' than in knowledge." Although the Code of Professional Responsibility prohibits false statements of fact or law in court, it is said that there is much "fiction weaving that customarily passes for argument to a jury."[e] As a result, there may be a gap between the principles and the actual practice of criminal defense.

CRITICAL THINKING QUESTIONS

1. What is a defense lawyer's role if not to represent "guilty people"?
2. Why do many people disapprove of defense attorneys or belittle their importance in criminal cases? Do you think this criticism is justified or not?
3. Give an example of a specific action or statement made by a defense attorney in a well-known case that leads you to believe that the attorney was acting inappropriately. In what sense was the behavior inappropriate?
4. What pressures do you think defense attorneys face that may lead them to act irresponsibly?

NOTES

a. Lisa J. McIntyre, *The Public Defender: The Practice of Law in the Shadows of Repute* (Chicago: University of Chicago Press, 1987), p. 139.
b. Ibid., p.145.
c. American Bar Association, *Standards for Criminal Justice*, Number 4-1.1.
d. *Nix v. Whiteside*, 475 U.S. 157 (1986).
e. H. Richard Uviller, *Virtual Justice: The Flawed Prosecution of Crime in America* (New Haven: Yale University Press, 1996), pp. 153, 155.

Summary

WHAT ARE THE RIGHTS OF THE ACCUSED?

- The Sixth Amendment to the U.S. Constitution guarantees the right of accused persons to have the assistance of counsel.
- The scope of the right to counsel has been expanded in a series of important Supreme Court cases, beginning with *Gideon v. Wainwright* in 1963.

■ In 1970 the Supreme Court ruled that defendants are entitled to *effective* assistance of counsel, but it is difficult to demonstrate that the outcome of a case would have been different without counsel's errors.

HOW ARE CASES SETTLED WITHOUT TRIAL?

■ Prosecutors have a great deal of discretion in deciding whether a case will be prosecuted and what charges will be pressed.

■ Prosecutors sometimes divert offenders to diversion programs, alternatives to the formal criminal justice process that attempt to achieve noncriminal disposition of cases.

■ Plea bargaining occurs when a prosecutor agrees to press a less serious charge, drop some charges, or recommend a less severe sentence if the defendant agrees to plead guilty.

■ Historical records show that plea bargaining has long been used in jurisdictions of all types.

WHAT ARE SOME PROBLEMS OF THE COURT SYSTEM?

■ A growing court caseload, combined with high case mortality, reveals that most cases end in guilty pleas.

■ Critics of plea bargaining point out that it takes place in private; the rights of the accused and the interests of the community are not adequately protected; and the public may believe that justice is not achieved. However, efforts to eliminate the practice have been unsuccessful.

■ Proposals to eliminate undesirable aspects of plea bargaining include time limits, more public negotiations, better case-screening procedures, and reviews of plea agreements by panels of judges.

■ A major issue for criminal defense is the tendency to focus on the offender rather than on the criminal act. This has led to the creation of new defenses that attempt to stretch the boundaries of concepts such as self-defense.

■ Another issue is whether the crime control model (which emphasizes the repression of criminal conduct) or the due process model (which emphasizes the preservation of individual liberties) will dominate the justice process in a particular case or jurisdiction.

Key Terms

right to counsel	caseloads
effective counsel	case mortality
necessarily included offenses	mandatory sentences
nolle prosequi	"three strikes" laws
diversion programs	pretrial settlement conference
pretrial intervention (PTI)	crime control model
plea bargaining	due process model
Speedy Trial Act	

Questions for Review and Discussion

1. What degree of discretion do prosecutors have in the disposition of cases? Explain.
2. What are diversion programs? Give an example of such a program.

3. What is plea bargaining? How long has it been used in the United States?
4. What are some undesirable features of plea bargaining?
5. What happens when mandatory sentences are combined with policies forbidding plea bargaining?
6. What are some proposed alternatives to plea bargaining?
7. What problems are caused by increasing court caseloads?
8. In what ways do the crime control and due process models conflict?

Notes

1. Patricia Hurtado, "Lost Control and Snapped: Defense Cites Stress in Social-Club Killings," *Newsday* (May 5, 1998), p. 7.
2. David Kocieniewski, "Appeal Is Denied for Death Row Inmate Who Had Asked for Speedy Execution," *New York Times* (July 28, 1999), p. B5.
3. Harry Charles, *The Palladium of Justice: Origins of Trial by Jury* (Reed, 1999); Nancy Jean King, "The American Criminal Jury," *Law and Contemporary Problems* 62 (spring 1999), pp. 41–67.
4. *Powell v. Alabama*, 287 U.S. 45 (1932).
5. *Johnson v. Zerbst*, 304 U.S. 458 (1938).
6. *Betts v. Brady*, 316 U.S. 455 (1942).
7. Anthony Lewis, *Gideon's Trumpet* (New York: Vintage, 1966), p. 59.
8. *Gideon v. Wainwright*, 83 S. Ct. 1340 (1963).
9. *Powell v. Alabama*, 287 U.S. 45 (1932).
10. *Escobedo v. Illinois*, 378 U.S. 478 (1963); *Miranda v. Arizona*, 384 U.S. 694 (1966).
11. *Coleman v. Alabama*, 399 U.S. 1 (1970).
12. *Douglas v. California*, 372 U.S. (1963).
13. *Gilbert v. California*, 388 U.S. (1967).
14. *In re Gault*, 38 U.S. 1 (1967).
15. See Jefferson Ingram, *Criminal Procedure: Cases and Materials* (Cincinnati: Anderson, 1995).
16. *Argersinger v. Hamlin*, 407 U.S. 25 (1972).
17. *McMann v. Richardson*, 397 U.S. 765 (1970).
18. Laurie S. Levenson, "Criminal Law; Effective Assistance," *The National Law Journal* 21 (February 22, 1999), p. B9.
19. *Strickland v. Washington*, 104 S. Ct. 2052 (1984).
20. 104 S. Ct. 2060.
21. Robert L. Spangenberg, Judy Kapucinski, and Patricia A. Smith, *Criminal Defense for the Poor* (Washington, DC: Bureau of Justice Statistics, 1988).
22. Richard Klein, "The Emperor *Gideon* Has No Clothes: The Empty Promise of the Constitutional Right to Effective Assistance of Counsel," *Hastings Constitutional Law Quarterly* 13 (1986), pp. 625–93.
23. David E. Rovella, "Unclogging Gideon's Trumpet; Mississippi Suits Are the Latest to Attack State Defense Funding," *The National Law Journal* 22 (January 10, 2000), p. A1.
24. Dallin H. Oaks and Warren Lehman, *A Criminal Justice System and the Indigent* (Chicago: University of Chicago Press, 1968).
25. David W. Neubauer, *Criminal Justice in Middle America* (Morristown, NJ: General Learning Press, 1974).
26. Dean J. Champion, "Private Counsel and Public Defenders: A Look at Weak Cases, Prior Records, and Leniency in Plea-Bargaining," *Journal of Criminal Justice* 17 (1989), pp. 253–63.
27. Roy B. Fleming, "Client Games: Defense Attorneys' Perspectives on Their Relations with Criminal Clients," in George S. Bridges, Joseph G. Weis, and Robert D. Crutchfield, eds., *Criminal Justice* (Thousand Oaks, CA: Pine Forge Press, 1996), pp. 276–82.
28. Laurie S. Levenson, "Criminal Law; Effective Assistance," *The National Law Journal* 21 (February 22, 1999), p. B9.
29. "Empowering Prosecutors: Movement to Allow Equal Right to Jury Trial Has Judges Fearing Overload," *ABA Journal* 85 (March, 1999), p. 28.
30. Peter Finn, *The Manhattan District Attorney's Narcotics Eviction Program* (Washington, DC: National Institute of Justice, 1995).
31. Richard Bloom, "Prosecutorial Discretion," *Georgetown Law Journal* 87 (1999).
32. Steven R. Donziger, ed., *The Real War on Crime: Report of the National Criminal Justice Commission* (New York: Harper Perennial, 1996), pp. 183–84.

33. Peter J. Henning, "Prosecutorial Misconduct and Constitutional Remedies," *Washington University Law Quarterly* 77 (Fall 1999).

34. Carol J. DeFrances, Steven K. Smith, and Louise van der Does, *Prosecutors in State Courts* (Washington, DC: Bureau of Justice Statistics, 1996).

35. Katherine Beckett and Theodore Sasson, *The Politics of Injustice* (Thousand Oaks, CA: Pine Forge Press, 2000); Daniel Glaser, *Profitable Penalties* (Thousand Oaks, CA: Pine Forge Press, 1997).

36. DeFrances et al., *Prosecutors in State Courts,* 1996, p. 4.

37. Timothy C. Hart and Brian A. Reaves, *Felony Defendants in Large Urban Counties* (Washington, DC: Bureau of Justice Statistics, 1999).

38. Milton Heumann, "A Note of Plea-Bargaining and Case Pressure," *Law and Society Review* 9 (Spring 1975).

39. Abraham S. Blumberg, *Criminal Justice: Issues and Ironies* (New York: New Viewpoints, 1979).

40. Barbara Boland and Brian Forst, *The Prevalence of Guilty Pleas* (Washington, DC: U.S. Bureau of Justice Statistics, 1984).

41. Brian A. Reaves and Pheny Z. Smith, *Felony Defendants in Large Urban Counties* (Washington, DC: Bureau of Justice Statistics, 1995).

42. Patrick A. Langan and Jodi M. Brown, *Felony Sentences in State Courts* (Washington, DC: Bureau of Justice Statistics, 1997), p. 7.

43. Heumann, p. 55; Boland and Forst.

44. Ted Gest, "Making a Case for Judges," *U.S. News & World Report* (January 12, 1998), p. 29.

45. National Center for State Courts, *Annual Report* (Washington, DC: National Center for State Courts, 1998).

46. "Clearing the Homolka Deal," *Maclean's* 109 (April 1, 1996), p. 27.

47. "Questioning Homolka's Deal," *Maclean's* 110 (April 28, 1997), p. 21.

48. "Beyond Misery," *People Weekly* (January 24, 2000), p. 125.

49. George B. Palermo, Maxine Aldridge White, Lew A. Wasserman, and William Hanrahan, "Plea Bargaining: Injustice for All?," *International Journal of Offender Therapy and Comparative Criminology* 42 (June 1998), p. 111.

50. Carol J. DeFrances and Greg W. Steadman, *Prosecutors in State Courts* (Washington, DC: Bureau of Justice Statistics, 1998).

51. Steven K. Smith and John Scalia, Jr., *Compendium of Federal Justice Statistics, 1997* (Washington, DC: Bureau of Justice Statistics, 1999).

52. Barbara Boland, E. Brady, H. Tyson, and J. Bassler, *The Prosecution of Felony Arrests* (Washington, DC: Bureau of Justice Statistics, 1983).

53. Steven K. Smith and John Scalia, Jr., *Compendium of Federal Justice Statistics* (Washington, DC: Bureau of Justice Statistics, 1999).

54. Vera Institute of Justice, *Felony Arrests,* revised ed. (New York: Longman, 1981).

55. Carol J. DeFrances, Steven K. Smith, and Louis van der Does, *Prosecutors in State Courts* (Washington, DC: Bureau of Justice Statistics, 1996).

56. Boland et al., *The Prosecution of Felony Arrests.*

57. See Nancy Jean King, "Priceless Process: Nonnegotiable Features of Criminal Litigation," *UCLA Law Review* 47 (October 1999); J. Shin, "Do Lesser Pleas Pay?: Accommodations in the Sentencing and Parole Process," *Journal of Criminal Justice* 1 (1973); T. Dungsworth, *Plea-Bargaining: Who Gains? Who Loses?* (Washington, DC: Institute for Law and Social Research, 1978).

58. Eric R. Komitee, "Bargains without Benefits: Do the Sentencing Guidelines Permit Upward Departures to Redress the Dismissal of Charges Pursuant to Plea Bargains?," *New York University Law Review* 70 (April 1995), pp. 166–95.

59. David E. Rovella, "Fake Plea Bargain in Death Case Raises Concerns," *The National Law Journal* 18 (October 9, 1995), p. 13.

60. Ty Alper, "The Danger of Winning: Contract Law Ramifications of Successful Bailey Challenges for Plea-Convicted Defendants," *New York University Law Review* 72 (October 1997), pp. 841–81.

61. Richard Birke, "Reconciling Loss Aversion and Guilty Pleas," *Utah Law Review* (1999), p. 205.

62. National Advisory Committee on Criminal Justice Standards and Goals, *A National Strategy to Reduce Crime* (New York: Avon, 1975).

63. Association of the Bar of the City of New York, *The Nation's Toughest Drug Law: Evaluating the New York Experience* (Washington, DC: Drug Abuse Council, 1977).

64. H. Lawrence Ross, "The Neutralization of Severe Penalties: Some Traffic Studies," *Law and Society Review* 10 (1976); David Rossman, Paul Froyd, Glen L. Pierce, John McDevitt, and William J. Bowers, "Massachusetts Mandatory Minimum Sentence Gun Law: Enforcement, Prosecution, and Defense Impact," *Criminal Law Bulletin* 16 (March–April 1980); Colin

Loftin, Milton Heumann, and David McDowall, "Mandatory Sentencing and Firearms Violence: Evaluating an Alternative to Gun Control," *Law and Society Review* 17 (1983); Michael L. Rubinstein, Steven H. Clarke, and Theresa J. White, *Alaska Bans Plea Bargaining* (Washington, DC: U.S. Government Printing Office, 1980).

65. Arthur Rosset and Donald R. Cressey, *Justice by Consent: Plea-Bargains in the American Courthouse* (Philadelphia: Lippincott, 1976), p. 161.

66. "New York Governor Offers Limited Revision of Mandatory Sentencing Laws," *Alcoholism and Drug Abuse Weekly* (May 17, 1999), p. 1.

67. Lisa Stolzenberg and Stewart J. D'Alessio, " 'Three Strikes and You're Out': The Impact of California's New Mandatory Sentencing Law on Serious Crime Rates," *Crime and Delinquency* 43 (October 1997), pp. 457–69.

68. John Cloud, "A Get-Tough Policy That Failed: Mandatory Sentencing Was Once America's Law-and-Order Panacea," *Time* (February 1, 1999), p. 48.

69. Marcus Dirk Dubber, "American Plea Bargains, German Lay Judges, and the Crisis of Criminal Procedure," *Stanford Law Review* 49 (February 1997), pp. 547–605.

70. Barbara Boland, *Felony Case-Processing Time* (Washington, DC: Bureau of Justice Statistics, 1986); Langan and Brown, *Felony Sentences in State Courts.*

71. Wayne A. Kerstetter and Anne M. Heinz, *Pre-Trial Settlement Conference: An Evaluation* (Washington, DC: U.S. Government Printing office, 1979); Debra S. Emmelman, "Trial by Plea Bargain: Case Settlement as a Product of Recursive Decisionmaking," *Law and Society Review* 30 (June 1996), pp. 335–60.

72. DeFrances et al., *Prosecutors in State Courts*, 1998, p. 5.

73. Langan and Brown, *Felony Sentences in State Courts.*

74. Kevin Johnson, "Train Gunman to Appeal, Use Incompetence Defense," *USA Today* (February 20, 1995), p. 2; Bruce Frankel, "New York Shooting Victims on the Stand: 'You' Did This," *USA Today* (February 9, 1995), p. 3.

75. Tony Mauro, "Child Abuse Becoming a Defense Trend," *USA Today* (September 24, 1993), p. 2.

76. See Faith McNulty, *The Burning Bed* (New York: Dell, 1980).

77. Susan Estrich, *Getting Away with Murder* (Cambridge, MA: Harvard University Press, 1998), pp. 119–30; Robert Schwaneberg, "The Legal Risks of 'Self-Defense'," *Atlantic City Press* (March 15, 1981), p. 1.

78. Steve Timko, "Murder Acquittal in 'Urban Fear' Trial," *USA Today* (April 12, 1995), p. 3.

79. M. L. Stein, "L. A. Courts Restrict Press: Proposed Courthouse Rules Force Reports to Wear Passes and Ban Hallway Interviews," *Editor & Publisher* 130 (November 8, 1997), p. 11.

80. Christian Berthelsen, "Guidelines for Lawyers in Court of Television," *New York Times* (April 20, 1998), p. 7.

81. William Glaberson, "Calm Returns to Brawley Case, but Punished Lawyer Doesn't," *New York Times* (May 1, 1998), p. 5.

82. Herbert L. Packer, *The Limits of the Criminal Sanction* (Stanford, CA: Stanford University Press, 1968).

83. Charles M. Sevilla, "Criminal Defense Lawyers and the Search for Truth," *Harvard Journal of Law and Public Policy* 20 (Winter 1997), pp. 519–28.

84. Alan M. Dershowitz, *The Best Defense* (New York: Vintage, 1983), p. xiv.

ten
Trials and Sentencing

The swearing in of a witness at

trial is a solemn moment that symbolizes the integrity of the criminal justice process. The inner workings of a trial are less visible but equally important to ensuring that justice occurs in the courtroom. The prosecution, defense, and judge represent the interests of the community, the defendant, and the law in a process that is designed to achieve justice in every case—although this goal sometimes is difficult to achieve in practice.

What Happens at Trial?

The trial is the centerpiece of the adjudication process; and this is true even through, as you have seen, most cases are decided without one. Trials serve an educational purpose, helping both jurors and the public understand how the balance is struck between protection of the community and protection of the rights of the individual. The detailed procedures of a criminal trial are designed to ensure that this balance is reached in every case.[1]

The system of criminal adjudication in the United States has often been criticized for the time it sometimes takes to proceed from arrest to disposition. Delays in the adjudication procedure cause the process to take even longer. Most felony cases are completed within three months of arrest, although cases involving trials take twice as long.[2] The total elapsed time from arrest through sentencing is about seven months nationwide.[3]

An example of a delay is a **continuance**—a court-authorized postponement of a case to allow the prosecution or defense more time to prepare its case. Judges have the discretion to grant continuances to allow the defense to locate a witness, prepare motions, or obtain medical reports, or for other reasons. Continuances ensure that the most complete information is available for a criminal proceeding. Prosecutors also can obtain continuances, but most states constitutionally require them to be ready for trial within six months. Exceptions are permitted only when the delays are caused by the defense for valid reasons. Most continuances are requested by, and granted to, the defense. By the time of indictment the prosecution already has prepared much of its case, but the defense has not begun to examine the evidence. Delays usually benefit the defendant more than the prosecution, because the memory and recall of witnesses often fades as time passes. Delays also may frustrate or disillusion victims and witnesses, or they may help to calm community sentiment in well-publicized cases. On the other hand, delays cause suffering for defendants who cannot make bail and must await trial in jail. Another cause of delays is a process called **discovery,** which entitles a suspect to see certain information gathered by the prosecutor. For example, suspects have the right to see the results of blood tests or transcripts of interrogations conducted by the police or the prosecutor in preparation for trial. In its examination of the prosecutor's evidence, the defense may find *exculpatory evidence* suggesting the defendant's innocence. For example, exculpatory evidence may consist of statements taken by police from victims or witnesses that show uncertainty about the identity of the offender. With this information defense counsel can assess the strength of the prosecution's case and decide whether the defendant will benefit more from going to trial or from pleading guilty. The steps in a criminal case are presented in Figure 10.1.

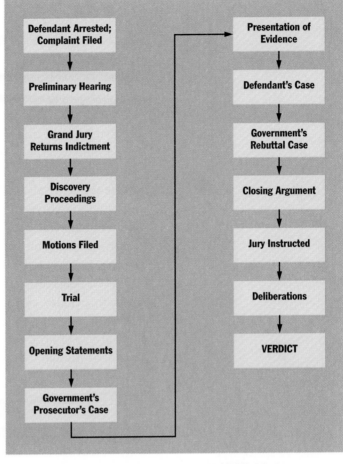

FIGURE 10.1
Progression of a Case through Trial

SOURCE: www.uscourts.gov/understanding_courts

Jury Selection

When a trial takes place, it begins with the selection of a jury. As explained in Chapter 8, the right to a jury dates from the signing of the Magna Carta in 1215 and is incorporated into both Article III of the Constitution and the Sixth Amendment, which states that "in all criminal prosecutions, the accused shall enjoy the right to a speedy and public trial by an impartial jury."[4] The jury pool is typically selected from voter registration records, tax rolls, or motor vehicle records.

After the jury pool is selected, the process of *voir dire* occurs, in which the judge, prosecution, and defense screen potential jurors by asking them questions. To prevent the inclusion of biased jurors, both the prosecution

DELAYS IN ADJUDICATION

■ **continuance**
A court-authorized postponement of a case to allow the prosecution or defense more time to prepare its case.

■ **discovery**
The process that entitles a suspect to review certain information gathered by the prosecutor.

VOIR DIRE

and the defense can challenge the selection of a certain number of jurors. These challenges, called *challenges for cause,* are used to disqualify jurors whose background or statements may be seen as prejudicial to the prosecution or the defense. In addition, both prosecution and defense have a specific number of *peremptory challenges,* which permit them to remove prospective jurors from consideration without cause. Although peremptory challenges have their origin in British common law, recent high-profile trials have featured the use of jury selection "consultants." These experts examine nonverbal cues such as body language, eye contact, and dress to predict whether a particular juror may be sympathetic to the prosecution or defense. Consultants' methods of juror selection have not been proved valid, but stereotypes persist regarding age, gender, religion, and other juror attributes and their likely impact on jurors' attitudes.[5] Critics of the practice of using jury consultants have proposed barring nonlawyers from giving jury selection advice to the prosecution or defense.[6]

JURY SIZE

The size of juries varies by state. All states require twelve-member juries in death penalty cases, although six states allow for juries of less than twelve jurors in other felony trials. Although the U.S. Supreme Court has left the size of juries up to the state, it has held that a five-member jury is unconstitutional.[7] Thus, states have juries that range in size from six to twelve members.

In rare circumstances the jury is *sequestered:* Jurors are housed in a hotel for the duration of the trial, and their access to newspapers, television, and other media is closely monitored. Sequestration is expensive and occurs only in cases in which public opinion is very strong or divisive or in which the security of jurors is in question (for example, when there are concerns about threats or bribes aimed at influencing jurors' votes).

After a jury has been selected, the prosecution makes an opening statement outlining its case against the defendant. At this time the state sum-

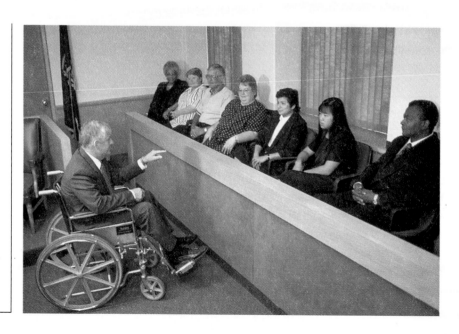

This lawyer is evaluating potential members on a jury in a criminal trial. What is this screening process called? On what grounds could the prosecutor exclude or disqualify a person from serving on the jury? On what grounds could the defense counsel do so? On what grounds could the judge do so? What instructions will the judge give to the jury at the beginning and end of the trial?

marizes the evidence it will use to show the defendant's guilt. Next, the defense counsel makes an opening argument stating why the defendant should be exonerated of the crime. The evidence to be used to support this position will be summarized.

Witness Testimony and Evidence

The body of the trial consists of the presentation of the prosecutor's evidence and the statements of witnesses, followed by the presentation of the case for the defense. Because the state is prosecuting an individual in a criminal case, the burden of proof is on the prosecution to prove guilt beyond a reasonable doubt.

STEPS OF A TRIAL

The steps of a trial are elaborate, because accuracy and the determination of the truth have been found to result most often when both sides have fair opportunity to present their views. Witnesses and physical evidence form the substance of all criminal cases. Witnesses are always sworn in by a court officer, usually a sheriff's deputy. *Swearing in* obliges the witness to be truthful; false statements about issues material to the case can result in a charge of perjury. The first round of questions the prosecutor asks his or her own witnesses in a criminal case are called the *direct examination.* Likewise, questions the defense counsel asks defense witnesses also are called direct examination. The types of witnesses and physical evidence that can be used are explicitly defined in the rules of evidence of each state. *Circumstantial evidence* is a form of indirect evidence often used in criminal trials and permits a jury to draw a conclusion by making a reasonable inference. For example, a witness who saw a person walking down the street with two sticks of dynamite just before an explosion offers circumstantial evidence that the person may have been involved in the incident. This form of evidence is very important when direct eyewitness evidence is lacking.

After the prosecution has conducted a direct examination of each of its witnesses, the defense may *cross-examine* those witnesses for inconsistencies, contradictions, or uncertainty. The prosecution may follow the defense cross-examination with a *redirect examination* to clarify issues that have been brought into doubt. Next, the defense may follow once against with a *recross-examination.* This procedure continues for each of the prosecution's witnesses.

The defense then calls its witnesses, and the process continues with prosecution cross-examination followed by redirect questioning by the defense and recross-examination by the prosecutor. At several points throughout the trial, the prosecution or the defense may raise *objections* to questions posed by the other side that seem to violate the rules of evidence. The judge rules on these objections according to the laws of the state. If the objection is *sustained,* the questioner must withdraw the question and the jury must disregard both the question and any response made by the witness. If the objection is *overruled,* the question is deemed proper and the questioning continues.

Defense Strategies

Certain **general defenses** are applicable to all criminal offenses. The two types of general defenses are justification and excuse. As you read in Chapter 4, **justification defenses** claim that the act was justified by over-whelming circumstances, such as self-defense. **Excuse defenses** argue the act should be excused because the defendant cannot be held responsible for it. Insanity and duress are examples of excuse defenses. The key distinction between justification and excuse defenses is that the former look to justify the offender's *conduct,* whereas the latter seek to excuse the *offender* as an individual.

As Chapter 4 described, there has been a trend toward attempting to create new types of justifications or excuses. In a Texas case, a man had shot two unarmed black men in the head. His lawyers argued that the defendant suffered from "a rational fear of other blacks in violent urban neighbor-hoods."[8] In another case, sleep apnea was said to have caused a man to kill his wife.[9] Bad chromosomes and multiple personalities (one of which committed a rape) have been put forth as excuses.[10] As defense attorney Alan Dershowitz has remarked, "If you can make it sound like an illness, people are much more sympathetic."[11]

Sometimes lawyers themselves can become defendants, and their claims of excuse are similar. In 1998 defense lawyer Gary Kleitman was sentenced to three to six years in prison for stealing more than $366,000 from his clients. He argued that his sentence was excessive because of the various physical disorders he must cope with and the fact that his wife was sched-uled to undergo cancer surgery. These medical problems created "crushing financial problems" that Kleitman could not handle and resulted in his stealing money from his own clients.[12]

INDIVIDUAL RESPONSIBILITY

These attempts to create new justifications and excuses for criminal conduct violate a fundamental assumption of criminal law: individual re-sponsibility. If individuals cannot be held responsible for their conduct but instead are victims of their circumstances, the punitive and deterrent pur-poses of the criminal law are undermined. Individual volition and personal accountability for one's actions must exist if punishment is to be mean-ingful. Historically, juveniles and people who are mentally ill have been treated as exceptions under the criminal law, because it cannot be assumed that such persons have enough rationality to understand the consequences of their actions. Apart from these exceptions, all people are held to a "rea-sonableness" standard in their conduct. Very few justifications and excuses for criminal conduct are recognized under law. Even so, cases involving these general defenses are growing in number and have generated a great deal of attention, although they are usually unsuccessful when presented to a trial jury.

Another common defense strategy is to attack the government's case. This strategy was accomplished most famously in the criminal trial of O. J. Simpson, in which the defense placed the conduct of the police at the cen-ter of its case rather than focusing on the alibi of the defendant. In some instances the government's case may also be vulnerable to attack because of the background of its informants. Juries are understandably reluctant to convict a defendant on the testimony of someone with a questionable history.[13] Several acquittals in the mob trials of the 1980s and 1990s occurred because juries disregarded the testimony of informants. During its deliberations in the trial of the alleged "godfather" John Gotti, the jury asked to reexamine a chart produced by the defense that displayed the backgrounds of seven prosecution witnesses. The chart listed sixty-nine crimes, including murder and kidnapping.[14] The jury acquitted Gotti, showing that close scrutiny of the government's case can be used successfully as a defense.

Arguments and Outcomes

When all the evidence has been presented, the prosecution and defense make their final arguments to the jury summarizing the evidence. Then the judge instructs the jury, explaining the elements of the alleged crime and the degree of proof required—that is, proof beyond a reasonable doubt. The jury then deliberates until it has agreed on a verdict. In order for a defendant to be found guilty, the jury must agree that guilt has been proved beyond a reasonable doubt. In nearly all states unanimous jury verdicts are required in criminal cases.

THE VERDICT

In rare cases (fewer than 6 percent) the jury is not able to agree on a decision of guilt or innocence.[15] This situation, called a *hung jury*, means that the defendant can be tried again before a different jury. In recent years **jury nullification** has occurred in some cases; that is, defendants have been acquitted despite facts that show guilt.[16] Some people believed that the jury that acquitted O. J. Simpson in his criminal trial engaged in jury nullification, but sloppy police evidence gathering and lies told by witnesses led some jurors to conclude that Simpson was not guilty beyond a reasonable doubt.

jury nullification
A jury's decision to acquit a defendant in the face of facts that show guilt.

When a jury reaches a verdict of guilty, the defendant stands convicted of the crime alleged. He or she then is sentenced within the limits established by law. Commonly both the prosecutor and defense counsel make recommendations to the judge regarding an appropriate sentence.

How Do Judges Decide on a Sentence?

Sentencing is subject to much criticism: Sentences often are seen as either too lenient or too severe. A sentence rarely is viewed as appropriate in a given case. However, judges do not decide on sentences in an arbitrary fashion. The degree of latitude given to judges is established by law. In most states, for example, a petty larceny (a misdemeanor) is punishable by up to one year in jail. In other words, a judge can choose any sentence from a fine (up to $1,000 in this kind of case) to probation or as much as a year in jail. The judge cannot sentence an offender to two years in jail or a fine of

This judge has just sentenced a convicted "three-strikes" felon to incarceration in a state prison for a maximum period of twenty-five years for purposes of incapacitation. What does this mean? How did the judge arrive at this sentence? What choices among purposes and sentencing options were involved? What legal constraints and public policies restricted those choices?

$10,000, for these sentences would fall outside the allowable range established by the legislature. This leeway is provided to allow judges to individualize sentences on the basis of the nature of the offender and the circumstances of the offense.

In South Carolina in 1995, a young mother, Susan Smith, killed her two children by leaving them in a car that rolled into a lake. Smith could have been convicted of involuntary manslaughter or murder and could have received a death sentence, or she could have been found guilty but mentally ill. In the trial the defense pointed out that she came from a troubled background. Her parents had divorced, and her father had committed suicide when she was six. She had been molested by her stepfather at age fifteen and later, even after she was married. The molestation was covered up by her mother. After her divorce Smith had been rejected by her new boyfriend because she had two children. She had a long history of depression. The defense also noted that she had confessed to her crime and showed deep remorse.[17]

Which of these factors should a jury consider in deciding on a sentence? And how should an appropriate sentence be determined? In the actual case, Smith was convicted of murder and sentenced to thirty years in prison. It is easy to see that other sentencing choices were available to the judge, and that other sentences could have been imposed and defended rationally. This case illustrates why it is important to understand the underlying rationale or philosophy of sentencing.

Retribution and Incapacitation

When a judge decides on a sentence, he or she first considers what the sentence should accomplish. The purposes of a sentence always consist of one or more of the following objectives: retribution, incapacitation, deterrence, and/or rehabilitation.

When a judge sentences for purposes of **retribution,** punishment is applied simply in proportion to the seriousness of the offense. The "eye for an eye" system of justice described in the Old Testament is an early form of retribution.[18] According to this concept, the more serious the crime, the more serious the punishment should be. What is the goal of retribution? As an objective of sentencing, retribution makes no effort to change the offender and provides nothing for society except a form of revenge. Nevertheless, as states have abandoned social reform as a purpose of sentencing in recent years, the use of retribution as a justification for punishment has become more popular. In the *just deserts* approach to retribution, using the sentencing process as a way to reform an offender or deter other offenders is seen as inappropriate, for it moves attention away from culpability for the past crime for which the offender was convicted.[19]

Sentences based on the concept of **incapacitation** are intended to prevent further criminal behavior by physically restraining the offender from engaging in future misconduct. The primary method of incapacitation in the United States is incarceration, although other methods also are used, such as suspension of the offender's license to practice law or medicine in cases of crimes committed by lawyers or physicians. Unfortunately, the use of incapacitation as a justification for punishment provides no clue as to how long it is necessary to incarcerate someone before he or she poses no further threat to society. It is not economical to lock up large numbers of offenders for long periods, because the burden on society is increased rather than lessened. Higher prison costs, the need to support families on welfare, and the inability to predict future criminal behavior make incapacitation both expensive and uncertain over the long term. Moreover, the incapacitation rationale can be used to justify incarceration for both trivial and serious offenses. A petty thief who steals many times could conceivably be incarcerated for as long as a one-time rapist.

It has been claimed that if repeat offenders could be identified and incarcerated for long periods, there would be a noticeable drop in crime rates.[20] A major problem with this idea is that some individuals might be identified as probable high-rate offenders who were not.[21] Thus, there is a risk of violating due process by punishing offenders for *predicted* future behavior rather than for criminal acts they have actually committed.[22] In addition, such a policy, termed **selective incapacitation,** would greatly increase prison populations.

Many states have **habitual offender laws** based on the notion of incapacitation. These laws can be applied to certain offenders who have committed two or more offenses within a certain period (usually ten years). Multiple offenders are subject to periods of incarceration ranging up to life imprisonment on the theory that these persons must be physically separated from society if crime is to be prevented. Under California's "three strikes" law, Jerry Williams faced a prison term of twenty-five years to life when he was tried for taking pizza from children at a beach. Williams's two prior robbery convictions made him a habitual offender and therefore subject to an extended sentence on grounds of incapacitation.[23] The rationale behind laws

■retribution
Punishment applied simply in proportion to the seriousness of the offense.

JUST DESERTS

■incapacitation
Physically restraining an offender (usually through incarceration) so as to prevent further criminal behavior.

■selective incapacitation
Incarceration of potential high-rate offenders for longer periods as a means of reducing crime.

■habitual offender laws
Laws that subject multiple offenders to periods of incarceration ranging up to life imprisonment, on the grounds that such persons must be physically separated from society if society is to be protected from their criminal conduct.

such as "three strikes" is that multiple offenders, who apparently have not been deterred or reformed by past convictions or incarceration, cannot be trusted to refrain from violating the law and must be separated from society. The popularity of incapacitation as a purpose of sentencing, despite the high costs of incarceration, remains high.

Deterrence and Rehabilitation

deterrence
Prevention of crime through the example of punishment of offenders.

Deterrence as a purpose of sentencing aims to prevent crime through the example of offenders' being punished. *General deterrence* is directed at preventing crime among the general population, while *special deterrence* is aimed at preventing future crimes by a particular offender. Unfortunately, the objectives of general and special deterrence are not always compatible. For example, a drunk driver who hits and kills a pedestrian may best be deterred from future drunk driving through participation in an alcohol treatment program. Such a disposition may not serve the purposes of general deterrence, however, if the penalty fails to deter other people from drunk driving. Another problem with the use of deterrence as a justification for punishment is the difficulty of proving its effectiveness; that is, only those who are *not* deterred come to the attention of the criminal justice system. To date, virtually no reliable evidence exists to suggest that penal sanctions can deter crime.[24]

DETERRENCE IS INEFFECTIVE

One reason that deterrence is ineffective is that it relies on certainty and speed of punishment.[25] If penalties are high but the chances of being caught are low, it is doubtful that potential offenders will be deterred. The very low clearance rates for serious crimes illustrate the low probability that offenders will be caught. Nevertheless, if in the mind of the would-be offender the perceived *risk of apprehension* is high, it is possible to achieve a deterrent effect.[26] For example, one study proved that mailing warning letters to illegal cable users deterred cable tampering.[27]

rehabilitation
Efforts to correct or treat individuals' social or psychological shortcomings so as to prevent future criminal behavior.

The **rehabilitation** or "reformation" approach sees criminal behavior as a consequence of social or psychological shortcomings. The purpose of the sentence, then, is to correct or treat these shortcomings in order to prevent future crimes. This approach assumes that we can identify and treat these shortcomings effectively. Also, it presumes that it is proper to sentence an offender based on the likelihood of reform in the future rather than on criminal conduct already committed. The results of rehabilitation efforts to date have been discouraging, with failures outnumbering successes. Nevertheless, some rehabilitation programs have been shown to work when treatment strategies and offender needs are matched effectively.[28] Successes have been document in cases in which offender needs have been screened carefully and treatments have been chosen to respond directly to those needs.[29]

The lack of empirical evidence to support the four basic purposes of sentencing has contributed to concern about disparity in sentences. Disparity occurs when offenders with similar histories commit similar crimes but receive widely different sentences. Disparity must be expected, of course, when there is little agreement regarding what a sentence should accomplish. A result of disparity has been a trend toward mandatory and fixed sentences. This move toward uniformity in sentencing can be attributed to the widespread adoption of retribution and incapacitation as guiding sentencing philosophies in most jurisdictions.

Probation, Restitution, and Incarceration

In addition to considering the various possible purposes of the sentence, the judge usually may choose among a number of sentencing options. As noted earlier, depending on the range of alternatives provided by law, a judge usually can fine an offender or impose a sentence of probation, incarceration, or restitution.

PAYMENT OF FINES

Fines can be used as punishment upon conviction for any offense. Statutes usually provide a maximum fine but allow the judge to impose any fine up to the maximum. Fines also are provided by law for serious crimes as an adjunct to a sentence of probation or incarceration. Fines obviously place a greater burden on the poor than on the wealthy, and in 1970 the U.S. Supreme Court ruled in *Williams v. Illinois* that offenders cannot be held in jail beyond the maximum sentence allowed by law merely because they are unable to pay the fine.[30] In 1971 the Court ruled in *Tate v. Short* that it is unconstitutional to imprison an offender who cannot pay a fine while not imprisoning offenders with the means to pay fines.[31] Several jurisdictions are now experimenting with *day fines*, or fines established according to the daily income of the offender. This system is designed to make the imposition of fines more equitable.

A probation sentence places the offender under the supervision of the court, allowing him or her to remain in the community. Probation is the most widely used form of criminal sentence, because most crimes are not violent and most offenders are not dangerous. Also, probation is much less expensive than incarceration; and probation does not permit the offender to associate with more serious offenders, as often occurs in prison.

Sometimes a judge orders an offender to make restitution as a condition of probation. This means that the offender must make compensation to the victim for any losses caused by the offense. Many states have laws that encourage restitution, but this approach is not utilized on a large scale. Most offenders are never caught, and those who are caught and convicted are often poor; restitution therefore is not feasible in many cases. This problem has led many states, as well as the federal government, to establish victim compensation programs in which the government reimburses victims for the costs of certain types of loss or injury due to crime. Although the concept of victim compensation is popular, in many states the programs are underfunded and have imposed burdensome paperwork requirements that discourage legitimate claims.

When an offender is sentenced to incarceration, he or she is physically separated from the community in a jail or a prison. Sentences of up to one

What alternatives to incarceration might this convict have received as a sentence? What kind of information in the probation officer's presentence report might possibly have resulted in a suspended sentence? What is a suspended sentence? What effect might a victim-impact statement have had on this inmate's sentence?

year are served in county jails; those of one year or more are served in state or federal prisons. Occasionally a judge delays—or suspends—the execution of a prison sentence and requires the offender to participate in an alcohol, drug, or gambling treatment program, or to pay restitution. This approach is called a **suspended sentence.** If an offender fails to fulfill the prescribed conditions, the court can incarcerate him or her immediately by imposing the suspended sentence. An offender who satisfactorily fulfills the conditions, however, avoids incarceration.

The Presentence Report

The **presentence report** is designed to help the judge decide on an appropriate sentence within the limits established by law. This report is written by a probation officer after an investigation of the offender's background (see Figure 10.2). A presentence investigation is carried out in virtually all felony cases and in some misdemeanor cases, because the sentence will have a significant impact on the offender. If there is any

■ **suspended sentence**
A delayed imposition of a prison sentence that requires the offender to fulfill special conditions such as alcohol, drug, or gambling treatment or payment of restitution.

■ **presentence report**
A report written by a probation officer after an investigation of an offender's background, to assist the judge in determining an appropriate sentence.

doubt about facts contained in the pre-sentence report, the U.S. Supreme Court has ruled that an offender must be given an opportunity to refute or explain information contained in the report, because his or her sentence will be based in part on that information.[32]

The probation officer's independent role at sentencing sometimes is impeded when prosecution or defense do not share important information about the circumstances of the offense or the offender. It is crucial that the probation officer obtain objective information to enable an appropriate sentencing decision to be made.[33] Studies have found a high correspondence between the probation officers' recommendations contained in presentence reports and the actual sentences imposed by judges.[34]

> **A typical presentence report includes the following information:**
>
> 1. **Personal information about the offender and his or her background**
> 2. **Detail description of the offense and its circumstances**
> 3. **A description of the offender's criminal record**
> 4. **Family information and current family status**
> 5. **Education history**
> 6. **Employment and military history**
> 7. **Health history and status (including drug history)**
> 8. **Financial status**
> 9. **Mental health status**
> 10. **Sentencing recommendation made by the probation officer**

FIGURE 10.2
Information in a
Presentence Report

PROBATION
OFFICER'S ROLE

How Do Sentencing Options Differ?

Two categories of sentencing are indeterminate and determinate. Indeterminate sentencing systems are based on the philosophy that a wide sentencing range gives an offender an incentive to reform and allows a parole board to determine whether the offender is ready for release prior to serving the maximum sentence. Determinate sentencing systems impose "fixed" sentences that provide little or no flexibility. This approach to sentencing rejects the notion of rehabilitation in favor of the philosophy of retribution, focusing on the seriousness of the crime and basing the sentence on the nature of the offense and the offender's prior record.

Indeterminate Sentencing

Indeterminate sentencing systems empower the judge to set a maximum amount of time (up to the limit set by the legislature), and sometimes a minimum amount as well, for the offender to serve in prison. During the sentence a parole board reviews the offender's progress toward rehabilitation to determine whether early release is justified. Therefore, the actual time to be served is set by the parole board. Indeterminate sentencing systems existed in most states until the 1970s, when growing criticism of criminal sentences became widespread. Consider the following points:

- Prison uprisings were found to result in part from disparity in sentences; offenders from similar backgrounds who had committed similar offenses received widely different sentences.

indeterminate sentencing
A sentencing system that empowers the judge to set a maximum amount of time (up to the limit set by the legislature), and sometimes a minimum amount as well, for the offender to serve in prison.

REASONS FOR
DETERMINATE
SENTENCING

- There were few serious rehabilitation efforts or programs in prisons. Reform of offenders took a back seat to concerns of custody and security.

- Parole boards could not tell whether an offender had actually been rehabilitated. They had to rely on the offender's word, which sometimes did not correspond with his or her actual behavior when released back into the community.

- In several widely publicized cases, offenders who had been released early from prison assaulted or killed again.

This series of incidents and events led to a dramatic shift in the philosophy of sentencing. Beginning in 1975, states began to change from indeterminate to determinate sentencing.

Determinate Sentencing

determinate sentencing
A sentencing system that permits judges to impose fixed terms of incarceration that cannot be altered by a parole board.

Determinate sentencing systems permit the judge to impose fixed sentences that cannot be altered by a parole board. In fourteen states parole board release has been abolished. In addition, allowable sentence ranges have been narrowed considerably, giving judges little room for discretion.[35] This has had the effect of treating offenders similarly, as long as the offense is similar. The needs, problems, and backgrounds of offenders are much less important in a determinate sentencing system, because the focus is on the crime that was committed rather than on the type of offender who committed it.

EFFECTS OF
DETERMINATE
SENTENCING

In practice, determinate sentencing has had a significant impact on sentence lengths and on the proportion of the sentence that is actually served in prison. In 1977, for example, 72 percent of offenders released from a state prison had served an indeterminate sentence and were released by a parole board. By 1997, fewer than 30 percent of prison releases were determined by a parole board.[36] In addition, the proportion of each sentence served in prison before release is increasing. Prisoners convicted of violent crimes and released from prison in 1996 had been sentenced to an average of seven years and had served about half of that time, but newly sentenced violent offenders today are receiving average prison sentences of more than eight and a half years and are expected to serve 85 percent of that time in most states.[37] This percentage will continue to rise with the escalation of political and public concern regarding truth in sentencing.[38]

truth in sentencing
A sentencing provision that requires offenders to serve the bulk of their sentence (usually 85 percent) before they can be released.

TRUTH IN SENTENCING **Truth in sentencing** refers to the establishment of a closer relationship between the sentence imposed and the actual time served in prison prior to release. The Violent Crime Control and Law Enforcement Act of 1994 requires states that wish to qualify for federal financial aid to change their laws so that offenders serve at least 85 percent of their sentences. The federal government offered large grants to states that adopted truth-in-sentencing laws. By 1998 twenty-nine states had truth-in-sentencing laws that met the federal government's guidelines. Another thirteen states adopted their own versions of truth-in-sentencing laws calling for offenders to serve a specific percentage of their sentence. The sentencing status of individual states is presented in Table 10.1. As of 1998 the states that met the federal 85 percent requirement had received more than $400 million in federal grants, a significant factor in a majority of the states that passed these laws.[39]

There are three major concerns associated with truth-in-sentencing laws and the federal government's push to have them implemented. These include the cost of truth in sentencing, the extension of these sentencing provisions to nonviolent crimes, and federal involvement in the states' rights to set sentences. The cost of implementing truth in sentencing is extremely high, because states must build new prisons to house offenders for longer periods. For example, the plan in Virginia to abolish parole and implement truth in sentencing called for construction of twenty-five new prisons at a

PROBLEMS WITH TRUTH IN SENTENCING

TABLE 10.1

Truth-in-Sentencing Laws by State

MEET FEDERAL 85% REQUIREMENT		50% REQUIREMENT	100% OF MINIMUM REQUIREMENT	OTHER REQUIREMENTS
Alaska	Missouri	Indiana	Idaho	Arkansas[c]
Arizona	New Jersey	Maryland	Nevada	Colorado[d]
California	New York	Nebraska	New Hampshire	Massachusetts[e]
Connecticut	North Carolina	Texas		Wisconsin[f]
Delaware	North Dakota			
District of Col.	Ohio			
Florida	Oklahoma[b]			
Georgia	Oregon			
Illinois[a]	Pennsylvania			
Iowa	South Carolina			
Kansas	Tennessee			
Kentucky	Utah			
Louisiana	Virginia			
Maine	Washington			
Michigan				
Minnesota				
Mississippi				

[a]Qualified for federal funding in 1996 only.
[b]Two-part sentence structure (2/3 in prison; 1/3 on parole); 100% of prison term required.
[c]Mandatory 70% of sentence for certain violent offenses and manufacture of methamphetamine.
[d]Violent offenders with 2 prior violent convictions serve 75%; 1 prior violent conviction, 56.25%.
[e]Requires 75% of a minimum prison sentence.
[f]Two-part sentence: Offenders serve 100% of the prison term and a sentence of extended supervision at 25% of the prison sentence.

BASED ON: Paula M. Ditton and Doris James Wilson, *Truth in Sentencing in State Prisons* (Washington, DC: Bureau of Justice Statistics, 1999).

cost of $2 billion.[40] Indeed, most of the states that have not adopted truth in sentencing cite the high cost of prison construction, even with the available federal grant money.[41]

A second concern is the extension of truth in sentencing beyond violent crimes. In some states these new sentencing provisions do not exclude property or drug offenders. In Virginia the governor's truth-in-sentencing plan projected that almost four times more nonviolent offenders than violent offenders would be incarcerated. This trend greatly increases the length of sentences and the costs of imprisonment without any offsetting benefit in protecting the public from violent offenders.

The third concern is the federal government's role in state lawmaking. Historically, states have set criminal penalties for most crimes. The intervention of the federal government in rewarding or penalizing states for adopting particular sentencing policies has been criticized. This federal involvement in the sentences to be served by violators of state law represents, one critic argued, "a significant shift in the traditional balance between the state and federal governments and a significant federalization of a traditionally local issue."[42] On the other hand, the federal government uses monetary incentives to encourage states to implement truth-in-sentencing laws that are seen as an improvement over current practice.

INCREASES IN PRISON POPULATIONS The impact of the trend toward determinacy and longer sentences is apparent when you examine data on correctional populations. As Figure 10.3 shows, the number of offenders sent to state and federal prisons rose dramatically from 1990 to 1998, reaching a record level of 1.3 million inmates. The fastest-growing segment of the prison population consists of drug offenders, who are sentenced to state prisons each year in greater numbers than are people convicted of violent crimes.[43]

These increases in prison populations outpace increases in the general U.S. population. As Table 10.2 indicates, the incarceration rate doubled between 1985 and 1996 as the number of adults in prison or jail mushroomed to 1.64 million, a rate of 618 per 100,000 population. If you add to the total those on probation or parole, the number of adults under correctional supervision in the United States in 1996 was 5.5 million, or 2.8 percent of the adult population, double the rate of a decade earlier.

The increase in prison populations is a direct result of an increase in the likelihood of offenders' being sent to prison; also, new incarcerations are occurring faster than releases from prison. In 1996 the rate of admissions into state prisons (per one hundred prisoners) was 55 per-

FIGURE 10.3

Number of State and Federal Prison Inmates, 1990–1998

SOURCE: Allen J. Beck and Christopher J. Mumola, *Prisoners in 1998* (Washington, DC: U.S. Bureau of Justice Statistics, 1999).

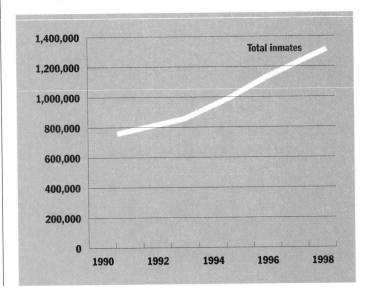

TABLE 10.2				
Trends in Numbers of Adults under Correctional Supervision (in Jail or Prison or on Probation or Parole)				
YEAR	TOTAL ADULTS IN JAIL OR PRISON	INCARCERATION RATE PER 100,000 U.S. POPULATION	TOTAL UNDER CORRECTIONAL SUPERVISION	PERCENTAGE OF U.S. ADULT POPULATION UNDER SUPERVISION
1985	0.74 million	312	3.01 million	1.7 %
1990	1.15 million	460	4.35 million	2.3 %
1995	1.58 million	598	5.37 million	2.8 %
1996	1.64 million	618	5.5 million	2.8 %

SOURCE: Compiled from Allen J. Beck et al., *Correctional Populations in the United States* (Washington, DC: U.S. Bureau of Justice Statistics, 1999).

cent; the release rate was 30.9 percent.[44] This difference of nearly 25 percent is a major cause of prison overcrowding and new prison construction in many jurisdictions. Prison crowding also reflects the decline of indeterminate sentencing and the shrinking power of parole boards in setting actual sentence lengths, and the corresponding rise in determinate sentencing and truth-in-sentencing laws.

MANDATORY SENTENCING Mandatory sentences are a form of determinate sentencing in which fixed sentences are imposed on individuals convicted of certain types of crimes. Most crimes subject to mandatory sentences are gun-related crimes, drug offenses, and drunk driving offenses. Mandatory sentences for certain crimes have been adopted in every state and by the federal government on the basis of their presumed deterrent and incapacitating effects. As noted in Chapter 9, mandatory sentences often shift decision-making discretion to the police and the prosecutor rather than eliminating discretion altogether. Mandatory sentencing disregards the fact that not all offenders are alike, even though they may commit the same crimes.[45] For example, a study of drug offenders sentenced to mandatory prison terms in Massachusetts found that nearly half of them had no prior record of violent crimes.[46] In New York State the governor reduced the sentences of three drug offenders because he believed their mandatory sentences were too long for the commission of nonviolent crimes.[47]

Moving discretion from sentencing to earlier stages of criminal procedure can be seen as an attempt to "correct" injustices that may arise when the system applies the same sentence to offenders from widely different backgrounds and to crimes of differing seriousness.[48] At the same time mandatory sentences reduce the visibility of discretionary decisions at the sentencing stage by shifting discretion to the arrest and charging stages of criminal procedure. Nevertheless, mandatory sentences remain popular as a mechanism to achieve "truth in sentencing," although at a high cost. These policies increase the number of inmates serving longer sentences and slow prison population turnover.[49] Extremely long mandatory sentences can

■**mandatory sentences**
Fixed sentences for offenders convicted of certain types of crimes, such as gun-related crimes, drug offenses, and drunk driving offenses.

PROBLEMS WITH
MANDATORY
SENTENCING

be counterproductive because they incarcerate offenders for long periods (at great expense) well past their late teens and early twenties, the ages when most violent crimes are committed.[50]

"Three strikes and you're out" laws, as mentioned earlier, are a form of mandatory sentencing, imposing mandatory minimum sentences of periods up to life in prison for repeat offenders. In a case ultimately decided by the U.S. Supreme Court, a homeless person, Michael Riggs, stole a bottle of vitamin pills from a supermarket. This petty theft was a misdemeanor, but under California law it was elevated to a felony because Riggs had at least two prior felony convictions. This placed him under the California three strikes law that imposed a mandatory minimum of twenty-five years to life imprisonment. Riggs appealed, arguing that such a long sentence was both disproportionate and excessive, violating the Eighth Amendment. In 1999 the U.S. Supreme Court denied a review of his sentence.[51] Yet a study of the three strikes law in California found that it did not reduce crime rates below preexisting levels and "was of no consequence in nine of the ten cities examined."[52] Nevertheless, concern over a perceived decline in morality in society appears to underlie strong public support for these laws.[53]

Sentencing Guidelines

Sentencing guidelines are a middle ground between indeterminate and determinate sentencing. They reduce disparity in sentencing by recommending **guideline sentences** that take into account the seriousness of crimes and the offenders' prior records. The guidelines are developed by commissions that examine averages of past sentences for various combinations of offenders and offenses. Guideline sentences achieve the goals of proportionality and uniformity without mandating specific sentences for certain crimes or offenders. Judges may deviate from the guideline sentence for a

■ guideline sentences
Sentences based on average past sentences for various combinations of offenders and offenses in an effort to achieve proportionality and uniformity without mandating specific sentences for certain crimes or offenders.

This parole board is meeting to consider applications for parole from a state prison. How will the board know if a prisoner has been sufficiently reformed or rehabilitated to be released on parole? What are the risks of granting parole? How do determinate sentencing, truth in sentencing, and mandatory sentencing reduce the discretionary power of parole boards?

given offense only if they provide written reasons for doing so. For example, if a sentence of five to seven years is typical for past robbery offenders, judges may sentence outside this range only if they state their reasons for doing so. These reasons might include a particularly serious prior record or severe injury to the victim.

The U.S. Sentencing Commission was created in 1984 to implement changes in the federal sentencing system. The primary thrust was to emphasize the offense, rather than the offender, in criminal sentencing.[54] In 1987 the commission implemented federal sentencing guidelines that apply to all federal offenses. By 1996 ten states also had adopted sentencing guidelines, and seven additional states had established voluntary sentencing guidelines.[55] Voluntary sentencing guidelines, created by a panel of judges, provide no mechanism for dealing with judges who ignore the guidelines. Nonvoluntary or presumptive sentencing guidelines are developed by sentencing commissions created by legislatures. These commissions often *prescribe* a sentencing policy, rather than merely summarizing past practice as is done with voluntary guidelines. It is presumptive guidelines that require the judge to hold a hearing and to provide written reasons for any departure from the sentencing guidelines.

Sentencing guidelines have several advantages and disadvantages, as summarized in Table 10.3. The primary advantage of sentencing guidelines is that they reduce disparity in sentencing while allowing greater flexibility than exists in mandatory sentencing schemes. Disparity is unwarranted when differences in sentences cannot be accounted for by the nature of crime or the background of the offender. A major concern, on the other hand, is that sentencing guidelines established by legislatures give the legislative branch of government control over a judicial function (sentencing). Perceived errors in judgment may result. For example, sentence guidelines established for federal drug offenses are so high that some federal judges have refused to impose them; about fifty judges have refused to take new drug cases. As one

ROLE OF SENTENCING COMMISSIONS

TABLE 10.3

Advantages and Disadvantages of Sentencing Guidelines

ADVANTAGES	DISADVANTAGES
1. Guidelines promote uniformity and proportionality in sentencing without the problems of mandatory sentences.	1. Sentence uniformity appears to deteriorate after a few years' experience with sentencing guidelines.
2. Guidelines allow for accurate projection and control of prison populations through the nature and length of the guideline sentences.	2. The purpose of sentencing should revolve around considerations of justice, not managing the prison population.
3. Prescribed sentences allow for departures from guidelines where necessary.	3. Guidelines violate constitutional separation of powers by permitting legislatures to set sentences, which is a judicial prerogative.

federal judge observed, "we're building prisons faster than we're building classrooms. . . . The whole thing doesn't seem to be very effective."[56]

In addition, guideline sentences that punish crack cocaine much more severely than powdered cocaine have been found to punish black offenders disproportionately over whites. First-time offenders caught with 5 grams of crack cocaine receive a mandatory minimum term of five years in prison, whereas a first-time powder cocaine offender must possess 500 grams of the drug to receive the same sentence. This 100 to 1 ratio has been called excessive and discriminatory, in light of the fact that the cheaper crack cocaine is used more often by blacks, whereas powdered cocaine is used more often by whites.[57] Nevertheless, sentencing guidelines generally have been shown to reduce discrimination on the basis of race or gender.[58]

Although sentencing guidelines have been found to increase uniformity in sentencing in many jurisdictions, this is not the case everywhere. After the first few years, uniformity tends to deteriorate.[59] Another argument for sentencing guidelines is that they make possible more accurate predictions of prison populations, and that jurisdictions can control prison populations by modifying the guidelines.[60] It can be argued that the size of prison populations should not be a factor in sentencing guidelines, because it is unrelated to any particular crime. Nevertheless, the public's fear of crime and willingness to support longer prison sentences has resulted in high prison expenses and new construction at a time when there also is pressure to reduce government spending. Sentencing guidelines may help to limit the use of incarceration so that available prison capacity can be restricted to serious offenders and habitual offenders, rather than being used for nonserious offenses.[61]

How Does the Eighth Amendment Restrict Sentencing?

The Eighth Amendment to the U.S. Constitution deals largely with the final stages of the criminal justice process. It is also one of the shortest amendments. It reads as follows: "Excessive bail shall not be required, nor excessive fines imposed, nor cruel and unusual punishment inflicted." As explained in Chapter 5, the purpose of bail is to ensure that a defendant will appear for trial. If the suspect cannot afford bail, he or she must stay in jail until the trial. It is important to note that the Eighth Amendment does not require bail; it only states that the amount cannot be excessive. In many states release on bail is not permitted in capital cases (i.e., those for which the death penalty applies). Otherwise, there are few restrictions on the amount of bail a judge may require. In a controversial 1987 decision, the U.S. Supreme Court held in *U.S. v. Salerno* that preventive detention without bail on grounds of predicted future dangerousness does not violate the Eighth Amendment. The Court did not consider such detention to be "punishment without trial."[62] This decision reflected the popular view that potentially

U.S. V. SALERNO

dangerous criminals should be confined—even though our ability to predict future criminality accurately is poor, a fact that raises the question whether offenders are being held for crimes they *might* commit in the future, rather than on the basis of the current charge.

The Eighth Amendment also states that fines cannot be excessive. The Supreme Court has not specified an amount that would constitute an excessive fine, but it has ruled that prison sentences imposed when offenders cannot pay fines discriminate against the poor and therefore are unconstitutional.[63] Other than this restriction, few conditions are placed on the imposition of fines. Maximum fines are, of course, fixed by the legislature and vary according to the seriousness of the crime.

The portion of the Eighth Amendment that has been most rigorously scrutinized is the prohibition of **cruel and unusual punishment.** A punishment is considered cruel and unusual if, in the words of the Supreme Court, it violates "evolving standards of decency that mark the progress of a maturing society."[64] Thus, torture is cruel and unusual punishment under the Eighth Amendment. Courts have sometimes held extreme cases of solitary confinement, corporal punishment, mechanical restraints, and poor medical or sanitary conditions for prisoners to be cruel and unusual.[65]

Under what circumstances could a death row inmate appeal his conviction? What four arguments are used to justify capital punishment? Which, if any, arguments seem to be supported by empirical evidence? Under what circumstances could a death row inmate win a stay of execution?

■**cruel and unusual punishment**
Criminal penalties that violate "evolving standards of decency that mark the progress of a maturing society"; such penalties are prohibited by the Eighth Amendment.

What Is the Answer to the Death Penalty Debate?

No penalty has received more attention than capital punishment—that is, the death penalty. The penalty of death for commission of murder is controversial, yet it is used with increasing frequency. Proponents argue that death serves as just retribution for murder, prevents future murders, and costs less than life imprisonment. Opponents argue the opposite: that capital punishment does not serve as retribution, does not deter murders, and costs more than life in prison. These are empirical arguments that can be resolved with the use of objective evidence. To what extent has the death penalty been used as retribution in the past? What impact does it have on homicide rates? How expensive are executions compared to life imprisonment? It is important that we answer these questions correctly, because a record number of prisoners await execution on death row, and the appeals process is being shortened, which will increase the pace of executions in the future.

The Legal Status of the Death Penalty

In 1977 the U.S. Supreme Court ruled that for the crime of rape the death penalty is excessive and disproportionate and therefore unconstitutional.[66]

Since then, capital punishment has been applied primarily to murder cases. During the 1930s there were nearly 200 executions in the United States each year. By the 1960s the number of offenders receiving the death penalty dropped to less than 50 per year. Because of growing uncertainty about the constitutionality of capital punishment, there was a virtual halt to executions in the mid-1960s. In two key decisions during the 1970s, however, the U.S. Supreme Court clarified the constitutionality of death sentences.

Media and Criminal Justice

erhaps no other sentencing issue is as controversial as the death penalty. More and more Americans favor capital punishment for convicted murderers. Opponents continue to point out that executions have not been proved to have a deterrent effect on crime. But many supporters of capital punishment counter that if nothing else, executions provide closure for the surviving families of the murder victims.

The 1995 film *Dead Man Walking* embraced all of these controversies in its story of a death row inmate who elicits the help of a nun as he faces the ultimate penalty for murder. Sister Helen Prejean assists this inmate, Matthew Poncelet, in filing a last-minute appeal that might bring him a reprieve. As Sister Prejean and Matthew discuss his plight in light of the impending execution, however, she becomes a spiritual counselor who is troubled by Matthew's lack of remorse for his crimes. She does not believe that Matthew should die for the brutal rapes and murders that he surely committed, but she hopes that the threat of death will cause him to take responsibility for his actions.

The great worth of *Dead Man Walking* is that it takes no position on the death penalty. Sister Prejean hopes to save Matthew from execution, but she also seeks to understand the ramifications of his crimes. She visits the families of Matthew's murder victims and is faced with the unrelenting heartache of each parent. They remind her that grief is compounded in knowing that their children, young people with such promising futures, suffered horribly in their final moments before death. The families insist that the depth of their tragedy is insulted by Matthew's very existence: It is unfair that the innocent victims are dead and that the murderer continues to live. Sister Prejean's understanding of their loss is made more acute by a visit with Matthew's

family; his mother clearly doesn't see the sense in the state's taking another life by executing her son. Do two wrongs make a right?

Dead Man Walking is a careful examination of the emotions and arguments claimed by all sides. The most important message of the movie is dramatized when Matthew, guided to the truth by Sister Prejean, actually breaks down and faces the ramifications of his murderous behavior. His remorse in painful and very genuine, but it comes too late. As he is strapped down for execution, the illogic and wastefulness in executing a truly remorseful person is made evident. Yet even as the lethal injection begins, the  poignant scene of execution is interspersed with shocking scenes of the actual rapes and murders of Matthew's innocent victims. The viewer is not allowed to forget the senseless, heinous crimes for which Matthew is dying. Retribution, not mere revenge or incapacitation, is communicated in his final moments.

The films brings a great deal of integrity to the discussion of the death penalty, but it does not attempt to convince the viewer of any particular stance. The theme of *Dead Man Walking* is one of careful contemplation, ensuring that both advocates and opponents of capital punishment understand each other's position.

Why was Matthew executed in *Dead Man Walking*? Which arguments and emotions concerning his death penalty do you find most compelling? In murder cases are there ways to recognize the victim's loss and hold the offender accountable without killing the offender?

FURMAN V. GEORGIA* AND *GREGG V. GEORGIA In 1972 the Court ruled in *Furman v. Georgia* that the administration of the death penalty in Georgia constituted cruel and unusual punishment. It was argued to the Court that death sentences were imposed in an arbitrary and discriminatory manner. In this case, Furman had been convicted of a murder that occurred during the course of a burglary attempt. It was left entirely up to the jury to decide, without any guidance in making that decision, whether Furman would receive a sentence of life imprisonment or death.

The Supreme Court's lack of consensus on the death penalty was apparent when each of the nine justices wrote a separate opinion in this case. The majority agreed, however, that Georgia's death penalty law provided for execution "without guidance or direction" as to whether life imprisonment, the death penalty, or other punishment was most appropriate in a given case of murder. The Supreme Court found the Georgia law to be unconstitutional, because offenders who receive the death penalty

CONSTITUTIONALITY
OF DEATH

> *are among a capriciously selected handful upon whom the sentence of death has in fact been imposed. . . . The Eighth and Fourteenth Amendments cannot tolerate the infliction of a sentence of death under legal systems that permit this unique penalty to be so wantonly and freakishly imposed.*[67]

The lack of guidance to judges and juries charged with determining when the death penalty should be imposed allowed for it to be imposed arbitrarily, and often selectively, against minorities. Under these circumstances the death penalty constituted cruel and unusual punishment and could not stand. The effect of this decision was to invalidate the death penalty laws of thirty-nine states.

By 1976, however, thirty-four states had enacted new death penalty statutes designed to meet the requirements of the *Furman* decision. These laws took one of two forms. Either they removed all judicial discretion by mandating capital punishment upon conviction for certain offenses, or they established specific guidelines for judges to use in deciding whether death was an appropriate sentence in a given case.

The Supreme Court assessed the validity of the new laws in 1976 in the case of *Gregg v. Georgia.* Two hitchhikers, Troy Gregg and Floyd Allen, had been picked up in Florida by Fred Simmons and Bob Moore. A third hitchhiker, Dennis Weaver, rode with them to Atlanta, where he got out of the car about 11:00 P.M. The four men remaining in the car later stopped to rest beside the highway. After Simmons and Moore left the car, Gregg told Allen that he was going to rob them. As Simmons and Moore came back toward the car, Gregg fired three shots at them and they fell to the ground. He then fired a shot into the head of each man at close range. He then robbed them and drove away with Allen. The bodies of Simmons and Moore were discovered the next morning.

Upon reading about the shootings in an Atlanta newspaper, Weaver (the third hitchhiker) contacted the police and described his journey with the victims, including a description of the car. The next afternoon Gregg and

Allen (still in Simmons's car) were arrested in Asheville, North Carolina. In the search incident to the arrest a .25-caliber pistol, later shown to be that used to kill Simmons and Moore, was found in Gregg's pocket. After receiving the warnings required by *Miranda v. Arizona* and signing a written waiver of his rights, Gregg signed a statement in which he admitted that he had shot and robbed Simmons and Moore but claimed that he had done so in self-defense. The next day, while being transferred to Lawrenceville, Georgia, Gregg and Allen were taken to the scene of the shootings, where Allen recounted the circumstances surrounding the killings.

The jury found Gregg guilty of two counts of armed robbery and two counts of murder. The judge instructed the jury that it could recommend either a death sentence or a life prison sentence on each count. The jury was free to consider any mitigating or aggravating facts and circumstances in recommending whether a death sentence or life imprisonment was most appropriate. The jury called for the death penalty on each count. The Supreme Court of Georgia affirmed the convictions and the death sentences, but the U.S. Supreme Court decided to hear Gregg's arguments to the effect that the new Georgia death penalty statute still constituted "cruel and unusual punishment" in violation of the Eighth Amendment.

This time, however, the Supreme Court upheld the Georgia law as constitutional, because the new statute requires the jury (which also has sentencing responsibility in some states) to focus

> on the particularized nature of the crime and the particularized characteristics of the individual defendant. While the jury is permitted to consider any aggravating or mitigating circumstances, it must find and identify at least one statutory aggravating factor before it may impose a penalty of death. In this way the jury's discretion is channeled. No longer can a jury wantonly and freakishly impose a death sentence; it is always circumscribed by the legislative guidelines.[68]

As a result, Gregg's death sentence was upheld. Nevertheless, this decision, together with two other death penalty cases decided the same day, struck down some state statutes, because they provided for mandatory death sentences in certain cases.[69] The Court felt that the standard of adequately guided discretion was not met when no discretion whatsoever was permitted. In addition, the Court held for the first time that as a form of punishment the death penalty is not inherently cruel and unusual.

JUDICIAL DISCRETION IN DEATH

The Supreme Court further refined its decision two years later when it struck down the Ohio death penalty statute, which did not permit a judge to consider mitigating factors such as a defendant's age, absence of prior record, or role in the crime. The Supreme Court concluded:

> The Eighth and Fourteenth Amendments require that the sentencer, in all but the rarest kind of capital case, not be precluded from considering as a mitigating factor, any aspect of a defendant's character or record and any of the circumstances of the offense that the defendant proffers as a ba-

sis for a sentence less than death. . . . The considerations that account for the wide acceptance of individualization of sentences in noncapital cases surely cannot be thought less important in capital cases.[70]

Therefore, courts must consider both aggravating *and* mitigating factors in determining the appropriateness of a particular sentence.

MCCLESKEY V. KEMP The death penalty was again called into question in 1987. The case of *McCleskey v. Kemp.*[71] made it clear that claims of alleged discrimination in the application of the death penalty had not been resolved. Warren McCleskey, a black man, was charged with armed robbery and murder for killing a white police officer who was answering a silent alarm during a store robbery in Georgia. After consideration of both aggravating and mitigating circumstances, McCleskey was convicted and sentenced to death. He appealed the sentence on the grounds that it was imposed in a racially discriminatory manner, presenting as evidence the findings of a statistical study that had examined more than 2,000 murder cases in Georgia during the 1970s. The investigators had looked at 230 factors that might have accounted for differences in sentences imposed in these cases. They had found that black defendants who killed white victims were much more likely to receive the death sentence than any other racial combination. The Supreme Court denied McCleskey's appeal on two grounds. First, the majority held that "to prevail under the equal protection clause [of the Fourteenth Amendment], McCleskey must prove that the decision-makers in his case acted with discriminatory purpose." On this basis, the statistical study was "insufficient" to prove discrimination in McCleskey's particular case.

Second, the majority held that McCleskey's treatment did not violate the Eighth Amendment prohibition of cruel and unusual punishment. It held that the statistical study "indicates a discrepancy that appears to correlate with race" but that this discrepancy is "a far cry from the major systemic defects identified in *Furman.*" The majority found that despite the imperfections identified by the study, "our consistent rule has been that constitutional guarantees are met when the mode for determining guilt or punishment has been surrounded with safeguards to make it as fair as possible."[72]

In a sharply worded dissent, four justices argued that proving discrimination in a particular case is irrelevant, because the Court "since *Furman* has been concerned with the risk of the imposition of an arbitrary sentence, rather than the proven fact of one." The dissent believed the Court's decision should address reducing the risk of arbitrary sentences and not await unfair results before intervening. The statistical study "produced striking evidence that the odds of being sentenced to death are significantly greater than average if a defendant is black and his or her victim is white." According to the dissent, such evidence calls into question the effectiveness of the legal standards established in *Furman* and *Gregg.*[73]

contemporary issues and trends

Victim's Race and Death Penalty Decisions

It has long been debated whether the death penalty can be imposed justly and also blindly with regard to race. Of the more than 3,400 prisoners under a sentence of death in the United States, 42 percent are black. Of the 500 persons executed since the U.S. Supreme Court approved the death penalty in 1976, 36 percent have been black.[a] In both cases, the percentage of blacks is far above their proportion in the general population; this imbalance has led to much speculation that black defendants are discriminated against in death penalty cases.

Less attention has been given to the impact of the race of the victim in murder cases. But in 1990 the U.S. General Accounting Office (GAO), the investigative arm of Congress, undertook an examination of the role of race in death penalty decisions. The researchers identified twenty-eight studies of the death penalty that included race as a variable, and they analyzed each study to determine whether race was a significant factor in death penalty cases.

The GAO's findings were remarkable, showing "a pattern of evidence indicating racial disparities in the charging, sentencing, and imposition of the death penalty."[b] In twenty-three of the twenty-eight studies, the race of the *victim* was associated with the decision to charge the offender with murder or to impose the death penalty. Legally relevant factors such as the offender's prior criminal record did not fully account for the racial disparities.

> The GAO researchers concluded that "The results show a strong race of victim influence."

Interestingly, there was mixed evidence regarding the impact of the *defendant's* race. A slight majority of the studies found the race of the defendant significant, but in some studies white defendants were more likely to be sentenced to death; in others it depended on urban–rural differences or on other factors.[c] The GAO researchers concluded that "The results show a strong race of victim influence: the death penalty sentence was more likely to be sought and imposed for an offender if the victim was white."[d] In contrast, the impact of the race of the defendant was not clear or uniform across the studies considered.

1. The typical offender on death row was arrested at age twenty-six, has a prior criminal record, and is from a southern state. How might you explain these findings?
2. What factors surrounding murder cases and trials might help explain the influence of the victim's race in death penalty decisions?
3. Why do you think the victim's race was more significant than the offender's race in cases in which the death penalty was imposed?

NOTES

a. Tracy L. Snell, *Capital Punishment* (Washington, DC: U.S. Bureau of Justice Statistics, 1999).
b. Lowell Dodge, Testimony before the Subcommittee on Civil and Constitutional Rights Committee on the Judiciary, U.S. House of Representatives, May 3, 1990, p. 4.
c. U.S. Comptroller General, *Death Penalty Sentencing: Research Indicates Pattern of Racial Disparity* (Washington, DC: U.S. General Accounting Office, 1990).
d. Dodge, Testimony, p. 6.

To sum up, under current law, the death penalty can be imposed so long as both aggravating and mitigating circumstances are considered by the judge or jury in a nonarbitrary manner.[74] Clearly, it is difficult to establish whether or not a sentence was imposed fairly in any given case, although evidence suggests that sentences are unfairly influenced by factors such as conduct of the prosecutor or defense attorney, juror comprehension, and race.[75]

The Death Penalty

By 1999 a total of thirty-eight states, as well as the federal government, had enacted capital punishment laws in accordance with the guidelines set forth by the U.S. Supreme Court. A record 3,452 people are now under sentence of death and awaiting execution. This reflects an upward trend that began in 1977 after the Supreme Court's ruling in *Gregg v. Georgia,* which specifically stated that capital punishment was not inherently cruel and unusual. Figure 10.4 graphically illustrates the rise in the number of persons sentenced to death from 1953 through 1998. There are now more people awaiting execution than at any time since 1930, when national statistics were first collected. Nearly 40 percent of the prisoners on death row are in only three states: California, Texas, and Florida.[76]

Support for the death penalty remains high, although there is some reluctance to carry out executions once a sentence of death has been pronounced.[77] Five hundred official executions have taken place since 1976, although the annual number is increasing. In 1998 alone there were 68 executions, reflecting the trend toward carrying out more death sentences in recent years. Since 1930, nearly 4,500 executions have been carried out.[78]

The most common methods used to carry out executions are lethal injection (thirty-four states) and electrocution (eleven states). Five states carry out death sentences with lethal gas; three by hanging (Delaware, New Hampshire, Washington); and three by firing squad (Idaho, Oklahoma, Utah). Sixteen states authorize the use of more than one method (lethal injection and an alternative method).[79] Federal offenders are executed by means of the method authorized in the state in which the execution takes place. Several states have provided an alternative to lethal injection because of concern that injection may be found unconstitutional in a court challenge (i.e., does it constitute cruel and unusual punishment in the manner in which it causes death?). There also has been controversy over whether electrocution is cruel and unusual punishment, but the U.S. Supreme Court has

**METHODS OF
EXECUTION**

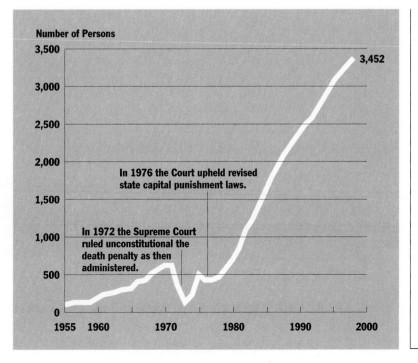

Number of Persons

In 1976 the Court upheld revised state capital punishment laws.

In 1972 the Supreme Court ruled unconstitutional the death penalty as then administered.

3,452

FIGURE 10.4

Persons under a Sentence of Death, 1953–1998

SOURCE: Tracy L. Snell, *Capital Punishment* (Washington, DC: U.S. Bureau of Justice Statistics, 1999).

TABLE 10.4

Methods of Execution by State

LETHAL INJECTION		ELECTROCUTION	LETHAL GAS	HANGING	FIRING SQUAD
Arizona[a,b]	New Hampshire[a]	Alabama	Arizona[a,b]	Delaware[a,c]	Idaho[a]
Arkansas[a,d]	New Jersey	Arkansas[a,d]	California[a]	New Hampshire[a,e]	Oklahoma[f]
California[a]	New Mexico	Florida	Missouri[a]	Washington[a]	Utah[a]
Colorado	New York	Georgia	North Carolina[a]		
Connecticut	North Carolina[a]	Kentucky[a,g]	Wyoming[a,h]		
Delaware[a,c]	Ohio[a]	Nebraska			
Idaho[a]	Oklahoma[a]	Ohio[a]			
Illinois	Oregon	Oklahoma[f]			
Indiana	Pennsylvania	South Carolina[a]			
Kansas	South Carolina[a]	Tennessee[a,i]			
Kentucky[a,g]	South Dakota	Virginia[a]			
Louisiana	Tennessee[a,i]				
Maryland	Texas				
Mississippi	Utah[a]				
Missouri[a]	Virginia[a]				
Montana	Washington[a]				
Nevada	Wyoming[a]				

[a]Authorizes 2 methods of execution.

[b]Arizona authorizes lethal injection for persons whose capital sentence was received after 11/15/92; for those sentenced before that date, the condemned may select lethal injection or lethal gas.

[c]Delaware authorizes lethal injection for those whose capital offense occurred after 6/13/86; for those whose capital offense occurred before that date, the condemned may select lethal injection or hanging.

[d]Arkansas authorizes lethal injection for those whose capital offense occurred on or after 7/4/83; for those whose offense occurred before that date, the condemned may select lethal injection or electocution.

[e]New Hampshire authorizes hanging only if lethal injection cannot be given.

[f]Oklahoma authorizes electrocution if lethal injection is ever held to be unconstitutional, and firing squad if both lethal injection and electrocution are held unconstitutional.

[g]Kentucky authorizes lethal injection for persons whose capital sentence was received on or after 3/31/98; for those sentenced before that date, the condemned may select lethal injection or electrocution.

[h]Wyoming authorizes lethal gas if lethal injection is ever held to be unconstitutional.

[i]Tennessee authorizes lethal injection for those whose capital offense occurred after 12/31/98; those whose offense occurred before that date may select lethal injection or electrocution.

NOTE: The method of execution of federal prisoners is lethal injection, pursuant to 28 CFR, Part 26. For offenses under the Violent Crime Control and Law Enforcement Act of 1994, the method is that of the state in which the conviction took place, pursuant to 18 U.S.C. 3596.

SOURCE: Tracy L. Snell, *Capital Punishment* (Washington, DC: U.S. Bureau of Justice Statistics, 1999).

not yet ruled on this issue.[80] Table 10.4 shows how methods of execution differ among the states.

Arguments for and against Capital Punishment

Those who support the death penalty usually base their argument on one of four grounds: (1) The death penalty is a necessary punishment as retribution for the life unlawfully taken; (2) the death penalty will deter others from committing murder; (3) the death penalty is less expensive to administer than life imprisonment; and (4) errors in executing innocent persons are rare. Let us examine the evidence that exists to support these claims.

CAPITAL PUNISHMENT AS RETRIBUTION The retributionist argument is perhaps the oldest of all justifications for punishment. It can be traced at least as far back as the Old Testament. The books of Exodus (21:12–25), Leviticus (24:17–21), Numbers (35:30–31), and Deuteronomy (19:11–12), all warn that

> *in case a man strikes any soul of mankind fatally, he should be put to death without fail. . . . And in case a man should cause a defect in his associate, then just as he has done, so it should be done to him. Fracture for fracture, eye for eye, tooth for tooth; the same sort of defect he may cause in the man that is what should be caused in him. And the fatal striker of a heart should make compensation for it, but the fatal striker of a man should be put to death.*

Although modern Israel, established in 1948, quickly abandoned the Mosaic law of "life for life" (except in cases of wartime treason or Nazi collaboration), many people continue to apply this notion of retribution in support of the death penalty. In fact, Christians sometimes use this justification for capital punishment despite Christ's teachings to the contrary. For example, the Gospel according to Matthew (5:38–39) recounts Jesus' stating, "You heard that it was said, 'Eye for eye and tooth for tooth.' However, I say to you: Do not resist him that is wicked; but whoever slaps you on the right cheek, turn the other also to him." Such teachings prompted the disciples of early Christianity to oppose capital punishment. Adherence to this principle wavered, however, when non-Christians came to be seen as heretics and deserving of death. This change of heart relied heavily on Paul's declaration to the Romans (13:1–2):

> *Let every soul be in subjection to the superior authorities, for there is no authority except by God; the existing authorities stand placed in their relative positions by God. Therefore he who opposes the authority has taken a stand against the arrangement of God.*

Some believed that Paul's statements meant that if the state permitted capital punishment, capital punishment must be God's will, because government exists only by God's will. This line of reasoning continues to be employed today by those who defend the death penalty on the basis of Biblical interpretation.

RETRIBUTION IS INEFFECTIVE

Regardless of the basis of the argument, there is little evidence that capital punishment has been effective as a form of retribution. Examinations of willful homicides in the United States have shown that fewer than half are murders involving premeditation or homicides committed during the course of a felony. Further, fewer than 25 percent of homicides are prosecuted as capital cases. In these capital cases males and blacks have been executed much more often than have females and whites convicted of the same crimes. Even when a person is prosecuted for murder, the defendant's odds of actually receiving retribution is extremely small.[81] For example, in Massachusetts between 1931 and 1950, a murder defendant faced a 29 percent chance of being convicted and a 4 percent chance of being put to death. In California between 1950 and 1975, only 29 percent of homicide convictions were capital cases; 6 percent of defendants were sentenced to death, and fewer than 2 percent were executed. In fact, the death penalty has been imposed on only a small minority of offenders convicted of homicide. During its greatest usage in the 1930s, death sentences were handed down in only 1 of 50 homicide convictions. And as criminologist Thorsten Sellin has pointed out, these examples actually *overestimate* the use of the death penalty as retribution:

> *Considering that these adjudicated murderers were only a part of a group that included the never-discovered offenders and those arrested but not prosecuted or convicted for lack of sufficient evidence, it is obvious that if retribution by death could be measured in relation to the number of actual murders, its failure would be even more evident.*[82]

Although in recent years supporters of retribution have succeeded in passing death penalty laws, it can be seen that only a small proportion of criminal homicides are actually subject to the death penalty. Moreover, the penalty is rarely imposed even in cases in which it is applicable. When it is applied, males and blacks receive a disproportionate share of the death sentences imposed.

It appears, therefore, that the goal of the retributionists has yet to be achieved. Even if the number of executions were to rise dramatically, it is unlikely that more than 2 percent of all homicide offenders sentenced would ever be executed. After all, the rate was 2 percent during the 1930s, when executions numbered more than 200 per year. Limits on appellate review of sentences in death penalty cases have resulted in more executions in recent years, but the numbers are quite small compared to those in the 1930s. Trends in the number of people executed in the United States from 1930 to 1998 are illustrated in Figure 10.5. It is clear that the increase in executions during the 1990s is dwarfed by the number of executions that took place each year from 1930 to 1950.

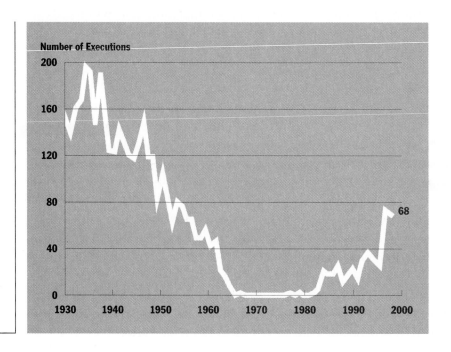

FIGURE 10.5
Persons Executed, 1930–1998

SOURCE: Tracy L. Snell, *Capital Punishment* (Washington, DC: U.S. Bureau of Justice Statistics, 1999).

THE DEATH PENALTY AS DETERRENCE The belief that the death penalty will prevent crime by deterring future murders is another common argument in support of capital punishment.[83] One aspect of this argument suggests that police officers in states without the death penalty are more likely to be killed than officers in states that provide for capital punishment for murder (or at least for murder of police officers). Studies consistently have found, however, that the numbers of police officers killed do not differ in death penalty and non–death penalty states.[84]

The deterrence argument also holds that capital punishment prevents the offender from committing another murder if released on parole. In the four-year period from 1969 to 1973, when no death sentences were carried out, 6,835 male offenders serving sentences for murder were released on parole from state prisons. Fewer than 5 percent of those released were returned to prison for additional crimes. Fewer than one-half of 1 percent committed willful homicides. From 1930 to 1962, when executions were more frequent, only 63 offenders convicted of first-degree murder in New York State were released on parole; of these, one person was returned to prison for committing an additional crime (a burglary). Other follow-up studies have had similar results.[85] It is clear that murderers are very rarely released on parole and that when they are, it is extremely uncommon for them to be involved in another homicide.

Another way to assess the deterrent effect of capital punishment is to determine whether homicide rates increase when states abolish capital punishment, or to examine the homicide rates in neighboring states, one of which has a death penalty while the other does not. Obviously, if capital punishment prevents murders, states without a death penalty law should have higher homicide rates than neighboring states that employ the death penalty. A comparison of homicide rates and use of the death penalty in Maryland, Delaware, and New Jersey from 1920 through 1974 found no difference in homicide rates, even though each of these states retained, abolished, and sometimes reinstituted capital punishment during this fifty-five-year period. The number of executions in these states varied from none to a high of twenty-six per year, but in no case was a higher number of executions accompanied by a lower homicide rate. Comparable findings were uncovered in tristate comparisons of Arizona, California, and New Mexico and of Indiana, Ohio, and Michigan, as well as of other states.[86] As Brian Forst concluded, "it is erroneous to view capital punishment as a means of reducing the homicide rate."[87] Likewise, Scott Decker and Carol Kohlfeld found that "several different methods of examining the deterrent effect of executions resulted in the same finding; there is no evidence of a deterrent effect of executions in the state of Texas."[88] These findings mirror the conclusions of other criminologists.[89]

Studies that appear to show a deterrent effect have been repudiated on methodological grounds.[90] In fact, there is evidence from two studies that there may be a slight *increase* in the number of homicides following a legal execution. These studies found a few more homicides after executions than one would normally expect to occur. It has been suggested that a legal

STUDIES ON
DETERRENT EFFECTS

execution may "provoke" homicides by conveying the message that vengeance by means of killing is justified.[91]

There are several important reasons that the death penalty is not a deterrent to criminal homicide. Most significant is that the offender must consider the consequences of his or her actions if deterrence is to take place. If a person does not not consider the possibility of being penalized for his or her actions, no penalty, however severe, will act as a deterrent. The crime of murder is rarely carried out in such a rational fashion. First, those who commit murder rarely set out to do it. Most homicides occur as an unplanned act during the commission of a robbery or other felony. Thus, the death penalty is not considered as a possible outcome because murder was not an anticipated part of the crime. Second, offenders rarely believe that they will be caught. Because police solve only a small percentage of all serious crimes, the likelihood of punishment is very low. Certainty of punishment is extremely important if deterrence is to work. The lower the chances of being caught, the lower the deterrent effect of any penalty. Third, when criminal homicides occur, they usually are committed during a moment of intense anger or emotion in which reason is distorted. Police estimate that about half of all homicides occur during arguments between an offender and a victim who know each other. Also, it is not unusual for the offender to be under the influence of alcohol or a drug, which certainly affects rational thinking. All these circumstances work against the exercise of rational behavior, which is pivotal to the notion of deterrence.

ECONOMICS AND CAPITAL PUNISHMENT Some claim that the death penalty is more economical than housing an offender in prison for life. A study conducted in New York State during the 1980s found that it would cost a total $648,560 to incarcerate a thirty-year-old murderer if he lived to age seventy. On the other hand, at that time the costs of the trials and multiple appeals involved in capital cases amounted to more than $1.8 million.[92] Currently, it costs $20,100 per year to imprison the average inmate, but the cost is usually higher on death row because of segregation practices for those awaiting execution.[93] The average inmate on death row is now twenty-eight years old, suggesting that living thirty or more years in prison is quite possible.[94] A 1998 study found that the cost of defending a federal death penalty case through trial was $269,139, plus the cost of subsequent appeals.[95] In Florida, each execution costs the state $3.2 million—six times the cost of life imprisonment.[96] The high cost of capital punishment cases arises from the fact that virtually all death penalty states provide for automatic appellate review of death sentences. To guard against the possibility of a mistake, states usually conduct this review regardless of the offender's wishes. Because of this time-consuming process, the average time between sentencing and execution of offenders executed since 1977 has been more than eight years.[97] Limitations on the right to appeal, enacted in 1996, will reduce the time between sentencing and execution; but it remains to be seen whether the difference will be significant.[98]

The economic argument for the use of the death penalty thus does not hold up under scrutiny. It also overlooks the fact that the proportion of offenders who ever face the death penalty is extremely small. As the New York State report concluded, "a criminal justice system with the death penalty is inordinately more expensive than a criminal justice system without the death penalty."[99]

ERRORS IN APPLYING THE DEATH PENALTY A major criticism of capital punishment is its finality. Proponents of the death penalty argue that errors are rare; but in a criminal justice system based on inexact legal standards such as "probable cause" and "proof beyond a reasonable doubt," there is always room for error.[100] There have been cases in which offenders who were executed have later been found to be innocent. In Illinois, for example, at least 13 offenders who were convicted of murder and sentenced to death later were found to be innocent.[101] A systematic nationwide study found 400 erroneous convictions in death penalty cases.[102] In 1999 and 2000, both Nebraska and Illinois put a hold on executions because of errors, and possible prosecution misconduct, that put innocent suspects on death row.[103] The 1996 Antiterrorism and Effective Death Penalty Act places restrictions on the appeals available to offenders sentenced to death. Some fear that these new limits will result in additional erroneous convictions in murder cases.[98]

Advances in testing for deoxyribonucleic acid (DNA) have been instrumental both in convicting and in exonerating suspects linked to serious crimes. Reliable DNA testing emerged during the late 1980s, and although testing procedures are still improving, DNA tests now are generally accepted as evidence in court.[104] DNA evidence has revealed that eyewitness testimony is sometimes mistaken, that jailhouse informants can be unreliable, and that those with criminal records often become suspects in criminal cases without strong evidence of their involvement in the crime. In one case a rape victim identified her assailant, but DNA evidence later showed she was mistaken. In another case a man was wrongly convicted in the rape of an eleven-year-old girl, even though eleven witnesses had testified he was 300 miles away at the time of the rape.[105] Errors like these are troubling, because they reveal that weak evidence sometimes results in erroneous criminal convictions. DNA samples taken from hair or body fluids from the victim or crime scene has revealed these errors to the shock of many, resulting in attempts to halt executions in eleven states in order to study the reasons for these errors.

From 1977, the year after the U.S. Supreme Court reinstated the death penalty in *Gregg v. Georgia*, through 1998, a total of 5,709 offenders were sentenced to death. Of these, 500 were executed, but 2,137 were removed from death row by appellate court review, sentence reductions, or death.[106] The large number of prisoners whose sentences are reduced or overturned, often because errors are discovered, has caused many to question the use of so final a penalty as capital punishment in so uncertain a process as the American criminal justice system.

critical thinking exercise

Is Life Imprisonment a More Severe Punishment Than the Death Penalty?

During the 1960s a majority of people in the United States opposed the death penalty, but today public opinion polls show widespread support for capital punishment. This support is manifested in the existence of death penalty laws in thirty-eight states and the federal government. The current support continues despite concerns about the deterrent effect of capital punishment and despite the fact that most other nations have abolished it. Even South Africa, which had used capital punishment for 350 years, abolished it in 1995.[a] This left the United States among the few developed nations that still carry out death sentences.

In death penalty cases a judge or jury usually may choose between the death penalty and life imprisonment. Supporters of capital punishment often argue that life imprisonment is a less severe penalty than death. An argument can be made, however, that life imprisonment is actually a *more* severe sentence than the death penalty. This argument was made most persuasively by Cesare Beccaria in his 1764 *Essay on Crimes and Punishments*. Beccaria argued that "it is not the terrible yet momentary spectacle of the death of a wretch, but the long and painful example of a man deprived of liberty . . . which is the strongest curb against crimes." He believed that the impression left by an execution is mitigated by a tendency to forget the event because of its brevity. In addition, some offenders may desire death because they are vain or fanatic, or because they wish to escape their misery. Beccaria goes on to argue that life imprisonment is a better deterrent to crime than the death penalty. An execution provides only a single deterrent example, whereas "the penalty of a lifetime of servitude for a single crime supplies frequent and lasting examples" to others. "Adding up all the moments of unhappiness and servitude," Beccaria concludes, life imprisonment "may well be even more cruel; [it is] drawn out over an entire lifetime, while the pain of death exerts its whole force in a moment."

Beccaria also states that the death penalty is not useful "because of the example of barbarity it gives men." He notes, "It seems to me absurd that the laws, which are an expression of the public will, which detest and punish homicide, should themselves commit it, and that to deter citizens from murder, they order a public one."[b]

Former New York State Governor Mario Cuomo opposed capital punishment on grounds similar to those set forth by Beccaria. His opposition to the death penalty was seen by many as a major cause of his failure to win reelection in 1994. During the previous year Cuomo had refused to send an inmate serving a life sentence from New York State to Oklahoma, where the inmate faced the death penalty, despite the inmate's stated wish to die. In 1994 the new governor sent the inmate to Oklahoma to be executed. Ironically, before his execution the inmate wrote a statement that said, "Let there be no mistake, Mario Cuomo is wright [sic]. . . . All jurors should remember this. Attica and Oklahoma State Penitentiary are living hells." Cuomo later remarked about the inmate, "He admitted that being allowed to die was an act of clemency for a double murderer, relieving him of the relentless confinement he dreaded more than death."[c]

CRITICAL THINKING QUESTIONS

1. Do you agree or disagree with Beccaria's argument about the severity of life imprisonment versus the death penalty? What are your reasons for doing so?

2. How would you respond to Beccaria's comment that it appears absurd for the state and its laws to express condemnation of homicide by committing it?

NOTES

a. Chris Eramus, "Death Penalty Is Abolished in South Africa," *USA Today* (June 7, 1995), p. 4.

b. Cesare Beccaria, *Essay on Crimes and Punishments* (1764) (Indianapolis: Bobbs-Merrill, 1984), ch. 16.

c. Doug Ferguson, "Grasso, Just Before Dying, Says Cuomo Is Right: Life in Prison Would Be Worse," *Buffalo News* (March 21, 1995), p. 14.

Summary

WHAT HAPPENS AT TRIAL?

- More than 90 percent of criminal cases are resolved through guilty pleas.
- When a trial takes place, it begins with the selection of a jury, usually consisting of twelve members.
- After a jury has been selected, the prosecution and defense counsel make opening statements. The body of the trial consists of the presentation of the prosecutor's evidence and the statements of witnesses, followed by the presentation of the case for the defense.
- A major issue in criminal defense is the new tendency to focus on the offender rather than on the criminal act. This has led to the creation of new defenses that attempt to go beyond the traditional boundaries of concepts such as self-defense.
- When all the evidence has been presented, the prosecution and defense make their final arguments to the jury. This stage is followed by the judge's instruction to the jury.
- In order for a defendant to be found guilty, the jury must agree unanimously that guilt has been proved beyond a reasonable doubt.

HOW DO JUDGES DECIDE ON A SENTENCE?

- In order to individualize sentences on the basis of the nature of the offender and the circumstances of the offense, judges may choose sentences within a range established by law.
- When a judge sentences for purposes of retribution, punishment is applied simply in proportion to the seriousness of the offense.
- Sentences based on the concept of incapacitation are intended to prevent further criminal behavior by the offender.
- Habitual offender laws such as "three strikes" statutes apply to offenders who have committed two or more offenses within a certain period.
- Deterrence aims to prevent crime through the example of offenders' being punished.
- The rehabilitation approach sees criminal behavior as stemming from social or psychological shortcomings. The purpose of a sentence aimed at rehabilitation is to correct or treat these shortcomings.
- Depending on the range of alternatives provided by law, a judge usually can fine an offender or impose a sentence of probation, incarceration, or restitution.
- Occasionally a judge suspends (delays) a prison sentence on condition that the offender participate in an alcohol, drug, or gambling treatment program or pay restitution.
- A presentence report is written by a probation officer after an investigation of the offender's background; the report is designed to help the judge decide on an appropriate sentence.

HOW DO SENTENCING OPTIONS DIFFER?

- Indeterminate sentencing systems empower the judge to set a maximum sentence; throughout the sentence a parole board reviews the offender's progress in order to determine whether early release is justified.
- Determinate sentencing systems permit the judge to impose fixed sentences that cannot be altered by a parole board.

- The trend toward determinate sentencing has produced significant increases in prison populations.
- Mandatory sentences are fixed sentences imposed on individuals convicted of certain types of crimes.
- Truth-in-sentencing laws endeavor to establish a closer relationship between sentence imposed and actual time served.
- Sentencing guidelines recommend a "guideline sentence" based on past average sentences and taking into account the seriousness of the crime and the offender's prior record.

HOW DOES THE EIGHTH AMENDMENT RESTRICT SENTENCING?

- The Eighth Amendment bars excessive bail, excessive fines, and cruel and unusual punishment.
- The Supreme Court has ruled that the death penalty is cruel and unusual punishment except in cases of murder.

WHAT IS THE ANSWER TO THE DEATH PENALTY DEBATE?

- There has been considerable controversy over how the death penalty is applied, with some critics claiming that it is imposed arbitrarily against minorities.
- Recent Supreme Court rulings require that courts consider both aggravating and mitigating factors in determining the appropriateness of a particular sentence, including the death sentence.
- Some supporters of the death penalty believe that it is a necessary punishment as retribution for the life unlawfully taken. There is little evidence that the death sentence has been effective as a form of retribution.
- Another common argument in support of capital punishment is that the death penalty will prevent crime by deterring future murders. Studies have found that there is no difference in homicide rates in states that have retained, abolished, and reinstituted capital punishment.
- Some death penalty proponents argue that execution is less costly to the state than life imprisonment, but studies show that this is not the case.
- Supporters of capital punishment contend that innocent persons are rarely executed, but studies have found numerous cases of erroneous convictions in death penalty cases. Analysis of DNA evidence has proved that suspects are convicted in error more often than was previously imagined.

Key Terms

continuance	deterrence
discovery	rehabilitation
general defenses	suspended sentence
justification defenses	presentence report
excuse defenses	indeterminate sentencing
jury nullification	determinate sentencing
retribution	truth in sentencing
incapacitation	mandatory sentences
selective incapacitation	guidelines sentences
habitual offender laws	cruel and unusual punishment

Questions for Review and Discussion

1. List the sequence of events in a typical criminal trial.
2. What is required if a jury is to reach a verdict of guilty?
3. What are some arguments for and against considering factors other than the crime in deciding on an appropriate sentence for a convicted offender?
4. Name and describe the four main purposes of sentencing.
5. What is a suspended sentence?
6. Distinguish between indeterminate and determinate sentencing systems.
7. What is meant by "truth in sentencing"?
8. What are sentencing guidelines? What effect have they had in the states where they have been adopted?
9. What protections are provided by the Eighth Amendment to the U.S. Constitution?
10. What is the current legal status of the death penalty?
11. Describe the main arguments in support of the death penalty.
12. How has DNA testing changed the way in which convicted criminals are viewed?

Notes

1. Michael E. Tigar, "Trials Teach Lessons of Rights and Responsibilities," *The National Law Journal* 19 (November 18, 1996), p. 19.
2. Timothy C. Hart and Brian A. Reaves, *Felony Defendants in Large Urban Counties* (Washington, DC: Bureau of Justice Statistics, 1999).
3. Jodi M. Brown, Patrick A. Langan, and David J. Levin, *Felony Sentences in the United States* (Washington, DC: Bureau of Justice Satistics, 1999), p. 8.
4. Leonard W. Levy, *The Palladium of Justice: Origins of Trial by Jury* (New York: Reed, 1999).
5. Rita J. Simon, *The Jury: Its Role in American Society* (Lexington, MA: Lexington Books, 1980); D. Suggs and B. D. Sales, "Using Communication Cues to Evaluate Prospective Jurors in the Voir Dire," *Arizona Law Review* 20 (1978), pp. 629–42.
6. Andrew Blum, "Jury Consultants Targeted: Illinois Bill Would Bar Non-Lawyers from Advising," *The National Law Journal* 18 (November 20, 1995), p. 6.
7. *Ballew v. Georgia*, 435 U.S. 223 (1978).
8. Robert Davis, "We Live in an Age of Exotic Defenses," *USA Today* (November 22, 1994), p. 2.
9. Davis, pp. 1–2.
10. Alan Dershowitz, *The Abuse Excuse* (New York: Random House, 1994).
11. Davis, p. 2.
12. Margaret Gibbons, "Kleitman Granted Second Chance to Ask for Freedom," *The Legal Intelligencer* (May 6, 1998), p. 5.
13. Margaret Cronin Fisk, "In Drug Defense, Stress Constitution," *The National Law Journal* 20 (September 22, 1997), p. 6.
14. Leonard Buder, "Gotti Is Acquitted in Conspiracy Case Involving the Mob," *New York Times* (March 14, 1987), p. 1.
15. Melvyn B. Zerman, *Beyond a Reasonable Doubt: Inside the American Jury System* (New York: Crowell, 1981).
16. Nancy S. Marder, "The Interplay of Race and False Claims of Jury Nullification," *University of Michigan Law Review* 32 (winter 1999); Nancy Jean King, "The American Criminal Jury," *Law and Contemporary Problems* 62 (spring 1999), pp. 41–67.
17. Susan Estrich, "A Just Sentence for Susan Smith," *USA Today* (August 3, 1995), p. 11.
18. Exodus 21:12–25; Leviticus 24:17–21; Numbers 35:30–31; Deuteronomy 19:11–12.
19. Andrew von Hirsch, *Doing Justice: The Choice of Punishments* (New York: Hill & Wang, 1976); Andrew von Hirsch, *Past or Future Crimes: Deservedness and Dangerousness in the Sentencing of Criminals* (New Brunswick, NJ: Rutgers University Press, 1985).

20. Reuel Shinnar and Shlomo Shinnar, "The Effects of the Criminal Justice System on the Control of Crime: A Quantitative Analysis," *Law and Society Review* 9 (1975), pp. 581–611; Peter W. Greenwood, *Selective Incapacitation* (Santa Monica, CA: Rand Corporation, 1978).

21. Kathleen Auerhahn, "Selective Incapacitation and the Problem of Prediction," *Criminology* 37 (November, 1999), p. 703.

22. Stephen D. Gottfredson and Don M. Gottfredson, "Selective Incapacitation?," *Annals* 478 (1985), pp. 135–49; Andrew von Hirsch, "Selective Incapacitation Reexamined," *Criminal Justice Ethics* 7 (1988), pp. 19–35.

23. "Costly Pizza," *USA Today* (August 4, 1994), p. 3.

24. See Alfred Blumstein, Jacqueline Cohen, and Daniel Nagin, eds., *Deterrence and Incapacitation: Estimating the Effects of Criminal Sanctions on Crime Rates* (Washington, DC: National Academy of Sciences, 1978); Michael L. Radelet and Ronald L. Akers, "Deterrence and the Death Penalty: The Views of the Experts," *Journal of Criminal Law and Criminology* 87 (Fall 1996), pp. 1–16; Neal Kumar Katyal, "Deterrence's Difficulty," *Michigan Law Review* 95 (August 1997), pp. 2385–476.

25. Scott H. Decker and Carol W. Kohlfeld, "Certainty, Severity, and the Probability of Crime," *Policy Studies Journal* 19 (1990), pp. 2–21; James J. Hennessy, Vincent P. Rao, Jennice S. Vilhauer, and Joyce N. Fensterstock, "Crime and Punishment: Infrequently Imposed Sanctions May Reinforce Criminal Behavior," *Journal of Offender Rehabilitation* 29 (March–April 1999), p. 65.

26. David Grosvenor, Traci L. Toomey, and Alexander C. Wagenaar, "Deterrence and the Adolescent Drinking Driver," *Journal of Safety Research* 30 (Fall 1999), p. 187; Daniel S. Nagin and Raymond Paternoster, "The Preventive Effects of the Perceived Risk of Arrest," *Criminology* 29 (1991), pp. 561–85.

27. Gary S. Green, "General Deterrence and Television Cable Crime," *Criminology* 23 (1985), pp. 629–45.

28. D. A. Andrews, Ivan Zinger, Robert D. Hoge, James Bonta, Paul Gendreau, and Francis T. Cullen, "Does Correctional Treatment Work?," *Criminology* 28 (1990), pp. 393–404; Daniele M. Polizzi, Doris Layton MacKenzie, and Laura J. Hickman, "What Works in Adult Sex Offender Treatment? A Review of Prison- and Non-Prison-Based Treatment Programs," *International Journal of Offender Therapy and Comparative Criminology* 43 (September, 1999), p. 357.

29. Gerald G. Gaes, Timothy J. Flanagan, Lawrence L. Motiuk, and Lynn Stewart, "Adult Correctional Treatment," *Crime and Justice* 26 (fall 1999), p. 361; Lee Sechrest, Susan O. White, and Elizabeth D. Brown, eds., *The Rehabilitation of Criminal Offenders* (Washington, DC: National Academy of Sciences, 1979).

30. *Williams v. Illinois*, 399 U.S. 235 (1970).

31. *Tate v. Short*, 401 U.S. 395 (1971).

32. *Gardner v. Florida*, 430 U.S. 349 (1977).

33. Catharine M. Goodwin, "The Independent Role of the Probation Officer at Sentencing and in Applying *Koon v. United States*," *Federal Probation* 60 (September 1996), pp. 71–79; S. Scott MacDonald and Cynthia Baroody-Hart, "Communication between Probation Officers and Judges: An Innovative Model," *Federal Probation* 63 (June 1999), p. 42.

34. Robert M. Carter and Leslie T. Wilkins, "Some Factors in Sentencing Policy," *Journal of Criminal Law, Criminology, and Police Science*, vol. 58 (1967), pp. 503–514; Curtis Campbell, Candace McCoy, and Chimezie Osigweh, "The Influence of Probation Recommendations on Sentencing Decisions and Their Predictive Accuracy," *Federal Probation* 54 (1990), pp. 13–21.

35. *1996 National Survey of State Sentencing Structures* (Washington, DC: Bureau of Justice Assistance, 1998).

36. Paula M. Ditton and Doris James Wilson, *Truth in Sentencing in State Prisons* (Washington, DC: Bureau of Justice Statistics, 1999); Lawrence A. Greenfeld, *Prison Sentences and Time Served for Violence* (Washington, DC: U.S. Bureau of Justice Statistics, 1995).

37. Ditton and Wilson; Greenfeld.

38. Pamala L. Griset, "Determinate Sentencing and Agenda Building: A Case Study of the Failure of a Reform," *Journal of Criminal Justice* 23 (July–August 1995), pp. 349–62.

39. U.S. Comptroller General, *Truth in Sentencing: Availability of Federal Grants Influenced Laws in Some States* (Washington, DC: U.S. General Accounting Office, 1998).

40. Virginia House Appropriations Committee Staff Report, *Analysis of Potential Costs under the Governor's Sentencing Reform Plan* (Richmond: Office of the Governor, 1994); Marc Mauer, "The Truth about Truth in Sentencing," *Corrections Today* 58 (February 1996), pp. 1–9.

41. U.S. Comptroller General, pp. 7–8; Lisa Stansky, "Breaking Up Prison Gridlock," *ABA Journal* 82 (May 1996), p. 70–76.

42. Steven R. Donziger, ed., *The Real War on Crime: The Report of the National Criminal Justice Commission* (New York: Harper Perennial, 1996), p. 24.

43. Allen J. Beck et al., *Correctional Populations in the United States* (Washington, DC: U.S. Bureau of Justice Statistics, 1999).

44. Beck et al., p. 13.

45. Paul Simon and Dave Kopel, "Restore Flexibility to U.S. Sentences," *The National Law Journal* 19 (December 16, 1996), p. 15.

46. Carey Goldberg, "Study Casts Doubt on Wisdom of Mandatory Terms for Drugs," *New York Times* (November 25, 1997), p. 11.

47. Raymond Hernandez, "Governor Commutes Sentences of 3 Convicted on Drug Charges: Clemencies Are Seen as Protest to Sentencing Laws," *New York Times* (December 25, 1997), p. B1.

48. Michael Tonry, *Sentencing Reform Impacts* (Washington, DC: National Institute of Justice, 1987).

49. Ditton and Wilson, *Truth in Sentencing in State Prisons*; John Wooldredge, "Research Notes: A State-Level Analysis of Sentencing Policies and Inmate Crowding in State Prisons," *Crime and Delinquency* 42 (July 1996), pp. 456–66.

50. Dale Parent, Terence Dunworth, Douglas McDonald, and William Rhodes, *Mandatory Sentencing* (Washington, DC: National Institute of Justice, 1997).

51. *Riggs v. California*, 1999 U.S. LEXIS 743; John Cloud, "A Get-Tough Policy That Failed," *Time* (February 1, 1999), p. 48.

52. Lisa Stolzenberg and Stewart J. D'Alessio, "Three Strikes and You're Out": The Impact of California's New Mandatory Sentencing Law on Serious Crime Rates," *Crime and Delinquency* 43 (October 1997), pp. 457–69.

53. Tom R. Tyler and Robert J. Boeckmann, "Three Strikes and You're Out, but Why?: The Psychology of Public Support for Punishing Rule Breakers," *Law and Society Review* 31 (June 1997), pp. 237–65; David Shichor, "Three Strikes as a Public Policy: The Convergence of the New Penology and the McDonaldization of Punishment," *Crime and Delinquency* 43 (October 1997), pp. 470–93; Daniel D. Ntanda Nsereko, "Minimum Sentences and Their Effect on Judicial Discretion," *Crime, Law and Social Change* 31 (June 1999), p. 363.

54. Richard P. Conaboy, "The United States Sentencing Commission: A New Component in the Federal Criminal Justice System," *Federal Probation* 61 (March 1997), pp. 58–62.

55. *1996 National Survey of Sentencing Structures* (Washington, DC: Bureau of Justice Assistance, 1998).

56. Bruce Frankel and Dennis Cauchon, "Judicial Revolt over Sentencing Picks Up Steam," *USA Today* (May 3, 1993), p. 9; "Hands Tied," *The National Law Journal* 18 (January 15, 1996), p. 18.

57. Dorothy K. Hatsukami and Marian W. Fischman, "Crack Cocaine and Cocaine Hydrochloride: Are the Differences Myth or Reality?," *Journal of the American Medical Association* 276 (1996), p. 1580; Kelly McMurry, "Researchers Criticize Cocaine Sentencing Guidelines," *Trial* 33 (April 1997), p. 17; Jeffrey L. Fisher, "When Discretion Leads to Distortion: Recognizing Pre-Arrest Sentence-Manipulation Claims under the Federal Sentencing Guidelines," *Michigan Law Review* 94 (June 1996), pp. 2385–421.

58. Dale Parent, Terence Dunworth, Douglas McDonald, and William Rhodes, *The Impact of Sentencing Guidelines* (Washington, DC: National Institute of Justice, 1996).

59. Michael Tonry, *Sentencing Matters* (New York: Oxford University Press, 1996); David Weisburd, "Sentencing Disparity and the Guidelines: Taking a Closer Look," *Federal Sentencing Reporter* 5 (1992), pp. 149–52; T. D. Miethe and C. A. Moore, "Socioeconomic Disparities under Determinate Sentencing Systems: A Comparison of Preguideline and Postguideline Practices in Minnesota," *Criminology* 23 (1985), pp. 337–63.

60. Don M. Gottfredson, *Effects of Judges' Sentencing Decisions on Criminal Careers* (Washington, DC: National Institute of Justice, 1999); Jeffrey Y. Ulmer and John H. Kramer, "The Use and Transformation of Formal Decision-Making Criteria: Sentencing Guidelines, Organizational Contexts, and Case Processing Strategies," *Social Problems* 45 (May 1998), p. 248.

61. Parent, Dunworth, McDonald, and Rhodes, *The Impact of Sentencing Guidelines*, p. 5.

62. *U.S. v. Salerno*, 107 S. Ct. 2095 (1987).

63. *Tate v. Short*, 91 S. Ct. 668 (1971).

64. *Thompson v. Oklahoma*, 108 S. Ct. 2687 (1988).

65. See *French v. Owens*, 777 F. 2d 1250 (7th Cir. 1985).

66. *Coker v. Georgia*, 97 S. Ct. 2861 (1977).

67. *Furman v. Georgia*, 92 S. Ct. 2726 (1972).

68. *Gregg v. Georgia*, 96 S. Ct. 2909 (1976).

69. *Roberts v. Louisiana* and *Woodson v. North Carolina*, 96 S. Ct. 3207 (1976).

70. *Lockett v. Ohio*, 98 S. Ct. 2954 (1978).

71. *McCleskey v. Kemp*, 107 S. Ct. 1756 (1987).

72. Id. at 1765.

73. Id. at 1770.

74. Jordan M. Steker, "The Limits of Legal Language: Decisionmaking in Capital Cases," *Michigan Law Review* 94 (August 1996), pp. 2590–624.

75. Benjamin P. Cooper, "Truth in Sentencing: The Prospective and Retroactive Application of *Simmons v. South Carolina*," *University of Chicago Law Review* 63 (fall 1996), pp. 1573–605; Ted Gest, "A House without a Blueprint: After 20 Years, the Death Penalty Is Still Being Meted

Out Unevenly," *U.S. News & World Report* (July 8, 1996), pp. 41–45; Marvin D. Free Jr., "The Impact of Federal Sentencing Reforms on African Americans," *Journal of Black Studies* 28 (November 1997), pp. 268–86; Linda A. Foley, Afesa M. Adams, and James L. Goodson Jr., "The Effect of Race on Decisions by Judges and Other Officers of the Court," *Journal of Applied Social Psychology* 26 (July 1996), pp. 1190–2113; Scott Burgins, "Jurors Ignore, Misunderstand Instructions," *ABA Journal* 81 (May 1995), pp. 30–32; Leigh B. Bienen, "The Proportionality Review of Capital Cases by State High Courts after *Gregg:* Only 'The Appearance of Justice'," *Journal of Criminal Law and Criminology* 87 (fall 1996), pp. 230–314.

76. Tracy L. Snell, *Capital Punishment 1995* (Washington, DC: U.S. Bureau of Justice Statistics, 1996), p. 6.

77. Marian J. Borg, "The Southern Subculture of Punitiveness?: Regional Variation in Support for Capital Punishment," *Journal of Research in Crime and Delinquency* 34 (February 1997), pp. 25–46; David A. Kaplan, "Life and Death Decisions," *Newsweek* (June 16, 1997), pp. 28–30.

78. Tracy L. Snell, *Capital Punishment* (Washington, DC: Bureau of Justice Statistics, 1999), p. 10.

79. Ibid., p. 4.

80. *Bryan v. Moore,* 120 S. Ct. 1003 (2000).

81. David A. Kaplan, "Life and Death Decisions," pp. 28–31.

82. Thorsten Sellin, *The Penalty of Death* (Beverly Hills, CA: Sage, 1980), p. 72.

83. "Death Penalty Debates Continue," *America* 176 (May 10, 1997), p. 3; George E. Pataki, "Death Penalty Is a Deterrent," *USA Today Magazine* (March 1997), pp. 52–54.

84. William C. Bailey, "Capital Punishment and Lethal Assaults against Police," *Criminology* 19 (February 1992).

85. Craig J. Albert, "Challenging Deterrence: New Insights on Capital Punishment Derived from Panel Data," *University of Pittsburgh Law Review* 60 (winter 1999); Sellin, *The Penalty of Death;* Brian Forst, "The Deterrent Effect of Capital Punishment: A Cross-State Analysis of the 1960s," *Minnesota Law Review* 61 (1977); Richard Lempert, "The Effect of Executions on Homicides: A New Look in an Old Light," *Crime and Delinquency* 29 (January 1983); Hans Zeisel, "The Deterrent Effect of the Death Penalty: Facts v. Faith," in P. B. Kirkland, ed., *The Supreme Court Review, 1976* (Chicago: University of Chicago Press, 1977).

86. See Charles L. Black Jr., *Capital Punishment: The Inevitability of Caprice and Mistake,* 2nd ed. (New York: Norton, 1981); Hugo A. Bedau, ed., *Capital Punishment in the United States,* 3rd ed. (New York: Oxford University Press, 1982); Sellin, *The Penalty of Death;* Dane Archer, Rosemary Gartner, and Marc Beittel, "Homicide and the Death Penalty: A Cross-National Test of a Deterrence Hypothesis," *Journal of Criminal Law and Criminology* 74 (1983), pp. 991–1013.

87. Forst, "The Deterrent Effect of Capital Punishment."

88. Scott H. Decker and Carol W. Kohlfeld, "Capital Punishment and Executions in the Lone Star State: A Deterrence Study," *Criminal Justice Research Bulletin* 3 (1988).

89. Michael L. Radelet and Ronald L. Akers, "Deterrence and the Death Penalty: The Views of the Experts," *Journal of Criminal Law and Criminology* 87 (fall 1996), pp. 1–16.

90. Decker and Kohlfeld, "Capital Punishment and Executions in the Lone Star State;" Samuel Walker, *Sense and Nonsense about Crime,* 3rd ed. (Pacific Grove, CA: Wadsworth, 1993).

91. William J. Bowers and Glenn L. Pierce, "Deterrence or Brutalization: What Is the Effect of Executions?," *Crime and Delinquency* 26 (October 1980); Brian Forst, "Capital Punishment and Deterrence: Conflicting Evidence?," *Journal of Criminal Law and Criminology* 74 (Fall 1983).

92. New York State Defender's Association, *Capital Losses: The Price of the Death Penalty for New York State* (Albany, NY: The Association, 1982).

93. James J. Stephan, *State Prison Expenditures* (Washington, DC: Bureau of Justice Statistics, 1999).

94. Tracy L. Snell, *Capital Punishment.*

95. Subcommittee on Federal Death Penalty Cases Committee on Defender Services, *Federal Death Penalty Cases: Recommendations Concerning the Cost and Quality of Defense Representation* (Washington, DC: Judicial Conference of the United States, 1998).

96. Eric M. Freedman, "The Case against the Death Penalty," *USA Today Magazine* (March 1997), pp. 48–50.

97. Tracy L. Snell, *Capital Punishment,* p. 10

98. Marcia Coyle, ""Innocent Dead Men Walking?," *The National Law Journal* 18 (May 20, 1996), p. 1.

99. New York State Defender's Association, p. 50.

100. David Stout, "Conviction for Child Abuse Overturned 10 Years Later," *New York Times* (September 30, 1997), p. B3.

101. Joseph P. Shapiro, "Rethinking Executions," *U.S. News & World Report* (February 14, 2000), p. 30.

102. Hugo A. Bedau and Michael L. Radelet, *Conviction of the Innocent* (Boston: Northeastern University Press, 1992); David E. Rovella, " Danger of Executing the Innocent on the Rise," *The*

National Law Journal 19 (August 4, 1997), p. 7.

103. Joseph P. Shapiro, "Rethinking Executions," *U.S. News & World Report* (February 14, 2000), p. 30; Warren Cohen, "Putting a Hold on Executions," *U.S. News & World Report* (May 31, 1999), p. 29; Richard Willing, "Illinois Prosecutors Accused of Framing an Innocent Man," *USA Today* (March 24, 1999), p. 9.

104. Lori Urs, "Commonwealth v. Joseph O'Dell: Truth and Justice or Confuse the Courts?: The DNA Controversy," *New England Journal on Criminal and Civil Confinement* 25 (winter 1999).

105. Barry Scheck, Peter Neufield, and Jim Dwyer, *Actual Innocence* (New York: Doubleday, 2000); Sharon Cohen, "Hard Work, DNA Advances Are Clearing Death Row Inmates," Associated Press (September 25, 1999).

106. Tracy L. Snell, *Capital Punishment,* p. 9.

Prisons

The Virginia State Penitentiary

was built in the shape of a horseshoe three stories high and housed men, women, and children. It opened in the year 1800. The cells had no heat, no light, and no plumbing. Solid oak doors made it impossible to see what was going on inside the cells. Sewage runoff ended in a ditch next to the James River, where a fierce odor lingered except when rain gave temporary relief. For the first thirty-eight years of the prison's existence, it was required by law that from 8 percent to 50 percent of a prisoner's sentence be served in solitary confinement. To meet this requirement, each prisoner was placed in a basement cell that was damp, unheated, and dark both day and night.[1]

In 1876 a Virginia State Penitentiary report listed an inmate's death as resulting from a fall into a tub of boiling coffee. The inmate was ten years old. An 1880 report listed 116 prisoners eleven to seventeen years of age.[2] The prison was refurbished several times during the twentieth century before being closed in 1990.

The purpose of prisons and their operating conditions have drawn concern from the very beginning. This chapter will take a closer look at U.S. prisons and their inmates.

How Are Correctional Institutions in the United States Organized?

Although many aspects of American criminal justice originated in England, the use of prisons as a method of dealing with law violators is largely an American invention. During the Middle Ages confinement of criminals was considered wasteful, so corporal punishment of criminals was common. In Europe during the sixteenth century, workhouses were established in an effort to instill a work ethic into the poor, who were considered lazy.[3] Workhouse inmates made furniture and other items; and although workhouses were never used to house criminal offenders, they were a precursor of prisons.

BEFORE PRISONS

Interestingly, prisons were established in response to concern for the humanitarian treatment of criminals. Before the invention of the prison, corporal punishment in the form of whipping and mutilation was the primary method of punishing criminals. Fines evolved as an alternative to corporal punishment, but poor offenders (the majority of criminals) could not afford to pay them. In Colonial America labor was scarce, so minor offenders often were sentenced to work for their victims for a specified period. Also, government structure and funding were weak, making long-term custody of offenders impractical. Jails were used for debtors and for those awaiting trial, as they were in Europe. Despite the obvious fact that jailed debtors were unable to earn money to repay their debts, it was not until the 1840s that imprisonment for debt was abolished in the United States.[4]

Incarceration became the primary form of sentence for poor offenders who could not afford to pay fines but whose offenses were not serious enough to deserve corporal punishment. Indeed, incarceration was seen as a humane alternative to corporal punishment. Physical punishment was associated with the Puritans, who believed that the doctrine of predestination made any attempt to rehabilitate offenders useless. The philosophers of the Enlightenment, however, advanced a more optimistic view. As stated in the Declaration of Independence, "We hold these truths to be self-evident, that all men are created equal, that they are endowed by their Creator with certain unalienable rights, that among these are life, liberty, and the pursuit of happiness." Rather than simply being part of human nature, crime and deviance came to be seen as a result of negative environmental influences. As a consequence, many humanitarian groups called for reform of the penal system.

The Invention of the Prison

The first of these humanitarian groups was the Philadelphia Society for Alleviating the Miseries of Public Prisons, formed in 1787 by Dr. Benjamin Rush. Rush urged that capital punishment and corporal punishment be replaced with incarceration. The Philadelphia Society, made up mostly of Quakers, believed that criminals could be reformed if they were placed in solitary confinement, where they could reflect on their deviant acts and repent. This is where the term *penitentiary* originated.

In 1790 the Pennsylvania legislature was persuaded to convert the Walnut Street Jail in Philadelphia into an institution for the solitary confinement of "hardened and atrocious offenders." Each cell was small and dark, with a small high window so that the offender "could perceive neither heaven nor earth." No communication with the offender was allowed. Later, additional institutions were built, beginning with the Eastern Penitentiary in 1829. This system of incarceration became known as the **Pennsylvania system.** According to its promoters, the Pennsylvania system promoted repentance through solitary confinement, was economical because it did not require long periods of confinement, and prevented offenders from being corrupted by mixing with other offenders. These principles soon fell prey to political and pragmatic considerations, however. The institutions quickly became overcrowded, and offenders were incarcerated for longer periods. As the French writers Gustave de Beaumont and Alexis de Tocqueville remarked in 1833, after visiting several U.S. penitentiaries:

> *Nowhere was this system of imprisonment crowned with the hoped-for success. In general it was ruinous to the public treasury; it never effected the reformation of prisoners. Every year the legislature of each state voted considerable funds toward the support of the penitentiaries, and the continued return of the same individuals into the prisons, proved the inefficiency of the system to which they were submitted.[5]*

In addition, most of these early prisons were "impersonal institutions marked by brutality and neglect," which defeated the underlying purpose of the confinement.[6] Beaumont and Tocqueville noted that in New York State twenty-six inmates in solitary confinement were pardoned by the governor, but that fourteen of them were returned to prison a short time later for new offenses.[7]

In 1819 a somewhat different system of incarceration was initiated in New York State. The **Auburn system** anticipated the Industrial Revolution with its emphasis on labor and meditation. Offenders worked in groups every day, but they did so in complete silence. The Auburn system spread throughout the country and was seen as a significant advance in the treatment of offenders.

During the second half of the nineteenth century, there was disillusionment with both the Auburn and Pennsylvania systems. Neither system effectively reformed prisoners, and neither appeared to have a deterrent effect on crime. As Beaumont and Tocqueville had observed in 1833, the silence and isolation of prisoners resulted in depression and death among both inmates and guards.

In 1877, believing that education was the key to rehabilitation, Zebulon Brockway developed a new approach to incarceration at the Elmira Reformatory in New York State. Brockway changed the purpose of incarceration

WALNUT STREET JAIL

■**Pennsylvania system**
A philosophy of imprisonment in which solitary confinement was expected to promote repentance and to prevent offenders from being corrupted by mixing with other offenders.

■**Auburn system**
A philosophy of imprisonment that emphasized labor and meditation; offenders worked every day, but in complete silence.

ELMIRA REFORMATORY

How did the prison system develop in the United States? Where did the term *penitentiary* come from, and what does it mean? What kinds of correctional institutions are there, and how are they organized? What are prisons really for anyway? What are the benefits and costs of prisons for inmates and their families? for communities and society in general? for the American criminal justice system?

■**reformatory movement**
Late nineteenth-century trend toward use of incarceration to reform through educating; inmates could be paroled when they showed substantial progress.

from custody to education. The Elmira Reformatory attempted to promote a school-like atmosphere in which inmates could progress at their own pace. The New York State legislature demonstrated its support for the program when it passed an indeterminate sentencing law that allowed for offenders to be released on parole when they showed signs of progress in the reformatory programs. By 1900 the **reformatory movement** had spread to many states.[8]

Disenchantment also arose with these education-based systems, however. Many prison administrators were reluctant to adopt the reform strategies and continued to emphasize discipline and control. Educational efforts often took a back seat to the more custodial demands of incarceration as punishment. Moreover, it was more difficult than expected to distinguish truly reformed prisoners from those who pretended to have changed. As a result, parole policies often were based on superficial indications of reform. Also working against prisoner rehabilitation were overcrowding and poor management of prisons.[9]

Today prisons lack a clear philosophical purpose. Most try to do a little of everything: punishment, work, and education. The results are equally mixed. The expectations of prisons and prisoners vary widely from one institution to another, leaving few people satisfied with the outcome. Meditation, labor, and education have not proved effective in stopping or deterring criminal behavior, causing some critics to argue that prisons should exist solely for purposes of punishment and should not make any effort to reform.[10] This view overlooks, however, the fact that the majority of inmates will someday return to society and that prisons can serve an important function in preparing inmates for release.

Levels of Custody

One of the newer prisons in the United States is the ultra–maximum security federal prison in Florence, Colorado. It holds more than 400 prisoners and cost $60 million to build. Dangerous inmates are confined in their cells twenty-three hours a day. This prison now holds some of the nation's most notorious criminals, including Ted Kaczynski (the Unabomber), Timothy McVeigh (the Oklahoma City bomber), and Ramzi Yousef (the World Trade Center attacker). When outside their cells, prisoners wear leg irons and handcuffs and are accompanied by guards.[11] The Florence prison has been called the "Alcatraz of the Rockies," after the prison on the island of Alcatraz in San Francisco Bay. Considered the toughest prison when it opened in the 1930s, Alcatraz was closed in 1963 because of the high cost of maintaining an island prison and a national shift toward rehabilitation as a model of punishment. The federal prison in Marion, Illinois, became the toughest prison in the mid-1980s, when it placed its violent inmates on permanent lockdown status after several assaults and deaths of staff and inmates.[12] The Colorado prison, designed exclusively for violent inmates, opened in 1994. Its inmates, all men, are serving sentences that average forty years; most will die in prison. The Florence prison also has its version of soli-

3 types of Prisons.

tary confinement, a unit that holds 184 prisoners who never come into physical contact with another human being.[13]

"Ultrasecure" prisons are reserved for the most violent inmates, especially those who have committed assaults while in other prisons or have records of escape or extreme violence or murder. Other types of prisons are distinguished by level of custody. **Maximum security prisons** often have a wall (eighteen to twenty-five feet high) surrounding the entire facility and house dangerous felons who have committed violent crimes or who have a history of escape attempts. About 26 percent of all inmates are incarcerated in such institutions. **Medium security prisons** often have some facilities outside the main enclosure. Usually there are two rows of chain-link fence, topped with barbed wire, around the main enclosure. Medium security prisons hold felony offenders who have not committed violent crimes or whose prior record and institutional conduct do not require a maximum security setting. About 49 percent of all inmates are serving time in these institutions. **Minimum security prisons** facilities usually have no fences but have locking outside doors and electronic surveillance devices around the perimeter of the institution. Inmates in these facilities are serving short sentences for nonviolent crimes or are near the end of longer sentences and at low risk for escape. About 23 percent of all inmates are in minimum security institutions.

maximum security prisons
Institutions that have a wall surrounding the entire facility and house dangerous felons; about 26 percent of all inmates are incarcerated in such prisons.

medium security prisons
Institutions that often have some facilities outside the main enclosure, which is usually surrounded by two rows of chain-link fence topped with barbed wire; about 49 percent of all inmates are serving time in these prisons. *holds largest portion*

minimum security prisons
Facilities that usually have no fences but have locking outside doors and electronic surveillance devices around the perimeter; about 23 percent of all inmates are in these institutions.

State and Federal Correctional Systems

State and federal prisons differ in number, size, and capacity. Table 11.1 summarizes some important differences between the numbers and populations of the state and federal systems. There are approximately 1,200 state and federal prisons in the United States, a number that is increasing as new prisons are being built. A total of 66 new maximum security prisons were added in the 1990s, as were 58 medium security and 91 minimum security prisons.[14] State and federal prisons now have a combined capacity of less than 1.1 million but hold more than 1.3 million inmates, for an occupancy rate of approximately 115 to 127 percent. These figures show that despite new prison construction during the 1990s, inmate populations still exceed prison capacity.

The federal correctional system is similar to the state systems, but it houses only federal offenders whose cases have been tried in federal courts. Maximum security federal institutions are called **penitentiaries;** medium security federal facilities are **correctional institutions;** and federal facilities for pretrial detention and for those serving short sentences

penitentiaries
Maximum security federal correctional institutions.

correctional institutions
Medium security federal correctional institutions.

TABLE 11.1		
State and Federal Prisons		
PRISON CHARACTERISTIC	STATE	FEDERAL
Number of prisons	1,084	112
Rated capacity	1,007,153	86,315
Inmates in custody	1,302,019	123,041
Percent capacity occupied	115%	127%
Maximum security prisons	289	9
Medium security prisons	438	25
Minimum security prisons	648	91

SOURCES: Allen J. Beck and Christopher J. Mumola, *Prisoners in 1998* (Washington, DC: Bureau of Justice Statistics, 1999); James J. Stephan, *Census of State and Federal Correctional Facilities, 1996* (Washington, DC: Bureau of Justice Statistics, 1999).

metropolitan correctional centers (detention centers) Federal jail facilities for pretrial detention and for those serving short sentences.

are called **metropolitan correctional centers** or **detention centers.** The federal corrections system also includes prison camps and community treatment centers.

An offender's assignment to a particular level of custody depends largely on whether the conviction was for a violent crime. For example, 62 percent of inmates in maximum security prisons were sentenced for a violent crime, compared to 45 percent of those in medium security and 34 percent of those in minimum security institutions. Conversely, there are more property and drug offenders in medium security prisons (47 percent of inmates) and minimum security prisons (60 percent of inmates) than in maximum security prisons (33 percent of inmates). Approximately 80 percent of all state prison inmates have a prior conviction and a record of probation or incarceration, but those with both a prior record and current conviction for a violent crime are most likely to be assigned to maximum security prisons.[15] The number of criminals incarcerated two or more times has been increasing steadily—rising, for example, from 18 percent of prison admissions in 1980 to 35 percent in 1995. This trend suggests that prisons are ineffective and may be losing their deterrent force.[16] As criminal justice researcher Al Blumstein has concluded, "we have now locked up so many people that we have lost the stigmatizing effect" of imprisonments.[17]

Problems with Jails

In August 1992 a black Mississippi teenager was discovered hanging by his shoelace in the Simpson County jail. This youth's death was one of 42 apparent suicides in Mississippi jails in a period of only five years. The U.S. Civil Rights Commission requested a federal investigation into this situation, raising questions not only about why there were so many suicides, but also about whether some inmates had been murdered and then hanged so their deaths would look like suicide.[18] In 1996 there were 146 jail and prison inmate suicides in the United States.[19]

jails Facilities operated by counties and municipalities to hold two main categories of inmates: those awaiting trial and those serving sentences of one year or less.

Although prisons attract more attention from the media and policymakers than jails do, the deplorable conditions in many jails have been highlighted in cases like these. **Jails** are operated by counties and municipalities. They hold two main categories of inmates: those awaiting trial and those serving sentences of one year or less. Jails also perform other functions, such as holding probation and parole violators and bail absconders. They also may hold mentally ill persons on a temporary basis. Jails often serve as transfer points between prisons and may also hold offenders who cannot be admitted to state or federal prisons because of overcrowding. Such a mixed bag of suspects, defendants, and offenders makes for a crowded and sometimes confusing jail environment.

JAIL POPULATIONS

The number of jail inmates more than doubled in the 1990s. The total number of jails remained about the same at 3,300, but jail space nearly doubled through new construction and renovation. Five states account for about half the total jail population of nearly 600,000 inmates. In 1998 the largest 25 jurisdictions in the United States accounted for 27 percent of all jail inmates.

The two jurisdictions with the most inmates, Los Angeles and New York City, together held nearly 40,000 inmates, or 7 percent of the national total.[20]

Local jails employ more than 165,000 persons, more than 70 percent of whom are corrections officers providing security services and inmate supervision. Because of rapid hiring, staff–inmate ratios have improved despite the dramatic growth in jail populations. There are approximately four inmates per corrections officer. Housing an inmate in jail costs just under $10,000 per year.[21] Table 11.2 describes some career opportunities in corrections and related fields—areas in which demand for new candidates will grow in the first part of the twenty-first century.

A 1996 study of jail inmates revealed that most were not new to the criminal justice system. More than half were on probation, on parole, or out on bail at the time of their arrest. More than 70 percent had a criminal history that included a prior probation or incarceration sentence, and more than 40 percent had served three or more prior sentences. In addition, about two-thirds of jail inmates were regular drug users, and 58 percent of these had

TABLE 11.2

Career Opportunities in Corrections and Related Fields

Probation officer http://www.communitycourts.org/ http://www.nyspoa.com/us.htm	Works for the courts of a particular county or city; conducts investigations to assist the judge in sentencing; supervises and monitors juvenile and adult offenders in the community. *Qualifications:* Bachelor's degree and relevant work experience.
Parole officer http://www.appa-net.org/ http://ajjdp.ncjrs.org/	State employee, often with police powers, responsible for supervising offenders after they are released from prison. *Qualifications:* Bachelor's degree and relevant experience.

Corrections officer
http://www.wco.com/~aerick/links.htm
http://database.corrections.com/career/
   index.asp
http://www.corrections.com/cjca/
http://www.sun.soci.niu.edu/!critcrim/
   prisons/prisons.html
http://www.nicic.org/inst/nicocjtp.htm
	State employee, sometimes with police powers; enforces laws in jails and prisons and transports prisoners.
	Qualifications: Competitive civil service examination; bachelor's degree preferred.

Counselor http://ssw.che.umn.edu/ctr4rjm/ http://www.darien.lib.ct.us/reentry/	Provides counseling and supervision in treatment programs for juvenile, adult, and family offenders, often in a detention center, shelter, reception or diagnostic center, training facility, treatment center, halfway house, or group home; helps offenders reintegrate into their communities and overcome problems that led to their arrest or incarceration. *Qualifications:* Master's degree in criminal justice, social work, or psychology preferred.
Criminologist http://www.jmu.edu/psyc/spcp/ http://www.ncjrs.org	Studies crime, criminals, and criminal behavior; conducts, analyzes, reports, and applies research on crime and social policies relating to crime; teaches courses in college; provides investigative or forensic or prison support services (e.g., ballistics). *Qualifications:* Master's degree or Ph.D. in, e.g., criminal justice, sociology, or psychology.

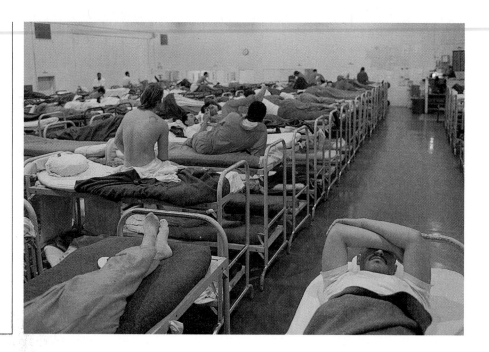

What problem of prisons today does this photograph suggest? How is this problem related to political issues? How is it related to issues of prison administration, security, violence, and health? What are some other problems of prisons? For example, how can gangs, organized crime, and corrupt correctional officers defeat the purposes of prisons? What prison reforms would you give top priority, and why?

never been in a substance abuse treatment program.[22] Thirty-six percent of inmates were unemployed at the time of their arrest. Thus, jail inmates have drug and employment problems that contribute to their criminal histories.

JAIL PROBLEMS

Reasons for the doubling of jail populations in ten years are similar to those for the increase in prison populations. The total number of arrests increased 20 percent over the same period to 14 million per year. This overall increase increased the numbers of offenders who received jail sentences. As with prisons, the largest source of growth was drug offenders. One consequence of overcrowding in both state and federal prisons is that by the late 1990s nearly 12 percent of jail inmates were people waiting for authorities to make room for them in prisons, more than triple the number a decade earlier.[23] National surveys of jail and prison administrators identified overcrowding and gangs as two primary problems. Jail administrators stated that improvement is needed in staffers' ability to identify gang members, which overcrowding makes difficult, and also in staff training on gang control.[24] In response to jail crowding, many states have developed alternatives for keeping more suspects, defendants, and offenders out of jail; these alternatives are discussed further in Chapter 12.

How Do Correctional Institutions Operate?

Correctional institutions have a difficult task. They must hold criminal offenders securely, in order to protect the public; at the same time, these institutions are supposed to promote behavior and attitude changes in inmates so that they become productive citizens upon release. Offenders' backgrounds often include long histories of criminal offending, drug and alcohol use, failure in school, and physical abuse. The difficulty of overcoming these problems has led to a debate over what correctional institutions should try to accomplish. This debate has centered on the degree to which punishment or reform should be at the center of correctional philosophy and operations.

Punishment

It is generally agreed that the purpose of imprisonment is to serve as punishment for a crime. There is less agreement as to what should occur *inside* prisons. The prevailing legal view is that deprivation of liberty through imprisonment *is* the punishment and that prison should not inflict additional punishment on offenders. For example, a prisoner in the Southern Ohio Correctional Facility sued the state, arguing that double-celling (housing two inmates in a single cell) violates the Eighth Amendment prohibition against cruel and unusual punishment. Studies recommended approximately six by nine feet of space for each inmate in a cell, but the Southern Ohio double-celling cut that space by 40 percent. Lower courts ruled in favor of the inmates, but the U.S. Supreme Court reversed the decision in *Rhodes v. Chapman*, holding that double-celling is not in itself cruel and unusual punishment. The Court stated that "such conditions are restrictive and even harsh, [but] they are part of the penalty that criminal offenders pay for offenses against society."[25] Therefore, "restrictive and even harsh" conditions in prison are permissible, although the Court indicated that deprivation of essential food, medical care, or sanitation is not permissible.

Numerous other challenges have been made to the conditions of confinement. Each case involved interpretation of the Eighth Amendment prohibition against cruel and unusual punishment. Under what conditions does punishment become cruel and unusual? In a landmark case, *Estelle v. Gamble*, the Supreme Court held that "deliberate indifference to serious medical needs of prisoners" violates the Eighth Amendment, because it permits "unnecessary and wanton infliction of pain" and offends "evolving standards of decency."[26] These phrases have become benchmarks in determining whether specific prison conditions, though harsh, exceed the limits imposed by the Constitution.

In a 1991 case, *Wilson v. Seiter*, an inmate at the Hocking Correctional Facility in Ohio filed suit, claiming that the conditions of his confinement violated the Eighth Amendment. Those conditions included excessive noise, overcrowding, inadequate heating and cooling, improper ventilation, unclean restrooms, unsanitary food preparation, and housing of healthy inmates among people who were mentally and physically ill. As in previous cases, the U.S. Supreme Court agreed that prison officials had shown "deliberate indifference," but the Court also held that inmates must

CONDITIONS OF CONFINEMENT

Liability Issues led
to private prisons.

contemporary issues and trends

Private Prisons and Liability

The failure of correctional institutions to deter offenders from committing further crimes has plagued the system throughout its history. During the 1980s this failure, combined with efforts to reduce the size of government, led to proposals that entire prisons be operated by private contractors. To date, more than fifty private correctional facilities housing adult prisoners have been established. Most are medium or minimum security facilities, and the majority are located in three states—Texas, Florida, and California, which also are the three states with the largest inmate populations.

Corrections Corporation of America is the largest private contractor in this field, followed by Wackenhut. These corporations bid on contracts to build or remodel prisons and to manage and operate them. Proponents of privatization contend that private contractors can operate prisons less expensively than the government while maintaining the

> Liability issues ultimately may determine the future of private prisons.

same level of custody and quality of service. Opponents argue both that it is improper for private contractors to supervise offenders sentenced by the state and that costs cannot be reduced significantly over the long term.[a]

Despite this debate, many states are currently under court order to reduce overcrowding or to improve conditions inside prisons. States are building new prisons to handle the exploding prison population and seeking ways to pay for them without raising taxes. Private contractors offer construction and supervision costs that initially appear lower than those the state has borne in the past.[b]

The investigative arm of Congress, the U.S. General Accounting Office (GAO), reviewed a series of studies that compared public and private correctional facilities in terms of cost of operation and quality of service. The studies' results were mixed: Some found that private facilities were cheaper and pro-

vided similar levels of service; one found private facilities more costly; others found no difference. The GAO concluded that the studies provided little guidance for jurisdictions seeking to reduce costs.[c] Privatization of prisons is likely to continue in the forseeable future, however, because it relieves states of the immediate burden of financing prisons on their own, which can cost $75,000 per bed. The long-term outlook is less clear.[d]

Liability issues ultimately may determine the future of private prisons. In its 1996 budget the Federal Bureau of Prisons had proposed to contract with private companies for the majority of its future minimum security and pretrial detention facilities. However, this decision was reversed when the Justice Department found that it was unable to reduce the risk of a strike or walkout by private corrections officers.[e] If corrections officers failed to appear for work, the result could be chaos in an unsupervised prison. Concerns about liability for any disorder that might occur if private prisons

show that prison officials had "intent" or a "culpable state of mind" in allowing these conditions to exist.[27] Simply demonstrating the existence of deplorable conditions, therefore, is not enough. It must be demonstrated that prison officials know about the conditions but fail to act. This burden of proof makes it difficult for claims regarding conditions of confinement to stand up in court.

Custody and Deterrence

Many people agree that prisons should not only punish offenders but also control crime. Some believe that incarceration controls crime merely through custody—by keeping the offender off the streets for a specified pe-

guards ever went on strike nixed the federal government's privatization plans—at least for now.

Operating even a minimum security prison is difficult. A corporation that runs a prison must be able to establish an entirely self-sufficient community and maintain security for the staff, inmates, and surrounding community. A private prison in Youngstown, Ohio, has been accused of staffing the institution with inexperienced guards, ignoring complaints of abuses against prisoners, and maintaining an unsafe prison environment.[f] A private prison in New Mexico experienced four inmate deaths and the killing of a guard within nine months, leading to doubts that private companies can handle high-risk inmates.[g]

In 1997 the U.S. Supreme Court ruled that private prison guards are not immune from allegations of civil rights violations. In the case in question, an inmate alleged that corrections officers at South Central Correctional Center in Tennessee, operated privately by Corrections Corporation of America, violated his Eighth Amendment rights by placing restraints on him that were too tight and caused injury serious enough to require hospitalization. The Supreme Court held the privately employed corrections officers responsible, stating that "mere performance of a governmental function does not support immunity for a private person, especially one who performs a job without government supervision or direction."[h] It will be interesting to see how the growth of private prisons is affected by the liability issues the industry has just begun to face.

1. How does disagreement over the purposes of incarceration complicate the privatization of prisons?
2. Why might a private company be expected to run a prison less expensively than the government?
3. Are there certain types of offenders that might be more amenable to handling by a private prison?
4. What do you think are the potential advantages and disadvantages of prison privatization for states? For inmates? For criminal justice?

NOTES

a Matt Bai, "On the Block," *Newsweek* (August 4, 1997), pp. 60–61; Norman Seabrook and Katherine Lapp, "Should Corporations Run the Jails?," *The Daily News* (August 23, 1995), p. 7.
b Sam Vincent Meddis and Deborah Sharp, "Prison Business in a Blockbuster," *USA Today* (December 13, 1994), p. 10.
c U.S. Comptroller General, *Private and Public Prisons* (Washington, DC: U.S. General Accounting Office, 1996), p. 3.
d Robbin S. Ogle, "Prison Privatization: An Environmental Catch-22," *Justice Quarterly* 16 (September 1999), pp. 579–600.
e Ibid., p. 1; Barbara Ann Stolz, "Privatizing Corrections: Changing the Corrections Policy-Making Subgovernment," *Prison Journal* 77 (March 1997), p. 92.
f Eric Bates, "CCA, the Sequel: The Largest Private Prison Firm Continues Its Pattern of Abuse and Profit," *The Nation* (June 7, 1999), p. 22; Anthony Lepore, "Prison Privatization Proposal Questioned," *Providence Business News* (June 21, 1999), p. 31.
g Ted Gest, "Private Prisons Suffer a Blow," *U.S. News & World Report* (September 13, 1999), p. 10.
h *Richardson v. McKnight*, No. 96-318 (1997).

riod. Others hope that prison will have a deterrent or reformative effect on the offender. The unpleasant experience of imprisonment might deter new criminal activity upon release, or the offender might come to see the error of his or her ways during imprisonment and make a genuine effort to reform. Statistical evidence shows, however, that the experience of imprisonment does not deter **recidivism**—reoffending—upon release. More than 60 percent of inmates in state prisons have been incarcerated before, and 94 percent of all inmates have been under some form of correctional supervision, counting probation, before their current incarceration.[28] Criminal justice researcher Don Gottfredson concludes that current incarceration policies are ineffective, do not contribute to public safety, and add to the burden shouldered by taxpayers.[29]

recidivism
Repeat offenses by an offender.

Rehabilitation and Reform

The average felony prison sentence is seven years; thus, the majority of offenders ultimately will be released. Efforts to rehabilitate or reform inmates while they serve their sentences could reduce recidivism and make prison more effective as a penal sanction. To succeed, rehabilitation and reform efforts do not necessarily require formal programs but do require an attitude change on the part of the offender. For example, some argue that family visitation and conjugal visits for inmates effectively reduce emotional stress on inmates and their families, resulting in more positive attitudes and behavior. Others believe that visits increase frustration and pose safety problems.[30] Studies of treatment programs for sex offenders, addicts, and victims of childhood sexual abuse reveal that rehabilitation programs can be effective in changing behavior.[31]

Models of Prison Administration

control model
Prison management approach characterized by strict enforcement of prison rules and few privileges for prisoners.

responsibility model
Prison management approach that gives inmates more autonomy; staff guides prisoners' decision making rather than making all decisions for them.

consensual model
Prison management approach that aims to maintain order by getting inmates and staff to agree on the validity of rules.

Prison administrators attempt to manage inmates in a way that will create the fewest problems for staff and other inmates during their term. Three major prison managerial approaches identified by John DiIulio are the control model, the responsibility model, and the consensus model.[32] The **control model** is characterized by strict enforcement of prison rules and few privileges for prisoners. This approach produces large numbers of rule violations and can increase the level of tension within a prison. Studies have suggested that formal management for control is not the most effective way to prevent prison disorder.[33] The **responsibility model** gives inmates more autonomy; staff guides prisoners' decision making rather than making all decisions for them. This approach employs minimal restraint except in cases requiring restraint for protection of staff or other inmates. The idea of the **consensual model** is to maintain order by getting inmates and staff to agree on the validity of rules, placing inmates in a position of participating in the operation of the prison—although DiIulio believes that this model is not effective, because inmates' self-interest leads them to attempt to manipulate the system. Debate continues over the optimum model of prison administration in terms of impacts on inmate conduct.[34] Nevertheless, each model could be applied in a prison environment, depending on the security level of the institution, the types of offenders involved, and the willingness of staff to support the management model employed.

A national survey of prison wardens and state corrections administrators identified three significant problems these officials face: prison overcrowding, gang-affiliated inmates, and understaffed treatment programs. The majority of survey respondents reported that their prisons were at or over capacity, making it difficult for them to maintain inmate and staff security and appropriate conditions of confinement. As with jail administrators, more than 70 percent of prison officials indicated that improvement is needed in the identification of gang-affiliated inmates and in training pro-

NATIONAL SURVEY
OF PRISON
WARDENS

What are the chances that one of these students will serve a prison term in the course of a lifetime? Who will it be? What characteristics of people and their backgrounds make them more likely to become incarcerated for committing felonies? What kinds of public policies, crime prevention programs, and prison reforms do these correlates of incarceration suggest to you?

grams designed to help staff control gang activities. Three-fourths of the wardens indicated a need for more staff to provide treatment for alcohol and substance abuse, mental health, parenting, and vocational education.[35] These problems suggest that even motivated inmates may find it difficult to obtain access to education or treatment to address their problems.

Who Is in Prison?

Many people believe that the sentences offenders currently receive are more lenient than ever before, but nothing could be farther from the truth. In fact, the number of offenders in state or federal prisons increased an average of 7 percent each year from 1990 to 1998, and the incarceration rate per 100,000 population increased more than 50 percent over this period. There are now more than 1.3 million inmates in state and federal institutions, more than at any other time in the nation's history.[36] The reason for this increase is simple: More people are being sent to prison than are being released. In 1996, 512,618 prisoners were admitted to state prisons, while only 467,200 were released. The rate of release also has dropped, reflecting a general increase in the length of time served.[37] This trend is merely an extension of the overall trend since 1925. Despite some fluctuations during the Great Depression (up), World War II (down), and the early 1960s (up), the rate of incarceration has been increasing steadily. This trend is illustrated in Figure 11.1.

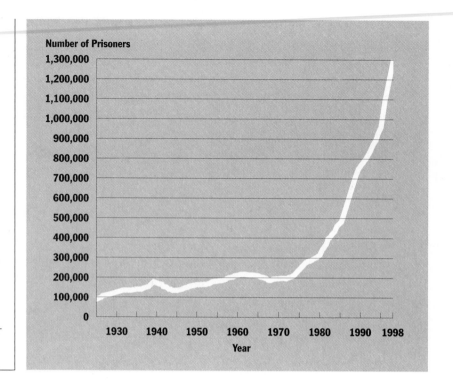

Number of Prisoners

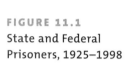

FIGURE 11.1

State and Federal
Prisoners, 1925–1998

SOURCES: Stephanie-Minor
Harper, *State and Federal Prisoners, 1925–1985* (Washington, DC: Bureau of Justice
Statistics, 1986) and Allen J.
Beck and Christopher J. Mumola, *Prisoners in 1998* (Washington, DC: Bureau of Justice
Statistics, 1999).

INMATE FAMILY
BACKGROUND

Correlates of Incarceration

The backgrounds of inmates reveal many factors found to be correlated with
crime, especially educational level, family background, age and race, and
drug use. Most people who commit felonies and are sentenced to state prisons are not highly educated. Approximately 20 percent have less than a
ninth-grade education, and another 50 percent did not graduate from high
school. Therefore, 70 percent of prison inmates in the United States lack a
high school education. Of those in jail awaiting trial or serving short sentences, 13 percent have less than a ninth-grade education and 50 percent did
not graduate from high school.[38]

The family backgrounds of adult inmates also are revealing. A large proportion of inmates (43 percent) were raised in a single-parent household, and
17 percent lived in a foster home or other institution at some time. Thirty
percent of inmates report that their parents abused either alcohol or drugs,
and 50 percent of inmates were under the influence of alcohol or drugs at
the time of their current offense. A striking 57 percent of female inmates
and 16 percent of males report that they were physically or sexually abused
in the past.[39] Thirty-nine percent of prisoners have an immediate family
member who has been incarcerated, and 94 percent have been convicted for
a violent crime *and/or* have a prior record of probation or incarceration.[40]
The high incidence of troubled backgrounds far exceeds national averages.

A significant problem in breaking families' cycles of crime and imprisonment is that fact that 43 percent of incarcerated women and 32 percent of
male inmates have two or more children under age eighteen. These children
usually live with the other parent or with grandparents, although 12 percent

live in foster homes or other institutions. In addition, 6 percent of women inmates are pregnant when they enter prison, and 32 percent of inmates sentenced for violent crimes victimized a relative, intimate, or person whom they knew well.[41] Victims often include children, who also are likely to become juvenile delinquents due to the absence of adequate parental supervision.

Two-thirds of inmates in state prison are under age thirty-five, although the prison population is aging. From 1991 to 1997 the proportion of inmates between the ages of thirty-five and forty-four rose from 23 to 30 percent. This aging reflects longer average prison sentences, truth-in-sentencing provisions, and a decrease in parole release. Approximately 48 percent of inmates are white and 49 percent black. In 1997 Hispanic inmates, who may be of any race, totaled 213,000 nationwide (or about 18 percent of all inmates), an increase of 64 percent from 1990. Stated in another way, about 7 percent of black males in their twenties and thirties are in prison, compared to 2.7 percent of Hispanic males and about 1 percent of white males. Racial disparity has resulted in criticism of the rate at which minorities are confined.[42] Disproportionate minority confinement occurs when a racial group is incarcerated at rates far above its proportion in the population, a pattern that raises questions of institutional discrimination by the criminal justice system. For example, the incarceration rate for white males is 369 per 100,000 in the U.S. population, but it is 1,273 per 100,000 Hispanic males and 3,209 per 100,000 black males.[43]

Drug offenders are a significant proportion of the prison population. Approximately 230,000 inmates are in prison for drug offenses, and they constitute 21 percent of the total prison population. Drug offenders also account for the largest total growth among female inmates between 1990 and 1997.[44] Sixty percent of convicted jail inmates were using drugs or alcohol at the time of the offense, and two-thirds reported regular drug use.[45] These statistics suggest a strong association between drug use and drug-related offenses.

The combination of family violence, substance abuse, lack of education, long criminal history, and incarcerated parents tends to perpetuate the cycle that places persons at risk of engaging in crime and becoming incarcerated. Even if effective measures could be implemented to improve education, provide substance abuse treatment, and restore family integrity, an entire generation of parents are now in prison and are unlikely to provide effective supervision for their children—who themselves are destined to become at risk for offending. Consider the incarcerated father and drug-abusing mother whose six-year-old son shot and killed a six-year-old classmate in school in March 2000.

DISPROPORTIONATE MINORITY CONFINEMENT

Incarceration of Women

In the last decade the number of women incarcerated in state or federal prisons or local jails in the United States has doubled. The rate of incarceration in prison increased from 27 per 100,000 women in 1985 to 57 per 100,000 in 1998. Men still outnumber women in the inmate population by a factor of about 14 to 1, but the gap is narrowing—from 17 to 1 a decade ago. Women constituted only 4 percent of the total prison and jail population in the United States in 1980 but more than 6 percent in 1998.[46] This trend

TABLE 11.3

Criminal History of Prison Inmates

	PERCENTAGE OF STATE PRISON INMATES	
CRIMINAL HISTORY	FEMALE	MALE
Past convictions		
None	35%	23%
Juvenile only	3	7
Adult only	46	39
Both adult and juvenile	16	31
Number of prior convictions		
0	35%	23%
1	17	17
2	16	16
3–5	19	25
6–10	8	12
11 or more	5	6
Status at arrest		
None	47%	53%
Probation	34	21
Parole	18	25
Escapee	1	1

SOURCE: Lawrence A. Greenfeld and Tracy L. Snell, *Women Offenders* (Washington, DC: Bureau of Justice Statistics, 1999).

INMATE MOTHERS

is due to increasing criminal activity by women, resulting in more arrests of women and an increase in the number of female defendants convicted of felonies; females' rate of conviction has grown at twice the rate of that of male defendants.[47] Table 11.3 indicates that women in state prisons are more likely than men to have been on probation at the time of their arrest, suggesting that women may have even higher recidivism rates than men.

The growing number of women inmates poses society with some unique challenges: dealing with the victims of women's crimes, their family histories, and child care issues. Women serving a sentence for a violent crime are twice as likely as men to have committed the crime against an intimate or relative. Half of all victims of male offenders were strangers, whereas only 35 percent of victims of females were strangers. These differences call for different approaches to treatment and custody of female inmates.[48]

Like male inmates, female inmates often grew up in single-parent homes (42 percent) or lived in a foster home or institution (17 percent). Women, however, are more likely to have a family member who has been incarcerated (47 percent versus 37 percent for men) and to have a parent or guardian who abused alcohol or drugs (34 percent versus 26 percent for men). Most significantly, 57 percent of women inmates were physically or sexually abused in the past (compared to 16 percent of men). For 37 percent of the women inmates this abuse took place before age eighteen. Table 11.4 indicates that for 61 percent of female inmates reporting physical or sexual abuse, the abuse was inflicted by an intimate; for 40 percent, by a family member.[49] The anger and pain caused by abuse and neglect often is a factor in assaults that occur within intimate relationships.

Approximately three-quarters of women in prison have at least one child, and two-thirds of female prisoners' children are under eighteen. These figures translate into nearly 200,000 children under age eighteen with mothers in prison or jail.[50] Half of women inmates' children live with a grandparent, 25 percent with the other parent, and 12 percent in foster homes or institutions. In addition, 6 percent of convicted women are pregnant upon admission to jail or prison.[51] In most cases the child is

TABLE 11.4

Prior Physical or Sexual Abuse of State Prison Inmates

RELATIONSHIP OF VICTIM TO ABUSER	MALE	FEMALE
Knew abuser	89.5%	90.6%
Family (parent or relative)	66.6%	40.1%
Intimate (spouse/ex-spouse or boyfriend/girlfriend)	5.8%	61.3%
Knew none of abusers	10.5%	9.4%

SOURCE: Caroline Wolf Harlow, *Prior Abuse Reported by Inmates and Probationers* (Washington, DC: Bureau of Justice Statistics, 1999).

taken from the mother at birth and is placed in custody of relatives or state welfare agencies until the mother is released from prison. Efforts to help maintain family contact and supervision of children of inmates might include pre- and postnatal training and care for the mothers. Travel to prison could be arranged for inmates' children, and more prisons could allow very young children to stay with their mothers for a specified period to encourage greater emotional bonding and parental responsibility.[52]

What percentage of the total jail and prison population today is female? How much of an increase is this compared to ten years ago? For what types of crimes are women incarcerated most often? How would you explain the causes of the dramatic increase in women's rates of arrest, conviction, and incarceration? What happens to the children of these women? In what sense are they victims in a system that is supposed to provide justice?

Prison Overcrowding

As you have read, the explosion in the prison population has led to overcrowding and new construction. As of 1998 state correctional facilities were operating at an average of 115 percent capacity, and federal prisons were at 127 percent capacity. Nearly 25,000 prisoners are being held in local jails because of lack of available prison space. Several hundred state correctional facilities are under court order to reduce overcrowding or correct conditions that violate the law, usually conditions involving health or safety. New construction has increased total prison capacity by 40 percent since 1990, but the number of inmates has increased faster. One-third of correctional facilities in the United States are less than twelve years old, although nearly a quarter are at least fifty years old.[53]

Prison overcrowding is a difficult political issue, because the public demands protection from criminals yet generally is reluctant to approve government spending. Nevertheless, public spending on prisons increased dramatically during the 1990s. The nationwide average annual cost to house each state prison inmate is $20,100, which includes facility construction and renovation, repair, wages of corrections employees, food service, medical care, transportation, and programs. Total state prison expenditures increased from $12 billion in 1990 to $22 billion in 1996. In constant dollars, state correctional expenses rose from $53 per U.S. resident in 1985 to $103 in 1996.[54] Critics allege that this money is not well spent; too many nonviolent offenders are sent to prison, and prisons are a "revolving door" for violent criminals who often recidivate.[55] Overcrowding must be addressed, as it leads to prison unrest, creating a dangerous situation for both corrections officers and inmates.

POLITICS OF PRISON OVERCROWDING

What Is Inmate Life Like?

Although opinions differ as to whether inmates should be treated harshly or humanely, no one argues that inmates should be idle or bored. Nevertheless, idleness and boredom are perhaps the conditions most typical of inmates in jails and prisons today. Inmates spend most of the day and night in their cells; depending on security level, they may leave the cell to eat (although most jail inmates eat in their cells) and to exercise. Most inmates are allowed to exercise outside their cells for several hours per day, usually walking, lifting weights, or playing basketball. Most prisoners are assigned a job to do each day, but in most cases the job is menial and lasts for only a few hours. Typical jobs include sweeping and polishing floors, washing dishes, and preparing food. Prisons usually have small libraries, but many prisoners cannot read. Prisoners seeking education or drug or alcohol treatment usually do not have access to programs or must wait for long periods before being admitted. Often the progress inmates make in these programs is quickly undone. For example, education in conflict resolution skills is undermined when the inmate returns to a general inmate population in which threats and violence are common or in which inmate or staff support for educational efforts is lacking. Major issues of inmate life can be grouped into eight categories: prison work, drugs and treatment, AIDS, prison gangs, and violence.

Prison Work

In a 1981 speech Supreme Court Chief Justice Warren Burger asked corrections agencies to establish "factories with fences" to provide inmates with the job skills they would need upon release.[56] This proposal was similar to the Auburn system described earlier in this chapter, in which prisoners worked in a workshop during the day and slept alone at night. The primary difference is that the Auburn system forbade any conversation among inmates for the duration of their sentence.[57]

INMATE WORK

Advantages

Disadvantages
- *forces people out of business.*
- *drives prices down.*

Nearly all observers have viewed inmate work favorably. Work can help inmates learn discipline, accountability, and job skills, and can sometimes enable them to earn money to pay compensation to victims. Nevertheless, starting in the 1930s and 1940s, prison-made products were banned from the open market in response to protests by businesses and labor unions, which feared unfair competition from low-wage inmate labor. In 1979 legislation was passed to restore the relationship between outside businesses and prison labor. Since then, a large number of successful inmate work programs have been created. In Kansas, for example, female inmates from the Topeka Correctional Facility perform housing renovation work in low-income homes. Operation Outward Reach is a nonprofit organization that contracts with five Pennsylvania prisons to provide vocational training in carpentry and masonry. Inmates also perform low-cost construction work for senior citizens and the poor. The Wisconsin Department of Corrections is engaged in the Recycled Mobile Home Project, which rehabilitates homes for the rural homeless and low-income families.[58] There are many other examples of prison and jail work programs that reduce the cost of operating correctional facilities and produce useful products or services.[59]

Media and Criminal Justice

THE SHAWSHANK REDEMPTION

Dozens of films have plots in which a truly innocent person is wrongfully accused of a crime he or she did not commit, but the 1994 Oscar winner for best picture is different from the rest. *The Shawshank Redemption*, unlike other movies about wrongfully convicted inmates in prison, is not really about the circumstances that land the innocent Andy Dufresne in prison for murdering his wife. The story suggests that some details of the crime don't add up, but it accepts the sentence for what it is; its focus is not on the questionable conviction but on the heart-wrenching realities of prison life in the 1940s.

The story is narrated by Red, a longtime prison inmate who has worked his way up to chief proprietor of the prison's smuggled contraband. As the inmates watch new prisoners unload from the bus, Red bets that the fragile-looking banker Andy will be the first to cry. When Andy proves himself to be far more determined and strong than anyone imagined, he and Red become trusted friends, but not before Red smirks at his story: "You're going to fit right in . . . you know that everybody in here's innocent."

Andy is a character study in survival. He refuses to kiss butt or back down, and he uses his formidable intelligence and confidence instead of violence. He gains the respect of all when he uses his accounting knowledge to barter with the recently audited warden in order to procure some cold beers for his fellow inmates during a roofing job.

The movie has no deep plot beyond the incredibly slow passage of time, as experienced by the inmates. Red measures time in terms of decades, for at the end of ten years (soon twenty, then thirty) he goes before the parole board, where he is asked if he has been rehabilitated. Each time he answers with a heartfelt "Oh, yes, surely!" But when he is never released, hope slowly fades away.

This process of succumbing to prison life as normal, even desirable for its stability and predictability, is referred to as *institutionalization*. Unlike the corrupt warden, disgusting conditions, or cruel predators of the prison, it is institutionalization that is the real enemy. As Red notes at one point, "These walls are funny. First you hate them. Then you get used to them. After time passes, you get so's you depend on them."

One of the most important facets of the movie involves Brooks, the elderly prison librarian who has been incarcerated for so long he has no real memory of life before prison. The highlight of his life as an inmate is domesticating an injured bird, which he keeps hidden in his pocket, feeding it the maggots found in his mashed potatoes. 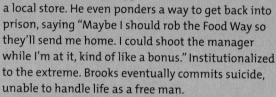 When he is finally paroled after more than fifty years in prison, Brooks finds himself at a loss as to how to deal with the loneliness of a rented room or cope with his nonintellectual job as a grocery bagger at a local store. He even ponders a way to get back into prison, saying "Maybe I should rob the Food Way so they'll send me home. I could shoot the manager while I'm at it, kind of like a bonus." Institutionalized to the extreme. Brooks eventually commits suicide, unable to handle life as a free man.

The Shawshank Redemption is indeed about redemption, as explored in the everyday existence of the lifers at Shawshank Penitentiary. Ironically, the oppressive gothic fortress that serves as the movie's setting was actually Ohio's Mansfield Reformatory, which was later closed down as unsuitable for today's prisoners. As an allegory about the personal worth of prisoners, the movie points out that life—even in prison—is what you make it. Whether prison's purpose is retribution, incapacitation, or reform, Andy sums up the prisoner's life in one simple philosophy: "Get busy living, or get busy dying."

Assuming that the depiction of prison life in *Shawshank* is accurate for the 1940s, discuss how prison life is the same or different today. Do you think that reform is possible in a prison setting that doesn't offer rehabilitative services? What can be done to combat the threat of institutionalization among inmates? And do you believe that the institutionalized mentality is a root cause of recidivism?

Nearly 70 percent of all inmates perform work in prison, but most tasks performed by inmates involve maintenance of the correctional facility itself. These tasks produce savings for the state, because it does not have to contract with outside firms for services. Only about two-thirds of inmates are paid for their work; the average wage is 56 cents per hour. Work involving farming, roadwork, or manufacturing accounts for only a small percentage of inmate work assignments. There are many more inmates than there are meaningful work opportunities.

Some businesspeople continue to fear that cheap prison labor will drive down prices and force them out of business. A Connecticut manufacturer of draperies complained that his sales to the government dropped by 50 percent because of competition from Federal Prison Industries.[60] Federal Prison Industries may bid on any government contract it can fulfill, and it can fulfill contracts more cheaply than most private companies because inmate labor is cheaper. As a result, labor unions, too, strongly oppose inmate labor. In recent years some prisons have used inmates to do data entry work or telemarketing work, usually for government agencies. Concerns that inmates might gain access to sensitive personal information via the telephone or the Internet prompted a study by the U.S. General Accounting Office, the investigative arm of Congress. The GAO found that 1,100 inmates nationwide had access to names, dates of birth, or social security numbers through the work they performed in prison. About 5,500 inmates had access to names and addresses or telephone numbers only. Information was safeguarded by means of close supervision of inmates, selective hiring, and security checks at exits from work areas. Nevertheless, there were nine documented incidents, summarized in Table 11.5, in which inmates misused this personal information. In five of the incidents the work programs were discontinued, even though poor supervision of the inmates was a primary factor. Work programs are viewed as privileges; even single incidents of inmate misconduct can cause entire programs to be terminated.

Most states permit inmate industries to supply only government agencies, so they do not compete against other businesses in the open market. Prison industry produces office furniture, clothing, textiles, bedding, electronic equipment, gloves, and optics.[61] Federal inmates employed in joint ventures with private firms have paid nearly $2 million in victim compensation, $2 million in family support payments, more than $3 million in taxes, and $5 million toward payment of the cost of their incarceration.[62] Nevertheless, an appropriate balance among the goals of preparing inmates for release, offsetting the costs of incarceration through inmate labor, and competing fairly with the private sector has yet to be achieved.

Drug Use and Treatment Programs

There is considerable evidence that drug use is rampant in prisons and jails. An inmate at the Marcy Correctional Facility in New York State, for example, relied on visitors to supply him with drugs. Some visitors smuggled drugs into prison in the heels of sneakers. Female friends passed small bal-

TABLE 11.5

Incidents of Misuse of Personal Information by Inmates

STATE	INCIDENT DESCRIPTION	HOW SAFEGUARDS FAILED	PROGRAM CONTINUED AFTER INCIDENT?
California	An inmate on parole used credit card numbers previously obtained in a prison telemarketing program (1991).	Unknown.	Yes, but discontinued in 1998
New Mexico	Inmate wrote a letter to a Medicare patient identified from information obtained in a data entry work program (1995).	Inmate was not searched when leaving work area.	No
New York	An inmate wrote a letter to a person whose name and address were provided by an inmate in a work program (1995).	Inmate left the premises with the information.	Yes
Oklahoma	An inmate wrote a letter to a person based on information obtained from a data entry program dealing with medical expenses (1990).	Inmate memorized the address.	Yes
Oklahoma	Two inmates attempted to smuggle copies of birth certificates obtained through a work program via U.S. mail (1995).	Papers removed despite secured work area.	Yes
South Carolina	Inmate continued to call a person identified through a work program that telemarketed local newspaper subscriptions (1995).	Inmate was not monitored while making calls.	No
South Dakota	An inmate used a credit card number obtained from a program that made motel reservations (1991).	Unknown.	No
Texas	Inmate wrote a letter to an individual identified through a data entry work program, including personal information (1992).	Unknown.	No
Washington	An inmate sent a Christmas card to a person identified through a 1-800 information line on state parks that inmates staffed (1997).	Lack of supervision.	No

SOURCE: U.S. Comptroller General, *Prison Work Programs: Inmates' Access to Personal Information* (Washington, DC: U.S. General Accounting Office, 1999).

loons filled with heroin from their mouths to his when they kissed in the visiting room. He then swallowed the balloons or hid them on his body. And sometimes corrupt prison employees would provide drugs. Since 1990, twenty-six corrections officers have been charged with smuggling drugs into Rikers Island jail in New York City. A convicted murderer was found dead of a cocaine overdose in his cell at Great Meadow Correctional Facility in New York, a hypodermic needle in his hand. Reports from Mississippi, the District of Columbia, Georgia, and other jurisdictions have found significant drug use in prisons, although such use is clearly prohibited.[63]

Most state departments of corrections deny that drugs are readily available in prison but admit that drugs are present. As one corrections official explains, "Unless you searched everyone going in and out, kept all packages out and locked all inmates in their cells for twenty-four hours a day, you're going to have contraband."[64]

PRISON CONTRABAND

Everything Done at Random

The effort to prevent drug use in prison has been called a cat-and-mouse game. Corrections officers resort to strip searches and unannounced cell searches, while prisoners become more inventive at smuggling drugs and use sophisticated techniques such as obtaining liquified LSD painted on the back of postage stamps. To combat the problem most state and federal prisons now use random urine testing of inmates. Those found using drugs have privileges taken away or are placed in solitary confinement. Because of overcrowding, however, most inmates are tested less than once a year, so little deterrent effect is achieved. Yet prison officials point to their drug testing findings to show that fewer than 10 percent of all inmates test positive for drugs.[65] In addition, because of its limited scope, this testing probably misses a great deal of drug usage.

High demand for drugs among prisoners has always existed. In fact, there are anecdotes of prisoners' making a form of wine from fruit juice and other substances long before drugs became widely popular. The increase in very long sentences adds to inmates' feelings of hopelessness and fear of forced sex and unprovoked fights in a population of desperate, angry, and frustrated prisoners. These feelings increase the tendency to seek a kind of temporary escape or relief from the prison environment through drug use.

A large number of inmates also exhibit high levels of anger, fear, and frustration *before* their crime and incarceration, which may account for the high rates of drug use among offenders. A majority of inmates report regular use of drugs in the month before their crime, and a majority committed their offense while under the influence of drugs or alcohol. In fact, 19 percent of state prison inmates committed their offense in order to obtain money to buy drugs.[66]

EFFECTIVE DRUG TREATMENT

Effective drug treatment would reduce the demand for drugs among both inmates and released prisoners and would have a long-term impact on prison drug smuggling and rates of reoffending. But few efforts to accomplish this goal have been effective. A review of a small number of successful prison-based drug treatment programs found that they shared several features. Each program had a special source of funds dedicated exclusively to drug treatment, which prevented the continual starting and discontinuing of programs that is typical in prison settings. All the successful programs were "guests" of the correctional institution and were not operated by the institution itself. Therefore, providers could focus on the program and not be concerned with custodial issues. In Delaware, a self-contained treatment environment was established inside a men's maximum security prison for drug-involved offenders. This **therapeutic community model** was based on the notion that a person's attitudes, values, and self-esteem must change together with the targeted drug use behavior if lasting change is to occur. The self-contained therapeutic community separated the inmates in the program from the drugs and violence that existed elsewhere in the prison. An evaluation of this program found that inmates who completed it were nearly 50 percent more likely to remain drug-free and arrest-free after six months than a comparison group of nonparticipating offenders.[67] Other characteristics of successful programs included using a variety of treatment strate-

■**therapeutic community model**
Prison drug treatment approach based on the notion that a person's attitudes, values, and self-esteem must change together with the targeted drug use behavior if lasting change is to occur.

gies, employing trained social workers and counselors rather than correctional officers, providing training in life skills, and contacting participants after the program ended.

AIDS in Prison

Approximately 2.1 percent (about 23,500) of inmates in state and federal prisons are known to be infected with HIV, the virus that causes AIDS. Of those HIV-positive inmates, more than a quarter have confirmed AIDS. This number rose from 1,682 confirmed AIDS cases in 1991 to 6,184 in 1997. The rate of confirmed AIDS among prison inmates is five and one-half times higher than in the general U.S. population.[68] And these figures understate the severity of the problem, because testing policies vary in different jurisdictions. The Federal Bureau of Prisons and eighteen states test all inmates for HIV upon admission or release. In most jurisdictions, however, an inmate is tested only if he or she exhibits HIV-related symptoms or requests a test. Requests are uncommon, because inmates who test positive for HIV often face discrimination. In Georgia, for example, a thirty-four-year-old inmate was placed in isolation in a city jail. He wanted to mop floors so that his six-month sentence for drunk driving would be reduced one day for each day of work, but he was denied this opportunity because he had HIV. As a result he was required to serve two extra months in jail. In Mississippi and Alabama, inmates with HIV are separated from all other prisoners and are denied equal access to prison jobs, early release, education, the chapel, and the library. As one inmate stated, "the stress, the depression, the boredom, the hopelessness—it's overwhelming."[69]

More than 500 prisoners die of AIDS-related diseases each year, accounting for a third of all prison deaths.[70] Many inmates and staff are afraid of contracting HIV through fights, sexual contact, or other involuntary exposure to blood or body fluids. The segregation of inmates with HIV reduces these fears. Nevertheless, prison administrators continue to fear that the disease will spread throughout a captive population, especially because the widespread sharing of hypodermic needles and other unsanitary practices promote the spread of HIV.[71]

Inmates have a right to medical treatment for AIDS-related illnesses. Treatment is expensive, however, and lawsuits have been filed by inmates claiming inadequate treatment of their medical conditions. The extent of treatment that prisons must provide in these cases remains unclear. Special custodial restrictions on inmates with HIV do sometimes interfere with medical treatment, but courts have generally upheld these restrictions when they are based on legitimate health, safety, and security considerations.

AIDS DEATHS

Prison Gangs

As mentioned earlier, surveys of jail and prison administrators have found that identifying gang members and training staff in how to handle gangs are pressing concerns. This issue of gangs in prisons first arose during the late

Gang	Percent
 Crips (various factions)	15.4
 Black Gangster Disciples	13.9
 Bloods/Piru factions	11.7
 Vice Lord factions	7.1
 Aryan Brotherhood	6.8
 Latin King factions	4.5

FIGURE 11.2

Percentage of Prisons in Which Gang Members Are Inmates

SOURCES: George W. Knox et al., "Preliminary Results of the 1995 Adult Corrections Survey," *Journal of Gang Research* 3 (Winter 1996), pp. 27–63; www.fredfarm.simplenet.com/pointman/pictures/tatoos

DEALING WITH PRISON GANGS

1980s, when cocaine and crack use became widespread and gangs formed to engage in narcotics trafficking.[72] Twenty percent of all male inmates are believed to be gang members, compared to only 3 percent of female inmates.[73] More than half of adult state correctional facilities report that racial conflicts are a problem and that these conflicts are aggravated by gang affiliations. Institutions with a high level of racial disturbances have been found to have a high rate of gang-related disturbances as well.[74]

Figure 11.2 lists the gangs that are among the most common in prisons. Members of the Crips, Black Gangster Disciples, and Bloods/Piru gangs are among the inmates in more than 40 percent of state correctional institutions. Gangs listed in Figure 11.2 are primarily drug-trafficking organizations, and their members are part of the fastest-growing segment of the prison population—those incarcerated for drug-related crimes. These inmates, not surprisingly, often engage in drug trafficking within the prison. Many are also involved in gambling, protection, and extortion rackets.

Current methods for dealing with prison gangs include formal staff training, but this training is not very extensive. A majority of jails and prisons have rules that prohibit gang recruitment; but, as noted earlier, it is difficult to identify gang members upon admission to prison. Many state prisons do not take gang membership into account as part of their inmate classification system,[75] although some states have enacted policies that segregate known gang members in high-security "supermax" prisons. These high-security prisons are generally reserved for those who have committed a serious assault while confined. Placement in a supermax facility based on the status of gang affiliation rather than because of violent behavior has been criticized on grounds of unfairness.[76]

Most wardens do not believe that solitary confinement or segregation effectively controls gang members, except possibly in a central federal facility. Both anger management training and mediation between gangs and racial groups in prison have been recommended as ways to change gang attitudes and behavior.[77] Currently wardens rely on transfers of gang members within the state prison system in an attempt to control the proliferation of gangs behind bars. Most troubling is the fact that 80 percent of prison administrators report that "gang members generally have a stronger affiliation with their gang after serving time."[78] The reason for the strengthening of gang ties in prison, in addition to the shared experience and mutual help, is that inmates have more opportunities to meet gang leaders and advance in the gang hierarchy in prison than on the street, where there is more competition. It appears that so long as drug trafficking is controlled by gangs, imprisoning gang members disrupts but does not end gang activity.

Violence in Prison

The number of violent incidents in prisons has increased sharply in recent years. Atlanta Federal Penitentiary, for example, had five inmate murders in sixteen months during the mid-1990s. The number of assaults on federal corrections officers also has increased throughout the prison system. Officials place some blame on mandatory sentences, which leave inmates with the feeling they have nothing to lose by being violent because their sentences are so long to begin with. Another factor is overcrowding: Prisons are susceptible to uprisings because inmates outnumber staff by three to one. In addition, many prisons are old, and inmates often move throughout the prison during the day, so locking an entire cellblock of inmates away from staff is not always feasible when trouble arises.

At Kirkland Correctional Institution in South Carolina, inmates seized control of the unit holding the most violent inmates. They climbed the fence around it and used construction tools left on the grounds to release 700 inmates. A riot squad responded and was able to end the disturbance in six hours. The Atlanta Federal Penitentiary had an uprising that lasted eleven days and involved more than a hundred hostages. That disturbance, which began when the government announced that 2,500 Cubans being held there would be sent back to Cuba, was resolved through extensive negotiations. A study sponsored by the National Institute of Justice analyzed eight prison riots and made recommendations for prison riot plans and prevention strategies. The most important elements in plans for responding to an actual riot situation include clearly defined lines of authority in the command structure, clear guidelines on the use of force, interagency cooperation, and adequate staff training. Long-term prevention strategies include supervision by experienced staff, sound security practices, good intelligence, appropriate tactics (i.e., negotiation versus force), and follow-up on staff morale after a riot has occurred.[79] Other studies have found that the personal characteristics of inmates and situational factors within prisons combine to form an organizational climate that can be conducive to prison violence.[80]

The frequency of prison riots increased during the 1990s.[81] In 1993 there were riots in three federal prisons over the crack cocaine law that imposes mandatory ten-year, no-parole sentences for possession of only fifty grams of crack. In 1995 prison uprisings in Alabama, Illinois, Pennsylvania, and Tennessee left twelve corrections officers injured and millions of dollars in damage.[82] Twenty-one percent of state prison administrators reported that a riot occurred in their facility during 1995.[83] In a riot at Pelican Bay State Prison in California in 2000, corrections officers shot sixteen prisoners, and another thirty-two prisoners were stabbed or slashed by fellow inmates. This event followed nine inmate deaths from fights with fellow inmates in 1997 and 1998.[84] The need for greater preparedness and appropriate responses to prison riots is apparent. The U.S. Supreme Court has held that shooting a prisoner without warning in an effort to suppress a prison riot is not cruel and unusual punishment.[85] Riot situations that are handled badly,

PRISON RIOTS

What are the constitutional rights of these prisoners? What rights do they forfeit? What kinds of prison rules are they typically held responsible for following? What economic and political issues are involved in the jobs they perform while prisoners? Could they be required to work without pay? In the 1990s what situations were associated with increases in prison riots? In a riot could these inmates be shot without warning?

such as the 1971 Attica uprising that resulted in the deaths of ten corrections officers and twenty-nine convicts, usually involve immediate forceful intervention. Most prison disturbances today are handled with more patience, because the inmates remain locked inside and there is no need for a quick resolution. Negotiations defuse anger over a period of hours and days, with the result that inmates and staff are less likely to engage in further violence. Also, violent responses to inmate uprisings lead to recriminations and lawsuits that last for many years after the incident, making it difficult to implement new prison procedures.[86]

What Are Prisoners' Rights and Responsibilities?

An inmate in a Texas prison was a Buddhist, but he was not permitted to use the prison chapel or to correspond with his Buddhist religious advisor. When he shared Buddhist religious material with other inmates, he was placed in solitary confinement on a diet of bread and water for two weeks for violating prison rules. The inmate alleged that his First Amendment right to freedom of religion had been violated.

The scope of prisoners' legal rights has been carved out by the courts in a large number of cases. Most of these cases involve alleged violations of the Eighth Amendment prohibition against cruel and unusual punishment. In this section we will consider important rights and responsibilities of prisoners under the First and Fourth Amendments. In every case the issues are the same: What rights does a prisoner surrender as a condition of his or her confinement, and what rights do all individuals have regardless of whether or not they are incarcerated?

Constitutional Rights

In the case of the Buddhist inmate, the Texas Department of Corrections argued that inmates with unconventional religious beliefs should not be guaranteed the right to practice their religion in prison. The U.S. Supreme Court disagreed, noting that although Buddhism may be unconventional in the United States, it was established in 600 B.C., long before Christianity. The Court held that Texas had violated the inmate's First Amendment protection of free exercise of religion.[87] The prison system provided chaplains for the Jewish and Christian faiths, as well as Bibles. By refusing to allow the inmate to practice Buddhism, the Texas Department of Corrections discriminated unfairly against the inmate and violated his First Amendment guarantee of freedom of religion.

In a subsequent case, however, the Court made it clear that there are limits on the freedom to practice religion in prison. Islamic inmates in a New Jersey prison were not permitted to attend a religious service on Friday afternoons. The prison did not permit inmates to attend services or meetings in buildings outside their housing unit unless they had "minimum" security status. Also, inmates who worked outside the prison were not allowed to return to prison buildings during the day for security reasons. The U.S. Supreme Court ruled against the inmates, stating that because there was a "rational connection to the legitimate governmental interest in institutional order and security," the decision by prison officials was reasonable and did not violate the First Amendment.[88] These cases are typical of court holdings in this area, recognizing the inmate's right to express religious belief within the limits imposed by a prison setting.[89]

ISLAMIC INMATES

The Fourth Amendment protects individuals from intrusions by the government in the absence of probable cause linking them to a crime. The extent to which inmates continue to enjoy the right to privacy was not clear or uniform until the 1980s. A landmark case began at Bland Correctional Center in Virginia, where two corrections officers conducted a warrantless search of an inmate's cell. The officers discovered a ripped pillow case in the trash basket and charged the inmate with destroying state property. The inmate filed suit, contending that the search of his cell violated the Fourth Amendment and had no purpose other than harassment.

The Supreme Court held in *Hudson v. Palmer* that "society is not prepared to recognize any subjective expectation of privacy that a prisoner might have in his prison cell . . . and the Fourth Amendment . . . does not apply within the confines of the prison cell." If inmates had such constitutional protection in their cells, it would contradict "the concept of incarceration and the needs and objectives of penal institutions" in maintaining custody and security.[90] This ruling makes clear that inmates have no rea-

HUDSON V. PALMER

sonable expectation of privacy in their cells. Therefore, no warrant or probable cause is required for searches.

These cases illustrate how the Supreme Court has weighed constitutional rights against the demands of running a prison in two important legal areas. It can be seen that the Court is sensitive to the requirements for operating a secure prison, while also attempting to address the appropriate scope of individual protections in the prison environment.

Prison Rules

A national survey of state prisons found that 53 percent of inmates had been charged with violating prison rules at least once. Examples of prison rules include regulations on maintaining a neat cell and rules governing dress, noise, foul language, littering, and responding appropriately to commands, among many others. The rate of rule violations in prison does not appear to change significantly over time, translating into an average of 1.5 rule violations per year per inmate.[91]

This rate of violations has led some to question the appropriateness of some prison rules for their supposed function of maintaining order and security. Prison administrators point to the fact that inmates outnumber corrections staff three to one and that numerous assaults on corrections officers have occurred.[92] Rules prohibiting extortion and assault also are needed to protect inmates from one another. Inmates complain, however, that some prison rules are petty, or not widely known and are misused to harass inmates. Rules prohibiting horseplay and certain sanitary regulations are examples.

The Supreme Court has held that inmates are entitled to due process (i.e., a hearing) and that some evidence of rule violation must be presented in cases in which penalties, such as solitary confinement, are possible.[93] However, inmates do not have the right to counsel or to cross-examination of witnesses against them in prison disciplinary hearings.[94] More than 90 percent of inmates charged with prison rule violations are found guilty.

Disciplinary procedures vary from one state to another. Penalties range from a notation of the violation in the inmate's file to a disciplinary hearing. The warden usually serves as the final avenue of appeal. If a serious rule violation is also a crime, the offense may be referred for prosecution. More than 30 percent of prison rule violators are placed in solitary confinement or otherwise separated from other prisoners. The second most common penalty is loss of "good time," or credit toward early release for good behavior; this is followed by loss of recreational privileges or confinement to the cell for some period of time.

Most rule violations are committed by inmates who have been in prison one to two years. Inmates who have served five years or more generally have the lowest incidence of violations. Younger inmates with a long criminal history and a history of drug use are most likely to violate prison rules. Rule violations are likely to increase, therefore, as increasing numbers of young drug offenders are sentenced to long prison terms in overcrowded prisons with little possibility for early release.

critical thinking exercise

The Elderly Inmate

Ilie Coleman had been in prison in Columbia, South Carolina, for nearly fifty-two years for killing his wife. At eighty-four years of age, he had heart problems and high blood pressure. A reporter for *USA Today* who interviewed Coleman in 1995 was his first visitor in thirty years. By the late 1990s there were more than 10,000 prisoners age sixty-five or older in the United States, a number that had doubled in ten years as a result of changes in sentencing and release policies.[a]

The average maximum federal prison sentence has increased by more than five years over the last decade. The average prison sentence for drug offenses has more than doubled over that period. As discussed in Chapter 10, the percentage of their sentences served by inmates before release also has increased steadily in recent years as states and the federal government have shifted to determinate sentencing systems, the abolition of parole release, and truth-in-sentencing laws.[b] During the 1990s the proportion of inmates over age forty rose from less than 20 percent to nearly 26 percent of all inmates.[c] It is predicted that by the year 2010 one-third of the prison population will consist of inmates age fifty-one or older.[d]

As the inmate population ages, there is concern about the higher health care costs that older people incur. Virginia announced in 1999 that it will set aside an entire prison solely for older and disabled inmates who need help with walking, dressing, bathing, and everyday routines.[e] Some have suggested releasing elderly offenders early, but victims and their families oppose early release; moreover, long-term elderly inmates often have no where to go upon release. They have no family members who would be willing to take care of them, and they are too old to compete in the workforce. In essence, they have aged out of their crime-prone years, passed middle age, and entered their retirement years, yet are still in prison. Prisons are having difficulty finding private care facilities that will take these inmates when they are eligible for parole. The result is a large number of elderly inmates who have been in prison for much of their lives, whose sentences are ending, but who have no place to go.

CRITICAL THINKING QUESTIONS

1. A person is incarcerated for twenty or thirty years and paroled at age sixty-five. The inmate has no money and no one to take him or her in. If you were a corrections administrator, what would you do?
2. Who should pay for medical care for inmates who require heart surgery, expensive medication, or help with physical or mental disabilities during their prison terms?
3. What are some possible long-term solutions to these problems?

NOTES

a. Tom Watson, "Prisons' Graying Inmates Exact a Price," *USA Today* (March 17, 1995), p. 12.
b. Paula M. Ditton and Doris James Wilson, *Truth in Sentencing in State Prisons* (Washington, DC: Bureau of Justice Statistics, 1999).
c. Allen J. Beck and Christopher J. Mumola, *Prisoners in 1998* (Washington, DC: Bureau of Justice Statistics, 1999).
d. Connie L. Neeley, Laura Addison, and Delores Craig-Moreland, "Addressing the Needs of Elderly Offenders," *Corrections Today* 59 (August 1997), pp. 120–24.
e. "Capron: A State Prison," *USA Today* (June 29, 1999), p. 13.

Summary

HOW ARE CORRECTIONAL INSTITUTIONS IN THE UNITED STATES ORGANIZED?

■ Before the invention of the prison, corporal punishment was the primary method of punishment of criminals.

- Incarceration was used for poor offenders who could not afford to pay fines but whose offenses were not serious enough to deserve corporal punishment.
- The Pennsylvania system of incarceration aimed to promote repentance through solitary confinement.
- The Auburn system emphasized labor and meditation.
- Various attempts to encourage education within prisons have been unsuccessful, and today prisons lack a clear philosophical purpose.
- Prisons are classified according to level of custody: maximum security, medium security, and minimum security.
- The assignment of an offender to an institution at a particular level of custody depends largely on whether the conviction was for a violent crime.
- Jails are operated by counties and municipalities. They hold inmates awaiting trial and those serving sentences of one year or less.

HOW DO CORRECTIONAL INSTITUTIONS OPERATE?

- Although many people believe that prisons should not only punish offenders but also deter crime, the evidence shows that imprisonment does not prevent offenders from committing further crimes upon release.
- Rehabilitation and reform are other objectives of imprisonment, but they often are superseded by concerns for custody and security.
- Three major managerial approaches in operating prisons are the control model, the responsibility model, and the consensus model.

WHO IS IN PRISON?

- The number of people in prisons has grown dramatically in recent decades, resulting in overcrowding.
- The proportion of prisoners who are women is growing rapidly.
- Prisoners tend to be poorly educated and to come from single-parent households where alcohol or drugs were used. Many were physically or sexually abused and have family members who have been incarcerated.

WHAT IS INMATE LIFE LIKE?

- Nearly all observers have viewed inmate work favorably, but businesspeople and labor organizations fear competition from cheap prison labor.
- Drug use is prohibited in prisons, yet is widespread.
- Many offenders who use drugs in prison were convicted of drug law violations or used drugs before being convicted on some other charge.
- Drug treatment programs in prisons have had little success.
- The growing number of women in prison poses challenges related to the nature of the women's crimes, their family histories, and child care issues.
- All federal and some state inmates are tested for HIV. Those who test positive are often discriminated against.
- Twenty percent of all male inmates are believed to be gang members. However, it is difficult to identify gang members upon admission to prison.
- The number of violent incidents in prison has increased sharply in recent years.
- The National Institute of Justice has made several recommendations regarding prison riot plans and prevention strategies. They include clearly defined lines of authority in the command structure, clear guidelines on the use of force, interagency cooperation, and training programs.

WHAT ARE PRISONERS' RIGHTS AND RESPONSIBILITIES?

- The Supreme Court has heard cases involving prisoners' rights in the areas of free exercise of religion and the right to privacy.

- The Supreme Court has held that inmates are entitled to due process in cases of violation of prison rules.
- Most rule violations are committed by younger inmates who have been in prison one to two years, have a history of drug use, and have a long criminal history.

Key Terms

Pennsylvania system
Auburn system
reformatory movement
maximum security prisons
medium security prisons
minimum security prisons
penitentiaries
correctional institutions
metropolitan correctional centers
  (detention centers)

jails
recidivism
control model
responsibility model
consensual model
therapeutic community
  model

Questions for Review and Discussion

1. What were the origins of the concept of incarceration?
2. What are the three main classifications of prisons?
3. What functions are performed by jails?
4. What is the debate between punishment or reform as the focus of correctional philosophy and operations?
5. What are the most typical characteristics of prison inmates?
6. What are the unique challenges associated with the growing numbers of women in prison?
7. What are the advantages and disadvantages of prison labor?
8. Why is drug use pervasive in prisons, and what factors interfere with efforts to prevent it?
9. What issues are raised by the presence of HIV and AIDS in prisons?
10. What are the implications of the presence of gang members in prisons?
11. What actions could be taken to prevent prison riots?
12. How has the Supreme Court ruled in major cases involving prisoners' rights?

Notes

1. Paul W. Keve, "Old Story," *Richmond Times-Dispatch* (July 6, 1986), pp. F1–2.
2. Ibid.
3. Luke Owen Pike, *A History of Crime in England* (Montclair, NJ: Patterson Smith, 1968); Harry Elmer Barnes, *The Story of Punishment* (Montclair, NJ: Patterson Smith, 1972).
4. Herbert A. Johnson and Nancy Travis Wolfe, *History of Criminal Justice*, 2nd ed. (Cincinnati: Anderson, 1996), p. 127.
5. Gustave de Beaumont and Alexis de Tocqueville, *On the Penitentiary System in the United States and Its Application in France* (1833) (Carbondale, IL: Southern Illinois University Press, 1979), pp. 39–40.

6. Robert Johnson, *Hard Time: Understanding and Reforming the Prison*, 2nd ed. (Belmont, CA: Wadsworth, 1996), p. 29.

7. Ibid., p. 41.

8. Lawrence M. Friedman, *Crime and Punishment in American History* (New York: Basic Books, 1993), pp. 160–61.

9. David J. Rothman, *The Discovery of the Asylum* (Boston: Little, Brown, 1971).

10. Ernest van den Haag, *Punishing Criminals* (New York: Basic Books, 1975).

11. Howard Chua-Eoan, "The Bomber Next Door: What Are the Most Dangerous Men in America Talking About at the Supermax Prison in Colorado?," *Time* (March 22, 1999), p. 55.

12. Gregory L. Hershberger, "To the Max: Supermax Facilities Provide Prison Administrators with More Security Options," *Corrections Today* 60 (February 1998), pp. 54–58.

13. Dennis Cauchon, "The Alcatraz of the Rockies," *USA Today* (November 16, 1994), p. 6.

14. James J. Stephan, *Census of State and Federal Correctional Facilities* (Washington, DC: Bureau of Justice Statistics, 1997).

15. Ibid.

16. Fox Butterfield, "Punitive Damages: Crime Keeps on Falling, but Prisons Keep on Filling," *New York Times* (September 28, 1997) p. 1.

17. Ibid.

18. Mark Mayfield and Tom Watson, "Jail Deaths Spark Call for Probe," *USA Today* (February 19, 1993), p. 3.

19. James J. Stephan, *Census of State and Federal Correctional Facilities, 1996* (Washington, DC: Bureau of Justice Statistics, 1999).

20. Darell K. Gilliard, *Prison and Jail Inmates at Midyear 1998* (Washington, DC: Bureau of Justice Statistics, 1999).

21. Craig A. Perkins, James J. Stephan, and Allen J. Beck, *Jails and Jail Inmates* (Washington, DC: Bureau of Justice Statistics, 1995), p. 4; Darrell K. Gilliard and Allen J. Beck, *Prison and Jail Inmates, 1995* (Washington, DC: Bureau of Justice Statistics, 1996).

22. Caroline Wolf Harlow, *Profile of Jail Inmates, 1996* (Washington, DC: Bureau of Justice Statistics, 1998).

23. Ibid., p. 14.

24. Tom McEwen, *National Assessment Program: Survey of Jail Administrators* (Washington, DC: National Institute of Justice, 1995).

25. *Rhodes v. Chapman*, 452 U.S. 337 (1981).

26. *Estelle v. Gamble*, 429 U.S. 97 (1976).

27. *Wilson v. Seiter*, 59 U.S. 4671 (1991).

28. Allen Beck et al., *Survey of State Prison Inmates* (Washington, DC: Bureau of Justice Statistics, 1993), p. 11.

29. Don M. Gottfredson, "Prison Is Not Enough," *Corrections Today* 57 (August 1995), pp. 16–20.

30. Jill Gordon and Elizabeth H. McConnell, "Are Conjugal Visits and Familial Visitations Effective Rehabilitative Concepts?," *Prison Journal* 79 (March 1999).

31. Danielle M. Polizzi, Doris Layton MacKenzie, and Laura J. Hickman, "What Works in Adult Sex Offender Treatment?: A Review of Prison- and Non-Prison-Based Treatment Programs," *International Journal of Offender Therapy and Comparative Criminology* 43 (September 1999); Serge Brochu, Louise Guyon, and Lynne Desjardins, "Comparative Profiles of Addicted Adult Populations in Rehabilitation and Correctional Services," *Journal of Substance Abuse Treatment* 16 (March 1999); Karen M. Fondacaro, John C. Holt, and Thomas A. Powell, "Psychological Impact of Childhood Sexual Abuse on Male Inmates: The Importance of Perception," *Child Abuse and Neglect* 23 (April 1999); Michael P. Hagan and Karyn L. Bust-Brey, "A Ten-Year Longitudinal Study of Adolescent Rapists upon Return to the Community," *International Journal of Offender Therapy and Comparative Criminology* 43 (December 1999).

32. John DiIulio, *Governing Prisons: A Comparative Study of Correctional Management* (New York: Free Press, 1987).

33. Michael D. Reisig, "Rates of Disorder in Higher-Custody State Prisons: A Comparative Analysis of Managerial Practices," *Crime and Delinquency* 44 (April 1998), pp. 229–45.

34. Mark Colvin, *The Penitentiary in Crisis: From Accommodation to Riot in New Mexico* (Albany, NY: SUNY Press, 1992).

35. Tom McEwen, *National Assessment Program: Wardens and State Commissioners of Corrections* (Washington, DC: National Institute of Justice, 1995).

36. Allen J. Beck and Christopher J. Mumola, *Prisoners in 1998* (Washington, DC: Bureau of Justice Statistics, 1999).

37. Paula M. Ditton and Doris James Wilson, *Truth in Sentencing in State Prisons* (Washington, DC: Bureau of Justice Statistics, 1999).

38. Harlow, *Profile of Jail Inmates.*

39. Caroline Wolf Harlow, *Prior Abuse Reported by Inmates and Probationers* (Washington, DC: Bureau of Justice Statistics, 1999).

40. James J. Stephan, *Census of State and Federal Correctional Facilities, 1996* (Washington, DC: Bureau of Justice Statistics, 1999).
41. Ibid., p. 16.
42. Heidi M. Hsia and Donna Hamparian, *Disproportionate Minority Confinement* (Washington, DC: Office of Juvenile Justice and Delinquency Prevention, 1998).
43. Beck and Mumola, *Prisoners in 1998*.
44. Ibid., p. 11
45. Harlow, *Profile of Jail Inmates.*
46. Beck and Mumola, *Prisoners in 1998*.
47. Lawrence A. Greenfield and Tracy L. Snell, *Women Offenders* (Washington, DC: Bureau of Justice Statistics, 1999).
48. Barbara A. Koons, John D. Burrow, Merry Morash, and Tim Bynum, "Expert and Offender Perceptions of Program Elements Linked to Successful Outcomes for Incarcerated Women," *Crime and Delinquency* 43 (October 1997), pp. 512–42.
49. Harlow, *Prior Abuse Reported.*
50. Toni Locy, "Like Mother, Like Daughter: Why More Young Women Follow Their Moms into Lives of Crime," *U.S. News & World Report* (October 4, 1999), pp. 18–21.
51. Greenfield and Snell, *Women Offenders,* pp. 8–9.
52. Catherine Conly, *The Women's Prison Association: Supporting Women Offenders and Their Families* (Washington, DC: National Institute of Justice, 1998); Meda Chesney-Lind, "Women in Prison: From Partial Justice to Vengeful Equity," *Corrections Today* 60 (December 1998).
53. Beck and Mumola, *Prisoners in 1998,* p. 5; Allen J. Beck, *Correctional Populations in the United States* (Washington, DC: Bureau of Justice Statistics, 1999), p. v.
54. James J. Stephan, *State Prison Expenditures, 1996* (Washington, DC: Bureau of Justice Statistics, 1999).
55. John Cloud, "A Get-Tough Policy That Failed," *Time* (Februry 1, 1999), p. 48.
56. Warren E. Burger, "More Warehouses or Factories with Fences?," *New England Journal of Prison Law* 8 (Winter 1982), pp. 111–20.
57. Rothman, *The Discovery of the Asylum,* p. 82.
58. Lee Roy Black, "Exemplary Programs Make All Participants Winners," *Corrections Today* (August 1996), pp. 84–87.
59. George E. Sexton, *Work in American Prisons: Joint Ventures with the Private Sector* (Washington, DC: National Institute of Justice, 1995); Rod Miller, George E. Sexton, and Victor J. Jacobsen, *Making Jails Productive* (Washington, DC: National Institute of Justice, 1991).
60. Harry Maier, "Some Businesses Fear Prison Labor," *USA Today* (January 10, 1991), p. 12B.
61. Aaron Epstein, "Study Shows Benefits of Prison Work Programs," *Buffalo News* (December 26, 1991), p. 8.
62. Sexton, *Work in American Prisons,* p. 13.
63. Matthew Purdy, "Bars Don't Stop Flow of Drugs into the Prisons," *New York Times* (July 2, 1995), p. 1.
64. Ibid., p. 28.
65. Ibid.
66. Christopher J. Mumola, *Substance Abuse and Treatment, State and Federal Prisoners, 1997* (Washington, DC: Bureau of Justice Statistics, 1999).
67. James A. Inciardi, *A Corrections-Based Continuum of Effective Drug Abuse Treatment* (Washington, DC: National Institute of Justice, 1996).
68. Laura M. Maruschak, *HIV in Prisons 1997* (Washington, DC: Bureau of Justice Statistics, 1999).
69. Dennis Cauchon, "AIDS in Prison: Locked Up and Locked Out," *USA Today* (March 31, 1995), p. 6.
70. Maruschak, *HIV in Prisons 1997.*
71. James W. Marquart, Victorio E. Brewer, Janet Mullings, and Ben Crouch, "The Implications of Crime Control Policy on HIV/AIDS-Related Risk among Women Prisoners," *Crime and Delinquency* 45 (January 1999).
72. Jay S. Albanese and Robert D. Pursley, *Crime in America: Some Existing and Emerging Issues* (Upper Saddle River, NJ: Prentice Hall, 1993), pp. 200–23.
73. George W. Knox et al., "Preliminary Results of the 1995 Adult Corrections Survey," *Journal of Gang Research* 3 (Winter 1996), pp. 27–63.
74. Ibid., p. 39.
75. Ibid., p. 47.
76. Scott N. Tachiki, "Indeterminate Sentences in Supermax Prisons Based upon Gang Affiliations," *California Law Review* 83 (July 1995), pp. 1115–49.
77. Eric Tischler, "Can Tolerance Be Taught?," *Corrections Today* 61 (August 1999).
78. Ibid., p. 37; George W. Knox, *An Introduction to Gangs* (Bristol, IN: Wyndham Hall Press, 1994).

79. Bert Useem, Camille Graham Camp, George M. Camp, and Renie Dugan, *Resolution of Prison Riots* (Washington, DC: National Institute of Justice, 1995).

80. Glenn D. Walters, "Time Series and Correlational Analyses of Inmate-Initiated Assaultive Incidents in a Large Correctional System," *International Journal of Offender Therapy and Comparative Criminology* 42 (June 1998); Paul Gendreau, Claire Goggin, and Moira A. Law, "Predicting Prison Misconduct," *Criminal Justice and Behavior* 24 (December 1997).

81. Steve Marshall, "Nine Guards Injured in Ohio Prison Riot," *USA Today* (April 12, 1993), p. 10; Paul Leavitt, "Five Montana Inmates Killed in Uprising," *USA Today* (September 23, 1991), p. 3; Dianne Barth and Roger Neumann, "New York Inmates Hold Three Hostages," *USA Today* (May 29, 1991), p. 3.

82. Kevin Johnson, "Rioting Inmates Locked Away," *USA Today* (October 23, 1995), p. 2.

83. Knox et al., "Preliminary Results of the 1995 Adult Corrections Survey," p. 42.

84. "Racial Violence: Fact of Life Inside Prisons," *USA Today* (February 26, 2000).

85. *Whitley v. Albers*, 106 S. Ct. 1078 (1986).

86. Bruce Porter, "Terror on an Eight-Hour Shift," *The New York Times Magazine* (November 26, 1995), p. 42; Bruce Frankel, "Attica Inmates' Suit to Begin," *USA Today* (September 9, 1991), p. 3.

87. *Cruz v. Beto*, 405 U.S. 319 (1972).

88. *O'Lone v. Estate of Shabazz*, 107 S. Ct. 2400 (1987).

89. See *Howard v. Smith*, 365 F. 2d 28 (4th Cir. 1966); *Hill v. Blackwell*, 774 F. 2d 338 (8th Cir. 1985).

90. *Hudson v. Palmer*, 468 U.S. 517 (1984).

91. James Stephan, *Prison Rule Violators* (Washington, DC: Bureau of Justice Statistics, 1989).

92. Frank Green, "Guards Say Reform Endangers Lives," *Richmond Times-Dispatch* (March 27, 1997), p. 1.

93. *Wolff v. McDonnell*, 418 U.S. 539 (1974); *Superintendent, Massachusetts Correctional Institution, Walpole v. Hill*, 37 Cr. L. 3107 (1985).

94. *Baxter v. Palmigiano*, 425 U.S. 308 (1976).

twelve
Corrections in the Community

What should be done with a

misdemeanor offender who commits a nonviolent offense? Vandalism, public drunkenness, disorderly conduct, and all the other lesser crimes against public order and property certainly deserve attention, but *how much* attention should they be given by the criminal justice system? Should the punishment be jail time? A fine? Something else?

These questions are not new. In 1841 a Boston bootmaker named John Augustus raised the same issues. A public drunk was sentenced to jail, but Augustus intervened by posting the man's bail on the promise he would stop drinking. From that point on, Augustus acted as a "private angel and guardian of men convicted of crime." By the time of his death in 1859 he had posted bail for 2,000 convicts.[1] His idea that a middle ground should exist between jail and freedom formed the basis for the invention of probation in the late 1800s. Today this idea seems little more than common sense and has been adopted by every state.

This middle ground, known as **community corrections,** has since grown to encompass two different types of **sanctions,** or ways to punish or place restrictions on offenders:

1. Sanctions that are *alternatives to incarceration* in jail or prison, such as monetary penalties, probation, intensive supervision, and home confinement with electronic monitoring.

2. Supervision in the community *after a sentence of incarceration* has been served. Here the goal is to promote a smooth transition from confinement to freedom. Parole, work release, furloughs, and halfway houses fall into this category.

This chapter examines each of these forms of community corrections from the perspective of the offender, the potential victims, and the goals of the criminal justice system.

What Are the Alternatives to Incarceration?

t is sometimes argued that the phrase *community corrections* is a contradiction in terms. The argument goes like this: The two primary purposes of corrections are to punish offenders and to protect the public. Allowing offenders to serve their sentences in the community violates both of these purposes, because nonprison sentences do not provide "enough" punishment and also create the risk of further offenses by criminals who are not incarcerated. Responses to this argument focus on either economics or rehabilitation:

1. Imprisonment is the most severe and expensive type of criminal sanction, so it should be reserved for offenders who commit the most serious crimes.

2. The vast majority of offenders commit nonviolent crimes and will eventually be released from prison. Imprisonment tends to change offenders for the worse, but in the long run public protection is best ensured when criminals reform. Community-based alternatives to imprisonment are the best way to accomplish this.

Both of these arguments are correct—but they are not generally accepted by the public, which believes that imprisonment is necessary if the public is to be protected.[2] The dramatic growth in community corrections in recent years, therefore, has not been due to a change of heart on the part of the public. Public views on crime, criminals, and punishment generally have hardened. Instead, the rapid growth in arrests and prison populations, combined with the soaring costs of building new prisons and operating them, has led to more careful consideration of community corrections.[3] One survey asked several hundred residents how they would sentence twenty convicted offenders, and virtually all thought prison was appropriate. But after the costs of incarceration and available alternatives to prison were explained, the respondents "resentenced" many offenders to community sanctions.[4]

Alternatives to incarceration take several forms. Among these are monetary penalties, probation, intensive supervision, and home confinement and electronic monitoring.

■ **community corrections**
Sanctions that are *alternatives to incarceration* in jail or prison (such as monetary penalties, probation, intensive supervision, and home confinement with electronic monitoring), or supervision in the community *after a sentence of incarceration* has been served (such as parole, work release, furloughs, and halfway houses).

■ **sanctions**
Ways to punish or place restrictions on offenders.

TWO TYPES OF SANCTIONS

serve the sentence in the public

Fines As a Form of Criminal Sanction

Fines and whippings were the two most common penalties during the eighteenth century. In Massachusetts in 1736, a thief was to be fined or whipped upon a first conviction. The next time he would pay triple damages, sit for an hour on the gallows platform with a noose around his neck, and then be taken to the whipping post for thirty lashes. A third conviction resulted in death by hanging. Likewise, a burglar would first be branded with the letter B on his forehead. If convicted a second time, he would sit on the gallows platform with a noose around his neck for an hour and then be whipped. Upon a third conviction, he was deemed "incorrigible" and hanged. The rationale of the colonists was apparent: "Anyone impervious to the fine and the whip, who did not mend his ways after an hour with a noose about him, was uncontrollable and therefore had to be executed."[5] Jail was reserved for suspects awaiting trial and for debtors.[6] Fines were effective when the offender had some wealth, whereas whipping could be applied more generally. There was no clear-cut division by type of crime that distinguished offenders who were fined from those who were whipped. The choice of punishment depended on the circumstances of the offender rather than on those of the offense.[7]

Fines continue to be the most common form of criminal sanction in the United States, although they are used primarily in cases involving minor crimes or as an adjunct to incarceration for more serious offenses. There are at least two problems in the current use of fines as a form of criminal sanction: *proportionality* and *collection*. In most states the maximum fine for an offense is set by law without regard for the wealth of the offender. As a result, fines often lack meaning for wealthy offenders, whereas poor offenders (the largest offender group) often cannot pay even a moderate fine. Second, many fines go uncollected because of the lack of effective enforcement and collection systems in many states.[8] The Justice Department keeps track of fines received by U.S. Attorneys' offices, but fines are also collected through courts by probation departments, or in the form of payments to the victim.[9] The U.S. Courts National Fine Center was established to centralize and better organize the fine-collection process in the federal courts and to improve coordination among agencies, but there is no analogous agency at the state or local level.

2 problems with the use of fines.

Day fines, which are commonly used in Europe, offer a solution to the problem of proportionality. They are called "day fines" because the amount of the fine is based on some percentage of an offender's daily earnings. The court attaches a "unit value" to the seriousness of the offense (usually between 5 and 120 units), then calculates the fine by multiplying these units of seriousness by a percentage of the offender's daily income. An offender who takes home $40 per day, for example, is able to keep 40 percent ($16) for housing, 20 percent ($8) for food and clothing, and up to 40 percent of the remainder ($6.40) to support dependents. In this case the fine (gauged to the seriousness of the offense) could range up to nearly $10 per day, or 25 percent of the offender's daily income. Therefore, the amount of the fine is proportional both to the offense and to the offender's ability to pay.

A test of day fines in Staten Island, New York, found that average fine amounts were higher under the day fine system but that collection rates were not affected. Significantly, fewer arrest warrants were issued for offenders' failure to appear at postsentencing hearings, suggesting a higher compliance rate.[10] Also, judges were more comfortable imposing monetary penalties under such an income-based system. Day fine programs have now been implemented in other states.[11] Despite their advantages, day fine systems are still rare in the United States, where traditional offense-based fines are still used in most jurisdictions. There is some concern that day fines are unconstitutional in that they allow for different fines for the same offense, thus violating the Fourteenth Amendment guarantee of equal protection of the laws; but there have not yet been court challenges to day fines.

Probation

Probation is a criminal sentence of community supervision of the offender that is conducted by a probation officer. The term *probation* was first used by John Augustus to describe his efforts to bail offenders out of jail and allow them to live under supervision in the community. Augustus worked without pay, and he often placed those he bailed out of jail in his own home. He was careful in whom he selected, taking into account "the previous character of the person, his age and the influences by which in the future he would likely be surrounded."[12] Augustus helped offenders of all kinds, and he reported only ten absconders among the 2,000 cases he handled. He worked as a volunteer for eighteen years. Massachusetts did not use paid probation officers until 1878, when it enacted the first probation statute. Other states soon copied Massachusetts's system for providing probation officers to investigate cases and recommend sentences. This growth in probation was aided by the invention of the juvenile court at the turn of the century. This step formally recognized that juveniles should be handled differently than adults, and probation supervision seemed appropriate in a large number of juvenile cases. The first directory of probation officers, published in 1907, identified 795 probation officers, who worked primarily in juvenile courts.[13] By 1920 every state had adopted probation for juveniles, and thirty-three states had provisions for adult probation.[14]

Today probation is administered in a variety of ways. In thirty-four states adult probation is part of the executive branch of government; in nineteen others it is part of the judicial branch at the state or local level. In half the states a central probation system operates throughout the state; in others probation is operated by the county government, and in the remainder it is administered by the municipality. This variation is similar to that among police agencies, which also exist at all levels of government. There is debate over whether probation is best administered at the state or local level and whether it is best administered by the executive or judicial branch of

PROBATION TODAY

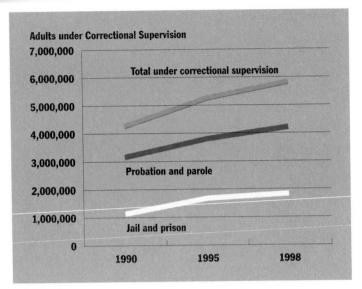

FIGURE 12.1

Adults under Correctional Supervision

SOURCE: Thomas P. Bonczar and Lauren E. Glaze, *Probation and Parole in the United States* (Washington, DC: Bureau of Justice Statistics, 1999).

government. A national commission concluded that probation is administered best at the state level by the executive branch of government, and there appears to be a trend in this direction, as several states have changed the way they administer probation in recent years.[15]

CLASSIFICATION OF OFFENDERS Most jurisdictions classify offenders to predict the likelihood of offenders' success on probation and the amount of supervision they will require. Classification or "risk prediction" scales summarize the outcomes in similar past cases and can be compared with a current case. These classification techniques have been used successfully to distinguish among high-, medium-, and low-risk offenders.[16] For example, offenders with substance abuse problems and prior felony records are much more likely than others to violate the conditions of probation and reoffend. Classification systems identify these and other risk factors so that high-risk offenders will receive more intensive supervision in order to reduce the risk of probation violations.

Probation is the most widely used form of correctional supervision in the United States. As Figure 12.1 illustrates, of the 5.9 million adults under correctional supervision in the United States in 1998 (2.9 percent of the adult population), 3.4 million were on probation.[17] Only eight years earlier, 4.3 million adult offenders were under some form of correctional supervision, including 2.7 million on probation; so the 1998 figures represent an increase of 36 percent in eight years. Of offenders serving probation sentences, 57 percent were convicted for felonies, 40 percent committed misdemeanors, and 17 percent were convicted for driving under the influence of alcohol.[18]

CONDITIONS OF PROBATION Offenders who are sentenced to probation usually have conditions attached to their sentences. These conditions are designed to control the offender's present behavior and to change it in the future. Conditions of control might include the following: no association with known criminals, no possession of weapons, no use of alcohol or drugs, and no leaving the jurisdiction. The conditions of control are designed to reduce the risk to the community while the offender is under supervision.

CONDITIONS TO CHANGE BEHAVIOR

– Curfew
– stay away from crowd.

Conditions designed to change behavior include mandatory drug/alcohol testing or treatment, education or employment requirements, community service, payment of fines, and/or restitution to the victim. The conditions seeking change are designed to produce conforming behavior once the probation sentence has ended. These changes are expected to result from treatment of addiction, steady employment, and greater understanding of the consequences of criminal behavior.

SUPERVISION OF OFFENDERS Supervision of offenders in the community poses a risk that prisons do not: People under correctional supervision might commit further crimes. This is the primary reason for negative public attitudes toward probation. Although probation is less expensive than incarceration, the huge prison construction programs in many states provide evidence that the public is willing to spend tax dollars in order to guarantee public safety.

The majority of probationers complete their sentence in the community without incident. According to figures compiled in 1999, probationers completing federal sentences show a success rate of 83 percent. Only five percent of federal probationers commit new crimes. Three percent test positive for drugs, and 2 percent become fugitives.[19] It has been found that misdemeanor offenders are much more likely than felons to complete probation successfully. Also, 21 percent of adult felons on probation were *not* recommended to the judge in the presentence report for placement on probation. These offenders were nearly twice as likely to have their sentence revoked as those recommended for probation.[20] This finding suggests that success rates on probation would be considerably higher if sentencing recommendations were more closely followed.

The impact of probation versus incarceration on the subsequent criminal careers of offenders has been debated for many years. Some believe that probation provides more opportunity for rehabilitation, whereas others believe incarceration has a greater deterrent effect. A twenty-year follow-up of nearly 1,000 felony sentences in New Jersey compared rearrests of offenders sentenced to confinement to rearrests of those sentenced to probation. Controlling for the age and criminal backgrounds of the offenders and the amount of time probationers spent in the community, the study found no difference in the proportion of offenders rearrested.[21] Approximately 55 percent of both groups had at least one new arrest after five years. This finding suggests that the impact of probation deteriorates after the end of the sentence and that the exclusive focus on felony offenders may mask the efficacy of probation for misdemeanor offenders. The difference in rearrests

EFFECTIVENESS OF PROBATION

What are this probation officer's primary concerns regarding his client? What are the client's responsibilities toward his probation officer? What kinds of felonies are typical in cases of probation? According to research, how effective is probation as a sentencing alternative to incarceration? How is probation similar to and different from parole?

10 min

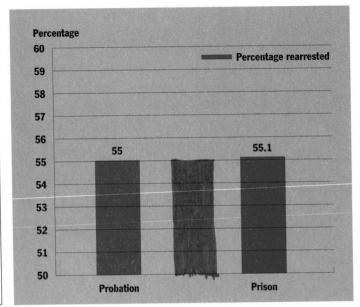

FIGURE 12.2
Percentage of Offenders with Any New Arrests Five years after a Sentence to Prison or Probation (adjusted for offender's risk and time spent in the community)

SOURCE: Don M. Gottfredson, *Effects of Judges' Sentencing Decisions on Criminal Careers* (Washington, DC: National Institute of Justice, 1999).

150 – 180 a probation officer has control over.

40 to 1 juvey

between offenders who were incarcerated and those placed on probation is summarized in Figure 12.2.

Intensive Supervision

intermediate sanctions
Sentences designed to provide more rigorous supervision than normal probation, yet something less expensive than incarceration.

Dissatisfaction with probation, combined with the need to use prison space more efficiently, has produced a movement toward **intermediate sanctions:** sentences designed to provide more rigorous supervision than normal probation, yet something less expensive than incarceration. These sanctions attempt to result in more punishment at less cost, but they raise three questions: (1) Are costs actually reduced? (2) Are these sanctions effective in controlling the growth of prison populations? And (3) do they protect the community?[22]

The oldest and most common form of intermediate sanction is intensive supervision programs for probationers and parolees. Jurisdictions achieve **intensive supervision** by maintaining small caseloads; making frequent contact with offenders under supervision; and requiring special conditions such as random drug tests, curfews, restitution to victims, electronic monitoring, or house arrest. Georgia was the first state to evaluate its intensive supervision program. It reported both reduced costs and lower recidivism.[23] Between 1980 and 1990 some form of intensive supervision was adopted in every state. Today about 5 percent of of probationers and parolees are in an intensive supervision program.[24]

intensive supervision
Probation or parole for which jurisdictions maintain small caseloads, make frequent contact with offenders under supervision, and require special conditions such as random drug tests, curfews, restitution to victims, electronic monitoring, or house arrest.

Evaluations of intensive supervision programs have shown mixed results. An evaluation of fourteen programs in nine states found that they provided effective surveillance of offenders but were costly and failed to reduce recidivism.[25] A study in England found a high rate of recidivism for offenders on intensive probation, but the rate was no higher than for offenders serving prison sentences.[26]

Media and Criminal Justice

SCARED STRAIGHT

In 1978 a film called *Scared Straight* not only won the Academy Award for best documentary; it also received such acclaim from policy makers and juvenile justice professionals that it was shown on television as a public service. This was highly controversial, because the film is rife with gratuitous profanity and graphic depictions of prison life. When the battle to show *Scared Straight* on public television was finally won in the late 1970s, the film could be shown only after 11:00 P.M., when children were presumably sleeping.

The irony is that over the years *Scared Straight* has become a such a classic in criminal justice and criminology that the film is now routinely shown to juveniles as a means of conveying the consequences of crime and the seriousness of incarceration. The documentary is a no-holds-barred look at the Lifer's Program at Rahway State Prison in New Jersey. This program, initiated and designed by prisoners serving life sentences for their crimes, involves having juvenile delinquents brought to Rahway for a full tour of the facility. Participants are not just guided through cells but they are locked in the cages and forced to experience the closed-in reality of a hard cot, filthy toilet, and pornographic graffiti. The cacophony of cell doors clanking shut and bells ringing is outdone only by the jeering and taunts of the inmates, who literally hurl spit and sexually explicit insults at the juveniles.

As the 1978 documentary shows, following the facility tour the teenage delinquents are locked in a prison room with a dozen lifers, who spend the next several hours enlightening them on the reality of prison life through plain talk, role-playing demonstrations, and direct threats. The prisoners steal the participants' shoes, to remind them of how the victims of their larcenies feel. One young man is challenged to attack an inmate to show how tough he is; when he chooses not to, that inmate suddenly "owns" the boy, then "sells" him to another inmate for a cigarette to show what happens to those who can't defend themselves. One double lifer threatens with genuine animosity to rip out the tearful eye of a young man "and squish it in front of your other good eye, so you can see what's happening to you as I do it."

The controversy surrounding the original *Scared Straight* revolved around its graphic nature and extreme profanity, but the point made by the documentary was that of the seventeen juvenile delinquents who went through the program that day, only one girl was arrested again in the following six months. The idea was that the Lifer's Program served as a tremendous deterrent to juvenile crime by focusing on still impressionable teens and literally "scaring them straight."

Critics would later argue that the *Scared Straight* documentary was premature in its claims of success, pointing out that long-term tracking of the Lifer's Program participants indicated a much higher rate of recidivism over time. To address such skeptics, the producers of the original documentary did their own longitudinal study, contacting the youths from the 1978 film ten years later, in 1988, and again ten years after that. The filmakers presented the true evidence in their 1998 made-for-television documentary *Scared Straight: 20 Years Later*.

The 1998 follow-up film provided tremendous qualitative data on how and why each youth came to be either a law-abiding citizen, a reformed criminal, or a chronic offender. The results were mixed. Quadir, who in 1978 had said that he planned to go to security school to learn how to dismantle locks and alarms in order to be a professional thief, was indeed incarcerated in 1998. The one girl who had reoffended within six months of her 1978 visit was now a working mother of three. One participant had died of an AIDS-related illness linked to his drug use; others had overcome drug addiction and alcoholism to become productive members of society. However, virtually every adult regarded his or her experience with the Lifer's Program as a pivotal point in the choice to avoid crime.

What factors do you think are involved in recidivism? What makes the Lifer's Program effective as an intervention? Do you think it should be continued? Why or why not? Do you think the Lifer's Program also could be used as a preventive measure? What might be some advantages and disadvantages of making the program mandatory for all youth rather than only to those with a record of delinquency? At what age would you recommend that youths participate?

It has been suggested that greater emphasis on treatment would lead to behavioral changes and result in lower recidivism. In California and Texas, offenders under intensive supervision who received substance abuse counseling, held jobs, paid restitution, and performed community service reoffended at a rate 10 to 20 percent lower than that of offenders who did not receive such treatment.[27] However, an evaluation concluded that there is little evidence that intensive supervision programs either rehabilitated offenders or deterred offenders from committing additional crimes more effectively than the sentencing options they replaced.[28] A 1999 study of day reporting in North Carolina, a program in which offenders are required to report daily in order to participate in treatment or employment programs, found the success rate to be low and questioned whether the program was cost-effective, given that most of those terminated returned to prison.[29] Thus, while intensive supervision programs have an intuitive appeal, they have not generally produced the anticipated outcomes. There are at least two reasons that may explain this lack of success: (1) The offenders chosen for intensive supervision are inappropriate, or (2) intensive supervision discovers more criminal activity. First, it is possible that a higher success rate could be achieved if offenders were more carefully screened before being assigned to intensive supervision programs. Substance abuse counseling, for example, works best for those motivated to kick the habit. Offenders not motivated in this way may be poor risks regardless of the level of supervision imposed. Second, it may be that closer supervision of offenders in the community is simply resulting in more discovery of recidivism. Offenders on intensive supervision may not be committing any more crimes than they did in the past, but probation officers may now be more aware of crimes because of more frequent contact with the offenders.

Confinement and Monitoring

An offender under home confinement is not permitted to leave his or her residence for purposes other than work, school, treatment, or other approved reasons. This form of punishment, sometimes called **house arrest,** can be a condition of probation or parole and is employed to varying degrees in every state.

A primary issue in home confinement is ensuring compliance. Increasingly this is being accomplished through **electronic monitoring,** in which offenders are monitored in the community by means of electronic devices such as radio and telephone transmitters. Such monitoring takes one of two forms: programmed or continuous contact. In programmed contact, the offender is called at home at random intervals and is required to verify his or her presence by voice or a code, or electronically through a device strapped to his or her wrist. In continuous contact, the offender wears an ankle bracelet that cannot be removed without setting off an electronic alarm. If the offender moves out of range of a receiver located in his or her telephone, the supervision office is notified electronically. In recent years house arrest has become synonymous with electronic monitoring, because manual mon-

house arrest
A condition of probation or parole in which an offender is not permitted to leave his or her residence for purposes other than work, school, treatment, or other approved reasons.

electronic monitoring
Surveillance of offenders in the community by means of electronic devices such as radio and telephone transmitters.

itoring requires more direct checks of offenders' whereabouts. The lower cost of electronic monitoring, combined with its more efficient surveillance of offenders in the community, has led to its widespread adoption.

The primary cost savings offered by home confinement are reduced jail or prison costs. If an offender can be supervised effectively in the community, the state does not have to pay for room, board, and round-the-clock supervision in jail or prison. In a 1998 study Virginia reported a total cost per day of $5.67 for an offender on home confinement with electronic monitoring, compared to an average jail cost of $47 per day.[30] On the other hand, if offenders under house arrest would normally have been placed on simple or intensive probation, costs are increased, because more resources are being devoted to surveillance of offenders in the community. This phenomenon is called **net widening.** This term refers to the process whereby more and more offenders end up being placed under supervision of the criminal justice system even though the intent of a program was to divert offenders out of the system.

The effectiveness of home confinement is not clear-cut; evidence from a growing number of jurisdictions has shown that it has both strengths and weaknesses as an intermediate sanction. Florida's home confinement program, the Community Control Program, placed more than 50,000 offenders under house arrest, mostly with manual monitoring. Each offender had a minimum of twenty-eight contacts a month with probation or parole officers. An evaluation found that about half of the offenders sentenced to house arrest would otherwise have been placed on probation, suggesting a net-widening effect.[31] But the other half would otherwise have been sentenced to prison; house arrest for these offenders may have had a positive effect on prison overcrowding. A follow-up study compared two groups of offenders matched by age, gender, type and severity of offense, and prior felony convictions, and found that reconviction rates for new offenses were slightly lower for those under house arrest (20 percent) than for those who had been sentenced to prison and then released (24 percent).

In many jurisdictions house arrest lasts no more than three months and is followed by regular probation. A seven-year study of offenders convicted of drunk driving or driving with a suspended license found that 97 percent successfully completed the electronic monitoring phase of their house arrest sentence. A third of these offenders, however, committed a new offense or technical violation while on regular probation.[32] This suggests that electronic monitoring may have only a temporary effect. An evaluation of three Canadian electronic monitoring programs concluded that "their effectiveness as a true alternative to incarceration and reducing recidivism has yet to be demonstrated."[33] House arrest may be effective for offenders with family members who do not mind the inconvenience of a homebound person who receives telephone monitoring calls or signals at all hours. But offenders can become bored and frustrated by their inability to engage in most behaviors, from doing the laundry to going for a walk. As a result, offenders view electronic monitoring as punitive, although better than jail,[34] and house arrest is more punitive than rehabilitative in nature. The build-

This offender is wearing an electronic monitoring device. What is the purpose of electronic surveillance? How is it used in house arrest? According to research, how effective is electronic monitoring as a deterrent against repeat offending in the short term? in the long term? What other means are available for supervising offenders in the community?

◼net widening
Process by which more offenders end up being placed under supervision of the criminal justice system even though the intent of a program was to divert offenders out of the system.

EFFECTIVENESS OF HOME CONFINEMENT

PROBLEMS WITH ELECTRONIC MONITORING

ing frustration with the limitations of life under house arrest may ultimately lead to violations of the supervision.

Another significant problem with electronic monitoring has to do with the imperfect technology of surveillance. Radio interference with electronic transmitters and receivers, mountainous terrain, and even cast-iron bathtubs have caused false alarms and alarm failures.[35] In one case a convict under house arrest was able to sell heroin from his apartment.[36] In another an offender was able to remove his bracelet and commit a homicide, causing New Jersey to drop its use of electronic monitoring for early parolees for three years.[37] Incidents like these give rise to concern over adequate protection of the community.[38] Electronics vendors are marketing new, improved electronic monitoring equipment that overcomes some of the flaws of earlier versions and improves the capabilities of probation and parole agencies to respond to violations.

How Can Ex-offenders Return to the Community after Prison?

Offenders convicted of murder and violent crimes receive the longest average sentences, but fewer than 2 percent of all felony convictions are for murder, and fewer than 17 percent for violent crimes.[39] Most offenders commit property crimes, and all but the most serious offenders eventually are released. Various kinds of programs have been developed to foster successful entry of offenders back into the community. These programs endeavor both to ensure that public safety is maintained and to improve the offenders' chances for rehabilitation.

PAROLE GUIDELINES

Some claim that unsuitable candidates have been released from prison and placed on parole; such releases reduce the effectiveness of parole and affect public safety. Parole guidelines have been adopted in many states and have contributed to more appropriate and consistent parole decisions.[40] These guidelines attempt to help jurisdictions make parole release decisions more uniform by employing standardized criteria. Nevertheless, public confidence in parole continues to erode, and fourteen states have abolished parole release altogether. Work/study release programs, furloughs, and halfway houses are examples of more restrictive forms of temporary release designed to promote successful transition from prison to freedom.

Parole

Parole is perhaps the least popular component of the criminal justice system. It consists of supervision in the community of offenders who were dangerous enough to have been sent to prison but are near the end of their sentences. Parole officers supervise the highest-risk offenders, and these offenders sometimes commit new crimes. The public is outraged when crimes are committed by parolees and cannot understand why dangerous offenders are allowed to go back into the community in the first place.

The logic behind parole is simple: Its goal is to provide a way for inmates to serve the last part of their sentence in the community under supervision in order to make a successful readjustment to freedom. Parole is one of three ways in which inmates are released. A second method is based on the accumulation of **good-time credits,** which are small reductions in the time to be served awarded to inmates for each day on which they obey prison rules. The third type of release is called **maxing out.** This occurs when the offender has served the entire sentence and has not been granted parole or accumulated enough good-time credits to justify early release. Parole is generally available only to prison inmates; jail inmates must serve their entire sentences, even though jail inmates are less serious offenders and presumably would be better candidates for parole.

PAROLE RELEASE DECISIONS In the United States parole is associated with indeterminate sentencing. Back in the 1870s Zebulon Brockway first included indeterminate sentencing and parole in his innovative program for youthful offenders. He persuaded the New York State legislature to adopt indeterminate sentencing and to shift the authority for prisoner release from the courts to corrections officials.[41] **Parole release** is decided by a parole board consisting of corrections officials and/or political appointees who evaluate the inmate's record and his or her behavior inside the prison. Using their discretion, they may release the inmate to serve the remainder of the sentence under community supervision. Parole thus is designed to provide supervised transition from prison to life in the community.

Offenders who are not released by the parole board can be granted supervised mandatory release if they accumulate enough good-time credits. These offenders are also supervised by parole officers. Inmates who max out and complete their sentences in prison are released, but because their sentence has ended they are not supervised in the community.

MANAGING HIGH-RISK OFFENDERS Managing high-risk offenders in the community is a difficult task under the best of circumstances. High caseloads, few resources for helping offenders make the transition into the community, and in some states poorly trained and educated parole officers are major issues. In many jurisdictions the caseloads of parole officers are too high to enable the officers to exercise meaningful supervision, a situation that suggests a lack of commitment to parole as a correctional strategy. Moreover, parole officers are not uniformly educated or trained. In some states a bachelor's degree and minimum training are required; in others there is no such standard. As a result, the quality of parole officers varies greatly. In many jurisdictions parole officers often lack the tools or resources necessary to help offenders adjust to life in the community. Parole officers need to be able to offer job training opportunities, job placement, training in basic skills, substance abuse treatment, and other resources if they are to intervene successfully in the lives of parolees. Despite all these

■**good-time credits**
Small reductions in the time to be served, awarded to inmates for each day on which they obey prison rules.

■**maxing out**
Release from incarceration after the offender has served the entire sentence without ever being granted parole or accumulating enough good-time credits to justify early release.

■**parole release**
Prisoner release decided by a parole board consisting of corrections officials and/or political appointees, who evaluate the inmate's record and his or her behavior in prison to determine whether the inmate will be released to serve the remainder of the sentence under community supervision.

shortcomings, however, approximately 60 percent of parolees have not returned to prison after three years. About half of those who do return are sent back for technical violations (e.g., drug test failure, curfew violations, or nonparticipation in required programs) rather than for new crimes.[42]

Work/Study Release and Furloughs

Prolonged incarceration can lead to a serious decline in inmates' capacity to function outside of prison. This decline is seen in several areas, including vocational and social skills, independence and self-esteem, and family support.[43] Temporary release programs are designed to reduce these effects by permitting inmates to enter the community on certain days for work, study, treatment programs, or family visitation. Given the increase in average sentence lengths in recent years, it is likely that temporary release will become even more important in the future.

Work release began as a way to encourage inmates' discipline and work ethic and as a response to complaints that offenders in prison were idle while free citizens had to work to support themselves. Today the reverse argument is employed: Paid employment for inmates is criticized at times when there is not enough work available for law-abiding citizens.[44] Depending on one's view, therefore, work release can be seen as a punitive consequence of incarceration or as a rehabilitative benefit.

Work release programs permit eligible inmates to work during the day at regular jobs outside the jail or prison, returning to the prison at night. Work release is generally not available in maximum security institutions; and even for inmates in medium or minimum security institutions, the ability to work is often affected by the location of the prison. Many prisons are located in rural areas where there are relatively few opportunities for employment.

The work release experience is designed to instill discipline, a routine, and work habits that closely resemble those found outside of prison. Inmates are paid the prevailing wage, although they are required to submit their earnings to the corrections authorities, who deduct 5 or 10 percent for room and board in the prison and payment of welfare agencies that may be supporting the inmate's family. The remainder of the inmate's earnings is placed in forced savings until the inmate is released. Approximately 65,000 inmates, fewer than 5 percent of the total inmate population, are involved in work release programs.

Study release is similar to work release, except that the inmate attends school by day and returns to the jail or prison at night. The study might consist of high school equivalency courses, vocational training, or college education. The inmate must meet the same entrance requirements as any other student, apply for admission, be accepted, and obtain permission from correctional authorities to attend the educational institution. Like work release, study release is feasible only for inmates in correctional facilities near educational institutions, which most prisons are not.

Two factors are most responsible for the limited use of study release: funding and public pressure. Unlike work release, study release costs money.

■ **work release**
Program that permits eligible inmates to work during the day at regular jobs in the outside world, returning to the jail or prison at night.

PURPOSES OF
WORK RELEASE

■ **study release**
Program similar to work release, in which an inmate attends school by day and returns to jail or prison at night.

Therefore, like any other student, an inmate must apply for financial aid to cover the cost of education. Funding is not always available, so most prison education is limited to that which takes place within prison walls. Public pressure also limits the use of study release. Concerns over public safety, along with complaints about inmates' being allowed to attend schools that many free citizens cannot afford, deter many corrections officials from allowing inmates to participate in study release. As a result, fewer than 500 inmates are currently participating in study release programs.[45]

Furloughs are unsupervised leaves from prison that are granted for only a few hours. The purpose of a furlough is to permit an eligible inmate to be present at a relative's funeral, visit loved ones, go to a job interview in preparation for release, or otherwise attend to personal or family matters. As with work release and study release, furloughs are designed to help the inmate prepare for a successful transition into free society.

This goal must be balanced, however, against the risk that the inmate might commit new crimes. The most infamous case of a furlough violation is that of Willie Horton. Horton was convicted of murder in Massachusetts and sentenced to life imprisonment. He was released on a furlough and did not return. He then kidnapped and raped a Maryland woman and assaulted her fiancé, and was arrested and tried for his new crimes. Shortly thereafter, the governor of Massachusetts, Michael Dukakis, ran against George Bush in the 1988 presidential election. The Bush campaign used the Horton case in commercials criticizing Dukakis for permitting furloughs for dangerous offenders. Furlough programs are permitted by state corrections policy or by state law, so Dukakis received criticism for a policy he did not implement. Even so, these ads hurt Dukakis's presidential ambitions; but, more important, they undoubtedly had an impact on the use of furloughs around the United States.

The available data suggest that furloughs are uncommon; fewer than 42,000 inmates (fewer than 3 percent of all inmates) are granted furloughs each year. In one year a total of 2,084 crimes were committed by inmates on furloughs, and 3,960 furloughed offenders absconded or returned late.[46] This is a failure rate of only 2 percent. Nevertheless, one sensational crime or violation can produce enough public and political outrage to kill a program, regardless of its merits.

furloughs
Unsupervised leaves from prison that are granted for only a few hours to permit an eligible inmate to be present at a relative's funeral, visit loved ones, go to a job interview, or otherwise attend to personal or family matters.

THE CASE OF
WILLIE HORTON

Halfway Houses

Halfway houses are residential centers for ex-offenders in the community. They originated with private efforts to help the homeless; houses established by the Quakers, the Salvation Army, and other religious and civic organizations to help the destitute and homeless emerged during the 1800s, and many of them are still in operation today.[47] Residents of halfway houses may be categorized as either halfway in or halfway out. Those who are "halfway in" have been sentenced to probation or diverted from the criminal justice system and are serving time in a halfway house as an alternative to incarceration. Those who are "halfway out" are near the end

halfway house
Residential centers for ex-offenders in the community. Most halfway house residents are parolees or similar inmates near the end of their sentence.

**PURPOSES OF
HALFWAY HOUSES**

of their prison sentences or are on parole.[48] Most halfway house residents are parolees or similar inmates near the end of their sentence.

There are nearly 500 halfway houses in the United States, with an average of twenty-five residents each. These facilities are located in multiple-family homes or apartment buildings, and residents spend from eight to sixteen weeks there. About 15,000 inmates, or about 2 percent of the total on parole, are living in halfway houses.[49] Halfway houses are considered a form of minimum custody correctional facility, and only offenders with that security status are eligible. The financial distinction between a halfway house and a minimum security prison is significant. A minimum security prison bed costs an average of $32,000 to build, whereas a maximum security bed costs $80,000.[50] Although there is no reliable estimate of the cost of halfway houses, they are considerably less expensive than prisons because of their lower security requirements. More than 90 percent of halfway houses are operated by private agencies that contract with the government to provide services for inmates.

Halfway houses refer residents for counseling, treatment, and employment services, and some provide these services themselves. Thus, halfway houses provide extra custody and services for offenders on probation, or less secure custody and services for offenders after prison. Offenders serving time in halfway houses often have no residence of their own and no family members who are willing to take them in. The halfway house provides food and shelter for a short period, enabling the offender to obtain a stable job and enough income to become self-sufficient.

There are no national data on the effectiveness of halfway houses, but individual reports have shown that they provide a useful, relatively low-cost transition for inmates returning to the community.[51] Their impact on recidivism has not been studied systematically, although it appears that recidivism rates for halfway house residents are comparable to those for offenders on parole.[52] This finding is significant, given that offenders in halfway houses are probably at higher basic risk of reoffending because of their lack of supportive family ties.

A continuing problem with halfway houses is public acceptance. Most people are reluctant to have ex-offenders living in their neighborhoods. Communities are more receptive, however, when they are given a voice in the usage and operation of the halfway house, when some space in the halfway house is available to community organizations, and when efforts are made to show how the residents might make a positive contribution to the neighborhood.[53] For example, halfway houses can help to stabilize a deteriorating neighborhood by establishing a visible presence of residents in a well-kept building that is open for community use.

Pardons and Commutations

pardon
A reprieve from a governor or from the president that excuses a convicted offender and allows him or her to be released from prison without any supervision.

A **pardon** is not actually a form of sentence, but it does allow a convicted offender to be released from prison without any supervision. Historically, pardons have been used as a form of parole to reward "reformed" offenders or those who in hindsight were deemed to have been given too severe a sentence. From the late 1700s to the late 1800s, for example, England sent its prisoners to Australia. The governor there could release convicts from their sentences by granting an *absolute pardon*, which restored all rights, including the right to return to England. A *conditional pardon* gave the convict Australian citizenship but not the right to return to England. A *ticket of leave* freed convicts from their obligation to work for the government or for a master and allowed them to work elsewhere.[54] The power to pardon resided in the king or queen. When the United States Constitution was drafted, the president was given the power to pardon. Article II states that the president "shall have power to grant reprieves and pardons for offenses against the United States, except in cases of impeachment."

There is considerable evidence that pardons were once used as a form of parole. During the mid-1800s more than 40 percent of offenders released from prisons were pardoned. In Ohio, pardons were granted to inmates to make room for new prisoners. Similar circumstances existed in other states until parole was adopted to make the release process more standardized and objective.[55]

Today pardons are acts of clemency rather than a kind of parole. They are entrusted to the chief executive: the governor in the case of state offenses, the president in the case of federal crimes. For example, in 2000 President Clinton pardoned a black man who had been a fugitive since 1961, after he fled after being sentenced to eighteen months in prison for draft evasion. The man refused to respond to an all-white draft board that would address him only by his first name after it learned he was black.[56] The pardon enabled the man, now sixty-three, to return to the United States without fear of arrest. A pardon excuses the offender from criminal penalties. Pardons are rare, and in most cases they are granted in order to remedy a miscarriage of justice. In many cases people serving prison sentences for murder have been pardoned when it was discovered that someone else committed the crime. On a less dramatic level, first offenders' criminal records are expunged if they complete special conditions and are not rearrested within a specified period; technically, this constitutes a pardon.

Pardon is distinguished from **commutation**, which modifies or reduces a sentence imposed on an offender. Commutations of death sentences to life imprisonment occur occasionally, especially during the holiday season. It is common for a governor to commute the sentence of a death row inmate as a sign of humane concern; this gesture is often made at the end of the governor's term and therefore cannot harm him or her politically.

CLEMENCY

▪commutation
A modification or reduction of a sentence imposed on an offender.

What Are Forms of Authentic and Restorative Justice?

n California an eighteen-year-old boy pleaded guilty to burning a cross on the lawn of a black family's home. No one was hurt, but a crime was committed. What would have been an appropriate sentence? Jail? Probation? A fine? The judge ordered the offender to read *The Diary of Anne Frank*, the journal of a young girl in hiding during the Nazi Holocaust. The offender had to submit a book report to the court.[57]

In a Maryland case, a teenager convicted of a drive-by shooting was required to read *The Ox-Bow Incident* and write a report on it while serving his jail sentence. The book describes people who take the law into their own hands and end up injuring the innocent.[58]

In Jacksonville, Florida, a seventeen-year-old girl pleaded guilty to manslaughter after having suffocated her newborn child and left it in a trash can. In addition to two years in prison, the judge imposed ten years on the contraceptive pill as part of the plea agreement.[59]

In each of these cases the judge, believing that no existing sanction was appropriate, invented an alternative sentence that fit the nature of the crime and the offender. The invention of new criminal sanctions became more common in the late twentieth century and has interesting implications both for society and for the criminal justice system.

Alternative sentences are of two general types: those that center on justice for the victim ("restorative") and those that attempt to punish the offender in accordance with the nature of the offense ("authentic"). In **restorative justice** the criminal justice process focuses primarily on "making the victim whole," or repairing the injury to the victim, rather than on the adversary relationship between the government and the offender. **Authentic justice** is based on the idea that sanctions should be more closely related to crimes and that offenders should be punished in ways that neutralize their gain.

Table 12.1 illustrates the differences between the elements of the restorative justice model and the traditional **retributive model of justice.** The role

> ■**restorative justice**
> Approach to criminal justice that focuses primarily on repairing the injury to the victim rather than on the adversary relationship between the government and the offender.
>
> ■**authentic justice**
> Approach to criminal justice that tries to relate sanctions closely to crimes and to punish offenders in ways that neutralize their gain.
>
> ■**retributive model of justice**
> Traditional approach to criminal justice that emphasizes the role of adversarial proceedings and punishment of offenders as retribution for their past acts.

TABLE 12.1

Characteristics of the Retributive and Restorative Models of Justice

RETRIBUTIVE JUSTICE	RESTORATIVE JUSTICE
Crimes are acts against the state.	Crimes are acts against another individual or the community.
Crime is controlled by the criminal justice system.	Crime control comes from the community.
Punishment holds offenders accountable.	Assuming responsibility and taking action to remedy harm results in accountability.
Victims are part of the community protected by the criminal justice system.	Victims are harmed by crime and are central in determining accountability.
Justice is pursued through the adversarial system.	Justice is pursued using dialogue and reconciliation, negotiation and reparation.
The focus is on punishing the crime that occurred in the past.	The focus is on the consequences of the crime and on how to make the victim and community whole again in the future.
Punishment changes behavior through retribution and deterrence.	Punishment alone is not effective, because it disrupts possibilities for harmony within the community.

of the community, the accountability of the offender, and the centrality of victims in the resolution of a case distinguish the restorative model; in contrast, the role of government, the adversarial relationship between the government and the offender, and punishment are featured in the retributive model, which underlies much of contemporary criminal justice.

RESTORATION VERSUS RETRIBUTION

Authentic justice attempts to link the nature of the penalty with the nature of the offense in a more explicit way than has traditionally been the case. Courts usually accomplish this by having the penalty mimic the crime to the extent possible. Examples of authentic justice, as this section will discuss, include shock incarceration, corporal punishment, public humiliation, and medical interventions for sex offenders.

Restitution and Repair

In the most common form of restorative justice, the offender provides **restitution** to the victim. Making restitution usually means paying money, but it can also include returning property or performing services for the victim. For example, an offender may be required to remove graffiti from a building or to earn money to replace stolen or damaged property. In such cases the offender compensates the victim for the loss either directly or indirectly. Restitution serves both as a way to restore the victim to his or her previous condition and as a way to punish the offender. Although there is widespread support for the concept of restitution, this approach is used infrequently in the criminal justice process. Most offenders are poor and have spent or lost any gain they received from the crime. They often possess few job skills and little education, disadvantages that reduce their access to money for restitution.

■restitution
Compensation for a victim's loss; a form of restorative justice that usually takes the form of money but can also include the return of property or services performed for the victim.

Community service is a way that offenders can be held accountable when direct restitution is not possible. As a condition of release, an offender can be required to work without pay for a civic, nonprofit, or government organization. Restoration of the grounds of public buildings and schools, conservation projects, and maintenance are among the community service tasks that have been performed by offenders. This form of restitution offers offenders the opportunity to make amends with dignity while providing needed services to the community.[60]

COMMUNITY SERVICE

Although restitution most often takes the form of monetary compensation, the harm caused to victims is very often physical, psychological, and/or emotional in nature. Also, many crimes have indirect victims such as the victim's family, which suffers from the victim's injury or loss of property. In an Alabama case a pregnant woman was killed, but her baby survived. The focus of the criminal case was exclusively on the culpability of the accused person.[61] Very little attention was given to the orphaned infant and the long-term impact of custody decisions. Similarly, there is a growing trend for police to make arrests in domestic violence cases, but less effort has been devoted to supporting the victims of such violence. In Georgia, for example, as many as half the women and children who seek shelter from abusive family members are turned away because of lack of space.[62] The restorative approach seeks to shift the focus of the justice process more toward repairing the harm done to the victim.[63] This is accomplished by direct involvement of victims and the community at large and by a justice process that relies on dialogue, negotiation, accountability, and reparation in achieving justice.

Mediation

After a crime has been committed, it is rare for the offender and the victim ever to speak to each other again. They may not even see each other, except in court. The prosecutor speaks on the behalf of the jurisdiction (which includes the victim), and the defense attorney speaks for the accused person. This arrangement further distances the offender from the victim and promotes an adversarial relationship.

Mediation programs provide a forum in which the offender and the victim meet in a neutral setting in an "atmosphere of structured informality."[64] At these meetings both the victim and the offender relate their versions of what happened and how it affected them. They can ask questions, communicate feelings of anger or remorse, and discuss ways in which the balance of justice can be restored in a fair and equitable manner. This may involve an apology, restitution, community service, or other alternative. An agreement is put in writing and the victim and offender discuss a restitution schedule, monitoring of the agreement, and follow-up procedures.[65]

Four benefits of mediation programs have been identified. First, mediation gives victims direct input into the justice process and lets them help determine an appropriate disposition. Second, mediation enables victims and offenders to communicate on a personal level, rather than through attorneys or not at all. Third, it allows victims to obtain closure on the trauma caused by the criminal event by exercising some control over its ultimate outcome. Fourth, mediation forces offenders to see victims as human beings with hopes, fears, and dreams similar to theirs. It thus leads offenders to understand and feel empathy for others. Studies have found that some victim–offender mediation programs do have these results. Victims are more likely to feel that justice has been done in mediated cases; in addition, higher rates of successful restitution and lower recidivism rates have been reported.[66]

A recent study found almost 300 mediation programs in the United States in which victims and offenders meet voluntarily with trained professionals.[67] The outcomes of these meetings often result in innovative dispositions, including help in refurbishing parks, installation of exterior lights, repair or demolition of deteriorated buildings, and community block watch patrols. When offenders participate in constructive efforts to make victims and neighborhoods safer, the goals of both restorative and authentic justice are served.

Shock Incarceration

At a boot camp for inmates in Florida, the regimen is not easy. One report summed it up: "Heads shaved. No phone calls for forty-four days, then just

■**mediation**
Process in which the offender and the victim meet in a neutral setting where they can ask questions, communicate feelings, and discuss ways in which the balance of justice can be restored; this may involve an apology, restitution, community service, or other alternative.

FOUR BENEFITS OF MEDIATION

These youthful offenders are undergoing shock incarceration in a military-style boot camp where they will learn to change the lifestyles that contributed to their criminal behavior. What makes this a form of authentic justice? What is the purpose of authentic justice? What might these youths be doing instead if they were engaged in restorative justice? If you were the victim of a theft perpetrated by one of these youths, what type of correction would you regard as most just?

to family. No TV, no recreation room. Marching in cadence. Obstacle courses. Spartan barracks. Psychological and substance abuse counseling. Five hours of classes. Homework. And a parade of victims, who tell the boys what it feels like on the other side of a gun."[68] This routine is much more severe and demanding than that experienced by most prisoners.

Many such **shock incarceration** programs were developed during the 1980s. They are short-term (three to six months) military-style boot camps designed primarily for nonviolent offenders. Although there is some variation in how boot camp programs are run, they all maintain a military atmosphere and strict discipline, and all are populated by young offenders for short terms. The extent of the camps' military atmosphere is manifested by the fact that the U.S. Army and Marine Corps train corrections officers to serve as drill sergeants in boot camps.[69]

Shock incarceration programs are examples of "authentic" justice because they attempt to mirror the nature of the crimes committed more closely than traditional incarceration does. That is, they try to re-create the shock of being victimized through a complete change in routine, attitude, behavior, and discipline. Boot camps are considered a better alternative than long-term imprisonment, where inmates are generally inactive. Shock incarceration forces inmates to engage in physical activity, drills, work, education, and counseling in order to change their attitudes and behavior patterns. The main characteristics of boot camp programs are summarized in Table 12.2.

Because of the rigorous physical activity they require, shock incarceration programs are designed for younger offenders. Most programs are designed for inmates who are serving sentences of less than five years or are in the second half of a longer sentence and have good records. Although originally designed for first offenders, a growing number of boot camp programs accept offenders with prior records of incarceration and convictions for violent crimes. There

■**shock incarceration**
Short-term military-style boot camp programs designed primarily for nonviolent young offenders and featuring a military atmosphere and strict discipline.

TABLE 12.2

Characteristics of Boot Camp Programs

CHARACTERISTICS	FEDERAL AND STATE* (N = 35)	LOCAL (N = 8)	JUVENILE (N = 9)
Year opened			
Before 1998	7	0	0
1988–1990	13	2	0
1991–1993	14	6	6
1994	1	0	3
Capacity			
Male	8,678	806	455
Female	626	102	0
Total capacity	9,304	908	455
Minimum length of residential boot camp			
<3 months	2	4	1
3 months	15	2	2
4 months	9	0	5
6 months	9	2	1

*There were 32 states known to operate boot camps at the time of the study.
SOURCE: Blair B. Bourque, Mei Han, and Sarah M. Hill, *A National Survey of Aftercare Provisions for Boot Camp Graduates* (Washington, DC: National Institute of Justice, 1996).

EVALUATIONS OF BOOT CAMPS

also are more than twenty-five jail boot camps that house inmates for two to four months in order to relieve jail overcrowding.[70]

Usually offenders volunteer to participate in boot camps rather than serving a longer sentence in a traditional prison. An underlying premise is that prisons have not been successful in deterring further crimes by offenders after release. The "shock" portion of shock incarceration, like basic training in the military, is designed to alter the offender's attitude, self-control, and lifestyle. Many inmates are not well prepared for shock incarceration. It is difficult to change a lifestyle that has developed over a period of years and is characterized by poor school attendance, drug use, lack of employment, and low levels of physical activity. Nevertheless, shock incarceration attempts to address these lifestyle issues; traditional incarceration, in contrast, tends to reinforce lethargic, unproductive behaviors, which often continue after release.

Evaluations of the impact of shock incarceration programs have revealed mixed results. These programs generally have not reduced recidivism compared to traditional incarceration. At the same time, offenders report that shock incarceration was a constructive experience.[71] In contrast, inmates who serve their sentences in prison do not view their experience as constructive. Part of the reason why boot camps have not had a stronger impact on recidivism is variation in the amount of time devoted to rehabilitative activities such as education; there is also a frequent lack of supervision or follow-up in the community after release. A national survey of fifty-two boot camp programs found that only thirteen had aftercare programs targeted at boot camp "graduates."[72] Therefore, most offenders completing boot camp programs are released to traditional probation or parole supervision, and the behaviors instilled in the boot camp program are not reinforced after release. Thus, offenders are, in essence, starting over when they reach the community. Boot camp graduates who are placed on intensive probation or parole supervision are under greater surveillance than traditional probationers and parolees, but more intensive services such as employment assistance and family counseling are not provided.

The possibility of long-term behavioral change through a short boot camp program has led to the development of similar programs for juveniles. Three demonstration programs were established in Cleveland, Denver, and Mobile, Alabama. An evaluation of these programs found offender completion rates to be high (between 80 and 94 percent). Committed youths also improved in educational skills, physical fitness, and behavior. Attitude surveys completed by youths after the program also showed improvements in respect for authority, self-discipline, teamwork, and personal appearance. The costs of shock incarceration per offender were lower than those of incarceration in traditional state or local corrections facilities.[73]

BOOT CAMP PROBLEMS

A continuing problem is how to keep offenders in aftercare services once the boot camp regimen is completed. Even though juveniles who remained in aftercare for at least five months reported positive changes in attitudes and behavior, nearly half of the juveniles dropped out of aftercare, were arrested for new offenses, or were removed from the program for rule violations.[74] There are many reasons for these failures in follow-up after release, but the major one is troubled home environments. Most youths in boot camp programs are from single-parent homes, half come from families receiving public assistance, and more than a third have one or more delinquent siblings. More than 30 percent of juveniles in boot camps have a parent or guardian who has been sent to court for child neglect or abuse, and more than a third of the parents have a criminal record. The lack of proper family support makes it difficult for a boot camp graduate to be successful in the community.

Another factor in ineffective boot camp programs is high staff turnover. In addition, staff members find it difficult to achieve a healthy balance between military discipline and remedial education and counseling.[75] The military discipline in boot camps is designed to build esteem, not simply to punish; but strict discipline and a hard physical regimen do not mix easily with education, counseling, and other rehabilitative services.[76]

Corporal Punishment and Public Humiliation

In 1994 an Ohio teenager, Michael Fay, committed acts of vandalism while visiting Singapore. Along with some friends, he spray-painted and threw eggs and bricks at eighteen cars over a ten-day period. Singapore police also found stolen flags and signs in Fay's Singapore apartment. Fay was sentenced to four months in prison, a $2,320 fine, and six lashes with a wet rattan cane. This kind of caning, administered by an expert in martial arts, breaks the skin and leaves permanent scars on the buttocks.[77] The sentence caused an uproar in the United States, with some people some defending it and others vehemently opposing it.

Corporal punishment is defined as physical punishment short of the death penalty. It has often been associated with torture and mutilation, and most forms of corporal punishment are illegal in the United States under the Eighth Amendment's prohibition against cruel and unusual punishment. In 1990, however, legislation was introduced in Texas that would have resulted in amputation of a finger for each conviction a drug dealer received.[78] This bill was an effort to imitate the penalty for theft in some Islamic countries, which is amputation of the offender's right hand.[79] Although such a penalty would seem to constitute a violation of the Eighth Amendment, it would be

■corporal punishment
Physical punishment short of the death penalty.

up to the courts to decide whether it was within the "limits of civilized standards" or "totally without penological justification."[80]

The U.S. State Department protested Michael Fay's punishment in Singapore, claiming that it was too severe. President Clinton called the punishment extreme and asked that it be reconsidered. This reaction is interesting in view of the long history of whipping as a form of punishment in America and elsewhere. Whipping was used as a form of punishment as far back as ancient Egypt, where Hebrew slaves were whipped by their Egyptian masters if they failed to produce enough bricks.[81] The Romans, and later the English, used whipping to punish slaves and vagrants. During the early 1800s England prohibited the whipping of women, but it was not until 1948 that whipping was abolished altogether as a form of punishment.[82] Whipping was employed for more offenses in the American colonies than it was in England. Lying, swearing, failure to attend church services, stealing, selling rum to Indians, adultery (for women), and drunkenness were among the crimes for which people could be whipped. After the American Revolution, incarceration came into use as an alternative to whipping. By 1900 all states except Maryland and Delaware had abolished whipping. The last known floggings occurred around 1950 in those two states, and the Delaware law was not repealed until 1972.[83]

Despite the American protests of the whipping in Singapore, the penalty is still used in many countries. A bill to permit whipping of drug dealers was introduced in the Delaware legislature in 1990 but was not passed. Legislation permitting whipping of vandals was introduced in California and in the cities of St. Louis and Sacramento in the early 1990s.[84] Amnesty International has reported that whipping is still legal in at least thirteen countries, including countries in the Middle East, Africa, the Caribbean, and the Far East.[85]

Singapore responded to criticism of its use of corporal punishment by stating that "it is because of our tough laws against antisocial crime . . . that we do not have a situation like, say, New York, where even police cars are not spared by vandals."[86] This leads to the question of whether whipping is effective as a deterrent to crime. An evaluation of the impact of whipping on subsequent criminal behavior of convicted offenders in the United States found that 62 percent of offenders who were whipped were later convicted of another offense. Further, 65 percent of those who were whipped twice were convicted a third time.[87] Despite the failure of flogging as a deterrent, whipping and other forms of corporal punishment, such as paddling of schoolchildren, continue to attract attention from the public and some policy makers.[88] There are two reasons for this: Corporal punishment more directly imitates the pain suffered by the victim, and it is of short duration and therefore much less expensive to administer than traditional incarceration.

Another ancient form of "authentic justice," public humiliation, also is newly popular. A judge in Pensacola, Florida, has given people convicted of minor crimes a choice: Serve jail time or buy an ad in the local newspaper that shows their photo and details of the crime.[89] A judge in Albany, New York, ordered a six-time drunken driving offender to place a fluorescent sticker saying "Convicted DWI" on his license plates.[90]

"Sentencing by public humiliation" has taken many different forms over its long history. In ancient Greece, deserters from the army were displayed in public wearing women's clothes. In England, public drunkards were walked through the streets wearing only a barrel.[91] Bridles were used on certain offenders in England and colonial America. These devices looked like cages that fit over the head with a metal plate that fit into the mouth. Any movement of the tongue was painful. Bridles were used primarily on "scolds," women who habitually lied or found fault with others.[92] Use of stocks, pillories, and the ducking stool continued in England, France, and America until the early 1800s. These devices held the offender in public view in extremely uncomfortable positions for the purpose of ridicule and punishment. Although the punishment itself was not painful, it was humiliating and exposed the offender to abusive remarks and to objects thrown by passersby. Offenders were sometimes seriously injured or killed when exposed in this manner.[93]

Branding of offenders through permanent scarring dates back to the beginnings of Western civilization. It was used in ancient Greece, and in fourth-century England offenders were branded on their thumbs (e.g., M for murderer) so that a judge could determine whether a person had a prior record. Branding was employed in the United States until the 1800s, and offenders were usually banished from the country.[94] Nathaniel Hawthorne's classic book, *The Scarlet Letter*, written in 1850, described the seventeenth-century practice of forcing offenders to sew letters on their clothing to represent the crimes they had committed. The letters (and sometimes complete descriptions of offenses, worn around the neck) were often used in the American colonies as punishments for blasphemy and public drunkenness.[95]

These sentences have been mimicked in recent years, although not duplicated. Some judges have required men caught soliciting prostitutes and those convicted of other minor crimes to pay to have their names and photos and descriptions of their crimes printed in local newspaper. Regency Cruises agreed to pay a $250,000 fine for dumping twenty plastic bags of garbage into the Gulf of Mexico, and the company was forced to run full-page ads in area newspapers stating that it had been convicted of the offense.[96] Are these authentic sanctions, or does public humiliation accomplish no purpose other than shaming? It has been argued that shaming is a useful form of sentencing, because it goes beyond mere punishment and instills feelings of guilt.[97] John Braithwaite claims that the criminal law is "too clumsy and costly a device to be a front-line assault weapon" for sanctioning and preventing crime.[98] He argues that consumer and professional groups, along with self-regulation, are better ways to deter corporate crime; and Braithwaite's argument may hold for the crimes of individuals as well. Just as media exposure of misdeeds and the resulting consumer distrust can do much to prevent repeat offenses by corporations, exposure of individual misdeeds to the media and to neighbors may have a similar impact outside the traditional sentencing process. In this way, public humiliation may exert a deterrent and preventive effect that traditional prison and probation criminal sentences have been unable to achieve with any consistency.

contemporary issues and trends

Registering Former Sex Offenders

he public has grave doubts about the ability of community corrections to control the conduct of ex-offenders. Nowhere is this more evident than in the case of sex offenders. Public concern reached a crescendo in 1994, when a seven-year-old New Jersey girl, Megan Kanka, was raped and murdered by a twice-convicted sex offender who was living across the street. Within six months of the incident, New Jersey passed "Megan's Law," a statute requiring former sex offenders on probation, parole, or furlough to register with police and for communities to be warned when such an offender was living there. The law also requires offenders to notify police of their location every ninety days and calls for penalties of seven months in jail and a fine if they do not comply.

Despite legal challenges, most states have followed New Jersey's lead. Once a sex offender has served his or her sentence, critics argue, the punishment has ended. Registration and notification laws allow a criminal sentence to continue as long as the offender lives, thereby punishing the offender again and again. The Supreme Court ruled in 1995, however, that it is constitutional to notify a community when a former sex offender lives there or moves into the area.[a] In 1998 the Court again rejected a challenge to New Jersey's Megan's Law, and the provisions of that law have now been adopted by thirty-seven states.[b] The Court did rule that judges must hold hearings to determine whether an individual sex offender is subject to

the notification law and to establish the extent of the warning to be given to the community. This due process provision is unlikely to make much difference, however. A CD–ROM has been released that lists the zip codes of California's 64,000 registered sex offenders. In fifteen states there are publicly accessible Internet sites that contain information on individual sex offenders, and five states are planning to add similar sites.[c]

The availability of this information to the public has led to vigilante behavior. Four days after one paroled child molester's name was listed, his car was fire-bombed; the crime was allegedly carried out by his neighbors.[d] A New Jersey man was attacked and beaten up by his son and two other men, who mistakenly believed that he was a child molester.[e] Five bullets were shot through the front window of the house of a former sex offender, after police circulated fliers in the area identifying him by name, address, and photograph.[f] Notification of the community regarding the release of sex offenders appears to produce panic rather than providing useful information. The notification itself implies that the state has some belief that the freed sex offender may still be dangerous, so it is not surprising that there have been some extreme reactions.

Even though fewer than 10 percent of all offenders are sex offenders, these cases are highly publicized, and public concern is quite high.[g] Nevertheless, few incarcerated sex offenders receive treatment, and the

> A New Jersey man was attacked and beaten up by his son and two other men, who mistakenly believed that he was a child molester.

treatment they do receive appears to be ineffective in many cases. Until more effective treatment of sex offenders occurs, notification will frustrate and aggravate people in communities rather than help them.

1. How is sex offender registration similar to house arrest or electronic monitoring of offenders?
2. Why do you believe sex offenders have been singled out for attention, rather than offenders who have committed murder, aggravated assault, or other serious crimes?
3. Under the guidelines set forth by the Supreme Court, in what way could a court hearing shed light on the necessity of notifying a community about the release or move of a former sex offender?

NOTES

a. Steve Marshall, "Megan's Law Upheld," *USA Today* (July 26, 1995), p. 2.
b. "New Jersey's Megan's Law on Sex Offenders Left Intact by Nation's Highest Court," *Buffalo News* (February 23, 1998), p. 4.
c. Devon B. Adam, *Summary of State Sex Offender Registry Dissemination Procedures* (Washington, DC: Bureau of Justice Statistics, 1999).
d. Arlyn Tobias Gajilan and Beth Glenn, "Sex-Crime Database," *Newsweek* (August 11, 1997), p. 12.
e. Paul Leavitt, "Sexual Predators," *USA Today* (August 28, 1993), p. 3.
f. Robert Hanley, "Shots Fired at House of Rapist," *New York Times* (June 17, 1998), p. B1.
g. Peter Finn, *Sex Offender Community Notification* (Washington, DC: National Institute of Justice, 1997).

Public humiliation sentences often are linked to reduced sentences or to no jail time, so they are rarely challenged in court. When they have been challenged, they have been found to be constitutional under most circumstances.[99] Public humiliation sentences are still rare, however, and no evaluation of their impact has been conducted. It will be interesting to see if public shaming has any greater effect than other forms of sentencing. Nevertheless, the line must be carefully drawn between sanctions that attempt to be more authentic in relation to the crime committed and those that are simply cruel or vindictive.

Why was the concept of chain gangs reintroduced during the 1990s? Why is this practice controversial? In what sense could you say that chained work gangs are related to community-based corrections? What are the main types of community-based corrections in lieu of incarceration? In what ways are offenders supervised in the community following incarceration?

Forced Birth Control and Chemical Castration

Darlene Johnson, the mother of four children and pregnant with a fifth, was convicted of three counts of child abuse. The Visalia, California, judge sentenced her to a year in jail, to be followed by implantation of a birth-control device that would prevent her from conceiving any more children. According to the judge, "It is not safe for her to have children."[100] Is such a sentence cruel and unusual, or is it authentic justice?

The contraceptive Norplant was approved for public use by the U.S. Food and Drug Administration in 1990. Norplant prevents conception when six small rods containing hormones are placed under the skin in a woman's arm. The rods can be implanted for a period up to five years.[101] The question for criminal justice is whether such a device can or should be used as a condition of sentencing in cases involving mistreatment of children. From the perspective of restorative justice, use of Norplant may prevent abuse of new victims, but it does not address the current or future harm done to present victims. Those who advocate authentic justice believe that use of Norplant is justified because it forces the offender to suffer the consequences of misconduct in the parental role and prevents the offender from continuing in that role in the future. Once again, however, *existing* victims are not protected, only *future* victims.

Norplant has been made available in school clinics in Baltimore in response to the city's high teenage pregnancy rate. A similar program was initiated in 1992 in Washington, D.C., where teenage mothers accounted for 18 percent of all births.[102] Although this use of Norplant outside the criminal justice system points to growing acceptance of this form of contraception, the coercion inherent in criminal sentencing poses important legal and social issues. Is forced birth control a weak technological attempt to solve a problem that is educational, social, and cultural in nature? Does the use of Norplant discriminate against women, inasmuch as it holds them entirely responsible for parenting and abuse, even though males also play a significant role in this process? Is this contraceptive used in discriminatory fashion against minorities and the poor? Can the use of Norplant be extended beyond the length of a normal jail or probation sentence? These questions

FORCED BIRTH CONTROL

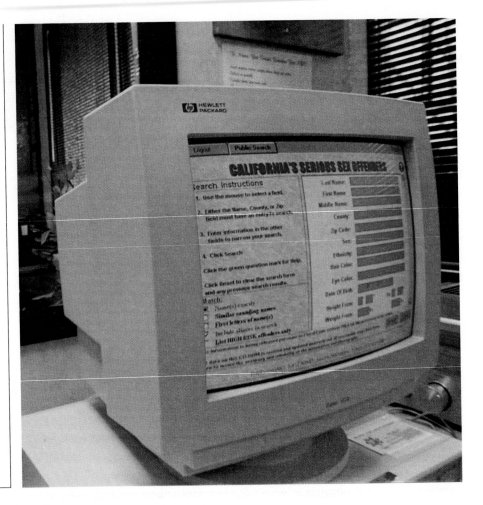

Some states require that convicted rapists and child molesters be registered with police and that the community be warned of their presence. What is the purpose of the sex offender registry? How do you think notification laws affect an ex-convict's reintegration into society? How have the courts responded to tests of states' notification laws? Are child molestation and rape caused by uncontrollable urges for sexual release? What treatments for sex offenders are based on this assumption? What arguments point to sociological rather than biological causes of sexual violence and sexual exploitation?

**CHEMICAL
CASTRATION**

have yet to be addressed by the criminal justice system as it looks for sentences that more directly mirror the nature of the harm inflicted by offenders.

Frustration over the difficulty of preventing sex offenses also has led to proposals for the use of hormones in sentencing. It has been estimated that rapists commit an average of seven rapes and that a child molester abuses an average of seventy-five children.[103] The State of Washington now requires male sex offenders to be given the option of castration in return for a 75 percent reduction in prison time.[104] In 1997 California enacted a law that requires "chemical castration" (by hormones) of parolees with more than one conviction for child molestation.[105] More common, however, are efforts to treat sex offenders with drugs that merely reduce their sex drive.

The compulsion of some sex offenders to seek out victims repeatedly, despite prior punishment for sex crimes, has led researchers to examine possible biological factors in this type of crime. Some researchers have concluded that there are rapists who suffer from an abnormally high level of the male sex hormone testosterone. As a result, these offenders have an "uncontrollable" urge to seek physical "release." Consider the case of Alcides Quiles, who escaped from a Connecticut prison while serving time for raping a six-year-old boy, only to be caught after raping a two-year-old girl.[106] Crimes such as these have led to the use of the drug Depo-Provera, which causes impotence. Sometimes referred to as "chemical castration," medication with Depo-Provera relieves the biological urge in sex offenders.[107] It does this through its active ingredient, a synthetic hormone similar to progesterone. (Depo-Provera is also used as a contraceptive, as one injection protects a woman against pregnancy for three months.[108])

Such drug treatments remain controversial. Richard Seeley, director of Minnesota's Intensive Treatment Program for Sexual Aggressiveness, argues that "what's wrong with a sex offender is what's between his ears, not his legs." Seeley claims that it is the rapist's thinking that is dysfunctional, not his sexuality. "Rapists are who they learn to be—it's not a product of their hormones."[109] Rape is often the result of anger and rage in which the offender seeks domination or control over the victim. This anger is not affected by Depo-Provera, leading to speculation that assaultive behavior will continue. This debate continues today. A Texas judge offered a sex offender the opportunity for physical castration (removal of the testicles) in exchange for his freedom. The possibility was abandoned when no physician would come forward to perform the procedure. But this will not always be the case. A Texas gubernatorial candidate supported chemical castration for sex offenders seeking parole.[110]

As with Norplant, the use of Depo-Provera as a sentencing option is an outgrowth of frustration over the ineffectiveness of traditional sentencing alternatives. The social and legal issues posed by Depo-Provera mirror those posed by Norplant, with the added concern that physical castration is a permanent condition. (Chemical castration can be reversed, however, by discontinuation of the drug.) Chemical castration through Depo-Provera has drawn support not because it is likely to be more effective than traditional sentencing—it is unclear what proportion of rapes have hormonal versus social causes—but because such a sentence more authentically reflects the nature of the crime committed.

Forfeitures and Fees

The "war on drugs" strives to reduce drug abuse and drug-related crime, but long prison sentences for drug offenders have not had a major impact on the drug trade.[111] An alternative to prison sentences is emphasis on a more authentic and restorative sanction: taking the profit out of the highly profitable drug market. The Organized Crime Drug Enforcement Task Force (OCDETF) program, established in 1983 to prosecute high-level drug traffickers, responds to the perception that drug offenders often consider prison sentences merely as a price to be paid for conducting their business. Consisting of members from the major federal law enforcement agencies, OCDETF attempts to seize the illicit assets of drug traffickers. Seizure involves a civil or criminal forfeiture of property if the government can prove that the property was acquired or used illegally. A criminal forfeiture occurs when property is seized after the owner has been convicted of certain crimes, such as drug trafficking or racketeering. A civil forfeiture requires only that the government show probable cause that the property was involved in criminal activity. The burden shifts to the property owner, who must show that such probable cause does not exist.[112] For example, when organized crime boss John Gotti was convicted of racketeering, the government filed a civil forfeiture suit against seven buildings and three businesses that it believed were involved in Gotti's illegal activities. These businesses included a social club, a bar, a restaurant, and a clothing manufacturer, among other enterprises.[113] Similarly, in a North Carolina case drug traffickers used their illicit profits to buy property within the state; they then sold that property and bought property in Florida. Using asset forfeiture, the government was able to seize the Florida property as "derivative proceeds" of crime.[114]

**PURPOSES OF
CIVIL FORFEITURE**

Cash, cars, boats, planes, jewelry, and weapons constitute 95 percent of all seized assets, although real estate has higher monetary value. Seized property is appraised, and each month the government lists forfeited property in *USA Today* to notify anyone who may hold a claim or lien on the property that the property will be put up for auction. Some jurisdictions allow law enforcement agencies to employ the seized property in combating crime by using seized cars as surveillance vehicles and cash for undercover drug purchases. Seizure of the proceeds of crime, especially the proceeds of high-profit drug crimes, can wipe out any financial gain achieved through illicit activities. Over the fifteen-year period from 1980 to 1995, the value of property seized by the federal government in asset forfeiture cases rose from $33 million to $2 billion.[115]

In 1996 the Supreme Court held that civil forfeitures are not excessive under the Eighth Amendment. The Court did not explain, however, when a forfeiture is considered excessive.[116] For example, a drug dealer who is found to have packaged drugs in his house, transported them in his car, and held drug-related telephone conversations from his boat can have his house, car, and boat seized under forfeiture provisions in addition to any criminal penalties he may face. In 1997 the Supreme Court ruled that civil forfeitures that occur together with criminal punishment do not violate the constitutional protection against double jeopardy.[117] Therefore, it is not considered double punishment for an offender to be convicted of a crime and incarcerated and then have the government pursue a civil forfeiture. Several instances in which innocent persons lost property and were injured in civil seizures based on false informant tips have resulted in closer scrutiny of the forfeiture process.[118] Nevertheless, asset forfeiture is an alternative sanction that attempts to address the motives behind profit-driven crimes and restore the balance of justice.

**OFFENDER FEE
PROGRAMS**

The rising cost of corrections has led many jurisdictions to impose offender fees. These fees are assessed to help pay for the cost of probation, parole, prison, or other forms of correctional supervision. Offender fees are now imposed in forty states, although not all states impose fees on all offenders. Some states restrict fees to probationers or jail inmates, or base the fee on the type of offense, the type of offender, or the offender's ability to pay.

Offender fee programs are based on the recognition that most offenders under community supervision are employed and can afford reasonable

critical thinking exercise

The Return of Chain Gangs

In 1995, Alabama and Florida became the first states to reintroduce chain gangs as a correctional technique. Chain gangs are groups of offenders, sometimes chained together at the ankle, who are taken out of prison to perform roadside cleanup tasks under the supervision of an armed guard. The inmates are returned to the prison at dusk.

On one hand, it can be argued that chain gangs are a part of community corrections. Inmates are on a form of "work release" (albeit under strict supervision) on which they are forced to perform work and returned to prison at the end of the day. Prison officials point out that one corrections officer can supervise up to forty chained prisoners, making chain gangs a cost-effective form of supervision. In addition, chain gangs, unlike inmates in prisons out of public view, serve as a visible deterrent to passersby. The wearing of leg irons has also been said to instill discipline and shame.[a,b,c]

On the other hand, chaining criminals together is a throwback to the past; one politician has called it "a return to slavery." Chain gangs were used to control African Americans in the South after the Civil War, and some believe they symbolize a legacy of racial injustice. Chain gangs are humiliating and can make an inmate "feel like an animal." The resulting anger may cause greater frustration and possibly more violence or vengefulness when offenders are released. Furthermore, there is no empirical evidence showing that chain gangs deter future criminal activity.[e,f,g]

Nevertheless, certain types of offenders, such as DUI (driving under the influence) offenders, have not responded well to existing forms of punishment. Since 1990 the number of DUI offenders under correctional supervision (jail, prison, probation, parole) has doubled to more than 500,000, but a third of DUI of-

fenders on probation and two-thirds of those in jail or prison had prior DUI sentences. Of DUI offenders in jail, more than half were out on probation, parole, or bail at the time of their new offense.[d] Even though many of these offenders were assessed fines or fees or were placed in alcohol or drug treatment programs, the high rate of recidivism has led to support for alternative sentences. Chain gains endeavor to change these offenders through shaming and supervision as well as to repair the harm caused.

CRITICAL THINKING QUESTIONS

1. In what ways are chain gangs similar to and different from work release and intensive supervision?
2. If jail and probation have not deterred repeat DUI offenders, why do you believe work on a chain gang would be any different?
3. How can it be argued that work on a chain gang is dehumanizing? Does this correctional technique violate the Eighth Amendment?

NOTES

a. "Florida Reintroduces Chain Gangs," *Harvard Law Review* 109 (February 1996), pp. 876–81.
b. Tessa M. Gorman, "Back on the Chain Gang: Why the Eighth Amendment and the History of Slavery Proscribe the Resurgence of Chain Gangs," *California Law Review* 85 (March 1997), pp. 441–78.
c. Adam Cohen, "Back on the Chain Gang," *Time* (May 15, 1995), p. 26.
d. Laura M. Maruschak, *DWI Offenders under Correctional Supervision* (Washington, DC: Bureau of Justice Statistics, 1999).
e. Marylee N. Reynolds, "Back on the Chain Gang," *Corrections Today* 58 (April 1996), pp. 108–5.
f. Emily S. Sanford, "The Propriety and Constitutionality of Chain Gangs," *Georgia State University Law Review* 13 (July 1997), pp. 1155–86.
g. Lori Sharn, "Chain Gangs Back in Alabama," *USA Today* (May 4, 1995), p. 3.

fees—and that the costs of operating state and local corrections systems are skyrocketing as correctional populations grow. In Texas, half of the total cost of probation supervision is paid by offender fees.[119] To be effective, such a program must be systematic, and jurisdictions must closely monitor collections to ensure compliance.[120]

Offender fee programs can be seen as a way to hold offenders accountable for their conduct and its long-term consequences. The fees offset the impact the offender has on the criminal justice system by providing compensation to the state. They attempt to reestablish the balance of justice in the community by helping to return the justice system to its previous status before the crime was committed.

Summary

WHAT ARE THE ALTERNATIVES TO INCARCERATION?

- Monetary fines are the most common form of criminal sanction in the United States. Fines are used primarily in cases involving minor crimes or as an adjunct to incarceration for more serious offenses.
- Fines have problems of proportionality and collection, which can be overcome to some extent by the use of "day fines" based on offenders' daily earnings.
- Probation is a system in which offenders are allowed to live in the community under supervision. Offenders who are sentenced to probation usually have conditions attached to their sentences.
- Supervision of offenders in the community poses the risk that these offenders may commit further crimes.
- Dissatisfaction with probation, combined with the need to use prison space more efficiently, has produced a movement toward intermediate sanctions, which provide more rigorous supervision than normal probation yet are less expensive than incarceration.
- Jurisdictions achieve intensive supervision by maintaining small caseloads, making frequent contact with offenders under supervision, and imposing special conditions such as random drug tests.
- An offender under home confinement or house arrest may leave his or her residence only for approved reasons. Compliance is increasingly ensured through electronic monitoring.

HOW CAN EX-OFFENDERS RETURN TO THE COMMUNITY AFTER PRISON?

- The purpose of parole is to allow inmates to serve the last part of their sentence in the community under supervision in order to readjust to freedom.
- Parole is associated with indeterminate sentencing. Parole release is decided by a parole board consisting of corrections officers.
- Offenders who are not released by a parole board can be granted supervised mandatory release if they accumulate enough good-time credits.
- Because prolonged incarceration can reduce inmates' capacity to function outside of prison, some states have temporary release programs that allow inmates to enter the community for work, study, or other purposes.
- Work or study release programs permit eligible inmates to work or take courses outside the prison during the day and return to the prison at night. Furloughs are unsupervised leaves from prison for specific purposes and are granted for only a few hours.
- Halfway houses are residential centers for ex-offenders in the community. These facilities refer residents for counseling, treatment, and employment services.

- A pardon allows a convicted offender to be released from prison without any supervision. A pardon excuses the offender from criminal penalties—unlike a commutation, which modifies or reduces a sentence.

WHAT ARE FORMS OF AUTHENTIC AND RESTORATIVE JUSTICE?

- Advocates of restorative justice believe that who wins the case is less important than "making the victim whole."
- In the most common form of restorative justice, the offender provides restitution to the victim.
- Mediation programs provide a neutral setting in which offenders and victims can ask each other questions and communicate their feelings about the offense.
- Some forms of restorative justice are designed to repair the physical or psychological harm done to the victim.
- Authentic justice seeks to link the nature of the penalty with the nature of the offense in a direct, tangible way.
- Shock incarceration creates a military-style boot camp atmosphere in which inmates are forced to engage in physical activity, drills, work, education, and counseling. Usually offenders volunteer to participate in boot camps rather than serving a longer sentence in a traditional prison.
- Corporal punishment is physical punishment short of the death penalty. It has a long history in the United States, and it is supported by some advocates of authentic justice because it imitates the pain suffered by the victim.
- Public humiliation also has a long history and can take many different forms. Although there is renewed interest in this approach, public humiliation sentences are still rare.
- Forced birth control has been used as a punishment in cases involving child abuse.
- Some jurisdictions have attempted to treat sex offenders with drugs that reduce their sex drive. These treatments are controversial, because some experts believe that the behavior of sex offenders is psychologically rather than biologically motivated.
- Forfeiture of assets is increasingly being used in cases involving drug trafficking.
- Some jurisdictions impose offender fees on offenders under community supervision who are employed and can afford reasonable fees.

Key Terms

community corrections
sanctions
intermediate sanctions
intensive supervision
house arrest
electronic monitoring
net widening
good-time credits
maxing out
parole release
work release
study release

furloughs
halfway houses
pardon
commutation
restorative justice
authentic justice
retributive model of justice
restitution
mediation
shock incarceration
corporal punishment

Questions for Review and Discussion

1. Why could it be said that the phrase *community corrections* is a contradiction in terms?
2. What do we mean when we say that there is a problem of proportionality in the use of fines as a criminal sanction?
3. What kinds of conditions are usually attached to the sentences of offenders on probation?
4. In what circumstances does probation appear to work best?
5. What are the advantages and disadvantages of house arrest?
6. What is parole, and why is it unpopular with the public?
7. Why are inmates sometimes permitted to participate in work release programs?
8. What is a halfway house?
9. What is the difference between a pardon and a commutation?
10. What legal issues are associated with probation and parole?
11. What is the philosophy underlying restorative justice?
12. What are the major forms of restorative justice?
13. What is meant by authentic justice?
14. What are the main features of shock incarceration, and what is their purpose?
15. What are some drawbacks of boot camp programs?
16. Briefly describe the history of corporal punishment in the United States.
17. Give an example of public humiliation as a criminal sanction.
18. What are some arguments against the use of forced birth control for child abusers?
19. Why is the use of drug treatments for sex offenders controversial?
20. What is the purpose of forfeiture of assets in drug trafficking cases?
21. What are offender fees?

Notes

1. Lawrence M. Friedman, *A History of American Law,* 2nd ed. (New York: Basic Books, 1985), p. 596.
2. Michael N. Castle, *Alternative Sentencing: Selling It to the Public* (Washington, DC: National Institute of Justice, 1991), p. 1; Dan M. Kahan, "What Do Alternative Sanctions Mean?," *University of Chicago Law Review* 63 (Spring 1996), pp. 591–653.
3. Leena Kurki, *Incorporating Restorative and Community Justice into American Sentencing and Corrections* (Washington, DC: National Institute of Justice, 1999); "If Not Jail, What?," *The Economist* 337 (December 9, 1995), p. 26.
4. Cited in Castle, *Alternative Sentencing,* p. 2; Laura A. Winterfield and Sally T. Hillsman, *The Staten Island Day-Fine Project* (Washington, DC: National Institute of Justice, 1993), p. 1.
5. David J. Rothman, *The Discovery of the Asylum* (Boston: Little, Brown, 1971), p. 52.
6. Ibid., p. 48.
7. Ibid., p. 49.
8. George F. Cole, *Innovations in Collecting and Enforcing Fines* (Washington, DC: National Institute of Justice, 1989).
9. U.S. Comptroller General, *National Fine Center* (Washington, DC: U.S. General Accounting Office, 1993).
10. Winterfield and Hillsman, *The Staten Island Day-Fine Project.*
11. Vera Institute of Justice, *How to Use Structured Fines (Day Fines) as an Intermediate Sanction* (Washington, DC: Bureau of Justice Assistance, 1996).
12. John Augustus, *John Augustus, First Probation Officer* (Montclair, NJ: Patterson Smith, 1972), p. 34.

13. Howard Abadinsky, *Probation and Parole: Theory and Practice* (Upper Saddle River, NJ: Prentice Hall, 1997), p. 33.

14. David Rothman, *Conscience and Convenience: The Asylum and Its Alternatives in Progressive America* (Boston: Little, Brown, 1980), p. 44.

15. National Institute of Corrections, *State and Local Probation Systems in the United States* (Washington, DC: U.S. Department of Justice, 1993); National Advisory Commission on Criminal Justice Standards and Goals, *Corrections* (Washington, DC: U.S. Government Printing Office, 1973), p. 316.

16. Jay S. Albanese, Bernadette A. Fiore, Jerie H. Powell, and Janet R. Storti, *Is Probation Working?: A Guide for Managers and Methodologists* (Lanham, MD: University Press of America, 1981).

17. Thomas P. Bonczar and Lauren E. Glaze, *Probation and Parole in the United States* (Washington, DC: Bureau of Justice Statistics, 1999).

18. Ibid.

19. Steven K. Smith and John Scalia, Jr., *Compendium of Federal Justice Statistics* (Washington, DC: Bureau of Justice Statistics, 1999).

20. Patrick A. Langan and Mark A. Cuniff, *Recidivism of Felons on Probation* (Washington, DC: Bureau of Justice Statistics, 1992); Thomas P. Bonczar, *Characteristics of Adults on Probation* (Washington, DC: Bureau of Justice Statistics, 1997).

21. Don M. Gottfredson, *Effect of Judges' Sentencing Decisions on Criminal Careers* (Washington, DC: National Institute of Justice, 1999).

22. Todd R. Clear and Patricia Hardyman, "The New Intensive Supervision Movement," *Crime and Delinquency* 36 (1990), pp. 42–60; Rebecca D. Petersen and Dennis J. Palumbo, "The Social Construction of Intermediate Punishments," *Prison Journal* 77 (March 1997), pp. 77–92.

23. Billie S. Irwin and Lawrence A. Bennett, *New Dimensions in Probation: Georgia's Experience with Intensive Probation Supervision* (Washington, DC: National Institute of Justice, 1987); Billie S. Irwin, "Turning Up the Heat on Probationers in Georgia," *Federal Probation* 50 (1986), p. 2.

24. Allen J. Beck, *Correctional Populations in the United States* (Washington, DC: Bureau of Justice Statistics, 1999).

25. Joan Petersilia and Susan Turner, *Evaluating Intensive Supervision Probation/Parole: Results of a Nationwide Experiment* (Washington, DC: National Institute of Justice, 1993).

26. Ian D. Brownlee, "Intensive Probation with Young Adult Offenders: A Short Reconviction Study," *British Journal of Criminology* 35 (autumn 1995), pp. 599–612.

27. Petersilia and Turner, *Evaluating Intensive Supervision Probation/Parole*, p. 9.

28. Dale Parent, Terence Dunworth, Douglas McDonald, and William Rhodes, *Intermediate Sanctions* (Washington, DC: National Institute of Justice, 1997), p. 4.

29. Liz Marie Marciniak, "The Use of Day Reporting as an Intermediate Sanction: A Study of Offender Targeting and Program Termination," *The Prison Journal* 79 (June 1999), pp. 205–25.

30. Virginia State Crime Commission, *The Use of Home Electronic Incarceration in Virginia* (Richmond: Commonwealth of Virginia, 1998).

31. Dennis Wagner and Christopher Baird, *Evaluation of the Florida Community Control Program* (Washington, DC: National Institute of Justice, 1993).

32. J. Robert Lilly, Richard A. Ball, David Curry, and John McMullen, "Electronic Monitoring of the Drunk Driver: A Seven Year Study of the Home Confinement Alternative," *Crime and Delinquency* 39 (1993), pp. 462–84.

33. James Bonta, Suzanne Wallace-Capretta, and Jennifer Rooney, "Can Electronic Monitoring Make a Difference? An Evaluation of Three Canadian programs," *Crime and Delinquency* 46 (January 2000), pp. 61–75.

34. Randy R. Gainey and Brian K. Payne, "Understanding the Experience of House Arrest with Electronic Monitoring: An Analysis of Quantitative and Qualitative Data," *International Journal of Offender Therapy and Comparative Criminology* 44 (2000), pp. 84–96; Terry L. Baumer and Robert I. Mendelsohn, "Electronically Monitored Home Confinement: Does It Work?," in James M. Byrne, Arthur J. Lurigio, and Joan Petersilia, eds., *Smart Sentencing: The Emergence of Intermediate Sanctions* (Newbury Park, CA: Sage, 1995), pp. 54–67.

35. Baumer and Mendelsohn, "Electronically Monitored Home Confinement."

36. "Paterson," *USA Today* (June 1, 1992), p. 8.

37. "Trenton," *USA Today* (October 9, 1992), p. 10; "Newark," *USA Today* (January 16, 1995), p. 6.

38. Daniel Ford and Anneseley K. Schmidt, *Electronically Monitored Home Confinement* (Washington, DC: National Institute of Justice, 1985).

39. Jodi M. Brown and Patrick A. Langan, *Felony Sentences in the United States* (Washington, DC: Bureau of Justice Statistics, 1999).

40. Don M. Gottfredson, Leslie T. Wilkins, and Peter B. Hoffman, *Guidelines for Parole and Sentencing* (Lexington, MA: Lexington Books, 1978).

41. Belinda Rodgers McCarthy and Bernard J. McCarthy Jr., *Community-Based Corrections*, 3rd ed. (Belmont, CA: Wadsworth, 1997), p. 270.

42. California and Oregon statistics cited in William M. DiMascio, *Seeking Justice: Crime and Punishment in America* (New York: Edna McConnell Clark Foundation, 1997), p. 23.

43. McCarthy and McCarthy, *Community-Based Corrections*, p. 294.

44. Linda Smith, "Intermediate Sanctions: Getting Tough in the Community," in Ira J. Silverman and Manuel Vega, eds., *Corrections: A Comprehensive View* (St. Paul, MN: West, 1996), p. 520.

45. Camille G. Camp and George Camp, *The Corrections Yearbook, 1997* (South Salem, NY: Criminal Justice Institute, 1997).

46. Ibid., p. 54.

47. Oliver J. Keller and Benedict S. Alper, *Halfway Houses: Community-Centered Correction and Treatment* (Lexington, MA: Lexington Books, 1970).

48. Donald J. Thalheimer, *Halfway Houses* (Washington, DC: U.S. Government Printing Office, 1975).

49. Camp and Camp, *The Corrections Yearbook, 1997.*

50. Ibid., p. 47.

51. Edward Latessa and Harry Allen, "Halfway Houses and Parole: A National Assessment," *Journal of Criminal Justice* 10 (1982), p. 161.

52. P. G. Connelly and B. R. Forschner, "Predictors of Success in a Co-Correctional Halfway House: A Discriminant Analysis," in T. Ellsworth, ed., *Contemporary Community Corrections* (Prospect Heights, IL: Waveland Press, 1992).

53. Margot C. Lindsay, *A Matter of Principle: Public Involvement in Residential Community Corrections* (Washington, DC: National Institute of Corrections, 1990).

54. Richard Hughes, *The Fatal Shore* (New York: Knopf, 1987).

55. Christopher Hibbert, *The Roots of Evil: A Social History of Crime and Punishment* (Boston: Little, Brown, 1968).

56. "Ex-Georgian Returns after Pardon," United Press International (February 23, 2000); "Homecoming King: After 39 Years, Preston King Gets a Presidential Pardon That Puts an End to His Exile," *People Weekly* (March 13, 2000), p. 89.

57. Cited in Marilyn D. McShane and Wesley Krause, *Community Corrections* (New York: Macmillan, 1993), p. 4.

58. "Judge Throws Book at Shooter," *Buffalo News* (April 14, 1995), p. 3.

59. Paul Leavitt, "Birth Control Sentence," *USA Today* (November 15, 1990), p. 3.

60. Richard J. Maher and Cheryl Holmes, "Community Service: A Way for Offenders to Make Amends," *Federal Probation* 61 (March 1997), pp. 26–28.

61. Etta F. Morgan and Ida M. Johnson, "Kidnapping and Murder for Motherhood," paper presented at the Annual Meeting of Southern Criminal Justice Association, Richmond, Virginia, 1997.

62. Elizabeth H. McConnell, "Issues in Family Violence in Georgia," paper presented at the Annual Meeting of the Southern Criminal Justice Association, Richmond, Virginia, 1997.

63. Sharon Levrant, Francis T. Cullen, Betsy Fulton, and John F. Wozniak, "Reconsidering Restorative Justice: The Corruption of Benevolence Revisited?," *Crime and Delinquency* 45 (January 1999).

64. Martin Wright and Burt Galway, eds., *Mediation and Criminal Justice: Victims, Offenders, and Community* (Newbury Park, CA: Sage, 1989), p. 2.

65. Robert Coates and John Gehm, "An Empirical Assessment," in Wright and Galway, eds., *Mediation and Criminal Justice*, pp. 251–56.

66. Mark S. Umbreit, "Victim–Offender Mediation in Canada: The Impact of an Emerging Social Work Intervention," *International Social Work* 42 (April 1999); Mark Umbreit et al., *Victim Meets Offender: The Impact of Restorative Justice and Mediation* (Monsey, NY: Criminal Justice Press, 1994); Mark S. Umbreit and Mike Niemeyer, "Victim–Offender Mediation: From the Margins toward the Mainstream," *Perspectives* (summer 1996), p. 28.

67. Catherine Edwards, "Paying for What They've Wrought," *Insight on the News*, (July 26, 1999), p. 46.

68. Deborah Sharp, "Boot Camps Try for Rehabilitation," *USA Today* (November 9, 1993), p. 3.

69. Doris Layton MacKenzie, "Boot Camp Programs Grow in Number and Scope," *NIJ Reports* (November–December, 1990), pp. 6–8; Jon R. Sorensen, "Shock Camps Get High Marks Despite Violent Incidents," *Buffalo News* (April 15, 1996), p. 8.

70. James Austin, Michael Jones, and Melissa Bolyard, *The Growing Use of Jail Boot Camps: The Current State of the Art* (Washington, DC: National Institute of Justice, 1993).

71. Michael Peters, David Thomas, and Christopher Zamberlan, *Boot Camps for Juvenile Offenders* (Washington, DC: Office of Juvenile Justice and Delinquency Prevention, 1997).

72. Blair B. Bourque, Mei Han, and Sarah M. Hill, *A National Survey of Aftercare Provisions for Boot Camp Graduates* (Washington, DC: National Institute of Justice, 1996).

73. Blair B. Bourque et al., *Boot Camps for Juvenile Offenders: An Implementation Evaluation of Three Demonstration Programs* (Washington, DC: National Institute of Justice, 1996).

74. Ibid.

75. Ibid., p. 2.

76. Cited in *NIJ Reports* (November–December, 1990), p. 5.

77. Andrea Stone, "Whipping Penalty Judged Too Harsh—by Some," *USA Today* (March 10, 1994), p. 3.

78. Tom Squitieri, "Proposals Seek More Drastic Punishments," *USA Today* (February 14, 1990), p. 3.

79. Sam S. Souryal and Dennis W. Potts, "The Penalty of Hand Amputation for Theft in Islamic Justice," *Journal of Criminal Justice* 22 (1994), pp. 249–65.

80. *Trop v. Dulles*, 356 U.S. 86, 1958; *Rhodes v. Chapman*, 452 U.S. 337, 1981.

81. W. M. Cooper, *A History of the Rod in all Countries* (London: John Camden Hotten, 1870).

82. L. A. Parry, *The History of Torture in England* (Montclair, NJ: Patterson Smith, 1934); Graham Newman, *The Punishment Response* (New York: Lippincott, 1978).

83. S. Rubin, *The Law of Criminal Correction* (St. Paul, MN: West, 1973).

84. Paul Leavitt, "Calls for Caning Keep on Coming," *USA Today* (May 25, 1994), p. 3.

85. Amnesty International, *1995 Report* (New York: Amnesty International, 1995).

86. Cited in Stone, "Whipping Penalty Judged Too Harsh—By Some."

87. R. G. Caldwell, *Criminology*, 2nd ed. (New York: Ronald Press, 1965).

88. Tamara Henry, "Groups Seek to Lay Down Law on Corporal Discipline," *USA Today* (March 8, 1994), p. 6D; Newman, *The Punishment Response.*

89. "Pensacola," *USA Today* (August 5, 1993), p. 9.

90. "Albany," *USA Today* (June 14, 1995), p. 11.

91. G. Ives, *A History of Penal Methods* (Montclair, NJ: Patterson Smith, 1914).

92. Newman, *The Punishment Response;* William Andrews, *Bygone Punishments* (London: William Andrews, 1899).

93. A. M. Earle, *Curious Punishments of Bygone Days* (Montclair, NJ: Patterson Smith, 1896).

94. H. Oppenheimer, *The Rationale of Punishment* (Montclair, NJ: Patterson Smith, 1913); Parry, *The History of Torture in England.*

95. *Curious Punishments of Bygone Days.*

96. Tony Mauro, "Judge Orders 'Humiliation' Ads: Papers Uneasy," *USA Today* (December 15, 1990), p. 3; "Albany," *USA Today* (June 14, 1995), p. 11; "Pensacola," *USA Today* (August 5, 1993), p. 9; "Tampa," *USA Today* (December 9, 1994), p. 6.

97. James Q. Whitman, "What Is Wrong with Inflicting Shame Sanctions?," *Yale Law Journal* 107 (January 1998), pp. 1055–92; Kelly McMurry, "For Shame," *Trial* 33 (May 1997), pp. 12–15.

98. John Braithwaite, "Restorative Justice: Assessing Optimistic and Pessimistic Accounts," *Crime and Justice* 25 (spring 1999); John Braithwaite, *Corporate Crime and the Pharmaceutical Industry* (London: Routledge & Kegan Paul, 1984); John Braithwaite, "Transnational Regulation of the Pharmaceutical Industry," *The Annals* 525 (January 1993).

99. Henry J. Reske, "Scarlet Letter Sentences," *ABA Journal* 82 (January 1996), pp. 16–18; Darryl van Duch, "State High Court Rejects Ridicule as Unreasonable," *The National Law Journal* 19 (May 5, 1997), p. 6.

100. Paul Leavitt, "Birth Control Sentence," *USA Today* (January 7, 1991), p. 3.

101. Kim Painter, "Norplant Gets a Shot in the Arm," *USA Today* (August, 22, 1995), p. 4D.

102. Paul Leavitt, "Baltimore Schools Offer Teens Norplant," *USA Today* (December 4, 1992), p. 3.

103. "Debate: Give Sex Offenders Longer Prison Terms," *USA Today* (March 7, 1990), p. 10.

104. "Castration Bill," *USA Today* (February 13, 1990), p. 3.

105. Kay-Frances Brody, "A Constitutional Analysis of California's Chemical Castration Statute," *Temple Political and Civil Rights Law Review* 7 (fall 1997), pp. 141–70.

106. "Tot Killing," *USA Today* (October 20, 1990), p. 3.

107. David Gelman, "The Mind of the Rapist," *Newsweek* (July 23, 1990), pp. 46–53.

108. Dori Stehlin, "Depo-Provera: The Quarterly Contraceptive," *FDA Consumer* (March 1993).

109. Ibid., p. 47.

110. Tom Squitieri, "Proposals Seek More Drastic Punishments."

111. U.S. Comptroller General, *Asset Forfeiture: Need for Stronger Marshals Service Oversight of Commercial Real Property* (Washington, DC: U.S. General Accounting Office, 1991).

112. George N. Aylesworth, *Forfeiture of Real Property: An Overview* (Washington, DC: Bureau of Justice Assistance, 1991).

113. Joseph P. Fried, "Government Sues to Seize Gotti's Ill-Gotten Assets," *New York Times* (January 15, 1993), p. B1.

114. *United States v. One Parcel of Real Estate*, 675 F. Supp. 645 (D. Fla. 1987).

115. Laurie E. Ekstrand, *Asset Forfeiture: Historical Perspective on Asset Forfeiture Issues* (Washington, DC: U.S. General Accounting Office, 1996).

116. *Austin v. United States*, 116 S. Ct. 994 (1996); Jerome Spencer, "Auspices of Austin: Examining Excessiveness of Civil Forfeitures under the Eighth Amendment," *American Criminal Law Review* 35 (fall 1997), pp. 163–89.

117. Matthew Costigan, "Go Directly to Jail, Do Not Pass Go, Do Not Keep House," *Journal of Criminal Law and Criminology* 87 (spring 1997), pp. 719–50; *U.S. v. Ursery*, 117 S. Ct. (1997).

118. Robert E. Bauman, "Take It Away," *National Review* 47 (February 20, 1995), pp. 34–38.

119. Peter Finn and Dale Parent, *Making the Offender Foot the Bill: A Texas Program* (Washington, DC: National Institute of Justice, 1992).

120. Dale Parent, *Recovering Correctional Costs through Offender Fees* (Washington, DC: National Institute of Justice, 1990).

Glossary

acquittal A finding of not guilty following a trial.

actual possession A condition in which a person has exclusive control over an object.

actus reus The behavior that must be committed to meet the definition of a crime.

administrative regulations Rules applied to organizations that are designed to protect public health, safety, and welfare in the marketplace.

aggravated assault A thrust against another person intended to cause serious bodily harm or death.

altruistic Selflessly helpful and giving toward others.

anomie A "normlessness" or lack of attachment felt by some people toward their society.

appeals Review of lower-court decisions by a higher court that looks for errors of law or procedure.

appellate jurisdiction The jurisdiction of courts that review specific legal issues raised in trial courts.

arraignment A hearing where the defendant is informed of the charges and of his or her rights and enters a plea.

arrest Process of taking a suspected law violator into custody for the purpose of prosecution.

arson Burning property of another without the lawful consent of the owner.

assigned counsel Private attorney appointed by the court on a case-by-case basis from a list of available defense attorneys.

Auburn system A philosophy of imprisonment that emphasized labor and meditation; offenders worked every day, but in complete silence.

authentic justice Approach to criminal justice that tries to relate sanctions closely to crimes and to punish offenders in ways that neutralize their gain.

authoritarianism A tendency to favor blind obedience to authority.

bail Money or property held by a court to ensure that an arrestee temporarily released before trial will appear for the trial.

battered woman syndrome An ongoing pattern of severe physical abuse that constitutes a continual threat of harm.

bench trial Trial in which the judge determines guilt or innocence.

Bill of Rights The first ten amendments to the Constitution, which detail many of the requirements for adjudication, such as arrests, warrants, searches, trials, lawyers, punishment, and other important aspects of criminal procedure.

biological determinism Positivistic view of criminal behavior as rooted in biological attributes.

blocked opportunity Theory that crime results from people's lack of access to legitimate means for achieving goals.

booking Procedure in which an official record of an arrest is made.

bribery Voluntary giving or receiving of anything of value with the intent of influencing the action of a public official.

burglary Unlawful entry into a building for the purpose of committing a crime while inside.

case law Judicial application and interpretation of law as it applies in a given case.

case mortality Case attrition, in which, for various reasons, arrests do not result in convictions.

caseloads The numbers of cases to be adjudicated in the courts of various jurisdictions.

civil law Formal rules that regulate disputes between private parties.

classical school Perspective in criminology that sees crime as resulting from the conscious exercise of an individual's free will.

clearance rate The proportion of crime cases that are "closed" or solved by an arrest.

common law The body of unrecorded decisions made by English judges in the Middle Ages, reflecting the values, customs, and beliefs of the period.

community corrections Sanctions that are *alternatives to incarceration* in jail or prison (such as monetary penalties, probation, intensive supervision, and home confinement with electronic monitoring), or supervision in the community *after a sentence of incarceration* has been served (such as parole, work release, furloughs, and halfway houses).

community courts Decentralized courts that respond to neighborhood conditions using citizen advisory committees, volunteers, and teen courts.

community policing A service-oriented style of law enforcement that focuses on disorder in the community, crime prevention, and fear reduction, as opposed to the traditional focus on prosecution of serious street crimes.

community prosecution A program in which prosecutors intervene in all disorderly behavior that affects the quality of life in neighborhood.

commutation A modification or reduction of a sentence imposed on an offender.

computer crime Crimes in which computers are used as the instrument of the offense, and crimes in which computers are the object of the offense.

conflict view The view that an act becomes a crime only when criminalizing it serves the interests of those in positions of power.

consensual model Prison management approach that aims to maintain order by getting inmates and staff to agree on the validity of rules.

consensus view The view that law reflects society's consensus regarding behavior that is harmful enough to warrant government intervention.

conspiracy Agreement between two or more persons to commit a crime or to carry out a legal act in an illegal manner.

constable A citizen in charge of weapons and equipment for one hundred families in his geographic area. In England constables were appointed by a local nobleman beginning around the year 900.

constitutions The fundamental principles of societies that guide the enactment of specific laws and the application of those laws by courts.

constructive possession A condition in which a person has the opportunity to exercise control over an object.

continuance A court-authorized postponement of a case to allow the prosecution or defense more time to prepare its case.

contract attorney programs Programs in which private attorneys, firms, or local bar associations provide legal representation to indigent defendants for a specific period under contract with the county.

control model Prison management approach characterized by strict enforcement of prison rules and few privileges for prisoners.

conviction A finding of guilt beyond a reasonable doubt.

corporal punishment Short-term military-style boot camp programs designed primarily for Physical punishment short of the death penalty.

corporate crimes Dangerous or unjust actions in the conduct of business, prompted by the desire for profits. Same as *regulatory offenses*.

correctional institutions Medium security federal correctional institutions.

courtroom work group The prosecutors, defense counsel, judges, and other courtroom personnel, who represent distinct interests but share the goal of shepherding large numbers of cases through the adjudication process.

crime commissions Commissions that focus on improved operation of the criminal justice system as the best way to reduce crime. Early twentieth-century crime commissions included the Chicago Crime Commission (1919), the National Crime Commission (1925), and the Wickersham Commission (1931).

crime control model The perspective that views the repression of criminal conduct as the most important function of the criminal justice system, thus calling for speed, efficiency, and finality in criminal justice processing.

crime rates The numbers of crimes committed in relation to the population at risk. Crime rates provide an indication of the risk of victimization per capita.

crime syndicate A system of loosely structured relationships among groups and individuals involved in organized crime.

crimes Forms of conduct that society prohibits in order to maintain order.

crimes against persons Violent crimes involving the use of physical force.

crimes against property Crimes in which property is taken unlawfully and misused.

crimes against public administration Attempts to impede government processes through bribery, obstruction of justice, official misconduct, or perjury.

crimes against public order Acts that disrupt the peace in a civil society.

crimes of fraud Embezzlement, extortion, forgery, and fraud.

criminal (penal) code A compilation of all the criminal laws of a jurisdiction.

criminal homicide Murder or manslaughter.

criminal justice system The more than 50,000 government agencies in the United States that deal with aspects of crime including criminal law enforcement, the courts, and corrections.

criminal law A code that categorizes all crimes and punishments by type.

criminal law Formal rules designed to maintain social control.

criminal liability Punishable responsibility for a crime, determined by the presence of the elements of a crime in a given case. Criminal liability subjects the accused person to criminal penalties.

criminal subcultures Different forms of deviance that result when youths cease to adhere to middle-class standards. Youths may become part of the adult *criminal* subculture, the *conflict* subculture, or the *retreatist* subculture.

criminalization The legislative decision to make a behavior a crime.

cruel and unusual punishment Criminal penalties that violate "evolving standards of decency that mark the progress of a maturing society"; such penalties are prohibited by the Eighth Amendment.

cynicism Belief that human conduct is motivated entirely by self-interest. A cynical person attributes all actions to selfish motives and has a pessimistic outlook on human behavior.

deadly force The use of lethal force by police against a suspect.

decriminalization The legislative decision to change a crime into a noncriminal act.

defense attorneys Attorneys who represent the legal rights of persons accused in criminal or civil proceedings.

determinate sentencing A sentencing system that permits judges to impose fixed terms of incarceration that cannot be altered by a parole board.

deterrence Prevention of crime through the example of punishment of offenders.

deviant police subculture hypothesis The view that some police departments have groups of officers who place loyalty to one another above obedience to the law.

differential association Theory that a person becomes criminal or delinquent when he or she associates more with people who condone violation of the law than with people who do not.

discovery The process that entitles a suspect to review certain information gathered by the prosecutor.

dispute resolution Method of handling complaints outside the judicial process through a mediator appointed by the court.

district attorneys City and county prosecutors (called by this title in many jurisdictions, but not in all).

diversion programs Alternatives to the formal criminal justice process that are implemented after charging but prior to adjudication; they attempt to achieve a noncriminal disposition of the case.

dogmatism An attitude characterized by tenacious adherence to one's opinions even though they may be unwarranted and based on insufficiently examined premises.

Drug Use Forecasting Program in many major U.S. cities in which police take urine specimens from a sample of arrestees to determine what proportion of those arrested have already used drugs.

due process model The perspective that considers preservation of individual liberties to be the most important function of the criminal justice system, thus emphasizing accuracy, fairness, and reliability in criminal procedure.

due process A legal protection included in the U.S. Constitution that guarantees all citizens the right to be adjudicated under established law and legal procedures.

duress Defense in which a person claims to have engaged in criminal conduct because of a threat of immediate and serious bodily harm by another person.

effective counsel Competent representation by a defense attorney. It is ineffective assistance of counsel when unprofessional errors would have changed the outcome of the case.

electronic monitoring Surveillance of offenders in the community by means of electronic devices such as radio and telephone transmitters.

embezzlement The purposeful misappropriation of property entrusted to one's care, custody, or control to which one is not entitled.

entrapment Defense designed to prevent the government from manufacturing crime by setting traps for unwary citizens.

ethical view Perspective in criminology that sees crime as a moral failure in decision making.

exclusionary rule Legal principle that holds that illegally seized evidence must be excluded from use in trials.

excuse defenses Defenses that claim that criminal conduct should be excused because the defendant cannot be held responsible for it; insanity and duress are examples.

expert witness A person called to testify because of his or her special expertise in an area at issue in a legal proceeding.

extortion Purposeful obtaining of property from another person when his or her consent has been induced through wrongful use of force or fear or under the guise of official authority.

FBI's Crime Index Tally of detailed reports on eight types of offenses: criminal homicide, forcible rape, robbery, aggravated assault, burglary, larceny, motor vehicle theft, and arson.

federal law enforcement Seventeen different agencies that investigate violations of federal law; most perform exclusively investigative functions.

felonies Serious crimes that are punishable by incarceration for more than one year.

felony drug courts Courts that handle only drug offenses and attempt to correct underlying causes of the illegal conduct.

Fifth Amendment The amendment to the Constitution that includes protection against self-incrimination.

"fleeing felon" rule The now obsolete common-law rule that police can use deadly force against any felon who flees the scene of a crime.

forgery False making or altering of an official document with the intent to defraud.

Fourth Amendment The amendment to the Constitution that prohibits searches without probable cause.

fraud Purposeful obtaining of the property of another person through deception.

frisk A patting down of the outer clothing of a suspect, based on reasonable suspicion; designed to protect a police officer from attack with a weapon while an inquiry is made.

furloughs Unsupervised leaves from prison that are granted for only a few hours to permit an eligible inmate to be present at a relative's funeral, visit loved ones, go to a job interview, or otherwise attend to personal or family matters.

general defenses Justifications or excuses for criminal conduct that are applicable to all criminal offenses.

general jurisdiction The jurisdiction of trial courts: courts where most trials for felonies occur, as well as trials in major civil cases.

good faith exception Exception to the exclusionary rule, stating that evidence seized with a defective warrant, not based on probable cause, is admissible in court if the police acted in good faith in presenting the evidence and the error was made by the judge.

good-time credits Small reductions in the time to be served, awarded to inmates for each day on which they obey prison rules.

grand jury A group of citizens who hear the evidence presented by a prosecutor to determine whether probable cause exists to hold a person for trial.

gross negligence Failure to perceive a substantial and unjustifiable risk when such failure is a gross deviation from the standard of care a reasonable person would observe.

guideline sentences Sentences based on average past sentences for various combi-

nations of offenders and offenses in an effort to achieve proportionality and uniformity without mandating specific sentences for certain crimes or offenders.

gun control Regulation of gun manufacturers, buyers, and sellers in an effort to minimize gun-related crime.

habitual offender laws Laws that subject multiple offenders to periods of incarceration ranging up to life imprisonment, on the grounds that such persons must be physically separated from society if society is to be protected from their criminal conduct.

halfway house Residential centers for ex-offenders in the community. Most halfway house residents are parolees or similar inmates near the end of their sentence.

hate crimes Offenses motivated by prejudice, usually against a particular race, religion, or sexual orientation.

house arrest A condition of probation or parole in which an offender is not permitted to leave his or her residence for purposes other than work, school, treatment, or other approved reasons.

identity fraud Manufacture and use of false identification and credit cards based on personal information stolen without the victim's knowledge.

ignorance of law Defense in which a defendant claims that a law is not widely known and that the person could not have been expected to be aware of it.

incapacitation Physically restraining an offender (usually through incarceration) so as to prevent further criminal behavior.

incarceration Segregation of offenders from the rest of the community in jails or prisons to rehabilitate, incapacitate, or punish them and to deter others from committing similar crimes.

indeterminate sentencing A sentencing system that empowers the judge to set a maximum amount of time (up to the limit set by the legislature), and sometimes a minimum amount as well, for the offender to serve in prison.

Index crimes The eight offenses tracked by the FBI's Crime Index.

indictment A formal accusation of a crime based on the vote of a grand jury.

information A formal accusation filed by a prosecutor based on the findings of a preliminary hearing.

insanity defense A claim that the defendant was not sane under law at the time of the act.

intensive supervision Probation or parole for which jurisdictions maintain small caseloads, make frequent contact with offenders under supervision, and require special conditions such as random drug tests, curfews, restitution to victims, electronic monitoring, or house arrest.

intention Conscious purposiveness in conduct; a factor in the determination of criminal responsibility.

intermediate sanctions Sentences designed to provide more rigorous supervision than normal probation, yet something less expensive than incarceration.

Interpol The International Criminal Police Organization, which assists 177 member nations' law enforcement agencies by providing information about crimes or criminals of a transnational nature.

jails Facilities operated by counties and municipalities to hold two main categories of inmates: those awaiting trial and those serving sentences of one year or less.

judge Person who objectively assesses the strength of a case, rules on issues of law and procedure, and in many cases determines the disposition of a case.

judicial review The U.S. Supreme Court's authority to review the constitutionality of acts of Congress.

jurisdiction The authority of a state, county, or city to apply its own laws within its own territory.

jury nullification A jury's decision to acquit a defendant in the face of facts that show guilt.

jury trial Trial in which the jury determines guilt or innocence.

justice of the peace An office established by Edward II in 1326 to assist the sheriff in enforcing the law. Eventually the role of the justice of the peace shifted to adjudication, while the sheriffs retained their local peacekeeping function.

justices Judges of an appellate court.

justification defenses Defenses that admit to the criminal conduct but claim it was justified by overwhelming circumstances, such as self-defense.

labeling theory The view that adjudicating a juvenile as a delinquent serves to encourage future delinquency by generating a negative public identity or changed self-image.

larceny Taking property of another person with the intent of depriving the owner.

Law Enforcement Assistance Administration (LEAA) Agency established in 1968 within the U.S. Department of Justice to allocate money to improve the efficiency and effectiveness of the criminal justice system. Between 1968 and 1977 the LEAA spent more than $6 billion on crime control programs and college education for police officers.

legalization Legislative action to remove a prohibited behavior from the criminal law.

limited jurisdiction The jurisdiction of courts that have narrow legal authority over specific types of matters (e.g., family courts, municipal courts, tax courts).

local jails Facilities used to detain adults awaiting trial and offenders serving sentences of one year or less.

local police Police departments of municipalities; local law enforcement also includes county sheriffs and special police agencies such as park, airport, transit, and university police.

mala in se Acts considered evil in themselves (e.g., assault and theft).

mala prohibita Acts considered undesirable although not inherently evil (e.g., drug use).

malfeasance A form of police corruption involving commission of an illegal act.

mandatory sentences Requirements that certain penalties be imposed upon conviction in order to guarantee that offenders do not escape punishment.

mandatory sentences Fixed sentences for offenders convicted of certain types of crimes, such as gun-related crimes, drug offenses, and drunk driving offenses.

manslaughter A mitigated murder: causing a death recklessly, or intentionally under extenuating circumstances.

maximum security prisons Institutions that have a wall surrounding the entire facility and house dangerous felons; about 26 percent of all inmates are incarcerated in such prisons.

maxing out Release from incarceration after the offender has served the entire sentence without ever being granted parole or accumulating enough good-time credits to justify early release.

mediation Process in which the offender and the victim meet in a neutral setting where they can ask questions, communicate feelings, and discuss ways in which the balance of justice can be restored; this may involve an apology, restitution, community service, or other alternative.

medium security prisons Institutions that often have some facilities outside the main enclosure, which is usually surrounded by two rows of chain-link fence topped with barbed wire; about 49 percent of all inmates are serving time in these prisons.

mens rea "Guilty mind": the conscious decision to commit a criminal act.

merit selection A method for selecting judges that involves a combination of appointment and election.

metropolitan correctional centers (detention centers) Federal jail facilities for pretrial detention and for those serving short sentences.

minimum security prisons Facilities that usually have no fences but have locking outside doors and electronic surveillance devices around the perimeter; about 23 percent of all inmates are in these institutions.

Miranda **warning** Five-point warning derived from the case of *Miranda v. Arizona*. Its purpose is to give crime suspects fair notice of their basic constitutional rights.

misdemeanors Less serious crimes that are punishable by imprisonment for one year or less.

misfeasance A form of police corruption involving failure to perform a legal duty in a proper manner.

mistake of fact Defense in which a person claims that honest ignorance rules out the presence of a "guilty mind."

mistrial A trial that has been declared invalid because of a substantial error in law or procedure.

money laundering "Washing" illegally obtained money (e.g., money from drug sales or gambling proceeds) by making it appear that the money was earned legally as part of a legitimate business.

multijurisdictional task forces Multi-agency efforts to combat multijurisdictional crimes through pooling of evidence, personnel, and expertise and to reduce unnecessary duplication of effort.

murder All intentional killings, as well as deaths that occur in the course of dangerous felonies.

mutual pledge system System of community self-responsibility that existed in Britain during the Middle Ages, in which residents were held responsible for the conduct of their neighbors.

National Crime Victimization Survey (NCVS) An annual survey of a representative sample of the U.S. population that assesses the extent of victimization and the extent to which these incidents were reported to police.

National Incident-Based Reporting System Data-collection program designed to gather information on victims, perpetrators, and circumstances of crime.

National Longitudinal Survey of Youth Self-report study investigating extent of delinquency among young people.

necessarily included offenses Offenses that are, by definition, included in a charge as part of another (more serious) offense; also called "lesser" included offenses.

necessity Defense in which a person claims to have engaged in otherwise criminal behavior because of the forces of nature.

negligence Failure to be aware of a substantial and unjustifiable risk.

net widening Process by which more offenders end up being placed under supervision of the criminal justice system even though the intent of a program was to divert offenders out of the system.

nolle prosequi Decision by a prosecutor not to press charges; also known as nol. pros.

nonfeasance A form of police corruption involving failure to perform a legal duty.

obstruction of justice Intentional prevention of a public servant from lawfully performing an official function.

offenses against morality Acts that are seen as immoral, such as adultery and fornication, prostitution, and gambling.

official misconduct A public official's unauthorized exercise of an official function with intent to benefit or injure another.

ordinances Laws that apply to a specific county, city, or town.

organized crime A continuing criminal enterprise that rationally works to profit from illicit activities that are often in great public demand. Its continuing existence is maintained through the use of force, threats, monopoly control, and/or the corruption of public officials.

overcriminalization Blurring of the distinction between crime and merely inappropriate or offensive behaviors.

pardon A reprieve from a governor or from the president that excuses a convicted offender and allows him or her to be released from prison without any supervision.

parole release Prisoner release decided by a parole board consisting of corrections officials and/or political appointees, who evaluate the inmate's record and his or her behavior in prison to determine whether the inmate will be released to serve the remainder of the sentence under community supervision.

parole Phase of the criminal justice process in which an offender completes the end of a prison sentence under supervision in the community.

penitentiaries Maximum security federal correctional institutions.

Pennsylvania system A philosophy of imprisonment in which solitary confinement was expected to promote repentance and to prevent offenders from being corrupted by mixing with other offenders.

perjury Making a false statement under oath in an official proceeding.

personal risk An individual's risk of being a victim of crime; determined through calculation of crime rates in relation to population.

plea A statement of innocence or guilt.

plea bargaining Agreement by a prosecutor to press a less serious charge, drop some charges, or recommend a less severe sentence if the defendant agrees to plead guilty.

police brutality Use of excessive physical force by police carrying out their duties.

police corruption Illegal acts or omissions by police officers in the line of duty who, by virtue of their official position, receive (or intend to receive) any gain for themselves or others.

police discretion An officer's ability to choose between arrest and nonarrest solely on the basis of his or her own judgment.

police pursuits Police chases of suspects immediately after crimes have been committed.

policing Traditionally, enforcing the law by apprehending violators and thereby protecting citizens. Crime prevention and social services such as education of

the public are more recent emphases in policing.

political crimes Acts viewed as a threat to the government.

positivism Perspective in criminology that sees human behavior as determined by internal and external influences, such as biological, psychological, and/or social factors.

precedents Previous court decisions that courts follow in current cases to ensure consistency in the application of the law.

predispositional model The view that the attitudes and values of police officers are developed before entry into the law enforcement profession.

presentence investigation An investigation by the probation department that seeks information regarding an offender's personal and social background, his or her criminal record, and any other information that may help the judge match the sentence to the offender.

presentence report A report written by a probation officer after an investigation of an offender's background, to assist the judge in determining an appropriate sentence.

pretrial intervention (PTI) A type of diversion program in which a prosecutor suspends prosecution of a case pending the fulfillment of special conditions by the defendant. If these conditions are met, the case is dismissed.

pretrial settlement conference A meeting of the prosecutor, the defendant, the defendant's counsel, and the judge to discuss a plea before a trial is held. No plea negotiations can take place outside this setting.

preventive police The first organized police department in London, established in 1829. The popular English name for police officers, "bobbies," comes from Sir Robert Peel, a founder of the Metropolitan Police.

private security Law enforcement agencies that protect private property and are paid by private individuals and corporations.

probable cause A reasonable link between a specific person and a particular crime; the legal threshold required before police can arrest or search an individual.

probation A system under which a person convicted of a crime serves a sentence in the community under the supervision of a probation officer.

procedural law Rules for adjudication of cases involving prohibited behaviors.

professionalization Changes in police organization, administration, and technology aimed at improving the efficiency of the police in the deterrence and apprehension of criminals.

progressivism Early twentieth-century era in policing that focused on efficiency, professionalism, and improved technology.

prosecutors Elected or appointed officials who represent the community in bringing charges against an accused person.

psychoanalytic theory Freudian theory that behavior results from the interaction of the three components of the personality: id, ego, and superego.

public defender Salaried attorney paid by the government to represent indigent persons charged with crimes.

public safety exception Rule stating that police do not have to provide the *Miranda* warning to suspects when circumstances indicate that public safety would be jeopardized.

racial profiling Alleged tacit or explicit police guidelines that lead officers to stop and search minorities for minor violations significantly more often than whites.

racketeering An ongoing criminal enterprise that is maintained through a pattern of criminal activity.

rape Sexual intercourse without effective consent.

reasonable suspicion A situation in which a police officer has good reason to believe that criminal activity may be occurring; this permits a brief investigative inquiry of the suspect.

reasonableness standard A standard under which persons are culpable for their actions if they rationally understand the consequences of those actions. Young children and mentally ill individuals are generally not held culpable, because of their inability to reason effectively.

recidivism Repeat offenses by an offender.

recklessness Conscious disregard of a substantial and unjustifiable risk.

reformatory movement Late nineteenth-century trend toward use of incarceration to reform through educating; inmates could be paroled when they showed substantial progress.

regulatory offenses Activities of a business or corporate nature that are viewed as a threat to public health, safety, or welfare.

regulatory offenses Attempts to circumvent regulations designed to ensure fairness and safety in the conduct of business; include administrative, environmental, labor, and manufacturing violations as well as unfair trade practices.

rehabilitation Efforts to correct or treat individuals' social or psychological shortcomings so as to prevent future criminal behavior.

responsibility model Prison management approach that gives inmates more autonomy; staff guides prisoners' decision making rather than making all decisions for them.

restitution Compensation for a victim's loss; a form of restorative justice that usually takes the form of money but can also include the return of property or services performed for the victim.

restorative justice Approach to criminal justice that focuses primarily on repairing the injury to the victim rather than on the adversary relationship between the government and the offender.

retribution Punishment applied simply in proportion to the seriousness of the offense.

retributive model of justice Traditional approach to criminal justice that emphasizes the role of adversarial proceedings and punishment of offenders as retribution for their past acts.

right to counsel A Sixth Amendment protection that guarantees suspects the right to representation by an attorney when their liberty is in jeopardy.

robbery Theft from a person involving threats or force.

sanctions Ways to punish or place restrictions on offenders.

search An exploratory inspection of a person or property, based on probable cause of law violation.

seizure Meaningful interference with an individual's possession of property.

selective enforcement An unwritten policy under which police are not required to fully enforce all laws as written.

selective incapacitation Incarceration of potential high-rate offenders for longer periods as a means of reducing crime.

sentencing A judge's decision as to the most appropriate punishment for a con-victed offender, within a specified range established by law, given the type of crime and type of offender.

sexual assault Forced sex, whether vaginal, anal, or oral.

shire reeve Official appointed by the British Crown who was responsible for overseeing the constables and several hundred families in a given area (called a "shire"). The modern word *sheriff* is derived from this term.

shock incarceration Short-term military-style boot camp programs designed primarily for nonviolent young offenders and featuring a military atmosphere and strict discipline.

simple assault A thrust against another person intended to injure that person.

social bond An individual's attachment to society, which has four primary elements: attachment to others, commitment to conventional activities, involvement in conventional activities, and belief in widely shared moral values.

socialization model The view that holds that police officers learn their attitudes and values from socializing experiences such as education and experience on the job.

Speedy Trial Act Legislation requiring that all criminal cases be brought to trial within one hundred days.

state police Agencies that enforce state laws exclusively. Primarily engaged in highway patrol activities; about half of state police agencies also have the authority to conduct investigative work.

statutes Specific laws passed by legislatures that prohibit or mandate certain acts.

statutory rape Nonforcible sexual intercourse with a minor.

structural/conflict view Perspective in criminology that sees the criminal law as reflecting the will of those in power and notes that behaviors that threaten the interests of the powerful are punished most severely.

study release Program similar to work release, in which an inmate attends school by day and returns to jail or prison at night.

substantive criminal law Law defining specific behaviors that are prohibited.

summons Written notice to appear in court; also called a citation.

surety Bail posted by a bondsman on behalf of an arrestee.

suspended sentence A delayed imposition of a prison sentence that requires the offender to fulfill special conditions such as alcohol, drug, or gambling treatment or payment of restitution.

terrorism Offenses designed to intimidate or coerce a government or civilians in furtherance of political or social objectives.

therapeutic community model Prison drug treatment approach based on the notion that a person's attitudes, values, and self-esteem must change together with the targeted drug use behavior if lasting change is to occur.

"three strikes" laws Laws under which conviction for a third felony results in an extended sentence, even life imprisonment.

transnational crime Organized crime that takes place across two or more countries.

transnational law enforcement International agreements and law enforcement efforts that attempt to serve the interests of all nations in the face of developments such as the growth of international travel, the transnational nature of the Internet, and the threat of international organized crime and terrorism.

truth in sentencing A sentencing provision that requires offenders to serve the bulk of their sentence (usually 85 percent) before they can be released.

U.S. courts of appeals Intermediate federal appellate courts.

U.S. district courts Federal trial courts of general jurisdiction.

U.S. magistrates Judges appointed by U.S. district court judges to conduct pretrial hearings and trials for minor civil and criminal offenses in federal court.

U.S. Supreme Court The highest court in the United States, which hears final appeals in cases involving federal law, suits between states, and interpretations of the U.S. Constitution.

Uniform Crime Reports (UCR) Annual FBI compilations of all crimes reported to the police in the United States.

victim impact statements Statements made by victims to the judge before sentencing about how the crime has harmed them.

Victim's Bill of Rights Legal changes that formally recognize the role and rights of victims in the justice process.

victimization Infliction of assault, theft, or other criminal behaviors on a person or household.

victimless crimes Offenses in which the "offender" and "victim" are the same individual or in which behavior is consensual.

warrant A sworn statement by police that attests to the existence of probable cause in a given case; it is signed by a judge who agrees with the officers' assessment of the facts.

watch and ward system System established in England in 1285 to aid constables in their law enforcement efforts. Men from each town were required to take turns standing watch at night. Crime suspects were turned over to the constable.

Weed and Seed Federal program that provides funds to help cities combine enforcement with community services in an effort to reduce crime in targeted neighborhoods.

white-collar crimes Crimes that are usually carried out during the course of a legitimate occupation; include crimes of fraud, crimes against public administration, and regulatory offenses.

work release Program that permits eligible inmates to work during the day at regular jobs in the outside world, returning to the jail or prison at night.

writ of certiorari A legal order from the U.S. Supreme Court stating that a lower court must forward the record of a particular case for review.

Name Index

Subject Index

Photo Credits

p. 70, Spencer Grant/PhotoEdit; **p. 76,** Khue Bui/AP/Wide World Photos; **p. 78,** Lee Snider/The Image Works; **p. 79,** © Touchstone Picture/David James/ Photofest; **p. 83,** Alan Tannenbaum/Corbis Sygma; **p. 93,** Jeff Christensen/Liaison Agency; **p. 95,** NBC News Today/AP/Wide World Photos; **p. 104,** David Young Wolff/ Stone; **p. 109,** Carolina Kroon/Impact Visuals; **p. 112,** North Wind Pictures Archives; **p. 115,** Photofest; **p. 119,** J. L. Atlan/Corbis Sygma; **p. 123,** Ron Edmonds/ AP/Wide World Photos; **p. 124,** Ansell Horn/Impact Visuals; **p. 135,** Lutz/Visum/ SABA Press Photos; **p. 138,** Brad Markel/Liaison Agency; **p. 143,** Bob Daemmrich/ The Image Works; **p. 154,** Photofest; **p. 156,** Lichtenstein/The Image Works; **p. 158,** Bob Daemmrich/The Image Works; **p. 161,** AP/Wide World Photos; **p. 173,** Atlan/ Corbis Sygma; **p. 178,** Photofest; **p. 182,** Owen Franken/Stock Boston; **p. 188,** Andrew Lichtenstein/Corbis Sygma; **p. 191,** Chris Brown/Stock Boston; **p. 193,** Photofest; **p. 196,** Bob Daemmrich/The Image Works; **p. 210,** Liaison Agency; **p. 213,** Steve Liss/Liaison Agency; **p. 214,** M. Reinstein/The Image Works; **p. 228,** AP/Wide World Photos; **p. 231,** Sam Emerson/Miramax/Shooting Star; **p. 233,** S. Agricola/ The Image Works; **p. 238,** Bill Swersey/Liaison Agency; **p. 247,** Bob Daemmrich/ The Image Works; **p. 252,** Sandra Baker/Liaison Agency; **p. 257,** Reed Saxon/AP/ Wide World Photos; **p. 261,** Springer/Liaison Agency; **p. 264,** J. Pickerell/The Image Works; **p. 266,** Carlos Osorio/AP/Wide World Photos; **p. 268,** Showtime/ Shooting Star; **p. 277,** Ruth Pollack/AP/Wide World Photos; **p. 281,** Bob Daemmrich/ The Image Works; **p. 284,** John/Chiasson/Liaison Agency; **p. 285,** Corbis Sygma; **p. 289,** Idaho State Journal, Chris Hunt/AP/Wide World Photos; **p. 299,** Nick Ut/AP/Wide World Photos; **p. 300,** Bob Daemmrich/The Image Works; **p. 307,** Keith Lanpher/Liaison Agency; **p. 310,** Dennis MacDonald/PhotoEdit; **p. 314,** Michael Newman/PhotoEdit; **p. 318,** Mark Foley/AP/Wide World Photos; **p. 324,** Bruce Ayres/Stone; **p. 327,** Andrew Lightenstein/Corbis Sygma; **p. 328,** Photofest; **p. 348,** Frank White/Liaison Agency; **p. 352,** Spencer Grant/ PhotoEdit; **p. 356,** Steve Lehman/SABA Press Photos; **p. 361,** Lawrence Migdale/ Stock Boston; **p. 365,** Benali/Liaison Agency; **p. 367,** Photofest; **p. 374,** Bill Swersey/Liaison Agency; **p. 383,** Mark Richards/PhotoEdit; **p. 389,** A. Ramsey/ PhotoEdit; **p. 391,** Courtesy of AIMS Multimedia; **p. 393,** J. Nubile/The Image Works; **p. 403,** Lester Sloan/Liaison Agency; **p. 409,** Jon Levy/Liaison Agency; **p. 410,** Denis Poroy/AP/Wide World Photos.